ELVIS & YOU

Your Guide to
the Pleasures
of Being
an Elvis Fan

LAURA VICTORIA LEVIN
AND JOHN O'HARA

A PERIGEE BOOK

A Perigee Book
Published by The Berkley Publishing Group
A division of Penguin Putnam Inc.
375 Hudson Street
New York, New York 10014

Copyright © 2000 by Laura Victoria Levin and John K. O'Hara
COVER DESIGN BY JOHN O'HARA
PRODUCED BY K&N BOOKWORKS INCORPORATED
Cover photo of Elvis courtesy of Showtime Archives
Cover photo of Elvis memorial vigil of August 16, 1982, © Brooks Draft/Sygma

First edition: July 2000

Published simultaneously in Canada.

The Penguin Putnam Inc. World Wide Web site address is
http://www.penguinputnam.com

Library of Congress Cataloging-in-Publication Data

Levin, Laura Victoria and John K. O'Hara
    Elvis & you : your guide to the pleasures of being an Elvis fan / Laura Victoria Levin and John O'Hara
            p.   cm.
    ISBN: 0-399-52565-3
    1. Presley, Elvis, 1935–1977 Miscellanea.   I. O'Hara, John, 1958–.

ML420.P96L48   2000
782.42166´092—dc21
[B]   99-39295
                                                   CIP

Printed in the United States of America
10 9 8 7 6 5 4 3 2 1

Most Perigee Books are available at special quantity discounts for bulk purchases for sales promotions, premiums, fund-raising, or educational use. Special books, or book excerpts, can also be created to fit specific needs.

For details, write: Special Markets, The Berkley Publishing Group, 375 Hudson Street, New York, New York 10014.

CONTENTS

Preface   v
Acknowledgments   xi

The Life of Elvis   1
The Death of Elvis   25
The Elvis Fan   39
The Music   73
Spirituality and Gospel   116
Elvis in Person   141
Television Elvis   163
Motion Picture Elvis   175
The Pilgrimage   198
Celebrating the Important Dates   237
Elvis Fan Clubs   251
Elvis and Charity   285
Collecting Elvis   297
Elvis and Art   315
Elvis and Style   333
Your Elvis Shrine   356
Elvis Impersonators   367

At Home with Elvis   401
Elvis and Family   425
Elvis and Romance   441
Elvis and Friendship   464
Elvis and Food   481
Elvis and Animals   496
Elvis and the Army   506
Elvis and Firearms   520
Elvis and Law Enforcement   534
Elvis and the Martial Arts   547
Elvis and the Motor Vehicle   559
Elvis and Air Travel   584
Elvis and Money   591
Elvis in Cyberspace   602
Elvis in the Future   618
What We Can Learn from Elvis   624

To Elvis.
Thank you for all the ways you've made our lives better.

PREFACE

As fans, we've always been fascinated by Elvis. Listening to his music and studying the vicissitudes of his life have held us in thrall for most of our own lives. But equally as fascinating are all the ripples his presence caused on Earth. Ripples is not quite powerful enough; it's been more like tidal waves. He retooled the entire landscape of the 1950s and no person since then, certainly no musician or entertainer, can function entirely outside of the consequences of what Elvis accomplished. That tidal wave continues—and we continue to be riveted. His fans, in unimaginable numbers, have never given up on Elvis and love him as much as they ever did. They have formed hundreds and hundreds of fan clubs and raised millions for charity in Elvis' name. The annual ritual of visiting Graceland on the anniversary of Elvis' death is newsworthy each time because of the tens of thousands of people who attend. New, and young, fans come under his spell at a surprising rate. To this day his music releases sometimes still make it onto top-ten lists around the world. A day rarely passes in which you don't hear his name. Remove any one element of Elvis' legacy and there'd be an enormous hole in our culture.

When we started to write *Elvis and You*, we intended to decipher it *all*, especially the relationship between Elvis and his fans. We wanted to capture what it is that attracts so many diverse individuals to Elvis and what it is that keeps this multitude faithful to him. There are so many questions whirling around the Elvis phenomenon: Why are some fans so zealously devoted? Why do some collect every single recording of his music? Why do so many fans raise money for charity in Elvis' name? Why are people compelled to visit his home, some every year? What motivates some to acquire almost anything Elvis: his CDs, films, books, his image on plates or velvet? Why do some seek out impersonators in the hopes of experiencing a vestige of Elvis thrill? Why do millions of people consider Elvis an important part of their everyday lives decades after his death. In short, what is it about Elvis?

We hope we've been able to shed at least some light on these questions. But ultimately it doesn't make sense to define Elvis and his fans anyway because the answers can't be neatly pinpointed, analyzed, or packaged. There will always be some mystery to it, and that's part of the appeal. Elvis is an experience that must be heard, seen, and felt. All people want excitement and pleasure in their lives. Some never find it. Elvis fans do. Something that could maybe be called magic flows back and forth between Elvis and each individual fan. He gave (and gives) to them and they give back. At this point in history, it's impossible to tell where Elvis ends and his fans begin. They're so intertwined, so associated in people's minds, that they form a kind of continuum.

The idea of *Elvis and You* is to give the reader a deeper appreciation of Elvis by getting to know some of the things that he enjoyed and loved. We celebrate all the characteristics that made Elvis who he was: musical, spiritual, quirky, daring, fun-loving, extreme. We suggest all kinds of ideas on how get a little (or a lot) more *Elvis* into your life, no matter what kind of fan you are. We've created a guide to visiting, navigating, understanding, and enjoying the world of the King by presenting information, activities, projects, and adventures to enhance your Elvis experiences.

Admittedly, we've written a biased look at the Elvis fan scene. We're not trying to hide the fact that we like Elvis. We like him a whole lot. And, needless to say, we like the other people who like him a lot.

We want to help destroy the pervasive negative stereotype of Elvis fans that reveals very little understanding of who we really are. Elvis fans wear their hearts on their sleeves and that's very easy to make fun of. The more extreme fans get all the media attention. We try to show all the different types of fans, their interests, and what turns them on and moves them about Elvis. Elvis may have created a rift between the young and old back in the fifties, but ever since he's been uniting people a lot more than dividing them.

If you only like Elvis' music and don't know a thing about the Elvis fan world, or if you've been wild about him since the fifties, belong to a fan club, and travel to Graceland twice a year—whatever type of fan you may be—come on and find out some more about the man and his fans.

One of the few things on which all of Elvis' friends and biographers agree is that Elvis Presley was known for his rollicking sense of humor and relentless pursuit of a good time. Elvis often used to ask the people around him, "Y'all havin' fun?"

Yeah, Elvis, wherever you may be, thanks to you, we are!

How *Elvis and You* Is Organized

Elvis and You is organized into chapters that distill Elvis' life and the Elvis fan experience into essential elements. Each chapter explores a subject that was important to Elvis or of interest to his fans.

The Essay

Each chapter begins with an essay giving an overview of the chapter subject. We've attempted to tell Elvis' story from the fan's perspective.

ESSENTIAL ELVISOLOGY

Here you'll find a collection of facts, stats, and trivia that every Elvis fan should know. Some of it will give you some real insight into Elvis and some of it is, well, pretty trivial.

YOUR ELVIS EDUCATION

A bibliography and guide to other media has been selected for each chapter. The books and videos are chosen because either in their entirety or in a good portion you can learn much more about the topic than we have space for. Books are listed by title and author only; most are available through major book stores or online providers, some you should try to trade with other fans for or seek out at fan conventions.

THE ELVIS AND YOU EXPERIENCE

In the final section of each chapter are our suggestions for more ways to enjoy yourself as an Elvis fan. There are things you can do, stuff to buy, places to go, and people to meet along the way. These suggested Elvis adventures range from serious and practical to extravagant and frivolous. Just like the man himself.

Please remember that Elvis Presley Enterprises owns the use of the words *Elvis*, *Elvis Presley*, *Graceland*, and *TCB*. All the ideas, projects, and things to make mentioned in the book are intended exclusively for your personal use and not for resale or profit. No Elvis product may be sold legally without first obtaining permission from EPE.

The Quote Boxes

Sprinkled throughout the chapters are quote boxes that contain comments and testimonials from fans. They were told to us directly, received by letter, or posted on the internet. Other boxes contain short excerpts from Elvis books that we think you should know about in the hope that you'll want to read more by the author. Together, these quotations represent a spectrum of feelings and give a fuller understanding of Elvis and his fans than the Elvis newbie may be aware of.

Concerning Errors and Omissions

Oh, believe us, we tried. But the Elvis world is an expanding, dynamic, and ever-changing place. We really want *Elvis and You* to be the definitive Elvis fan resource guide, so whatever we've missed or gotten wrong, we want to rectify in future editions. Please don't hesitate to let us know about any corrections and additions. If you're a fan club, memorabilia dealer, Elvis impersonator, or any Elvis-related place or service and you'd like to be listed in the next edition, please feel free to write to us in care of our publisher or e-mail us directly at ELandYOU@aol.com.

About the Resources Provided

In some cases a video or book is listed with ordering information. This is because that may be the only source for that title at this time.

Some entries are listed without a zip code and some are listed with no phone number, and some with no address, just a phone. That's because there are people featured in the book who requested that only a portion of their contact information to be provided, or that was all the information that was available to us.

About Us

We'll be in Memphis for Tribute Weeks every year, most Elvis birthday celebrations, and at as many fan conventions around the country as we can. We love to meet fellow fans so we hope to see you out there in Elvis world. We're lifelong Elvis devotees, defenders of the truth, and, above all, Elvis adventurers. To learn even more about us, visit the *Elvis and You* web site. It's a portal to the world of the Elvis fan on the internet. From there you'll be able to hyperlink to many of the places, businesses, stuff for sale, and other web sites mentioned in the book. It's also a great launchpad to meet other Elvis fans from all over the world.

http://www.elvisandyou.com

About Graceland

Elvis Presley Enterprises, Inc. (EPE) is the corporate entity that was created by the Presley Estate to conduct business and manage its assets. It is wholly owned by the Elvis Presley Trust. The Graceland operation in Memphis is the Graceland Division of Elvis Presley Enterprises, Inc. EPE also has an office in Los Angeles.

Priscilla Presley is the president of EPE and is based in the Los Angeles office. Jack Soden is the chief executive officer of Elvis Presley Enterprises, Inc., and is based in Memphis.

Graceland's e-mail address: Graceland@icomm.com
Graceland's web site: http://www.elvis-presley.com
For questions about Elvis, e-mail: Elvis@icomm.com
For a Graceland catalog, call: (888) 358-4776
Mailing address:
  Elvis Presley's Graceland
  P.O. Box 16508
  Memphis, Tennessee 38186-0508

Street address:
   Elvis Presley's Graceland
   3717 Elvis Presley Boulevard
   Memphis, Tennessee 38186-0508
   (800) 238-2000 toll free
   (901) 332-3322 direct dial
Ticket office hours of operation:
   Seven days a week, except for New Year's,
Thanksgiving, and Christmas
   7:30 A.M.–6 P.M. Memorial Day through
Labor Day
   8:30 A.M.–5 P.M. the rest of the year
Jack Soden
   Chief Executive Officer
Todd Morgan
   Director of Creative Resources
Patsy Anderson
   Fan Relations Manager

"Don't ask why, don't ask how. Our devotion cannot be explained. Our love for [Elvis] has no beginning, it has no end. The love Elvis invoked is magical, beyond definition. He was not just a man but a phenomenon, a space in this life, a space in our hearts and a space in our collective consciousness. And here he'll stay until it's time for us to go."
   —Excerpt from the Elvis Country Fan Club reading, from the August 1999 Candlelight Vigil

"When we go seeking Elvis we most often find ourselves."
   —Dave Marsh, *Elvis*

ACKNOWLEDGMENTS

So many people helped us, with such generosity, during the writing of this book that we were often in awe. In addition to countless individuals, there were hundreds of fan club members from every corner of the globe who provided us with their newsletters, told us their stories, and sent us their photos. These wonderful people made us both laugh (and one of us cry) and it is to all the Elvis fans we met during this project that we owe all the pleasure we had from this experience.

We are grateful to Sandi Miller, who is very close to a miracle, for her kindness, trust, humor, and glorious Elvis stories. It's perfectly clear to us why Elvis considered her a friend and fun to have around. We are very happy and honored to know the friendship of this extraordinary woman as well. Her stories and the photos she took of Elvis and, amazingly, decided to share with all of us can be found throughout this book.

We are grateful to Lex Raaphorst and Jordan Ritchie for being our internet geniuses and for sharing that knowledge with us directly and through their incredible web sites. Others on the internet whose web sites we are indebted to are Willem Kaauw, Haruo Hirose, David Troedson, Christophe Jouanne, Sami Niemelainen, and Oven Egeland.

We are grateful to Mary McLaughlin and Joanne and Jimmy Digilio, as well as Megan Murphy and Rich Wilson, for their help in showing us the ropes of the local fan scene here in New York and New Jersey. They opened their homes and hearts to us and now, many good meals and parties later, we consider them all friends.

Most special thanks to Ian Mackay for his fearsome knowledge of Elvis and his frequent willingness to share his perspective on the differences between European and American fans. And to Julian Grant and Paul Downie, also from Scotland, for their help.

There were so many people we met in person and online who contributed to this book that we must honestly admit it wouldn't exist without them. To Margaret Freisinger of New Mexico; Gabe and Betty Rodriguez of Florida; Bobbie Cunningham of Elvis Friends Hollywood; Phylis Collas, Bev Campbell, Alex Watson from New Zealand; Andy Hearn from England; Steve Braun, Rick Rennie, Donna K. Deen, and her friend Kathy Holloway; Mary and Daniel Young, Shane Peterson, and Bill Dufour of New Hampshire; Jon Are Jensaas, Celia Carvalho from Portugal; Maurice and Maureen Colgan of Ireland; all our buddies at elvis@coollist.com; Priscilla Parker of the We Remember Elvis Fan Club; Sue Manuszak, Chris Dashner, Jean-Marie Pouzenc; Crystal Drake Milne and Dr. Emil Verban, Jr., DDS; Kathy Ferguson, Kay and Paul Lipps, Alice Franco, Henrik Knudsen; Richard Palmer and Paul Milliot and all the rest of the gang on alt.elvis.king newsgroup (damn, you guys are funny); Carol Light of the Memories of Elvis store in Memphis; Peggy Sue Sosebee, Steve Curtis, and Cathy Rogers; Jane Ng at Columbia, Terry Davis, and Sharon Collins—you all made this book infinitely better.

There were Elvis artists, photographers, collectors, and raconteurs who helped us along our way, to every one of whom we owe our deepest thanks. Pamela Wood, for being phenomenally generous with her time, photos, impressive knowledge of the Elvis world, and her provocative artistic creations. Her connection with and insights into Elvis were an inspiration to us and we couldn't have gotten the project under way without her. We hope to see an Elvis book by her in the near future. Kata Billups, whose art we love, is a generous and gentle person who we count ourselves lucky to know. Johnny Ace, talented and funny, provided us with his extraordinary artwork that you will find in these pages. Bob Klein, for sharing his vast and humbling knowledge about Elvis with us and for opening his breathtaking collection of photos to us. We consider him a good friend. Levi Morgan of Butterfield and Butterfield auction house, for all his effort in providing us with photos from their excellent auction catalogs—for his enthusiasm and help, he was one of the more amazing people we encountered during this project. Lew and Ron Eliot from Super Cycle who told us great stories and shared numerous photos. Karl Lindroos for supplying us with photos of his spectacular Elvis collection. Mike Schreiber for their excellent photos of Tribute Week 1999. Simon Vega for his army-days stories and his photos of Little Graceland. Claude Jones of the *Commercial Appeal*, who helped us gain access to the paper's vast Elvis photo archives. To Bob Heis, Robin Rosaaen, Keith Alverson, Stephen Christopher, Betty Harper, Patty Carroll, Gloria Pall, thank you all for your help and contributions.

In the world of Elvis impersonators we also have many people to thank. Gene Lane for his thoughtful and untiring help and insight. Frankie Castro for all the entertainment he has provided—another person we are extremely grateful to count among our friends. Brendan Paul and Trent Carlini in Las Vegas: Wow. Jamie Aaron Kelley, Robert Washington, Travis Morris, Kenny Wyatt for his kindness, Joel Harris, Rich Wilson, Quentin Flagg, Elvis Junior from Belgium, Irv Cass, Johnny Thompson, Douglas Roy, Darrell Dunhill, Steve Davis as well as Nance Fox and Alice Dickey for their unflagging interest and help.

Many luminaries from the Elvis world took time to talk with us, help us with details and information; some we are also grateful to for their example as chroniclers, historians, and defenders of Elvis. Becky Martin and John Brown of Tupelo we can hardly thank enough for all they shared with us. Ernst Jorgensen graciously called us from Norway and shared his insights about Elvis' musical legacy, for which he has done immeasurable good through his own works and efforts at RCA. Cindy Hazen and Mike Freeman, authors of *Memphis Elvis-Style* and *The Best of Elvis*, opened their home (which also happens to have been Elvis') to us, told us incredible stories, and turned out to be our good friends. Larry Geller, who we believe gave his genuine friendship and caring to Elvis, shared his stories and gave us encouragement. Richard Davis, who it was great pleasure to meet and get to know. Kang Rhee for the time he kindly spent with us, and for his photos and stories. Bill Burk and Darwin Lamm for their excellent publications, which were an enormous help to us. And the late Mike McGregor, for his humor and affection for Elvis. To all of you we give our sincerest thanks.

Everyone at Graceland was unbelievably kind, helpful, and encouraging. We want to thank them for allowing us to take photos all around Elvis' beautiful home and grounds so that we could share them with Elvis fans everywhere. To Patsy Anderson, Greg Howell, Todd Morgan, Todd Anderson, and Jack Soden, we admire you and thank you for all your efforts to protect Elvis' history. To Priscilla Beaulieu Presley, thank you for your decision to open Graceland to the fans, and for all the things you do to preserve Elvis' memory.

To John Duff, our publisher, for your confidence in our book and our ideas (and for the great ideas you contributed); we count ourselves incredibly fortunate to have our first book published by Perigee and by you. And to Katharine Sands who agented, nursed, buoyed, endorsed, goosed, pumped up, and supported this project every waking moment since its first light—we are grateful for the patience, thoughtfulness, and inspirational energy you brought to it. Your belief in us is what carried us through 640 pages.

Laura would like to additionally thank Francesca Reigler, for being the kind of mother I wanted and needed while writing a book. Richard Schurkamp, for friendship for which no amount of thanks can ever be enough. Brian Campbell, Steve Schreiber, and Dan Connelly, for keeping me laughing. Stanislav Jonas, for helping me to keep my head above water. My partner, John O'Hara, for being the only person in the universe I could have accomplished this with—you're a monstrously talented man and I thank the stars for having been able to team up with you. Finally, I would really like to thank Pete Jones for giving me something I think actually no one else has.

John would like to especially thank the following people. To my coauthor Laura Levin for her inspired lunacy. To Amy who helped me endure what was one of the more challenging episodes in my life. To Anna for her German translations. To Uncle Hooney who made possible one of my most important research missions to Memphis. To "Pistol Gal" Lisah Nicholsen for photographing the Guernsey's Elvis auction in Las Vegas. To Carolyn van Hifjte who didn't hesitate to leave her cozy home in Amsterdam and travel to Germany to shoot some excellent photographs of

Elvis landmarks. To William Forsythe who shares some of Elvis' best qualities like loyalty, generosity, and a fierce lust for life. To Papa Joe Delaney, my fellow Nazarene brother, there aren't enough pages in this book to list the number of times he has showered me with his kindness. To his son Andrew for his mathematical prowess and swimming abilites. To David Jeandhour who helped keep my computers functioning, both the one on my desk and the one in my head. To Finnbar Winterson who created the illustrated Presley Family Tree. He's shared many an adventure with me and my life has been enriched by knowing him. To my "Brutha" Gerard Downey who created the architectural drawings in this book. He has been my friend since I was a small child and if I'm lucky will be my friend when I am an old man. To Charlie Soto whose friendship I cherish. To my "nice" brother Danny for always being ri-i-i-ght. To my sister Maureen who has been an inspiration to me my whole life. To my brother-in-law Bill Lloyd whose extraordinary talents are only eclipsed by the goodness of his heart. And last and most important, to my beloved mother, Delia, my greatest blessing in life.

THE LIFE OF ELVIS

It was a relatively short life; Elvis walked among us for only 42 years. But there are few who don't know his story. The events of his life are so familiar because they were lived—both the peaks and the valleys—in front of our eyes. More biographies have been written about him than about any other entertainer and perhaps any other person of this century. Forests have been felled so that his friends, family, lovers, and hangers-on could commit their memories to print. We've even learned about him from his cooks, army pals, nurse, and karate instructors.

Instead of focusing on the image of and mythology surrounding Elvis, it's important to remember to see him as a man. His life, like a good drama, was brimming with contradictions. He rose from dismal poverty to great riches. He grew up in the segregationist South yet he helped disrupt the separation of black and white culture by combining country music with rhythm and blues. He was a rebel who became an ideal soldier. He was a profoundly religious churchgoer who kick-started the sexual revolution. He was both Yin and Yang.

Elvis has far transcended his original role as a singer and movie star. He was one of the few people who could truly be called a legend in his own time. He is a modern

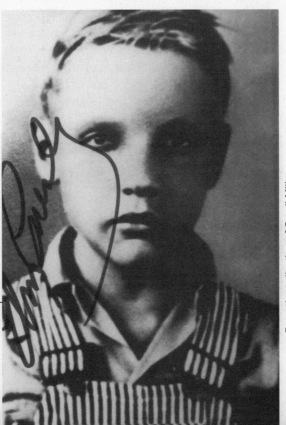

Autographed photo of Elvis as a young boy

1

Commercial Appeal

folk hero and for many people the embodiment of the American dream— the belief that in a meritocracy it's possible for those who have courage, ambition, and talent to make their dreams come true.

If the value of a person's life is measured by the impact he has had on other people, then Elvis' life remains one of the more extraordinary, and positive, lives of modern times. The world is a different place because he passed this way and his influence on the lives of others is still being felt. His story resonates because it says so much about the human condition: how those at the bottom can ascend and how the mighty at the top can fall. The story of Elvis' life is the second greatest story ever told.

Many Elvis fans feel compelled to study his life to get to know him better, to try and solve the enigma of his powerful hold and lasting appeal. They become amateur historians who go to see the places of his life and talk to the people who knew him. Our entire culture has not been able to forget him and no one has been able adequately to explain why. To better understand and enjoy Elvis, this book organizes his life thematically, according to the things that were important to him and therefore important to his fans. The timeline below will give the reader an overview of some of the events of that extraordinary life.

John O'Hara

Lifeline

January 8, 1935

Elvis Aron Presley was born in a two-room shack to Gladys and Vernon Presley in East Tupelo, Mississippi, at approximately 4:35 A.M. His twin brother, Jesse Garon

The Presley family bedroom in the house where Elvis was born, Tupelo, Mississippi

Priceville Cemetery in Tupelo, where many Presleys, including Jesse Garon, are buried

John O'Hara

Presley, had been delivered stillborn shortly before. Vernon later told of a blue glowing light over their house that night.

April 5, 1936

A tornado rips through Tupelo killing more than 200 people and injuring many more. Gladys and Elvis take shelter at grandfather Jessie Presley's home.

March 25, 1938

Vernon Presley is sentenced to three years at Parchman State Penitentiary for the crime of altering a check.

February   6, 1939

Vernon Presley is released from prison.

August 1945

Elvis' grandmother Minnie Mae moves in with Elvis and his family. She will live with them for the rest of her life and outlive them all.

October 3, 1945

Ten-year-old Elvis sings in front of hundreds of people at the Mississippi–Alabama Fair and Dairy Show at the Tupelo Fairgrounds. He sings "Old Shep," without music, for the Children's Day Talent Show but doesn't win. (Some versions of this story say he came in fifth place.)

January 8, 1946

Elvis' mother, Gladys, buys Elvis his first guitar as a birthday present at the Tupelo Hardware Store.

Author's collection

Elvis' sixth-grade class photo, Milam School; Elvis is in the third row, far right

November 6, 1948

The Presley family arrives in Memphis in search of a better life. They initially move into a place where they cook, eat, and sleep in the same room and share a bathroom with several other families.

September 1949

Elvis enters L. C. Humes High School.

September 20, 1949

The Presleys move into a government subsidized housing complex called Lauderdale Courts and their living conditions improve. They have a bum car and still no telephone.

June 3, 1951

Elvis gets a job at Precision Tool but is forced to quit a month later when it is discovered he is underage.

April 17, 1952

Elvis starts a part-time job as an usher at the Loew's State Theater. Five weeks later he is fired for fighting with a coworker.

August 6, 1952

Elvis starts work at Upholsteries Specialties Company. This job lasts about a month.

September 1952

Elvis starts work at Marl Metal Products. He works an after-school shift from 3:30 to 11:30 P.M. Gladys forces him to quit because he was too tired for school.

"My opinion is that Elvis is the most important cultural revolutionary figure in Western culture in the last fifty years (screw Time magazine) and that the fact that he unwittingly changed the way we look and think and its subsequent effects on him personally is a subject deserving of more scrutiny.

"The fact that this cultural religion was achieved primarily though the channels of marketing and commerce, as opposed to, say, a Sermon on the Mount, or a march on the courtyard, is also significant in that it reveals something about us as a society (good, bad, you tell me) if we've reached the place where our spiritual fulfillment can be purchased....

"Elvis was much more than a great musician, of course. He's a mirror of ourselves and reflects the best and worst of our dreams. That's why he's still significant."
—John Brown, on the alt.elvis.king newsgroup

April 9, 1953

Elvis performs for his classmates at the L. C. Humes High School minstrel show.

June 3, 1953

Elvis graduates from L. C. Humes High School. The commencement exercises take place at 8 P.M. in Ellis Auditorium and he is awarded his diploma by a Mr. E. C. Ball. George Klein, Elvis' life-long friend, is class president.

July 1953

Elvis begins working at Crown Electric as a delivery truck driver.

July 18, 1953

Elvis pays to make his own record at Sam Phillips's Memphis Recording Service. He sings "My Happiness" and "That's When Your Heartaches Begin," claiming he is making the record for his mother for her birthday (which is months away). For the first time he meets Marion Keisker, who plays a role in bringing his potential to Sam Phillips's attention.

January 4, 1954

Elvis meets Sam Phillips briefly for the first time and once again pays to make a recording, this time "Casual Love Affair" and "I'll Never Stand in Your Way."

June 26, 1954

Trying to find a fit for a potentially talented young man, Sam Phillips has Elvis called in to Sun Studio to tape him singing "Without You."

July 4, 1954

Sam Phillips hooks Elvis up with Scotty Moore for the first time. They get to know each other and rehearse some songs with an eye to recording for Sun.

July 5, 1954

Elvis, Scotty, and Bill show up at Sun Studio. After just a few hours of singing moony ballads and rehearsal that didn't produce anything great, everyone takes a break. During this time Elvis goofs around, riffing on a song called "That's All Right." Bill Black jumps in, clowning with his bass. Scotty Moore joins on guitar. Sam Phillips perks up and asks them to repeat what they had just done so he can tape it. This is essentially the official beginning.

July 7, 1954

Sam Phillips cuts the acetate in the afternoon and brings it to local DJ Dewey Phillips at WHBQ, who plays it on his radio show "Red, Hot, & Blue" that night around 9:30 or 10 P.M. He plays the song 14 times in a row. Elvis sits in a movie theater, too nervous to listen to himself on the radio.

July 9, 1954

Elvis returns to Sun to record a second side in order to be able to release "That's All Right." Within the next few nights' sessions they had created a new version of "Blue Moon of Kentucky." With Sam Phillips's "slapback" echo effect and the same kind of spirited, anything-on-a-dare mood of their first song together, Elvis and the Blue Moon Boys do something absolutely original. Elvis is 19 years old.

From the collection of Bob Klein

July 12, 1954

Elvis and his parents sign a one-year contract with Scotty Moore to be Elvis' manager.

July 17, 1954

Elvis and the Blue Moon Boys perform at the Bon Air Club. This is their first public performance.

July 19, 1954

Elvis' first recording, Sun Record #209, "That's All Right"/"Blue Moon of Kentucky," is officially released.

July 28, 1954

Elvis gives his first print interview to Edwin Howard of the Memphis *Press-Scimitar.*

July 30, 1954

Elvis performs at the Overton Park Shell in Memphis. A large crowd who had heard, and liked, Elvis on the radio turns out to get a gander at him.

September 9, 1954

Marion Keisker of Sun Records organizes the first Elvis fan club.

September 25, 1954

Elvis' second recording, Sun Record #210, "Good Rockin' Tonight"/"I Don't Care if the Sun Don't Shine," is released.

October 2, 1954

Elvis performs at the Grand Ole Opry. It's becoming plain that one branch of country music is morphing into something else in Elvis' hands. This launches what would become a long-term disgruntlement on the part of the country music establishment.

October 16, 1954

Elvis makes his first performance on *Louisiana Hayride* radio show out of Shreveport.

November 1954

Elvis quits his day job at Crown Electric to devote his full attention to being a singer.

November 6, 1954

Elvis makes the only commercial of his career—for Southern Made Doughnuts.

January 1, 1955

Elvis signs on with Bob Neal, a local Memphis DJ, as manager.

February 6, 1955

Elvis meets Colonel Parker for the first time. This event takes place at Palumbo's Café on 85 Poplar Avenue in Memphis.

March 1955

Elvis flies to New York to audition for *Arthur Godfrey's Talent Scouts* and is turned down.

March 5, 1955

Elvis makes his first television appearance on Shreveport television station KWKH-TV.

May 13, 1955

The first "Elvis riot" occurs at the Gator Bowl in Jacksonville, Florida. Elvis is mobbed by fans intent on getting a piece of him.

August 15, 1955

The Colonel begins his business relationship with Elvis as "special adviser."

November 21, 1955

RCA Records buys Elvis' contract from Sam Phillips. The Colonel negotiates an unheard of payment of about $40,000. There's a $5,000 signing bonus for Elvis.

January 10, 1956

Elvis records "Heartbreak Hotel" at RCA Studios in Nashville. It will be the number-one hit in the country by April.

January 27, 1956

RCA releases "Heartbreak Hotel," which goes on to become Elvis' first

> "Elvis' retreat was ironic. The world was his oyster—he opened it, got inside, and closed the shell. The sixties art that was about to explode was kinetic, pop, raw, sex-based, black-inspired—as was Elvis' art. You could say he was the father of the sixties."
>
> —Jill Pearlman, from *Elvis for Beginners*

gold record. "I Was the One" is the second side.

January 28, 1956

Elvis and the Blue Moon Boys (Scotty, Bill, D. J.) make their first network television appearance on *Stage Show* hosted by the Dorsey Brothers and produced by Jackie Gleason. He appears again on February 4, 11, and 18.

February 23, 1956

Elvis collapses from exhaustion after a show at the Gator Bowl in Florida. He gets out of the hospital the next day and does another performance that night.

March 26, 1956

Colonel Parker officially becomes Elvis' sole manager.

March 13, 1956

Elvis Presley, Elvis' first album, is released by RCA. It goes to number one on Billboard's Pop Album Chart for ten weeks, hits $1 million in sales, and becomes his first gold album.

April 1, 1956

Paramount Studios screen tests Elvis in Hollywood. He reads for *The Rainmaker* and lip-synchs to his song "Blue Suede Shoes."

April 3, 1956

Elvis makes his first *Milton Berle Show* appearance, broadcast from the deck of the aircraft carrier USS *Hancock*.

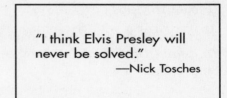

"I think Elvis Presley will never be solved."
—Nick Tosches

April 6, 1956

Elvis signs his first movie contract: Paramount Pictures, seven years, Hal Wallis producer.

April 23, 1956

Elvis plays in Las Vegas for the first time at the Venus Room at the New Frontier Hotel. He more or less bombs and does not play Vegas again until 13 years later.

April 30, 1956

The first story on Elvis in a national magazine runs in *Life*.

May 11, 1956

Elvis and his family move into the first home he buys with his success earnings. The ranch-style house at 1034 Audubon Drive costs $40,000.

July 1, 1956

The Steve Allen Show appearance: Elvis is forced to wear white tie and tails and to sing to a basset hound. Elvis is cheesed but he goes along.

July 2, 1956

Elvis records "Hound Dog," "Don't Be Cruel," and "Any Way You Want Me" at RCA Studios in New York. It's his first recording with the Jordanaires.

August 23, 1956

Shooting begins on Elvis' first movie, *Love Me Tender*.

September 3, 1956

Elvis buys his mother the now famous pink Cadillac even though she can't drive.

September 9, 1956

Elvis makes the first of his three appearances on *The Ed Sullivan Show*. The show garners the highest rating to that date for any variety show.

September 26, 1956

An official Elvis Presley Day is declared in Elvis' hometown of Tupelo, Mississippi, and Elvis performs at the fairgrounds where he once sang as a boy.

November 15, 1956

Love Me Tender, Elvis' first movie, premieres at the Paramount Theater in New York City.

December 4, 1956

An impromptu recording session at Sun Studio produces the "Million Dollar Quartet" that includes Elvis, Carl Perkins, and Jerry Lee Lewis. (Johnny Cash, who was present only for a photo session, left to go shopping before the singing commenced.)

December 11, 1956

Elvis is given the honorary commission of a Louisiana colonel by Louisiana Governor Earl K. Long.

December 15, 1956

Elvis makes his final *Louisiana Hayride* appearance.

January 6, 1957

"This is a decent, fine boy," Ed Sullivan gushes about Elvis during his third appearance on the Sullivan show. Memorably, this is the show where Elvis is shot from the waist up through all of his five songs *including* the traditional gospel song "Peace in the Valley."

February 3, 1957

A *New York Times* article says that bootleg Elvis recordings have reached the Soviet Union, where they are not available legally. They are being cut on discarded X-ray plates and sold on the black market.

March 25, 1957

Elvis' purchase of a 23-room mansion called Graceland is finalized.

> "You never heard anybody ask 'Elvis who?'"
> —Charles Kuralt

April 2 and 3, 1957

Elvis performs in Canada. It's the first time he stages an official concert outside of the U.S.

June 26, 1957

Elvis spends his first night at Graceland. It is the home where he will spend the rest of his life while in Memphis.

July 9, 1957

Loving You premieres and reaches top ten at the box office.

August 31, 1957

Elvis performs for the third time in Canada. This is the last time he ever performs in concert outside of the U.S.

October 17, 1957

Elvis' third movie, *Jailhouse Rock*, premieres in Memphis and reaches top five at the box office.

November 10, 1957

Elvis performs in Hawaii for the first time and begins a lifelong love affair with the state.

December 19, 1957

Elvis receives his draft notice.

December 25, 1957

Elvis spends his first Christmas at Graceland and his last with Gladys.

March 24, 1958

Elvis reports to the Memphis draft board for induction into the U.S. Army. He is assigned serial number is 53310761.

March 25, 1958

Elvis is shorn for his GI haircut by barber James Peterson at Fort Chaffee.

March 29, 1957

Basic training starts for Private Presley. He is stationed at Ford Hood, Texas, for six months.

August 14, 1958

Gladys Presley dies; her funeral is held the next day.

Entrance to Tupelo Fairgrounds, January 1999

John O'Hara

September 22, 1958

Elvis sails for Germany aboard the USS *Randall*.

October 1, 1958

The USS *Randall* troop ship docks in West Germany with Elvis on board.

November 27, 1958

Elvis is very well regarded by fellow soldiers and his commanding officers. He is promoted to private first class.

June 1, 1959

Elvis earns a promotion to specialist fourth class.

September 13, 1959

Priscilla Beaulieu arrives in Elvis' life.

January 20, 1960

Elvis is promoted to sergeant.

March 1, 1960

Elvis leaves West Germany.

March 5, 1960

Elvis receives his official discharge from active duty.

March 21, 1960

Elvis receives his first-degree black belt in karate.

March 26, 1960

Frank Sinatra swallows his previous vitriol about rock and roll and hosts the "Welcome Home Elvis" variety show.

July 3, 1960

Vernon Presley weds Dee Stanley in a ceremony that Elvis does not attend.

December 25, 1960

Priscilla spends her first Christmas at Graceland.

March 25, 1961

Elvis performs at the Bloch Arena at Pearl Harbor. This is a benefit performance to raise money for building a memorial for the USS *Arizona*. It will be his last live performance for eight years.

December 19, 1962

Priscilla arrives stateside to celebrate Christmas with Elvis at Graceland.

February 13, 1964

Elvis presents the St. Jude Children's Research Hospital in Memphis with the *Potomac*, which had been President Franklin Roosevelt's presidential yacht.

August 27, 1965

The Beatles visit Elvis at his Bel Air home. Not *one* single person has the presence of mind to take a photo or tape their jam session.

February 9, 1967

Elvis acquires a 163-acre ranch in Walls, Mississippi, and names it the Flying Circle G Ranch.

May 1, 1967

Fourteen Colonel-picked guests attend Elvis and Priscilla's eight-minute nuptials at the Aladdin Hotel in Las Vegas.

May 29, 1967

Elvis and Priscilla have a second wedding reception at Graceland for family and friends who had not been invited to the Las Vegas event.

February 1, 1968

Lisa Marie Presley is born to Elvis and Priscilla.

June 27, 1968

Taping begins for the "'68 Comeback Special."

December 3, 1968

The "'68 Comeback Special" airs on NBC.

July 31–August 28, 1969

Elvis performs a four-week standing-room-only engagement at the International Hotel in Las Vegas.

"The first thing Elvis had to learn to transcend, after all, was the failure and obscurity he was born to; he had to find some way to set himself apart, to escape the limits that could well have given his story a very different ending. The ambition and genius that took him out and brought him back is there in that first music...."
—Greil Marcus,
from *Mystery Train Images of America in Rock 'n' Roll Music*

August 26, 1969

"Suspicious Minds" is released. It will turn out to be Elvis' last number-one hit.

October 10, 1970

Elvis receives a commission as special deputy sheriff of Shelby County, giving him *full* police powers and the legal right to carry concealed weapons.

December 21, 1970

Elvis meets with President Nixon at the White House and receives the federal narcotics agent badge he went there seeking.

January 16, 1971

The United States Junior Chamber of Commerce (Jaycees) votes Elvis one of the Ten Outstanding Young Men of America.

Elvis in rare two-piece stage outfit, Las Vegas

Sandi Miller

February 20, 1971

"Also Sprach Zarathustra" is used for the first time to herald Elvis' arrival on stage.

March 29, 1971

Elvis receives his fourth-degree black belt from Master Kang Rhee.

August 9–September 6, 1971

Elvis returns to Las Vegas for another International Hotel gig. He continues to break all attendance records. During this stand he is presented with a Grammy Award for Lifetime Achievement (called the Bing Crosby Award at the time) in his dressing room.

January 19, 1972

Highway 51 South in Memphis is renamed Elvis Presley Boulevard.

July 5, 1972

Elvis meets Linda Thompson and begins a romantic involvement that lasts until 1976.

January 14, 1973

Elvis performs the "Elvis: Aloha from Hawaii via Satellite" special from the Honolulu International Center Arena. It is broadcast live to Australia, South Korea, Japan, Thailand, the Philippines, South Vietnam, and several other countries. (It will be seen later in Europe and the States.) In the end, it's seen in at least 40 countries by an estimated 1.5 billion people. The soundtrack from the show reaches number one on the Billboard Pop Album Chart and continues to chart for one whole year.

October 1973

A divorce is granted to Elvis and Priscilla.

Courtesy of Butterfield & Butterfield

Diamond, enamel, and gold astrology pendant necklace, given to Elvis Christmas 1976 from the Las Vegas Hilton

October 15–November 1, 1973

Elvis is hospitalized for several health problems including pneumonia, pleurisy, and hepatitis.

August 29, 1974

Elvis is presented with his eighth-degree black belt in Kenpo karate.

January 29–February 14, 1975

Elvis is hospitalized with recurring health problems.

December 31, 1975

Elvis sets single-performance attendance and income records in Pontiac, Michigan.

October 30, 1976

Elvis makes the last "studio" recording of his life in the Jungle Room at Graceland.

November 19, 1976

Elvis meets Ginger Alden.

December 12, 1976

Elvis' last Las Vegas appearance.

March 3, 1976

Elvis writes his final will.

April 1–April 5, 1977

Elvis is hospitalized and his scheduled tour is canceled.

June 26, 1977

Market Square Arena in Indianapolis, Indiana, is Elvis' last concert.

August 1, 1977

Elvis, What Happened?, written by several former members of the Memphis Mafia purporting to help Elvis by exposing their opinions of his private life to the world, is released.

August 8, 1977

Elvis rents the Fairgrounds amusement park for the last time.

August 16, 1977

Elvis dies at Graceland.

ESSENTIAL ELVISOLOGY

The Number of Days Elvis Lived
15,197

Elvis' Astrological Sign
Capricorn

I Am and I Was
This enigmatic phrase that Elvis was known to say occasionally during his later concerts has been interpreted by some fans as having a mystical meaning and as a portent of his impending death. More likely it was just taken out of context. It was spoken after announcing the title of "Are You Lonesome Tonight?" and Elvis was just responding to the question the song asks: "I am and I was" lonesome tonight.

Present at Elvis' Birth
Dr. William Robert Hunt
Mrs. Edna Robinson, midwife

Elvis' Schools

East Tupelo Consolidated, Tupelo   Milam School, Tupelo
Lawhon School, Tupelo   L. C. Humes High School, Memphis

University Courses on Elvis

University of Iowa
    Elvis as Anthology
University of Mississippi
    Blue Hawaii: The Polynesian Novels and Hawaiian Movies of Melville and Elvis

Elvis' and Jesse Garon's birth record documents, handwritten by delivering physician Dr. William Robert Hunt

Georgetown University
  Icons of Popular Culture 1: Elvis and Marilyn
University of Tennessee
  The Cultural Phenomenon of Elvis Presley: The Making of a Folk Hero
University of Mississippi
  Vernon Chadwick's International Conference on Elvis

The Jaycee Award

On January 16, 1971, Elvis was named one of the ten outstanding young men of America by the Jaycee civic organization. To Elvis, it was the greatest honor and for the rest of his life the award traveled with him wherever he went.

The Jaycee Award Inscription

"The hope of mankind lies in the hands of youth and action."

Elvis' Acceptance Speech

"When I was a child, ladies and gentlemen, I was a dreamer. I read comic books, and I was the hero of the comic book. I saw movies, and I was the hero of the movie. So every dream I've ever dreamed has come true a hundred times.

  "[Referring to his fellow nominees] See, these are the type of people who care. They're dedicated. You realize, they might be building the kingdom of heaven right here. It's not too farfetched to believe that.

  "I'd like to say that I learned, very early in life that, without a song the day would never end, without a song, a man ain't got a friend, without a song, the road would never bend, without a song, so I'll keep singing the song."

Some Fellow Jaycee Award Winners throughout the Years

Richard Nixon	Jesse Jackson	Ted Kennedy
Nelson Rockefeller	Leonard Bernstein	John F. Kennedy
Orson Welles	Ralph Nader	Robert Kennedy
Howard Hughes		

Elvis' Aliases

Elvis used various aliases over the years to protect his anonymity when making hotel or airline reservations and for hospital stays and private correspondence.

Aaron Sivle (*Sivle* spelled backward is *Elvis*.)	Deke Rivers
Dr. John Carpenter	Arthur Hooten
Colonel Jon Burrows	

Elvis' Blood Type
O positive

YOUR ELVIS EDUCATION

Books

Elvis Day by Day: The Definitive Record of His Life and Music
    Peter Guralnick and Ernst Jorgensen
Early Elvis: The Tupelo Years
    Bill E. Burk
Early Elvis: The Sun Years
    Bill E. Burk
Elvis: The Concert Years
    Bill E. Burk
Elvis: A 30-Year Chronicle: Columns, Stories, Articles & Features Exactly as Originally Reported 1954–1983
    Bill E. Burk
Elvis: Through My Eyes
    Bill E. Burk
✗ *Last Train to Memphis: The Rise of Elvis Presley*
    Peter Guralnick
✗ *Careless Love: The Unmaking of Elvis Presley*
    Peter Guralnick
✗ *Elvis*
    text by Dave Marsh; art direction by Bea Feitler
Memphis Elvis-Style
    Cindy Hazen and Mike Freeman

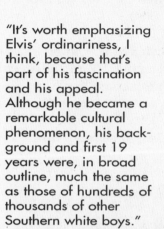

"It's worth emphasizing Elvis' ordinariness, I think, because that's part of his fascination and his appeal. Although he became a remarkable cultural phenomenon, his background and first 19 years were, in broad outline, much the same as those of hundreds of thousands of other Southern white boys."
—John Shelton Reed, from *In Search of Elvis*

Phil Gelormine, publisher of Gelormine's *Elvis World*, meeting Elvis biographer Peter Guralnick at book signing for *Careless Love* in New York City

John O'Hara

All Shook Up: Day by Day with Elvis Presley
  Lee Cotton
The Early Years Elvis: A 2001 Fact Odyssey (first of seven volumes)
  Jim Curtin
X *Elvis: His Life From A to Z*
  Fred L. Worth and Steve D. Tamerius
X *Elvis: A Biography*
  Jerry Hopkins
X *Elvis: The Final Years*
  Jerry Hopkins
Elvis Presley References Guide and Discography
  John A. Whisler
Elvis: A Bio-bibligraphy
  Patsy Guy Hammontree
X *Down at the End of Lonely Street: The Life and Death of Elvis Presley*
  Pat Broeske and Peter Harry Brown
The Ultimate Elvis: Elvis Presley Day by Day
  Patricia Joe Pierce
Elvis: His Life in Pictures
  text by Todd Morgan with Laura Kath
Elvis: A Celebration in Pictures
  Charles Hirshberg and the editors of *Life*
Elvis Up Close, In the Words of Those Who Knew Him Best
  edited by Rose Clayton and Dick Heard
Elvis: Unknown Stories Behind the Legend
  Jim Curtin
The Hitchhiker's Guide to Elvis
  Mick Farren

The Inner Elvis: A Psychological Biography of Elvis Aaron Presley
  Peter Whitmer
Elvis: Portrait of the King
  Susan Doll
Best of Elvis
  Susan Doll
Elvis: A Tribute to His Life
  Susan Doll
Understanding Elvis: Southern Roots vs. Star Image
  Susan Doll
Elvis: Images and Fancies
  Jack L. Tharpe
Elvis for Beginners
  Jill Pearlman; illustrated by Wayne White
The Quotable King
  Elizabeth McKeon and Linda Everett
The Official Elvis Presley Fan Club Commemorative Album 1935–1977
  edited by Julie Mundy
The Complete Idiot's Guide to Elvis
  Frank Coffey
Amazing But True Elvis Facts
  Bruce Nash and Allan Zullo with John McGran
The Complete Elvis
  Martin Torgroff, editor
Unseen Elvis
  compiled by Jim Curtin
Elvis: Thank You Very Much
  Paul Lichter
Elvis Album
  Susan Doll
Wise Men Say: An Incomparable Collection of Little-Known Facts about Elvis
  Jesse Fonatana

Shake Rag: From the Life of Elvis Presley
(for children ages four to eight)
Amy Littlesugar and Floyd Cooper
Elvis: The Last Word: The 328 Best (and Worst) Things Anyone Ever Said

about "The King"
Sandra Choron and Bob Oskam
The Elvis Encyclopedia
David Stanley with Frank Coffey

Video
"Elvis"
1979 ABC TV bio-pic
Rare Moments with the King
Documentary: MSG and 1970
Houston Astrodome interviews
This Is Elvis
Elvis '56
Cinemax
Presley: Tenth Anniversary Tribute Documentary
Elvis docudrama TV series (ABC)
February 6, 1990, to May 26, 1990

A&E Biography: Elvis Presley
May be purchased by calling
(800) 423-1212 from the U.S. or
Canada.
The Lost Films of Elvis
Available through M. T.
Productions, 2785 East Foothill
Boulevard, Pasadena, California
91107 (877) 401-1095.
Elvis, the Echo Will Never Die

Web Sites
http://www.interbooking.no/elvis/day
byday.html
Elvis day-by-day Database
http://www.geocities.com/~arpt/az/
Elvis Presley Encyclopaedia
http://elvistyle.com/elvistyl.html
Memphis Elvis-Style; Memphis
Explorations
http://www.cnn.com/
SHOWBIZ/9708/elvis/
CNN's Elvis site; lots of good info
and activities
http://www.geocities.com/Nashville/
8605/thanks.html
The Elvis Presley diary; his where-
abouts everyday of his career
http://www.jerryosborne.com/word4
word.html
Elvis, Word for Word

http://www.gomemphis.com/elvis/
elvis.html
The *Commercial Appeal* Elvis
archive
http://www.dafridge.com.
Elvis Artifacts Collector Box Sets
http://www.fiftiesweb.com/elvis.htm
The Early Years
http://www.multimania.com/fancho/
Olivier Bruaux's site specializing in
1950s culture.
http://www.pathfinder.com/people/
960819/photogallery/king00.html
People magazine's Elvis site with
real audio and tons of photos

THE ELVIS AND YOU EXPERIENCE

Read the Elvis Biographies

There are dozens and dozens of biographies about Elvis already and more are published every year. There are so many books about Elvis that if you want to learn more about any aspect of his life, you won't be struggling to find material. (But, alas, no autobiographies.) Fans have relied on books by friends, "*friends*," relatives, lovers (real and imagined), neighbors, employees, guys who served in the army with him, rock critics, music specialists, sessionographers, science fiction writers, and creeps. (The biggest creep being Albert Goldman, who spat out what was nominally a biography of Elvis in 1980. The book reads more like the notes from one of Goldman's therapy sessions; he reveals more about his hang-ups and prejudices than he does about Elvis. Not worth reading in our opinion but serves as a dandy fund-raiser if you auction off the pages for fans to destroy as they see fit.)

In each chapter we've included a list of books relating to the subject discussed, but here we want to provide an overarching, though *highly subjective*, list of the books we consider fundamental reading. There are a gazillion—try to read some of them. You can make a game out of finding all the inconsistencies.

Elvis and You's Essential Booklist for Elvis Fans

Elvis
  Text by Dave Marsh; art direction by Bea Feitler
Dead Elvis
  Greil Marcus
  Greil Marcus and Dave Marsh have done more for Elvis' artistic reputation with their writings than anyone else anywhere, maybe including EPE. Not for the fainthearted; thought-provoking, insightful writing.
The Best of Elvis: Recollections of a Great Humanitarian
  Cindy Hazen and Mike Freeman
  Hazen and Freeman have written several books about Elvis, including *Memphis, Elvis-Style*. In *The Best of Elvis* they tell so many beautiful stories about Elvis' kindness, gentleness, and warmth that you'll feel like you know the man.

Last Train to Memphis: The Rise of Elvis Presley
Careless Love: The Unmaking of Elvis Presley
  Peter Guralnick's two-volume biography came along as the anti-venom, the cure, to earlier negative, distasteful, sensation-ized rubbish. His books are considered as gen-

> "Elvis and his revolution were vulnerability disguised as bravado."
> —M. Orth, *Newsweek*

erally reliable as it gets outside of having been an eyewitness yourself.

Anything written by Bill E. Burk
  Bill Burk was a Memphis journalist who was on the front lines all during Elvis' career. His stories and anecdotes about Elvis are scrupulously researched and well told.

Elvis Presley: A Life in Music: The Complete Recording Sessions
  Ernst Jorgensen
  This book is the last word on the history/sessionography of Elvis' musical career.

The Concert Years 1969–1977
  Stein Erik Skar
  No other book comes close to covering every live performance Elvis gave during these years and conveying a real sense of what it was like to see Elvis live.

Elvis and Gladys
  Elaine Dundy
  This is an intelligent, well-researched book about Elvis' mother, her life, and their love for each other; a stimulating read.

The Death of Elvis
  Charles C. Thompson II and James P. Cole

When Elvis Died: Media Overload & the Origins of the Elvis Cult
  Neal and Janice Gregory
  These two books cover every aspect of Elvis' death, the media coverage, and the worldwide response to it; excellent, exhaustive, and meticulous.

Images of Elvis Presley in American Culture 1977–1997: The Mystery Terrain
  George Plasketes
  Very interesting book about the wake Elvis left behind; ample proof that he hasn't been forgotten by a long shot.

The Best of Elvis
  Susan Doll

The Official Elvis Presley Fan Club Commemorative Album
  Julie Mundy
  These are excellent photo books covering Elvis' life from beginning to end.

Graceland: The Living Legacy of Elvis Presley
  text by Chet Flippo
  This book covers every aspect of Elvis' home and much of his life with great photos and quite good writing.

> "Elvis was the firstest with the mostest."
> —Roy Orbison

> "*Time*, in a tradition they started the week Elvis died, alone among national newsmagazines, failed to put him on the cover. (Anybody here still remember Bert Lance? I didn't think so.) 'Elitist bastards' is as good an explanation as to why they failed to include him among their list of the most influential entertainers. There's always been a class-based bias against Elvis in the mainstream media. Elvis endured it throughout his life, certainly. I'll go on a limb and say that more people, whether they realize it or not, have been affected by the fact that Elvis ever existed than have been by either T. S. Eliot or Le Corbusier."
> —John, about Elvis not being included on *Time*'s editors "Most Influential Entertainers of the Twentieth Century" list, on alt.elivs.king

Elvis Day by Day: The Definitive Record of His Life and Music
　　Peter Guralnick and Ernst Jorgensen
　　Covers Elvis' life on every day that it is known what he was doing or where he was; thorough and fascinating.

Write Your Own Elvis Biography

If you're literarily inclined, you might enjoy putting your thoughts, interpretations, analyses, theories—whatever it is you have to say about the life of Elvis—into print. Everybody has a personal perspective on Elvis. You may already know tons about him, or it may be the perfect excuse to do more research about the man and his life. There's a couple of ways to go about doing this. You can submit your work to an established publisher, self-publish it, contribute it to a fan club newsletter or other Elvis publications, or post it on the internet to share with other Elvis fans.

Walk a Mile in His Shoes

Do like the Elvis song says: "walk a mile in his shoes" by retracing some of the steps of Elvis' life. See the things that he saw, breathe the air that he breathed. It'll give you a personal connection and maybe a more profound understanding of the King.

Record an Elvis Oral History

Seek out those who knew Elvis. Ask them to tell you Elvis stories. Everyone who knew him has one. There's a finite number of people who had personal contact with him and unfortunately the passage of time robs us of these precious resources.

Acknowledge Meeting Elvis Insiders

Leave or send a thank you note. Include a small token of appreciation with your note. It's the right thing to do. Their time is valuable and it gives Elvis fans a good name.

Get an Elvis Research Kit

Graceland provides an Elvis Research Kit to students who call or write the Graceland Communications Department. The kit contains information about Elvis' life and career and a suggested reading list to learn more.

> "The world seems more alive at night ... it's like God ain't watchin'."
> —Elvis Presley

Subscribe to *Elvis International Forum*

It's the most entertaining, informative, exciting magazine on the newsstand today! Why? It's all about Elvis. This quarterly magazine has all the current news on the Elvis front, but you can also count on testimonials and stories about Elvis, by people who were there, in every issue. It has the imprimatur of Elvis Presley Enterprises. See "The Elvis Fan" chapter for information on subscribing to other publications.

Elvis International Forum
P.O. Box 3373,
Thousand Oaks, California 91359
(818) 991-3892
Fax: (818) 991-3894

Get Answers to Your Questions about Elvis

Graceland is one place to turn, whether by phone or on the internet, with Elvis questions. Elsewhere on the internet sites offer to answer any questions you might have. *Elvis International Forum* magazine has a Q&A section; you might want to include one in your club's newsletter too. Attend fan conventions; there are often Elvis intimates as invited guests who speak at these events. You can try this site when you're online:
http://www.geocities.com/Nashville/4402/index.html

"If [the books written about Elvis] were completely fact, then I really wouldn't have any argument (other than, is it *really* anyone's business?) but, although most of the stories are rooted in an incident that actually did happen, they take off on a wild journey and develop a life of their own, and what are the fans left with? Some distorted weirdo picture of Elvis Presley.

"No, it's not going to stop the new fans from enjoying his music, it's not going to stop them from becoming fans, but it does *him* a disservice that he does *not* deserve and that irritates the begeezes out of me! I'll be the first to admit that Elvis could be a tad strange at times (actually that was part of his appeal to me—normal–eccentric I call it) but I don't think everyone needs to know his bathroom habits, among other things.

"Elvis' life did, after all, consist of more than shooting out a TV set, cussing, firing and rehiring, and buying cars. He most definitely consisted of more than the sad, pathetic, angry, drug-riddled legacy that *his friends* have left the world with. *Where* is that gentle, caring, funny, hardworking, and hard-loving little boy? So far, he's only been in a few books and I have a real problem with that.

"I think fans who've been around a long time can pretty much figure out what's probably fact and what's not but it's the *new* fans I worry about. I can't tell you how many times [new fans] have said, 'But why would they lie; they were his friends?' How do I answer that? So, as long as these guys are supported in what they write and what they say, they're going to keep right on putting this stuff out."

—Sandi Miller, a good friend to Elvis, on the Memphis Mafia and other negative writings about Elvis, from the *Young and Beautiful Friends of Elvis, New Jersey* fan club newsletter (now called *Elvis Now*)

THE DEATH OF ELVIS

August 16, 1977. On that stiflingly hot and humid Tuesday, Elvis Presley died in the home he loved in Memphis at the age of 42. His sudden death came as a total shock to millions of people. What happened afterward, the enormity of the reaction to his death, came as an even greater shock. It illustrated the profound depth of feeling that so many people had for this man. The international convulsion of grief in response to Elvis' death revealed to the world that he was much more than just an entertainer. How much more is proven every day by his fans everywhere. On that sad day in August, Elvis left this mortal realm and was transformed into a legend. It's a legend that continues to grow and probably always will.

Like much of his life, Elvis' death is surrounded by controversy and rumor. There were no witnesses to his final moments and Elvis Presley's complete autopsy records are protected, at his family's request, by the privacy laws of Tennessee for 50 years (until 2027). According to Shelby County medical examiner Dr. Jerry Francisco's official announcement on the cause of death, it was cardiac arrhythmia due to undetermined causes that killed Elvis; in laymen's terms, a heart attack. Subsequent investigations have asserted that Elvis died from an

Elvis' grave, January 8, 1999

John O'Hara

Interior of racquetball building, at Graceland

John O'Hara

allergic reaction to codeine. Others maintain he died as a result of polypharmacy, in this case a lethal combination of prescription drugs. There are those who believe he committed suicide and even a few who theorize that there was foul play involved. Most bizarre are the theories that he never died at all and that Elvis faked his demise and is now living in happy anonymity. The total truth may never be known. Be that as it may, there is general agreement as to the events of the last 24 hours that led up to Elvis' death.

Elvis woke up around 4:00 in the afternoon on the fifteenth of August. He ate breakfast and sent for his cousin Billy Smith around 7:00 P.M. The two watched television while they tried unsuccessfully to get a copy of either the film *Star Wars* or *MacArthur* for viewing later. Elvis played with his daughter, Lisa Marie, until she went to bed at 9:30. A little later he drove out of Graceland in his Stutz Blackhawk accompanied by Ginger Alden, Billy Smith, and Charlie Hodge for an 11:00 P.M. dental appointment with his dentist, Lester Hofman. He had his teeth cleaned and a couple of small cavities filled. At 12:28 A.M. on the sixteenth, he drove back through the gates of Graceland. At that moment, a fan at the gates snapped the last photo ever shot of Elvis alive. He went up to his bedroom and after making a few calls to his staff about the upcoming tour he went out to the racquetball court behind the house and played with Billy Smith until around 4:00 A.M. Then Elvis sat at the piano in the lounge area next to the court and sang what would be the last songs he would ever sing. He ended with "Blue Eyes Crying

John O'Hara

Window to Elvis' bathroom on the second floor, at Graceland

in the Rain." They went back to the house where Billy washed Elvis' hair. After Billy left, Elvis' stepbrother Ricky Stanley delivered a packet of sleeping medication and Elvis and Ginger went to bed. A couple of hours later Elvis requested a second packet and Ricky obliged. Elvis, battling insomnia, lay in bed reading a book while Ginger slept. Different versions of the story mention different titles of the book he was reading. One version claims it was *The Scientific Search for the Face of Jesus*; another claims it was actually *Sex and Psychic Energy*. At about 8:30 A.M. Elvis requested a third dose of sleep medication and his aunt Delta Mae Biggs brought it to him. Ginger woke briefly around 9:00 A.M. and Elvis, still not asleep, went into the bathroom with his book. In response to Ginger's reminder not to fall asleep in the bathroom, his last words, according to her, were "Okay, I won't."

Around 1:30 P.M. Ginger woke up from her own pill-enhanced sleep and called her mother. Realizing that Elvis had not come back to bed, she got up and with no sense of alarm, showered and put on her make-up. At long last, she called out his name and when there was no answer she opened the door to find him face down on the thick red carpet. She called downstairs and summoned help. Al Strada was first upstairs followed by Joe Esposito. Soon the bathroom was filled with people. Elvis' father along with household staff and security personnel created a chaotic scene. Lisa Marie was trying to see what was going on but was led away by Ginger Alden. Joe Esposito summoned an ambulance and contacted Dr. Nick, Elvis' physician.

Fire station No. 29 at 2147 Elvis Presley Boulevard dispatched an ambulance driven by Charlie Crosby. With him was an emergency medical technician named

> "Without the friendship, camaraderie, and shared emotions of those who also admire [Elvis], I could not have borne the sorrow of losing him so unexpectedly, too soon.... Overwhelming sorrow over the loss of a loved one was compounded tenfold by the harsh and cruel press. It wasn't easy anymore to be an Elvis fan. The pain of loss plus the lies of the media and so many thoughtless, cruel and stupid comments from a variety of people have been a wicked combination these last 21 years.
>
> "To have been alone in my mourning would have been unendurable. I hope that everyone who deeply loved Elvis has had at least one person to commiserate with over the loss.... To be understood in one's grief is so important. I thank my many friends for this invaluable gift."
>
> —part of Diana Maguire's beautiful letter to fellow Elvis friends in the *We Remember Elvis* newsletter, January 30, 1999

John O'Hara

Ulysses S. Jones, Jr. They carried Elvis into the waiting ambulance and sped to Baptist Memorial Hospital. After futile attempts at resuscitation by the hospital Harvey Team of cardiac specialists, Dr. Nick, who was present, officially declared Elvis dead at 3:30 P.M.

The news of Elvis' death was announced by hospital administrator Maurice Elliot. Instantly people started to gather outside of Graceland. Thousands of people, on hearing the news, made spontaneous voyages to Memphis from wherever they were. Some people who had heard the news on their car radios didn't even bother to go home first. They just pointed their cars in the direction of Memphis and drove until they got there. Every flight arriving at Memphis International Airport was filled. The huge crowd of mourners, a blend of surprisingly different types of people of varying ages, was so dense that those who passed out in the intense heat could not fall down. The weeping and the wailing combined with the harrowing sounds of the helicopters overhead and the sirens of police cars and ambulances all merged with the Elvis music that poured out of every radio in the crowd.

Every flower available in Memphis was sold by noon Wednesday. Bouquets in the shape of guitars, musical notes, and lightning bolts flooded Graceland. Flowers had to be shipped in from other cities to meet the demand, making it the biggest day in FTD history. All over the world radio stations played Elvis' music and fielded phone calls from devastated and heartbroken fans. Record stores sold out of Elvis' records as they stocked each new batch.

After spending the night at the Memphis Funeral Home, the site of his mother Gladys's funeral, Elvis' body was brought back to Graceland. Elvis was dressed in a white suit that had been a gift from his father and his coffin was placed in the arch-

"Vernon and several of us were standing by as the casket lid was being lowered. Joe Esposito reached over and took the TCB ring off Elvis' finger and handed it to Vernon. Just before the lid closed I had an overwhelming urge to reach in and touch his forehead to say good-bye. It was simply an emotional response, knowing I would never see him again."

— Larry Geller,
Elvis' good friend

Fans from all over the world gathered at Graceland after after hearing the news of Elvis' death

Sandi Miller

way between the music room and the living room.

After friends and family had paid their respects, Vernon, aware of the fans' immense grief and in acknowledgment of their importance to his son, decided to give them the opportunity to view the body. The mourners, many of whom had spent the sweltering day and a half with little food or water, lined up at the gate to make the journey up the hill to the house. After being searched twice for hidden cameras, each person was allowed to swiftly pass the copper casket, which had been moved to the foyer just inside the door. Upon leaving the house many mourners "looked like they had been punched in the stomach," to quote journalist Bob Greene. As the gates of Graceland were closed, the screams of those who realized they would never see Elvis again filled that awful summer night.

Roughly 200 people attended the funeral service that began with "Danny Boy" played on the organ. Television evangelist Rex Humbard, comedian Jackie Kahane, and Reverend C. W. Bradley all eulogized Elvis. Some of Elvis' favorite singers and gospel performers—J. D. Sumner and the Stamps, Jake Hess and the Statesmen, and Kathy Westmoreland—filled the air with the music that Elvis loved best.

The three-and-a-half-mile route between Graceland and the cemetery was lined with more than 20,000 people. The column of cars was led by a silver Cadillac followed by a police motorcycle escort, the white hearse, and then 17 white limos. Vernon and Priscilla rode in limo number one, Ginger Alden and her family in limo number 5, and Linda Thompson in limo number 16.

"God bless you Elvis. Wherever you are, I hope you, Momma, Daddy, and Jesse are singing a quiet spiritual with the rest of that great choir. I will be thinking of you today, playing your music in my car and at home as so many of your fans will be doing. Thanks for the memories, the laughs, the tears. But most of all, thanks for being the artist that you were and still are to me and thanks for the music. You will *always* be The King!"
—Ben Milano, reflecting on Elvis on the anniversary of his death

John O'Hara

Elvis was buried in Forest Hill Cemetery in a 9-by-27-foot gray marble crypt. In a kind gesture to Elvis' fans, Vernon decided to allow them to take the floral arrangements that were left at the cemetery. By noon the next day 50,000 people had visited the grave to collect the cherished mementos. In the month after Elvis was entombed more than a million people visited the cemetery. Among them were four people who were arrested for attempting to steal the body. They claimed that they only wanted to see if his body was actually there and the judge believed them. The charges were dismissed in October. Later that month in response to such incidents, Elvis and his mother were exhumed and reburied in the Meditation Garden at Graceland. There is a rumor among some fans that instead of being buried beneath his grave marker, Elvis actually lies buried closer to his mother beneath the statue of Jesus inscribed with the Presley name.

For a while the most pervasive and peculiar rumor concerning Elvis' death was that it never happened at all. Perhaps because of some fans' refusal to accept the reality of his passing, the notion that Elvis faked his demise and is now living in seclusion gained a foothold in an extremely small segment of the fan community. Author Gail Brewer-Giorgio contributed to the controversy with her book *Is Elvis Alive?* Her exposé found many interested readers and sold more than a million copies, fueling the rash of Elvis "sightings" that continue to this day only as a very tired joke.

For many fans the death of Elvis was a personal tragedy of massive proportions as painful as the loss of a friend or family member. Every year in August tens of thousands of people gather in Memphis for a week of commemorative festivities that culminates in a candlelit

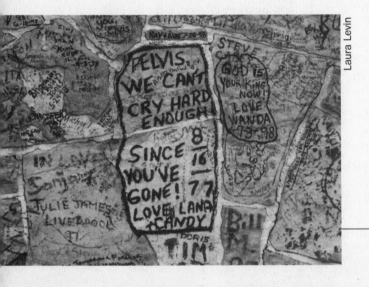

Laura Levin

Graffitti from the Wall of Love, at Graceland

Some of the millions of fans who've filed past Elvis's grave in the Meditation Garden, at Graceland

John O'Hara

visit to Elvis' final resting place on the anniversary of the eve of his death. To be in Memphis in August, among the Elvis fans outside the gates of Graceland waiting to pay their respects to Elvis, in many ways re-creates the emotion of that awful August day in 1977. The difference now is that the atmosphere is not that of a sudden tragic loss; instead it's more of a collective expression of love and appreciation for the man and the legacy of music, compassion, and fun that he left for us.

We often don't know what we have until it's gone. Sadly, it wasn't until his death that the world could fully appreciate Elvis and his impact on so many people's lives. Our culture's continuing fascination with him only seems to increase with each year that passes from that terrible date in August. It proves what his fans always instinctively knew: when Elvis died we knew that it was the end of something unique and special because there will never be anyone like him again.

ESSENTIAL ELVISOLOGY

Elvis' Grave Inscription, by Vernon Presley

Elvis' father was called upon to do one of the hardest things in this life: to bury his child. He wrote a beautiful tribute to Elvis, a portion of which is quoted below. It marks the grave at Graceland where Elvis is buried.

He was a precious gift from God
We cherished and loved dearly

He had a God-given talent that he shared
With the world, and without a doubt;
Capturing the hearts of young and old alike

He was admired not only as an entertainer,
But as the great humanitarian that he was:

"All along the six-mile route to the cemetery, we could see people lined two and three deep on either side of the road. Many people were crying, some looked stunned; others sad; and others showed quiet reverence. Law enforcement officers saluted as Elvis passed. People from all walks of life were there to pay their last respects."

—Ed Parker,
from *Inside Elvis*

For his generosity, and his kind feelings
For his fellow man

God saw that he needed some rest and
Called him home to be with Him

We miss you, Son and Daddy, I thank God
That he gave us you as our son.

President Carter's Statement
August 17, 1977

"Elvis Presley's death deprives our country of a part of itself. He was unique; and irreplaceable. More than twenty years ago he burst upon the scene with an impact that was unprecedented and will probably never be equaled. His music and his personality, fusing the styles of white country and black rhythm and blues, permanently changed the face of American popular culture. His following was immense and he was a symbol to people the world over, of the vitality, rebelliousness, and good humor of his country."

The Funeral Motorcade

1 silver Cadillac: The first car of the procession
12 police motorcycle escorts
1 white Cadillac hearse: License # 1-cf653; it was driven by Trent Webb.
17 white Cadillac limos
49 other cars

Autopsy Physicians

Dr. E. Eric Muirhead
Dr. Noel Florendo
Dr. Harold Sexton
Dr. Thomas Chesney
Dr. George Bale

Dr. Raul Lamin
Dr. James Holbert
Dr. J. A. Pitcock
Dr. Roger Haggit
Dr. Jerry Francisco

The Pallbearers

Charlie Hodge
Joe Esposito
Billy Smith
Gene Smith
Jerry Schilling

George Klein
Dr. George Nichopoulos
Lamar Fike
Felton Jarvis

The Casket
Nine-hundred-pound copper casket made by National Casket Company of Oklahoma City

The Burial Vault
Made by the Wilburt Vault Company of Memphis

The Grave Marker
The bronze ledger on the grave was made by the James H. Matthews Company of Pittsburgh.

The Funeral Director
Bob Kendall

Elvis' Burial Outfit
Elvis was buried in a white suit, a light blue shirt, and a white tie.

Songs Sung at Elvis' Funeral
Jake Hess and the Statesmen
"Known Only to Him"

James Blackwood
"How Great Thou Art"

The Stamps
"Sweet Sweet Spirit"
"His Hand in Mine"

Bill Baize
"When It's My Turn"

Kathy Westmoreland
"My Heavenly Father Watches Over Me"

The Suspected "Grave Robbers"
Ronnie Lee Adkins, Bruce Eugene Nelson, Raymond Martin Green, Gary Oscar Travis

"I can guarantee you one thing, we will never agree on anything as we agreed on Elvis."
—Lester Bangs, music critic in his obituary on Elvis

"Hello Elvis Friends, Twenty-one years ago on August 17th in the morning, I heard the terrible news on the radio that Elvis had died on August 16th of a heart attack. At first the words did not get through to me, but then after they played 'Heartbreak Hotel,' they repeated the words. At that moment, I really lost a part of my youth. Although I'd never seen Elvis on stage, or met him in person, it felt like I was losing a friend or a relative. And I felt so sad that I never had been to the States to see an Elvis concert. If there is a heaven I surely believe that Elvis is there."
—Norbert, from Belgium

The *National Enquirer* Cover Photo
The photo of Elvis in his coffin that ran on the front page of the September 7, 1977, *National Enquirer* was reportedly shot by one of Elvis' cousins, Bobby Mann.

YOUR ELVIS EDUCATION

Books
When Elvis Died: Media Overload & the Origins of the Elvis Cult
   Neal and Janice Gregory
True Disbelievers: The Elvis Contagion
   R. Serge Denisoff and George Plasketes
The King Is Dead
   Robert Kendall
   (Available through Katco Literary
   Group, 30185 Stetson Drive,
   Coarsegold, CA 93614.
   Fax: (559) 645-4002)
The Death of Elvis: What Really Happened
   Charles C. Thompson II and James P. Cole
Down at the End of Lonely Street: The Life and Death of Elvis Presley
   Pat Broeske and Peter Harry Brown
Elvis: The Final Years
   Jerry Hopkins
Elvis after Elvis: The Posthumous Career of a Living Legend
   Gilbert B. Rodman
Elvis: The Inventory of the Estate of Elvis A. Presley
   edited by Richard Singer
Images of Elvis Presley in American Culture 1977 to 1997
   George Plasketes
Dead Elvis: A Chronicle of a Cultural Obsession
   Greil Marcus
The Elvis Conspiracy?
   Dick Grob
Elvis through My Eyes
   Bill E. Burk

"I was playing my Elvis Ten on a little tape recorder I had. Number One was playing, 'For the Millionth and Last Time,' when my dad came in, tears and all, 'I'm sorry but I have some bad news. Elvis is dead.' Unlike many people, I did not doubt for a minute what I had just heard. I picked up my shoe and threw it at my dad. He came over and hugged me and we both wept openly."
   —Julian Grant, Scottish fan, of the Memphis Mafia Fan Club in Edinburgh

Elvis after Life: Unusual Psychic Experiences Surrounding the Death of a Superstar
    Raymond A. Moody, Jr., M.D.

Video
20/20, ABC news magazine, "The Elvis Cover-Up"
    September 13, 1979
The Elvis Files
    Media Home Entertainment (1990)
Have You Heard the News?
    Documentary made by OEPFC about the media's response to Elvis' death.
E! True Hollywood Story: "The Last Days of Elvis"

> "We at Graceland try to keep Elvis Week an upbeat celebration of Elvis's life culminating in one solemn event, the candlelight vigil at the grave site."
> —Todd Anderson, Graceland spokesman

Web Sites
http://www.gomemphis.com/elvis/
    elvis.html
    The *Commercial Appeal* Elvis archive.
http://www.stevecox.com/elvis/
    Wreath-1.html
Elvis' funeral wreath from a private collection.

http://moranandcompany.simplenet.com/elvispage.html
    Mickey Moran's site—for people who believe Elvis is alive. He also hosts a web ring along the same lines.

THE ELVIS AND YOU EXPERIENCE

Remember the Anniversary of Elvis' Death and Reach Out
August 16 is a dark day for Elvis fans. Comfort a fellow fan in need of consolation. Invite people over to watch Elvis' movies and reminisce. Go on to one of the Elvis chat rooms or newsgroups and share your feelings.

Send Flowers to Graceland
Many individual fans and fan clubs have flowers delivered to Elvis' grave. Some of the floral arrangements are works of folk art incorporating photos of Elvis, poetry, or objects such as teddy bears or flags. You can also request that your bouquet be placed in a specific area other than at the grave site. Graceland makes every attempt

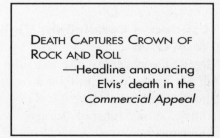

DEATH CAPTURES CROWN OF ROCK AND ROLL
    —Headline announcing Elvis' death in the *Commercial Appeal*

to accommodate these requests. For example, some fans ask that their floral arrangements be left near the piano in the racquetball building, the place where Elvis sang his last song. Send your bouquets to:

Graceland
3734 Elvis Presley Boulevard
Memphis, Tennessee 38116

Donate to Bouquets of Love from All Around the World

This international flower fund was established to send flowers to Elvis' grave every month on behalf of Elvis fans from all over the world. These two people collect donations for the fund:

Priscilla Parker
1215 Tennessee Avenue
Pittsburgh, Pennsylvania 15216-2511
or
Jane Anderson
2501 Captain Sawyer Drive
Shreveport, Louisiana 71104-2801

Place an "In Memoriam" in Your Local Newspaper

Remind your community of Elvis' legacy. Don't be afraid to express how much he is missed.

Conduct a Candlelight Vigil of Your Own

Even if you can't make it to the one in Memphis, you can light a candle at home and play your favorite Elvis music. Elvis' gospel songs set the right mood.

"I cried like a baby when Elvis died. But did he actually die or leave with the FBI or CIA? Did anyone see him in the coffin? Was that him? I wish I saw it myself. I wanted to go to Memphis but my family thought it was too much—too many people and too hard. I heard about it at 4:00 P.M. Chicago time and I cried and cried till 11:00 P.M. when my parents consoled me and put me in bed. I was 16 years old. I will always think of him. My home is filled with Elvis pictures. But I mourn for his loss and wish him to be alive. But his legend lives forever and in me as well as in you and you all."

—Tom, on an internet loop

Arrange to Have a Theme Casket

Patrick Fant, Elvis fan and entrepreneur, makes artistic caskets including one that is sort of Elvis related. One of his clients ordered a casket decorated as a parcel and stamped "Return to Sender," and he is planning on using the same idea for himself. Custom-designed caskets can be ordered from White Light in Dallas. You can reach them at (214) 373-2011 for more information.

Buy a Crypt at Forest Hill Cemetery

The crypt just across the hall from the mausoleum room where Elvis and Gladys Presley were entombed has been offered for sale; minimum bid $5,000.
Mrs. Hugh Smith
3170 Southern Avenue
Memphis, Tennessee 38111

"I have always felt Elvis was singing about his own life and Priscilla leaving in certain songs; I feel the power of his voice, and I believe his pain. I have told my family and my priest, if they are around at the time when I die, that 'You Gave Me a Mountain' is the one song I want sung *by Elvis* at my funeral."
—Elisa,
on the TLC mail loop

"I enjoy reliving all of my Elvis memories even though a few of them are painful. I have beautiful memories and even the painful ones are beautiful. It's been a while since I talked about his death and the months following. I remember Harold [Loyd, Graceland gatekeeper] slipping me up to the grave in the snow when he was not supposed to let anyone up because of the chance of accidents. It was late at night and there was a big snow on the ground. Harold said he would take me up but for me to walk in his footprints so there would be only one set. If you ever saw Harold you know he is a tall man with long legs. It was so funny, me trying to stay in his wide strides. It was so beautiful in the Meditation Garden at night, just me and him.
"I love looking back on my Elvis memories. They make the gospel song 'Precious Memories' have so much meaning."
—Linda, one of the original Memphis gate people

A LONELY LIFE ENDS ON ELVIS PRESLEY BOULEVARD
—Headline announcing Elvis' death in the Memphis *Press-Scimitar*

Imagine a world with no
Elvis
How bleak and how dim
without him

Imagine songs not sung
by Elvis
With no love, so grim
without him

But he is here
in our hearts and minds
and that's his legacy,
left behind,
We never will be
without him.
                    —by Mary McLaughlin

THE ELVIS FAN

Well over one billion Elvis Presley records have been purchased the world over. More people tuned in to Elvis' "Aloha from Hawaii" concert than watched the moon landing. More than 600 official Elvis Presley fan clubs exist—including some that were clandestinely formed in countries where it was forbidden, such as Pakistan and the former Soviet Union, and that figure continues to grow. Two separate surveys conducted in the U.S. (*48 Hours* television news magazine and CNN/*USA Today* Gallup poll) show similar results: roughly 45 percent of Americans consider themselves Elvis fans. It's estimated that as many as 60,000 mourners converged on Memphis immediately following Elvis' death and nearly one million people visited his original burial place during the following month. Tons upon tons of flowers were sent in remembrance of his passing. An estimated 750,000 visitors arrive at the doorsteps of Graceland every year. When the United States Post Office asked the citizenry to vote for their choice of Elvis stamp, more people—1.2 million— voted than in the presidential primary of that same year. As the twentieth century came to a close, poll after poll selected Elvis' as being one of the most popular and influential personalities of the

Elvis with a group of young fans
in 1957

From the collection of Bob Klein

past century. The editors of *Time* magazine selected Albert Einstein as man of the century. The readers of *Time* magazine, and Elvis fans everywhere however, overwhelmingly selected Elvis for this honor in an on-line vote the magazine conducted. It's indisputable: No other entertainer, living or dead, can match the numbers, longevity, or level of devotion

of Elvis' fandom. By any definition this is one of the most extensive fan populations of any one person in recent memory, probably ever. Elvis seems to have tapped into something primordial that exists in the hearts of people all over the world.

It's apparent by this time that the Elvis fan phenomenon transcends every boundary and distinction that separates people: culture, class, race, economics, age. While there are Elvis fans who exclusively prefer the raw, young Hillbilly Cat as well as those who primarily prefer the regal, jumpsuited Vegas uber-Elvis, the vast majority love him from beginning to end and, as is now amply obvious, beyond. There are fans who saw Elvis perform hundreds of times and ones who were born after his death (way more than most people realize—we bet there are considerably more teenagers who are fans of Elvis than of the Beatles). There are fans who are blinkered to Elvis' shortcomings and those who are bluntly honest about his faults. There are fans from the South like Elvis who understand exactly where he was coming from and those who don't even understand the words of his songs. A big surprise for many is the number of male Elvis fans. They also fall outside of the stereotype yet make up an impressive percentage of the fan population. Many fan club presidents and founders are men; and they are considerably more likely than women to have Elvis CD collections that are hundreds strong.

It doesn't seem to matter how widespread the fan phenomenon is because even with all this evidence, there is an irreconcilable chasm between the perception of an Elvis fan and the reality of who Elvis fans actually are. The stereotype of the

Sandi Miller

Elvis with fans on the set of *Charro!*

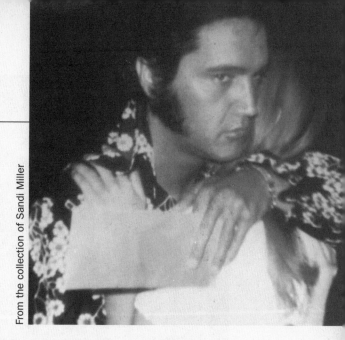

Elvis was warm and affectionate with his fans. Here he is with Sandi Miller

From the collection of Sandi Miller

eccentric Elvis fan makes for good copy but is simply inaccurate. A drive past Graceland's bus-staging area or a cursory perusal of an on-line Elvis newsgroup yields an unexpected array of humanity—the sort of diversity one would find in a group without a common interest. However, the common interest, and that's putting it mildly, is the powerful bond that connects this incredibly disparate collection of people. The media are the main offenders in characterizing the fans as 300-pound, big-haired, toothless, wide-eyed zealots with trailer park home addresses who share about one marble among them. Every year there are journalists who descend on Graceland to cover the festivities of Tribute Week with the sole purpose of singling out the looniest of the crowd to represent all the rest of the fans who are by and large normal, happy, fun folks who enjoy Elvis, his music, and each other. The feeling of being misunderstood creates a sense of community and cohesion among the fans that is one of the pillars on which the Elvis world stands.

In *E: Reflections on the Birth of the Elvis Faith*, John Strausbaugh refers to "the constant need to defend the King and themselves against all the detractors" as "one of the primary adhesives that give Elvis' dispersed and increasingly diverse following a sense of community." Fans have reason to feel somewhat defensive. They remember or have seen documentary footage of the scurrilous attacks on Elvis, his music, and his singing ability. And they have had to put up with relentless derision of themselves as fans.

Few people can forget the hatchet job that was done on Elvis by the media after his passing and in the years immediately following. The unashamed and very public grieving of his fans following his death may also have alienated those who did not comprehend the Elvis mystique. Now that Elvis' place in history is entirely secure, his reputation has shifted somewhat over the last decade. With his musical and cultural legacy better understood and appreciated, his image is starting to be rehabilitated and there's been a marked growth in his popularity. The fans

> "Elvis the rockabilly vies with Elvis the patriot and Elvis the philanthropist for fan favoritism."
> —Erika Doss, in
> *Elvis Culture:
> Fans, Faith & Image*

Sandi Miller

Sandi Miller

haven't fared quite as well and it's been frustrating for them as the media continues to portray them as marginal and obsessed.

There are some fundamental rifts among fans. One of the main ones is between those who appreciate or enjoy Elvis impersonators and those who *don't*. There are fans who actually participate in fan clubs for individual impersonators and those who don't have a moment's patience for the whole scene. The extremists in the fan community are generally looked down upon as reflecting badly on other fans. The people who only collect Elvis' music and don't go in for any other aspects of fandom are not even considered real fans by some others. The infighting over these sort of issues can get rather fractious, especially on the internet. There, cloaked behind an e-mail handle, fans of differing camps and persuasions at times grumble and snipe at each other. In person, though, Elvis fans are usually thrilled to find a compadre and the judgments tend to fall away.

Vis-à-vis the rest of the world, Elvis fans often find themselves bucking the snobbery against them. It seems strange that if someone were passionate about classical music or deeply into Coltrane

Elvis posing with fans backstage
in Las Vegas

Sandi Miller

they'd be considered highbrow or even intellectual. But admit that you adore Elvis Presley and watch out. Some people assume you believe he's still alive.

There are stories, thousands of them, that reveal Elvis' special relationship with his fans, not only through his music, but directly with them in person. It's impossible to name another star who has had as intensely close a relationship to his fans as Elvis. He was incredibly kind and patient about signing autographs and almost always stopped for at least a few minutes to speak to people who had been waiting to see him. He thanked and acknowledged his fans publicly on a regular basis with true sincerity. There's a sense that he cared for the people who gave him his popularity and their love—and even an impression that he identified more with them than the snobs he ran into in Hollywood. Especially early in his career, Elvis welcomed fans into his homes and offered a kind of access that is unheard of for stars of his caliber; for fans, this was one of his most endearing qualities. Elvis loved to help people and his fans were often the recipients of his largesse. When informed that some fans at the Graceland gates had spent all their money to come to see him and had nothing left to get home, Elvis was known to provide bus fare for their return trip. On very hot days while fans waited for him outside of one of his Los Angles homes, Elvis would call down to the gates on the intercom and offer everyone sodas. He took their orders and then came down and delivered the drinks himself.

In addition to the lucky few who were recipients of his kindness in person, Elvis connected very powerfully with his concert audiences on an emotional plane and certainly they reciprocated. Elvis fans feel an enormous gratitude toward him because they sense he really shared himself with them, really gave his all. But somehow the fans' constancy and unswerving loyalty is

"He was bigger than anything in terms of the emotions he caused. Kids didn't run around him as much as he got into us. I think every kid my age thought of Elvis Presley as a major part of their life."
—Chris Matthews, host of
CNBC's *Hardball*

Elvis with Sandi Miller

often turned against them: that they continue to love Elvis makes outsiders perceive them as bizarre. Several books try to make the case that many if not most Elvis fans see him as a sort of god. These claims are offensive to fans and, as usual, fans feel, miss the point of what they're about.

Elvis fans often feel compelled to visit the important places of his life, such as Memphis and Tupelo, to better understand and enjoy him. To grasp how unique this is, look at other adored music stars like Frank Sinatra and count the number of people running to make a pilgrimage to Hoboken, where he was born.

There are some fans who aren't wild about EPE and Graceland. Among the biggest complaints is the positioning of the Graceland brand on the same level as Elvis, as if the house by itself is on a par with its owner. Some fans feel that EPE tries to impose too many restrictions on clubs and newsletters (such as their approval). They find Graceland's litigiousness too extreme. And even though Elvis fans are reputed to be willing to buy anything, most people feel

Jimmy Digilio scattering the ashes of a good friend and fellow Elvis fan at Elvis' grave site

Graffitti on the Wall of Love, at Graceland

Laura Levin

that the marketing department isn't staying awake nights thinking of cool, special, or beautiful things to sell. Fans worry if EPE appeals to younger fans, about the future of Elvis' image in their hands, and if they're genuinely attempting to understand the fans and their concerns. Of course everyone acknowledges that without EPE we wouldn't have Graceland to visit.

As diverse as Elvis fans truly are, there are some constants among them. They generally accept, even embrace, the inexplicability of their love for Elvis. They give an absolute, unquestioning *yes* to the pleasures of Elvis. And there's a faithfulness in their attachment to him and his music. Elvis is generally not a hobby or pastime that one moves on from, it seems. If anything, the opposite is true; and for many fans the depth of involvement increases.

What kinds of people are Elvis fans? Why do they still care? Why do they spend a week's vacation in Memphis so they can visit his grave? How can they love him with undiminished emotion after all these years? How can some of them have absolutely no one other than Elvis in their music collections? No matter what it looks like to observers, Elvis brings beauty, meaning, maybe even grandeur to the lives of his fans. The power of his voice cheers, uplifts, invigorates, heals, turns on, and liberates. His looks have inspired countless fantasies. His faith leads some fans to find or renew their own.

"There is no in-depth interview with you. Early on you said you wanted to be Dino and you weren't being sarcastic. What are we to think.... We have your work. The movement from the exciting to the most mundane. A movement from polar opposites. You became exactly what we had all imagined you despised. But maybe you didn't. Maybe you wanted to be a crooner. You say you really wanted to 'act' and you became the Flying Nun. No wonder you wanted out.... You did have talent. That excitement. We know the effect you had on future singers and players. I ran out and bought a guitar after I saw you."

—from an essay by Lou Reed to Elvis, from *The King Is Dead*

How to explain all this? Here follows a list of some of Elvis fans' characteristics, motivations, actions, and beliefs. It goes a woefully short way to explaining who the people are who become and remain Elvis fans. Every fan, of course, fits into several categories. And with Elvis meaning so many different things to different people, there's a million more aspects that could be covered.

The Original Circa 1950s Fans

The first fans were there at the beginning of Elvis' career and most of them are now in their fifties. In those days a lot of young girls went very nearly wild (puberty and 1956 Elvis are a combustible combo) when they went to see him perform at the concerts in the '50s. They participated in what have been described as "orgiastic scrimmages" in their attempts to express the effect Elvis was having on them. It's been reported that the FBI checked with the Graceland Gates security whenever a runaway was reported. Desperation ran so high early on that two girls even mailed themselves to Graceland in a large package. These are fans who have been listening to the same Elvis albums for 40 years and have never tired of him or the music.

The Gate-People Fans

Throughout Elvis' career, wherever he lived gate people flocked to his homes in hope of just soaking in his environment, getting a glimpse of him or an autograph, befriending him, or more. Over the years the gate people did do all these things.

The Rebel Fans

People of all ages are attracted to Elvis' rebel image: the black leather, the motorcycles, the

John O'Hara

Memphian Beth Pease, one of the original gate people, at Graceland, January 1999

"If you're looking for trouble, you came to the right place" attitude. Elvis is the leader of this pack.

The "I Was Catapulted into Puberty by Elvis" Fans

Many people who were young teenagers in the 1950s claim to have been unceremoniously ushered into sexual awakening by Elvis' music and his performances on television and in movies. Both male and female. And, of course, we always remember our first … Elvis song.

"Long live Elvis Presley!"
—15 Elvis fans in Leipzig, East Germany, who were jailed for six months to 4½ years for their anti-regime slogan, November 2, 1959

The Still Young—And Not Just at Heart—Fans

Fans who are starting to get a little older often comment that having Elvis in their lives keeps them young. They kick up their heels at sock hops; they dress all in black like the "bad kids" in high school; some of these fans also dye their hair black to this day—not because they're frozen in time, but as a physical, visible allegiance to their rocker image.

The Concert-Years Fans

A lot of the fans who liked Elvis since the beginning of his career still liked him during the concert years in the 1970s. However, the Elvis style during that period—the patriotism, the decorative jumpsuits, the ballads—resonated with an expanded group of people. Many of these fans are amazingly knowledgeable about jumpsuit styles, concert dates, and song programs.

The Collector Fans

Some people just love to collect stuff. If they're Elvis fans too, they're in luck. There probably isn't a household product, article of clothing, or tchotchke that hasn't been reproduced with Elvis' image on it.

From the collection of Bob Klein

Sylvia Perera, fan from Sri Lanka

John O'Hara

The Follow-in-His-Footsteps Fans

Some fans choose to travel the same roads he did. They visit Elvis' birthplace, his homes, his relatives, his movie locations, his favorite restaurants, even his podiatrist in order to glean a deeper understanding of Elvis as a man.

The From-Outside-the-U.S. Fans

In spite of Elvis being the ultimate symbol of American culture, or more likely because of it, there are millions of Elvis fans all over the world. There is a whole segment of people who listen to Elvis' music without understanding the language he is singing in.

The More-Hip-than-Thou Fans

In advertising agencies, art studios, and college dorms, there is a new breed of fan who's drawn to Elvis because he was the embodiment of cool. He's a guilty or maybe even secret pleasure for them; and they're likely to look down on the Elvis of the 1960s and 1970s and even on traditional fans.

The Music Fans

Every Elvis fan loves Elvis' music, that's a given. Most enjoy hearing him sing anytime and use his music as their mood-altering method of choice. It seems some, especially Europeans, are quite vociferous about collecting, comparing, and opining. A good guess as to why this might be is that the releases outside the States aren't always the same-old, same-old "10 Greatest Hits" all the time.

The Music-Only Fans

Then there are the fans who whatever their preferences from rockabilly to ballads, love the music and admire Elvis as an artist but not for his other traits. They are often committed to the 1950s Elvis canon.

Sandi Miller

Laura Levin

Elvis signing one of the countless autographs he gave to his fans during his lifetime

The Nonpracticing Fans

These are casual Elvis fans who aren't involved in the scene; they're probably not even aware of the goings-on, much less the extent, of the fan community. They might have an Elvis postcard tucked into a mirror frame or one refrigerator magnet—but they do feel something special when an Elvis song comes on the radio.

The Closet Elvis Fans

Closet fans feel they have to hide their interest in or affection for Elvis. They're often school kids or white-collar professionals and think admitting to a passion for Elvis would not be seen as acceptable.

The "Elvis Saved My Life" Fans

Some fans tell of the time when they were ill, seriously depressed, or grieving and Elvis' voice and music helped carry them through. The presence of Elvis in their lives is consoling and nurturing. A few among them feel that in a way, Elvis watches over them.

The "I'm Gonna See Elvis in Heaven" Fans

Surveys show that a high percentage of people believe in an afterlife. The Elvis fans among these people are looking for-

Nothing can stop a devoted Elvis Fan from visiting Graceland

"I was born in 1961. By that time, according to popular (retrospective) opinion, and/or John Lennon, you decide which party you put your faith in, Elvis was already taking baby-steps on the road to being Crap.

"That's Crap with a capital C, that rhymes with P, and that stands for PRESLEY. Of course at the tender age of zero I had no opinion with regard to musically castrated rock and roll singers. It would be ten long years before I could finally come out of the closet, stand up and say to the world I AM AN ELVIS FAN. Six more years (of the intense record-buying kind, the kind that only the obsessed teenage gadget-loving male can truly sympathise with) before it all came to a head at 10 P.M. U.K. time, on the day that will forever be known around here as 'Black Tuesday.'

"And this is at the heart of my dilemma: how did a sixteen-year-old red-blooded male, living at the height of Punk Rock, (the only person in his class at school with a copy of the Sex Pistols *Never Mind the Bollocks* album) come to be crying himself to sleep that night, over the death of an obese, long-past-his-best, Las Vegas cabaret artist? Hell, am I a fan or a critic?

"I often wondered over the years, who had the hardest job: Elvis Presley, standing on a stage in Vegas for a regulation 50 minutes, thousands of screaming fans crying out for a piece of him while banks of spotlights shone down and picked him out like a character in a religious painting, and him, all the while in total denial of his vast drug intake, being paid sums of money most mortals will never have access to; or me, standing in a cold wet schoolyard on a winter morning, defending his honour to a bunch of acne-ridden kids, knowing one false word on my part could lead to a beating the likes of which were seldom seen outside of a boxing ring, before trotting off to the local record store to relieve myself of what little money I had, and at the same time inadvertently funding Mr. P's prescription drug habit.

"All I can say is that few things have genuinely changed my life: discovering girls—that's a biggie; buying my own house; getting married and having kids—hell, don't get me started on that one; and finally, discovering Elvis Presley. I've spent more money, more time, more effort and more sleepless nights, reading about, listening to, watching and daydreaming over that guy's voice/looks/talent/charisma/style/charm/laugh—well, you get the idea? Summing up me 'n' Elvis on one page? Forget it, you'd need more than a page, you'd need a lifetime—I should know, I've spent one and I'm no nearer to knowing the definitive answer to his appeal. And I hope I never find out, because if I do, I'm screwed. What will there be left for me to search for?"

—Richard Palmer, England

ward to being united with departed family and friends, and of course Elvis.

The Make-the-Pilgrimage Fans

A large segment of fans want more than anything to go to Graceland to see where Elvis lived and is buried—and many of them do. Fans from the far side of the globe plan their trips years in advance and many people scrimp for a long time to accomplish this. The subsets of this group are: the people who go every year, or even twice a year (for Elvis' birthday and during Tribute Week); the kind of fan who just wants to go once during a lifetime; and the tiny portion of fans who go way beyond making the Pilgrimage to Graceland and actually make a permanent move to Memphis to be there year-round.

> "Elvis' musical output in the late '60s is largely overlooked by the music industry and the media. The focus always seems to be on either the young rockin' pre-army Elvis or the declining Elvis of the late '70s. I've always favored the late '60s— Elvis looked his best and sang his best."
> —D. K. Deen, on alt.elvis.king

The Refuse-to-Make-the-Pilgrimage Fans

There's also a good segment of the fan community who refuse to go to Graceland. Some object very strongly to his home and grave being used as a profit generator and some don't want to be associated with the types of fans who go there.

The Taking-Care-of-Elvis Fans

For all the bravado and flash, Elvis was very vulnerable. Fans respond to this quality like a mother protecting her child. They let everyone know that he is still loved. These fans are the Hallelujah Chorus of the fan community.

The Rose-Colored-Glasses Brigade

For these fans Elvis can do no wrong. They may be aware of the negative things said about him but they don't want to hear about them or dwell on them. These people do not buy the Elvis exposé books.

The Burst-Everyone-Else's-Bubble Fans

These fans are a fascinating crowd. They love Elvis for various reasons, but they are brutally realistic about the man and they love to raz other fans for their devotion. The rose-colored-glasses brigade and the bursters are locked in a mortal struggle.

The "I Don't Drink, Smoke, Gamble, or Cuss Because of Elvis" Fans

There are those who say they have led better lives because of Elvis' example. These fans aren't exactly modeling themselves on Elvis' now-revealed reputation; they are responding to the impression of goodness and decency that he emanated while he was alive.

The Elvis Couple Fans

There are two types of Elvis couples: ones in which both are prior fans and meet through him, and ones where an Elvis fan brings the significant other into the fold.

> "It is sad that so many people hide the fact that they like Elvis. I have always been proud to be a Elvis fan and have been one for 43 years. I'm just as crazy today about him as I was the first day I ever heard of him. Where would we be musically today if it were not for Elvis? He gave us something of our own to identify with. We should all be proud to say 'I'm an Elvis fan.'"
>
> —Bev

The Impersonator Fans

The men who do an Elvis impersonation as an act or for a living are, most often, hard-core fans. Impersonators, to have a chance at being good, have to immerse themselves in Elvis and they do this because they love him.

The Elvis Is Still Alive Fans

During the 1980s, amid all the "sightings," some folks (perhaps through a strong desire for it to be true) started to believe that Elvis might still be alive. And coming back. This group accounts for a minuscule fraction of the fan community yet gets a disproportionate amount of the media attention.

The "I Didn't Realize I Was a Fan Until He Was Gone" Fans

These fans weren't paying too much attention to Elvis during the 1970s and were shocked to find how they felt when he died. The ones who are old enough are kicking themselves for not seeing him in concert when they *could have*.

The "I-Became-a-Fan-After-1977" Fans

This group only discovered Elvis well after he died. During the late '70s, '80s, and '90s Elvis acquired millions of these new fans.

The No-Jumpsuits-Please Fans

There are actually several web sites— good ones—based on this attitude and there are a lot of fans who are of this mind. Impersonators leave them cold because the singing, the looks, the routine, can never be good enough for these purists. Why would anyone listen to an Elvis impersonator when he can hear the real thing? And don't get this type of fan started about other Elvis fans who idolize impersonators or who wear jumpsuits themselves.

The Join-a-Fan-Club Fans

Along with the internet, fan clubs are the social hubs of Elvis fans. Club members make friends and participate in local meetings and events. They are very often charity minded and committed to continuing Elvis' legacy of charitable donations.

The Cyberspace Fans

Apart from the gazillions of sites about Elvis on the internet, there are several main gathering places where Elvis fans meet to talk about Elvis and issues in the Elvis world. (Refer to "Elvis in Cyberspace.") A lot of fans spend a good deal of time socializing and sharing their feelings about everything from BMG Elvis CD-release policies to the bloopers in his movies. An interesting group of cyberspace fans are the ones who spend a large percentage of their leisure time creating, updating, and maintaining their own Elvis web pages.

The Dang, He Was the Best-Looking Man Ever Fans

There is virtually no fan who doesn't think Elvis was handsome, but some initially *became* fans by their attraction to his looks.

Photo reprinted with permission

Elvis with fan and friend Carol Jacobs, backstage in Las Vegas

"Hello. My name is Bill and I'm a ... a ... Beatles fan. Wait, don't turn the page. It is possible to be both an Elvis fan and a Beatles fan and I am living proof of it. I mean, how can I choose one over the other when it comes to my listening time, not to mention my spending money? The truth is, I can't. The genius that is Elvis and the Beatles is not the genius taught in the classrooms of NYU or the Berkley School of Music. It is the genius forged in endless one-night stands on the country fair circuit throughout the South and in long ten-hour sets, night after night in a smoky Hamburg nightclub. It is taking all of the various musical influences that they were exposed to and not just aping them, but dissecting them, twisting them into something so unique that it becomes known as simply Elvis Music or Beatles Music. Pushing the limits so far that those who follow still are trying to reach them. Exhausting so much of your soul that you end up a sad, lonely man in a big mansion or break up, clawing at each other's throats with insults and lawsuits. But that's for another chapter, the one we don't like to read. So let's remember the good times when two amazing entities walked the earth. One, a hip-shaking king who taught the world to rock, and four moptop princes who taught the world that all you need is love. Hello. My name is Bill and I'm a Beatles and Elvis fan."

—Bill Dufour, fan from New Hampshire

The Trivia Expert Fans

A lot of fans have made something of an in-depth study of Elvis. These fans have a formidable knowledge of his life and it is to them that others turn for answers.

The Celebrity, World Leader, and Musician Fans

This list goes on forever and includes many notable and illustrious names. Sophia Loren, Woody Harrelson, William Forsythe, and Eddie Murphy have all made it known they are Elvis fans. Salman Rushdie cites Elvis as one of his major influences. Ernest Hemingway said Elvis was his favorite singer. Raisa Gorbachev, the King and Queen of Thailand, and according to some reports, even the Ayatollah Khomeini have all made their admiration public. Jerry Glanville, former Houston Oilers coach, left tickets at the box office for Elvis for every game long after he was gone.

As for musicians, it can be said that everyone who came after Elvis is either influenced or affected by him directly or by other musicians who were. He is mentioned over and over in interviews as the driving impetus that made musicians want to go into music. Bruce Springsteen says Elvis was one of his big-time

A young next-generation fan named Preslee

influences and closed many of his own concerts with "Can't Help Falling in Love" like Elvis did. He said that he felt like he was busting out of jail the first time he heard him. The Boss once even leapt over the wall at Graceland in hope of being able to meet the King.

John Lennon and Paul McCartney, Lou Reed, Trisha Yearwood, Engelbert Humperdinck, Chris Isaak, Barry White, Melissa Etheridge, Iggy Pop, Tom Jones, Jon Bon Jovi—all huge fans. Jim Morrison patterned himself after Elvis. Bob Dylan became a fan when he first heard Elvis and it made him feel that he knew "no one would ever be [his] boss." He later said, "Elvis recorded a song of mine that's the record I treasure the most." The liberating effect he had, not only on the population in general, but on artists everywhere, is undeniable.

The Next-Generation Fans

It may be assumed that very young fans are introduced to Elvis by adults in their family but this is not necessarily true. They might catch Elvis on TV and respond to him on their own. Each successive generation carries Elvis a little further into the future, ensuring that he and his fans are here to stay.

ESSENTIAL ELVISOLOGY

The King's Royal Connections

Here are a few of the real royals who had an audience with the King.

The King holds his own with European princesses as he greets them on the set of *GI Blues.*

King Bumiphol of Thailand
Queen Sirikit of Thailand
Princess Margretha of Denmark
Princess Astrid of Norway
Princess Margaretha of Sweden

The King's Presidential Connections

John F. Kennedy
Elvis was invited to President Kennedy's inauguration but did not attend.

Lyndon B. Johnson
Elvis met LBJ on the set of *Spinout*. Johnson invited E to his inauguration but he did not attend.

Nelson Rockefeller
Elvis met the former vice president June 21, 1967, at a recording session for *Speedway*.

Richard Milhouse Nixon
Elvis had a famous, spontaneous presidential summit with Nixon in 1970. Nixon also called Elvis with get-well wishes when Elvis was in the hospital. They forged a friendship of sorts.

Jimmy Carter
Elvis met then-Governor Carter in Atlanta on June 29, 1973, backstage at a concert in Atlanta. On June 13, 1977, Elvis called the White House to ask Carter to intervene on behalf of his friend George Klein who was in some legal trouble.

George Bush
Bush, then U.S. ambassador to the United Nations, was the keynote speaker at the Jaycees award presentation on January 16, 1971, when Elvis was voted one of the Ten Most Outstanding Young Men in America. Also, in his acceptance speech at the 1992 Republican convention, Bush mentioned Elvis twice.

William Jefferson Clinton
Nicknamed "Elvis" by the Secret Service. He mentioned Elvis shamelessly often during his campaign. He actually sang "Don't Be Cruel" on *Charlie Rose* and played "Heartbreak Hotel" on his sax on the *Arsenio Hall Show*.

The "Elvis Gang" Remembers Margie Woods, Georgia's #1 Elvis Fan

"Our dear friend Margie left this earth August 9, 1994, at the age of 47 just before Tribute Week, doing what she loved best—being in Memphis, to be with our 'Elvis Gang' and other friends and paying tribute to Elvis. We, and all who knew her, loved her dearly for the kind and caring person she was and will always be remembered as. Our gang included Margie, Jack Myers, Dennis Pledger, and Beverly Powers, though there are many more friends whose lives were also touched by her spirit. Although we had met during Elvis concerts and went to Memphis regularly several years before 1985, it was then that we formed our gang and became a group. Even though we lived in different areas of Georgia, we faithfully went to Memphis together at those special times of the year—except for Margie, who went a few days earlier to spend more time there, as she did in August of 1994. Over the years we became like a closely knit family and felt like sisters and brothers. We each took names from Elvis' movies: Jack was Jess Wade from Charro!; Dennis was Vince from Jailhouse Rock; Beverly was Lonnie Beale from Tickle Me; and Margie was Doc from Change of Habit. We all had special shirts made with our movie name and a picture of Elvis from that movie.

"In 1992 Margie inherited money and became a millionairess; boy, did she have a good time spending it and making up for lost time! She bought every kind of Elvis item she could find, including articles of his clothing and other valuable items at Elvis auctions. She traveled to places where Elvis had been, including Germany, Hawaii, and California, and often brought friends along to share the joy.

"Margie died suddenly in Memphis in 1994. She had made her wishes known about how she wanted things to be handled after her death: at her funeral, have only Elvis gospel music played, be dressed in her favorite Elvis dress, ride in a white hearse, and have her Elvis stand-up be at her side and buried with her. All of this was carried out. Margie was a fan for the same reasons most of us are fans, in addition to being a humanitarian like Elvis. She wanted most of her Elvis collection to be auctioned for charity and given to the Memphis charities she had chosen, which was also done. Our Elvis World is no longer the same without Margie here, nor is the rest of the world; it was a better place with her in it."

YOUR ELVIS EDUCATION

Books
Elvis
  text by Dave Marsh; art direction by Bea Feitler
Elvis, You're Unforgettable: Memoirs of a Fan
  Frances Keenan
Elvis People—The Cult of the King
  Ted Harrison
Elvis Culture: Fans, Faith & Image
  Erika Doss
True Disbelievers: The Elvis Contagion
  R. Serge Denisoff and George Plasketes
E: Reflections on the Birth of the Elvis Faith
  John Strausbaugh
Elvis Is Everywhere
  photographs by Rowland Scherman
Elvis Up Close, In the Words of Those Who Knew Him Best
  edited by Rose Clayton and Dick Heard
Dead Elvis: A Chronicle of a Cultural Obsession
  Greil Marcus
When Elvis Died: Media Overload & the Birth of the Elvis Cult
  Neal and Janice Gregory
Elvis after Elvis: The Posthumous Career of a Living Legend
  Gilbert B. Rodman
Hurry Home Elvis (Volumes One and Two)
  Donna Lewis
Dear Elvis: Graffiti from Graceland
  Daniel Wright
Letters to Elvis: Real Fan Letters Written by His Faithful Fans
  P. K. McLemore
Elvis: Portrait of the King
  Susan Doll

"Some of my favorite stories with Elvis are ones where he was interacting with the fans. There are a lot of celebrities in California but not ever has there been another person who would take the time with their fans the way Elvis did and on such a consistent basis. He was always very generous with his time! If he could not stop and visit, he took the time to explain why and usually apologized on top of it. He got to know a lot of the fans personally; remembered their names and general information that he could *and would* recall months later. This always amazed me since half the time I can't remember what I walked into the next room for! If someone who was a regular didn't come around for a while, he'd ask about them. I wonder sometimes if there wasn't a certain comfort in familiar faces for him. Also, if it was a group of fans he knew, he'd really cut loose and get goofy ... if there were a lot of new faces, he'd be more reserved but the little mischievous devil in his eyes never completely left his expression."

—Sandi Miller

To Elvis with Love
  Lena Canada
Return to Sender: A Collection of Poems for Elvis Presley
  various authors
Le King et Moi
  Pierre Efratas

Video
CBS News *48 Hours*, "Crazy about Elvis,"
  August 12, 1992
The Woman Who Loved Elvis
  TV Movie starring Roseanne Arnold
Eat the Peach (1986)
  Columbia Pictures
Out of the Blue (1980)
  directed by Dennis Hopper
Elvis Presley's America
Riding with the King
Ten Thousand Points of Light
Why Elvis?
Elvis: He Touched Their Lives (1980)
  Documentary by OEPFC
Mondo Elvis (1990)
Disciples of Rock
Mystery Train

"We all know that as far as their-graceland is concerned Elvis died in 1973. Graceland has always hidden him from the world and since the early '80s set out to hide the real Elvis. Is that love? We all know what Elvis said don't criticize what you don't understand, son, you never walked in that man's shoes. I have tried to understand Graceland, Lisa, Priscilla. But I can't."

—Memphis fan

"I don't know about you, but I think he sure had nice buns even at his heaviest."

—Becky, on the internet

Web Sites
http://www.geocities.com/~arpt/
  elvex.html
  Lex Raaphorst's ELVEX Site
http://jordanselvisworld.simplenet.
  com/index.html
  Jordan's Elvis World and the world's
  largest Elvis music library
http://www.noord.bart.nl/~kaauw/
  import20.html
  Dutch import site
http://www.noord.bart.nl/~kaauw/
  index2.html
  Willem's Kaauw's For CD Fans Only

http://www.geocities.com/~arpt/
  ieteng/216inl.html
  Ger Rijff's It's Elvis Time, jumpsuit-
  free zone
http://www.kolumbus.fi.samini/
  Sami's Finnish web site
http://www.uio.no/~ovene/
  Oven Egeland's Elvis Is Still Active
  In Norway site
http://www.perso.wanadoo.fr/ch.
  jouanne/index.htm
  Elvis en Bourgogne/in Burgundy
  Christophe Jouane's site

http://members.tripod.com/~Crazy_
    Canuck/elvisworld.html
    Elvis World
http://www.biwa.ne.jp/~presley/
    Haruo Hirose's Elvis World of Japan
http://www.elvis.com.au/
    Elvis Information Network
http://www.geocities.com/SunsetStrip/
    8200/events.html
    Site listing upcoming Elvis events
http://www.fansites.com/elvis_
    presley.html
    ElvisPresley@Fansites.com links
    page
http://www.metronet.com/~elvis/
    personal/trivia.html
    Elvis Trivia Contest
http://www.fansites.com
    Listings of fan sites
http://www.geocities.com/Nashville/
    8575/
    Elvis central; Dana's Elvis site
http://expage.com/page/elvisletters
    Irish couple's web site showing the
    letters they received from Elvis.
http://www.komet.teuto.de
    German Elvis Pages has, among
    other things, a posting page where
    fans can post questions and mes-
    sages to other fans.
http://elvis.htmlplanet.com
    Yuri Nikulin's site
http://www.home.wxs.nl/~hruyter
    de Ruyter's Elvis home page
http://ourworld.compuserve.com/
    homepages/elvis/
    Bringin' It Back—The Elvis Presley
    E-zine
http://www.dsr.kvl.dk/~jakobpo/
    index.html

Jakob Ottesen's On a Surfin' Safari
    with Elvis Presley
http://community.webtv.net/Elvis
    3577/ElvisLives
    Personal fan site
http://www.thekingsrealm.com/
    Brian Harnish's the King's Realm
    site
http://www.geocities.com/Hollywood/
    Location/9763/elvislady.html
    Marianne's tribute to Elvis
http://members.xoom.com/teenytg/
    Teresa's Safe Haven for Elvis
http://victorian.fortunecity.com/
    barchester/524/index.htm
    Personal site
http://www.elvissightings.com
    Elvis Ain't Dead site
http://members.aol.com/kyepfan/
    index.htm
    John's It's only Elvis page
http://www.geocities.com/Hollywood/
    Hills/8915/elvis.html
    Don's Elvis Presley page
http://www.geocities.com/
    ~elviscentral
    Dana's Elvis site
http://elvisnews.com
    Excellent Elvis News and info site
http://www.angelfire.com/ar/tcb4ep/
    main.html
    Timmy and Brandon's trading page
http://www.aha.ru/~hse/
    Russian fan site
http://home.sol.no/~tlidsoe/
    Tormod's Elvis pages
http://www.netcom.ca/~sumner/elvis.
    html
    Paul's Elvis page

http://www.inos.com/users/pebbles/
Becky's home page

http://www.westword.com/extra/elvis/
index.html
Elvis: The Postmortem Scrapbook

http://cnn.com/SHOWBIZ/9708/elvis/
index.html
CNN Viva Elvis! site

http://welcome.to/tigerman-elvis
Tigerman Elvis

http://www.apachelvis.simplenet.com/
Pete Smith's Apache Elvis site

http://www.elvismovie.com/
Stephanie Beck's "Elvis Movie" site

http://www.house.gov/writerep/
Write-to-your-congressperson site
about any Elvis-related concerns or
requests you have.

http://www.gomemphis.com
The *Commercial Appeal* newspaper,
great photo archives

http://members.aol.com/just4elvis/
circle.htm
Circle of Memories Annual Elvis
Weekend hosted by Elvis friends
Hollywood Fan Club site

THE ELVIS AND YOU EXPERIENCE

Subscribe to Fan Publications

There are some great magazines and publications, as well as fan club and even online newsletters that are outstanding. You can subscribe to them to get updates on news about Elvis music releases, activities, new books, stuff for sale, all sorts of information that is of interest to Elvis fans. We've included a few here that we think people would enjoy. Please contact them directly for subscription information and prices. The newsletters are associated with individual fan clubs and are a benefit of membership.

Elvis International Forum

Elvis International Forum, or EIF, is the official magazine of the Elvis fan community. This quarterly has glossy, beautiful photos and stories about Elvis.

P.O. Box 3373

Thousand Oaks, California 91359

(818) 991-3892

Fax: (818) 991-3894

http://www.mwnet.com/EIFmagazine

From the collection of Bob Klein

Elvis World
Bill Burk's Elvis World can always be counted on for interesting, accurate, and up-to-date info that the fans want to know.
Burk Enterprises
Box 16792
Memphis, Tennessee 38186-0792
(901) 327-1128
Fax: (901) 323-1528
E-mail: beb7@juno.com

Elvis, The Man and His Music
The publication of choice among hard-core, long-time fans and music collectors.
Now Dig This
19 South Hill Road
Bensham, Gateshead
Tyne and Wear NE8 2XZ United Kingdom

Elvis News Digest
Mitchell Enterprises
721 North 17 Street
Frederick, Oklahoma 73542

Elvis Only Newsletter
P.O. Box 15650
Boston, Massachusetts 02215
(800) 349-5484
E-mail: elvisp@tiac.net

Essential Elvis Fan Club Newsletter (UK)
P.O. Box 4176
Worthing BN14 9DW, England
E-mail: elvisfanclub@compuserve.com
http://ourworld.compuserve.com/
homepages/elvisfanclub/

Memphis Mafia, Edinburgh Fan Club
Magazine
Official Elvis Presley Fan Club,
Edinburgh Branch

> "None of us wear jumpsuits or any other strange attire—we're all normal folks who just have an appreciation of the King and his music and want to enjoy it in the company of other fans. Over the years there have been at least a dozen marriages and countless young Elvises as a result of fan club events. We've always objected strongly to Elvis and his fans being portrayed in a negative light and we'll do anything we can to ensure that it doesn't happen. It's easy to make a fool of the King and his fans, who tend to fall for any press story, invented or otherwise. We see it as our job to promote Elvis' name, his music to all sections of the press and broadcast media—that's why our club principle is 'Keeping Elvis Number One.'
> —Memphis Mafia Club, Edinburgh Branch of OEPFC

> "The fans claimed Elvis, and he was theirs."
> —Priscilla Beaulieu Presley, in *Memphis* magazine, July/August 1998

P.O. Box 710
NWDO Edinburgh, EH4 Scotland
E-mail: memphis.mafia@dial.pipex.com
httpp://dialspace.dial.pipex.com

Jailhouse Rockers of California Fan Club
P.O. Box 16423
Irvine, California 92623
Fax: (714) 505-6758
E-mail: sanjeans@ptw.com

Elvis Unlimited (in English) Danish Fan
Club
Tranevej 10
Stevnstrup
DK-8870 Langaa, Denmark
E-mail: elvis@post7.tele.dk
http://home7.inet.tele.dk/elvis/index.htm
or
Records and Books
P.O. Box 2042
8900 Randers, Denmark

Flaming Star (in Norwegian), Norwegian
Fan Club
P.O. Box 38 Lambertseter
N-1101 Oslo, Norway

It's Elvis Time (in Dutch), Dutch Fan Club
They have some plans to do an English-
language newsletter if there is enough
demand. It would be worth encouraging
them to do this.
Postbus 27015
3003 LA Rotterdam, Holland

Memphis Flash
P.O. Box 1548
N-2401 Elverum, Norway
(47) 62-42-56-23
Fax: (47) 62-42-56-24

"I am from Russia, and I first *met* Elvis in 1989 when I was 4 years old, while the Soviet Union was still active. I saw his picture on the door to my sister's room. I liked the man from the first look, I think that it was a photo from the '60s. And only a year after I first heard Elvis. My sister was doing her homework and I've heard that she was playing the song 'I Don't Care if the Sun Don't Shine' which was a real revolution to me. I don't know where did she get these tapes from but I've listened to them lots of times until I began collecting Elvis. The King is surely the best thing that has ever happened to the music history. Even now, 22 years after his death, he is still loved by millions, and he surely always will."
—Yuri Nikulin

"I get angry at those who speak out against Elvis for they have not taken the time to know the talent, or how he changed the music world, or to learn about the giant of a MAN inside that jumpsuit. He has left us a legacy to treasure."
—Bev Caldwell

"The Father, Son, and Holy Ghost picked me up at the West End. I got into the back seat beside Andy Kane, the patriarch of the Fan Club in Scotland. No compromise on Elvis with Andy and I didn't know how he'd take the man dying. Gerry in front was the boy of the group. He'd not come through the hard times of the '60s but he knew his stuff, he was a smart Elvis fan in a world not overflowing with them and he was the future. Robert, driving, was the Scottish Sean Shaver: cool, poised and, in my little Elvis world, a legend. He'd not only seen Elvis in Vegas, he'd met him, with the pictures to prove it.

"This had been arranged for weeks, since before the 16th. 'You've never seen it before Ian?' How could I have? I was only 10 when NBC was new, and I'd been so excited about going to see it—and now no more Elvis. I felt privileged—well, normally I would—but now?

"None of us knew, how would Andy, who had lost everything, take it? The silence was broken twice on the way to Newcastle. 'You're really going to enjoy this Ian' and then finally, 'You know, they've froze Walt Disney's body.'

"The four of us have never been together again and we may well never be but I love them now as much as I did 22 years ago. Andy Kane, Gerry McLafferty and Robert Maxwell are what being an Elvis fan is about. I feel like digging up my mother and saying 'See, I never did grow out of Elvis.' But she was cremated."

—Ian Mackay, Scotland via New Jersey

http://www.memphisflash.com
E-mail: frniels@online.no

Elvis Monthly
Glenda Pickering
27 Abbott Street
Heanor, Derbyshire DE75 7QD England

Elvis Now
Excellent newsletter from a relatively small club. It's not high-gloss, but it has great writing and editorials, and a very cool attitude.
Megan Murphy
34 West 29 Street
Bayonne, New Jersey 07002

We Remember Elvis Fan Club Newlsetter
Priscilla Parker

"He still is the King no matter what. I get so tired of people making jokes about him. Elvis Presley was a human like anyone else."
—Fan, on the internet

"With the Elvis fan, quite the reverse [from the usual] would seem to be true. To paraphrase JFK, they 'ask not what Elvis can do for them, but what they can do for Elvis.'"
—Mick Farren, from *The Hitchhiker's Guide to Elvis*

> "Every time I felt low, I just put on an Elvis record and I'd feel great, beautiful."
>
> —Paul McCartney

> "I've been an Elvis fan for as long as I can remember. When I was 2½ years old, it was the summer of 1977, and I heard all of these people talking on TV. I didn't know who they were reporting on, so I asked my mom, 'Why are they talking?' She said 'Elvis Presley has passed away.' I knew that he was a singer, but that really got me interested in Elvis. I would have never imagined, years later, Elvis Presley would become part of my day-to-day activities as a fan club president. I am more than happy to be associated with Elvis and everything he did as a person and an entertainer. The influence he has on me is something that I would never trade. Elvis Presley was the world's biggest overnight success but he never forgot his roots or what made him a star. From his generosity to his pink Cadillac, there is and always will be only one Elvis."
>
> —Charle Reeves, president, Elvis Fans of Oklahoma

1215 Tennessee Avenue
Pittsburgh, Pennsylvania 15216-2511
http://ourworld.compuserve.com/home-pages/elvis/we.htm

E. P. Continentals of Florida Fan Club
Sue Manuszak
P.O. Box 568082
Orlando, Florida 32856
Fax: (407) 889-0300
E-mail:manuszaksb@juno.com
http://www.jordanselvisworld.
    simplenet.com/Epcont/htm

That's the Way It Is Fan Club of Chicago
P.O. Box 189
Franklin Park, Illinois 60131

Blue Hawaiians Fan Club Newsletter
Sue Wiegert
P.O. Box 69834
Los Angeles, California 90069

Elvis Information Network Fan Club
They have an excellent web site that provides Elvis news over the internet. Go to their web site to sign up for regular updates.
E-mail: david@elvis.com.au
http://www.elvis.com.au/

ElvisNews.com
Independent weekly online news magazine
E-mail: editor@elvisnews.com
http://elvisnews.findhere.com/

Haruo Hirose's Elvis World Online News Page
http://www.biwa.ne.jp/~presley/elnews.htm

Seek Out Other Fans

Looking for an Elvis pen pal, friendship, or … more? Some fan club newsletters have a "Pen Pal

"Everyone remembers one of Elvis' most-quoted statements: 'The image is one thing, the human being is another.' I think this applies not only to Elvis, but to his fans as well. The books, TV programs, movies, etc., have dealt with the *image* of Elvis fans and not with Elvis fans as human beings. When I first got into the Elvis world in 1993, you might say I had a bit of an identity crisis—I didn't fit the image of an Elvis fan, and at that time, I didn't want to be associated with them! I bought into the image that all Elvis fans were basically trailer park trash. Male Elvis fans dyed their hair black, wore lots of jewelry and said, 'Thankya, thankyaverramuch.' Female Elvis fans were fat women in their fifties with overpermed hair and wore too much make-up. And of course, Elvis fans believed Elvis was alive and hiding out in Hawaii or Kalamazoo or wherever.

"I am a college graduate who grew up in the suburbs. I wasn't 'raised on Elvis,' though I do recall as a teenager thinking, after reading about yet another exploit in the newspaper, that Elvis was some sort of Southern-fried Superman because he was always doing things for other people, whether it was buying Cadillacs or breaking up fights or raising money for charity.

"I got into all of this after visiting Graceland in 1993 with a friend. My life has certainly taken a different turn since then! I've traveled to Memphis, Tupelo, Las Vegas, Palm Springs, L.A., and all over Texas (I've made friends with Elvis fans all over the world). I've written articles for several fan club newsletters and for *Elvis International* magazine. I've met and become friends with people who knew Elvis. Reading about Elvis' spiritual quest caused me to consider my own beliefs about God, and has brought me closer to God.

"Sometimes there does seem to be pressure not to delve too deeply or talk too much about Elvis' mistakes and faults, though. There are fans who seem to take a perverse interest in Elvis' weaknesses—they like to throw it in the faces of fans who they perceive are wearing rose-colored glasses. And there are fans who don't want to deal with Elvis' lifestyle and decline and prefer to blame everyone else (Colonel Parker, Priscilla, Memphis Mafia) for it. Every once in a while, I go through 'Elvis crises'— when I ask myself, 'How can I possibly be an Elvis fan, since I don't approve of his lifestyle?' But as distressing as those times are, I do think they remind me that no human being should be put on a pedestal and that I can learn from his mistakes. And I realize that I don't know what he went through, so maybe I shouldn't judge him too harshly."

—Donna Deen

"I was not quite fifteen years old when I first heard Elvis singing 'Mystery Train' on the radio that was on an open windowsill and I was instantly drawn to it. So much so, that even though I was riding on the back of my friend's bike, I jumped off and stumbled toward the radio trying to get to Elvis' voice. I had no earthly idea who he was or anything else about him. I became an instant fan from that day forward and here I am, 44 years later, still an Elvis-only fan."

—Margaret Freisinger, New Mexico

"I'm fifteen years old (soon) and come from Sweden, but I still understand what Elvis is saying and singing. How? It isn't the words that send the messages, it is the voice. And Elvis had that voice that could send hope and love to everybody, even those who don't understand English!"

—Linda G., on the internet

"Songs like 'It's Midnight,' 'You Gave Me a Mountain,' 'I Miss You,' told exactly how I felt. And hearing your voice and being able to appreciate it, even when I was in that much pain, showed me that I wasn't alone. You too had gone through this. I just wish that I could have been there for you as you had been there for me so many times before."

—letter from Beth Radtke to Elvis, in *Letters to Elvis*

"I'm from Barcelona, Spain. When Elvis died I was eight years old. One Sunday my parents and I were listening to the radio when Elvis began to sing 'In the Ghetto.' I thought *what a strong and deep voice....* I don't know why but I was moved by this song and my tears were falling. I didn't understand the lyrics but the power of Elvis' voice hooked me."

—Francesc Lopez

"My approach to Elvis evolved from a romanticized view to a more academic one several years ago. And when I took that step I began to resent the romantic image I always had of Elvis ... as if it was a lie, and actually diminished his standing as a man and an artist. I spend much of my time on the newsgroup attempting to destroy the 'image' and rediscover the 'artist' ... with mixed success to be certain."

—Dennis Rodgers, on alt.elvis.king

Wanted" section and Elvis International runs a long list of names and addresses of fans who are looking to correspond in every issue. The internet, if you have access, is chock full of people who want to get in touch and converse with other fans. A couple of sites are set up specifically with Elvis personals and pen pal listings. Visit:
http://elvis-is-still-the king.simplenet.com/
    Personals_Page/Personals.html

http://members.aol.com/Kingbee25/
    personals.html

Meet Other Fans Whenever Traveling

Make a point of contacting a fan club in the place where you are traveling to. You may be able to meet up with some fans during your vacations or business trips—it'll be like already having friends wherever you go. (See "Elvis Fan Clubs" for a list of clubs.)

Offer to Be a Host to a Traveling Elvis Fan

Many fans already do this. You can put a listing in your fan club newsletter saying that you'd be willing to host a fellow fan visiting your town. It's a great way to form friendships with people from all over.

Start a Letter-Writing Campaign to the Post Office

Request other Elvis stamps, reissues, phone cards, and more stamp-related products. Tell them issuing another Elvis stamp will be so lucrative that it will prevent stamp price hikes. Write to the address below or call them at (800) STAMP-24.
USPS Citizen's Stamp Advisory Committee
Room 5301
475 L'Enfant Plaza West, S.W.
Washington, D.C. 20260-2420

"Elvis knew love was to be spread around—he soaked it up from all around him and he gave it back in spades to everyone. If he'd never become famous and never made a million and never lived in a mansion, I believe Elvis would still have been a 'success' because he knew the importance and the power of *love* .... The profit, the spotlight, the power trip, that isn't part of *love*; let others take the short cut. We Elvis fans will always know the deepest success in life, because we had the best and most loving teacher in the world: Elvis and his heart. Amen!!!"
    —Sue Wiegert, president of the Blue Hawaiians Fan Club from Winter 1998 newsletter

"Elvis fans have this horrible sense of guilt like they are cheating on him if they even play another artist's music. Some might cheat on a spouse, but never on Elvis. I find this a little twisted."
    —Dutch fan

> "Elvis came along, the coolest, best looking thing I had ever seen, singing 'I Just Can't Help Believing.' ... I realized Elvis was not American after all, he was one of the genuinely few world citizens—bigger than America, free from its prejudices, appealing across age groups, nationalities, and languages. From this came Elvis friends, Elvis vacations, an Elvis lifestyle, and 100 percent Elvis music. Though I wouldn't be seen dead with some fans, others are friends for life when Elvis is all we have in common."
> —editorial from the Young and Beautiful Friends of Elvis New Jersey newsletter (now called Elvis Now)

Send a Letter to or E-Mail Graceland

We strongly urge fans to contact Graceland to tell them how you feel, what you would hope to see in the future from them, and your opinions and thoughts on anything related to Elvis. Graceland used to get ten thousand letters a week while Elvis was alive; now it's more like ten thousand a year. It's important for the fans to be heard.

Send Your Elvis Friends Free Postcards over the Internet

See "Elvis in Cyberspace" for a long list of sites that offer Elvis photo postcards for free; many have Elvis songs you can attach.

Create Your Own Motto to Live By

Elvis' motto was "Takin' Care of Business—in a Flash." His "TCB" was accompanied by a lightning bolt, representing the flash. It's copyrighted by Graceland, so think of your own and have it printed on a T-shirt. Let the world know the philosophy you live by.

Sponsor a Trip to Graceland for a Fellow Fan

If you can swing it, this is about the best gift you could give someone. Join them yourself for a special vacation together.

Get an Elvis Telephone

Graceland catalog carries a working telephone for purchase. What better way to gab with your Elvis friends.

Put an Elvis Message on Your Answering Machine

You have several choices if you'd like to have an Elvis message to greet your callers. You can obviously tape a song snippet from one of your CDs, tape a message in your best Elvis voice, or download something from the computer. Try: http://www.answeringmachine.co.uk

Buy or Make Your Own Elvis Stationery

There are Elvis cards and stationery for sale, but why not make your own? It can be as simple as photocopying your favorite Elvis photo onto a blank page— or as elaborate as your artistic talents will take you.

Be a Defender of Elvis

The best weapon against the negative image of Elvis, and his fans, is to contact the media with accurate information whenever you see them perpetuating a wrong.

Take Every Opportunity to Be a Proactive Fan

Call radio stations and the press around the time of Elvis' birthday and the anniversary of his death to offer your assistance with information for anything they might want to report on about Elvis.

Wear Elvis T-Shirts

Yeah, it may be corny, but it'll attract smiles, and even initiate conversation, with fellow fans. Be an Elvis goodwill ambassador, especially when you travel.

"… a week of Elvis, dancing, drinking, dancing, drinking, Elvising, drinking, Elvising and dancing and all of that stuff where you think you've gone to paradise."
—A fan describing the Mablethorpe, England, Elvis Week convention and party

"I buy his music and videos, I read books about him, and if he was alive and thought I was a nasty little s**t, then who gives a f**k? Just because I supported his career and helped pay for his lifestyle doesn't mean I have to watch my every step in case I might do something that would have offended him."
—Richard, on alt.elvis.king

"It was the opening lines of 'Heartbreak Hotel' that did it for me, back in 1977 as an eight-year-old. It was my first introduction to music with real energy.
"I never knew who he was when he was alive but since then he's become my life. I believe that Elvis Presley is alive in everyone who has ever seen him or heard his music."
—Fan, on the internet

"Elvis always provided me with something to look forward to and he kept me from boredom. His loyalty to me must be repaid with my everlasting loyalty to him."
—Rick, on the internet

Join an Elvis Fan Club or Start Your Own

See "Elvis Fan Clubs" for a list of clubs and tips on how to get your own off the ground.

Throw an Elvis Obscure-Music Party

This is the best way to expose your friends to Elvis music that they may not have heard before—the songs that are off the beaten path. *Everyone* knows the top ten so if you've got bootlegs, this is the time to share them. No one we know has listened to the laughing version of "Are You Lonesome Tonight?" and not been won over.

Help to Create the Next Generation of Elvis Fans

We'll leave this completely open to your interpretation.

Send Elvis Picture Postcards

Elvis postcards are available in most card shops, at Graceland, at fan conventions, and you can make your own with the make-a-postcard kits (stick postcard backing on photos).
MagTech
10850 Switzer #111
Dallas, Texas 75238
(800) 278-9458
Fax: (214) 340-4983
http://www.magtech.com
http://www.magtechmagnets.com

> "I tell you, if I could give up my life for Elvis Presley to be alive here today, I'd be dead and you'd be looking at him right now."
>
> —Paul MacLeod, owner of Graceland Too

> "That's my idol, Elvis Presley. If you went into my house, you'd see pictures all over of Elvis. He's just the greatest entertainer who ever lived. I think it's because he had so much presence. When Elvis Presley walked into a room, Elvis Presley was in the f—king room. I don't give a f—k who was in the room with him, Bogart, Marilyn Monroe."
>
> —Eddie Murphy

> "I am a huge fan, know all about his life, and love his music. However, I don't wear Elvis T-shirts, don't sport mutton-chop sideburns, haven't moved to Memphis or drive around in a pink Cadillac. In fact I sometimes wonder why the hell I have this unexplainable passion for Elvis, the man and his music. I don't know why, it's just there. I listen to Elvis, I watch him on stage, and I think, 'well, I get it'; those who don't like him just don't get it. Too bad for them."
>
> Paul Pollock

Use Elvis Expressions in Your Correspondence

You can express your Elvis fanship with a phrase at the close of your letters and e-mails. Here are some Elvis salutations fans use:

That special love that Elvis fans share is a celebration of the heart

Keeping Elvis #1

Love through Elvis

Elvis means the same in every language

Love 'n' Elvis

Elvis Heals

Taking it on the chin for Elvis

TCB in eternity

TCB4EAP

Always Elvis

Always for Elvis

With Burning Love

IWAN2BLVIS

(Very) soft spot for Elvis

EEEE L   VV I SSS

EE   L   VV I SSSS

EEEE LLLL V   I SSS

Sandi Miller

Blue Hawaii was first to hook
   me
All Shook Up really shook
   me
One Night with You made
   me dream
Burning Love made me steam
But then the man himself
   shone through
And made me realize,
Rock or Gospel, Soul or
   Country
His soul is in his eyes!!
           —By Kay
   on the TLC mail loop

Elvis signing autographs backstage in Las Vegas.

THE MUSIC

Elvis' post-death image has evolved in many unexpected, and sometimes strange, directions. Elvis has come to represent drastically different things: he's an icon of cool, a symbol of America, a tragic hero, a savior, a subject of tabloid ridicule, a mass-market commodity, a cultural catchphrase. The revolution he helped launch was so powerful—affecting sexual mores, race relations, and other aspects of our lives even to this day—that people tend to forget how the whole thing began. His universal fame and ubiquity as a pop icon sometimes tend to obscure the very thing that started it all: the music; the voice; the feeling. Before he was *Elvis, the King,* he was Elvis, a singer of songs.

Elvis grew up listening to the different styles of music that would eventually merge to form rock and roll. On the radio he listened to the country and bluegrass music of the Grand Ole Opry, while in church he was engulfed by the passion of gospel. When his budding talent was noticed by one of his teachers, he was persuaded to enter the Mississippi Alabama Fair children's talent contest. At ten years old he stood on a chair and sang Red Foley's "Old Shep." That feeling, of singing in front of a huge

Vintage RCA microphone used by Elvis at RCA Studios

Courtesy of Butterfield & Butterfield

This old and very rare photo shows the contestants of the Mississippi Alabama Fair children's talent contest; In spite of its poor condition you can see Elvis is second from right wearing eyeglasses

"I remember my childhood dreams. The intense longing for something to happen, for my life to be somehow different from all its predictable elements, its guarantee of what appeared to be a safe, boring future as a child growing up in Denmark. Riding to school on my bicycle through the snow at five-thirty in the morning I had plenty of time to dream. What I dreamed was that somehow I would get involved with Elvis Presley's music; that I would come to understand how, when, and why it was made; and that someday, finally, I might come to understand why it seemed to have a greater effect on the world than any other music I knew."

—Ernst Jorgensen

crowd for the first time and getting a response from them, may have been among Elvis' motivations when he established the goal of making music his life. On his next birthday his mother took him to the Tupelo Hardware Store and bought him a guitar. Elvis and that guitar became joined at the hip and it soon became a tangible statement to those around him of his nascent musical aspirations.

When Elvis was 13 his family moved from Tupelo to Memphis, a musical melting pot, where his education continued. He soaked up the many influences that permeated the air of that unique place and time. He listened to the radio stations that played "race music," the term used for rhythm and blues in those days, and he frequented the blues venues that were within walking distance of his home. He attended all-night gospel sings that showcased the up-tempo jubilee tradition of white gospel quartets and went to black churches to hear their flamboyant and uninhibited gospel style. He also modeled his vocal style on the pop ballad singers of the day like Bing Crosby, Dean Martin, and Eddy Arnold. He taught himself how to play the piano and was often heard crooning ballads in the laundry room of

The legendary Sun Studio in Memphis

John O'Hara

the housing complex where he lived. In his senior year he entered his high school's talent show and thoroughly impressed his schoolmates. The day after he graduated he hitchhiked to Meridian, Mississippi, and competed in the Jimmie Rodgers music contest where he took second place. His confidence was growing as well as his ambition.

On a Saturday in July of 1953 an 18-year-old Elvis, fresh out of high school and emboldened by his limited success in talent contests, walked into the small office of the Memphis Recording Service, paid his three dollars and ninety-eight cents plus tax, and recorded his voice for the first time. Accompanied by the rudimentary strumming of his guitar, he sang "My Happiness," a slow, sentimental ballad. On that day *The Voice* was first introduced to the medium that it would so radically change. The mysterious quality of Elvis' voice that seems to touch people universally existed, in its raw form, there in that first record. It was appropriate that Elvis chose "My Happiness" as his first song because singing truly was his happiness. On the flip side he recorded "That's When Your Heartaches Begin." Like so many other things in Elvis' life, even the titles of his first record were a paradox.

Elvis could have made his recording in any number of studios in the Memphis area but he chose the Memphis Recording Service because it was also the home to Sun Records, the label that musical visionary Sam Phillips had established to record the black R&B scene. Although Elvis lore claims he was making a record for his mother's birthday (which was many months away), Elvis was auditioning and he knew it. On that momentous day Marion Keisker, Sam's assistant, engaged the nervous young man in what has now become a legendary conversation. She asked him, "What kind of singer are you?" He replied, "I sing all kinds." His answer was prophetic; it was an accurate description of his future career. Although Elvis is most associated with rock and roll, he did in fact sing all kinds. Marion made a note to herself about the young man that read, "good ballad singer, hold."

"Before Elvis there was nothing."
—John Lennon

"And after him not much."
—Lex Raaphorst, Dutch fan

With no response to his "audition," Elvis returned to Sun for another shot almost six months later on January 4, 1954. He recorded "I'll Never Stand in Your Way" and "It Wouldn't Be the Same without You." Still no reaction from Phillips. Finally on June 26 Elvis got the call that every artist dreams of. At Marion's suggestion Sam called in Elvis to try him out with a ballad called "Without You." For whatever reason Elvis just couldn't nail it the way Sam wanted but Sam recognized in Elvis' voice that same indefinable magic that millions of people continue to hear today. Sam took Elvis on and hooked him up with Scotty Moore and Bill Black. It was a Sunday, the Fourth of July, when the three aspiring musicians all got together for the first time at Scotty's house. It was appropriate that the three of them should get together on Independence Day, a holiday that celebrates freedom and self-determination. That day Elvis, Scotty, and Bill—the rockabilly holy trinity—rehearsed a little on the eve of what would become the most important recording session of their lives and maybe even in twentieth-century music history.

Like many Memphis summertime days it was over 100 degrees on July 5, 1954, when Elvis, Scotty, and Bill started working with Sam in the tiny nonair-conditioned studio. The trio tried all afternoon but just couldn't seem to get anything that impressed Sam. While Scotty and Bill were taking a break, sipping cokes in the heat, Elvis launched into "That's All Right," an old blues song by Arthur "Big Boy" Crudup. According to Scotty Moore, "Elvis just started singing this song and acting the fool, and then Bill picked up his bass and he started acting the fool, too, and I started playing with

From the collection of Bob Klein

Elvis performing with a custom-made leather cover on his guitar them." When Sam heard them he asked what they were doing. Scotty said, "We don't know." "Well back up, try to find a place to start, and do it again," said Sam.

"That's All Right" became an instant megahit. The Blue Moon Boys, as the trio came to be called, eventually released nine other songs on the Sun label. Those songs, among them "Blue Moon of Kentucky," "Mystery Train," "Milk Cow Blues Boogie," "Good Rockin' Tonight," and "Baby Let's Play House," are the cornerstone on which a revolutionary new musical style would be built.

It was at this point that Elvis would meet the most significant, though ultimately detrimental, person to his career. Colonel Tom Parker was a country music promoter who was immensely proud of his talents as a con man and his past as a carny worker. He witnessed Elvis' ascent and instead of hearing music heard only one thing: Kaching! Like a bird of prey he set his sights on the young singer.

Elvis needed national exposure and Sam Phillips needed cash so Sam sold Elvis' contract to RCA on November 21, 1955, in a deal brokered by the Colonel. Elvis remained with RCA for the rest of his life. In his first sessions with his new label Elvis recorded his first number-one record, "Heartbreak Hotel," at RCA Studios in Nashville. A few weeks later at RCA Studios in New York he recorded "Blue Suede Shoes." He was a perfectionist in the studio, often recording 30 or more takes before he decided it felt right. His instinctive talent as a producer was as evident in these sessions as his talent as a singer. In between recording sessions for RCA Elvis made close to a dozen TV appearances that fueled his popularity and his records' continuing ascension up the charts. His TV appearances led to film roles and with the films came a new reason for recording: movie soundtracks. In his first few movies Elvis resisted having to sing, hoping instead to be taken seriously as an actor. But in the end he did as the Colonel dictated. Because some of his early movies tended to mimic Elvis' life as a rock and roll idol, some of the soundtracks are really no different from the material he was already singing. "Jailhouse Rock," "(You're So Square)

> "Nobody could sing the varied styles of Elvis."
>
> —Jerry Leiber

From the collection of Bob Klein

Baby I Don't Care," and "Teddy Bear" are all soundtrack songs and great Elvis music.

Elvis' musical career took an unexpected turn in 1958 when he was drafted into the army. During a two-week furlough in June of 1958 before he shipped out, Elvis recorded enough "product," as the Colonel referred to it, to keep Elvis fans happy until he finished his army stint. While Elvis was overseas, the Colonel took the two-year break as a chance to transform Elvis from a music star to primarily a movie star. The only recordings of Elvis in Germany are the home recordings of him at the piano singing the songs he loved, mostly gospel and ballads. These recordings capture an unguarded Elvis singing for the pure joy of it.

When Elvis got out of the army he wasted little time before he was back in the RCA Studios. The result of his efforts were *Elvis Is Back*, an artistic and commercial success that yielded such gems as "Such a Night," "Fever," "Like a Baby," and "Reconsider Baby."

Some people think of the next stage of Elvis' career as the Dark Ages of his music. In April of 1960 he recorded the soundtrack for *Blue Hawaii*. With the exception of his two gospel albums (see "Spirituality and Gospel" to learn more about these two amazing recordings), virtually the only music Elvis recorded until the end of the decade were movie soundtracks. John Lennon's famous statement that "Elvis died when he went into the army" was made as a result of this abrupt change in musical direction.

"It is often said that if Elvis had not come along to set off the changes in American music and American life that followed his triumph, someone very much like him would have done the job as well. But there is no reason to think this is true, either in strictly musical terms, or in any broader cultural sense. It is vital to remember that Elvis was the first young Southern white to sing rock and roll, something he copied from no one but made up on the spot; and to know that even though other singers would have come up with a white version of the new black music acceptable to teenage America, of all that did emerge in Elvis' wake, none sang as powerfully, or with more than a touch of magic."
—Greil Marcus, from *Mystery Train: Images of America in Rock 'n' Roll Music*

Two things conspired against the quality of Elvis' music at this time. One, the sheer volume of material needed to fill the soundtracks of three movies a year made finding consistently good songs difficult. And two, the Colonel insisted that songwriters enter into publishing deals that denied them full earnings from their songs. They were basically being asked for a kickback and the best songwriters in the business balked at such tactics. In spite of the Colonel's shortsightedness, some good stuff did manage to squeak through. "Return to Sender," "Viva Las Vegas," "Little Sister," "Bossa Nova Baby," and "King of the Whole Wide World" are all classic Elvis pop songs. But for every one of those there were many more, like "No Room to Rhumba in a Sports Car," "Song of the Shrimp," "Do the Clam," and "Slicin' Sand."

While Elvis was recording a long string of movie soundtracks, pop music was going through one of its most creative phases. The British invasion, led by the Beatles, was sweeping America. How far had Elvis' musical career gone off track? Consider the historic meeting between the Beatles and Elvis, their musical idol, that took place on August 27, 1965, at Elvis' house at Perugia Way in Bel Air. Elvis was said to be shy, almost indifferent, when he met the fab four. Could his reluctance

> "Rock and Roll smells phony and false. It is sung, played, and written for the most part by cretinous goons, and by means of its almost imbecilic reiteration, and sly, lewd, in plain fact, dirty lyrics, it manages to be the martial music of every sideburned delinquent on the face of the Earth. It is the most brutal, ugly, desperate, vicious form of expression it has been my misfortune to hear."
> —Frank Sinatra, press statement 1957

have been because he was embarrassed about the type of music he was making in contrast to the artistically and commercially successful Beatles hits? Exactly one month prior to meeting the Beatles, on July 27, Elvis was in a studio in Hollywood recording for posterity such classics as "Queenie Wahine's Papaya," "House of Sand," and "A Dog's Life." The same artist who revolutionized music was now reduced to covering songs like "Old MacDonald."

A turning point in Elvis' musical revival was his introduction to RCA producer Felton Jarvis while recording the Grammy award winning gospel album *How Great Thou Art*. Felton, young, flamboyant, and a long-time Elvis fan, immediately hit it off with Elvis.

Thankfully for Elvis the public had started to grow almost as tired of his movies as he had. The Colonel once again looked to the medium that had launched Elvis to superstardom and started to plan a Christmas television special as a career boost. The Colonel wanted a traditional Christmas show of Elvis singing nothing but schmaltzy holiday music. Elvis was lucky to work with two producers, Bones Howe and Steve Binder, who were given the freedom to present Elvis as they saw him—the King of rock and roll ready to reclaim his throne. The special used Elvis' own career as its concept by showcasing some of his early hits interspersed with his strongest new material. It featured gospel, production numbers, even a karate fight scene. But the most important parts of the show were Elvis' live performances. Elvis was given free rein to do what he did best: connect with his audience. The "unplugged" jam session sequence with Elvis on a small square stage with a few of his friends and two of the musicians from his Sun Records days was a prototype of the Elvis stage shows to come: Elvis in a stunning costume holding our attention not only with his music but with his charisma. The show ended with Elvis singing "If I Can Dream," a passionate gospel-influenced plea for peace and brotherhood. Elvis recorded it in a darkened studio while in a fetal position on the floor. It was after hearing this song that he said, "I'm never going to sing another song I don't believe in."

Revitalized by the "'68 Comeback Special," Elvis returned to Memphis to record for the first time in his hometown since Sun Records. In 1969 he recorded with producer Chips Moman, the head of American Studios in Memphis. American Studios and their roster of musicians were responsible for a uniquely Memphis style of funk that had produced more than 100 hit records. They were said to have eaten a lot of fried chicken that week and you can almost hear it in the music. Elvis created some of the best work of his career during these sessions, producing such classics as "Stranger in My Own Hometown," "Don't Cry Daddy," and "Suspicious Minds," the last of which would go on to become a number-one hit. Elvis said that he never worked as hard as he did at these sessions and it shows in the work.

> "If Elvis had simply stolen rhythm and blues from Negro culture, as pop music ignoramuses have for years maintained, there would be no reason for Southern outrage over his new music. (No one complained about Benny Goodman's or Johnny Ray's expropriation of black styles.) But Elvis did something more daring and dangerous: He not only 'sounded like a nigger,' he was actively and clearly engaged in race-mixing. The crime of Elvis' rock and roll was that he proved that black and white tendencies could coexist and that the product of their coexistence was not just palatable but thrilling."
> —Dave Marsh, from *Elvis*

To capitalize on the enthusiastic response to the television special and his reemergence on the charts, Elvis embarked on the next phase of his career. He assembled a handpicked team of musicians led by guitarist James Burton and named them the TCB (Taking Care of Business) Band. He hired the white gospel group the Imperials and the black female vocal group the Sweet Inspirations to be part of his act. He assembled on stage with him essentially all his musical influences.

On July 31, 1969, Elvis opened at the International Hotel in Las Vegas and began a series of live performances that would continue until the end of his life. The documentary *Elvis, That's the Way It Is* gives us a look at the preparations leading up to one of the Las Vegas engagements. It remains one of the few visual records of Elvis working in a studio situation at that time: confident, relaxed, funny, and focused. Many of Elvis' recordings in the 1970s emerged from his live performances. He performed an eclectic repertoire of songs from his early rockabilly hits and gentle ballads to bombastic vocal tours de force like "Unchained Melody" and "American Trilogy." His Madison Square Garden concert in 1972 was released as an album eight days after his appearance and went gold within weeks. The "Aloha from Hawaii" special was another successful concert album that represents Elvis in his prime.

In 1973 Elvis and his wife, Priscilla, were divorced and Elvis' choice of material left little doubt about the pain he felt. He selected songs such as "Good Time Charlie's Got the Blues," "My Boy," "We Had It All," and "Softly As I Leave You." Red West, in addition to his role as Elvis' friend and bodyguard at the time, wrote the breaking up song "Separate Ways" in response to what he was witnessing in Elvis' life.

Toward the end of his life Elvis fell into a depression fueled by his failed marriage, poor health, prescription drug problem, and the betrayal by some of his former friends. But he continued to tour and record until the very end and his music seemed to reflect his state of mind. Because of his reluctance to leave his home, RCA set up a recording studio in the Jungle Room at Graceland. It was from these final recording sessions that Elvis cut his last hit, the appropriately titled "Moody Blue." In June of 1977, just six weeks before his death, Elvis' final concerts were taped as part of a CBS television special. It's hard to believe that it was just four years after the "Aloha from Hawaii" concert that the clearly ill Elvis gave what would be his last performance. The voice, that feeling, his magical ability to drive us wild and touch our hearts remained with him to the very end. Listen to Elvis sing "My Way" in that final concert and we defy you to not be moved. Just hours before he died, Elvis did what he had so often in his life; he sat at a piano, the upright Schimmel in the racquetball court at Graceland, and did what he

Keith Alverson

Elvis bringing the house down with "Unchained Melody"

From the collection of Bob Klein

loved to do best, that which brought him his happiness. He sang his song.

As he told Marion Keisker on that July day back at Sun Studio, he did indeed sing all kinds. And he sang it all like no one else. Elvis left us with a huge and amazing body of work. There's something there to please almost anyone.

Since Elvis' death his music has been freshly evaluated. Instead of the focus being on his groundbreaking early work of the fifties, his career is being reexamined as a whole. RCA/BMG finally has people managing the vast Presley catalog with insight and passion for the music. Ernst Jorgensen—Elvis scholar, musical historian, and rock and roll detective—is largely responsible for the Grammy-nominated compilations of Elvis' music that have been released in recent years.

Now that the dust is finally starting to settle from the cultural big bang that Elvis ignited, his contributions to the world of music can be better assessed. He not only possessed a spectacular voice, he possessed an encyclopedic knowledge of American musical traditions making him a musicologist and a master vocalist.

If there's one thing that doesn't need to be repeated to an Elvis fan it's "Listen to the music." But for everyone else out there—unfamiliar with Elvis' vast range—seek out the stuff you haven't heard before, unjam your frequencies, sing along, dance along, let the music get to you. Prepare to be wowed.

ESSENTIAL ELVISOLOGY

Elvis' Roster of Songs

"A Big Hunk o' Love"
"A Boy Like Me, a Girl Like You"
"A Cane and a High Starched Collar"
"A Dog's Life"
"(Now and Then There's) A Fool Such As I"
"A House that Has Everything"
"A Hundred Years from Now"
"A Little Bit of Green"
"A Little Less Conversation"
"A Mess of Blues"
"A Thing Called Love"
"A Whistling Tune"
"A World of Our Own"
"Adam and Evil"
"After Loving You"
"Ain't that Loving You Baby"
"All I Needed Was the Rain"
"All Shook Up"
"All that I Am"
"Alla en el Rancho Grande"
"Almost"
"Almost Always True"
"Almost in Love"
"Aloha Oe"
"Always on My Mind"
"Am I Ready"
"Amazing Grace"

"America the Beautiful"
"American Trilogy"
"An Evening Prayer"
"And I Love You So"
"And the Grass Won't Pay No Mind"
"Angel"
"Animal Instinct"
"Any Day Now"
"Any Way You Want Me"
"Anyone (Could Fall in Love with You)"
"Anyplace Is Paradise"
"Anything that's Part of You"
"Are You Lonesome Tonight?"
"Are You Sincere"
"As Long As I Have You"
"As We Travel Along the Jericho Road"
"Ask Me"
"(You're So Square) Baby I Don't Care"
"Baby, If You'll Give Me All of Your Love"
"Baby, Let's Play House"
"Baby, What You Want Me to Do"
"Bad Nauheim Medley"
"Barefoot Ballad"
"Beach Boy Blues"
"Beach Shack"
"Because of Love"
"Beginner's Luck"
"Beyond the Bend"

"Beyond the Reef"
"Big Boots"
"Big Boss Man"
"Big Love, Big Heartache"
"Bitter They Are, Harder They Fall"
"Black Star"
"Blessed Jesus Hold My Hand"
"Blowin' in the Wind"
"Blueberry Hill"
"Blue Christmas"
"Blue Eyes Crying in the Rain"
"Blue Hawaii"
"Blue Moon"
"Blue Moon of Kentucky"
"Blue River"
"Blue Suede Shoes"
"Bosom of Abraham"
"Bossa Nova, Baby"
"Bridge over Troubled Water"
"Bringin' It Back"
"Britches"
"Burning Love"
"By and By"
"Can't Help Falling in Love"
"Carny Town"
"Catchin' on Fast"
"Change of Habit"
"Charro"
"Chesay"
"Cindy, Cindy"

"City by Night"
"Clambake"
"Clean Up Your Own Backyard"
"C'mon Everybody"
"Come Along"
"Come What May (You Are Mine)"
"Confidence"
"Cotton Candy Land"
"Could I Fall in Love"
"Crawfish"
"Cross My Heart and Hope to Die"
"Crying in the Chapel"
"Danny"
"Danny Boy"
"Dainty Little Moonbeams"
"Dark Moon"
"Datin'"
"(You're the) Devil in Disguise"
"Didja' Ever"
"Dirty, Dirty Feeling"
"Dixieland Rock"
"Doin' the Best I Can"
"Dominic"
"Do Not Disturb"
"Do the Clam"
"Do the Vega"
"Do You Know Who I Am"
"Doncha Think It's Time"
"Don't"
"Don't Ask Me Why"
"Don't Be Cruel"
"Don't Cry Daddy"
"Don't Forbid Me"

"Don't Leave Me Now"
"Don't Think Twice It's All Right"
"Double Trouble"
"Down by the Riverside"
"Down in the Alley"
"Drums of the Islands"
"Early Mornin' Rain"
"Earth Angel"
"Earth Boy"
"Easy Come, Easy Go"
"(Such an) Easy Question"
"Echoes of Love"
"Edge of Reality"
"El Toro"
"Everybody Come Aboard"
"Faded Love"
"Fairytale"
"Fame and Fortune"
"Farther Along"
"Fever"
"Finders Keepers, Losers Weepers"
"Find Out What's Happening"
"First in Line"
"Five Sleepy Heads"
"Flaming Star"
"Follow that Dream"
"Fool"
"Fool, Fool, Fool"
"Fools Fall in Love"
"Fools Rush In"
"(That's What You Get) For Lovin' Me"
"For Ol' Times Sake"
"For the Good Times"
"For the Heart"

"For the Millionth and the Last Time"
"Forget Me Never"
"Fort Lauderdale Chamber of Commerce"
"Fountain of Love"
"Frankfurt Special"
"Frankie and Johnny"
"Froggy Went a Courtin'"
"From a Jack to a King"
"Funny How Time Slips Away"
"Fun in Acapulco"
"Gentle on My Mind"
"Gently"
"GI Blues"
"Girl Happy"
"Girl Next Door Went a-Walking"
"Girl of Mine"
"Girls! Girls! Girls!"
"Give Me the Right"
"Go East, Young Man"
"Goin' Home"
"Golden Coins"
"Gonna Get Back Home Somehow"
"Good Luck Charm"
"Good Rockin' Tonight"
"Good Time Charlie's Got the Blues"
"Got a Lot o' Livin' to Do"
"Got My Mojo Working/Keep Your Hands Off of It"
"Green, Green Grass of Home"
"Guadalajara"

"Guitar Man"
"Happy Ending"
"Harbor Lights"
"Hard Headed Woman"
"Hard Knocks"
"Hard Luck"
"Harem Holiday"
"Have a Happy"
"Have I Told You Lately that I Love You?"
"Hawaiian Sunset"
"Hawaiian Wedding Song"
"Heart of Rome"
"Heartbreak Hotel"
"He Is My Everything"
"He Knows Just What I Need"
"He Touched Me"
"He'll Have to Go"
"Help Me"
"Help Me Make It through the Night"
"Here Comes Santa Claus"
"He's Only a Prayer Away"
"He's Your Uncle, Not Your Dad"
"Hey Little Girl"
"Hey, Hey, Hey"
"Hey Jude"
"Hi Heel Sneakers"
"His Hand in Mine"
"(Marie's the Name of) His Latest Flame"
"Holly Leaves and Christmas Trees"
"Home Is Where the Heart Is"

"Hot Dog"
"Hound Dog"
"House of Sand"
"How Can You Lose What You Never Had"
"How Do You Think I Feel"
"How Great Thou Art"
"How the Web Was Woven"
"How Would You Like to Be?"
"How's the World Treating You?"
"Hurt"
"I Beg of You"
"I Believe"
"I Believe in the Man in the Sky"
"I Can Help"
"I Can't Help It (If I'm Still in Love with You)"
"I Can't Stop Loving You"
"I Don't Care if the Sun Don't Shine"
"I Don't Wanna Be Tied"
"I Don't Want To"
"I Feel So Bad"
"I Feel that I've Known You Forever"
"I Forgot to Remember to Forget"
"I Got a Feelin' in My Body"
"I Got a Woman"
"I Got Lucky"
"I Got Stung"
"I Gotta Know"

"I, John"
"I Just Can't Help Believin'"
"I Just Can't Make It By Myself"
"I Love Only One Girl"
"I Love You Because"
"I Met Her Today"
"I Miss You"
"I Need Somebody to Lean On"
"I Need Your Love Tonight"
"I Need You So"
"I Really Don't Want to Know"
"I Shall Be Released"
"I Shall Not Be Moved"
"I Slipped, I Stumbled, I Fell"
"I Think I'm Gonna Like It Here"
"I Want to Be Free"
"I Want You, I Need You, I Love You"
"I Want You with Me"
"I Was Born about Ten Thousand Years Ago"
"I Washed My Hands in Muddy Water"
"I Was the One"
"I Will Be Home Again"
"I Will Be True"
"If Every Day Was Like Christmas"
"If I Can Dream"
"If I Get Home on Christmas Day"
"If I Were You"

"If I'm a Fool (For Loving You)"
"If that Isn't Love"
"If the Lord Wasn't Walking by My Side"
"If We Never Meet Again"
"If You Don't Come Back"
"If You Love Me (Let Me Know)"
"If You Talk in Your Sleep"
"If You Think I Don't Need You"
"I'll Be Back"
"I'll Be Home for Christmas"
"I'll Be There"
"I'll Hold You in My Heart"
"I'll Never Fall in Love Again"
"I'll Never Know"
"I'll Never Let You Go"
"I'll Never Stand in Your Way"
"I'll Remember You"
"I'll Take Love"
"I'll Take You Home Again Kathleen"
"I'm Beginning to Forget You"
"I'm Coming Home"
"I'm Countin' on You"
"I'm Falling in Love Tonight"
"I'm Gonna Sit Right Down and Cry (Over You)"

"I'm Gonna Walk Dem Golden Stairs"
"I'm Leavin'"
"I'm Left, You're Right, She's Gone"
"I'm Movin' On"
"I'm Not the Marrying Kind"
"I'm So Lonesome I Could Cry"
"I'm with a Crowd but Oh So Alone"
"I'm Yours"
"Indescribably Blue"
"In My Father's House"
"In My Way"
"In the Garden"
"In the Ghetto"
"In Your Arms"
"Inherit the Wind"
"Is It So Strange"
"Island of Love"
"It Ain't No Big Thing but It's Growing"
"It Feels So Right"
"It Hurts Me"
"It Is No Secret (What God Can Do)"
"It Keeps Right on a-Hurtin'"
"It Won't Be Long"
"It Won't Seem Like Christmas"
"Ito Eats"
"It's a Matter of Time"
"It's a Sin"
"It's a Wonderful World"
"It's Carnival Time"
"It's Diff'rent Now"
"It's Easy for You"

"It's Impossible"
"It's Midnight"
"It's Now or Never"
"It's Only Love"
"It's Over"
"It's Still Here"
"It's Your Baby, You Rock It"
"I've Got a Thing about You Baby"
"I've Got Confidence"
"I've Got to Find My Baby"
"I've Lost You"
"Jailhouse Rock"
"Jesus Walked that Lonesome Valley"
"Johnny B. Good"
"Joshua Fit the Battle"
"Judy"
"Just a Little Bit"
"Just a Little Talk with Jesus"
"Just Because"
"Just Call Me Lonesome"
"Just for Old Time Sake"
"Just Pretend"
"Just Tell Her Jim Said Hello"
"Kentucky Rain"
"King Creole"
"King of the Whole Wide World"
"Kismet"
"Kiss Me Quick"
"Kissin' Cousins"
"Known Only to Him"
"Ku-u-i-po"
"Lady Madonna"
"Lawdy Miss Clawdy"

"Lead Me, Guide Me"
"Let It Be Me"
"Let Me"
"Let Me Be There"
"Let Us Pray"
"Let Yourself Go"
"Let's Be Friends"
"Let's Forget about the Stars"
"Life"
"Like a Baby"
"Little Cabin on the Hill"
"Little Darlin'"
"Little Egypt"
"Little Sister"
"Lonely Man"
"Lonesome Cowboy"
"Long Black Limousine"
"Long-Legged Girl (with a Short Dress On)"
"Long Lonely Highway"
"Long Tall Sally"
"Look Out Broadway"
"Love Coming Down"
"Love Letters"
"Love Me"
"Love Me, Love the Life I Lead"
"Love Me Tender"
"Love Me Tonight"
"Love Song of the Year"
"Lover Doll"
"Lovin' Arms"
"Loving You"
"Make Me Know It"
"Make the World Go Away"
"Mama Liked the Roses"
"Mansion Over the Hilltop"

"Marguerita"
"Mary in the Morning"
"Maybellene"
"Mean Woman Blues"
"Memories"
"Memphis Tennessee"
"Merry Christmas Baby"
"Mexico"
"Milkcow Blues Boogie"
"Milky White Way"
"Mine"
"Miracle of the Rosary"
"Mirage"
"Mona Lisa"
"Money Honey"
"Moody Blue"
"Moonlight Swim"
"Mr. Songman"
"My Babe"
"My Baby Left Me"
"My Baby's Gone"
"My Boy"
"My Desert Serenade"
"My Happiness"
"My Heart Cries for You"
"My Little Friend"
"My Way"
"My Wish Came True"
"Mystery Train"
"Never Again"
"Never Been to Spain"
"Never Ending"
"Never Say Yes"
"New Orleans"
"Night Life"
"Night Rider"
"No More"
"(There's) No Room to Rhumba in a Sports Car"

"Nothingville"
"O Come, All Ye Faithful"
"O Little Town of Bethlehem"
"Oh How I Love Jesus"
"Old MacDonald"
"Old Shep"
"On a Snowy Christmas Night"
"Once Is Enough"
"One Boy Two Little Girls"
"One Broken Heart for Sale"
"One Night"
"One Night of Sin"
"One-Sided Love Affair"
"One-Track Heart"
"Only Believe"
"Only the Strong Survive"
"Padre"
"Paradise, Hawaiian Style"
"Paralyzed"
"Party"
"Patch It Up"
"Peace in the Valley"
"Petunia the Gardener's Daughter"
"Pieces of My Life"
"Plantation Rock"
"Playing for Keeps"
"Please Don't Drag that String Around"
"Please Don't Stop Loving Me"
"Pledging My Love"
"Pocketful of Rainbows"

"Poison Ivy League"
"Polk Salad Annie"
"Poor Boy"
"Power of My Love"
"Promised Land"
"Proud Mary"
"Puppet on a String"
"Put the Blame on Me"
"Put Your Hand in the Hand"
"Queenie Wahine's Papaya"
"Rags to Riches"
"Raised on Rock"
"Reach Out to Jesus"
"Ready Teddy"
"Reconsider Baby"
"Relax"
"Release Me"
"Return to Sender"
"Riding the Rainbow"
"Rip It Up"
"Rock-a-Hula Baby"
"Roustabout"
"Rubberneckin'"
"Run On"
"Runaway"
"Sand Castles"
"Santa Bring My Baby Back to Me"
"Santa Claus Is Back in Town"
"Santa Lucia"
"Saved"
"Scratch My Back"
"Seeing Is Believing"
"See See Rider"
"Sentimental Me"
"Separate Ways"
"Shake a Hand"
"Shake, Rattle and Roll"

"Shake That Tambourine"
"She Thinks I Still Care"
"She Wears My Ring"
"She's a Machine"
"She's Not You"
"Shoppin' Around"
"Shout It Out"
"Silent Night"
"Silver Bells"
"Singing Tree"
"Sing You Children"
"Slicin' Sand"
"Slowly but Surely"
"Smokey Mountain Boy"
"Smorgasbord"
"Snowbird"
"So Close, Yet So Far"
"So Glad You're Mine"
"So High"
"Softly as I Leave You"
"Soldier Boy"
"Solitaire"
"Somebody Bigger than You and I"
"Something"
"Something Blue"
"Song of the Shrimp"
"Sound Advice"
"Spanish Eyes"
"Speedway"
"Spinout"
"Spring Fever"
"Stand by Me"
"Starting Today"
"Startin' Tonight"
"Stay Away"
"Stay Away Joe"
"Steadfast, Loyal and True"
"Steamroller Blues"

"Steppin' Out of Line"
"Stop, Look and Listen"
"Stop Where You Are"
"Stranger in My Own Home Town"
"Stranger in the Crowd"
"Stuck on You"
"Such a Night"
"Summer Kisses, Winter Tears"
"Suppose"
"Surrender"
"Susan When She Tried"
"Suspicion"
"Suspicious Minds"
"Sweet Angeline"
"Sweet Caroline"
"Swing Down Sweet Chariot"
"Sylvia"
"Take Good Care of Her"
"Take Me to the Fair"
"Take My Hand, Precious Lord"
"Talk about the Good Times"
"Teddy Bear"
"Tell Me Why"
"Tender Feeling"
"Tennessee Waltz"
"Thanks to the Rolling Sea"
"That's All Right"
"That's Someone You Never Forget"
"That's When Your Heartaches Begin"
"The Bullfighter Was a Lady"
"The Fair's Moving On"

"The First Noel"
"The First Time Ever I
Saw Your Face"
"The Fool"
"The Girl I Never Loved"
"The Girl of My Best
Friend"
"The Impossible Dream"
"The Lady Loves Me"
"The Last Farewell"
"The Lord's Prayer"
"The Love Machine"
"The Meanest Girl in
Town"
"The Next Step Is Love"
"The Sound of Your Cry"
"The Twelfth of Never"
"The Walls Have Ears"
"The Whiffenpoof Song"
"The Wonderful World
of Christmas"
"The Wonder of You"
"The Yellow Rose of
Texas/The Eyes of Texas"
"There Ain't Nothing
Like a Song"
"There Goes My
Everything"
"There Is No God but
God"
"There Is So Much
World to See"
"There's a Brand New
Day on the Horizon"
"There's a Honky Tonk
Angel"
"There's Always Me"
"There's Gold in the
Mountains"
"There's No Place Like
Home"

"They Remind Me Too
Much of You"
"Thinking about You"
"This Is Living"
"This Is My Heaven"
"This Is Our Dance"
"This Is the Story"
"This Time"
"Three Corn Patches"
"Thrill of Your Love"
"Tiger Man"
"Today, Tomorrow and
Forever"
"Tomorrow Is a Long
Time"
"Tomorrow Never
Comes"
"Tomorrow Night"
"Tonight Is So Right for
Love"
"Tonight's All Right for
Love"
"Too Much"
"Too Much Monkey
Business"
"Treat Me Nice"
"Trouble"
"T-R-O-U-B-L-E"
"True Love"
"True Love Travels on a
Gravel Road"
"Tryin' to Get to You"
"Turn Your Eyes Upon
Jesus/Nearer My God
to Thee"
"Tutti Frutti"
"Tweedle Dee"
"Twenty Days and
Twenty Nights"
"Unchained Melody"

"Until It's Time for You
to Go"
"Up Above My Head"
"U.S. Male"
"Vino, Dinero y Amor"
"Violet"
"Viva Las Vegas"
"Walk a Mile in My
Shoes"
"Way Down"
"We Call on Him"
"We Can Make the
Morning"
"Wear My Ring Around
Your Neck"
"Wearin' That Loved-On
Look"
"Welcome to My World"
"We'll Be Together"
"We're Coming in
Loaded"
"We're Gonna Move"
"Western Union"
"What a Wonderful Life"
"What Every Woman
Lives For"
"What Now My Love"
"What Now, What Next,
Where To"
"What'd I Say"
"What's She Really Like"
"Wheels on My Heels"
"When I'm Over You"
"When It Rains, It Really
Pours"
"When My Blue Moon
Turns to Gold Again"
"When the Saints Go
Marchin' In"
"Where Could I Go but
to the Lord"

"Where Did They Go Lord"
"Where Do I Go from Here?"
"Where Do You Come From?"
"Where No One Stands Alone"
"White Christmas"
"Who Am I?"
"Who Are You (Who Am I?)"
"Who Needs Money"
"Whole Lotta Shakin' Goin' On"
"Why Me Lord?"
"Wild in the Country"
"Winter Wonderland"
"Wisdom of the Ages"
"Witchcraft"
"Without Him"

"Without Love (There Is Nothing)"
"Wolf Call"
"Woman Without Love"
"Wooden Heart"
"Words"
"Working on the Building"
"Write to Me from Naples"
"Yesterday"
"Yoga Is as Yoga Does"
"You Asked Me To"
"You Belong to My Heart"
"You Better Run"
"You Can't Say No in Acapulco"
"You Don't Have to Say You Love Me"
"You Don't Know Me"

"You Gave Me a Mountain"
"You Gotta Stop"
"You'll Be Gone"
"You'll Never Walk Alone"
"You'll Think of Me"
"Young and Beautiful"
"Young Dreams"
"Your Cheatin' Heart"
"Your Love's Been a Long Time Coming"
"Your Time Hasn't Come Yet Baby"
"You're a Heartbreaker"
"You're the Boss"
"You're the Only Star in My Blue Heaven"
"You've Lost that Lovin' Feelin'"

A Few Import and Bootleg CD Titles

Absent without Leave
Adios, the Final Performance
All Things Are Possible
American Crown Jewels
America the Beautiful
As Recorded in Stereo 57
Behind Closed Doors!
Best of the Lost Binaural Takes
Brightest Star On Sunset Boulevard (Volumes 1 and 2)
Burning in Birmingham
By Special Request, Vegas 1975
Café Europa Sessions GI Blues Outtakes
Candid Elvis on Camera, Omaha '77
Colonel's Collection
Come What May
Complete Bonus Songs 1960/1967

Complete On Tour Sessions (Volumes 1, 2, and 3)
Complete Spinout Sessions (2-CD set)
Cut 'Em Down to Size
Deep Down South
Desert Storm (2-CD set)
A Dinner Date with Elvis
Electrifying
Face to Face
Finding the Way Home
From Sunset Blvd. to Paradise Road (2-CD set)
Get Down and Get with It
Girl Happy at the World's Fair
Goodbye Memphis (2-CD set)
Good Times Never Seemed So Good
Greetings from Germany

Guaranteed to Blow Your Mind
Hang Loose
Hawaii USA
Hello Memphis
Here I Go Again!
Holding Back the Years
Hot Winter Night in Dallas
If You Talk in Your Sleep
I Got Stung
Lean, Mean & Kickin' Butt
Let Me Take You Home
Live in Virginia
Louisiana Hayride Archives
Loving You Recording Sessions
Make the World Go Away
Moody Blue & Other Great
    Performances
More Pure Elvis
My, It's Been a Long, Long Time
Old Times They Are Not Forgotten
Opening Night '69
Opening Night 1972
One Night in Portland
The Power of Shazam!

Pure Diamonds
Rockin' Rebel
Rockin' with Elvis April Fool's Day
Running for President
Season's Greetings from Elvis
Sold Out in Dixie
Something Complete (2-CD set)
Songs to Sing!
South Bound
Stand by Me (Volumes 1 and 2)
Stereo '57 (Volumes 1 and 2)
Surrender by Elvis
Sweet Carolina
Teenage Rage
Tiger Man: An Anthology
There's Always Me
There's a Whole Lotta Shakin' Goin' On
Tuscaloosa Night!
True Love Travels on a Gravel Road
Unissued Elvis '56–'57
Walk a Mile in My Shoes
Welcome to San Antone
With a Song in My Heart

The Only Song Elvis Composed
"You'll Be Gone"
Red West and Charlie Hodge, cowriters.

Songs Elvis Sang in Languages other than English

"Alla en el Rancho Grande"   "Havanagila"   "Santa Lucia"
"Aloha Oe"   "Ku-u-i-Po"   "We'll Be Together"
"El Toro"   "Marguerita"   "Wooden Heart"
"Guadalajara"   "O Sole Mio"

Elvis' Grammy Awards and Award Nominations
1959 Record of the Year
   "A Fool Such As I"—Nominated
1959 Best Performance by a Top 40 Artist
   "A Big Hunk O' Love"—Nominated

1959 Best Rhythm and Blues Performance
"A Big Hunk O' Love"—Nominated
1960 Record of the Year
"Are You Lonesome Tonight?"—
Nominated
1960 Best Vocal Performance, Male
"Are You Lonesome Tonight?"—
Nominated
1960 Best Performance by a Pop Singles
Artist
"Are You Lonesome Tonight?"—
Nominated
1960 Best Vocal Performance, Male, Album
GI Blues—Nominated
1960 Best Soundtrack Album
GI Blues—Nominated
1961 Best Soundtrack Album
Blue Hawaii—Nominated
1967 Best Sacred Performance
"How Great Thou Art"—Won
1968 Best Sacred Performance
"You'll Never Walk Alone"—Nominated
1972 Best Inspirational Performance
"He Touched Me"—Won
1974 Best Inspirational Performance
"How Great Thou Art"—Won
1978 Best Country Vocal Performance
"Softly as I Leave You"—Nominated
National Academy of Recording Arts and
Sciences (NARAS)
Bing Crosby Award 1971
Now called the Lifetime Achievement Award

> "Elvis had a range of about two octaves and a third. Most pop singers have about a one-octave range. He was a high baritone. He could nail high Gs and As full-voiced. That was just his natural ability. But in the army, practicing with Charlie [Hodge], he made his voice stronger. He sang more from the diaphragm, and with some power, rather than just from the throat. He'd say, 'It's the same music, just with more balls.'"
> —Billy Smith, Elvis' cousin, from *Elvis Aaron Presley: Revelations from the Memphis Mafia*

Elvis' Very First Review
Marion Keisker noted on his very first recording at Sun: "Good ballad singer. Hold."

The Day the Soviet Union Lifted Its Ban on Elvis' Music
December 29, 1988

The Company that Made the First Elvis Records
Buster Williams Plastic Products, Memphis

The First Elvis Record Purchased

Eldene Beard bought the very first copy of "That's All Right" at Charles Records on Main Street in Memphis.

Studios Where Elvis Recorded

Sun Studio, Memphis
American Studio, Memphis
RCA Studio, Nashville
RCA Studio, New York
RCA Studio, Hollywood
Samuel Goldwyn Studio, Hollywood
United Artist Recorders, Hollywood
Fox Soundstage, Hollywood
Decca Universal Studio, Hollywood
MGM Studios, Culver City
Radio Recorders, Los Angeles
MGM Soundstage, Hollywood
Stax Studio, Memphis
Paramount Soundstage, Hollywood
Western Recorders, Burbank

> "I have been studying Elvis' high notes and vocal range. He hits *B* below high *C* on most 'Hurt' second endings as well as the 12/31/76 'Rags to Riches'. On the 'Hurt' in Hot Winter's Night in Dallas, he hits a bit of a *C* sharp. His main big high note was a high *B*, though. I am going to check some of the live 'It's Now or Never's. On the 1960 'Surrender' he does a *B* flat at the end. Most of the Trilogy endings are *B* to *A*. I have been studying this and trying to hit these notes myself."
> —Vince,
> on alt.elvis.king newsgroup

The Blue Moon Boys

Bill Black on bass
Scotty Moore on lead guitar
D. J. Fontana on drums

The Core TCB Band Members

James Burton on lead guitar
Glen Hardin on piano
Ronnie Tutt on drums
John Wilkinson on rhythm guitar
Jerry Scheff on bass

Line-Up Changes and Replacements

Larry Muhoberac on piano
Hal Blaine on drums
Marty Harrell on trombone
Shane Kiester on keyboards
Larry Londin on drums
Duke Bardwell on bass

Elvis' Backup Singers

The Jordanaires:
  Hoyt Hawkins
  Hugh Jarrett
  Ray Walker, replacement
  Neal Matthews
  Gordon Stoker

J. D. Sumner and the Stamps Quartet
The Imperials:
   Jake Hess
   Sherrill Nielsen
   Greg Gordon
   Gary McSpadden
   Joe Moscheo
   Terry Blackwood
The Sweet Inspirations:
   Estelle Brown
   Cissy Houston (Whitney Houston's mother)
   Sylvia Shemwell
   Myrna Smith
Voice
   Tim Baty
   Donnie Sumner
   Sherrill Neilsen
The Amigos
The Anita Kerr Singers
The Blossoms
The Carole Lombard Trio (then Quartet)
The Jubilee Four
The Ken Darby Trio
Lea Jane Berineti Singers
The Mello Men
The Nashville Edition
The Surfers
The Hugh Jarrett Singers

> "In 1985 when it was Elvis' 50th birthday and Michael Jackson was at his 'peak,' a reporter wanted to put Elvis' popularity into perspective. She said, 'If Michael Jackson continues to sell 35,000,000 records a year, it would take him 25 years to equal Elvis' numbers. That is if Elvis doesn't sell another record until then.'"
>
> —Julie Niarchos, on elviscoollist.com

Some of Elvis' Producers

Sam Phillips
Thorne Nogar
Chips Momam

Chet Atkins
Felton Jarvis

Elvis' Classical Piano Repertoire

In addition to the hundreds of gospel and pop songs that Elvis taught himself to play on the piano, many fans are surprised to learn he could also perform these two classical pieces:

Beethoven's "Moonlight Sonata"
Debussy's "Clair de Lune"

Some of Elvis' Different Styles of Singing

Soft, Airy, Falsetto-Like

Many of the ballads from the mid-'60s had this sound. If you're singing in a rock or blues band, this sound is forbidden! In classic singing it is also avoided, because the air passing through your nose muffles the sound of your voice. Vocally this sound is created by letting much air through your nose during the high notes while keeping your larynx high up in your throat. The sound is prominent on songs like "Mine," "I'll Remember You" (1966 version, in 1972–73 the sound is much darker and more dramatic), "Suppose," and "Sand Castles."

Macho, Dark, and Solemn

This is how most people sing when they try to imitate Elvis. The sound is very prominent on several of the songs on the *How Great Thou Art* album. To create this dark sound, one lowers the larynx down the throat (in singers' jargon this is called "swallowing"). Try "swallowing" while holding the same tone, and you'll notice how the sound becomes darker! The effect is strongest on medium-level tones. Elvis used the technique in the '50s, adding this macho sound to songs like "I Got Stung," "I Was the One" (the verses), "Somebody Bigger than You and I," and especially "Peace in the Valley."

Classic (Italian) Tenor

In many concert pictures of Elvis, his mouth is wide open—like Pavarotti. Demanding songs from the '70s like the "Wonder of You," "Rags to Riches," "American Trilogy," and (the best-known one, from 1960) "It's Now or Never" show Elvis using classic technique—putting theatrical drama to the songs. Using classic technique makes it easier to reach the high notes and reduces the risk of throat ache and damage. The sound is created by opening the mouth wide up, shutting the nose completely, and (when reaching for the high notes) swallowing. To make the heroic Italian sound you have to add power by pushing with your diaphragm. Professional singers always take great care to warm up properly. If you don't warm up, your technique might fail, resulting in throat problems and canceled shows. This may have happened to Elvis in Vegas. Performing two shows a night, his voice wouldn't have the time to recover if it needed to.

Aggressive, Rasping

Examples of this sound can be found on "Long Tall Sally" from Elvis' Little Rock concert in '56, the "'68 Comeback Special" Sitdown Segment: "Trying to Get to

You" and "Lawdy Miss Clawdy." On some occasions he also put this rasping sound to parts of some ballads, for example "Release Me," "You've Lost that Lovin' Feelin'," "It Hurts Me," "I'll Hold You in My Heart," and "If I Can Dream."

—Compiled with the generous help of Jon Are Jensaas

From the collection of Bob Klein

First Studio Recording
"My Happiness"
Memphis Recording Service, July 1953

Last Studio Recording
"He'll Have to Go"
The Jungle Room at Graceland, November 1, 1976

Last Song Sung in Concert
"Can't Help Falling in Love"

Singers Who Influenced Elvis at Various Points in His Life

Arthur "Big Boy" Crudup	Ink Spots
Big Joe Turner	Ray Charles
Roy Brown	Roy Orbison
Fats Domino	Righteous Brothers
Martha Carson	Dean Martin
Little Junior Parker	Johnny Cash
Willie Mae "Big Mama" Thornton	Tom Jones
Joe Turner	Marty Robbins
Muddy Waters	Dusty Springfield
Rufus Thomas	Jackie Wilson
Johnny Ace	The Platters
Blackwood Brothers	The Weavers
LaVern Baker	Peggy Lee
Roy Hamilton	Jimmy Reed
Kay Starr	Eddy Arnold
Teresa Brewer	Billy Eckstine
Joni James	Blackwood Brothers
Hank Snow	Arthur Prysock
Bing Crosby	Robert Merrill
Eddie Fisher	Jimmy Reed
Perry Como	Ike and Tina Turner
Hank Williams	Gary Puckett and the Union Gap

Elvis' Least Favorite Singers
Robert Goulet
Mel Tormé

Some Elvis Cover Records
Pat Boone
  Pat Boone Sings Guess Who?
Albert King
  King Does the King's Thing
Bugs Bunny
  Bugs and Friends Sing Elvis

Some Singers Who've Cited Elvis as a Major Influence
John Lennon
Paul Simon
David Bowie
Paul McCartney
Neil Diamond
Mick Fleetwood
Barry White
Joe Cocker

Gary Glitter
Phil Ochs
Eric Clapton
Bruce Springstein
Chris Isaak
K. D. Lang
Bono

Microphones Elvis Used
Shure Unidyne III Dynamic Model 545G
Neumann (67) Directional Mike

Elvis' Home Recording Equipment
Grundig tape recorder

Musical Instruments Elvis Owned

Keyboards

Stroud 1911–1912 upright piano
  Elvis' first piano, bought in 1955.
Story & Clark baby grand piano
  In the music room of Graceland.
Wm. Knabe & Co. grand piano—gold and white
  Originally the stage piano of Ellis Auditorium. Elvis owned this piano for twelve years.

> "Most people do not realize how Elvis still sells records at a phenomenal rate. Last year [1997] Elvis sold eight million records worldwide."
> —Ernst Jorgensen

> "Elvis served as our entry point into the world of music. For me, personally, Elvis was the *only* singer worth hearing throughout much of my youth (1970s). During the late '70s when groups like the Sex Pistols and the Clash came to the fore, I was attracted to that music and attitude not because it sounded like Elvis, but because it reminded me of Elvis at his best and gave me the same emotional impact that Elvis always had."
> —John Brown, on alt.elvis.king

Kimball 1928 gold-leafed grand piano
Now on display at The Country Music Hall of Fame.

Lowrey brass and string symphonizer
Elvis played this at his Chino Canyon Drive home in Palm Springs.

Sterling Clark piano
Bought from Palm Springs Music and used at Elvis' Chino Canyon Drive.

Lowrey manual electric organ
Elvis played this in his upstairs office at Graceland.

Allen organette
With mandolin repeat. Bought at Jack Marshall Pianos and Organs in Memphis.

Baldwin grand piano

Schimmel Mahogany Spinet piano
The last instrument Elvis ever played. Bought at Jack Marshall Pianos and Organs in Memphis.

Guitars

Flat top round hole Martin D-18
Used during the Sun sessions. Sold at auction in 1993 for $152,000.

NBN acoustic guitar
Six-string steel guitar. Elvis received it as a gift.

Giannini acoustic guitar
Model 900, made in Brazil. Elvis used this on tour.

Hagstrom V-2 acoustic/electric guitar
Cherryred six-string guitar. Used in the "'68 Comeback Special."

Burns of London double six guitar
Green, twelve-string used in *Spinout*.

1973–1975 Gibson dove acoustic guitar
Six-string with sunburst design on body and dove design on pick guard.

Estrella acoustic guitar
Nylon six-string acoustic made in Japan,

Megan Murphy

Stroud piano

Courtesy of Butterfield & Butterfield

Wm. Knabe & Co. grand piano

Courtesy of Butterfield & Butterfield

(Left to right) Martin O-18, Estrella acoustic, Fransiscan Model A-580 guitars ideal for Spanish music. "Estrella Guitara Classico de Espana" imprinted inside.

August Julius Ziegle guitar

1956 Gibson J-200
Used on stage in the fifties with a leather cover. Used in the "'68 Comeback Special."

1960 Gibson J-200
With "Elvis Presley" inset into the neck.

Personalized Gibson
Gift from Jim Curtin; decorated with crown.

Gibson double-neck guitar
Red guitar seen in *Girl Happy*.

1967 Gibson S. G. Jr.
Bought from Amro Music Store, Memphis.

Martin 0-18
Mahogany six-steel-string acoustic guitar. Gift from Elvis to Charlie Hodge.

Franciscan Acoustic Guitar
Six-nylon-string acoustic, model A-580.

Fender electric bass
White and tan.

Gretsch Chet Atkins
Country Gentleman electric guitar
Mahogany-colored six string.

Martin D-28 acoustic
Used in concerts in 1977.

NBN acoustic guitar

Courtesy of Butterfield & Butterfield

Hagstrom V-2 acoustic/electric guitar

Courtesy of Butterfield & Butterfield

Gibson Dove acoustic guitar

Courtesy of Butterfield & Butterfield

Gibson J-200

Courtesy of Butterfield & Butterfield

Banjos

Olson Gibson banjo
  Five string.

Violins

Stradivarius SP copy

Scotty Moore's Guitars
Fender Esquire
Gibson Model ES 295
  Blond f-hole noncutaway used in the Sun
  sessions.
Gibson L5 CES (blond)
  Used 1955–1957.
Gibson Super 400 CESN
  Used 1957–1963.
Gibson Super 400 (Sunburst)
  Used 1963–1986.
Gibson Super 100 CESN
Gibson L5 CES (blond)

YOUR ELVIS EDUCATION

Books
Elvis Presley: A Life in Music
  Ernst Jorgensen
*The Complete Guide to the Music of Elvis
Presley*
John Robertson
Elvis Day by Day: The Definitive Record of His Life and Music
  Peter Guralnick and Ernst Jorgensen
Last Train to Memphis
  Peter Guralnick
Careless Love
  Peter Guralnick
Elvis: The Concert Years 1969–1977
  Stein-Erik Skar, Flaming Star Publishers
Lost Highway
  Peter Guralnik

"When I first heard Elvis' voice I just knew that I wasn't going to work for anybody; and nobody was going to be my boss. He is the deity supreme of rock and roll religion as it exists in today's form. Hearing him for the first time was like busting out of jail.... I thank God for Elvis Presley."
—Bob Dylan

"Black record customers saw Presley as a kind of black stepchild. Even as the general market saw him as a modified country/rock singer, many blacks regarded him as a modified blues singer."
—*Billboard* magazine,
August 1977

Good Rockin' Tonight: Sun Records and the Birth of Rock 'n' Roll
  Colin Escott with Martin Hawkins
That's Alright, Elvis
  Scotty Moore as told to James Dickerson
Elvis, Hank, and Me: Making Musical History on the Louisiana Hayride
  Horace Logan with Bill Sloan
Country
  Nick Tosches
Elvis: His Life From A to Z
  Fred Worth and Steve Tamerius
Elvis
  text by Dave Marsh, art Direction by Bea Feitler
The Essential Elvis: The Life and Legacy of the King as Revealed through 112 of His Most Significant Songs
  Samuel Roy and Tom Aspell
Elvis: The Ultimate Album Cover Book
  Paul Dowling
For CD Fans Only
  Available through Worldwide Elvis, Box 17998, Sarasota, Florida 34276. Go to their web site http:www.worldwideelvis.com or phone (941) 346-1930.
Elvis Presley: Songs of Inspiration
  Collection of gospel and inspirational sheet music for vocal, guitar, and piano published by Hal Leonard Corporation, Milwaukee, Wisconsin.
Best of Elvis
  Susan Doll
Heartbreak Hotel: The Life and Music of Elvis Presley
  Robert Matthew Walker

Elvis Presley Anthology
  Music Sales Ltd.
Elvis: The Sun Years, The Story of Elvis Presley in the Fifties
  Howard A. Dewitt
Mystery Train: Images of America in Rock 'n' Roll Music
  Greil Marcus
Rhythm Oil
  Stanley Booth
Bootleg
  Clinton Heylin
Elvis—Standing Room Only
  Joseph A. Tunzi, JAT Productions
Elvis Meets the Beatles
  Chris Hutchins and Peter Thompson
In Search of Elvis: Music, Race, Art, Religion
  edited by Vernon Chadwick
Elvis Presley Anthology (Volumes One and Two)
  Vocal, guitar, and piano sheet music for 203 songs published by Hal Leonard Corporation, Milwaukee, Wisconsin.
Elvis: Portrait of the King
  Susan Doll
Solid Gold Elvis: The Elvis Presley Collectors Manual
  David Petrelle
  Order from Timewind Publishing, 7756 Silverweed Way, Lonetree, Colorado 80124 (877) 395-6775. Or visit their web site at http://www2.csn.net/petrelle/elvis2.htm.
Elvis: Melody Line, Chords and Lyrics for Keyboard-Guitar-Vocal
  Hal Leonard

Tennessee Music: Its People and Places
Peter Zimmerman
http://www.total.net/~pinker/
BookandMusicStore.html
The Sound of the City
Charlie Gillett
Elvis: The Music Lives On
Richard Peters

Elvis Presley: A Study in Music
Robert Matthew-Walker
Guitar Signature Licks: The Guitars of Elvis
Wolf Marshall
The Boy Who Dared to Rock: The Definitive Elvis
Paul Lichter

Video

Elvis '56
One Night with You
Elvis, That's the Way It Is
Elvis on Tour
The Great Performances

All the King's Men video collection
Sun Days with Elvis
"Baby, That's Rock and Roll: A Celebration of the Songs of Leiber & Stoller"

Web Sites

http://www.geocities.com/~arpt/elvex.html
ELVEX site
http://apachelvis.simplenet.com/
Pete Smith's Apache Elvis site.
http://www.virginmega.com
Virgin's web site for music, movies, books, and software.
http://www.tunes.com
Music hub; MP3s
http://www.biwa.ne.jp/~presley/cdnews.htm
Haruo Hirose's Japan World CD news
http://www.bmg.com
BMG RCA web site
http://www.amisg.com
Music links site

http://www.noord.bart.nl/~kaauw/
bootleg_news.html
Import News
http://jordanselvisworld.simplenet.com/index.html
Home of the world's largest Elvis music library!
http://w1.866.telia.com/~u86600188/
elvis/index2.html
The Elvis Presley albums and singles page
http://listen.to/elvis-presley-superstar
Elvis Superstar: Elvis at his best site; RealAudio.
http://www.members.tripod.com/
~wbroekman
Wouter Broekman's site; lyrics

http://www.casema.net/~arpt/
elvisbotn.html
Elvis music library
http://www.geocities.com/~arpt/az/
Elvis Presley Encyclopaedia
http://www.elvisnews.com
Excellent source for Elvis music
news
http://www.rockhall.com/induct/
preselvi.html
Rock and Roll Hall of Fame
http://www.sunstudio.com/
Sun Records, Memphis
http://www.geocities.com/
~aaltonen/elvis.html
Music of Elvis Presley site
http://www.rockabillyhall.com/
ElvisLetters.html
Rockabilly Hall of Fame
http://www.geocities.com/Bourbon
Street/Delta/7095/
Site where you can find the lyrics
to Elvis' songs
http://www.geocities.com/
bourbonstreet/quarter/5733
Site for Elvis song guitar chords
http://home.gelrevision.nl/~bakeenei/
CD database
http://www.geocities.com/SunsetStrip/
Balcony/1441/index.html
Elvis Country; lyrics, discography,
and much more
http://members.home.nl/rfrieser/index.
html
Elvis Memphis sound 1969;
American Sound Studios music site
http://www.geocities.com/SunsetStrip/
Stadium/4309
De Ruyter's Elvis import RealAudio
page

http://www.geocities.com/SunsetStrip/
Stadium/1204
De Ruyter's Elvis RCA RealAudio
page
http://www.biwa.ne.jp/~presley/
index1.htm
Haruo Hirose's Elvis World site
http://www.biwa.or.jp/~presley/gold.
htm
Haruo Hirose's gold and platinum
list site
http://www.geocities.com/~arpt/
igottaknow/
Lex Raaphorst's Elvis page
http://www.noord.bart.nl/~kaauw/
index2.html
For Elvis CD collectors only;
Willem Kaauw's site
http://www.metronet.com/~elvis/
personal/lyrics.html
Mike Hernandez's lyrics site
http://lyrics.astraweb.com
Lyrics site
http://w1.866.telia.com/~u86600188/
elvis/index.html
Elvis Internet Times; guide to
albums and singles of the hillbilly
cat
http://members.aol.com/eonair/
index.html
Stephen Christoper's Elvis on the
air site
http://w1.383.telia.com/~38300150/
Per's Elvis site with RealAudio
http://www.total.net/~pinker/Bookand
MusicStore.html
Elvis, blues, country music, and
Tennessee travel books and CDs
http://www.resoftlinks.com/musica

Internet music site

http://members.aol.com/RockinEd1/index.html
Rockin' Ed's Rockin Roots Ranch, rockabilly, hillbilly, western swing, R&B, blues, doo wop, gospel, '50s, '60s rock and roll

http://www.nb.net/~glarkin/index.html
Oldies Unlimited—home of doo wop, rock and roll, and rhythm and blues; you can listen to Gary Larkin's Elvis radio show on this site

http://www.geocities.com/bourbon-street/quarter/5733
Elvis site with guitar chords

http://www.welcome.to/elvispresley
Great Swedish site with guitar chords

http://www.riaa.com
RIAA home page; find their latest version of Elvis' record sales and world standing

http://www.grammy.org
Grammy Awards site

http://www.oldiesauction.com
Buy or sell your records here

http://www.promisedland.com
Promised Land records and collectibles site

http://www.biwa.or.jp/~presley/audio/index.html
From the record collection of Haruo Hirose

http://www.informatik.uni-konstanz.de/~nissen/elvis_songlist.html
Elvis song list A to Z

http://www.uio.no/~ovene/
Oven Egelan's Elvis Is Still Active in Norway

http://www.elvis.com.ar/03/home.html
Elvis Line, from South America

THE ELVIS AND YOU EXPERIENCE

Music Every Elvis Fan Should Have

Many excellent boxed sets of Elvis' music have been released, usually compiled and organized around a theme or period of time. The '50s, '60s, and '70s Masters are a great way to jump-start or expand an Elvis music collection. Try and buy them chronologically and see the evolution of Elvis' music.

Sunrise (RCA 67675)
Always begin with Sun. This compilation contains all of the Sun sessions including alternative takes.

The King of Rock 'n' Roll: The Complete 50's Masters (5 CDs) (RCA 66050)
Studio masters of everything Elvis recorded during the 1950s.

Elvis from Nashville to Memphis: The Essential 60's Masters (5CDs) (RCA 66160)
Studio masters from the '60s.

Walk a Mile in My Shoes: The Essential 70's Masters (5CDs) (66670)
Studio masters from the '70s.

Amazing Grace (2CDs) (RCA 66421)
A definitive collection of Elvis' gospel music.

The Million Dollar Quartet (RCA 2023)
   The legendary impromptu jam session at Sun Records is a piece of history, great music, and an insight into the unguarded Elvis.
Elvis Is Back (RCA 67737)
   Elvis' first album after the army and one of his best.
Elvis NBC/TV Special (RCA 61021)
   Soundtrack of the "'68 Comeback Special."
Tiger Man (RCA 67611)
   The second live sit-down show of the "'68 Comeback Special."
Suspicious Minds (RCA 67677)
   Contains all the masters from the American Studio sessions of 1969.
Platinum: A Life in Music (4 CDs)
   A very good overview of Elvis' entire career that includes many home recordings only recently discovered at Graceland. Many exclusives.
Elvis Aron Presley Silver Box
   Contains the '61 USS *Arizona* Benefit Show, the Vegas Venus Room appearance in '56, and many exclusives.
He Touched Me: The Gospel Music of Elvis Presley (2 CDs)
   Bill Gaither Collections, definitive collection of gospel

Listen to the Music Elvis Listened To
This is an album that contains the original versions of songs that Elvis covered and made into hits.
The King's Record Collection (Volumes 1 and 2) (Hip-O 40082 and 40083)

Where to Buy Elvis Music

Join a Music-Buying Club

Columbia House
1400 North Fruitridge Avenue
Terre Haute, Indiana 47812
http://www.columbiahouse.com
BMG Music Service
6550 East 30th Street
Indianapolis, Indiana 46219
http://www.bmg.com

> "'That's All Right'" was a tremendous hit with teenagers, and in Memphis, where the record broke first, the current greeting among the teenagers is still a rhythmical line from the song: 'Ta dee dah dee dee dah.'
> —The *Memphis Press-Scimitar*, 1954

Internet Sources

In addition to the opportunity to shop in your underwear, internet shopping sites frequently offer pretty good discounts. Go to some of the fan music sites listed above to see what new releases are coming up.

http:www.everycd.com
  EveryCD site, or phone: (800)
  EVERY-CD
http://www.amazon.com
  Amazon.com site
http://www.barnesandnoble.com
  Barnes & Noble site
http:www.cdnow.com
  CD Now site
http:www.soundstone.com
  Soundstone Music site
http:www.musicblvd.com/gifts
  Music Boulevard site

http://freespace.virgin.net/vinyl.
  music/
  Virgin Music site; E-mail:
  vinyl.music@virgin.net
http://www.allmusic.com/
  Music and book source
http://cduniverse.com
  CD Universe site
http://www.musicmaniacom
  Music Mania site
http://www.mbnet.mb.ca/~hobson/
  bkbillbrd.html
  In association with Amazon.com

Other Sources

Promised Land Records and
Collectibles Catalog
They also sell memorabilia and guitars.
P.O. Box 516
Imperial, Missouri 63052
(314) 287-1968
http://www.promisedland.com

River Records
822 South Highland
Memphis, Tennessee 38111
(901) 324-1757

D&J Records
When you contact D&J Records ask
for "Beans." He has more than
1,000,000 records in stock from the
forties to the nineties. They also buy
record collections.
212 East Main Street
Carnegie, Pennsylvania 15106
(412) 279-8888
Fax: (412) 279-5538

Jewel, Paula, Ronn Records
They don't carry Elvis records per se
but they carry all the stuff he would
have listened to when he was young:
R&B, gospel.
1700 Century Boulevard
Shreveport, Louisiana 71101
or
P.O. Box 1125
Shreveport, Louisiana 71163-1125
(800) 446-2865
(318) 227-2228
Fax: (318) 227-0304
Audio Collections
P.O. Box 1474
Bolingbrook, Illinois 60440
(630) 759-2273
Fax: (630) 759-2430
E-mail: audicoll@aol.com
http://www.audiocollections.com

Imports and Elvis rarities

King Collectibles
B. Allward & Associates Inc.
141 King Road
P.O. Box 2792
Richmond Hill, Ontario, L4E 1A7 Canada
(905) PRESLEY
Fax: (905) 773-2842

RPM Records
10054 Culver Boulevard #2

Culver City, California 90232
(310) 838-8RPM
Fax: (310) 836-3795

The King's Connection
Connie Boles
147 Milton Road
Rochester, New Hampshire 03868
E-mail: cgboles@worldpath.net

European CDs

E-mail: elvis@post7.tele.dk
http:/www.elvismyhappiness.com/
http://www.elvisnow.com

South American CDs

Carlos R. Ares
Florida 520, Local 15
1005 Buenos Aires, Argentina
Fax: (54) 11-4394-5216
E-mail: ares@elvis.com.ar

Worldwide Elvis
Paul Dowling puts together CDs, books, and memorabilia into collectible pack-
aged sets.
Box 17998
Sarasota, Florida 34276-0998
(800) 55-ELVIS
(941) 346-1930
Fax: (941) 346-8139
E-mail: wwelvis@gte.net
http://www.worldwideelvis.com

Rowe's Rare Records
P.O. Box 28384
San Jose, California 95159

"10-inch shellac, the 45, the EP,
the 8-track tape, the cassette
tape, the LP, the CD, the DAT,
the VHS, and the laser. Elvis has
lasted through all these."
—Don Wardell,
RCA executive

The Elvis Presley Unique Record Club
Paul Lichter
(602) 984-5026

Japan Allround Music, Inc.
Yuri Yasuda
4-11-8 Sendagaya Shibuya-ku Tokyo, 151-0051 Japan.
TEL : 813-3408-6711
FAX : 813-3404-0147
E-mail : jtr@rrm.co.jp
http://www.rrm.co.jp/world

Recycled Music
Collectible and out-of-print vinyl. Recycled Music also has turntables for sale.
E-mail: jimeukey@execpc.com
http://www.execpccom/~jimeukey

The Time Life Music Hall Catalog
East Parham Road
P.O. Box 85535, Department MHK
Richmond, Virginia 23285
(800) 382-2348
Fax: (888) 853-8681
Heartland Music
Country and gospel music catalog
East Parham Road
P.O. Box 85535
Richmond, Virginia 23285-5535

Get Special Fan Club Only Releases
RCA has launched a new BMG collectors label for the kind of material fans are interested in—not just the repackaged top-ten hits. There are four CD releases a year. The CDs are only available through certain Elvis fan clubs and from Graceland. For information about upcoming releases contact Graceland.

British fan, Simon Harris, visiting Sun Studio

Retire Your Old Records to the Walls
This company makes frames that fit precisely around your old album covers so you can hang them on the walls as art.
Worldwide Marketing
(800) 640-0306
http://www.albumframes.com

Request Elvis Songs as Often as Possible
When a band or DJ asks for requests, you know what to do. Try to request the more obscure Elvis songs. Educate the masses.

Visit the Place Where the Sound Began
Sun Studio, Elvis' original label, is open for tours. It's the most famous recording studio in the world and, of course, ground zero of the big bang. The visit is fascinating. There's a tour, gallery of memorabilia, and shop. You can even cut a record there like Elvis did! Ringo Starr, Tom Petty, U2, John Fogerty, Bonnie Raitt, Paul Simon, and countless Elvis impersonators have all recorded at Sun.
Sun Studio
706 Union Avenue
Memphis, Tennessee 38103
(800) 441-6249
(901) 521-0664
http://www.sunstudio.com
E-mail: sun@wspice.com

John O'Hara

Other Musical Meccas
Graceland
Many of Elvis' guitars are on display.

Memphis Music Hall of Fame Museum
97 South Second Street
Memphis, Tennessee 38103
(901) 525-4007

Poplar Tunes
This is the store where Elvis bought most of his records throughout his life and it remains pretty much unchanged to this day. Some Elvis memorabilia is displayed.
308 Poplar Avenue
Memphis, Tennessee 38103
(901) 525-6348

The Country Music Hall of Fame Museum
The guitar that Elvis used during the Sun Sessions is here.
Four Music Square East
Nashville, Tennessee 37203
(615) 256-1639
(615) 255-5333

Hard Rock Hotel and Casino
This rock and roll themed casino has several of E's guitars on display.
Hard Rock Hotel and Casino
4455 Paradise Road
Las Vegas, Nevada 89109
(702) 693-5000
(800) 473-ROCK

All-Elvis Radio Shows

Stephen Christopher's Elvis on the Air *radio program*

Stephen Christopher travels all over North America with his radio show *Elvis on the Air*. He specializes in playing the rarer Elvis recordings to expose them to a wider audience. The show has live interviews with people who knew Elvis, trivia games, prizes. If you can name a song he can't play, you win a car. Steve makes frequent appearances at Elvis fan gatherings. For information about having *Elvis on the Air* in your hometown call:
(334) 277-3166
http://members.aol.com/eonair/index.html
E-mail: elvisonair@aol.com

Jay Gordon's Elvis Only Radio Show

Jay is the founding member of If I Can Dream Elvis Fan Club of Massachusetts. His show is not nationally syndicated but you can call to find the station near you that carries it. He also publishes the *Elvis Only* newsletter.
(800) 349-5484
(617) 787-7510
http://www.tiac.net/users/subzero/elvis/join.htm

If I Can Dream Fan Club of Massachusetts
Gary Larkin's Internet Radio House of Wax Oldies Show
Contact him for more information.
E-mail: glarkin@nb.net
http://www.nb.net/~glarkin/

Predominately Presley Computer Radio

Bryan Gruska hosts an all-Elvis radio program, *Predominately Presley*, which can now be heard live around the world via RealAudio. All you need is a computer, the RealAudio program, and a modem.
E-mail: PPresley@juno.com
http://www.angelfire.com/il/
   ElvisToday/PPresley
http://www.flamesradio.com

Special Elvis Songs for Special Occasions

No matter what's happening in your life, good times or bad, there's an Elvis song that fits the occasion. Here's a few examples.
When you need to wake up in the morning.
   "See See Rider"
When you need to persevere.
   "This Time You Gave Me a Mountain"
When you quit your job.
   "Big Boss Man"
When you've reached rock bottom.
   "You'll Never Walk Alone"
When things are going great for you.
   "King of the Whole Wide World"
When things aren't going quite so great.
   "Bridge Over Troubled Water"
When you're trying to win someone's heart.
   "Rags to Riches"
When you want to be alone.
   "Make the World Go Away"
When you need to be inspired.
   "If I Can Dream"
When your dog goes to heaven.
   "Old Shep"
When you want to "you know."
   "Let's Play House"

Sandi Miller

"I thank God for Elvis Presley. I thank the Lord for sending Elvis to open the door so I could walk down the road...."
   —Little Richard

Record Your Own Voice
Test your own singing ability. Find a recording studio near you that you can rent by the hour. It will probably give you a renewed appreciation for Elvis' talents.

Build a Replica of Sun Studio
It was only a 17-by-28-foot room, probably not much bigger than the average garage. So why not build one in your garage? Use it as a listening room for your Elvis music. The soundproofing will let you play your music as loud as you want. Go to Sun, take a tour, take some pictures, get to work. Try to equip it with antique recording equipment for full effect.

How to Create the Sun Slapback Sound
Slapback was an echo effect that Sam Phillips created by running the original recording through a second Ampex 350C recorder machine creating a phased effect.

How to Get D. J. Fontana Autographed Drumsticks
To get information about how to order a set of autographed drumsticks from Elvis' drummer, send a self-addressed, stamped envelope to:
D. J. Fontana
4815 Trousdale Drive 3412
Nashville, Tennessee 37220-1324

Tell 'Em What You Think at RCA
All questions, comments, requests, complaints, and opinions should be sent to RCA at the following address. They do not have an e-mail address that is available to the public.
RCA Records, Strategic Marketing
1540 Broadway, 35th Floor
New York, New York 10036

Buy the Type of Guitar Strings Elvis Used
Graceland Catalog carries Gibson acoustic and electric guitar strings made of phosphor bronze like Elvis preferred for his own guitars.

Buy a Jukebox
Elvis had a jukebox at Graceland, and so should you! Wurlitzer makes an Elvis Presley Limited Edition jukebox. Stock it with all Elvis records.
Wurlitzer
(800) 987-5480
Fax: (847) 662-1212
http://www.wurlitzerjukebox.com/showroom.html

Rig Your Property with Outdoor Speakers

Just like they have at Graceland. Great for parties. If your neighbors are Elvis fans they'll love it, too. If they're not Elvis fans, maybe it will encourage them to move. (Who wants to live next door to someone who's not an Elvis fan?)

Get an Elvis Presley Signature Gibson Guitar

Gibson's Epiphone division has a cutaway acoustic/electric guitar for sale that's decorated with Elvis' name and picture. They can send you a catalog with a photo of the guitar if you contact them.

Gibson Musical Instruments
645 Massman Drive,
Nashville, Tennessee 37210
(800) 444-2766
http://www.gibson.net

Learn to Play the Guitar

It was Elvis' first instrument and because of that it's considered *the* instrument of rock and roll. Try to buy it from a hardware store like Elvis did.

Learn to Play the Piano

Elvis always made sure he had access to a piano even when he was young and money was scarce. He would often gather friends and family around the piano for sing-alongs. He was self-taught and much more proficient on the ivories than he was on guitar.

Get a Vintage Turntable

Play your vintage vinyl on a vintage turntable. The snaps, pops, and hisses are part of the experience.

Find Your Local Radio Station that Plays the Most Elvis

There are a lot of oldies stations around and if they don't play enough Elvis for your taste: call in ... often.

Listen to the Music of Elvis' Backup Groups

Many of Elvis' backup singers and groups are recording artists in their own right. The Sweet Inspirations have several records, as do the Stamps, J. D. Sumner, Jake Hess.

> "... rockabilly fixed the crucial image of rock and roll: the sexy, half-crazed fool standing on stage singing his guts out."
>
> —Greil Marcus

How to Avoid Elvis Burnout

You may think it's impossible to burn out on Elvis—but it's a good idea to occasionally take an Elvis fast. Listen to some longhair music or some Michael Bolton. We predict you'll soon be screaming for Elvis.

Use Guerrilla Tactics in Record Stores

When Elvis' CDs are released these days, record stores often put them in their oldies section, unlike new releases of artists like Hendrix or the Beatles. To help promote Elvis music in the same way, why not move Elvis' CDs from the oldies (or wherever they have the nerve to put them) to the new releases section. If this seems too bold, then you can always just politely request that they do it.

Create an Elvis Influence Tape

Make a tape mix of Bill Monroe, Hank Williams, Mississippi Slim, Dean Martin, Mario Lanza, or the many others who influenced Elvis early on. See what it inspires *you* to do.

Whenever Possible, Replace Muzak with Elvis Music

The world would be a better place if elevator, office, mall, and telephone-hold muzak all were replaced with Elvis. If you're in charge of music choice in a public place, go with Elvis. Otherwise make your Elvis requests.

Give Elvis Music as Gifts

Turn someone onto Elvis and perhaps change their lives. For your friends who are already Elvis fans, try to find them the rarer stuff.

Elvis on a Boombox

Boomboxes let you bring quality sound to unusual places, so Elvis really can be everywhere.

Take Singing Lessons

Learn at least one Elvis song really well. Sing it often.

Visit the Museum that Traces Southern Music through Elvis

Mississippi River Museum
The museum has five galleries devoted to the evolution of music in the South from slave songs to rock and roll. One Elvis gallery has a costume of Elvis' and other special related exhibitions during Tribute Week.
125 North Front Street
Mud Island River Park
Memphis, Tennessee 38103

(901) 576-7205
(800) 507-6507

Give to a Music-Related Charity

The MusiCares Foundation was established by the National Academy of Recording Arts and Sciences, Inc., with the objective of focusing the attention and resources of the music industry on the health, human service, and welfare needs of all music people. MusiCares provides a lifeline to music people in need of financial or other assistance. Their long-term goals include the creation of health clinics and retirement facilities for members of the music community.

MusiCares Foundation
3402 Pico Boulevard
Santa Monica, California 90405
(800) MusiCares (687-4227)
http://grammy.org/musicares/contact.html

Play It Again Memphis
They accept donations of musical instruments (used or not) to give to kids who can't afford them. Drop off point in Memphis is the Amro Music Store

Amro Music Store
2918 Poplar Avenue
Memphis, Tennessee
(901) 323-8888

Give to the University of Memphis Elvis Presley Scholarship for Music Students

This endowment was created to aide gifted music students at the University of Memphis and it is partially funded by EPE. You can get information from Graceland or the university.
(888) 867-8636
(901) 678-4438

Find Audio Sites on the Internet to Jam with other Fans

For those with a mike and one would hope some talent, there are sites where you can plug in and jam with other Elvis fans. There are many; here's one:
http://www.mplayer.com

"Pat Boone covered Black music while Elvis delivered Black music."
—Steve Braun

SPIRITUALITY AND GOSPEL

Gladys Love Presley had the kind of life that made a person need to believe in the promise of a better place. When she wasn't working or taking care of her family, she took refuge in her faith. She spent hours singing and praying in a small wooden church built by her uncle Gains Smith, the church's first pastor. It was a fire and brimstone fundamentalist Pentecostal denomination that believed in speaking in tongues, faith healing, and letting the spirit move you. And move you it did. It was soul-stirring music and its power to touch the heart and move the feet was a powerful influence on Elvis for his entire life. It was most likely in this tiny church that Elvis both sang in public for the first time and first heard the guitar—the inex-

pensive and portable instrument of choice for the preachers who ministered to the poor in much of the South. (Years later Elvis was among the forerunners who made the guitar the defining instrument of rock and roll.)

As a toddler, even before Elvis could speak, he tried to sing along with the rest of the congregation. He didn't need to know the words because he already knew the feeling. When the Presleys moved to

This building was Elvis' first church. It was moved around the corner from its original location and is now a private residence.

John O'Hara

The Jordanaires performing at the 1999 Elvis birthday festivities in Memphis

John O'Hara

Memphis, the capital of both white and black forms of gospel, Elvis was able to further indulge his ever-growing passion for spiritual music. Several local radio stations played all-gospel formats.

The Blackwood Brothers, one of Elvis' favorite gospel groups, were members of the Assembly of God Church where Elvis attended and regularly took part in bible study classes. Elvis looked up to them as musical heroes and remained in awe of them his entire life. He also often slipped into East Triggs Baptist Church to hear some of the most stirring black gospel in the South. At Ellis Auditorium he attended all-night sings, marathon performances by up to a dozen professional gospel groups that began at 8:00 P.M. and went on till early the next morning. He was a gospel groupie. Elvis even auditioned to replace a member of a gospel quartet, the Songfellows. He was turned down either because they felt he just couldn't help himself from singing lead instead of harmony or the person he would have replaced returned, as two different versions go. In spite of how little money his family had during these years, Elvis made it a priority to rent a piano so he could practice his spirituals.

Before Elvis could fulfill his dream of becoming a member of a gospel quartet, he strolled into Sun Studio and instead of becoming a harmonizing baritone, became a star of a very different kind of music—a sort of hybrid offspring of gospel that would come to be called rock and roll. Although Elvis reached unprecedented levels of stardom as the flag bearer of this daring new music, he never strayed far from his roots. On his third Ed Sullivan appearance, after igniting a firestorm of controversy for his shockingly uninhibited performance style, he performed "Peace in the Valley" backed by the gospel group the Jordanaires. He was condemned by conservatives, unaware of Elvis' religious background, as cynically trying to calm his critics and

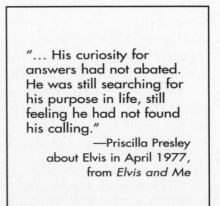

"... His curiosity for answers had not abated. He was still searching for his purpose in life, still feeling he had not found his calling."
—Priscilla Presley about Elvis in April 1977, from *Elvis and Me*

broaden his market. His fans saw it differently and the response to the performance was so great that RCA released "Peace in the Valley" as an EP with four other songs. It became a million seller and the best-selling gospel record in history.

No matter what kind of song he was scheduled to record, whether a gut-busting rocker or a lilting ballad, Elvis began every session warming up, usually accompanying himself at the piano, singing gospel music as if he needed to return to the source of his talent and recalibrate his heart. One of the few times Elvis ever exercised his clout as a star was when he walked out of one of his first RCA recording sessions in protest when an RCA representative suggested he stop wasting time playing gospel and get down to the business at hand. They soon learned how important and essential the music of his youth was to conjuring Elvis' magic. It was truly sacred to him.

It was around this time that Elvis started another lifelong habit of his spiritual development. In 1956 June Juanico, a girlfriend of Elvis', gave him a copy of *The Prophet* by Kahlil Gibran. Elvis devoured the philosophy of the book—he had never been exposed to anything like it before—and it remained one of his favorite. It was a foreshadowing of things to come: years later, Elvis acquired a library of more than a thousand books related to spiritual matters and often gave inspirational books as gifts.

Not long after he was inducted into the army, Elvis suffered the worst tragedy of his life when his mother, Gladys, died suddenly at the age of 46. In this darkest hour, Elvis turned to the healing power of gospel music. He arranged to have the Blackwood Brothers flown in to perform at his mother's funeral and, among many other songs, they sang Gladys's favorite, "Precious Memories." As they finished each song, Elvis sent them a note with another request until they had sung a dozen or so of his favorites. The death of his mother had a profound impact on Elvis. Just as he was reaching unprecedented levels of success he lost the person whom he most wanted to share it all

John O'Hara

The statue of Jesus in the Meditation Garden that was originally Gladys's grave marker in Forest Lawn Cemetery

"Elvis Presley—the charmer of fans, the favorite of many—and yet, an enigma to some. People loved his music, marveled at his endless gyrations, yet puzzled over the stories of his private conduct and his sometimes inexplicable behavior. But I loved the Elvis who showed himself through his music. Being a musician myself, I know that art has countless outlets. Presley's artistic expressions took many forms. My favorite was his gospel music. I think that the message proclaimed in his spiritual songs portrayed a man who, behind that sometimes wild exterior, had a kind and loving heart, and who gave generously to the poor and the needy."

—Sister Anna Rose

with. Her death caused him to question the meaning of life and to ponder the mysteries of death and he embarked on a lifelong search for answers to the big questions.

Wherever he was stationed while in the army, he made sure there was a piano in the house. And when not on duty Elvis spent a good deal of his time sitting at that piano, singing his favorite gospel songs, and harmonizing with friends. Although he spent much of his time in Germany in the comfortable cocoon of his transplanted entourage, his horizons did broaden somewhat. It was during this time that he became an enthusiastic student of the martial arts. Elvis was further exposed to Eastern philosophy, meditation, and the concept of mind-body unity by his karate teachers.

When he returned home, it was to a Graceland without Gladys and her absence was a gnawing emptiness in his life. He kept a poster-sized blowup of a photo of them together on an easel beside his bed as a reminder of the question he always asked: *Why would a loving God permit this to happen?* The inscription chosen by him for her gravestone was an almost defiant and certainly defeated, "Not mine but Thy will be done."

In the fall of 1960, perhaps in response to the pain of his mother's death, he recorded his first full-length gospel album, *His Hand in Mine*. It was a labor of love and a tribute to the quartet music of his youth. He thoughtfully selected each song and had almost total control over the project. Many of the songs were among the ones he requested at his mother's funeral. On one of the songs Elvis sings are the lyrics "Known Only to Him Are the Great

John O'Hara

Larry Geller being interviewed at the Circle of Memories fan event in Palm Springs, 1999

Hidden Secrets." For Elvis, it expressed his quest to know those secrets.

Elvis soon fell into a pattern of making three movies a year then retreating behind the walls of Graceland. He was rich, famous, talented, and bored out of his skull. He had everything but the serenity he sought. One of the few things that continued to keep his interest was his karate training. On April 30, 1964, a 24-year-old hairstylist working at Jay Sebring's salon in Los Angeles was summoned to Elvis' Bel Air home to replace Elvis' former haircutter Sal Orifice. The saying goes, "When the student is ready a teacher will appear...." In this case the teacher also cut and dyed hair. Larry Geller was a self-styled guru with a soothing manner who was well versed in the knowledge of the dawning New Age. During that first haircut he and Elvis talked for more than four hours. Elvis was intrigued by Geller and immediately hired him as a full-time employee. Larry introduced Elvis to a new world of books on spiritual matters, cosmology, numerology, and metaphysics. They spent hours discussing various philosophies of life.

Courtesy of Butterfield & Butterfield

AND YE SHALL KNOW
THE TRUTH AND THE
TRUTH SHALL MAKE
· YOU FREE ·

כִּי תַשְׂכִּילָה אֶת הַמַּדָּע
תֵּעָשֶׂה הַחָכְמָה וְהַדַּעַת
וְהָאֱמֶת

· ET · COGNOSCETIS ·
VERITATEM · ET · VERITAS
LIBERABIT · VOS

The rest of Elvis' entourage became suspicious and resentful of Larry's monopoly of his attention. Larry was insultingly nicknamed "Swami," "Rasputin," or the "Wandering Jew" by some of the members of the Memphis Mafia. In reluctant recognition of Elvis' spiritual yearnings, the guys gave Elvis a deluxe leather-bound Bible as a gift for Christmas in 1965. Printed on the front of the book was a drawing of a tree of life with Elvis' name on the

The Tree of Life gold pendant presented to Elvis by the Memphis Mafia

The star of David/cross watch made by Harry Levitch Jewelers

trunk and the names of his inner circle written on the branches. Also inscribed in the Bible was "The truth shall make you free" in English, Hebrew, and Latin. Conspicuously missing among the branches was Larry's name. Elvis refused to accept the gift until Larry's name was added. For his next birthday in January, they gave Elvis a gold medallion version of the tree of life. This time Larry was included.

Larry revealed new ways of thinking to Elvis. As a result of Larry's influence, Elvis started to take great interest and pride in being part Jewish. He was told by his mother that her maternal grandmother, Martha Tackett, was Jewish as if it were a family secret. Elvis now flaunted it. He had the Jewish star carved on his mother's gravestone at Forest Hills Cemetery. He started to wear a *chai*, the Hebrew symbol of life around his neck. He designed a watch that alternately flashed every thirty seconds between the cross and the Star of David. Elvis had hundreds of these made and gave them out to encourage brotherhood.

After a year of study under Larry's tutelage, he felt he had finally made some progress. In 1965, while making one of the road trips home from Hollywood, Elvis and his entourage were crossing the desert on Route 66 near the south rim of the Grand Canyon when Elvis had a spiritual breakthrough, of sorts. A cloud in the distance appeared to him to have formed into the face of Joseph Stalin and then seemed to morph into the face of Jesus. Elvis interpreted this as having great significance. Whether it was a vision of God, the power of suggestion, or just a cumulonimbus Rorschach test, it served as a turning point for Elvis. For a short period thereafter, Elvis entertained a desire to become a monk.

Around this time, Larry brought Elvis to the Self-Realization Fellowship Lake Shrine, a yoga ashram in Pacific Palisades. It was founded in 1920 by Yogi Paramahansa Yogananda who was sent

Elvis in *Harum Scarum*

to America as an emissary of Sri Yukteswar Giri to spread the principles of kiri yoga. Elvis had read Yogananda's book *Autobiography of a Yogi* and was impressed by his teachings. Yogananda had died in 1952 and when Elvis visited the fellowship it was being run by one of his disciples, Sister Daya Mata. Elvis often met with Daya Mata and called her "Ma." He spoke candidly about his fears and desires for peace of mind to the benevolent Ma, who he said reminded him of his own mother, his other confessor. He also spent many hours discussing life with an octogenarian monk named Brother Adolph and another named Brahma Chari Josef. The Lake Shrine was later the inspiration for the Meditation Garden at Graceland.

His personal quest for meaning was in stark contrast to what was happening in his professional life. At the time he was visiting the Lake Shrine and actually contemplating joining a monastery, he was shooting movies like *Harum Scarum*. He was in the midst of his spiritual journey while he was making some of his more fluffy films. When watching some of these movies, think of Elvis in his trailer between takes delving into a spiritual tract or discussing philosophy with Larry or a costar while still in costume. After filming was finished on some of these movies Elvis gave out the Star of David/cross watches to the cast and crew.

Elvis decided that one of the best ways to express his new-found fervor would be with another gospel album. In May of 1966 he recorded *How Great Thou Art* in Nashville. After three years of nothing but skillfully tossed-off movie soundtracks he once again got the chance to do something he really cared about and he fully invested himself in the project. In his eyes, he was on a mission from God. He assembled a handpicked and extraordinary group of voices. Among them was his vocal idol Jake Hess. The Jordanaires, the Imperials, and four female studio singers including Millie Kirkham supplied the choir sound that he was looking for. Elvis' talent was to sing all songs with feeling; even if he didn't really care about

"One of my favorite moments of all time was an Easter morning in Palm Springs. Elvis had been up all night and the sun was rising over the mountains ... all but a couple of people had gone to bed. He quietly sat down at the piano and started singing gospel songs ... just him, and the piano, and his thoughts.... He threw his head back, closed his eyes, and just sang his heart out all by himself. We had tears streaming down our faces and so did he ... it was a religious experience if ever there was one! Those people snoring in their rooms down the hall never had any idea what they missed out on!"
—Sandi Miller, friend of Elvis

This statue of Jesus was a gift to Elvis from the Memphis Mafia

John O'Hara

a song he could make you believe he did. But when he sang gospel music, he sang it with true conviction. Elvis put so much of himself into this album, particularly the title song, that when it was over he almost collapsed. "Something really happened to Elvis," said Jerry Schilling, who witnessed the recording session. In 1967 it won Elvis his first Grammy Award for Best Sacred Performance.

The Colonel increasingly saw Larry as a threat to his control over Elvis. Spiritual fulfillment was not the Colonel's goal. Wallet fulfillment was. He didn't like the changes he witnessed in Elvis. He was getting too independent, too hard to control. Only when it threatened the Colonel's income did he ever address Elvis' personal life. The Colonel had a rare face-to-face meeting with Elvis to discuss the "religious kick" he was on. Elvis was infuriated with his manager's meddling. The Colonel let his feelings be known in other ways also. As technical adviser on Elvis' film, the Colonel had a scene inserted into *Easy Come Easy Go* specifically designed to belittle Elvis' new interests. Elvis' character in the movie stumbles into a yoga class populated by beatniks and other "weirdos." After his character ridicules yoga, he sings a duet with the instructor played by Elsa Lanchester (of *Bride of Frankenstein* fame). Let's just say "Yoga Is as Yoga Does" is not a high point in Elvis' musical career.

After each break between films Elvis reluctantly returned to Hollywood to shoot the next movie. As if subconsciously refusing to participate in another humiliating film, Elvis fell, hit his head, and suffered a concussion on the eve of the start of production on the film *Clambake*. The Colonel took this as his chance to reassert himself over Elvis. After keeping Elvis in seclusion for a few days, the Colonel called a meeting at which he issued edicts establishing the "new Elvis world order," with Elvis sheepishly kowtowing. Among the Colonel's new rules were that Larry was no longer allowed to be alone with Elvis and Elvis was not to read

"In the Pentecostal South, heaven is not a concept, it is a destination."
—Peter Whitmer, from *The Inner Elvis: A Psychological Biography of Elvis Aaron Presley*

The Circle G Ranch, Walls, Mississippi

any more of his books or even to discuss religion. During the meeting the Colonel, looking directly at Larry, said, "Some of you think maybe he's Jesus Christ, who should wear robes and walk down the street helping people. But that's not who he is."

Who, exactly, Elvis *was* now, according to the Colonel, remained unclear. There was a change in him after the meeting. Two weeks later, production began on *Clambake*. As Larry described the atmosphere at the time, "It was open season on the swami." Larry saw the writing on the wall and soon quit. Once filming was completed, Elvis married Priscilla in a wedding organized by the Colonel that left many of Elvis' friends uninvited. Shortly after the marriage, at his new wife's behest, Elvis and Priscilla burned much of his forbidden library of spiritual books in a well.

When the movies were finally behind him, Elvis made his historic musical rebirth with the "'68 Comeback Special." Since the theme of the show came from Elvis' own life, and tells (loosely) his story through song, gospel was a big part of the show.

The success of the "'68 Comeback Special" launched Elvis' return to live performance. For his new backup singers he once again assembled a superb group of voices to take the stage with him. His choir included the Imperials, J. D. Sumner (listed in the *Guinness Book of Records* as the world's lowest bass singer at double-low *C*) and the Stamps, the Sweet Inspirations, and Voice. The film *Elvis on Tour* shows the kind of backstage gospel jams that Elvis would have before and after shows. When you look at the footage, don't just take note of how Elvis sings; take note of how he listens. To Elvis, gospel was more than music; it went right to his core. He often sang gospel with his eyes closed as if better able to concentrate on the vision he was seeing so clearly in his mind.

It was at one of the Las Vegas shows in 1972 that Larry Geller reunited with Elvis and remained in his life until he did Elvis' hair in preparation of his funeral. Elvis continued his spiritual education during this time and always traveled with a personal library of several hundred books that were loaded on the *Lisa Marie* so he could have them at hand.

At Elvis' funeral, Jake Hess, Elvis' lifelong musical idol, once again sang the song he sang at Gladys's funeral. This time when the words were sung "Known Only to Him Are the Great Hidden Secrets," Elvis had finally found his answers and understood.

Elvis boarding the *Lisa Marie* carrying one of the many books from his collection that always traveled with him.

Sandi Miller

Certainly during the '60s and '70s there was increased interest in alternate religions and philosophies and expanding one's consciousness was everyone's bag. Lots of people were searching for answers. What made Elvis' search different, and so urgent, was that the question that troubled his heart was one that no one else on the planet could answer, much less ask. Elvis wanted to know why God had chosen him to be Elvis Presley—and what was he meant to do with this gift.

Understanding Elvis' search for meaning and purpose in his life is vital to knowing the real man. Elvis Presley was a sincerely and profoundly religious man. He was a spiritual seeker. This is one of the aspects of Elvis that resonated deeply with many fans, and still does, while at the same time generating some skepticism among his critics. It didn't matter to him. Elvis incorporated gospel into his performances as his way of witnessing. To many of his fans, gospel is the music that inspires not only worship of God, but also offers a more profound appreciation of Elvis.

ESSENTIAL ELVISOLOGY

Elvis' Gospel Grammy Awards
1967 Winner Best Sacred Performance
  How Great Thou Art—album
1972 Winner Best Inspirational Performance
  He Touched Me—album
1974 Winner Best Inspirational Performance
  "How Great Thou Art"—live version

> "I know practically every religious song that's ever been written."
> —Elvis Presley

Guitar-Playing Pastors Who Influenced Elvis
Reverend Edward Parks
Reverend James Ballard
Reverend Frank Smith

Gospel Singers and Groups Who Influenced Elvis

The Blackwood Brothers
Jake Hess
Sister Rosetta Tharpe
The Clara Ward Singers
The Harmoneers
The Happy Goodman Family

The Jordanaire
Golden Gate Quartet
Harmonizing Four
Reverend Jimmy Jones
The Statesmen Quartet
The Sunshine Boys

Gospel Songs Elvis Recorded

Elvis, who once claimed to know every religious song ever written, handpicked these songs to record. These are the songs that he most loved.

"I Believe"
"Peace in the Valley"
"Take My Hand, Precious Lord"
"It Is No Secret What God Can Do"
"Milky White Way"
"His Hand in Mine"
"I Believe in the Man in the Sky"
"He Knows Just What I Need"
"Mansion over the Hilltop"
"In My Father's House"
"Joshua Fit the Battle"
"Swing Down Sweet Chariot"
"I'm Gonna Walk Dem Golden Stairs"
"If We Never Meet Again"
"Known Only to Him"
"Working on the Building"
"Crying in the Chapel"
"Run On"
"How Great Thou Art"
"Stand by Me"
"Where No One Stands Alone"
"So High"
"Farther Along"
"By and By"
"In the Garden"
"Somebody Bigger Than You and I"
"Without Him"
"Reach Out to Jesus"

"If the Lord Wasn't Walking by My
   Side"
"Where Could I Go But to the Lord"
"We Call on Him"
"You'll Never Walk Alone"
"Only Believe"
"Amazing Grace"
"Miracle of the Rosary"
"Lead Me, Guide Me"
"He Touched Me"
"I've Got Confidence"
"An Evening Prayer"
"Seeing Is Believing"
"A Thing Called Love"
"Put Your Hand in the Hand"
"He Is My Everything"
There Is No God but God"
"I, John"
"Bosom of Abraham"
"Help Me"
"If That Isn't Love"
"Why Me Lord"
"You Better Run"
"Lead Me Guide Me"
"Turn Your Eyes upon Jesus"
"Nearer My God to Thee"
"Sweet, Sweet Spirit"

Gospel Music at Elvis' Funeral

Jake Hess and the Statesmen
    "Known Only to Him"
James Blackwood
    "How Great Thou Art"
J. D Sumner and the Stamps
    "Sweet, Sweet Spirit"
    "His Hand in Mine"
Bill Baize
    "When It's My Turn"
Kathy Westmoreland
    "My Heavenly Father Watches Over Me"

Gospel in Elvis' Films

The Trouble With Girls
    "Swing Low Sweet Chariot"
Frankie And Johnny
    "When the Saints Go Marching In"
Easy Come, Easy Go
    "Sing You Children"
Change of Habit
    "Let Us Pray"
Elvis On Tour
    "I, John"
    "Lead Me, Guide Me"
    "Amen"
    "Bosom of Abraham"
    "You Gave Me a Mountain"

Elvis' Favorite Bible Quotation

Book of Revelations
Chapter 21, Verses 2–27

Elvis' Favorite Section of the Bible

Book of John

Elvis' Library of Spiritual Books

Elvis' favorite reading matter was his Bible and spiritual and philosophical books of all sorts. He surrounded himself with these books—on his bedside table, scattered around his room. Wherever Elvis went, so did a selection of more than 300 books in trunks so they'd always be at hand. Many photos of Elvis climbing the

> "For those who place some credence in astrology [his birth date] meant Elvis was a Capricorn, a cardinal earthy sign whose key words were ambitious, persevering, diplomatic, and reserved—the sign of the priest, ambassador, or scientist."
> —Jerry Hopkins, from *Elvis: A Biography*

> "How can anyone go through life without God and Elvis?"
> —from an episode of *Touched by an Angel*

Jeweled caftans designed for Elvis were inspired by his studies of spiritual masters.

Courtesy of Butterfield & Butterfield

stairs to the *Lisa Marie* show him carrying a book.

The very first book that exposed Elvis to different spiritual horizons was Kahlil Gibran's *The Prophet*, which he read in 1956. Elvis was bowled over by the Eastern concepts conveyed in the book. Elvis read and reread this book for years making notations, underlining, and above all, sharing it. If you want to follow his spiritual path, *The Prophet* would be the place to start. These are some of the many books that were never more than an arm's length from him.

The Bible
  Old and New Testaments, King James Version
The Prophet
  Kahlil Gibran
The Impersonal Life
  Joseph Benner
The Initiation of the World
  Vera Stanley Adler
The Fifth Dimension
  Vera Stanley Adler
Through the Eyes of the Masters
  David Anrias
Siddhartha
  Herman Hesse
The Shroud of Turin
  Ian Wilson
The Secret Teachings of All Ages
  Manly P. Hall

The Secret Doctrine
  Helena Blavatsky
The Infinite Way
  Joel Goldsmith
Elvis Unveiled
  Helena Petrovna Blavatsky
Wisdom of the Overself
  Paul Brunton
Cheiro's Book of Numbers
  Count Louis Hammon (Cheiro)
Beyond the Himalayas
  Murdo MacDonald-Bayne
Man, Grand Symbol of the Mysteries
  Manly Palmer Hall
The Rosicrucian Cosmo-Conception
  Max Heindal
America's Invisible Guidance
  Corinne Heline

Only Love
　Sri Daya Mata
Leaves of Morya's Garden
　Morya
Autobiography of a Yogi
　Paramahansa Yogananda
New Mansions for New Men
　Dane Rudhyar
The Changing Condition of Your World
　J. W. of Jupiter

Billy Graham Presents Man in the 5th Dimension
　Billy Graham
Psychedelic Experience
　Timothy Leary
Doors of Perception
　Aldous Huxley
The Power of Positive Thinking
　Dr. Norman Vincent Peale
How to Live 365 Days a Year
　Dr. John A. Schindler

The First Books

Elvis' friend Larry Geller gave Elvis books that had moved and enlightened him. The day after Elvis and Larry met, Larry brought Elvis these books:

The Impersonal Life
　Joseph Benner
Autobiography of a Yogi
　Paramahansa Yogananda
The Initiation of the World and *Beyond the Himalayas*
　M. MacDonald-Bayne

The Last Books

The night before Elvis died Larry Geller brought him these three books.

The Scientific Search for the Face of Jesus
　Frank O. Adams
The Second Birth
　O. Mikhail Aivanhv
Music: The Keynote of Human Evolution
　Corinne Heline

Elvis' Numerology Number

8

Stone Corresponding to the Number 8

Black Sapphire

Elvis' Stage Prayer

"Lord, send me some light, I need it bad."

"He liked Kahlil Gibran's books. Not only would he read to you, he'd recite a passage from one book or another. He'd deliver some long passage from memory, and he always had something that he wanted to spiritually relate to you."
　—Myrna Smith, one of Elvis' backup singers, from *Elvis Up Close*, edited by Rose Clayton and Dick Heard

Elvis and 2001

Because of Elvis' interest in numerology, and his choice of the 2001 theme to open his concerts, Elvis fans have given the number 2001 special significance. These equations show how different combinations of important dates from Elvis' life add up to 2001.

$8 + 16 + 1977 = 2001$

$8 + 16 + 42 + 1935 = 2001$

YOUR ELVIS EDUCATION

Books

Elvis' Search for God
  Larry Geller and Jess Stearn
The Truth about Elvis
  Larry Geller and Jess Stearn
If I Can Dream: Elvis' Own Story
  Larry Geller
Elvis: His Spiritual Journey
  Jess Stearn
Elvis and Gladys
  Elaine Dundy
In Search of Elvis: Music, Race, Art, Religion
  Edited by Vernon Chadwick
Elvis: The Messiah
  Jack D. Malley and Warren Vaughn
Elvis: Prophet of Power
  Samuel Roy
Nothin' but Fine
  Jake Hess
The Best of Elvis: Recollections of a Great Humanitarian
  Cindy Hazen and Mike Freeman
Elvis After Life: Unusual Psychic Experiences Surrounding the Death of a Superstar
  Raymond A. Moody
Elvis Aaron Presley: His Growth and Development as a Soul Spirit within the Universe
  Paula Farmer
The Gospel of Elvis : Containing the Testament and Apocrypha Including All the Greater Themes of the King
  Edited by Solomon B. T. Church
Elvis: His Love for Gospel Music and J. D. Sumner
  J. D. Sumner

Video

The '68 Comeback Special
Elvis—Docudrama TV Series (ABC)
  February 6, 1990 to May 26, 1990
"This is Elvis"
Elvis on Tour
Elvis, That's the Way It Is
Singing in My Soul
  This video, packaged by Bill Gaither, features
  200 gospel greats including many who influenced and performed with Elvis
  like J. D. Sumner, Jake Hess, and Hovie Lister.
Change of Habit
Live a Little, Love a Little

Web Sites

http://jordanselvisworld.simplenet.com/Jordanaires/home.htm
  The Official Jordanaires homepage on Jordan's Elvis World site.
http://www.bestjerusalem.co.il/food/cafe/elvis/
  Jerusalem Inn site
http://www.whatwouldelvisdo.com
  "What would Elvis do?" web site
http://rrq.simplenet.com/music/Elvis_Presley/
  Russell Reed Quartet's Elvis gospel Links page
http://www.gospelsinging.com
  Site where you can purchase Elvis gospel music
http://schlbus.belmont.edu/mb/sumner.html
  J. D. Sumner's Elvis CD page with sound files
http://chelsea.ios.com/~hkarlin1/welcom.html
  First Presleyterian Church
http://www.gaithermusic.com
  Gaither Collection site; gospel music source

THE ELVIS AND YOU EXPERIENCE

Visit the Elvis Presley Memorial Chapel

Elvis was once asked what he would want done in his memory after he was gone. The story goes that he suggested a chapel be built so his fans could go and meditate and reflect on their own lives, just as he had. The Elvis Presley Memorial Chapel was dedicated August 17, 1979. Inside is the original pulpit from the Assembly of God church and the Presley family Bible.

Elvis Presley Memorial Chapel, Tupelo, Mississippi

Elvis Presley Memorial Chapel
306 Elvis Presley Drive
Tupelo Mississippi 38801
(601) 841-1245

John O'Hara

Visit One of Elvis' Churches

Tupelo

First Assembly Church of God
It was inside this building that Elvis first heard gospel music. Built by his great uncle Gains Smith, it is now a private home that has been moved from its original location just around the corner. Another church currently stands on the original site.
206 Adams Street (site during Elvis' time in Tupelo)
909 Berry Street (current location of the original church building)
Tupelo, Mississippi 38801
(601) 844-5841

Memphis

First Assembly of God
It was inside this church that Elvis met his girl-friend Dixie Locke. The Blackwoods were also members of the congregation.
1084 McLemore (original building)
255 North Highland (present location)
Memphis, Tennessee
(901) 324-3585

Attend a Gospel Service
Check your yellow pages to find a church with gospel services near you and call ahead to find out when they are and if guests are allowed to join the congregation in song.

> "[Gospel] resembles the cocky, brash, exuberant sound of early rock far more than the heavier and more sophisticated emotions of the blues; Gospel also shares with rock its beat, its drama, its demand for honesty of emotion, and its emphasis on participation."
> —Neal and Janice Gregory, from *When Elvis Died*

Attend the Annual Elvis Gospel Mass

Every year the Elvis Chicago Style Fan Club sponsors a gospel mass at St. Paul's Church in Memphis during Tribute Week. A Catholic priest conducts an Elvis-centric mass for the faithful that incorporates Elvis' gospel music. No matter what your religion, the afternoon is a unique way to feel the potency of this deeply emotional music. The church is located at 1425 East Shelby Drive in Memphis. You can get more information by writing to the club president, Mike Keating, at P.O. Box 388554, Chicago, Illinois 60638 or calling (312) 494-2626

Introduce Elvis Gospel Music at Your Own Church

No matter what denomination your church is, there's an Elvis gospel song that could be incorporated into any service. To get sheet music to some of Elvis' gospel songs you can buy this book from Graceland's bookshop or catalog.
Elvis Presley: Songs of Inspiration
Collection of gospel and inspirational sheet music for vocal, guitar, and piano published by Hal Leonard Corporation, Milwaukee, Wisconsin.

Join a Choir

If you really want to feel the glory of this music don't just listen to it, sing it! With as many other people as possible.

Don't Wear Black to a Funeral

Elvis said he didn't want anyone to wear black at his funeral. His spiritual readings suggested purple or violet instead. His ex-girlfriend Linda Thompson was one of the few people who followed his advice and wore a lavender dress.

Make Arrangements to Have Elvis Gospel at Your own Funeral

Choose some of the songs that were performed at Elvis' funeral. Too bad you'll miss it.

Commission Elvis-Themed Stained Glass

Why not design your own? You can hire the same company that created the stained glass at Graceland and in the Memorial Chapel in Tupelo.
Laukhuff Stained Glass of Memphis
2585 Summer Avenue
Memphis, Tennessee 38112
(901) 320-9206

> "... Oh God, it's the way he touched my heart that I truly miss the most. So, Lord, could you do one thing just for me? Please hold Elvis close to you and let him know I miss him so and tell him I never said good-bye and I wanted him to know."
> —Linda, with a late-night prayer, on the TLC mail loop

Elvis-themed stained glass at the Hard Rock Café, Atlantic City, New Jersey

Subscribe to *The Singing News*

This is monthly publication, sold at many religious book stores, and is a must for true gospel lovers. Send them letters to the editor about Elvis' gospel music and what it means to you.

The Singing News
P.O. Box 2810
Boone, North Carolina 28607
(800) 255-2810

Learn about Elvis through Astrology

This extremely insightful limited-edition magazine gives a detailed profile of Elvis' place in the cosmos complete with a biorhythm analysis. The author states that "reading this publication will give the reader a deeper, fuller, and better insight into Elvis' personality and inner being." They also offer a compatibility profile between you and Elvis that you can send away for. Contact them for information about this.

Elvis' Astrological and Psychological Profile
Lifestyles International
1691 Columbia Road
Berkley, Michigan 48072
(800) 987-5544
E-mail: lifeintl@wwnet.com
http://www.lifeintl.com

Have Your Astrological Chart Done in Relation to Elvis'

Matt Tilton, New York City-based astrologist, will do your own chart in relation to Elvis'. Just send your birth date, time of birth, and place of birth, along with a check or money order for $20 and he'll write you back with information on how the planets line up for your and Elvis' natal charts.

> "I know this—all good things come from God. You don't have to go to church to know right from wrong. Sure, church helps, but you can be a Christian so long as you have a Christian heart."
> —Elvis Presley

Matt Tilton
P.O. Box 1645
Old Chelsea Station
New York, New York 10011

Where to Get Gospel Recordings

Gaither Family Resources

This is your resource for Elvis' gospel and Elvis' favorite gospel singers. They carry CDs and videos of gospel singing jubilees like Elvis loved to attend as a young man. You can also find books such as *Nothin' but Fine*, Jake Hess' autobiography, which includes anecdotes about Elvis.

Gaither Family Resources store
1617 South Park Avenue
Alexandria, Indiana 46001

Gaither Collection Catalog
P.O. Box 178
Alexandria, Indiana 46001
(800) 520-4664
(765) 724-8222
http://www.gaithermusic.com

Jewel, Paula, Ronn Records

They don't carry Elvis records per se but they carry all the stuff he would have listened to when he was young.

Jewel, Paula, Ronn Records
1700 Century Boulevard
Shreveport, Louisiana 71101
or
P.O. Box 1125
Shreveport, Louisiana 71163-1125
(800) 446-2865
(318) 227-2228
Fax: (318) 227-0304

Become a Fan of Elvis' Favorite Gospel Group

Elvis admired J. D. Sumner and the Stamps, who performed with him from 1970 to 1977. He would often close his eyes onstage and just listen to their beautiful harmonizing. He

> "Elvis brings out a special depth and understanding between Steve and myself as a couple, and individually as well. Elvis once stated, 'I want to awaken in all these young people a close relationship with God.' Steve and I feel he is, inspirationally, a conduit to a higher awareness."
>
> —Cathy Rogers and Steve Curtis

was especially in awe of that unbeliev-able double-low *C* that J. D. reached, which won him a place in the *Guinness Book of Records* as the world's lowest bass singer.

You can hear them singing on many of Elvis' records such as "Burning Love," "American Trilogy," and "Way Down." They also recorded a tribute album, *Memories of Our Friend Elvis.*

Since J. D.'s death, the Stamps (which was a registered trademark of his) are now called Ed Enoch and the Golden Covenant. They still perform and you can be transported like Elvis was by their wonderful voices.

Hear the J. D. Sumner Gospel Interview

J. D. Sumner, one of Elvis' great friends and gospel mentors, released an inter-view on two cassettes recorded at Belmont University in Nashville on July 26, 1995. He talks about Elvis' love of gospel and calls Elvis the most spiritual man he ever met. The special treat is the recording included by the Stamps and J. D. of five of Elvis' favorite gospel songs.

Southern Marketing Association
9 Music Square South
Drawer A—Suite 118
Nashville, Tennessee 37203

Get an Elvis Fish Symbol

This company sells a unique Elvis product. The word *Elvis* is shaped into a metal logo in the style of the ancient Christian fish symbol.

Dark Carnival Imaginative Fiction Book Store
3086 Claremont Avenue
Berkeley, California 94705
(510) 654-7323

"According to the Chinese concept of *chi* (basically a life force) people who talk a lot or sing for a living often die young because they burn up their *chi*, or burn themselves out. I don't think there's any doubt that Elvis, even in cruise mode, had *chi* explod-ing in him like the Fourth of July. Chinese medicinal the-ory seems to conclude that the saying about the brightest stars burning the shortest time is true."

—Shane, on alt.elvis.king

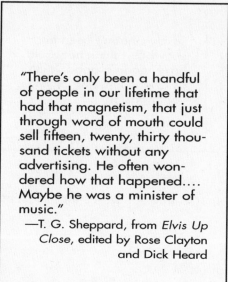

"There's only been a handful of people in our lifetime that had that magnetism, that just through word of mouth could sell fifteen, twenty, thirty thousand tickets without any advertising. He often wondered how that happened.... Maybe he was a minister of music."
—T. G. Sheppard, from *Elvis Up Close*, edited by Rose Clayton and Dick Heard

Get to Know Elvis' Guru

Larry Geller, Elvis' former hairstylist and spiritual adviser, often makes personal appearances at fan conventions. This sensitive man, who is a fan of Elvis fans, was a good friend to Elvis.
To order his books contact:
Greenleaf Publications
P.O. Box 8152
Murfreesboro, Tennessee 37133
(800) 905-8367
(615) 896-1356
E-mail: marc@
greenleafpublications.com

The New Age Voice magazine
edited by Larry Geller
This magazine only had one edition so it's quite a collector's item.

Drive Down Elvis' "Road to Damascus"

While heading east on his bus through the desert on Highway 66, Elvis was said to have experienced a religious vision. In the Bible, Saul was hit by a bolt of lightning when he was converted on the road to Damascus. For Elvis it was a cloud. Drive this road and see what you see. Coincidentally, Larry Geller also claims to have had a spiritual awakening at the same place years earlier.

Highway 66—25 miles from the south rim of the Grand Canyon just outside of Flagstaff, Arizona

Read Some of Elvis' Favorite Books

To gain some insight into Elvis and maybe yourself, read some of the books from Elvis' extensive library. Consult the list of books in "Your Elvis Education" above.

Where to Find Some of Elvis' Favorite Books

The Bodhi Tree
8585 Melrose Avenue
Los Angeles, California 90069
(310) 659-1733
Fax: (310) 659-0178
E-mail: bodhitree@bodhitree.com

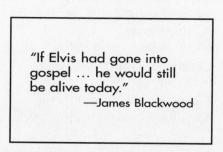

"If Elvis had gone into gospel ... he would still be alive today."
—James Blackwood

Wear a Star of David, a Cross, and a Chai

As Elvis was known to say, "Don't want to miss heaven on a technicality."

Meditate

Meditation was so important to Elvis that he had a garden created just for that purpose. Everyone can benefit from daily meditation.

> "If Elvis hadn't been in showbiz, I think he would have made a good youth or grief counselor, or youth pastor."
>
> —Fan

Practice Yoga

Beside being the inspiration for one of Elvis' more lame songs, it's an excellent form of exercise.

Find Your Own Guru

Seek out a spiritual adviser. Ask your hairstylist for advice.

Light a Candle for Elvis

Maybe because Elvis has become so associated with the Candlelight Vigil, lighting a candle in Elvis' memory has become a fan tradition.

Take an Elvis Retreat

Get away from your daily routine. Unplug your phone. Set up an easel next to your bed with a picture of Elvis on it. Spend a weekend listening exclusively to Elvis gospel.

Spread the Good Word

Give Elvis' gospel recordings to a friend in need of inspiration or salvation. It's guaranteed to lift the spirits of even the most jaded.

Evangelical Elvis Impersonator

Gary Stone is an Elvis impersonator who specializes in Elvis gospel music. His mission is to focus on the spiritual side of Elvis and follow his example by exposing people to Elvis' inspirational music. He performs benefits at churches and nursing homes.
Gary Stone
Cincinnati, Ohio
(513) 867-1007
E-mail: gstone2814@aol.com
http://hometown.aol.com/gstone2814/index.htm

Elvis Gospel Ministries

An evangelical group that had its inception in June of 1997, that in their words "has grasped the God-given opportunity of the continuing popularity of Elvis Presley, to make available to many thousands of people, the good news of Jesus Christ." Their web site states, "Many people have given their life to Christ as a direct result of listening to gospel sung by Elvis. As a result of our activities we are contacted by the media and have had the opportunity to talk about Jesus to thousands of people via radio and television interviews."

> "The main difference between Elvis and God is that nations don't go to war over Elvis."
> —Richard, on alt.elvis.king

About Their Elvis Gospel Prayer Letter

"Elvis Gospel Ministries regularly pray for Elvis fans and people in the 'Elvis' world. We would be very pleased to hear from anyone who feels called into this area of ministry. We have established a 'Graceland Fund' to offer practical help for Elvis fans in need. We now produce a regular prayer letter. If you would like to receive that by e-mail, please let us have your e-mail address and put 'Elvis Gospel Prayer letter' in the subject line. God bless you!"
Peter and Madeleine Wilson
107 Coniston Road
Wolverhampton, West Midlands WV6 9DT England
(44-1)902829424
E-mail: elvisgospel@rocketmail.com
http://www.elvisgospel.com.
http://netministries.org/see/charmin.exe/CM00784

Hear Elvis in Latin

Jukka Ammondt, a Finnish academic, translated Elvis' songs into Latin and produced a CD, *The Legend Lives Forever in Latin*. He has also translated Elvis' songs into Sumerian, which is a Babylonian cuneiform language that died out around 2000 BC. The Sumerian version of "Blue Suede Shoes" presented a problem: the Sumerians did not exactly have shoes, much less suede—so

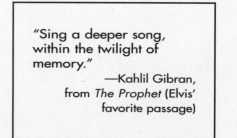

> "Sing a deeper song, within the twilight of memory."
> —Kahlil Gibran, from *The Prophet* (Elvis' favorite passage)

you end up with "sandals of leather the color of a blue gem." "Esir kus za-gin." Look for Jukka's titles on the internet.
ViihdeSallap, Ltd./Stop Records
P.O. Box 252
SF-40101 Jyvaskyla, Finland
(358) 41-666-771
Fax: (358) 0-41-666-773
E-mail: viihdesallap@co.inet.fi

Doctor Jukka Ammondt
E-mail: ammondt@cc.jyu.fi
http://www.drammondt.com/yhteys.html

Explore Some of the Same Paths that Elvis Did

Elvis delved into theosophy, ancient teachings about death and the afterworld, and the writings of Madame Blavatsky. Free leaflets on H. P. Blavatsky and theosophy in general are available from:
The Theosophical Society in America
P.O. Box 270
Wheaton, Illinois 60189

Buy Birthstone Rings for Your Friends

Elvis often made it a point to give rings and other jewelry set with the birthstone of the recipient. Most places that sell jewelry can provide you with specific birthstone information.

> "Dear God: Bolton and Cyrus for Presley?!? Let's trade!!!"
> —Graffiti on the Wall of Love, from *Dear Elvis: Graffiti from Graceland*

> "I believe I will meet Elvis Presley in Heaven."
> —Reverend Billy Graham

ELVIS IN PERSON

You're in a $10 seat close to the stage. The warm-up acts that just ended were less than spectacular but it doesn't matter because you really didn't hear one word. Everyone present is growing thrillingly restless. People start stamping their feet and chanting, "Elvis! Elvis! Elvis!" You hear the orchestra start to tune their instruments and then you pick it out in all the discordant rumbling—it's the first few notes of the tone poem you recognize as "Also Spach Zarathustra." It builds to a crescendo and you think the concert hall is going to explode, and then explode it does as Elvis strides onto the stage to the blinding strobe-light effect of thousands of flashbulbs popping. Every single man, woman, and child gives voice to the elation they are feeling. You're in the same building as Elvis! Elvis prowls the stage letting everyone soak in the sight of him and then he grabs the microphone … and you'll never be the same again.

Elvis Presley started touring in the southern states in 1954, sometimes singing to audiences as small as a few dozen. By 1955, a mere one year later, he had audiences topping 14,000 clamoring to see the new rocker, bebop, country, hillbilly, Western sensation. People may not have known what to make of the young Elvis Presley quite yet, but he was already a star.

That original touring show with Elvis backed by the Blue

Sandi Miller

From the collection of Bob Klein

Moon Boys—Scotty Moore on guitar and Bill Black on bass—was much more than the sexual tour de force that it is remembered as today. Mixed in with those early rock and roll anthems such as "Mystery Train," "Blue Suede Shoes," "Money Honey," "Tutti Frutti," and "I Got a Woman" were some unexpected spiritual and gospel songs. Elvis would sometimes stun an audience of frenzied teenagers with "Silent Night." Once when he followed two of his favorite gospel acts, the Statesmen and the Blackwood Brothers, Elvis had been so moved he decided to sing exclusively gospel during his own set, much to the chagrin of an audience prepared to cut loose.

Elvis' association with Colonel Parker in 1955 may have changed the publicity, merchandising, and overall slickness of the roadshow, but it didn't change it fundamentally. Everything Elvis did was a product of his own imagination, from his musical phrasing to the way he moved his body onstage. Critics may have been saying things like "his facial expressions [suggest] an acute appendix condition," "contortionist exhibition," and "nightmare of bad taste," but Elvis instinctively knew that if he just stood still and sang, people might figure that they could stay home and listen to his records. He wanted to give them a real performance and something to talk about.

It wasn't only Elvis' extraordinary sexual presence and charisma that had fans storming the stage. Elvis may have been initially baffled and alarmed by the reaction he was get-

From the collection of Bob Klein

Elvis with the Blue Moon Boys

ting from his audiences when he wangled his legs around while singing—a lot of people who were there at the time have reported that he was. But as soon as he caught on and figured out what got the responses from his fans, he played it to the absolute hilt. He provoked them endlessly with invitations onstage: "I usually have the Jordanaires sing along [on "I Was the One,"] but if anyone wants to come up and help, they're welcome." Not surprisingly, hundreds of fans immediately clamored to the stage. And by claiming that his pants were too large and might fall down at any moment; by asking his maniacally screaming audiences, "Do you love me?" or by moving only his little finger when he was ordered by the local constabulary to cease wiggling upon threat of arrest. The reaction he created? Utter pandemonium.

It's not surprising that the mayhem followed him everywhere. It often took a flying wedge of local policemen and bodyguards to deliver Elvis safely to his car after a show. Some local newspapers seized on this image and erroneously reported that Elvis had been arrested. But a man dressed in pink trousers, bright green jackets—not to mention gold suits and lace or velvet shirts open to the waist—was bound to cause some uproar.

"It has been said that [Elvis] was the first white to sing like a black person, which is untrue in terms of hard facts but totally true in terms of cultural impact. But what's more crucial is that when Elvis started wiggling his hips and Ed Sullivan refused to show it, the entire country went into a paroxysm of sexual frustration leading to abiding discontent which culminated in the explosion of psychedelic-militant folklore which was the sixties.

"I mean, … Elvis was not hip at all, Elvis was a goddamn truck driver who worshipped his mother and would never say shit or fuck around her, and Elvis alerted America to the fact that it had a groin with imperatives that had to be stifled. Lenny Bruce demonstrated how far you could push a society as repressed as ours and how much you could get away with, but Elvis kicked 'How Much Is that Doggie in the Window' out the window and replaced it with 'Let's fuck.' The rest of us are still reeling from the impact. Sexual chaos reigns currently, but out of chaos may flow true understanding and harmony, and either way Elvis almost singlehandedly opened the floodgates. That night in Detroit, a night I will never forget, he had but to ever so slightly move one shoulder muscle, not even a shrug, and the girls in the gallery hit by its ray screamed, fainted, howled in heat. Literally, every time this man moved any part of his body the slightest centimeter, tens or tens of thousands of people went berserk. Not Sinatra, not Jagger, not the Beatles, nobody you can come up with ever solicited such hysteria among so many."
—Lester Bangs's *Village Voice* obituary of Elvis Presley August 29, 1977

Even with a police presence, those wild clothes were often ripped to smithereens backstage or in the parking lot melees. "The kids took my watch, my ring, coat, shirt, and shoes. I got out with my pants but the cuffs were gone," Elvis told a reporter after one incident. His cars were covered with love notes and phone numbers written in lipstick or scratched into the paint.

Elvis' humor was already very much in evidence during the first few years he performed. He introduced his hit "Heartbreak Hotel" as "Heartburn Motel." At the end of one show he earnestly asked that his audience stand and place their right hands over their hearts, that he was going to sing the national anthem. He then broke into "Hound Dog." Elvis always improvised a great deal and was playful with his audiences. It was apparent he was enjoying himself onstage and many reviewers commented on how infectious this was to everyone present. Later on, friends would confirm this about Elvis in everyday life as well—another of those extraordinary qualities of his.

By the fall of 1956, just two short years after he started touring, Elvis' popularity was so remarkable that his hometown of Tupelo, Mississippi, named an official day after him and he returned triumphantly to perform in the same fairgrounds where he started his "public" singing life eleven years earlier at a Children's Day competition. Then, he placed either fifth or not at all according to local legend. For his return engagement, Elvis sang to tens of thousands of frenzied fans who were separated from their idol by 100 special police plus highway patrol officers and national guardsmen.

By 1956–57, the merchandising bonanza that would accompany Elvis' entire career was well under way through the dealings of Colonel Parker. Photos, records, and Elvis paraphernalia were available at live appearances, on occasion sold by the Colonel himself. On April 23, 1956, Elvis started a gig in the Venus

From the collection of Bob Klein

Elvis at a press conference in Las Vegas, 1969

Elvis having a "it's good to be the king" moment while basking in the adulation of his fans

Sandi Miller

Room at the New Frontier Hotel in Las Vegas. Colonel Parker billed Elvis as the "atomic-powered singer," but this booking appears to have been a miscalculation. The audience was largely conventional and middle-aged and Elvis' reception was nowhere near as enthusiastic as it was to become during the performances of the 1970s. However, the rumor that his engagement there was cut short is false. He was booked and he played for two weeks.

The army and Hollywood intervened during the late 1950s and 1960s. Some people find this period in Elvis' career an extremely regrettable detour, but perhaps it made his return to performing live even more stunning. When Elvis returned to the stage he surrounded himself with some of the best musicians in the business such as James Burton on electric guitar and Ronnie Tutt on drums. Gone were the days when the boys drove themselves from gig to gig with the bass attached to the roof of the car. Taking the Elvis stage show tour on the road in the 1970s was a masterpiece of logistics and precision planning. The show consisted of several opening acts, up to a 24-plus-piece orchestra, and custom lighting and sound systems. It took up to 5 planes to move all this plus Elvis' entourage, musicians, backup singers, technicians, costumes, and everyone's luggage from city to city from one day to the next.

Unlike the ill-fated brush with Vegas at the beginning of his career, his return in 1969 was victorious. He was being paid $1,000,000 per year for two four-week gigs in Las Vegas alone. During the first month back onstage, Elvis broke Las Vegas records for attendance and receipts and he continued this trend almost everywhere he went, breaking local records (and fire code laws) with packed beyond capacity crowds across the country. He received giddily good reviews and per-

"... graying grandmothers and halter-topped teenyboppers stood side by side and screamed their ever-livin' lungs out."
—Louisville reviewer

formed to celebrity-studded audiences. The normally staid and tactful *New York Times* entitled one review of him "A White Boy with Black Hips."

As soon as Elvis' show was booked in a venue, tickets went on sale. Fans invariably showed up at the box offices, which was the most common way to buy tickets, a minimum of 24 hours in advance. If local promoters decided to make tickets available through mail order, they had to contend with thousands of refunds once the ticket supply was quickly exhausted. Fans flew in from around the world; Japanese fan clubs chartered 8 to 10 planes and came 3000-strong at a time.

Instead of rebellion as his aim, Elvis went for style and comfort when it came to stage clothes of the 1970s. His very first stage outfits were created based on an idea of his to wear a sort of modified two-piece karate *gi*. They came in black or white, which Elvis alternated throughout that first Las Vegas stand with different color sash belts.

Elvis didn't perform his shows for the critics, the reporters, or chroniclers of history—he performed them as if they were his gift to his fans. Fans were known to put off needed operations until after his appearances in their hometowns and one or two attended his concerts in body casts. By his fans he did right, encouraging them to approach him, joking with them, shaking hands, bestowing scarves, kissing them, remembering the names of the regulars, and singing "Happy Birthday" to some lucky ones. Elvis' nimble sense of humor and mischievousness was always apparent in his concerts and he talked directly to his audiences about any sort of thing he was thinking about, things that were written about him in reviews. He introduced segments of his show saying "I'd like to do a medley of Turkish folk songs." He did imitations of Johnny Cash, Shirley Bassey, and Edward G. Robinson—and even of himself from the '50s (while holding his nose to capture the nasal quality). He yodeled and did splits. The fans threw all manner of gifts onstage and Elvis returned the favor by throwing teddy bears, rubber chickens, guitars, rings, the occasional cape, even chain loops from his belts back at them.

He put on hats that were thrown to him (police, straw, cowboy), wore gorilla and clown masks, feather boas, Mickey Mouse

Sandi Miller

ears, fake noses, and inflatable prank feet. He had water fights with band members. Elvis was so relaxed with his audience, he laughed at his own mistakes without embarrassment. But when he wasn't satisfied with any element of the show, missed cue of the backup singers, musical accompaniment, or a flub of his own, he would start a whole song over again. He was famous for changing the lyrics and singing saltier versions of his songs. Most of all he was in perpetual motion.

Keith Alverson

In 1971, "Also Spach Zarathustra" (the *2001: A Space Odyssey* theme song) was introduced to open Elvis' shows and immediately became the defining moment of what's been called "the most electrifying minute in the pop concert business"—when Elvis appeared onstage. A few such rituals could be counted on at virtually every performance. When Elvis sang "Can't Help Falling in Love," it indicated that the show would be over soon. The stage-side ceremony of grabbing scarves *and kisses* from Elvis was one the fans would never do without.

For Elvis, there was an extreme downside to touring. Death threats came in every so often and several measures were instituted over the years to protect him. With FBI involvement, at certain performances arrangements were made for Elvis to be fitted with an electronic monitoring device for his wrist, a we-mean-business security team and a doctor were stationed in the wings, and an ambulance was kept on hand. Smaller indignities such as having his tooth chipped trying to escape the

Keith Alverson

Both Elvis and his audience were often physically drained after a show.

Keith Alverson

attentions of a fan and having to calculate exactly how to stand so that he wouldn't be dragged off the stage were among the negative experiences that wore Elvis down over the years.

From the beginning of his career until the end, hysteria reigned at Elvis' performances. It didn't take anything overt on his part—a flick of his hair, a lowering of his eyes— and the fans acted as if they felt it go right through them. He could create the feeling that a performance in the largest arena was a cozy and intimate experience. If it was Elvis' aura, presence, or magic, we'll never really know, but it's undeniable that he had an incandescence that eclipsed everything else and affected everyone who saw him perform.

To have seen Elvis in person was an experience that no one would ever forget. And it is worn like a merit badge in the fan community. It is among the first questions asked in any gathering of fans: Did you ever see him? The rest of the group must rely on the concert and bootleg videos, and the lovingly retold reminiscences of the fortunate.

Keith Alverson

ESSENTIAL ELVISOLOGY

Some of Elvis' Classic Showstoppers
Everyone has different favorite Elvis songs, but certain songs stand out above others for being particularly memorable in his live performances.

"How Great Thou Art"
It's impossible to have heard Elvis sing this song and not come to understand a

Elvis leaving the stage to deafening applause

lot about him, his sincerity, and his faith. It is a challenging, vocally near operatic, tour de force.

"Suspicious Minds"

Elvis sometimes extended this crowd pleaser to more than ten minutes. Although some people read a lot into the lyrics because of his divorce, there was nothing melancholy about the athleticism and exuberance he exhibited during this song.

"Hurt"

Fans still debate which version of this emotionally wrenching song they love best. The New Year's Eve 1976 performance in Pittsburgh gets the most votes.

"Are You Lonesome Tonight"

For the next 20 years Elvis had to sing many songs that had launched his career. Many just got tempo and orchestration changes; this song got a humorous overhaul and became a sort of improv and running comedy bit between Elvis and Charlie Hodge.

"Polk Salad Annie"

Elvis did some powerfully sexy moves when he sang this song. Afterward, he would sometimes lie down on the floor to rest—like we said, *very* sexy.

"American Trilogy"

"Dixie," the "Battle Hymn of the Republic," "All My Trials": another one of Elvis' signature performance pieces and always rousing and emotional.

"Unchained Melody"

Elvis often accompanied himself at the piano when he sang this song. Potent and dramatic—it's Elvis distilled down to his most elemental—incredibly beautiful.

Keith Alverson

Sandi Miller

Keith Alverson

Keith Alverson

Keith Alverson

Keith Alverson

Keith Alverson

Keith Alverson

Keith Alverson

Keith Alverson

From the collection of Bob Klein

"My Way"

Other people have sung this song … but everyone we know agrees that Elvis owned it.

"Bridge Over Troubled Water"

A good measure for the success of a song is that so many people feel that Elvis was singing it directly to them. Fans still turn to this song for comfort when they feel low.

"You Gave Me a Mountain"

Another song that Elvis sang from his heart, sometimes dedicating it to a fan in the audience who was ill or troubled. It is impossible to listen to without knowing that Elvis had seen some pain in his own life.

"Can't Help Falling in Love"

This one was literally a show-stopper—it was often the last song Elvis sang before leaving the stage. It had the added bene-fit of being one of the songs during which Elvis distributed kisses to women who approached him.

Number of Live Performances between 1969 and 1977

During those first years of touring in the late 1950s, no exact record was kept of all the performances Elvis gave. But from 1969, when he returned to live performing after years of making movies, until 1977, when he died, there's a more reliable record.

1,128 concerts

Comedians Who Opened for Elvis

Nipsy Russell

Sammy Shore

Bob Melvin

Jackie Kahane

Musicians Who Performed with Elvis Onstage

From the mid- to late '50s, Elvis toured with the Blue Moon Boys, first across the South and then over a good portion of the rest of the country. The original members were Scotty and Bill, with whom Elvis created "the sound." D. J. joined on, and at times other musicians played with them as well.

The Blue Moon Boys

 Bill Black on bass

 Scotty Moore on lead guitar

 D. J. Fontana on drums

 Floyd Cramer on piano

 James Clayton "Jimmy" Day on steel guitar

From 1969 through 1977 Elvis had a large and ever expanding and contracting stage show. The list below is a good number of the talented people who shared the stage with Elvis—but they weren't all on at the same time.

The Awesome Core TCB Band

 James Burton on lead guitar

 Glen Hardin on piano

 Ronnie Tutt on drums

 Jerry Scheff on rhythm guitar

Other Musicians Who Toured with Elvis

Larry Muhoberac on keyboards

Hal Blaine on drums

Joe Osborne on bass

John Wilkinson on rhythm guitar

Pat Houston on trumpet

Marty Harrell on trombone

David Briggs on electric piano

Bobby Ogdin on electric piano

Shane Kiester on piano

Tony Brown on piano

Larry Londin on drums

Bob Lanning on drums

Emory Gordy on bass

Duke Bradwell on bass

Joe Guerico, conductor

The Joe Guerico Orchestra

The Tony Bruno Orchestra

Elvis' Stage Backup Singers

These people sang behind Elvis, and often soloed at his request, at various points during the touring years.

Kathy Westmoreland

Millie Kirkham

Charlie Hodge

The Jordanaires
- Gordon Stoker
- Neal Matthews
- Hoyt Hawkins
- Hugh Jarret

J. D. Sumner and the Stamps Quartet
- Bill Baize
- Ed Enoch
- Ed Hill
- Richard Sterban
- Donnie Sumner
- Dave Rowland
- Larry Strickland

The Imperials
- Jake Hess
- Armond Morales
- Gary McSpadden
- Jim Murray

The Sweet Inspirations
- Estelle Brown
- Emily "Cissy" Houston
  (Whitney Houston's mother)
- Myrna Smith
- Ann Williams
- Sylvia Shemwell

Voice
- Shaun Neilsen
- Tim Baty
- Per-Erik Hallin
- Donnie Sumner
  (after being in the Stamps)

The Hugh Jarrett Singers

Historic Live Performances

The Mississippi Alabama Dairy Show—October 3, 1945
Elvis sang "Old Shep" in a talent competition at this Tupelo, Mississippi fair.

L. C. Humes High School Minstrel Show—April 9, 1953
As a high school senior Elvis performed in front of a large audience of his peers for the first time and was enthusiastically cheered.

The Mississippi Alabama Dairy Show—September 26, 1956
Elvis returned to Tupelo to give this benefit performance.

Overton Park Band Shell—July 30, 1954
Elvis' first concert appearance before a paying audience, in Memphis.

Bloch Arena—March 25, 1961
This benefit performance in Hawaii was his last live performance until 1968.

International Hotel, Las Vegas—July 31, 1969
Elvis returned triumphantly to Vegas.

Houston Astrodome—February 27, 1970
This concert marked the beginning the touring years.

The Los Angeles Forum—November 14, 1970
Among the best shows Elvis ever gave.

Elvis entering the Houston Astrodome before his concert on February 27, 1970, the concert that kicked off the touring years of the '70s

From the collection of Bob Klein

Dallas Auditorium—
    November 13, 1971
Honolulu International
    Center—January 14,
    1973
    The "Aloha from
Hawaii" benefit performance was seen by more than a billion people.
Keil Auditorium, St. Louis, Missouri—June 28, 1973
    Said by many fans to be among the absolutely best performances Elvis ever
    gave.
Detroit Pontiac Silverdome—December 31, 1975
    Elvis set the record for single-
    performance gate receipts.
Dallas Memorial Auditorium—December
    28, 1976
Birmingham, Alambama—December 29,
    1976
Market Square Arena, Indianapolis,
    Indiana—June 26, 1977
    Elvis' last performance onstage.

Noteworthy Live Performances on Official Release

One could argue that all of Elvis' concerts were noteworthy but here are some of the more important career performances and some of the recordings on which you can hear them. There are hundreds of bootlegs in addition to these of course.
Louisiana Hayride
    Elvis: The First Live Recordings
    The Hillbilly Cat
    The Complete Fifties Masters

"I've just been to the Elvis World Tour concert last night in Belgium and the Americans who said it was awesome, impressive, and emotional were right. From the moment the show started all hell broke loose. I'm not a foolish fan and I never expected to be so moved but I really felt I was at an Elvis concert. The show is fantastic, the lights and sounds are overwhelming, and trust me for those of you who are yet to be going, you will be crying."
—Dutch fan, on the day after attending *Elvis: The Concert* in 1999

"In 1972, my sister and I started the day as we usually did when Elvis was in town. We rode around until we found where he was staying. My sister kept saying she felt we were going to meet him. She had always had this image of him and she was afraid that when we met him he wouldn't be as she thought. When we found the hotel, we spent the day riding up and down the elevator. After seeing him in concert a few times we started going outside during the last song so we could see him drive away. That year, standing outside, as the car with Elvis drove by, my sister and I were knocked around pretty bad by the cops holding people back. We hobbled up to the hotel. Red West was in the lobby and asked if my sister got hurt. Well, that meant Elvis had seen it too because Red was sitting right next to Elvis in the car. Red said Elvis was concerned if she was all right. We were invited up to Elvis' room where we met his father, Tom Parker, and the others who traveled with him. We were invited to sit down (Elvis was not in the room at the time) and told not to take any pictures and not to ask about his wife. I was looking down at the floor when out of nowhere, standing in front of me was a pair of legs. I heard him say, 'Is anyone going to introduce me to these two young ladies?' God! It was really him standing there, beautiful as everything. I swallowed my tongue. He had on black pants and a Tom Jones-type white shirt. He didn't come in with the attitude 'Hey, I'm Elvis.' He was so nice. We were the only fans in the room and we had to act normal as we were afraid of being thrown out. He sat down next to us and we sat there looking at him and feeling in shock. Every time he moved someone would ask him where he was going. He asked me if I had liked the song he had added that night and I asked him which one. Imagine my shock when he started singing 'The first time ever I saw your face.' He sang the first two lines and all I could do was say 'Oh, yeah, that one! Loved it.' I felt like I was in a trance. At one point everyone disappeared and we were left alone with him and my sister sat next to him and started patting him on the leg. I stood up in front of him and held his hand. He had Band-Aids on his knuckles and cuts. I reached over and rubbed my fingers along his cheek and sideburns. His skin was flawless. He was absolutely gorgeous! He just sat there and let us touch him. We spent at least two hours there. We were supposed to act like we were at a normal little get together and I guess for them it was. One final note, remember when I said my sister had been scared Elvis wouldn't be as wonderful as she had imagined? Well, he was and more! He was the sweetest, kindest, most gentlemanly person we have ever met!!"

—Carolyn, on the internet

Eagle's Hall, Houston Texas
  The First Year
1956 Tupelo Fairgrounds Performance
  RCA: A Golden Celebration
  New Frontier Hotel, Las Vegas
  The Complete Fifties Masters
  Elvis Aron Presley Boxed Set
The Arizona Memorial Benefit
  Elvis Aron Presley Boxed Set
The Vegas Years
  Elvis in Person at the International Hotel
  Collector's Gold Boxed Set
  On Stage
  Elvis: That's the Way It Is

The Seventies Tours
  Elvis as Recorded at Madison Square Garden
  An Afternoon in the Garden
  Aloha from Hawaii
  The Alternate Aloha
  Elvis as Recorded Live On Stage in Memphis
  Elvis Aron Presley Boxed Set
  Elvis in Concert
  Walk a Mile in My Shoes: Essential 70s Masters
  Welcome to My World

The "Elvis Has Left the Building" Guy

Al Dvorin was a promoter who was recruited by the Colonel to be the announcer who would end Elvis concerts with the now famous line, "Elvis has left the building." Although many other people uttered these words at the end of Elvis' performances to prevent pandemonium when Dvorin wasn't there, he is the person most associated with the phrase. Today he makes appearances at fan conventions telling stories of the time he toured with Elvis.

The Tour that Was Never Made

Elvis died right before he was about to start a concert tour in August of 1977. To the shock of arena managers and critics in the media, virtually everyone who had tickets kept them.

8/17/77—Portland, Maine
8/18/77—Portland, Maine
8/19/77—Utica, New York
8/20/77—Syracuse, New York
8/21/77—Hartford, Connecticut
8/22/77—Uniondale, New York
8/23/77—Lexington, Kentucky
8/24/77—Roanoke, Virginia
8/25/77—Fayettville, North Carolina
8/26/77—Asheville, North Carolina
8/27/77—Memphis, Tennessee
8/28/77—Memphis, Tennessee

Al Dvorin

John O'Hara

YOUR ELVIS EDUCATION

Books

Elvis: The Concert Years 1969–1977
   Stein Erik Skar, Flaming Star Publishers
Did Elvis Play in Your Home Town?
   Volumes One and Two
   Lee Cotton
Elvis: His Life in Pictures
   text by Todd Morgan with Laura Kath
Last Train to Memphis: The Rise of Elvis Presley
   Peter Guralnick
Careless Love: The Unmaking of Elvis Presley
   Peter Guralnick
The Official Elvis Presley Fan Club Commemorative Album 1935–1977
   edited by Julie Mundy
The King on the Road: Elvis Live on Tour 1954 to 1977
   Robert Gordon
The Elvis Atlas: A Journey through Elvis Presley's America
   Michael Gray and Roger Osborne
That's Alright, Elvis
   Scotty Moore as told to James Dickerson
Me 'n' Elvis
   Charlie Hodge with Charles Goodman
Early Elvis: The Sun Years
   Bill E. Burk
Elvis: The Concert Years
   Bill E. Burk
Elvis in Canada
   Bill E. Burk
Steamrolling over Texas
   Ger Rijff
   Can be purchased through From This Old House, Box 468, Almont, Michigan 48003, (810) 798-3581
The Field Guide to Elvis Shrines
   Bill Yenne

"Elvis! You're not a *$A&N star. You're a *SA&N GALAXY!"
—Chuck Connors, "The Rifleman," to Elvis after seeing him perform, from *Me 'n' Elvis* by Charlie Hodge with Charles Goodman

"I know very well how difficult it is to play Las Vegas."
—Richard Nixon to Elvis

"... I never danced vulgar in my life. I've just been jigglin'."
—Elvis

Bringing It Back: San Bernardino
Mickey Pfleger
Aloha via Satellite
Joe Tunzi
Available from JAT Publishing, P.O. Box
56372, Chicago, Illinois 60656.

Films Available on Videotape
Elvis on Tour
Elvis, That's The Way It Is
Elvis '56
The Lost Performances
The Great Performances
Aloha from Hawaii
Alternate Aloha
"Elvis in Concert"
CBS TV (1977)
Elvis, August 7th, 1955 or *First-Ever Elvis*
Available through EIF, P.O. Box 3373, Thousand Oaks, California 91359
(818) 991-3892
Fax: (818) 991-3894

Web Sites
http://userzweb.lightspeed.net/~mimii/elvis/index.htm
Elvis Presley in Concert site by Francesc Lopez
http://userzweb.lightspeed.net/~mimii/elvis/form.htm
Elvis concert site
http://www.casema.net/~arpt/elvis.html
Lex Raaphort's Elvis Presley page
http://www.casema.net/~arpt/elvisbotn.html
Lex Raaphort's Elvis music library
http://jordanselvisworld.simplenet.com/index.html
Jordan's Elvis World
http://www.biwa.ne.jp/~presley/index1.htm
Haruo Hirose's Elvis World site
http://listen.to/elvis-presley-superstar
Elvis Superstar: Elvis at his best site
http://www.fortunecity.com/tinpan/morrissey/273/camera.htm
Candid Elvis on Camera; concert site
http://www.fortunecity.com/tinpan/floyd/597
Elvis in Hawaii site

"So, there was total darkness, then this blinding flash of light. I'm not talking about the super trooper—the big spotlight—but the 15,000 flashbulbs from the Instamatics going off simultaneously."
—Bob Abel, filmmaker of *Elvis on Tour*, about Elvis' arrival onstage, from *Elvis: The Final Years*

http://www.noord.bart.nl/~kaauw/index2.html
   For Elvis CD Collectors Only; Willem Kaauw's site
http://home.sol.no/~tlidsoe/
   Elvis: the Las Vegas Years site
http://tor-pw1.netcom.ca/~sumner/elvisphotos.html
   Elvis photographs on Jumpsuit Junkies
http://www2.arkansas.net/~larryp/
   E-mail: larryp@arkansas.net
   To purchase videos
http://www.blackdogweb.com/elvis/
   To purchase videos

THE ELVIS AND YOU EXPERIENCE

See *Elvis the Concert*

The TCB band takes the stage, and many of Elvis' original backup singers perform live to huge video-screen images of Elvis performing. This is absolutely as close as it gets to having seen Elvis perform live. *Elvis the Concert* has played all over the U.S. and in Europe, the Far East, and Australia. There is universal agreement among fans that this concert tour is the best experience there is left to be had on earth. Graceland came up with the finest concept they have ever had—and people all over the world are grateful for it. Kudos to EPE.

Attend an Elvis Impersonator Event

Not everyone likes the idea of Elvis impersonators, but some of the good ones really do capture a fraction of the original Elvis magic. The audience can fill in the blanks. (See "Elvis Impersonators" for lots more information.)

Where to Buy Photos of Elvis in Concert

The photographers listed below sell the photographs they took of Elvis performing live. Some have photo-of-the-month clubs; others sell on an individual basis. Write to them for information and prices. (Photographs taken by Bob Heis and Keith Alverson appear throughout this book.)
Bob Heis
   P.O. Box 354
   Miamisburg, Ohio 45343-0354
   E-mail: BHEISTCB@aol.com
Keith Alverson
   P.O. Box 1666
   Palmetto, Georgia 30268

Rosemarie Leech
  P.O. Box 2633
  Vincentown, New Jersey 08088
Sean Shaver
  P.O. Box 9100
  Kansas City, Missouri 64168
Ed Bonja Enterprises
  P.O. Box 156
  San Dimas, California 91773-0156
Bob Klein
  Bob has an extraordinary collection of Elvis
  concert shots.
  140-10 84th Drive
  Briarwood, New Jersey 11435
  (718) 523-5013
Steve Barile
  P.O. Box 61059
  Bronx, New York 10461-059
  (718) 798-3571

Keith Alverson

Help Preserve Important Elvis Venues

The historical significance of some of Elvis' venues is sometimes overlooked by the people who now run them. Over the years, many have been torn down or been allowed to fall into disrepair. Elvis fans may contact the managements and offer to help in a preservation effort. This is a good fan club activity.

Overton Park Shell Tours and Charity
The Overton Park Shell, where Elvis gave one of his earliest professional performances, is located at 1928 Poplar Avenue in Memphis. In addition to the tours that are conducted there (backstage area included), you're welcome to bring your guitar and play and sing on the stage. "Save our Shell" is involved in preserving this Elvis site. For more information about the tour or donations contact: Joel Hurley, Save Our Shell, Inc., P.O. Box 820409, Memphis, Tennessee 38182. (901) 274-6046

"The scarves came in different colors, and with Elvis' name on them they obviously had some fetish value. Women fell out of balconies leaning over for them. Some got into fierce tugs of war after grabbing a scarf simultaneously in midair. Others grimly held onto opposite ends for an entire show, until some Solomon-like Larry [Geller] came along to cut the cloth in two."
  —from *Elvis' Search for God*
    by Larry Geller and
    Jess Stearn

John O'Hara

A carved totem pole of Elvis looks down at the Overton Park shell

The Tupelo fairgrounds grandstands, May 1999; note the single white shoe left by a fan in remembrance of Elvis

John O'Hara

Tupelo Fairgrounds
This important site has been used for town storage and otherwise neglected. Write to the Tupelo Convention and Visitors Bureau and remind them of its significance.
P.O. Box 1485, Tupelo, Mississippi 38802.
(601) 841-6521

Other Elvis Performance Venues You Can Visit
Polk Theater
Elvis performed here on August 6, 1956. He put his signature on the wall of his dressing room and it's still there—preserved under glass.
121 South Florida Avenue
Lakeland, Florida 33801
(941) 682-8227

Bloch Arena
Elvis gave a charity performance here March 25, 1961, to raise money to create a permanent memorial to the USS *Arizona* that was sunk during WWII.
Naval Base Building 161
Pearl Harbor, Hawaii 96860
(808) 474-6156

> "With astonishing cultural illiteracy, New York critics of the 1950s mistook Elvis Presley's leg-shaking rock and roll as an obscene striptease, when in fact his moves stemmed from the provincial sub-worlds of southern gospel, country, and blues that combined spiritual exaltation with bodily release."
> —Vernon Chadwick, Director of Annual International Conference on Elvis Presley

Mid-South Coliseum
This is the site of the last performance Elvis gave in his hometown on July 5, 1976. During Tribute Week, events are sometimes held here.
996 Early Maxwell Boulevard
Memphis, Tennessee 38104
(901) 274-3982
Market Square Arena
Elvis gave his last performance here on June 26, 1977. The Arena is being torn down but a plaque on this site commemorates this historic concert.

300 East Market Street
Indianapolis, Indiana 46204
(317) 639-6411

Eagle's Nest
Now called the Americana Club
This nightclub was the locale of some of
the first gigs Elvis had in 1954, perhaps as
early as 1953. It was a rockabilly joint in
those days. Not entirely the same place
anymore.
4090 Winchester Road at Lamar and
Clearpool Avenues
Memphis, Tennessee 38118
(901) 368-0994

Hampton Coliseum
The Friends through Elvis Fan Club erected
a commemorative plaque to Elvis here.
Hampton, Virginia

The Myriad
A plaque commemorates Elvis' 1973, 1975,
and 1976 performances here.
Oklahoma City, Oklahoma

Mabee Center, Oral Roberts University
A plaque commemorates Elvis' 1974 and
1976 performances here.
Tulsa, Oklahoma

Lloyd Noble Center, Oklahoma University
A plaque commemorates Elvis' 1977 per-
formance here.
Norman, Oklahoma

Pittsburg Civic Center
A plaque commemorates Elvis' 1973 and
1976 performances here.
Pittsburg, Pennsylvania

"[The Colonel] would go
in and buy thirty-second
radio spots on Elvis to
advertise his show. They'd
go 'Elvis, Elvis, Elvis,' with
an echo, a three-second
delay. That's all it was.
Then a voice-over would
say, 'Appearing in such-
and-such city. Tickets —.'
Very effective."
—Lamar Fike on Colonel
Parker, from *Revelations from
the Memphis Mafia*

"Extraordinarily untal-
ented" ... "no discernible
singing ability" ... "he
can't last" ... "Elvis is
mostly nightmare" ... "he
can't sing a lick" ... "Elvis
Presley is morally insane"
... "he's *too* hot" ... "his
vibrato annoy[s] me."
—Early Critics

"We were the only band
in history that was
directed by an ass."
—Scotty Moore, Elvis' original guitarist, about having to
take his cue from Elvis' butt
because he couldn't hear
over the fans' screams

Elvis and James Burton

Keith Iverson

Hear Elvis Kidding around Onstage
"Having Fun Onstage with Elvis"
A recording of stage intros and live performance tomfoolery with Elvis.

"Between Takes with Elvis"
Nothing but stage antics and Elvis fun, including "The Complete Water Fight."
Available from Jerry Osborne and Creative Radio Shows, P.O. Box 11203, Burbank, California 91510

Join the James Burton Fan Club
James Burton International Fan Club
P.O. Box 51475
Jacksonville Beach, Florida 32240

Share your Comments and Impressions of E's Concerts
Visit this web site and add your own story if you have seen Elvis in concert and check out the other comments from people who saw him.
http://userzweb.lightspeed.net/~mimii/elvis/form.htm

Get a Souvenir Scrapbook of Elvis at Madison Square Garden
Copies of *Elvis at Madison Square Garden* by Phil Gelormine's Elvis World are available for sale. This magazine-style book has many unpublished photos and the whole story about Elvis' four legendary concerts at Madison Square Garden in 1972. It's a chance to relive the appearances for those who saw him in New York, and a genuine glimpse into an Elvis concert. Please look for their next issue that is centered around the "'68 Comeback Special" titled *The '68 Special Scrapbook.*
    Elvis World Souvenir Scrapbook
    P.O. Box 388
    Bound Brook, New Jersey 08805
    E-mail: gelormine@aol.com

> "I was lucky enough to go to his first performance at the International Hotel. He was awesome and I screamed at him 'You are gorgeous' several times. My big mouth got his attention but when I was introduced to him I couldn't make any intelligible sounds. He was the most glorious thing I ever saw. I witnessed greatness and then it was gone."
> —Buttons

TELEVISION ELVIS

America 1956 is placid, peaceful, and predictable. Perry Como is a singing sensation, Pat Boone is considered a hottie, and Lawrence Welk has a popular television show. Suddenly the country is introduced to, stunned, and dazzled by a young singer from the South who appears in their living rooms who "don't sound (or look) like nobody else." By the end of that year, the changes brought about by this new type of music, propelled by Elvis Presley's teasing and provocative way of performing it, had actually done nothing less than bring the entire world to the point of no return. And it was the new medium of television that had delivered this agent of change.

Although everyone who is old enough seems to remember having seen Elvis for the first time on *The Ed Sullivan Show*, he had already appeared on national television more than a half dozen times throughout 1956. By the time of the Ed Sullivan appearances, the puritans already had their panties in a knot about rock and roll. They were inconsolable about this terrible influence on the nation's youth and intractable in their condemnation of the person they saw as the main cause of the breakdown of the nation's moral structure. Hearing Elvis Presley on the radio and listening to his records was bad enough, according to them, but watching the way he moved on stage was beyond the pale!

Elvis first went from regional act to national figure when he performed on Stage Show

Courtesy of Butterfield & Butterfield

Elvis and Sinatra

hosted by the Dorsey Brothers on January 28. Peter Guralnick describes the very first moment Elvis arrived on our television sets: "[He] came out looking like he had been shot out of a cannon." He was initially booked for four performances, but considering the audience response and the boost he gave to the ratings, he was signed on for two more. A national audience got its first look at Elvis Presley and he has never left our hearts and minds since.

Elvis then went on to do *The Milton Berle Show* in June. Mr. Television created several comedic skits about Elvis' sex appeal and the frenzied reaction he was generating in women. The big moment came when Elvis sang "Hound Dog" for the first time on television. Without his guitar, he moved around the stage unencumbered with that incredible chaotic abandon that was the hallmark of his early performances. This display only increased the consternation of the starched-shirt set and the thrills for his fans. At the time, nothing remotely like him had ever been seen by a mass audience.

Elvis' *Steve Allen Show* appearance is generally considered the nadir of his early career and to his fans, a low point in television history. In the name of family entertainment, Allen set out to tame Elvis' performance. It is from this show that we have the famous Elvis in tuxedo singing to a basset hound. In spite of all the efforts to make Elvis the butt of every lame joke of the evening, he proved himself to be good natured and good humored and won even more fans.

And finally, there was the most notorious of Elvis' television appearances, *The Ed Sullivan Show*. During these three shows Elvis made more than just television his-

"This isn't so much an 'act' as an exposé of the emptiness not only of most entertainment but of most *lives*. In the process of watching him, lives are changed."
—Dave Marsh, on Elvis' television performances during the 1950s, from his fabulous book *Elvis*

The room where Elvis' parents watched his television appearances while living at Audubon Drive

John O'Hara

tory—he made world history. More people saw him than had watched anything else on television to that date, launching what Quincy Jones referred to as the "emotional revolution of white America." Essentially Elvis flicked what had been passing for entertainment right out the window with that first snap of his legs. When he shook his entire body looking like he was about to fly out of control and sang songs directly to the soul of a new generation, he replaced the blandness of the songsters of the 1950s and gave us an extremely stimulating alternative. The abandon and lack of inhibition of Elvis' early television performances were such a powerful image for young people that he has been credited with providing the detour off the road of lockstep conformity that led to the sexual revolution of the '60s.

After getting out of the army, Elvis made a television appearance on the Frank Sinatra–Timex Special, "Welcome Home Elvis." It aired on ABC on May 12, 1960, and Elvis was paid the then-unheard of sum of $125,000 for singing two songs—eight minutes of airtime. Along with Frank Sinatra, fellow Rat Packers Peter Lawford, Joey Bishop, and Sammy Davis, Jr., shared the billing. Here was an Elvis who had just returned from Europe, subtly

From the collection of Bob Klein

Elvis appearing on Frank Sinatra's "Welcome Home Elvis" television special

> "It was the finest music of his life. If ever there was music that bleeds, this was it. Nothing came easy that night, and he gave everything he had—more than anyone knew was there."
>
> —Greil Marcus, about Elvis' performance in the "'68 Comeback Special," from *Mystery Train Images of America in Rock 'n' Roll Music*

changed and less frenetic. All those magnificent contradictions that made up Elvis, self-conscious and smooth, humble and confident, promise and denial, were still in evidence; but now he didn't look at all out of his element in a tuxedo—he was suavely elegant, hair piled so high it posed a direct challenge to gravity. Elvis and Sinatra sang each other's hits and then harmonized together. Elvis delivered a beautiful and haunting "Witchcraft" while Frank Sinatra mugged through "Love Me Tender," jerking his shoulders in an awkward, unsexy way.

Perhaps the most significant television appearance of Elvis' entire career occurred in 1968. Colonel Parker arranged with NBC for Elvis to do his own special. It was to air in December and the Colonel envisioned a Christmas show containing little more than Elvis singing traditional Christmas carols and bidding the audience a merry Christmas. Steve Binder, the producer of the show, wanted to do something more hip. He convinced Elvis to pass on the Christmas theme and return to his own strengths in rock, gospel, and rhythm and blues.

The show consisted of production numbers, concert sequences, and an informal jam session. Here was an impassioned and potent Elvis demolishing with each note he sang every saccharine moment he had spent on the big screen over the past decade. This performance redeemed Elvis in the eyes of everyone who felt betrayed by the music that came out of the Hollywood soundtracks. Elvis could still rock. He proved he still had it in every sense of the word. Here was a black-leather-clad Elvis singing on an intimate stage with his original band members, D. J. Fontana and Scotty Moore, prowling and looking like a man who was gonna bust out of any restraints

From the collection of Bob Klein

put on him. In an emotional finale, Elvis, looking impossibly beautiful dressed in a white suit, sang an inspirational "If I Can Dream."

The show, officially called "Singer Presents Elvis," has come to be known as the "'68 Comeback Special." It's been said that Elvis' performance in this special formed the conceptual basis for music videos and MTV's popular "Unplugged" series.

In 1973 Elvis again made television history with "Elvis: Aloha from Hawaii," a benefit concert for the Kuiokalani Lee Cancer Fund that was broadcast by the Intelsat IV satellite to 40 different countries and seen by *at least* one billion people. A large percentage of the planet saw Elvis Presley in that white jumpsuit with the American eagle design belting out "American Trilogy," creating one of our more enduring images of Elvis.

In June 1977, CBS filmed Elvis during two live concerts in Omaha and Indianapolis that were to be broadcast as a television special later that year. In the end, they proved to be Elvis' final performances. They were taped just six weeks before his death and he was in apparent poor health and physical distress. It is a heartbreaking record of those final months of Elvis' life and many people think it was an inexcusable decision on the part of Vernon Presley to allow the broadcast of the show after Elvis died. It's sometimes cited among the reasons why the media, in the years immediately following Elvis death, focused on those final, troubled years instead of seeing his life in its entirety. To this day EPE refuses to permit the release of the videotape of the CBS show and because of this it's become a much sought-after bootleg item. Although the performance may not have been Elvis in his prime, he still managed to do what he always did better than any other performer. He sang with passion and depth and as always made a powerful connection with his audience.

Elvis was a voracious television viewer (there were 14 television sets at Graceland) and he watched with a great deal of emotion and involvement— enough to cause him to commit "telecide" on several occasions by shooting out the screen of the offending set when he saw something he didn't appreciate.

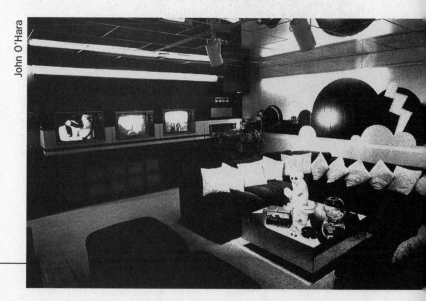

John O'Hara

The TV room at Graceland

He had three sets rigged up side-by-side for simultaneous viewing in a comfortable room in the basement of Graceland and three in his bedroom: one at the foot of his bed and two mounted in the ceiling above it.

These days, it's nearly impossible to sit through an evening of television without hearing Elvis' name mentioned. Some shows have even had an Elvis theme: *Alf, Designing Women, X-Files, WKRP in Cincinnati, Murphy Brown.* Unfortunately, these brief moments don't add up to anywhere near the kind of thrill it was to see Elvis on television for the very first time. But for Elvis fans, there are still many ways to enjoy that exciting combination of Elvis and TV.

ESSENTIAL ELVISOLOGY

Some of Elvis' Favorite TV Shows
Hawaii 5-0
The Tonight Show
Shindig
I Love Lucy
Sgt. Bilko
The Dick Van Dyke Show
The Millionaire
The Mary Tyler Moore Show
The Carol Burnett Show
Monday Night Football

Elvis' Television Performances, Appearances, and Interviews
Louisiana Hayride
  March 5, 1955
Town and Country Jubilee
  March 14, 1955
Grand Prize Saturday Night Jamboree
  March 19, 1955
The Roy Orbison Show
  May 31, 1955
Stage Show
  January 28, 1956
  February 4, 1956
  February 11, 1956
  February 18, 1956

March 17, 1956
March 24, 1956
The Milton Berle Show
April 3, 1956
June 5, 1956
Dance Party
June 20, 1956
The Steve Allen Show
July 1, 1956
Hy Gardner Calling
July 1, 1956
The Ed Sullivan Show
September 9, 1956
October 28, 1956
January 6, 1957
Holiday Hop
December 31, 1956
American Bandstand
Transatlantic phone interview with Dick Clark
January 8, 1959
Frank Sinatra–Timex Special
"Welcome Home Elvis"
May 12, 1960
"Singer Presents Elvis"
Also called the "Comeback" or "'68 Special"
December 3, 1968
"Elvis: Aloha from Hawaii"
January 14 and 15, 1973
April 4, 1973
"Elvis Live"
CBS Special 1977

> "Denim was the big thing among the hippies. I was doing embroidery and all kinds of things to jeans to make them look different. I said, 'Why don't I take a jean jacket and a pair of jeans and duplicate those in black leather.'"
> —Costume designer Bill Belew, on the famous black leather outfit he created for the "'68 Comeback Special"

Elvis' Commercials
This excludes promos for shows, albums, and the never-used photo shots for a Memphis furniture shop.
Southern-Made Doughnuts
November 6, 1954 (aired on radio during *Louisiana Hayride*)
Pizza Hut
1998 Super Bowl (computer-spliced Elvis movie footage into a new television commercial)

Energizer Batteries
   1999 (television commercial using a short clip of Elvis' face)

Songs that Mention Elvis Shooting Out Televisions
Bruce Springsteen
   "57 Channels and Nothing On"
Bob Dylan
   "TV Talkin' Song"

A Few Recordings on which You Can Hear the TV Performances
Memories
"'68 Comeback Special," entire evening
Tiger Man
Live show segment of the "'68 Comeback Special"
RCA: A Golden Celebration
1956 television performances
From Nashville to Memphis
"The Frank Sinatra Special"

Television Studios Where Elvis Performed
Ed Sullivan Theater
   Majestic, gothic, vaulted-ceilinged theater between 53rd and 54th Streets on
   Broadway in New York City, now home to the *Late Show with David
   Letterman.*
CBS Television City
   In Studio 33 on September 9, 1956, Elvis performed on *The Ed Sullivan Show*
   via remote feed from Los Angeles.
NBC Studios
   It was here in Burbank at Studio 4 that Elvis taped the "'68 Comeback
   Special."

YOUR ELVIS EDUCATION

Books
Images of Elvis Presley in American Culture 1977–1997
   George Plasketes
Elvis After Elvis: The Posthumous Career of a Living Legend
   Gilbert B. Rodman
Last Train to Memphis
   Peter Guralnick

Careless Love
  Peter Guralnick

Video

Elvis '56
Elvis and the Colonel
Elvis and the Beauty Queen
Elvis and Me
Elvis, the Early Years
Elvis and Nixon
This Is Elvis
"Elvis"
Elvis
Elvis Great Performances
The Century
"Famous Families' The Presleys: Rock and Roll Royalty"

> "Was Elvis, on first contact, able to impart some indestructible energy to his fans that would remain with them for the rest of their lives and actually outlive the man himself?"
> —Mick Farren, on the effect of seeing Elvis on television for the first time, in *The Hitchhiker's Guide to Elvis*

Web Sites

http://www.tv-now.com/stars/stars.html
  Television schedule information about Elvis appearances for the upcoming month
http://www.geocities.com/~arpt/az/
  Elvis Presley Encyclopaedia
http://www2.arkansas.net/~larryp/relvis.html
  E-mail: larryp@arkansas.net
  For a catalog of videos for sale

http://www.members.tripod.com/~wbroekman
  Elvis the King site; for Elvis television references
http://www.mtr.org
  The Museum of Television and Radio
http://www.geocities.com/Nashville/8575/ecindex.html
  List of Elvis' television performances

THE ELVIS AND YOU EXPERIENCE

How to Watch Television Elvis-Style

Watch Three Televisions Simultaneously

In the basement of Graceland is the TV Room where Elvis did some big-time television watching—on three side-by-side sets. Inspired by President Johnson.

Mount a Television in the Ceiling over Your Bed

Elvis' had two televisions mounted over his bed. You can do the same in your own bedroom. It's indulgent and relaxing.

Install Video Surveillance Cameras around Your House

Elvis often watched the monitors that displayed the people outside the gates. It's good security and sometimes good entertainment. Just look at the popularity of web cams on the internet.

How to Safely Shoot a Television Set

Refer to "Elvis and Firearms."

Keep a Special "Elvis Sightings" Tape in Your VCR

This will really pay off if you are trying to increase your Elvis video library because he crops up on television unexpectedly all the time. VH1 does an outstanding job of keeping Elvis in the public eye by showing his concerts fairly regularly.

Have an Elvis Historic TV Appearance Party

Play video of one of Elvis' historic TV performances on your VCR. Invite friends over and make believe the show is being broadcast live. Go back in time to when you first saw Elvis on the Sullivan show or play the "Aloha from Hawaii" concert and relive the seventies. Dress for the period. If you have a vintage TV set and an unedited tape with the period commercials, it'll really add to the experience.

Create a Cable-Access Elvis Fan TV Show

Start a cable-access Elvis talk show. Each show can feature different guests from the Elvis world, like Elvis collectors, or fan club presidents, even authors. Local tribute artists can perform.

"For weeks before the airing of the Aloha special in 1973, I bugged my two aunts to make sure they were going to be home *that* night. They had just bought a new 25-inch color television set and I wasn't going to get stuck watching Elvis on my 13-inch black-and-white set. The night Aloha aired I was nervous as hell. My aunt laughs when she now tells the story of how many trips to the bathroom I made in between songs and during commercials. Elvis was *the* thing for me. I had finally found something I could grab onto and have for my very own—his music. I was about 12 years old and that one night literally changed my life forever. I always sang and had even joined the chorus at school when I was eight. But now things were different. I wanted to be in front of an audience so I could hear the applause and the shouting out of requests. I sang in nursing homes and outdoor stages—anyplace that would let me. I guess I was pretty good."

—Ben Milano

Lobby for an All-Elvis Cable Channel

If they can find an audience for all-sports, all-history, all-science fiction, all-cooking, and all-weather channels then there should surely be an all-Elvis channel.

Use an Old Television as an Elvis Shrine

Find an old set; it doesn't have to work. Remove the tube and build a diorama to display your memorabilia.

Where to Get Collectible Elvis-Cover TV Guides

Jay-Bee Magazines
150 West 28 Street
New York, New York 10001
(212) 675-1600

Where to See Elvis' Television Appearances

There are several broadcast museums across the U.S. that are phenomenal resources for viewing and hearing Elvis, even shows in which Elvis was only the topic. They provide drop-in service; you don't need to call in advance. Simply request the performances you would like to see from a list provided on computer terminals and they set you up at private consoles.

They have scores of radio recordings and TV appearances to choose from starting with a 1954 *Louisiana Hayride* tape of "That's All Right" to the *Dorsey Brothers, Milton Berle, Steve Allen,* and three *Ed Sullivan Show*s (where you'll see for yourself that the myth of him being filmed only from the waist up isn't entirely true; there's plenty of glorious head-to-toe Elvis in these performances). You can have the pleasure of seeing Frank Sinatra passing the teen-idol mantle to Elvis and watch him totally out-cool the members of the Ratpack. The "'68 Comeback Special," the "Aloha from Hawaii," Elvis' very last performance in Indianapolis, the various made-for-TV movies, Bruce Springsteen discussing Elvis, and the networks' coverage of his death—it's all here.

There's so much incredible footage of Elvis, you could spend days in one of these museums. But if you have only a limited amount of time we highly recommend you go straight to the Milton Berle shows, the Ed Sullivan appearances, and if you can stand the heartbreak, the final performances in June 1977.
The Museum of Television and Radio
25 West 52 Street
New York, New York 10019
http://www.mtr.org
(212) 621-6600

The Museum of Television and Radio
465 North Beverly Drive
Beverly Hills, California 90210
(310) 786-1000

The Museums of Television and Radio in New York and Beverly Hills have an adopt-a-program. For $350 per half-hour of program, you can "adopt" a piece of historic Elvis film. The money goes toward preserving the film and your name will be permanently associated with the program as the sponsor. Contact Richard Teller at (212) 621-6755, by fax at (212) 621-6632, or write to him at the New York museum.

Television News Archives
This archive is where you can find all television news pertaining to Elvis.
Vanderbilt University Library
West End Avenue
Nashville, Tennessee 37212
(615) 322-2927

Lobby Graceland to Release the ABC TV Miniseries

This excellent television series about Elvis' early life is unavailable for sale. Contact Graceland and request that they make it available.

Where to Buy Videos of Elvis' Ed Sullivan Performances

Whether you missed them the first time around or want to take a wild trip down memory lane, they make a good addition to any video collection.
(800) 263-2006
http://www.edsullivan.com/order.html

Tell VH1 What a Great Job They're Doing

VH1 is the one channel where you can see the most Elvis. Several times a year, they run Elvis movies, concerts, and videos. Write to them to say how much Elvis fans appreciate this and take the chance to tell them we want more!
VH1 Viewer Services
1515 Broadway
New York, New York 10036
(212) 258-7819
E-mail: VH1POSTAL@aol.com

"The anticipation of seeing Elvis on the screen was unlike anything I had ever experienced. It was an event, and I remember carrying my chair and putting it right in front of the television as if closer was better."

—Margaret

MOTION PICTURE ELVIS

Elvis just plain loved the movies. As a boy he would sit in the magical darkness of the Lyric Theatre in Tupelo and dream of being one of the larger-than-life heroes he saw up on the screen. It was a refuge from the reality of an impoverished childhood. Years later as an impressionable teenager he had the perfect job for a budding movie buff when he worked as an usher at the Loews State Theatre in Memphis. The job gave him ample opportunity to study the matinee idols of the day and imagine himself in their place. In July of 1954, when he was nervous about having his first record played on the radio, Elvis retreated into the familiar darkness of the Suzore Theatre until he was summoned to the radio station to be interviewed by DJ Dewey Phillips. Little did he know when he walked out of the theater on that summer night he was taking his very first step toward making his dream of being a movie star a reality.

Elvis' desire to be a movie star, like many of his other dreams, came true. He succeeded in being the highest paid actor of the 1960s and every film he ever made was profitable. At first his films were valid endeavors made with the best intentions by some of Hollywood's top talents. But then, through poor choices and the Colonel's shortsighted and often uncouth management, the films evolved into a genre unto

John O'Hara

Lyric Theatre, Tupelo, Mississippi

Elvis getting made up on the set of *Love Me Tender*

themselves—"The Elvis Movie." Boy meets girl. Boy sings. Boy chases girl. Boy sings. Boy beats up boy. Boy sings. Boy wins race. Boy sings. Boy gets girl. Boy sings. And all this unfurls in some exotic locale.

Elvis' film career is a bittersweet part of his legacy. Many of his movies were lamentable and yet they still packed theaters. It was said his fans would pay to watch him saw wood. They weren't intended as art and shouldn't be held to a standard other than popular entertainment. And popular they were; at the time, Elvis was just about the only sure thing in Hollywood. His films remain both a testament to his star power and a reminder of the lost opportunity to see it reach its full potential.

Elvis was discovered by Hollywood in the same way he was discovered by the rest of America. One of the many millions of people watching his extraordinary performance on the Dorsey Brothers' television show was producer Hal Wallis. The next day he called Elvis' manager, Colonel Parker, to set up a screen test. On April Fool's Day, 1956, Elvis made a screen test at Paramount Studios and six days later he signed a three-picture contract.

Elvis juggling a knife on the set of *Love Me Tender*

Elvis' first film, *Love Me Tender*, had its debut in New York City on November 15, 1956. An army of police was employed to restrain the mob of frenzied fans as a huge cutout silhouette of Elvis straddling the marquee was unveiled to the crowd. At the end of this Civil War era Western, Elvis' character is shot to death. So intense was the negative reaction of his fans to the news of his death scene, the studio felt compelled to add additional footage of Elvis singing from beyond the grave. Even as a piece of fiction his death was hard for his fans to accept. The movie opened to mixed reviews yet recouped its entire investment within three days of its national debut.

Elvis made three more films before he was drafted into the army—*Loving You*, *Jailhouse Rock*, and *King Creole*. Each had plots that mirrored Elvis' own life story in some way. These are generally considered the best of the Elvis movies. They were challenging roles that captured the rebel Elvis in his youth and served as a showcase for his raw talent.

While Elvis was in Germany, his manager plotted the path of his post-army career. The Colonel, deigning rock and roll to be a passing fad, had begun his nefarious master plan to transform Elvis into the next Bing Crosby, to make him into a mainstream artist with an appeal that went beyond the fickle teenybopper audience. His first film after his army stint, *GI Blues*, capitalized on Elvis' new all-American boy image. The lighthearted musical was wildly successful. Elvis followed it up with two more films, *Flaming Star* and *Wild in the Country*. They were both attempts at promoting Elvis as a serious actor with very little singing done by their star. When these two films proved to be somewhat less successful than *GI Blues*, the Colonel decided to revert to the more-musical and therefore more profitable formula.

Elvis' next film, *Blue Hawaii*, more or less drove the nails into the coffin of Elvis' potential, serious film career. Originally titled "Hawaiian Beach Boy," it was part of the trend of popular beach-themed youth movies of the early sixties. Its success spawned a series of musical travelogues with similar plot lines and minimal production values. One studio executive said that Elvis films didn't even need titles, they could be numbered. Elvis movie #8 would differ little from Elvis movie #12 or #22, and yet they would still make money.

Elvis in Hawaii while shooting
Blue Hawaii

Sandi Miller

Sandi Miller

Elvis on the set of *Clambake* wearing his "baseball suit"

When the Colonel realized he had a money machine, he attempted to preserve the winning formula by locking Elvis into a series of multipicture contracts that kept him busy making movies, and little else, until 1969.

Because of the Colonel's strategy not to saturate the market with too much "product," Elvis' recording career during the movie years was limited almost exclusively to soundtracks for his movies. Although there were some true gems among them, for the most part they were inferior songs written by uninspired and unhip songwriters. Elvis, whose great talent was to sing with feeling and make the listener share that feeling, couldn't bring much sincerity to songs like "Queenie Wahine's Papaya" or "Yoga Is as Yoga Does." Reflecting his disgust with the quality of material, Elvis would record an entire soundtrack in one or two nights of quick work. But to the Colonel, who it seems wouldn't recognize a good song if it bit him on his corpulent gluteus maximus, the situation was perfect. The soundtrack albums and the movies promoted each other and the money continued to roll in with minimal effort.

For most of the 1960s, Elvis would shoot three films a year that were scheduled for a Christmas, Easter, and Summer release to coincide with school vacations so the kids would have plenty of time for multiple viewing. Life for Elvis during those years centered around the thrice-yearly migration from Memphis to Los

Sandi Miller

Elvis reviewing a script on his way to the studio

Elvis and Vernon in Hollywood on
the set of *Live a Little, Love a
Little* in Spring of 1968

Sandi Miller

Angeles. He and his men would travel between home base and Hollywood, with the occasional side trip to Vegas or Palm Springs, in a caravan of cars led by Elvis at the wheel of his customized Greyhound bus. In L.A., Elvis would keep largely to himself ensconced behind the gates of various rented houses, as he counted the days until he could get back to Memphis.

Elvis was well aware that most of these movies fell far short of his aspirations and he became extremely disillusioned with his Hollywood career. Eventually, the movies became just a job to him. A very well-paying job. Elvis knew show biz was a notoriously fickle business, and his Tupelo beginnings were never far from his memory. It was hard to turn down a million dollar payday for a couple of weeks of easy work. After making his last dramatic feature, *A Change of Habit,* Elvis finally had had enough of the Elvis-ploitation movies and refused to make any more.

The last two movies of Elvis' film career were rockumentaries. *Elvis, That's the Way It Is* showcased Elvis' 1970 summer appearance at the International Hotel in Las Vegas. *Elvis on Tour* followed Elvis on a 15-city tour in the spring of 1972. In contrast to some of the talent who worked on Elvis' previous films, the young Martin Scorcese was an edi-

Elvis on the set of *Stay Away Joe*

Sandi Miller

Elvis at the gates of his home at 1174 Hillcrest Drive sporting a beard for his role in *Charro!*

Sandi Miller

tor for *Elvis on Tour.* The film won a Golden Globe Award as Best Documentary of 1972. When Elvis found out the film had won the award, he let out a justifiable hoot of prideful joy.

Of the thousands of live performances he gave during his lifetime, very few were officially recorded on film. There are bootlegs that were clandestinely shot by fans of practically every show Elvis did, but these two films remain the only official documentation of the Elvis concert experience of the seventies.

Though critics have tripped over themselves to lambaste his films, to an Elvis fan they're an integral part of his body of work. His movies preserve a visual record of one of the world's most photogenic men in his prime; we get to watch him growing up from age 21 to 34. They capture something of his essence in a way no still photo can—his walk, his laugh, his charisma, his specialness, and even his goofiness. Rewind and take another look. Is this guy cool or what?

These days his films are often the medium through which many people get their first exposure to Elvis. Some appear on television fairly often and probably always will. His films serve as time capsules for future generations of Elvis fans, in which Elvis is frozen in perpetual youth and amiability.

Elvis never lost his love of the movies. Even in the last few weeks of his life he rented out an entire theater in Memphis for himself and his friends and watched three or

"We went to the Sheriffs' Youth Ranch in Live Oak, Florida. In August of 1961, Elvis and Colonel Parker donated the house that was used in the movie (the one with the grass roof in *Follow That Dream*). It is still in there and they use it for a meeting room for the kids. It has pictures of Elvis and the Colonel on the walls and there's a guest book to sign with signatures dating back to 1971. It sits in a heavily shaded (drooping cypress trees) area all by itself. Very pretty area, and they welcome visitors. As we walked up the path I just pictured in my mind, Elvis lying on that cot on the porch waiting for Anne Helm to come out while he sang 'Angel.'"
—Sandi Miller

more movies in a single night. One has to wonder as Elvis sat there in the darkness, surrounded by his entourage, did he look up at the screen and continue to dream?

ESSENTIAL ELVISOLOGY

The Elvis Movies
They have been cited as formulaic, harmless, even embarrassing, but they've got Elvis-a-plenty and a lot of the songs are surprisingly good.

Love Me Tender (1956)

Elvis' screen debut, and the first and last film in which Elvis does not have top billing. It's a Civil War period drama in which Elvis marries the girlfriend (Deborah Paget) of his brother (Richard Egan) who everyone believes to have been killed in battle. When the brother shows back up, much guilt and unhappiness ensues. When the studio making the film tested the original ending with Elvis being killed, the fans were highly distressed; this was remedied with a specter of Elvis singing over the closing credits.

   Songs: "Love Me Tender"; "We're Gonna Move"; "Let Me"; "Poor Boy"

Loving You (1957)

Elvis plays Deke Rivers, a country boy who joins a band. A highly motivated press agent (Lizabeth Scott) orchestrates Deke's rock and roll career. There's a love quadrangle with Dolores Hart and Wendell Corey. Elvis' mother appeared as an extra in this film and after her death, he never watched this film again.

   Songs: "Loving You"; "Got a Lot of Livin' to Do"; "Let's Have a Party"; "Teddy Bear"; "Hot Dog"; "Lonesome Cowboy"; "Mean Woman Blues"

Jailhouse Rock (1957)

Elvis as Vince Everett gets jail time for a barroom fracas. There he learns to polish his singing and guitar playing from a fellow inmate played by Mickey Shaughnessy. When Vince gets outs of jail, his singing career is promoted by Judy Tyler—until he gets to the top and turns into a crumb. Love wins out.

   Songs: "Jailhouse Rock"; "Young and Beautiful"; "I Want to Be Free"; "Treat Me Nice"; "Don't Leave Me Now"; "(You're So Square) Baby I Don't Care"

King Creole (1958)

Elvis plays Danny Fisher, a New Orleans kid with family and high school problems. He falls in with some local thugs and two nightclubs vie for his talents; there's gunplay, several love interests, betrayals, and beatings. Directed by Michael Curtiz, based on a Harold Robbins book—this movie is often cited as Elvis' best performance. Elvis told many people it was his own favorite.

   Songs: "Trouble"; "Hard Headed Woman"; "Crawfish"; "Steadfast, Loyal and True"; "Lover Doll"; "Dixieland Rock"; "Young Dreams"; "New Orleans"; "King Creole"; "Don't Ask Me Why"; "As Long As I Have You"

GI Blues (1960)

Benefiting from Elvis' recently ended stint in the army, the movie is about a $300 bet among a group of soldiers that Elvis' character, Tulsa McLean, could get the club dancer, played by Juliet Prowse, to spend the night with him. He succeeds in melting the frosty dancer, but they spend their night together baby-sitting for a friend's tot.

Songs: "GI Blues"; "Blue Suede Shoes"; "What's She Really Like"; "Doin' the Best I Can"; "Frankfurt Special"; "Shoppin' Around"; "Tonight Is So Right for Love"; "Wooden Heart"; "Pocketful of Rainbows"; "Big Boots"; "Didja Ever"

Flaming Star (1960)

Elvis plays Pacer Burton, a half-American Indian, half-white character who suffers from torn allegiances. Dolores Del Rio plays his Kiowa Indian mother who is killed by a white man in revenge for an Indian attack on him and his family.

Songs: "Flaming Star"; "A Cane and a High Starched Collar"

Wild in the Country (1961)

Elvis plays Glenn Tyler, a troubled character who is torn between three women: the easy girl who's his cousin (Tuesday Weld), his regular girlfriend (Millie Perkins), and a lady court psychiatrist (Hope Lange). This was the last "legit" movie of Elvis' career.

Songs: "Wild in the Country"; "I Slipped, I Stumbled, I Fell"; "In My Way"; "Husky Dusky Day"

Blue Hawaii (1961)

Elvis plays Chad Gates, heir to a Hawaiian pineapple fortune who turns his back on the track laid out for him by family and obligation in order to work as a tour guide. Angela Lansbury plays Elvis' colorful but snobby mother who disapproves of his island allegiances and Joan Blackman, his long-time girlfriend.

Songs: "Blue Hawaii"; "Can't Help Falling in Love"; "Ito Eats"; "Almost Always True"; "Aloha Oe"; "No More"; "Rock-a-Hula Baby"; "Ku-u-i-Po"; "Slicin' Sand"; "Hawaiian Sunset"; "Beach Boy Blues"; "Island of Love"; "Moonlight Swim"; "Hawaiian Wedding Song"

Follow That Dream (1962)

A family of Southerners decides to homestead on a Florida beach. Gangsters and welfare bureaucrats all have a stake and much mayhem follows. Elvis's acting is quite competent and funny considering the material.

Songs: "Follow That Dream"; "What a Wonderful Life"; "I'm Not the Marrying Kind"; "Sound Advice"; "On Top of Old Smokey"; "Angel"

Kid Galahad (1962)

Elvis plays Walter Gulick, who starts out as a sparring partner/punching bag then turns pro and is exploited by his manager, portrayed by Gig Young. Walter fights a final bout for the purse at the end so he can quit the fight game, get married, and open a chain of garages. Other than bobbing and weaving in the ring, Elvis has a scene where he does the sexiest Twist *ever*.

Songs: "King of the Whole Wide World"; "I Got Lucky"; "This Is Living"; "Riding the Rainbow"; "Home Is Where the Heart Is"; "A Whistling Tune"

Girls! Girls! Girls! (1962)

Elvis as Ross Carpenter, a boat captain who sings by night to save money for his own boat. As usual, Elvis has his choice of girls—a glamour girl (in this case Stella Stevens) or a good girl (Lauren Goodwin). There's a Hawaiian location and many bikini-clad females.

Songs: "Girls! Girls! Girls!"; "I Don't Wanna Be Tied"; "We'll Be Tied Together"; "A Boy Like Me, a Girl Like You"; "Return to Sender"; "Earth Boy"; "Because of Love"; "Thanks to the Rolling Sea"; "Song of the Shrimp"; "The Walls Have Ears"; "We're Coming in Loaded"; "Dainty Little Moonbeams"

It Happened at the World's Fair (1963)

This time he's Mike Edwards, a crop-dusting bush pilot. Gambling debts cause him and his partner to lose their plane. Elvis heads off to the Seattle World's Fair where he becomes the baby-sitter/ward of a little girl and romances a nurse. This movie is not commercially available, so for the time being you can only get it from another fan who has it on tape.

Songs: "I'm Falling in Love Tonight"; "Take Me to the Fair"; "Cotton Candy Land"; "How Would You Like to Be"; "Beyond the Bend"; "Relax"; "They Remind Me Too Much of You"; "One Broken Heart for Sale"; "A World of Our Own"; "Happy Ending"

Fun in Acapulco (1963)

Would you believe, trapeze artist? Former trapeze artist, actually, who can't face the heights because his brother, who was in the act with him, was accidentally killed. Off to Acapulco where he sings and lifeguards and finally cliff dives and overcomes his fears. There are entanglements with a lady bullfighter (Elsa Cardenas) and a yummy hotel social director (Ursula Andress).

Songs: "Fun in Acapulco"; "(There's) No Room to Rhumba in a Sports Car"; "Bossa Nova Baby"; "Vino, Dinero, y Amor"; "I Think I'm Gonna Like It Here"; "Mexico"; "El Toro"; "Marguerita"; "The Bullfighter Was a Lady"; "You Can't Say No in Acapulco"

Kissin' Cousins (1964)

Elvis plays two parts: Air Force Lieutenant Josh Morgan and hillbilly Jodie Tatum, long-lost cousins. One role involved wearing a blond wig which made him pretty unhappy. Morgan is on a mission to get his cousin's family to sign over rights to build a missile base on their mountain. There's much pawing by men-starved womenfolk of Elvis and the other enlisted men.

Songs: "Kissin' Cousins"; "Barefoot Ballad"; "Smokey Mountain Boy"; "There's Gold in the Mountains"; "One Boy, Two Little Girls"; "Catchin' On Fast"; "Tender Feeling"; "Once Is Enough"

Viva Las Vegas (1964)

Two breathtakingly beautiful lead characters. Chemistry-a-plenty. Sixties camp. Ga-roovy Vegas backdrop. Elvis is a race car driver named Lucky Johnson, who needs to work as a waiter to work off a hotel bill and falls for the hotel swimming instructor (Ann-Margret). The dramatic tension comes in the form of the annual employees' talent contest in which both Elvis and Ann-Margret tie for first place.

Songs: "Viva Las Vegas"; "C'mon Everybody"; "The Lady Loves Me"; "What I'd Say"; "The Yellow Rose of Texas"; "The Eyes of Texas"; "Today, Tomorrow, and Forever"; "Santa Lucia"; "If You Think I Don't Love You"; "I Need Somebody to Lean On"

IT'S THAT "GO-GO" GUY AND THAT "BYE-BYE" GAL IN THE FUN CAPITAL OF THE WORLD!

METRO-GOLDWYN-MAYER PRESENTS
ELVIS PRESLEY & ANN-MARGRET
in A JACK CUMMINGS-GEORGE SIDNEY PRODUCTION
VIVA LAS VEGAS
PANAVISION & METROCOLOR
CESARE DANOVA · WILLIAM DEMAREST · NICKY BLAIR
SALLY BENSON · GEORGE SIDNEY

Roustabout (1964)

Good girl Joan Freeman and vixen Sue Ann Langdon vie for Elvis' (as Charlie Rogers) affections. Action takes place at a carnival where Elvis is hired as a roustabout, then singing sensation, by the owner played by Barbara Stanwyck. Dicey issues like indebtedness and drunkenness are treated here. Nice karate demonstration by Elvis in opening scenes.

Songs: "Roustabout"; "Little Egypt"; "Big Love, Big Heartache"; "Poison Ivy League"; "Wheels on My Heels"; "It's a Wonderful World"; "There's a Brand New Day on the Horizon"; "It's Carnival Time"; "Carny Town"; "One-Track Heart"; "Hard Knocks"

Girl Happy (1965)

Elvis, as Rusty Wells, chaperones his boss's daughter, played by Shelley Fabares, during her spring break in Fort Lauderdale. The romantic foil is played by Mary Ann Mobley. In spite of the song "Do the Clam," *Girl Happy* has a good soundtrack.

Songs: "Girl Happy"; "Do Not Disturb"; "Puppet on a String"; "Spring Fever"; "Fort Lauderdale Chamber of Commerce"; "Startin' Tonight"; "Wolf Call"; "Cross My Heart and Hope to Die"; "The Meanest Girl in Town"; "Do the Clam"; "I've Got to Find My Baby"

Tickle Me (1965)

This movie has an unsalvageable script and plot—really the absolute final turning point for Elvis' films from amusing and entertaining to beyond the pale. Elvis is Lonnie Beal, a rodeo rider moonlighting at a health spa/dude ranch until the rodeo season starts up. There's some intrigue over some hidden gold and a haunted ghost town.

Songs: "Slowly but Surely"; "Long Lonely Highway"; "Dirty Dirty Feeling"; "It Feels So Right"; "Such an Easy Question"; "Put the Blame on Me"; "I'm Yours"; "Night Rider"; "I Feel that I've Known You Forever"

Harum Scarum (1965)

Elvis plays a matinee idol, Johnny Tyrone, kidnapped and embroiled in a plot to murder an enemy of the Lord of the Assassins. There's lots of *tsuris* and, most notably, Cecil B. DeMille's *King of Kings* recycled set and costumes left over from *Kismet* are used for color and local atmosphere in this production.

Songs: "Harem Holiday"; "My Desert Serenade"; "Mirage"; "Kismet"; "Go East Young Man"; "Shake that Tambourine"; "Hey Little Girl"; "Golden Coins"; "So Close Yet So Far"

Frankie and Johnny (1966)

In this Mississippi riverboat scenario set during olden times, Donna Douglas (Frankie) won't marry Elvis (Johnny) until he gives up gambling and schmoozing with the ladies. Trouble is, a little redhead shows up and turns out to be a good luck charm when Johnny gambles.

Songs: "Frankie and Johnny"; "Petunia, the Gardener's Daughter"; "Chesay"; "Come Along"; "What Every Woman Lives For"; "Look Out Broadway"; "Beginner's

Author's collection

Luck, Hard Luck"; "Down by the Riverside"; "When the Saints Go Marching In"; "Shout It Out"; "Please Don't Stop Loving Me"; "Everybody Come Aboard"

Paradise, Hawaiian Style (1966)

Elvis plays Rick Richards, a pilot who's out of work, in his third Hawaii-set scenario. He hooks up with an old friend and they form a helicopter charter service around the islands with his various lady friends recommending the customers. Problems arise when the helicopter Elvis is piloting spins out of control because of some unruly dogs he is carrying, forcing a car off the road below—with a bigwig from the FAA at the wheel.

Songs: "Paradise Hawaiian Style"; "A Dog's Life"; "Queenie Wahine's Papaya"; "Scratch My Back"; "Drums of the Islands"; "This Is My Heaven"; "Datin'"; "House of Sand"; "Stop Where You Are"

Spinout (1966)

Elvis plays Mike McCoy, a race car driver and singer being pursued by at least three women looking for a husband. For an expert driver, he has a lot of car trouble—running into mud pits, dead batteries. In the end, the three women marry other guys and Elvis meets up with a girl who doesn't want to marry till she's 50.

Songs: "Spinout"; "Stop, Look, and Listen"; "I'll Be Back"; "Smorgasbord"; "Never Say Yes"; "Adam and Evil"; "All That I Am"; "Am I Ready"; "Beach Shack"

Easy Come, Easy Go (1967)

Former Navy frogman Elvis (Ted Jackson) dives for sunken treasure. He hooks up with a hippie chick who is the descendant of the owner of the downed boat that has the gold on it. She wants the whole haul to go toward an art center.

Songs: "Easy Come, Easy Go"; "Yoga Is as Yoga Does"; "The Love Machine"; "You Gotta Stop"; "Sing, You Children"; "I'll Take Love"

Double Trouble (1967)

Elvis plays Guy Lambert, a society singer, supported by an English cast, including Annette Day as an underage girl who falls for him. She's an heiress whose uncle has been spending her money and is now trying to have her killed.

Songs: "Double Trouble"; "Baby, If You'll Give Me All Your Love"; "Could I Fall in Love"; "Old MacDonald"; "City by Night"; "Long-Legged Girl with the Short Dress On"; "I Love Only One Girl"; "There Is So Much World to See"

Clambake (1967)

One of the few films where Elvis plays a rich guy, Scott Hayward. He switches roles with a waterskiing instructor in order to taste life as he never knew it. He gives lessons to Shelley Fabares, who confesses to him that she is exclusively interested in securing a rich hubby. During a powerboat race, Elvis wins the day with the help of some glue and the bankrolling of his father. The gold digger realizes she loves him and has abandoned her quest for a loaded husband when he comes up with a proposal and a bi-i-i-g ring.

Songs: "Clambake"; "Hey, Hey, Hey"; "Who Needs Money"; "Confidence"; "A House that Has Everything"; "You Don't Know Me"; "The Girl I Never Loved"

Stay Away, Joe (1968)

Elvis plays a Navajo Indian bull rider, Joe Lightcloud. Elvis must sing to a bull named Dominick who is refusing to make hay with the cows, thereby causing problems with his plan to raise a herd. Turns out Dominick is a bucking bull and Elvis raises money to increase the herd by staying on his back at the rodeo.

Songs: "Stay Away, Joe"; "Stay Away"; "Lovely Mamie"; "Dominick"; "All I Needed Was Rain"

Speedway (1968)

Elvis plays Steve Grayson, a wildly generous and frivolous stock car race champion who has tax trouble because his manager (Bill Bixby) wasn't keeping their books properly. Nancy Sinatra plays the IRS agent called in to sort it all out.

Songs: "Speedway"; "Let Yourself Go"; "Your Time Hasn't Come Yet, Baby"; "He's Your Uncle, Not Your Dad"; "Who Are You?"; "There Ain't Nothing Like a Song"

Live a Little, Love a Little (1968)

Elvis plays Greg Nolan, a photographer holding down two advertising jobs. Elvis' own Great Dane, Brutus, played Albert in this film. A ditsy girl played by Michele Carey alternately chases him and retreats. This movie included Elvis' first bed scene with a woman.

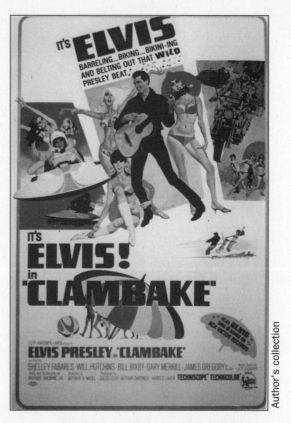

Author's collection

Songs: "A Little Less Conversation"; "Wonderful World"; "Almost in Love"; "Edge of Reality"

Charro! (1968)

Elvis, sporting a fabulous, rugged bearded look, plays a reformed gunslinger who's framed by his ex-gang, a nasty bunch of outlaws, for a murder and the theft of a prized Mexican cannon. One title originally considered for *Charro!* was "Come Hell, Come Sundown!"

Songs: "Charro" (sung over the opening credits)

The Trouble With Girls (And How to Get into It) (1969)

Elvis, as Walter Hale, manager of a 1927 traveling troupe of entertainers, has tons of trouble—from a union organizer and a murderess. When the wrong person is arrested for the crime, Elvis plots to get the lady who dealt the deadly blow to confess onstage during the show.

Songs: "The Whiffenpoof Song"; "Swing Down, Sweet Chariot"; "Violet"; "Clean Up Your Own Backyard"; "Sign of the Zodiac"; "Almost"

Change of Habit (1969)

In his final feature film for Hollywood, Elvis plays Dr. John Carpenter. He runs a ghetto clinic where three undercover nuns are assigned to help him out as a nursing staff. The film is very sixties in mood and attire and it deals with such hot contemporary issues as racism and social problems. Elvis gives a great performance and has great hair in this film. Mary Tyler Moore is just about the only costar Elvis doesn't get to snog.

Songs: "Change of Habit"; "Rubberneckin'"; "Let Us Pray"; "Have a Happy"

Elvis during the filming of *Stay Away Joe*

Sandi Miller

Elvis in *Speedway*

Author's collection

Elvis on the set of *Live a Little, Love a Little*

Sandi Miller

Elvis, That's the Way It Is (1970)

This film documents Elvis' preparation for his opening night at the International Hotel in Las Vegas. It includes celebrity, hotel management, and fan interviews.

Songs (alphabetically): "All Shook Up"; "Blue Suede Shoes"; "Bridge Over Troubled Water"; "Can't Help Falling in Love"; "Crying Time"; "Heartbreak Hotel"; "How the Web Was Woven"; "I Just Can't Help Believin'"; "I've Lost You"; "Little Sister"; "Love Me Tender"; "Mary in the Morning"; "Mystery Train"; "The Next Step Is Love"; "One Night"; "Patch It Up"; "Polk Salad Annie"; "Stranger in the Crowd"; "Suspicious Minds"; "Sweet Caroline"; "That's All Right"; "Tiger Man"; "What I'd Say"; "Words"; "You Don't Have to Say You Love Me"; "You've Lost that Lovin' Feelin'"

Elvis on Tour (1972)

This is a rockumentary about Elvis on a 15-city tour around the U.S. There's also footage of him from the 1950s. *Elvis on Tour* won the Golden Globe Award for Best Documentary in 1973.

Songs (alphabetically): "Amen"; "American Trilogy"; "Big Hunk o' Love"; "Bridge Over Troubled Water"; "Bosom of Abraham"; "Burnin' Love"; "Can't Help Falling in Love"; "Don't Be Cruel"; "Funny How Time Slips Away"; "I Got a Woman"; "I, John"; "Johnny B. Goode"; "Lawdy Miss Clawdy"; "Lead Me", "Guide Me"; "Love Me Tender"; "Memories"; "Mystery Train"; "Never Been to Spain"; "Polk Salad Annie"; "Proud Mary"; "Ready Teddy"; "See See Rider"; "Separate Ways"; "Suspicious Minds"; "That's All Right"; "Until It's Time for You to Go"; "You Gave Me a Mountain"

This Is Elvis (1981) (released posthumously)

This bio-pic produced by Dick Clark incorporates real footage of Elvis and reenactments by actors portraying him.

Paul Boenish III plays Elvis as a child.
David Scott plays Elvis at 18.
Dana MacKay plays an infirm Elvis.
Johnny Hara plays Elvis at 42.
Ray Donner did Elvis' vocals.

Elvis' Screen Test

Elvis spent three days making a screen test in which he played the role of Jimmy Curry in scenes from *The Rainmaker*. As part of the test, Elvis also lip-synched "Blue Suede Shoes."

Movies Elvis Didn't Make

There's a handful of roles that Elvis never got to perform. Some were turned down by the Colonel and some didn't work out for *good* reasons.

Kiss of Death
Remake of 1947 hard-boiled gangster film.
Rope Law
Remake of *The Mississippi Gambler*.
The Girl Can't Help It
Colonel asked for $50,000 for one song.
The Way to the Gold
Jeffrey Hunter got the part.
The Love Maniac
He was to costar with Jayne Mansfield in 1957.
The Defiant Ones
Tony Curtis got the role.
Thunder Road
Robert Mitchum wanted Elvis to play his moonshining brother.
West Side Story
Robert Wise wanted Elvis to play Tony.
The Rainmaker
Elvis was considered for two roles, including Starbuck.
The Threepenny Opera
Would have been a real departure for Elvis in 1961.
Too Late Blues
Bobby Darin got the role of jazz musician John Wakefield.
Sweet Bird of Youth
Colonel turned down the role because the character was a gigolo; Paul Newman got the role instead.
Your Cheatin' Heart
Hank Williams's wife vetoed Elvis for the role in his bio-pic; George Hamilton got the part.
The Fastest Guitar Alive
Roy Orbison got the part in 1968.
Midnight Cowboy
Elvis was up for Jon Voigt's 1969 role as Texas stud.
A Star Is Born
Barbra Streisand wanted Elvis but the Colonel wanted top billing and $1 million.

Some of Elvis' Favorite Movies

Wuthering Heights	*Patton*
It's a Wonderful Life	*The Party*
Miracle on 34th Street	*Village of the Damned*
To Kill a Mockingbird	*The Wild Bunch*
Dr. Strangelove	*Across 110th Street*

Rebel without a Cause
A Streetcar Named Desire
The Wild One
The Way of All Flesh
One Flew over the Cuckoo's Nest
The Pink Panther

Lawrence of Arabia
Deathwish
Monty Python and the Holy Grail
Diamonds Are Forever
Straw Dogs
Dirty Harry

Elvis' Favorite Movie that He Made
King Creole

Elvis's Friends and Family's Movie Cameos
Vernon and Gladys Presley
   Both appear in *Loving You* when Elvis is singing "Got a Lot of Livin' to Do."
   When he jumps out into the crowd, both can be seen sitting.
Vernon Presley
   In *Live a Little, Love a Little*, when Elvis goes to take a photograph of the girl
   in the mermaid outfit eating a sandwich, he's sitting in a chair to the left. In
   Viva Las Vegas, Vernon is standing at the back when Elvis is singing "Yellow
   Rose of Texas" and trying to get everyone out of the dance hall.
Joe Esposito
   It Happened at the World's Fair; *Kissin' Cousins*; *Spinout*; *Clambake*; *Stay
   Away, Joe*; *The Trouble with Girls*
Jerry Schilling
   The Trouble with Girls
Charlie Hodge
   Clambake; *Speedway*; *Charro!*
Raymond Sitton
   Follow That Dream and *Kid Galahad*
Bill Black
   Loving You; *Jailhouse Rock*; *GI Blues*
D. J. Fontana
   Loving You; *Jailhouse Rock*; *GI Blues*
Scotty Moore
   Loving You; *Jailhouse Rock*; *GI Blues*
Red West
   Flaming Star; *Wild in the Country*; *Follow That Dream*; *Girls! Girls! Girls!*; *It
   Happened at the World's Fair*; *Fun in Acapulco*; *Viva Las Vegas*; *Roustabout*;
   Girl Happy; *Tickle Me*; *Harum Scarum*; *Paradise, Hawaiian Style*; *Spinout*;
   Live a Little, Love a Little
Sonny West
   Kid Galahad and *Stay Away, Joe*

Marty Lacker
Extra in 13 films including the part of the chef turning the spit while Elvis sang "Clambake" in *Clambake*
George Klein
Frankie and Johnny and *Double Trouble*
The Jordanaires
Loving You and vocals credits for 18 other movies
Bitsy Mott
Bit parts in *GI Blues* and *Wild in the Country*

Stand-Ins and Doubles for Elvis
Lance LeGault
Tom Creel
Billy Smith
Stood in for one of Elvis' female costars.

Some of the Famous Actors Who Costarred with Elvis

Richard Egan	Kurt Russell
Ed Asner	Rudy Vallee
Bill Bixby	Angela Lansbury
Charles Bronson	Barbara Eden
John Carradine	Dolores Del Rio
Dabney Coleman	Ann-Margret
Walter Matthau	Hope Lange
Gig Young	Ursula Andress
Burgess Meredith	Barbara Stanwyck
Vic Morrow	Elsa Lanchester
Vincent Price	Joan Blondell

Some Movie Bloopers
Love Me Tender
In a scene where female lead Deborah Paget is crying by a window, it is possible to see a car in the background of the frame. Unfortunately, the film is set during the Civil War.
Jailhouse Rock
Elvis' prison uniform changes numbers between one scene and the next.
Clambake
There's a mountain range in the background of several scenes, obviously not Florida (California as it turns out) where the film is supposed to be set.

Change of Habit

At the beginning, under the opening credits, a bus drives by with an ad panel advertising a Los Angeles radio station. The film is set in New York City.

Elvis' First Words on Screen

"Whoa! … Brett, Vance. They told us you were dead!"

Elvis' Last Movie Night Out

The Spy Who Loved Me

Privately screened at the General Cinema Whitehaven in Memphis.

YOUR ELVIS EDUCATION

"When I sat down to write a book about Elvis Presley, I watched all 33 of his movies—including the ones that are all but unwatchable. I felt that to understand what happened to Elvis, I really had to look at what happened to his career. And those movies are undeniable proof of Hollywood's general disdain for his talents…."
—Pat H. Broeske, author of *Down at the End of Lonely Street*, in *Writer's Digest* magazine

Books

Elvis! Elvis! Elvis! The King and His Movies
    Peter Guttmacher
The Elvis Film Encyclopedia: An Impartial Guide to the Films of Elvis
    Eric Braun
Reel Elvis! The Ultimate Trivia Guide to the King's Movies
    Pauline Bartel
The Elvis Encyclopedia
    David E. Stanley with Frank Coffey
Elvis in Hollywood: Celluloid Sellout
    Gerry McLafferty
Time Out Film Guide
    edited by *Time Out* magazine

Video

Elvis in Hollywood   *This is Elvis*
Wild in Hollywood   *All the King's Men*

Video Sources

Your neighborhood video store may have a limited selection of Elvis movies. In fact, some are no longer being distributed at all such as *It Happened at the World's Fair*. Graceland's stores and phone order are a safe bet and there's no end to online sources for Elvis' movies. The two places below will mail videos anywhere.

Eddie Brandt's Saturday Matinee
6310 Colfax Avenue
North Hollywood, California 91606
(818) 506-4242 or (818) 506-7722
Fax: (818) 506-5649

Critic's Choice Video
P.O. Box 749
Itasca, Illinois 60143
(800) 367-7765

Web Sites

http://www.geocities.com/~arpt/az/
  Elvis Presley Encyclopaedia
http://www.imdb.com
  Internet movie database
http://www.members.tripod.com/
  ~wbroekman
  Elvis the King site; for Elvis film
  references
http://www.videoflicks.com
  Video Flicks; site to purchase videos
http://www.bigstar.com
  Bigstar; site to purchase videos
http://www.mgm.com/elvis/
  MGM Home Entertainment; Elvis
  Commemorative Collection for sale

http://www.geocities.com/~arpt/
  hollywood/
  Lex Raaphorst's movie Database
  site; information, posters
http://greggers.granitecity.com/elvis/
  women/
  Elvis' Women, in the movies, that is
http://www.imdb.com
  Internet movie database
http://www.reel.com
  To buy or rent Elvis films
http://www.gloriapall.com
  Costar from *Jailhouse Rock* Gloria
  Pall's site

THE ELVIS AND YOU EXPERIENCE

Join a Video Purchasing Club

Jump-start your Elvis movie collection by joining a video club. Most offer several movies for an extremely low fee to begin your membership and then discounts on films after that.
Columbia House Video Club
1400 Fruitridge Avenue
Terre Haute, Indiana 47811
(800) 457-0866
http://www.colombiahouse.com

Take an Elvis-in-Hollywood Tour

See where Elvis lived during the movie years. His former homes listed below are not open to the public, but you can drive by and soak in the atmosphere.

The Hollywood Knickerbocker Hotel
1714 North Ivar Avenue
Los Angeles, California 90210
The Regent Beverly Wilshire Hotel
(formerly the Beverly Wilshire)
9500 Wilshire Boulevard
Beverly Hills, California 90212
565 Perugia Way, Bel Air
Former home of the Shah of Iran and Rita Hayworth. The Beatles had the famous meeting with Elvis here.
10539 Bellagio Road, Bel Air
1963 until 1965
10550 Rocca Place
Stone canyon rental 1965-67
1174 Hillcrest Drive, Bel Air
First house purchased in L.A. in May 1967
144 Monovale, Holmby Hills
Purchased late '67; Priscilla lived here after the divorce.

See Elvis' Hawaiian Movie Locations

This company leads tours of movie locations, including Elvis,' on the islands.
Hawaii Movie Tours
356 Kuhio Highway
Kapaa, Hawaii 96746
(800) 628-8432
(808) 822-1192

Put Yourself in an Elvis Movie

Edit yourself into your favorite Elvis movie scene. There are very affordable video editing programs available for your home computer.

A fan photographs Elvis as he pulls out of 1174 Hillcrest Drive on one of his many motorcycles

Albuquerque fan Margaret Freisinger at 1174 Hillcrest in May 1999

144 Monovale, Holmby Hills home

10550 Rocca Place

Elvis relaxing on the set of *Blue Hawaii*

Elvis Repertory Theater
Do a live version of an Elvis movie script as a play. Do not charge admission or you'll have to pay royalties.

When You Go to the Movies, Sit in the "Elvis Seat"
Elvis usually insisted on sitting in the center of the fifth row.

Rent a Movie Theater for You and Your Friends
Like Elvis did, it is possible to rent a movie theater after hours for a private movie party. Show a print of an Elvis movie or show one of Elvis' favorites. A great thing to do as a fan club event.

Rent One of Elvis' Favorite Theaters
The Playhouse on the Square (formerly The Memphian Theater)
51 South Cooper Street
Memphis, Tennessee
(901) 726-4656

Malco Theatres
This company managed many of the theaters Elvis frequented. They still have 24 theaters in the Memphis area.
Orpheum Theatre (formerly The Malco)

203 South Main Street
Memphis, Tennessee 38103
(901) 525-3000
Corporate Headquarters
5851 Ridgeway
Center Parkway, Tennessee 38120

The Lyric Theatre
This is where Elvis saw his first movies as a boy.
P.O. Box 1094
Tupelo, Mississippi 38802
(601)-844-1935

Give to a Movie-Related Charity
Make a donation to the Motion Picture Relief Fund through the Screen Actors Guild. Elvis gave $50,000 at one time. When the hat is passed around at the movie theater, pitch in in the spirit of Elvis.

Where to Get Elvis Movie Posters
Vintage Movie Posters
LeMay Movie Poster Gallery
6333 West 3 Street #150-36
Los Angeles, California 90036
Fax: (213) 933-4465
E-mail: LeMayCo@aol.com

Jerry Ohlingers Movie Material
242 West 14 Street
New York, New York 10011
(212) 989-0869

Request Elvis Movies Be Carried by Your Local Video Store
Whenever you see that a video store doesn't carry Elvis' movies, let them hear about it. For instance, the national chain Blockbuster carries a fairly paltry selection. You can ask them to stock more by contacting them at:
Blockbuster Video
3000 Redbud Boulevard
McKinney, Texas 75069
(800) 800-6767

THE PILGRIMAGE

Because Elvis' life was so anchored to this one place, Graceland has become a focal point of the fans' interest: the Elvis World capital. It's where Elvis lived most of his life as well as where he died and now remains, both in body and in spirit. Graceland is both a king's palace and his tomb. It's one of the few monuments where you can visit a great man's kitchen and his grave on the same tour.

Elvis spent more time at Graceland than anywhere else and many of the significant events in his life happened there. He mourned the loss of his mother, he lived with his wife, he raised a child, and he went through a divorce. He had a lot of fun there and some pain, too. And in 1977, he died and was buried there. Graceland is the most concentrated dose of physical Elvis essence you can get on Earth.

A visit to Graceland is sometimes referred to as a *pilgrimage* because the intensity of some of the fans who flock there invites a comparison to the religious faithful visiting the Holy Land. Most fans don't feel comfortable with the religious implications of the term because it's been used by critics to mock the people who make the trip to Memphis. It seems to imply a level of fanaticism that very, very few fans actually subscribe to. The 750,000 people who visit Graceland any given year don't go there because they believe Elvis to be a god or a saint. There are as many reasons to visit Graceland as there are Elvis fans, but there's no denying the emotional, and for some

Graceland street sign circa 1978

Courtesy of Butterfield & Butterfield

John O'Hara

people the deeply spiritual, aspects of making the journey to Memphis.

When you finally see Graceland with your own eyes and experience its scale, it affects how you perceive the stories you've heard about Elvis. Maybe everyone just expects things to be bigger, to be King-sized. But instead, the intimacy humanizes the icon. You come away from Graceland knowing a little bit more about Elvis. It makes real an unreal life.

People have been flocking to Elvis ever since he started singing for us in the 1950s. Fans felt compelled to appear outside his homes throughout his career. Girls would sneak up to the windows of his Audubon Drive house hoping to hear, see, touch, smell, or taste him. It was partly to avoid these invasions of privacy that Elvis bought Graceland. He needed a place where he could retreat behind a wall and have some control over his contact with fans.

From the day Elvis installed those famous music gates, there has seldom been a moment when there has not been a crowd outside them. There's a rumor that in the fifties when a teenage girl ran away from home, FBI agents checked outside the gates of Graceland as a routine part of their search. During Elvis' lifetime, people came to Graceland attracted by the possibility that they might have a chance to meet him. Elvis would often come down from the house to the gates, sometimes by horse, sometimes by golf cart, and sign autographs and pose for pictures. When Elvis wasn't home, his Uncle Vester, the head gatekeeper, would allow fans onto the grounds for short tours.

After Elvis' death, Graceland took on perhaps even more significance for Elvis fans, if that's

Laura Levin

The Wall of Love undergoing some sandblasted censorship

Holding a torch for Elvis during the Tribute Week candlelight vigil

possible. His body and his mother's were moved to Graceland and interred in the Meditation Garden. With part of the estate rezoned as a cemetery, a clause in municipal law required that the grave site must be open to the public. On November 27, 1977, the grave site was opened and 8,000 people visited on that first day alone. On the anniversary of Elvis death in 1978, tens of thousands of fans appeared in Memphis and a new tradition was born. The interest in visiting Graceland increased more dramatically when the house was opened to the public on June 7, 1982.

The emphasis of the pilgrimage is, of course, on Graceland itself. Early in the morning, before the tours begin, fans take part in the Morning Walkup. Between 6:30 and 8:30 A.M., fans are allowed, free of charge, to walk up from the gates to spend some quiet time in the Meditation Garden. This is when you're likely to meet the most emotional and, perhaps, devoted fans. Among the regulars in the morning walkups are the fans who've moved to Memphis to be near Elvis year-round.

The wall in front of Graceland is an attraction in itself. Nicknamed the "Wall of Love," it's filled with graffiti written by people expressing their love for Elvis, their grief that he's gone, their gratitude for his talent, or even their puzzlement of the whole phenomenon. In some ways, the wall was the original Elvis chat room.

The tour itself begins across the street from the house in Graceland Plaza where tickets are sold among the gift shops, restaurants, museums, and other attractions. Small buses shuttle people back and forth between the plaza and the mansion across the street. Each person is given a Walkman with a pre-recorded tour available in several languages. (The details of the house itself and the tour are explored thoroughly in the "At Home

Graffiti from the Wall of Love

with Elvis" chapter.) After the tour people are brought back across the street and strategically dropped off in front of the gift shops.

Other attractions at Graceland Plaza include: the Bijou Theater, which shows a 22-minute film about Elvis' life; the Sincerely Elvis Museum, a small museum containing some of his personal items and other exhibits; and the Elvis Presley Automobile Museum, which displays many of Elvis' favorite motor vehicles. The Airplane tour features two of Elvis' private jets, the sleek Jetstar *Hound Dog II* and the huge Convair 880, named after Lisa Marie. There are restaurants — the Chrome Grille; Rockabilly's Diner; and Shake, Split & Dip — and of course places to buy Elvis stuff, Elvis Threads, Gallery Elvis, and Good Rockin' Tonight.

The rest of the fans' time in Memphis is spent visiting as many other significant places from Elvis' life as possible in the time available. His schools, churches, recording studios, places of employment, former homes, performing venues, and favorite restaurants and hangouts are sought out by fans to gain insight into the man. Friends and associates are tracked down for precious oral histories. It seems like almost everybody in Memphis has an Elvis story.

As part of their pilgrimage to Memphis some fans do charity work in Elvis' name. Some donate blood at the Elvis Presley Trauma Center, others present the fruits of their fund-raising efforts from back home to one of Elvis' favorite Memphis charities. (See "Elvis and Charity" for more details.)

As the years have passed, the number of people visiting Graceland has continued to grow. It reaches its apex every August around the anniversary of Elvis' death when the faithful, and the curious, converge on Memphis for a full week of activities that has come to be known as Tribute Week. In 1993, 45,000 people visited Memphis during that one week alone. In 1997, it was 60,000. A visit to Graceland is an emotionally satisfying experience any time of the year, but during Tribute Week it's the most Elvis-centric experience you can possibly have. Tribute Week, or Death Week as the Elvis-jaded local cynics refer to it, has evolved into a unique festival with its own rituals and traditions.

During Tribute Week there's a wide range of special activities and events. Every year, certain fan clubs hold conventions and throw parties in nearby hotels. In the

Laura Levin

On line for the Candlelight Vigil, August 1998

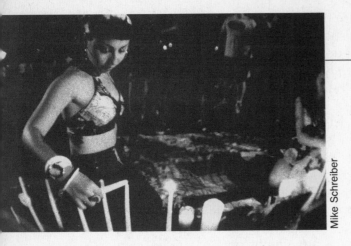

Some fans, like this one from New York City, set up temporary "shrines" in front of Graceland on the anniversary of Elvis' death

past there have been concerts, memorabilia conventions, auctions, karate tournaments, 5K races, discussion panels and seminars, impersonator contests, window decorating contests, art exhibits and contests, Elvis-themed river cruises, and special events at amusement parks and casinos. The week builds to an emotional crescendo on the eve of the anniversary of Elvis' death with the Candlelight Vigil to his grave. It is the peak experience for an Elvis fan, the night when Graceland truly becomes Amazing Graceland.

On the afternoon of August 15 fans start to gather outside the gates. Police close Elvis Presley Boulevard to traffic and a line that snakes back and forth in front of the wall starts to form. Elvis music plays from loudspeakers. News and police helicopters circle overhead. The heat lessens only slightly as night falls and the humidity hangs in the air. Medical technicians and ambulances stand by to tend those who are overwhelmed either by the heat, their emotions, or a combination of the two.

At around 9:00 P.M. the ceremony begins with prayers, some short words, and the sound of Elvis' sweet voice. The mood is sad, subdued, and reflective. A friend or relative from the Elvis world, or a representative from Elvis Presley Enterprises, lights a torch from the eternal flame at Elvis' grave and walks down to the gates to light the candles of the fans as they stroll slowly, single file, up the driveway. Elvis Presley Enterprises even provides some advice in their brochure on the proper way to act. "Please avoid loud talking or laughter or any behavior that might be offensive to, or unappreciated by, those who take this tribute seriously. The Candlelight Vigil is intended to be a solemn, respectful tribute." The spectacular procession of thousands of candles flicker in the thick

Veteran fans attending the Candlelight Vigil get in line early and come well prepared

Mike Schreiber

Memphis night as Elvis' soothing voice sings songs of peace and hope from speakers mounted around the Graceland grounds.

Many fans carry gifts to be left at the grave—a flower, a teddy bear, a poem, a photo, or an artwork made especially for Elvis with their love. After filing past Elvis' grave they make the long walk down the driveway, many of them in tears. Some fans schedule their Walkup after dawn to coincide with the approximate time of Elvis' early morning death.

It's rumored that some years Lisa Marie has watched the candlelight procession from the window of Elvis' bedroom. One has to wonder what must have gone through her mind as she witnessed the level of emotion devoted to her father.

To fully appreciate Elvis' extraordinary life you have to see where it began, and Graceland is only a part of that story. A visit to Elvis' birthplace in Tupelo, Mississippi, is essential to grasping what he achieved in his 42 years. Elvis himself used to make frequent trips back to the shotgun shack he was born in. He understood the need to visit the places of his childhood to better understand himself and gain perspective on his life.

The Graceland pilgrimage has become part of the American experience. It has worked its way into pop culture in songs, plays, movies, and TV shows. When Paul Simon sang that he has "reason to believe that we will all be received at Graceland," he voiced a collective feeling that many people have, that Graceland is not just a home to Elvis but a home of the heart for his fans. In an episode of *The X-Files,* FBI Agent Fox Mulder tells his partner he's going on a spiritual journey to a special place. The episode ends with Agent Mulder at Graceland wearing Elvis shades. In a 1988 *Designing Women* episode, Charlene and her reluctant costars make the pilgrimage, the "nonbelievers" in the bunch leaving as the

John O'Hara

converted. In the film *Rattle and Hum*, the Irish rock band U2 makes an emotional stop at Graceland (and records some songs at Sun Studio). And in *Finding Graceland* Harvey Keitel plays a man who believes he's Elvis and travels to Graceland in the hope of consolation and a redemptive reunion with his past.

Visiting Memphis and meeting all the other fans feels like coming home to a family that understands you. The first time fans go to Graceland they go to see Elvis. Each time after that they also go to see each other. The trip to Graceland becomes a reunion in which the family gets together on a regular basis to remember one of its lost members.

Laura Levin

"How do I begin to express my feelings about my first trip to Memphis. My emotions ran the gamut from the depths of unhappiness to a mountain high: I would be laughing one minute, crying my eyes out the next.

"The night of the candlelight services made me realize, if I had not already, the reason I was here. It was not just a night of beauty and love; but to me, it was almost like being in church. I felt like this was sort of a religious pilgrimage we were all going on, and not just a mere visit to the grave site of one of the greatest performers who ever lived.

"The true meaning of Elvis came to pass on the morning of August 17. The Japanese girls were getting ready to leave for home; there were tears all around. As we left the grave site, the Japanese girls bowed and placed their gifts on the stone. One of the English girls was standing by the pillars sobbing. As we walked down the driveway we were linked arm and arm: Japan, America, United Kingdom, Germany, Holland, and Canada. It was the saddest but also one of the most beautiful moments of my life. To me, at that moment, that is what coming here to Memphis and Graceland is all about. I never felt so loved, or felt like giving love in return as I did that morning. My life will be forever enriched by it for it will surely never be the same again. We hugged and kissed the girls from Japan—they speak little or no English, but for the love, no words were needed.

"If we now all would go home to our respective towns and countries and carry back with us Elvis' love for mankind, maybe we as Elvis fans can in some small way make this world just a little better place to live in. Elvis gave us all his great love. Let us go now and share it with the world."

—Joanne Digilio

ESSENTIAL ELVISOLOGY

The Year Graceland Opened for Tours
1982

The Year the *Lisa Marie* and *Hound Dog II* Opened for Tours
1984

The Year the Elvis Presley Automobile Museum Opened
1989

The Only House in America Visited by More People
The White House

National Register of Historic Places
Graceland was placed on this prestigious list in 1991

Number of Visitors Annually
600,000 visitors each year and growing

The Peak Season for Visitors
Memorial Day through Labor Day

Number of Visitors Daily
2,000 to 3,500 visitors a day in the spring and early summer with more than 4,000 a day in July at the height of the travel season; in contrast, only a few hundred visitors on a weekday in the dead of winter

Graceland's Economic Impact on Memphis
Estimated at more than $150 million per year

Number of Graceland Employees
450 during the summer season
350 people the rest of the year

Graceland Visitor Demographics
Visitors are typical of most any major attraction. They come from all walks of life, all ages, all musical tastes, all classes, all levels of education, and all parts of the world. More than half of Graceland's visitors are under the age of 35. Graceland has become a must-see for visiting dignitaries, touring Broadway show casts, touring rock stars, and people of virtually every description coming to Memphis.

YOUR ELVIS EDUCATION

Books

The Field Guide to Elvis Shrines
  Bill Yenne
Memphis Elvis-Style
  Cindy Hazen and Mike Freeman
The Elvis Atlas: A Journey through Elvis Presley's America
  Michael Gray and Roger Osborne
Did Elvis Sing in Your Hometown? (Volumes One and Two)
  Lee Cotton
Roadside Elvis: The Complete State-by-State Travel Guide for Elvis Presley Fans
  Jack Barth
Graceland: The Living Legacy of Elvis Presley
  Chet Flippo
Graceland: Going Home With Elvis
  Karal Ann Marling
Placing Elvis: A Tour Guide to the Kingdom
  Sharon Colette Urquhart

Video

Elvis Presley's Graceland
  hosted by Priscilla Beaulieu Presley
Mystery Train
  directed by Jim Jarmusch
U2: Rattle and Hum
Finding Graceland

CD ROM

  Virtual Graceland: Your Personal Tour of Elvis' Life and Home

Web Sites

http://www.elvis-presley.com
  Graceland; official web site
http://www.memphisguide.com/
  "The Memphis Guide"; request free
  guidebook
http://www.geocities.com/~arpt/az/
  Elvis Presley Encyclopaedia
http://elvistyle.com/elvistyl.htm

Memphis Elvis-Style; Memphis
Explorations
http://tupelo.net/calendar.html
Tupelo, Mississippi Calendar of
Events
http://www.epmemphis.com
Elvis Presley's Memphis Restaurant;
events, schedule, menu

http://www.fortunecity.com/tinpan/
  floyd/597/
    Martin Nolet's Elvis in Hawaii site
http://www.total.net/~pinker/Bookand
  MusicStore.html
    Elvis, blues, country music;
    Tennessee travel books; CDs
http://www.lasvegas.com
    Las Vegas information site

http://www.geocities.com/~mygraceland/
    My Graceland; sights and sounds of
    the King
http://www.apeculture.com/ELVISWK.
  HTM
    Fan's trip to Graceland site
http://www.gomemphis.com/elvis/
  elvis.html
    The *Commercial Appeal* Elvis
    archive

THE ELVIS AND YOU EXPERIENCE

Graceland is the epicenter of the Elvis universe of course but there are many
other places to find Elvis. Enjoy your journey wherever it takes you. The
Memphis Visitor Information Bureau can help you plan your trip.
Memphis Visitor Information Bureau
(901) 543-5333
Fax: (901) 543-5335
http://www.memphistravel.com

Booking a Flight to Memphis
Be sure to ask about any special Tribute Week fares.
Northwest Airlines
(800) 328-1111
(800) 225-2525
http://www.nwa.com
Ask for the worldwide file code number for Tribute Week travel; it changes every
year. This code applies to travel to Memphis from August 5–21 and provides a 5
percent discount on the lowest applicable fare. For tickets reserved 60 days or
more in advance, the discount is 10 percent.

American Airlines
(800) 433-7300
http://www.aa.com

Decorate Your Luggage
Don't forget to bring an extra piece of luggage with you to haul home all your
Elvis loot. Decorate it in an Elvis theme, with buttons or sewn-on material. Or
you can buy Elvis carryalls at the gift shops at Graceland and carry your souvenirs
in a souvenir.

What to Pack for Your Pilgrimage

This book and other guide books

Spare hankies (emotions tend to run high)

Container for holding relics (bring back a piece of Elvis' world)

Smelling salts (he can still make 'em faint)

Extra candles and candle holders

Portable water bottle

Portable fan

Polaroid camera (for autographed photos)

Tape recorder

Video camera

Address book (to record all the new friends you'll make)

Autograph book

Sun block

Your eyeglass prescription (for your new Elvis sunglasses)

Special Things to Pack in January

Warm clothes

Umbrella

Nonskid shoes

Keep a Pilgrimage Journal

Record your thoughts in a journal. Share your pilgrimage experience with other fans when you get back. Post your Memphis journal entries on the internet.

'50s Elvis style

'60s Elvis style

'70s Elvis style

From the collection of Bob Klen

Sandi Miller

Sandi Miller

Pack an Elvis-Style Picnic when Visiting Sites
(Refer to the "Elvis and Food" chapter.)

Tips for Making the Pilgrimage as a Fan Club or Group of Elvis Friends
Travel agents often arrange special discounts and package deals for groups. Booking a bus or even chartering a plane is a great way to get to Memphis with your friends. You can play Elvis movies and music the whole way there. Affix decorations with an Elvis message to the side of your bus.

Rent a Motorcoach
American Charters & Tours
5702 Summer Avenue
Memphis, Tennessee 39134
(888) 836-3678
(901) 382-6366
Fax: (901) 382-7496
http://www.3act.com

Rent an Apartment in Memphis
Rents are relatively inexpensive in Memphis. Rent an apartment in July and August. Use it as your Tribute Week fan club headquarters or work out a timeshare with other fans. Write or call for Memphis apartment listings in:
Memphis Apartment Blue Book
4746 Spottswood Avenue, Suite 347
Memphis, Tennessee 38117
(901) 323-5207
Fax: (901) 323-5242
(877) 323-5207

Rent a Plane or Helicopter
Get an aerial view of Graceland and don't forget your camera. Or fly to Tupelo and get the lay of the land.
Palm Air
2432 Winchester Road
Hanger 15
Memphis, Tennessee 38116
(901) 398-6900
(888) 398-7256

Elvis spending the day tooling around Lake McKellor in his speedboat on July 8, 1960

Memphis East Aviation
5793 Airline Road
Arlington, Tennessee 38117
(901) 867-9464

Rent a Vintage Car

Rent a car similar to one that Elvis would have driven. Consult "The Presley Motor Pool" in "Elvis and the Motor Vehicle" for makes and models. The best way to see Memphis is in an old Cadillac or Lincoln.
Rent-a-Wreck
1780 Bartlett Road
Memphis, Tennessee 38116
(901) 384-4800
(800) 535-1391

Rent a Boat

Elvis used to tool around McKellor Lake in one of his two speedboats. Why not rent a boat for the day? Be sure to wear a yachting cap like he did.
Lakeview Boat Dock
(601) 781-1550

Go to the Movies While in Memphis

Elvis loved going to the movies and would rent out entire theaters for all-night moviethons for himself and his friends. While you're in Memphis, why not take a break from the heat and catch a flick in the air-conditioned darkness like Elvis did. During Tribute Week some theaters even show special Elvis programs. Here are two theaters that Elvis rented.

Elvis leaving a movie theater in Memphis

Playhouse on the Square (formerly the Memphian Theatre)
51 South Cooper Street
Memphis, Tennessee 38103
(901) 726-4656

Orpheum Theatre (formerly the Malco)
203 South Main Street
Memphis, Tennessee 38103
(901) 525-3000

Write Your Message on Graceland's Wall of Love
You may still feel the need to communicate with Elvis somehow. The Wall of Love
acts as a wailing wall where fans write messages of love, humor, and longing.

Submit Your Wall of Love Graffiti for a Book
Send a photo of something you've written on the Wall of Love to be considered
for inclusion in the sequel to *Dear Elvis: Graffiti from Graceland*. If your photo
is used, the author will send you a free copy of the book. (Photos cannot be
returned.) Send them to:
Dear Elvis: Graffiti from Graceland
c/o Mustang Publishing Company
P.O. Box 3004
Memphis, Tennessee 38173

Graceland Information
3764 Elvis Presley Boulevard
Memphis, Tennessee 38116

Mailing address:
P.O. Box 16508
Memphis, Tennessee 38186-0508
(901) 332-3322
TTY (901) 344-3146
(800) 238-2000

Mail-order department:
(888) 358-4776
http://www.elvis-presley.com

Graceland Tour

The 60–90 minute tour includes all this:

Living room	Poolroom	Kitchen
Music room	Jungle Room	Business office
Dining room	Trophy hall	Shooting range
Gladys's room	Racquetball building	TV room
Meditation Garden		

Elvis Presley Automobile Museum

Refer to "Elvis and the Motor Vehicle" for more information.

Airplane Tour

Refer to the "Elvis and Air Travel" chapter for more information.

Sincerely Elvis Museum

Candid photos, home movie clips, off-stage clothing, home furnishings, books, horseback riding, and sports gear

Walk a Mile in My Shoes

Theater showing a 22-minute film on Elvis presented every half hour

Gift Shops

Good Rockin', Elvis Threads, Gallery Elvis, Elvis Kids, Welcome to My World, and "Walk a Mile" (See "Collecting Elvis" for more information.)

Post Office

For that enviable mailed-from-Graceland postmark and shipping memorabilia.

Restaurants

Rockabilly's Diner; Chrome Grill; Shake, Split & Dip

Visitor Center

Pavilion with hotel reservations, one-hour photo developing and translation (either written or for the recorded tour) services

Private Events at Graceland

The Graceland Special Events department can arrange for parties, receptions,

meetings and other special events at Graceland Plaza. Package may include a private off-hours tour of the mansion and museums.
Graceland Special Events Department
(800) 238-2010
(901) 344-3146

Visit Elvis' Other Homes in Memphis
See "Elvis at Home,"

Some Other Memphis Points of Interest
Please note that these are now private homes and not open to the general public.
Ginger Alden's Home
   The home of Elvis' last girlfriend
   4152 Royal Crest Place
   Memphis, Tennessee 38103
Linda Thompson's Home
   Linda was Elvis' girlfriend during the early to mid-1970s. She sold the house
   to Elvis collector Jimmy Velvet in 1981. It has since changed hands.
   1254 Old Hickory Road
   Memphis, Tennessee 38103
Gary Pepper's Home
   Elvis bought this house for Gary Pepper, fan club president. It is now owned
   by Elvis fan Phylis Collas.
   1260 Dolan Drive
   Memphis, Tennessee 38103
Vernon and Dee's Home
   Elvis bought this home for Vernon and his new wife Dee Stanley and her
   three children. It had a passage in back of
   the house onto the Graceland grounds.
   1266 Dolan Drive
   Memphis, Tennessee 38103
First Assembly of God
Originally at 1084 East McLemore Avenue, this
is where Elvis first heard fellow church members the Blackwood Brothers. This also where
he met Dixie Locke, one of his girlfriends.
   255 North Highland
   Memphis, Tennessee 38103
   (901) 324-3585

John O'Hara

Vernon's former home on Dolan Drive

John O'Hara

L. C. Humes High School
The auditorium of Elvis' high
school has been renamed the Elvis
A. Presley Auditorium in honor of
his first performances. To arrange
a tour contact Mrs. Jackson.
659 North Manassas Street
Memphis, Tennessee 38107
(901)-579-3226

Elvis Presley Plaza
A statue of Elvis stands here facing
the lights of Beale Street as Elvis himself so often did.
Intersection of Beale and Second
Memphis, Tennessee 38103

Poplar Records
The store where Elvis bought his first records.
308 Poplar Avenue
Memphis, Tennessee 38103
(901) 525-6348

Sun Studio
It's the most famous recording studio in the world, surely, and the visit is fascinating. There's a tour, gallery of memorabilia, and shop. You can even cut
a recording if you want.
706 Union Avenue
Memphis, Tennessee 38103
(800) 441-6249
(901) 521-0664
http://www.sunstudio.com
E-mail: sun@wspice.com

Blue Light Studio
Elvis had publicity photos shot here. His parents and Priscilla also posed for
portraits. You can still be photographed with the same camera and on the
same stool where he sat.
510 South Main Street
Memphis, Tennessee 38103
(901) 523-8678

Peabody Hotel
Elvis' high school prom was held here in 1953.
149 Union Avenue

Memphis, Tennessee 38103
(901) 529-4000

Lamar Airways
Elvis performed from a flatbed truck on September 9, 1954, in this parking lot.
2256 Lamar Avenue at Airways Boulevard

Bel Air Motel
The site of one of Elvis' first paid performances.
1850 Elvis Presley Boulevard

Overton Park Municipal Band Shell
This open band shell was the site of one of Elvis' first live performances on July 30, 1954.
Overton Park Shell
1928 Poplar Avenue in Overton Park
Memphis, Tennessee 38112

Mid-South Coliseum and Fairgrounds (Libertyland)
These are the sites of Elvis' hometown concerts and the amusement park that Elvis would often rent. The Fairgrounds, now called Libertyland, still runs the Zippin' Pippin', Elvis' favorite ride.
940-996 Early Maxwell Boulevard
Memphis, Tennessee 38104
(901) 274-3982
(901) 274-1776

Forest Hill Cemetery
Elvis was buried here for 11 days before his body was moved to Graceland.
1661 Elvis Presley Boulevard
Memphis, Tennessee 38106
(901) 775-0310

Memphis Funeral Home
This is where Elvis was prepared for his burial and where his mother's funeral took place.
1177 Union Avenue
Memphis, Tennessee 38114
(901) 725-0100

Dr. Nick's Office
The former site of Doctor George Nichopolous, Elvis' personal physician's office.

The Zippin' Pippin'

John O'Hara

1734 Madison Avenue
Memphis, Tennessee 38104
Prescription House
Right across the street from Dr. Nick's, this is where the pharmacy Elvis most often used was located.
1737 Madison Avenue
Memphis, Tennessee 38104
Baptist Memorial Hospital
Lisa Marie was born here and Elvis was a frequent patient later in his life. The day he died he was brought here by paramedics and declared dead in trauma room two.
899 Madison Avenue
Memphis, Tennessee 38105
(901) 227-2727
St. Joseph Hospital
Gladys worked at this hospital.
264 Jackson Avenue
Memphis, Tennessee 38105
(901) 577-2833
St. Jude Children's Research Hospital
Elvis helped in fund-raising activities at this hospital founded by Danny Thomas.
332 North Lauderdale Street
Memphis, Tennessee 38105
(901) 495-3306
Methodist Hospital
The hospital where Gladys died on August 14, 1958.
1265 Union Avenue
Memphis, Tennessee 38104
(901) 726-7000
Behavioral Health Center
(Former site of Mid-South Hospital)
Elvis had a facelift performed here in 1975.
135 North Pauline Street
Memphis, Tennessee 38103
(901) 448-2400
Elvis Presley Trauma Center
One of the corridor walls displays plaques commemorating the donations from Elvis fans and clubs.
877 Jefferson Avenue
Memphis, Tennessee 38103
(901) 227-2727

Lowell G. Hayes and Sons
   This jeweler used to make TCB jewelry for
   Elvis and now makes it for his fans.
   4872 Poplar Avenue
   Memphis, Tennessee 38117
   (901) 767-2840

Harry Levitch Jewelers
   Another of Elvis' jewelers.
   5100 Poplar Avenue, Suite 111
   Memphis, Tennessee 38137
   (901) 761-1188

John O'Hara

Immaculate Conception
   This is where Priscilla finished high school.
   1725 Central Avenue
   Memphis, Tennessee 38104
   (901) 276-6341

Hotel Chisca
   This is where radio station WMPS was located. It was here that Dewey Phillips
   on July 7, 1954, played "That's All Right" for the first time.
   272 South Main Street
   Memphis, Tennessee 38103

National Bank of Commerce
   This is where Elvis kept at least $1 million in his checking account at all
   times.
   3338 Elvis Presley Boulevard
   Memphis, Tennessee 38116
   (901) 346-6100

Memphis Music Hall of Fame
   They have a large collection of Elvis stuff.
   97 South Second Street
   Memphis, Tennessee 38103
   (901) 525-4007

Mississippi River Museum
   This museum presents the story of the music of the Mississippi Delta from the
   origins of the blues through rock and roll. Artifacts include the original Stax
   Records recording equipment, various radios, a 1950s juke box, numerous LPs
   and 45 rpm records, photos, and a video biography of Sam Phillips. The galleries conclude with the Elvis Room complete with an audio program, photographs, and an authentic Elvis Presley jumpsuit.

Mud Island River Park
125 North Front Street
Memphis, Tennessee 38103
(901) 576-7230
Super Cycle
Refer to "Elvis and the Motor Vehicle" for more information.
624 South Bellevue Boulevard
Memphis, Tennessee 38104
(901) 725-5991
Kang Rhee Institute
Refer to "Elvis and the Martial Arts" for more information.
706 Germantown Parkway
Memphis, Tennessee 38018
(901) 757-5000

Tribute Week

Tribute Week is the festival of Elvis held during the week leading to the anniversary of his death on August 16. The schedule of events changes from year to year. However, some events have become Tribute Week traditions and are almost always a part of the week's activities. For more information and a brochure about Graceland-sponsored annual events call (800) 238-2000.

Photo reprinted with permission

Elvis Tribute Week Roster of Events

Elvis Art Contest and Exhibit
  Elvis-themed artwork created by amateur and professional artists from around the world are displayed in the Graceland ticket office pavilion. To receive an art contest entry form and further information contact:
  Amy Silberberg at Graceland
  (800) 238-2010
  (901) 332-3322

Fans often get to meet Elvis celebrities while visiting Graceland. Here Barbara Digilio meets Elvis' cousin Harold Loyd and his former army sergeant Ira Jones during Tribute Week

Live Entertainment at Elvis Presley's Memphis Restaurant
  All week long there's great entertainment at this new Memphis landmark.
  Elvis Presley's Memphis
  126 Beale Street
  Memphis, Tennessee 38103
  (901) 527-6900
Elvis' Legacy in Light Laser Concert
  Every year, a laser-light concert set to Elvis music, with hundreds of photos of
  Elvis, takes place at the Sharpe Planetarium.
  Memphis Pink Palace Museum
  3050 Central Avenue
  Memphis, Tennessee 38111
  (901) 320-6362
Tupelo Birthplace Tours by Blues City Tours
  Daily trips during Elvis Week to the birthplace home of Elvis also include the
  hardware store where Elvis' mother purchased his first guitar and the
  McDonald's restaurant where Elvis memorabilia is on display.
  Melvin or Linda Bledsoe
  (901) 522-9229
  Fax: (901) 522-8492
  E-mail: Bluestours@aol.com
Sun Studio Block Party
  Every year Sun Studio throws a free concert in the street in front of Sun Studio.
  Sun Studio
  706 Union Avenue
  Memphis, Tennessee 38103
  (901) 521-0664
  (800) 441-6249
Marion Cocke's Annual E. P. Memorial Dinner Charity Event
  This annual event, hosted by Elvis' friend and nurse Marian Cocke, is held at
  the Peabody Hotel in thanksgiving for the life of Elvis Presley. Several chari-
  ties benefit each year.
  Marian Cocke
  784 Pecan Garden Circle East
  Memphis, Tennessee 38122
  (901) 324-9612
Elvis Moonlight Cruise
  An Elvis cruise on the mighty Mississippi.
  Memphis Showboat
  (901) 527-5694
  (800) 221-6197

Record and Memorabilia Convention
   This convention is sponsored by Promised Land Records & Collectibles, a worldwide mail-order dealership with thousands of rare Elvis records and memorabilia, owned by world-renowned Elvis fan and collector Steven Banas.
   Elvis Presley's Heartbreak Hotel
   Lobby Conference Room
   3677 Elvis Presley Boulevard
   Memphis, Tennessee 38116
   (877) 777-0606
   (901) 322-1000
Reflections of Elvis at Libertyland
   There are events every year honoring Elvis at this amusement park that he used to rent for his friends.
   Libertyland Amusement Park
   Mid-South Fairgrounds
   940 Early Maxwell Boulevard
   Memphis, Tennessee 38104
   (901) 274-1776
Betty Harper Art Exhibit
   An exhibit of the work of internationally known Elvis artist Betty Harper is held every year.
   The Ramada Inn
   1471 East Brooks Road
   Memphis, Tennessee 38116
   (901) 332-3500
Elvis Presley International 5K Run and Fun Walk
   This 5K run and fun walk is a lot of fun and all for a good cause: as a benefit for United Cerebral Palsy. The finish line is in front of the Graceland gates and many participants run in Elvis-related costumes.
   Jeannie Townshend
   United Cerebral Palsy of the Mid-South
   4189 Leroy Avenue
   Memphis, Tennessee 38108
   (901) 761-4277
   Fax: (901) 761-7876
   http://www.ucpmemphis.org
George Klein's Memphis Mafia Reunion
   Members of Elvis' entourage, the Memphis Mafia, reminisce and answer questions. It's usually held at Alfred's restaurant.
   Alfred's
   197 Beale Street

Memphis, Tennessee 38103
(901) 525-3711

George Klein's Elvis Memorial Gathering
This annual event is also hosted by George Klein. Speakers traditionally include friends and relatives of Elvis and a celebrity guest. It's usually held at The University of Memphis.

Elvis Week Blood Drive
Anyone donating blood gets a special Elvis T-shirt.
American Red Cross Blood Services
7505 Stage Road, Suite 109
Bartlett, Tennessee 38134

Annual Elvis Gospel Mass
The perfect prelude to the actual candlelight service later in the evening, it's held at St. Paul's Church on 1425 E. Shelby Drive

Contact Mike Keating
Elvis Chicago Style
P.O. Box 388554
Chicago, Illinois 60638
(312) 494-2626
E-mail: ElvisChgoStyle@webtv.net

Candlelight Vigil
There's a brief opening ceremony at 9:00 P.M. every year on August 15. Gates remain open until all who wish to participate have completed the procession up to Elvis' grave site at Graceland

Gospel Brunch at Elvis Presley's Memphis
There's usually a Sunday morning brunch with live gospel music at this EPE-run restaurant that's a great way to end Tribute Week.
Elvis Presley's Memphis
126 Beale Street
Memphis, Tennessee 38103
(901) 527-6900
Jennifer Dorman ext. 104

Tour Guides
Memphis Elvis-Style
This tour is personally run and conducted by the authors of *The Best of Elvis: Recollections of a*

Photo reprinted with permission

Japanese fans in Memphis for Tribute Week

Great Humanitarian and one of the best guidebooks yet written, *Memphis Elvis-Style*, Mike Freeman and Cindy Hazen. They lead downtown walking tours called "Downtown Elvis" and also frequently host customized driving tours. If there is a site or story associated with Elvis in Memphis, there's a 99.9 percent chance that Mike and Cindy know it. And they own and live in Elvis' first-success home before Graceland on Audubon Drive. Talk about great stories!

Memphis Explorations
P.O. Box 41134
Memphis, Tennessee 38174
http://www.elvistyle.com
(901) 274-7187

Unique Tours
88 Union Avenue, Suite 107
Memphis, Tennessee 38103
(901) 527-8876
Blues City Tours
Melvin and Linda Bledsoe
(901) 522-9229
Fax: (901) 522-8492
E-mail: Bluestours@aol.com
Grayline Tours
3677 Elvis Presley Boulevard
Memphis, Tennessee 38116
(901) 384-3474
(800) 948-8680
Memphis Tour and Travel Service
Sharon Parker
E-mail: elvis77presley@webtv.net

Memphis Hotels

Elvis Presley's Heartbreak Hotel
This 128-room theme hotel run by EPE is located at the end of Lonely Street across the street from and within walking distance of Graceland. Black-and-white photos of Elvis by Alfred Wertheimer decorate the walls. Each guest room includes a kitchenette with refrigerator and microwave. They offer four special theme suites each nearly 1,100 square feet with two bedrooms and baths, two sitting parlors, two kitchenettes, and a living room/dining room. There's a heart-shaped swimming pool and free Elvis movies in every room.
3677 Elvis Presley Boulevard

Memphis, Tennessee 38186
(877) 777-0606
(901) 322-1000
http://www.heartbreakhotel.net

Days Inn at Graceland

This is another great place to stay if at all possible, but they book up well in advance. It's across the street from Graceland. They have a guitar-shaped pool and an Elvis-themed breakfast nook. During Tribute Week fans decorate the windows of their rooms here and it's really something to see.

3839 Elvis Presley Boulevard
Memphis, Tennessee 38116
(800) DAYS-INN
901) 346-5500
Fax: (901) 345-7452

Days Inn Brooks Road
1533 East Brooks Road
Memphis, Tennessee 38116
(901) 345-2470
Fax: (901) 345-1371

HoJo Inn Graceland
3265 Elvis Presley Boulevard
Memphis, Tennessee 38116
(901) 398-9999
Fax: (901) 345-6736

Comfort Inn Graceland
1581 Brooks Road
Memphis, Tennessee 38128
(800) 221-2222
(901) 345-3344

Ramada Inn, Southwest Airport
1471 East Brooks Road
Memphis, Tennessee 38116
(901) 332-3500
(800) 272-6232
Fax: (901) 346-0017

Four Points Memphis Airport
2240 Democrat
Memphis, Tennessee 38132

John O'Hara

Guitar-shaped swimming pool at Days
Inn Graceland

(901) 332-1130
Fax: (901) 398-5206
Embassy Suites
  1022 S. Shady Grove Road
  Memphis, Tennesse 38120
  (800) 362-2779
  (901) 684-1777

Follow Tribute Week Activities on the Internet

Memphis newspapers such as the *Commercial Appeal* have web sites that cover the events and news of Tribute Week. Their site is at http://www.gomemphis.com. See "Elvis in Cyberspace" for chatrooms and other ways to find out what's going on if you can't make the trip.

Keep Up with News from Memphis

Subscribe to newspapers and magazines from Elvis' hometown to keep up on what's going on. To an Elvis fan, Memphis is sort of a hometown, too. They usually publish special Tribute Week sections that are not only useful, they're collector's items.

Memphis Magazine
  460 Tennessee Street
  Memphis, Tennessee 38103
  (901) 575-9494
The *Commercial Appeal*
  Home Delivery
  495 Union Avenue
  Memphis Tennessee 38103
  (901) 529-2666

Visit Tupelo

Tupelo Convention and Visitors Bureau
P.O. Drawer 47
Tupelo, Mississippi 38802-0047
(601) 841-6558 Fax
(601) 841-6521
(800) 533-0611
E-mail: tour20@tsixroads.com
http://www.tupelo.com

Annual Elvis Presley Festival
Tupelo has finally seen the light and now organizes an annual Elvis Festival to honor their native son. It usually precedes Tribute Week festivities in Memphis by a few days so you can start off in Tupelo and then take the trip up to Memphis (just like Elvis).
For festival information call (888) 273-7798.

Some Tupelo Hotels
All American Coliseum Motel
767 East Main Street
Tupelo, Mississippi 38802
(601) 844-5610

Days Inn
1015 North Gloster
Tupelo, Mississippi 38802
(800) DAYS-INN
(601) 842-0088

Holiday Inn Express
923 North Gloster
Tupelo, Mississippi 38802
(601) 842-8811
(800) 465-4329

Ramada Inn
854 North Gloster
Tupelo, Mississippi 38802
(601) 844-4111
(800) 228-2828

> "His music has always been there for me. Good times and bad, Elvis has never let me down. When my plans for a trip to Las Vegas were finalized I danced around to 'Viva Las Vegas' for a half hour nonstop."
> —Marcy L. Taranto, in the We Remember Elvis Fan Club newsletter, July 30, 1998

Elvis Presley's Birthplace
306 Elvis Presley Drive (formerly Old Saltillo Road)
Tupelo Mississippi 38801
(601) 841-1245

Elvis Presley Memorial Chapel
Built with donations from fans and friends, the chapel contains the Presley family Bible and the original pulpit from the First Assembly of God Church where Elvis and his family attended services.

Elvis would sometimes drive from Graceland to Tupelo and park outside his former home and contemplate his life. Renting a limo and recreating that drive is a fun way for Elvis fans to share the feeling he must have felt as he revisited his humble beginnings.

John O'Hara

The Elvis Presley Center
A souvenir shop and museum opened in 1992.

Vernon Vale
The name given to the patch of land between the house and the chapel.

Gladys's Glen
The area outside of the chapel named after Elvis' mother.

Elvis' Other Homes in Tupelo
Refer to "At Home with Elvis."

Other Tupelo Points of Interest
Priceville Cemetery
Here Elvis' stillborn twin brother lies buried in an unmarked grave. Elvis was known to visit here throughout his life.
Feemster Lake Road, three miles outside of Tupelo along Elvis Presley Drive

Lawhon School
Elvis attended grades one through five here. The school's auditorium was the site of one of Elvis' first appearances in front of an audience.
140 Lake Street
Tupelo Mississippi 38801
(601) 841-8910

Elvis Presley Lake and Campground
This scenic 850-acre lake and park is about five miles from Elvis' birthplace. It's for campers, boaters, waterskiers, swimmers, fishermen, and Elvis fans. Open from March through September.
(601) 841-1304

John O'Hara

First Assembly of God Church
Elvis was baptized in 1944 at age nine by the guitar-playing pastor Rev. W. Frank Smith in this church and sang maybe for the first time as a toddler here. Vernon was deacon.
206 Adams Street (site during Elvis' time in Tupelo)
909 Berry Street (current location of the original church building)
Tupelo, Mississippi 38801
(601) 844-5841

Tupelo Hardware Company
Owned by George H. Booth at the time of the guitar purchase January 1946. It's now owned by his son. This is where Elvis' mother bought him his first guitar. There is a guitar case painted on the floor at the site of the transaction. Elvis also purchased guitar picks here in 1956 and 1957.
114 West Main Street
P.O. Box 1040
Tupelo, Mississippi 38802
(601) 842-4637

Tupelo Fairgrounds
The site of the Mississippi–Alabama Fair and Dairy Show on October 3, 1945, in which Elvis' principal, J. D. Cole, entered him in singing contest. Elvis sang "Old Shep." Years later he had a triumphant homecoming performance here on what was declared Elvis Presley Day, September 26, 1956. His third and final performance here was a benefit on September 27, 1957.
East Main Street (at Cockerall Street Intersection)
Tupelo, Mississippi 38801

John O'Hara

William T. Booth, Tupelo Hardware Company president, is happy to share with fans the story of how Elvis bought his first guitar in his store

Milam Intermediate School
During E's time it was called Milam Junior High School. He spent his 6th, 7th, and part of the 8th grade here before moving to Memphis in November 1948. His teachers were Mrs. Quay Web Camp and Virginia Plumb.
720 West Jefferson Street
Tupelo, Mississippi 38801
(601) 841-8920

McDonald's Restaurant
A McDonald's loaded with memorabilia of Tupelo's favorite son.
372 South Gloster Street
Tupelo, Mississippi 38801
(601) 844-5505

Other Points of Interest in Mississippi
Circle G Ranch
This 163-acre cattle ranch was purchased by Elvis on February 9, 1967. He built a 10- foot-high fence around the property (the wood has since been sold as souvenirs). Elvis lost his wedding ring here and it has never been found. If it was permitted, someone could run a booming concession renting metal detectors here.
Mississippi Highway 301
(at Goodman Road)
Walls, Mississippi 38680

Mike McGregor's Custom Jewelry & Leatherwork
The late Mike McGregor was a much-loved figure in the Elvis world. He was befriended by Elvis and Elvis fans. This is his store where he made jewelry and leather goods after working at Graceland for many years taking care of Elvis' horses. The store has a gallery that includes Elvis memorabilia.
793 Highway 7 South
Oxford, Mississippi 38655
(662) 234-6970

Graceland Too
Both Tupelo and Memphis are within spitting distance so set aside the time to stop at Graceland Too while you're on your way from one to the

"I am going on 68 come November but I'm hanging in there. I'll be in Memphis August 9 through 16. I will go till I can't. I made a promise to Elvis to visit him every year to say 'Hi, and thank you for the entertainment you give me each day.' When the heart is sad, he perks up the day (always)."
—Terry Davis, fan from Pittsburgh

other. This shrine-like museum to Elvis' memory and glory is a very worthwhile detour if you're interested in total Elvis-immersion. Paul MacLeod, who's been described as Elvis' number-one chronicler, has been collecting Elvis memorabilia, recordings, costumes, and photos since he was 13. To quote him, "If it's not pertaining to Elvis, we don't keep it on this property." And he, along with his son Elvis Aaron Presley MacLeod, welcomes the public to their wall-to-wall, floor-to-ceiling tribute to the King 24 hours a day, 365 days a year. The hour-plus tour costs approximately $5. They play and let you tape recordings (if it's not too busy), barter collectibles, and regale you with stories collected during a lifetime's devotion to Elvis.
200 East Gholson Avenue
Holly Springs, Mississippi 38655
(601) 252-7954

Nashville
The Country Music Hall of Fame Museum
Elvis memorabilia and the infamous Gold Limo are here. RCA Studio B, where Elvis recorded his first work for RCA, is part of the museum.
Four Music Square East
Nashville, Tennessee 37203
(615) 256-1639
(615) 255-5333

Ryman Auditorium
Early in his career Elvis performed here, the former site of the Grand Ole Opry, only once and was not asked back.
116 Fifth Avenue North
Nashville, Tennessee 37219
(615) 254-1445

Las Vegas
Las Vegas Convention and Visitors Bureau
5191 South Las Vegas Boulevard
Las Vegas, Nevada 89109
(702) 739-1482
http://www.lasvegas.com

Frontier Hotel (formerly the New Frontier)
Elvis performed here for the first time in Las Vegas on April 23, 1956. He shared the marquee with the Freddie Martin Band and Shecky Greene, the comedian. He bombed with the older out-of-it crowd. Thirteen years later he returned to Vegas and basically saved its beans.

3120 Las Vegas Boulevard South
Las Vegas, Nevada 89109
(702) 794-8200
(800) 634-6966

John O'Hara

Las Vegas Hilton Hotel (formerly the International Hotel)
On July 29, 1969, Elvis started his run as the most popular act in the history of Las Vegas. Elvis appeared here more often than at any other venue and because of that he is linked forever to Vegas. A statue and plaque in the lobby commemorates his achievements.
3000 Paradise Road
Las Vegas, Nevada 89109
(702) 732-5111
(800) 732-7111

Imperial Palace
This is the site of the "Legends in Concert" show that always features some of the most talented Elvis impersonators. Also, the auto museum here has several Elvis vehicles.
3535 Las Vegas Boulevard
Las Vegas, Nevada 89109
(702) 731-3311
(800) 634-6441

Elvis-o-Rama
This Elvis museum has a large inventory of Elvis' personal belongings on display including some of his clothes, the famous peacock stage suit worn in '74, some of his cars, and other cool stuff.
3401 Industrial Boulevard
Las Vegas, Nevada 89109
(702)-309-7200

Country Rock & Roll Store
This place has a lot of Elvis things: photographs, T-shirts, and various Elvis knickknacks.
Stratosphere Tower
2000 South Las Vegas Boulevard
Las Vegas, Nevada 89014
(702) 366-0362 or (702) 380-7777
http://www.countryrocknroll.com

Hawaii
The Movie Locations
Refer to "Motion Picture Elvis."

Performance Venues in Hawaii
Neal S. Blaisdell Center (formerly Honolulu International Center)
The "Aloha from Hawaii" concert was broadcast to the world from here.
777 Ward Avenue
Honolulu, Hawaii 96814
(808) 527-5400

Old Stadium Park (formerly Honolulu Stadium)
The site of an Elvis performance in 1957.
2237 South King Street
Honolulu, Hawaii 96826

Schofield Barracks
Elvis entertained U.S. troops here on November 11, 1957.
U.S. Army 25th Infantry Division
Schofield Barracks
Schofield Hawaii 96857
(808) 471-7110

Bloch Arena
Elvis gave a charity performance here March 25, 1961, that raised $62,000 to create a permanent memorial to the USS *Arizona,* which had been sunk during WWII.
Building 161 Naval Base
Pearl Harbor, Hawaii 96860
(808) 474-6156

The USS *Arizona* Memorial
This is the memorial that Elvis helped fund.
One Arizona Memorial Place
Honolulu, Hawaii 96818
(808) 422-0561
(808) 422-2771

Los Angeles
Refer to "Motion Picture Elvis."

Cleveland
Rock and Roll Hall of Fame and Museum
One Key Plaza
Cleveland, Ohio 44144
(888) 764-ROCK
http://www.rockhall.com

Stay at an Elvis-Related Hotel
Here are some hotels where Elvis stayed or that have Elvis rooms.
Brickyard Crossing Golf Resort and Inn (formerly the Stouffers Indianapolis Inn)
Elvis stayed here when he was in Indianapolis to give his final performance at
the nearby Market Arena. It was probably the last rented hotel room of Elvis life.
4400 West 16 Street
Indianapolis, Indiana 46222
(317) 241-2500

Ramada Governor's House (formerly the Sheraton South Motor Inn)
Elvis stayed here and sulked over troubles with his girlfriend Ginger instead of
going to a recording session.
737 Harding Place
Nashville, Tennessee 37211
(615) 834-5000

The Spence Manor Suites
Elvis stayed here when he recorded at RCA's Studio B on Music Row. They have
a guitar-shaped swimming pool.
11 Music Square East
Nashville, Tennessee 37203
(615) 259-4400
Fax: (615) 259-2148
http://www.songnet.com/SpenceManor/elvis.htm

Jefferson Hotel
Elvis stayed here in 1956.
101 West Franklin at Adams
Richmond, Virginia 23220
(804) 788-8000

Quality Inn (formerly the Holiday Inn)
Elvis stayed here while he taped his 1977 "Elvis in Concert" TV special.
1902 La Crosse Street

Rapid City, South Dakota 57701
(605) 348-1230

Quality Inn (formerly the Sheraton)
Elvis stayed here in suite 214–216.
2727 Ferndale Drive NW
Roanoke, Virginia 24014
(703) 562-1912

Tradewinds Courtyard Inn and Restaurant
Room 215 is now the Elvis Presley Suite.
2128 West Gary Boulevard
Clinton, Oklahoma 73601
(580) 323-2610

The Washington Hotel
This is where Elvis stayed, in Room 506, when he visited Nixon.
515 15 Street, N.W.
Washington, DC 20004
(202) 638-5900

The Fountainbleau Hilton
This is where Elvis stayed while making the "Welcome Home Elvis" TV special
that was broadcast from here.
4441 Collins Avenue
Miami Beach, Florida 33140
(305) 538-2000

Warwick Hotel
This is where Elvis stayed when he came to New York for his television appearances in the fifties and his Madison Square Garden appearances in the seventies.
His room, 527, has been converted into other rooms.
65 West 54 Street
New York, New York 10019
(212) 247-2700

The Columbia Inn
It Happened at the World's Fair was filmed near here and Elvis stayed at this inn
while he was in Washington. They've made it sort of a shrine to him and they sell
souvenirs. His likeness can be seen painted on the building from the freeway.
602 Frontage Road

Kalama, Washington 98625
(360) 673-2855

Fairmount Hotel (formerly the Roosevelt)
Elvis stayed on the tenth floor while filming *King Creole*.
123 Baronne
New Orleans, Louisiana 700112
(504) 529-7111

The Atrium Inn (formerly Howard Johnson's)
Elvis stayed here while on his last tour.
2550 North Glenstone
Springfield, Missouri 65803
(417) 866-5253

The Superstition Inn
Elvis stayed here on the second floor while filming *Charro!* in July and August
of 1968.
1342 South Power Road
Mesa, Arizona 85206
(800) 780-7234
(602) 641-1164

Ink House
Elvis slept here while filming *Wild in the Country* in Napa Valley. Ask for the
French Room.
1575 St. Helena Highway
St. Helena, California 94574
(707) 963-3890

Daytona Beach Travelers Inn
They have an Elvis Presley theme room.
735 North Atlantic Avenue
Daytona Beach, Florida 32118
(800) 417-6466

Port Paradise Resort
Elvis stayed here while filming *Follow that Dream*.
1610 Southeast Paradise Circle
Crystal River, Florida 34429
(352) 795-3111

Fall Creek Falls Bed & Breakfast
Die-hard Elvis fan owner Rita Pruett has created a sort of Elvis Presley Boulevard corridor that leads to the guest rooms. They also provide Elvis videos to watch during your stay.
Deweese Road
Pikeville, Tennessee 37367
(423) 881-5494

The Illikai Hotel Nikko Waikiki (formerly The Illikai Hotel)
In August of 1965 Elvis stayed here while filming *Paradise Hawaiian Style* in rooms 2426 and 2425. The entire 24th floor was booked by his entourage. The hotel is pictured behind the opening credits of the TV series *Hawaii Five-0*.
1777 Ala Moana Boulevard
Honolulu, Hawaii 96815
(808) 949-3811

Hilton Hawaiian Village
In 1957 Elvis stayed here in room 14a. He also stayed during 1962 while filming *Girls, Girls, Girls.* In 1972 he stayed in the hotel's Rainbow Towers penthouse.
2005 Kalia Road
Honolulu, Hawaii 96815
(808) 949-4321

Coco Palms Resort
Elvis stayed in cottage 56 while filming and vacationing.
4241 Kuhio Highway
Kapaa, Hawaii 96746
(808) 822-4921

In Germany, France, Scotland
Refer to "Elvis and the Army."

Take an Elvis Theme Cruise
Callaway Cruises
This company organizes an Elvis-themed cruise down the Mississippi from Memphis to New Orleans on the *American Queen.*
(800) 667-4523

Elvis and Priscilla vacationing in Hawaii

Sandi Miller

(800) 535-5772
http://www.callawaycruises.com

Norwegian Cruise Line
Norwegian runs an Elvis-themed cruise aboard the *Norway*. Past guests have included Joe Guerico, original TCB band members, Jackie Kahane, and the Flying Elvi. A portion of each cruise fare is contributed to the Elvis Presley Memorial Foundation. For information call (800) 327-7030.

Pleasure Travel Unlimited
This company organizes Elvis-themed cruises.
55 East Monroe Street
Chicago, Illinois 60603
(800) 225-7185
Fax: (312) 726-8662

Travel Tips for Elvis Fans

Elvis really is everywhere. No matter where you're traveling to and for whatever reason, try to find the nearest Elvis-related spot. There are places all over the world that have significance to Elvis and his fans. Do some research before you make your trip. Consult the fan club list to find a local fan club near your destination. Try to stay in a hotel that Elvis stayed in.

CELEBRATING
THE IMPORTANT DATES

The most amazing thing that's happening with Elvis these days is that people are not forgetting him. It may even be said that his popularity is gaining new dimensions, moving into younger generations, proliferating in cyberspace, and affecting cultures near and far. A small part of the explanation may be the attention given to the emotion and sincerity with which Elvis fans commemorate the two most important anniversaries in the Elvis world, his birth and death. At these times Elvis fans gather at Graceland like a meeting of the tribes and Elvis birthday parties and candlelight vigils take place around the globe. Disc jockeys, media planners, and television programmers take this opportunity to feature Elvis tributes, schedule his movies, and fill the airwaves with Elvis tunes.

While these two dates—January 8, 1935, and August 16, 1977—give the Elvis fan community and a good part of the rest of the world the chance to enjoy and recognize Elvis together, hard-core fans also like to celebrate and remember the thousands of days that fell in between. They sometimes choose a day that has some personal significance, such as the day they saw him concert, and commemorate it in their own special way.

Anniversaries and holidays had special significance for Elvis as well. Each

Gold and diamond pendant, a birthday
gift to Elvis from Priscilla

Courtesy of Butterfield & Butterfield

237

Elvis and Priscilla in front of the Graceland Christmas decorations

Sandi Miller

year on August 14, the anniversary of his mother's death, he arranged to have her grave covered with flowers. Even though he was known more as a spontaneous gift giver, he made a lot of friends' birthdays occasions they would never forget. He embraced the Christmas season and always made a point of being home for the holidays. Elvis became the essence of holiday spirit not only to those close to him, but to the dozens of charities to which he made donations. It meant a great deal to Elvis that the house and front lawn of Graceland were decorated and made festive for the pleasure of fans and family and those traditions he started continue to this day. From the day after Thanksgiving until January 8, the grounds of Graceland are decorated with the original life-sized nativity scene and "Merry Christmas to all, Elvis" sign and hundreds of blue lights lining the driveway.

In addition to his birthday and the day he died, several states currently have official Elvis Presley days, a few cities stage

John O'Hara

Todd Anderson of Graceland's staff speaking at Elvis' birthday celebration in January of 1999

Graceland Christmas
decorations at night

John O'Hara

annual Elvis parades, and fans continue to lobby to have a national day of recognition declared.

For Elvis fans, the number 2001 has a special significance. If you add the numerals of the day, 16, month, 8, and year, 1977, that Elvis died, it totals 2001. And if you add the day that he was born, 8, to the year that he was born, 1935, plus the day he died, 16, and the age that he was when he died, 42, it also totals 2001. And, of course, it was the glorious earth-shaking theme from *2001* that used to herald Elvis' appearance onstage during his touring years.

The focus on Elvis in January and August has become a self-perpetuating phenomenon, creating new fans who in turn will usher in future celebrations commemorating these dates. Twice a year the world gets reacquainted with Elvis. The media covers the anniversaries, some seeking to smirk at the ardor of the fans, some bemused, some confused, but all covering what is a cultural event of undeniable noteworthiness. And somewhere, some young kid watching television or listening to the radio who hasn't discovered Elvis yet sees all the attention and says, "Hey, this guy is cool," and a new fan is born—a fan who will have a new day to celebrate in the future: the day he or she first heard Elvis Presley.

ESSENTIAL ELVISOLOGY

The Most Important Dates on the Elvis Calendar

Elvis' Birthday: January 8
Mother's Day

Tribute Week: August 8–16
Christmas: December 25

Official Elvis Presley Day Declarations

Some states already have Elvis Presley days; this list shows when they were declared. If your state doesn't, look below to see what you can do about it.

September 26, 1956—Tupelo, Mississippi
February 25, 1961—Tennessee
September 29, 1967—Tennessee
November 11, 1970—Oregon
January 13, 1973—Honolulu, Hawaii

January 8, 1974—Georgia
October 19, 1976—Wisconsin
January 8, 1981—South Carolina
January 8, 1981—Alabama
January 8, 1981—Florida

January 8, 1981—Illinois
January 8, 1981—Georgia
January 8, 1981—Kansas
January 8, 1981—North Carolina

January 8, 1981—Pennsylvania
January 8, 1981—Virginia
January 8, 1982—Tennessee
January 8, 1992—Tennessee

YOUR ELVIS EDUCATION

Books
Elvis Day by Day: The Definitive Record of His Life and Music
    Peter Guralnick and Ernst Jorgensen
All Shook Up: Elvis Day-by-Day 1954–1977
    Lee Cotton
Complete Idiot's Guide to Elvis
    Frank Coffey
The Elvis Atlas: A Journey through Elvis Presley's America
    Michael Gray and Roger Osborne
The Ultimate Elvis: Elvis Presley Day by Day
    Patricia Jobe Pierce
Elvis: His Life In Pictures
    text by Todd Morgan with Laura Kath
Christmas with Elvis
    Jim Curtin and Renata Ginter

Web Sites
http://www.elvis-presley.com
    Graceland's web site for events and
    activities
http://perso.wanadoo.fr/ch.jouanne/
    index.htm
    Christophe Jouanne's site; excellent
    links; to request a free Elvis calen-
    dar e-mail:
    christophe.jouanne@wanadoo.fr
http://www.geocities.com/SunsetStrip/
    8200/events.html
    Elvis events calendar
http://www.biwa.ne.jp/~presley/
    christmas/index.html

Haruo Hirose's Merry Christmas
page on Elvis World Japan
http:www.vegaslounge.com/elvis/
    postcards.html
    Send Elvis-photo postcard to fellow
    Elvis friends over the internet for
    free; choice of nine designs
http://www.americangreetings.com
    Use those important dates to send
    Elvis postcard with sound over the
    internet
http://www.gomemphis.com/elvis/
    elvis.html
    The *Commercial Appeal* Elvis archive

THE ELVIS AND YOU EXPERIENCE

Celebrate Elvis' Birthday, January 8

This is certainly the most celebrated nonofficial birthday in the world. Several days of activities to commemorate Elvis' birthday occur each year at Graceland in Memphis. While there aren't as many people as there are during August for Tribute Week, the atmosphere and mood—and being able to wish happy birthday to Elvis—make this a worthwhile time to go. Don't forget about little brother Jesse; it's his birthday too.

Throw a Birthday Party for Elvis

Pick a decade—make it a theme. Send out fun Elvis invitations. Decorate the house with Elvis posters and make Elvis party favors. Hire a band. Or even better, get out that karaoke machine. Or get Elvis' latest CDs and share the music with your friends. If you are so inclined, hire an Elvis impersonator. Make a guitar-shaped birthday cake and have everyone make an Elvis wish when the candles are blown out. This is definitely a time to celebrate!

The Birthday Party Menu

Cheeseburgers
Coconut cake
Pork chops with sauerkraut
Chocolate malted shakes
Mashed potatoes with gravy
Pepsi
Fried peanut butter and mashed
banana sandwiches

Elvis Party Games

Elvis bingo (Make your own bingo cards using Elvis songs or movies instead of numbers in each box of the grid.)
Elvis trivia contests (Have a prize for the winner.)

> "After the tour of the house, we went through the Meditation Garden in the night, with the stained glass windows and the statues all lit up. Elvis' grave had frost on it and this just tore me up. I can't even express how cold and sad this scene was to me. I had to remind myself that this was Elvis' birthday celebration and he deserved our happiest thoughts."
> —Fan, January 1998

> "Christmas is about the only time they get really loud up at the mansion, and that's because they always have those fireworks. Elvis spends $1,200 to $1,500 on fireworks at Christmas."
> —Vester Presley, Elvis' uncle, in *A Presley Speaks*

Elvisopoly (Play this board game, which is available through Graceland shops, after everyone is tuckered out from dancing.)
Pin the microphone on the Elvis Albert Goldman piñata

Send Flowers from Elvis
Send a bouquet anonymously to a fan on her birthday. Let her think, for a moment, that it's from Elvis.

Mother's Day

Send Flowers to Graceland

Send your flowers or floral arrangements to the attention of Sheila James at Graceland Corporate Office:
3734 Elvis Presley Boulevard
Memphis, Tennessee 38116

Do Something Nice for Your Own Mother

Elvis would've liked that.

Add Something Gladys-Related to Your Shrine

Place a photo of Gladys and Elvis together, a rose, or something else that Gladys might've appreciated in your shrine.

Tribute Week, August 8–16

Send a Floral Arrangement to Graceland

A touching fan tradition is to send wreaths to Graceland. They are placed all around the Meditation Garden and on the road leading up to it. Club members design arrangements to represent their club each year and there are also some phenomenal floral designers in Memphis who can create an amazing tribute to Elvis for you.

Flowers by Sandy
2015 Union Avenue
Memphis, Tennessee 38104
(901) 276-4495

Piano's
4532 Elvis Presley Boulevard
Memphis, Tennessee 38116
(901) 345-7670

Attend Tribute Week in Memphis

See "The Pilgrimage" for more details about this event.

Go to a Concert in Your Area

No matter where you live, some bar or musical venue will be having an Elvis tribute or event and playing his music. Look for listings in your local papers.

Have Your Own Candlelight Vigil

If you can't get to Memphis, conduct a small memorial for Elvis at home. Invite some other Elvis fans, light some candles, put on the music, and remember the man.

Christmas, December 25

Christmas was real big with Elvis. He loved the season and always went overboard with decorations and gifts. Here are some ideas on how to have yourself a merry Elvis Christmas.

Spend Christmas at Graceland

Decorations, including the life-sized nativity scene, go up the day after Thanksgiving and stay up through January 8. For the most part, they are the original decorations that adorned the lawns of Graceland while Elvis was alive.

Contribute to the Graceland Poinsettia Campaign

Your contribution will go to the Memphis Chapter of the National Hemophilia Campaign and for decorating Elvis' home for the holidays with poinsettias. Make check payable to the National Hemophilia Foundation and send it to:
Graceland-Poinsettia Campaign
Attn: Beth Farrelly
P.O. Box 16508
Memphis, Tennessee 38186-0508

Hire an Elvis Santa

Instead of Santa, why not hire an Elvis impersonator to appear at a Christmas party? The impersonator could sing songs from Elvis' Christmas repertoire and then have photos taken with the kids. We're guessing some moms will want photos with him too.

Make Your Own Personalized Elvis Christmas Cards

Every Christmas holiday Elvis and the Colonel sent thousands of cards, often depicting Parker dressed as Santa. With a personal computer and a photo scanner, or even just scissors and glue, it's easy to create customized greeting cards.

You can try to recreate some of the Colonel and Elvis Christmas cards. Replace the Colonel with yourself. There's specific computer software that enables you to create cards easily.

Elvis Christmas Tree

Elvis liked a white tree with red ornaments. There are commemorative decorations for sale every year with Elvis' picture or photo on them. The best, though, are homemade ornaments. For quick ones, you could use color photocopies of Elvis photos or your own Elvis drawings glued onto spray-painted, cut-out cardboard or ready-made ornaments. Put Elvis photos in tiny frames with little looped ribbons to hang them from.

Elvis Christmas Gifts

Remember the Elvis fans on your Christmas list and think of giving them a collectible they've been hankering for—a framed photo of Elvis, an Elvis book, or, for the extravagant, an all-expense-paid trip to Graceland.

Here's how Ken Terry of the Elvis Club of Albuquerque decorated for the club's latest Halloween party:

On the porch there was a crime-scene chalk outline of a dead body with spilled fake blood. On the outside wall was a skeleton with a saying, "Are You Gruesome Tonight?" Also standing guard on the front porch was an inflatable skeleton with a black wig, sideburns, and a guitar. At the front door a skeleton greeted you with, "If You're Looking for Trouble, You Came to the Right Place." Once inside, all over the walls, there are frightful creatures with sayings: Frankenstein saying "I'll Dismember You"; a ghost saying "I Will Spend My Whole Death through, Haunting You, Haunting You"; another ghost saying, "Come Back Baby, I Wanna Haunt a House With You"; Dracula saying "Well, I Heard the News, There's Bloodsucking Tonight," "I Don't Care If the Sun Don't Shine," and "Got a Lot of Killing to Do"; a mummy saying, "That's All Right, Mummy" and "There's a Freak in This Old Building"; a skeleton saying, "Nothing's Quite as Pretty As Mary in the Morgue" and "Lay Your Skull Upon My Pillow," "Do Be Cruel," and "I Gotta Mess of BOOS"; and a bat suspended from the ceiling saying "You Saw Me Flying in the Chapel."

Ken very cleverly ties in the Elvis song titles with the Halloween theme. A plastic heart in a dish stating "One Broken Heart for Sale" round out the decorations.

—Submitted by Margaret Freisinger,
the Elvis Club of Albuquerque secretary

Elvis Wrapping Paper

You can make your own really easily if you have Elvis ink stamps and a couple of different color ink pads. Or glue photos or photocopies of Elvis on plain white wrapping paper and decorate it with magic markers, glitter pens, or rhinestones. Graceland's catalogs and shops carry beautiful Elvis-photo wrapping paper also.

Plan Christmas Activities as a Club

At one of your fan club's meetings around Christmastime, why not undertake some Elvis-crafts projects together to give to children in a local foundling home, hospital, or your favorite charity. Handmade stockings decorated with Elvis fabric would be nice.

> "One year on Halloween at his Beverly Hills house, Elvis was out at the gates which were wide open. He had on a gorilla mask and he was handing out candy himself. No one had any clue it was him until I drove up with my daughter who had seen him enough to recognize him with or without a mask. Thankfully no one really noticed when she yelled out! By the way, he was giving out Butterfinger candy bars."
> —Sandi Miller

Give Elvis Christmas Music or Gospel CDs to Your Nonfan Friends

Fellow fans will probably have these recordings, but for someone new to Elvis we really can't think of a better gift.

Where to Find Collectible Elvis Christmas Ornaments

Long Island Treasures
Jim Voesack
1024 North Hamilton Avenue
Lindenhurst, New York 11757
(516) 226-8078
E-mail: voesack@interport.net
http://www.users.interport.net/~voesack

Choose a Letter from the Post Office Listings

During the holidays, the post office makes available letters written to Santa by children. Brighten up the holidays for others and get a child what he asks for in the letter *and* introduce him to Elvis with a small inexpensive Walkman and an Elvis cassette.

Consult the Elvis Calendar to Find Your Lucky Days

Elvis was a big believer in numerology. He sometimes consulted his many numerology books before planning his schedule. Consult the Elvis dates before you plan your schedule. Choose a date from his life and plan an activity accordingly. It's possible to make some connection between the events of his life and the events of yours. It might bring you luck. Then again it might not. But it's a fun way to test your knowledge of his life and keep in practice for trivia contests.

Choose Your Own Elvis Day to Celebrate

There are several exhaustive sources chronicling Elvis' life, virtually every moment of the way. You can mine these sources for dates of events that strike a note for you—maybe the anniversary of a movie opening, the performance when you first saw Elvis, or the date he recorded your favorite song.

February 6, 1966—Elvis' pet chimp Scatter died. Visit a local zoo and play some Elvis music near the monkey cage.

February 13, 1948—Elvis got his first library card. Spend the day reading a book from Elvis' library. (Refer to the "Spirituality and Gospel" chapter for a list of Elvis' favorite books.)

March 6, 1954—Elvis filed his first federal income taxes. Good day to file your taxes.

March 7, 1957—Elvis bought Graceland. Auspicious day to go house or apartment hunting.

March 25, 1958—Elvis got his GI haircut. Bad day to change your hairstyle.

April 10, 1957—Presley family moved into Graceland. Good day to move.

May 1, 1967—Elvis got married. Wouldn't it be nice to get married on this day and share Elvis and Priscilla's anniversary?

July 5, 1954—Elvis recorded his first hit record. Lucky day to start a new career.

August 15, 1955—Tom Parker undertook Elvis' management. Avoid any new business dealings. Don't sign any contracts.

August 27, 1965—Beatles visited Elvis. Invite some friends from abroad over for a jam session.

October 9, 1973—Elvis got divorced. Good time to get out of a relationship that has gone belly up.

December 4, 1956—Million Dollar Quartet recorded at Sun. Perfect time for collaboration.

August 21, 1957—Elvis buys the lion statues for Graceland. Good day to buy ornamental lawn sculpture.

Celebrate a Special Event at One of Elvis' Homes

Celebrate a date from Elvis' life or your own in one of Elvis' homes. Some of them are available to rent. There's a sense of magic at these places and it'll definitely rub off on your party.

The Audubon House
Cindy Hazen and Mike Freeman, authors of *Memphis Elvis-Style*, are planning to open their Audubon home, where Elvis lived for the year before buying Graceland, to private parties. Call to confirm availibility.
Memphis Explorations
P.O. Box 41134
Memphis, Tennessee 38174
(901) 274-7187
http://www.elvistyle.com

The Honeymoon Hideaway, Palm Springs
The Hideaway was Elvis' futuristic desert home where he and Priscilla spent the first part of their honeymoon. It is available to rent.
The Honeymoon Hideaway
1350 Ladera Circle
Palm Springs, California 92262
(619) 322-1192

Royal Oak King's Hideaway, Palm Springs
Elvis' former 5,000-square-foot home is available to rent by private guests, fan clubs, or corporate groups. For information, call them at (760) 327-3359.

Graceland
Have a party across from the Graceland mansion! Graceland allows parties, even weddings, in most of the shops and museums across the street from the Graceland mansion. They offer full catering and event-planning services. Packages may include private evening tours of the mansion and other Graceland sites.
Graceland Special Events Department
(800) 238-2010
(901) 344-3146

Get an Elvis Picture Calendar or Make Your Own
A calendar can serve as a daily reminder of the important dates. You can make it part of your shrine if you have one. Most bookstores have calendars for sale at the end of each year or you could order one from Graceland. Also, many photo shops and catalogs offer custom-made calendars with your own photos. And you can always make your own by gluing photos of Elvis over one of those "kitten calendars."

An Elvis fan from France, Christophe Jouanne, offers to fellow fans, free of charge, a calendar he designed. You only have to write to him or contact him

online. Ask for an international reply coupon at the post office, then send it to him so he can mail the calendar back to you.
Christophe Jouanne
1, Rue des Prévôts
21600 Longvic, France
E-mail: christophe.jouanne@wanadoo.fr
http://www.perso.wanadoo.fr/ch.jouanne/index.htm

Lobby for a National Elvis Presley Holiday

It's been brought up and defeated twice in Congress, but we all know if this were put to a popular vote it would be a done deal. So fans should keep the heat turned up on their elected representatives until a National Elvis Presley Day becomes a reality. Contact your local congressperson or senator and let them know how you feel about Elvis.
Addressing correspondence:
To a Senator:
The Honorable (full name)
United States Senate
Washington, DC 20510
Senate Directory
http://www.policy.net.capweb.senate

To a Representative:
The Honorable (full name)
United States House of Representatives
Washington, DC 20515
Congress Capital Directory
http://www.congress.org/main.html

Celebrate Your Local Elvis Presley Day

Many places all over the world celebrate a local Elvis Presley Day. If your town has one, then whoop it up on that day. If you don't have an official one where you live, contact your mayor's office and find out why the hell not. Campaign to establish an Elvis Presley Day with local authorities.

Organize an Elvis Parade

There are parades for every special interest under the sun, and we think Elvis is real special and real interesting. Imagine Elvis floats, marching bands playing Elvis music, impersonator drill teams, rockabilly musicians performing on flatbed trucks, a vintage car procession, bagpipes playing Elvis music. Fans should try to persuade EPE to throw an Elvis parade in Memphis.

Make It an Elvis Valentine's Day

Of all the days of the year that beg to be celebrated thinking of Elvis, none can beat Valentine's Day. You can decorate your house with valentine-red roses. Bake a heart-shaped cake and write I LOVE ELVIS on it. Get out those Elvis mugs, light some rose-scented candles, put on those Elvis love songs, put the *Lost Loves* video or your favorite E movie on the VCR, and invite some good friends—or that one special someone—to share it all with you.

Take Off from Work for an Elvis Holiday

Take a break from your daily routine and have an Elvis-immersion day. Unplug your phone, blast his music, indulge in some 'nana pudding. His birthday would be perfect, but any day would be lovely.

Eat Russell Stover Chocolates

For Valentine's Day, Mother's Day, and Christmas, Russell Stover comes out with several different Elvis commemorative tins and heart-shaped boxes filled with chocolates. The chocolates are good and the tins collectible—great combination.

The Christmas Miracle

'Twas the night before Christmas
And all through my place
Elvis music is playing
On each wall is his face.
My stocking was hung
On the TV with care
In hopes that an Elvis item
Soon would be there!

And I in my nightgown
With the cat in my lap
Had just settled down
For an evening nap.

When all of a sudden
I heard such a clatter
I jumped to my feet
To see what was the matter!

And what to my wondering
Eyes should appear
But Elvis in person
With those he held dear!

There was Gladys and Vernon
And little Lisa Marie
The "Dodger" and Priscilla
Sat at his knee!

There was the Colonel and Joe
And his drummer D. J.
And the big wheels were there
From RCA.

The Memphis Mafia
Came of course
The band and the singers
Were there in full force.

Then Elvis stood up
And began to sing

The songs about Christmas
And what Santa would bring!

His eyes were so clear
And as blue as can be
And he walked over and came
Directly to me!
He reached for my hand
And said, "My dear Sue
I've come to deliver
This message to you!"

"Tell all of my fans
To be of good cheer
I'm with you in spirit
Tho my body's not here!

"Tell all that I love them
To carry on in my name
What the fans do for me
Is all that remains!"

As he kissed my hand gently
He shed a single, wet tear
Then said, "Good-bye"
And "Merry Christmas, my dear!"
Then all of a sudden
I awoke with a start
And though I'd been dreaming
His tear touched my heart.

As I sat up in dismay
What do you suppose?
On the table beside me
Lay a single, red rose.

A card lay beside it
And I opened to see
A message that said
"Merry Christmas," signed "E"!
　　　　　—by Sue Manuszak, president
　　　　　　of the E.P. Continentals

ELVIS FAN CLUBS

There's no arguing that the greatest pleasure of being an Elvis fan centers on each individual's personal relationship with Elvis—reveling in the music and thrilling to his multitude of charms. But for many fans there's the added benefit and pleasure of their relationship with each other. For those interested, there's a huge selection of fan clubs that anyone can join (Graceland's latest official worldwide tally: 600-plus and counting). Participating in a fan club is the most fun way to meet and party with other like-minded people and to network news and information from the Elvis world. People share stories, experiences, and photos through newsletters and at club meetings. Among Elvis fans, there's no need to be defensive about loving Elvis as is sometimes the case with the rest of the population. Above all, though, many fan clubs have as their primary mission to do good works in Elvis' memory and name. They tirelessly raise money for the same charities that Elvis made donations to during his lifetime and other worthy causes in their regions. Graceland acknowledges that millions of dollars have been raised and donated in Elvis' name. Fans have committed themselves to carrying on the charity tradition *for* Elvis.

Club members are at times very inventive when it comes

Photo reprinted with permission

The Elvis Country Fan Club

251

The Elvis Forever Fan Club of Greece

to charitable works. Members from the Memories of Elvis Fan Club of New Zealand bring their Elvis collections to a local nursing home, share their memorabilia with the people there, and conduct sing-alongs of Elvis songs. Our favorite story is what one of the branches of the Official Elvis Presley Fan Club of England did when Albert Goldman's vicious biography of Elvis came out. They sold off individual pages of the book to raise money for charity—for a small fee you got to rip out a page and destroy it in any way you saw fit.

In order to form your own official Elvis Presley fan club you should get in touch with Graceland's fan relations manager, Patsy Andersen, and ask for the fan club start-up package. You'll receive a thick mailing with a letter from Patsy; 16 pages of ideas for newsletters, membership campaigns, charity ventures, and event planning; about 80 pages that include an Elvis biography, career chronology, statistics, Elvis Presley Estate history, coloring book pages, suggested reading, information about Graceland and a "guided tour"; and tons more information explaining basically everything you need to do to start and run a club.

In the package, you'll also receive an admonishment from Graceland saying that by forming a club you have the honor of helping to maintain Elvis' memory, and to conduct yourself with honor, dignity, integrity, and honesty—that, essentially, you'll be carrying on the name of Elvis Presley. This seems like it may be

Darwin Lamm, editor of *Elvis International Forum,* speaking at the 1999 Circle of Memories, the annual event sponsored by the Elvis Friends Hollywood fan club

Gang Elvis Fan Club from Brazil

unnecessary, at least among fan club members, because the sincerity with which they strive to protect and preserve Elvis' image doesn't appear to need much encouragement.

Certain Elvis fan clubs are famous for a variety of reasons such as organizing or conducting some of the big Elvis events and conventions. The Elvis Country Fan Club leads the Candlelight Vigil to Elvis' grave every year during Tribute Week and the Chicago Elvis-Style Fan Club organizes the Elvis Gospel Mass held every August 15 in Memphis. The Presley-ites Fan Club in Florida has organized the campaign for an official National Elvis Presley Day. Every May, Elvis Friends Hollywood puts on the Circle of Memories Honeymoon Weekend at the house in Palm Springs where Elvis and Priscilla spent their honeymoon. The We Remember Elvis, the Taking Care of Presley along with the Elvis Fans from Hoosierland, and the E. P. Continentals clubs hold large yearly fan festivals, as do many other clubs too numerous to mention. If you go to any Elvis-related get-together, the first thing you'll feel is that the mood, the whole vibe, is wonderful. Everywhere are fun-loving people; there's a sense of warmth, affection, and camaraderie; and of course, plenty of rock and roll.

Elvis fans think of themselves, in a way, as "friends" of Elvis. And fan clubs are the focal points where these friends can associate and have fun; get together through activities such as holiday parties, dances, fundraisers, and trips to Graceland; and share

International Elvis Presley Fan Club, Hong Kong

stories and experiences, and stay in touch throughout the year with newsletters. There is a fan club for every type of fan in every spot on the globe. We strongly recommend joining at least two if you can swing it—one locally and one in a place where you vacation every year. Or the second one could be in the place where your family was originally from. How about a foreign club where they speak a language you already know or one you would like to learn? Joining a club connects you to a grassroots network of people united in their feelings for Elvis, love for great music, and the desire to do good things and keep the momentum of Elvis' popularity growing.

ESSENTIAL ELVISOLOGY

Some Fan Club Testimonials and Mission Statements

Club founders usually come up with some sort of philosophy or mission statement that defines the club's personality and tone. For the most part, they all boil down to Taking Care of Elvis (TCE).

Society of Admiration for Elvis

Society of Admiration for Elvis was established to give the local (and distant) Elvis fans of all ages a realm in which to honor Elvis and share in their admiration for the King of Rock and Roll. We will work together in keeping his name and reputation "SAFE" whenever necessary and free of degradation. Keeping his image and honor alive is the most important aspect of our club. Coming together in love, sharing past and present Elvis experiences, and enjoying the music and movies from his career we have all grown to love and cherish.

Universally Elvis Fan Club

Goals:
1. Bring Elvis back to #1 in the public eye.
   We will do this by taking an aggressive approach to all forms of media. By starting an online and domestic family larger than ever before. By bringing tapes/CDs to area radio stations, and asking them to give E some much-needed airtime, not just "Hound Dog"! Get E's status with *Billboard* fixed, so he can chart again in the U.S. Prepare articles for local newspapers with Elvis-related news.
2. Promote Elvis as a humanitarian.
   Promote Elvis' philanthropic ways through all media. Dispel rumors related to racist remarks. Publicize Elvis' work with various ethnic groups and his work with charities.

3. Be aggressive toward all negative media.
   We will contact all negative media with correct information.

"Talk About the Good Times" Elvis Fan Club

"Talk About the Good Times" Elvis Fan Club will support those who speak positively about Elvis and defend him against all criticism, while maintaining a worldwide membership of all ages. Elvis gave 100 percent of himself to entertaining his fans and we feel we can do no less in return to perpetuate his memory.

Jailhouse Rockers of California

Jailhouse Rockers of California is an Elvis Presley Fan Club formed … to promote the memory of Elvis Presley in positive ways, to raise and donate funds to charities in Elvis Presley's memory, to foster the sharing of experiences related to Elvis Presley among the members of the club and others, and to organize and hold special events, activities, and field trips for our members to have fun and socialize.

The E. P. Foundation of New York

The E. P. Foundation of New York was founded in 1980. Our goals have been to join with others who appreciate Elvis' talent and charisma, and contribute in every way to continuing his legacy of charity and good works. We welcome anyone traveling to New York to contact us and join in our meetings or parties. Some of us are first generation Elvis fans and we realize that the younger generations are the ones to carry on his legacy. That tells us to keep initiating younger fans to continue doing good in his name. His memory will carry us through. —Joanne Digilio, president, and Mary McLaughlin, vice president

We Remember Elvis Fan Club

On August 16, 1977, I made a promise to Elvis and myself that the world would not forget this great man. I was not sure just how to keep that promise but it soon became clear. In August 1982, the We Remember Elvis Fan Club came to life. It is through our works of charity and our club newsletters that we fulfill our promise to not let the world forget Elvis. —Priscilla Parker, president

It's Only Love for Elvis Fan Club

It was always my intention to form yet another Elvis Presley fan club and share as much with other fans as I could. Our newsletters go around the world and our web site (http://visitweb.com/ELVIS) is a popular stop for web surfers. The most remarkable thing is that we have so many teenagers from all walks of life who contact us with questions about Elvis and tell us how much they love him. It is refreshing and encouraging to know that the music and influence of Elvis still touches people every day and will continue to do so for "Today, Tomorrow, and Forever." —Rich Wilson, president

Memphis Mafia club, Edinburg Branch, OEPFC

Since 1973, the Memphis Mafia club has held over 500 events, including a regular monthly dance for more than 20 years, video nights, skittles, bowling and snooker nights, barbecues, picnics, and kids events. Over the past year, the Memphis Mafia have run an eight-a-side football team, Elvis FC, who play in an Edinburgh Sunday League. In addition, eight big conventions have been staged in Edinburgh, some of the most ambitious events ever to be organised by an Elvis fan club, bringing rare movies, items of Elvis' clothing, stage plays, cabaret acts, and even Elvis' friends from the U.S. to Edinburgh and a Scottish audience. Our dances are reckoned by many to be the best in the U.K., if not the world, and introduce fans to much recorded and video material previously unknown to them. A large number of Elvis' songs are shown for dancing via large video screen. With competitions, a featured year from the King's career at every dance, and a friendly club atmosphere, our fans have a great time.

Elvis Friends Hollywood

Our club was formed in 1993 to honor Elvis' memory and to perpetuate the memory of the greatest entertainer who ever lived in a very positive and loving way. We also follow Elvis' example of charitable giving by donating funds raised from club events to charities that Elvis would have supported—especially children's charities such as Centers for Abused Children, Special Olympics, Pediatric Cancer Research, the Elvis Presley Memorial Trauma Center, and others. —Bobbie Cunningham, president

List of Fan Clubs Worldwide

Here's a list of Elvis fan clubs all over the world. Contact the ones that interest you and find out about their membership dues, newsletters, meetings, and whatever else is important to you in a prospective club. Most clubs don't have a postage budget just for inquiries, so if you are writing don't forget to send a self-addressed stamped envelope for the response.

Note: There is an official fan club in Great Britain (listed as OEPFC). It was formed in 1957 and now has approximately 20,000 members in a network of 25 branches throughout England, Scotland, Wales, etc. We have listed a few of the many branches by their individual names.

Always Elvis Fan Club

Attn: Rob Nekich, 5728 Tulip Drive, Allentown, Pennsylvania 18104

America's Legend Elvis Presley Fan Club
    Attn: Ruth Mercer, 21660 State Road 120, Elkhart, Indiana 46516
    E-mail: AMLEGEND1@aol.com

Assembly of Elvis Fan Club
    Attn: Pam Wood, 776 North Parkwood Road, Decatur, Georgia 30030
    E-mail: p.wood@mindspring.com

Association Elvis pour Toujours
    Attn: Jean Philippe Camusat, 8 Rue Marc Sangnier, 21000 Dijon, France

Austrian Elvis Presley Fan Club of Modling
    Attn: Walter Richter, Krongasse 14/12 A 1050 Vienna 5 Austria

Because of Elvis Fan Club
    8880 Bellaire, Box 359, Houston, Texas 77036

Bedfordshire Branch of OEPFC
    Attn: Bill Hyde, 38 Dordans Road, Leagrave, Luton, Bedfordshire LU4 9BS England

Berkshire Branch of OEPFC
    Attn: Jenny Milbourne, 100 Blandford Road North, Langley, Berkshire SL3 7TA England

Blue Hawaiians
    Attn: Sue Wiegert, P.O. Box 69834, Los Angeles, California 90069

Bromsgrove Branch of OEPFC
    Attn: Helen Tipton, 87 Perryfields Road, Sidemoor, Bromsgrove, Worcestershire B61 8SZ England

Burning Love Fan Club
    P.O. Box 649, Okemah, Oklahoma 74859

California Fans All Shook Up
    83 Lynwood Place, Watsonville, California 95076

California's Graceland Fan Club
    Attn: Ramona Robert, P.O. Box 1010, Port Hueneme, California 93041

Canadian Federation of Elvis Friends
    Attn: Allan Bunn, 59 Briarwood Crest, Hamilton, Ontario L9C 4C3 Canada

Can't Get Enough Elvis
    4794 Glen Bonnie Court, Doraville, Georgia 30340

Author's collection

Author's collection

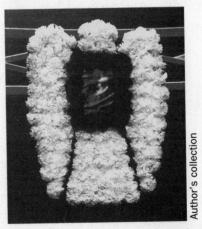
Author's collection

Capital Elvis, London Branch of OEPFC
    Attn: John Talbot, 59 Beadnell Road, Forest Hill,
    London SE23 1AA England
Cleveland Branch of OEPFC
    Attn: Stuart Colley, 69 Walter Street, Cleveland,
    Stockton, England
Club Elvis
    Apdo de Correos 347, SP-08910 Barcelona,
    Spain
Clube Oficial de Elvis "Burning Star"
    Attn: Celia Carvalho, Apartado 111, 2800 Cova da
    Piedade, Portugal
Collector Fan Club
    P.O. Box 1027, Sutter Creek, California 95685
    E-mail: ELVISLADY@aol.com
Collingwood Rocks with Elvis Fan Club
    Attn: K.A. DeNike, P.O. Box 2346, R.R. #2,
    Collingwood, Ontario L9Y 3Z1 Canada
    E-mail: kdenike@the-rocket.net
Colorado Graceland Elvis Always Fan Club
    Attn: Annette Wall, #204-16731 East Iliff, Aurora,
    Colorado 80013
Club Elvis
    Attn: Joaquin Luque, Aptdo de Correos 347,
    08910 Barcelona, Spain
Don't Forget Elvis Fan Club
    Attn: Phyllis Presnell, 2210 Glenside Drive,
    Greensboro, North Carolina 27405
Elvis Always Fan Club
    Attn: Ann Morrison, Route 3, Box 1200, Folkston,
    Georgia 31537
Elvis and Friends
    4017 Route 413, Levittown, Pennsylvania 19056
Elvis' Angels Fan Club
    Attn: Dianne Patrick, P.O. Box 776, Shreveport,
    Louisiana 71162
    E-mail: dianne@jewel-paula.com
    http://www.jewel-paula.com
Elvis Archives Fan Club
    Attn: John Lombard, P.O. Box 27501, Milwaukee,
    Wisconsin 53227

Author's collection

Author's collection

Author's collection

Elvis Arkansas-Style Fan Club
    Attn: Beverly Rook, 1130 Donnie Drive, Mabelvale, Arkansas 72103
Elvis Brazilian Friends
    Attn: Rosoleta Esteves, Caixa Postal 31, Eng. Dentro, Rio de Janeiro 20, 730 Brazil
Elvis Business Fan Club
    Attn: Matt Swanson, P.O. Box 663, Mt. Prospect, Illinois 60056
    E-mail: mtselvis1@aol.com

Elvis Capital of Canada Fan Club
    Attn: Marc Bruneau, 547-3 Gilmour Street, Ottowa, Ontario, Canada K1R 5L5
Elvis Chicago Style Fan Club
    Attn: Mike Keating, P.O. Box 388554, Chicago, Illinois 60638
    (312) 494-2626
    E-mail: ElvisChgoStyle@webtv.net
    http://www.angelfire.com/il/CHICAGOSTYLEHOMEPAGE
    They sponsor the annual Elvis Gospel Mass during Tribute Week.
Elvis Club Berlin
    Attn: Werner Strube, Landsberger Allee 200, Berlin 0-1156 Germany
Elvis Connection Fan Club
    Attn: Mary Danks, P.O. Box 45941, Madison, Wisconsin 53719
    E-mail: sunitwin@terracom.net
Elvis Connections
    Attn: Pat Clemins, 716 Broadway #11, El Cajon, California 92021
    E-mail Mompac@aol.com
    http://www.members.aol.com/mompac/epfc.htm

Elvis Country Fan Club
    6203 Shoalwood Avenue, Austin, Texas 78757
    (512) 452-8245
    E-mail: Elvisfc@aol.com
    Sponsors of the annual Candlelight Vigil which is held every August 15 at Graceland in Memphis.
Elvis Cross the Mersey

THE WORLD UNITED THRU ELVIS

ELVIS IN THE HEART OF DIXIE

Attn: Terry Bellis, 43 Brownlow Road, New Ferry Wirral, Merseyside L62 1AU England

Elvis Dixieland Fan Club
1306 Rosedale Drive, Demopolis, Florida 34203

Elvis Echoes of Love
5903 Montibello, Imperial, Missouri 63052

Elvis en Chile
Attn: Hugh Reyes, Av. Frei #3221-F d.21, Viña del Mar, Chile
(56) 9 3365393
E-mail: wmelvis@usa.net
http://www.geocities.com/sunsetstrip/venue/5350

Elvis Extravaganza Fan Club
Attn: Kitty Wood, P.O. Box 272014, Columbus, Ohio 43227

Elvis Fan Club
Box 4537, Corpus Christi, Texas 78469

Elvis Fans Club
Chevy Radio, Jalan Pasir Kaliki 59, Bandung, Indonesia, Post Code 40172
(62) 22-6013304

Elvis Fans from Hoosierland
Attn: Sharon Ott, 37 South Lynhurst Drive, Indianapolis, Indiana 46241

Elvis Fans United
110 Graston Avenue, Syracuse, New York 13219

Elvis Fever Fan Club
Attn: Anna Mae Meyers, 4014 Keeners Road, Baltimore, Maryland 21220

Elvis Fever Fan Club
Attn: Joann Smith, 3545-1 St. Johns Bluff Road South, PMB 253, Jacksonville, Florida 32224

Elvis Forever Fan Club of Athens, Greece
Attn: Anna E. Proios, P.O. Box 70139, GR. 1610 Glyfada, Greece

Elvis 4-Ever King Fan Club
Attn: Kaye Hollingsworth, 130 Bobsled Drive, West Columbia, South Carolina 29170
E-mail: steveboni@mindspring.com

Elvis Forever TCB Fan Club
Attn: Bob and Susan Still, Box 1066, Pinellas Park, Florida 34665

Elvis for Everyone International
Attn: Andrew Leach, 59 Stotfold Road, Hitchin, Herts SG4 0QW England

Elvis Friends Are the Best Friendship Circle
Attn: Sandy Warehime, 3007 Southpoet Avenue, Chesapeake, Virginia 23324

Elvis Friends Fan Club of Milan
Attn: Rapillo Fraco, c/o Memphis Cafè, Via Altaguardia, 17, IT-20135 Milano 99000 Italy

Elvis Friends International Fan Club
Attn: Richard Denning. P.O. Box 1201, Lawton, Oklahoma 73502

Elvis Friendship Circle
2908 Juen Lane, Bossier City, Louisiana 71112

Elvis-Friends Hollywood
Attn: Bobbie Cunningham and Suzanne Philips, 333 N. Screenland Drive #142, Burbank, California 91505
E-mail: BOBBIETCB@aol.com
Fax: (213) 953-8566

Elvis History World of the King of Hofing
Hannes Pum, Gstatter Boden 2-3 Gesause, A8913, Styria, Austria

Elvis' Hometown Fans Fan Club
Attn: Mary Etta Stonebraker, 3767 Charles Drive, Memphis, Tennessee 38116

Elvisians from Another Planet
Attn: Marjorie Wilkinson, 133 Sunnyside Avenue, Mill Valley, California 94941
E-mail: bev@bigtimedesign.com
http://www.bigtimedesign.com/

Elvis in Astrodome Fan Club Brazil
Attn: Maria Augusta Mendes, Al. Princesa Isabel, 1378, Curitiba, PR Brazil
(80) 730-080
http://mais.sul.com.br/epkingd/astro.htm

Elvis in Canada
Attn: Fran Roberts, Box 6065, Station F, Hamilton, Ontario L9C 5S2 Canada

Elvis Information Network
   Attn: David Troedson, P.O. Box 1, Lyons ACT
   Australia 2606
   E-mail: david@elvis.com.au
   http://www.elvis.com.au/
Elvis in My Heart Fan Club
   Attn: Cindy Hubka, P.O. Box 614, Clarksville,
   Iowa, 50619
Elvis in the Heart of Dixie Fan Club of Alabama
   Attn: Ronnie Bewsey, 39 Dunn Street,
   Somerville, Alabama 35670
Elvis in the Heart of Kent
   Attn: Kevan Gray, 49 West Dumpton Lane,
   Ramsgate, Kent CT11 7DF England
Elvis Is King Fan Club
   Attn: David Trotter, 59 Cambridge Road, New
   Silksworth, Sunderland SR3 2DQ England
Elvis It's Now And Forever
   BP 12, 67110 Niederbronn les Bains, France
   (03) 88-80-36-26
   Fax: (03) 88-77-80-00
   E-mail: Gobersch@aol.com
Elvis Land Fan Club
   Attn: Jaqueline Manzano, R. Rondonopolis 148
   Cidade Alta, Cuiba Mt, Brazil 78025
Elvis Little Sister Fan Club
   Attn: Yesenia Sandoval, 6941 Walker Avenue,
   Bell, California 90201
Elvis Lives!
   Attn: Jeff Mudalia, 31 Holland Close, #10-229,
   Singapore 270031 Singapore
Elvis Lives On
   13658 SE 192 Street, Renton, Washington 98058
Elvis Lives Worldwide Fan Club
   Attn: Brian Presley, P.O. box 62018, 6491 Jeanne
   D'Arc, Orleans, Canada K1C 7HA
Elvis Love's Burning
   Box 7462, Shreveport, Louisiana 71107
Elvis Lucky 7 Fan Club
   P.O. Box 337, Sta. Cruz Post Office, Metro
   Manila, Philippines

Author's collection

Author's collection

Author's collection

Elvis Memorial Fan Club of Hawaii
Attn: Charlie Ross, P.O. Box 11295, Honolulu, Hawaii 96828
Elvis Memories
Sylvain Vertez, Statiestraat 124-126, B-2070 Zwijndrecht, Belgium
Elvis Memories
Box 2401, Livermore, California 94550
Elvis Memphis Style
Attn: Cyndi Sylvia, 286 Firelight Cove, Southaven, Mississippi 38671
(601) 208-5430
E-mail: user284316@aol.com

Elvis My Happiness
Attn: Jean-Marie Pouzenc, PB 68, 78321 Le Mesnil Saint Denis Cedex, France
(01) 34-61-24-06/http://www.elvismyhappiness.com
ElvisNet Online Fan Club (Taking Care of Elvis Online)
http://www.elvisnet.com
Elvis Presley Burning Love Fan Club
Attn: Bill DeNight, 1904 Williamsburg Drive, Streamwood, Illinois 60103
Elvis Presley Club of Italy in France
Attn: Luca Barbonaglia, 24, Avenue de France, 06190 Roquebrune Cap Martin, France
E-mail: Elvisclub@aol.com
http://perso.infonie.fr/elvisclub
http://members.aol.com/elvisclub/index.html
Elvis Presley Fan Club
Attn: Egon Setznagel, Einoed 18, A-5580 Tamsweg, Austria
Elvis Presley Fan Club
P.O. Box 82, Elsternwick, Victoria 3185 Australia
Elvis Presley Fan Club
Attn: Jayaretne Perera, 113/1 Pirivena Road, Mount Lavinia, Sri Lanka
Elvis Presley Fan Club
Attn: Francine Dumong, 25 Avenue Berchem, L-1231, Howald, Luxembourg
Elvis Presley Fan Club Interessen-gemeinschaft Germany

Attn: Claudia Agnes Nenn, Pestalozzistr. 19, Eberbach 69412 Germany

Elvis Presley Fan Club Official de Argentina
Florida 520, Local 15, (1005) Bs. As., Argentina

Elvis Presley Fan Club of Australia
Attn: Jim Porter, P.O. Box 436, Mount Druitt, South Wales 2770, Australia
E-mail: micomp@ozemail.com.au

Elvis Presley Fan Club of Austria
Offenes Fach 543, A/1101 Vienna, Austria

Elivs Presley Fan Club of the Capital District
392 Rynex Corners Road, Schenectady, New York 12306
http://www.serve.com/music/elvis/

Author's collection

Elvis Presley Fan Club of Denmark
Claus Hansen, Postbox 871, DK-2400 Copenhagen NV, Denmark

Elvis Presley Fan Club of Florida
Attn: John Beach, 6761 Candlewood Drive South, Jacksonville, Florida 32244

Elvis Presley Fan Club of Israel
Attn: Arye Ne'eman, 36 Yehuda Hanasie Street, Kiryat Tiron 36000 Israel

Elvis Presley Fan Club of Italy
Attn: Sebastiano Cecere, Piazza Cirene 10A, IT-10151 Torino, Italy

Elvis Presley Fan Club of Macedonia
Attn: Julie G. Damjanovska, Bujurestka 69, MK 91000, Skopje, Macedonia

Elvis Presley Fan Club of Norway
Boks 52, 1470 Lorenskog, Norway

Elvis Presley Fan Club of Oklahoma
Attn: Charle Reeves, Route 2, Box 239-A, Okemah, Oklahoma 74859
E-mail: Cmarch75@yahoo.com
http://www.clubhomepage.com/elvispresleyok

Elvis Presley Fan Club of Queensland
Attn: Katrina Searle, P.O. Box 151, Chermside, Queensland 4032 Australia

Elvis Presley Fan Club of Tasmania
Attn: Elaine Green, P.O. Box 165, Sorrell 7172, Tasmania, Australia

Elvis Presley Fan Club of Tokyo
   P.O. Box 5, Kasai, Tokyo 134, Japan
Elvis Presley Fan Club of Victoria
   Attn: Wayne Hawthorne, P.O. Box 301, Heidelberg, Victoria 3084, Australia
Elvis Presley Fan Club (Northampton Branch)
   7 Faraday Close, Northampton NN5 4AE England
Elvis Presley Fan Club of Old Hickory/Hermitage, Tennessee
   Attn: J. Stone, 432 Rolling Mill Road, Old Hickory, Tennessee 37138
   E-mail: rock43@bellsouth.net
Elvis Presley Fan Club of South Africa
   Attn: Andre and Annatjie, P.O. Box 4466, Kempton Park, 1620 Gauteng, South Africa
Elvis Presley Fan Club of Tokyo, Japan
   Attn: B.J. Remi, P.O. Box 820143, Memphis, Tennessee 38182
   (901) 726-5012
   Fax: (901) 726-4983
   or
   Attn: B. J. Remi, New Sendagaya Mansion #302, 1-28-8 Sandagaya, Shibuya-Ku
   Tokyo 151 Japan
Elvis Presley Fan Club of Victoria
   Attn: Wayne Hawthorne, P.O. Box 301, Heidelberg, Victoria 3084, Australia
Elvis Presley Foundation
   Box 1352, Norfolk, Virginia 23501
Elvis Presley Foundation of New York
   Attn: Joanne and Jimmy Digilio, 1220 Park Avenue, New York, New York 10128
   http://members.tripod.com/~ep4me/epfofny.htm
Elvis Presley Gesellschaft E.V.
   Attn: Peter Kranzler, Postfach 229, D-35616 Braunfels, Germany
Elvis Presley International Fan Club
   Attn: Luuk Bonthond, Bevelandsestrast 15A, 3083 NA Rotterdam, The Netherlands
Elvis Presley International Fan Club Worldwide
   Attn: Georgia King, P.O. Box 3770, Memphis, Tennessee 38173
   E-mail: dtspangler@aol.com
Elvis Presley's Kingdom, Official EP Fan Club of Curitaba, Brazil
   http://www.bbs1.sul.com.br/
Elvis Presley King "O" Mania Fan Club
   Attn: Mario Grenier, 552 Croteau Quest, Thetford Mones, PQ Canada G6G 6W7
Elvis Presley Love Me Tender Fan Club
   Attn: Marlene Potieter, Kathu 8845, South Africa
Elvis Presley Memorial Society of Syracuse
   Attn: Sue Fetcho, 411 Mallard Drive, Camillus, New York 13031

Elvis Presley Rock Fan Club
   Via Brunamonti 2, 62019, Recanati, Italy
Elvis Presley's Kingdom Fan Club, Brazil
   Attn: Renate Ursula Lampe, Caixa Postal 6844, Curitiba, PR Brazil
   http://mais.sul.com.br/epkingd/index.htm
Elvis Presley Sun Dial Fan Club
   118 Rue De Lagney, 75020 Paris, France
The Elvis Presley TCB Fan Club of Chicago
   Attn: Jeanna Kalweit, 4939 Spring Road, Oak Lawn, Illinois 60453
Elvis Presley Today Society
   Attn: Nico Declerck
   E-mail: nicodeclerck@planetinternet.be
Elvis Presley Today, Tomorrow, and Forever Fan Club of Malaysia
   Attn: H. T. Long, P.O. Box 32, 41700 Klang, Selangor D.E. Malaysia
Elvis Rock-a-Hula Baby Fan Club
   Attn: Cle Medler, P.O. Box 1641, Kea-au, Puna, Hawaii 96749
Elvis the One and Only King of Rock and Roll Fan Club
   8010 West Gregory Street, Norwood Park Township, Illinois 60656
Elvis Show Fan Club
   Attn: Jacqueline Raphael, P.O. Box 430 CH-4020, Basel, Switzerland
   E-mail: elvisshowfanclub@datacomm.ch
Elvis Social Club, Irish Branch of the OEPFC of Great Britian
   43 Bernard Curtis House, Bluebell, Dublin 12 Ireland
Elvis Still Rockin' Fan Club
   Attn: Debbie Reeves, 348 Trotters Ridge, Lawrenceville, Georgia 30043
The Elvis Teddy Bears
   744 Caliente Drive, Brandon, Florida 33511
Elvis That's the Way It Is Fan Club of Chicago
   Attn: Carol Hopp, 8730 S. Newland, Oak Lawn, Illinois 60453
Elvis the King Fan Club
   4714 Dundee Drive, Jacksonville, Florida 32210
Elvis, This One's For You Fan Club
   Attn: Casey Korenek, 7601 Cameron Road, #1036, Austin, Texas 78752
Elvis Till We Meet Again Fan Club
   Attn: Doreen Oldroyd, 124 Rankin Road, Sault Ste. Marie, Ontario, Canada
   P6A 4R8
Elvis Today, Tomorrow & Forever
   Attn: Diana & Ray Hill, Box 41, Gloucester GL1 2LN England
Elvis Touch Glasgow
   Attn: Paul Downie, 95 Gottries Road, Harbourside, Irvine, KA12 8QH Scotland

Elvis 2001 Fan Club
Attn: Michelle Rivers, 11, Bondfield Close, Southborough, Tunbridge Wells, Kent TN4 0BF England
E-mail: Elvisa2001@netscape.net

Elvis Worldwide Fan Club
Attn: Will "Bardhol" McDaniel, 3081 Sunrise, Memphis, Tennessee 38127

E. P Continentals of Florida
Attn: Sue Manuszak, P.O. Box 568082, Orlando, Florida 32856
(407) 381-3739 or (407) 889-3696
Fax: (407) 889-0300
E-mail: manuszaksb@juno.com
http://www.jordanselvisworld.simplenet.com/Epcont.htm
The E. P. Continentals club was formed in Memphis in the mid-fifties and Elvis actually picked the name.

Essential Elvis (UK)
Attn: Andrew Hearn, 62 Shandon Road, Worthing, Sussex BN14 9DX England

Eternal Elvis
Attn: Lyn and Les Dean, 185 Landlands, Overhill Road, Dulwich London SW22 England

Eternally Elvis TCB, Inc.
2251 N.W. 93rd Avenue, Pembroke Pines, Florida 33024

Expresley Elvis
2456 South Zenobia Street, Denver, Colorado 80219

Fans of Elvis Fan Club Rhode Island
593 Woodward Road, North Providence, Rhode Island 02904

50s Remember Elvis
Attn: Billie LeJuene, Rt. 10, Box 201 #2, Lake City, Florida 32025

Fit for a King Fan Club
Attn: Karen Spiers, 1505 Heritage Cove, Acworth, Georgia 30102

Flaming Star Official Elvis Presley Fan Club of Norway
P.O. Box 38 Lambertseter, N-1101 Oslo, Norway

Follow That Dream Elvis Fans of Florida
Attn: Anne O'Hear, 224 Down East Lane, Lake Worth, Florida 33467

"The Elvis Forever Fan Club of Greece was started in 1977 by husband and wife Anna and Evaggelos Proios, and we still run it. Many of our members come from countries other than Greece, so we publish our newsletter in English and it contains not only Greek but up-to-date international Elvis news, too.

"Like most other clubs, Elvis Forever offers various articles for sale and exchange, including books, magazines, postcards, Greek and other Elvis releases, etc. Given the number of items produced in Greece over the years that bear Elvis' name, this might well be a source of some interesting memorabilia."
—Anna and Evaggelos Proios

For the Heart Fan Club
    5004 Lyngail Drive, Huntsville, Alabama 35810
From Memphis to Philly
    Attn: Tom Larson, 1925 Berkshire Street, Philadelphia, Pennsylvania 19124-4618
Gang Elvis
    Terciani, Caixa Postal 532-09000, Santo Andre, Sao Paulo, Brazil
Good Luck Charms Fan Club
    Attn: Pat Viall, 452 Old Farm Drive, Birmingham, Alabama 35215
Graceland Express
    Box 16508, Memphis, Tennessee 38186
Graceland's Rising Sun
    Attn: Marie Nersesian, 1254 Old Hickory Road, Memphis, Tennessee 38116
Greater New Orleans Elvis Fan Club
    Attn: Jud Ergle, 7520 Hayne Blvd, New Orleans, Louisiana 70126
    E-mail: wlergle@datasync.com
Having Fun with Elvis
    Attn: Judy Dial, 5310 Binz-Engleman Road, San Antonio, Texas 78219
Heartbreak Hotel Elvis Fan Club
    Attn: Marsene Emert, 210 Mildmay Road, College Station, Texas 77840
House of Elvis
    Attn: Mick Haywood, 40 Hawthorne Street, Leicester LE3 9FQ England
If I Can Dream Elvis Fan Club
    Attn: Charla Volkov, 847 East Le Marche Avenue, Phoenix, Arizona 85022
If I Can Dream Elvis Fan Club of Massachusetts
    Attn: Marsha Hammond, 4 Solar Road, Billerica, Massachusetts 01821-3430
    http://www.tiac.net/users/subzero/
    elvis/mag.htm
    E-mail: ificandream@aol.com
If I Can Dream Elvis In Alabama Fan Club
    Attn: Ida Sue Sutherland, P.O. BOX 581, Haleyville, Alabama 35565
International Elvis Presley Club of Italy
    http://perso.club-internet.fr/epresley/
International Elvis Presley Fan Club
    Chaussee de Boendail, Brussels, Belgium
International Elvis Presley Fan Club, Hong Kong
    Attn: Tommy Ooi, P.O. Box 20720, Hennessy Road Post Office, Wanchai, Hong
    Kong
    Fax: (852) 2337 3951
    E-mail: mabellee@hknet.com
It's Elvis Time Official Dutch Fan Club
    Attn: Peter Haan, Postbus 27015, 3003 LA Rotterdam, Holland

http://www.geocities.com/~arpt/iet/
It's Now and Forever Fan Club
    39A Rue St. Urbain, Strasbourg 67100
    France
It's Only Love For Elvis Fan Club
    Attn: Rich Wilson, P.O. Box 65, Huguenot,
    New York 12746
    E-mail: rawill@orn.net
    http://visitweb.com/ELVIS
    http://www.geocities.com/Nashville/4402/
I Was—I Am "Searching" Elvis Fan Club
    Attn: Nancy Newman, 832 Benjamin Court,
    Franklin, Tennessee 27064
Jailhouse Rockers of California
    Attn: Christine Dashner, P.O. Box 16423,
    Irvine, California 92623
    Fax: (714) 505-6758
    E-mail: sanjeans@ptw.com
Japanese Heart For Elvis
    Attn: B. J. Remi, P.O. Box 820143, Memphis, Tennessee 38182
    (901) 726-5012
    Fax: (901) 726-4983
    or
    Attn: B. J. Remi, New Sendagaya Mansion #302, 1-28-8 Sandagaya, Shibuya-Ku
    Tokyo 151 Japan
King Creole Fan Club
    Attn: Mike Castano, 314 Lafayette, Chateaguay, Quebec, Canada J6J 1V8
Kingmania EPFC
    Bukurestka 69, MK-91000, Skopje, Macedonia
Lancashire Branch of OEPFC
    Attn: Paul Smith, 47 Carrington Road, Adlington, Chorley, Lancashire PR7 4RN England
The Legend Continues Fan Club
    Attn: David Lewis, 4221 Crestview Drive, Chattanooga, Tennessee 37415
Les Amis D'Elvis
    Attn: Jean Marc Gargiulo, Boite Postale 69, 75961 Paris, Cedex 20, France
    Tel/Fax: (331) 43-64-23-64
    http://perso.wanadoo.fr/elvispresley/
    They are the only club in the world that has a meeting every Saturday after-
    noon.
Little Presley Rascals
    Attn: Theresa Smith, P.O. Box 1168, Crystal Springs, Florida 33524

"All U.S. fan clubs need their arses kicked. I went back to Scotland last weekend and timed my visit to coincide with one of the two monthly fan club dances. There's been two Elvis dances a month, every month, in Scotland since 1977."
—Ian Mackay, Scottish fan who's been displaced to the States

London Branch of the OEPFC
  Attn: Clive Robson, 76 Pretoria Road, Leytonstone, London E11 4BD England
Looking For Elvis Fan Club
  Attn: Joan Clark, P.O. Box 501002, Mobile, Alabama 36605
Love 4 Elvis Fan Club
  Attn: Fran Colvin, Box 2271, Clifton, New Jersey 07015
Love Me Tender Elvis Fan Club
  Attn: Carmen Bode, Str. Panselelor 2 B1 446, Sc. A4etJ5, Apt.29, Sector 4,
  Bucuresti, Romania
Loving You Elvis Fan Club
  Attn: Pam Hendricks, 1222 Northeast Monroe, Topeka, Kansas 66608
Loving You Elvis Fan Club
  Attn: Judy French & Dot Johnson, P.O. Box 444, Rolling Fork, Mississippi 39159
Memories of Elvis Express
  Attn: Betty Roloson, 302 Whitman Court, Glen Burnie, Maryland 21061
Memories of Elvis Fan Club of Auckland
  Attn: Susan Brennan-Hodgson, P.O. Box 99-818, Newmarket Auckland, New
  Zealand
  E-mail: elvisnz@iconz.co.nz
Memphis Flash
  Attn: Frode Nielsen, Munkebekken 432B, N-1061 Oslo, Norway
Memphis King
  Attn: June Clark, 60 Northcote Drive, Leeds LS11 6NH England
Memphis Mafia Fan Club, Edinburgh Branch of OEPFC
  P.O. Box 710 NWDO, Edinburgh EH4 Scotland
  http://dialspace.dial.pipex.com/memphis.mafia
  E-mail: rcs40@dial.pipex.com
Memphis Sideburns
  Attn: Randy Keller, P.O. Box 991, Rocklin, California 95677
Mile High on Elvis Fan Club
  Box 2332, Arvada, Colorado 80001
"My Wish Came True" Elvis Fan Club
  Attn: Carol Miller, 5393 Mooretown Road, Williamsburg, Virginia 23188
  E-mail: grangraw@widowmaker.com
Networking for Elvis
  Attn: Connie J. Michel 2205 Johnson Avenue NW, Cedar Rapids, Iowa 52405
  Fax: (319)398-0569
  E-mail: CJMichel@worldnet.att.net
Never Ending Elvis Presley Fan Club
  Attn: Toni Thompson, 214 Pattee Canyon Drive, Missoula, Montana 59803
  E-mail: osage1@mssl.uswest.net

New Jersey Stage Association for Elvis
    Attn: Robert Job, 304 Carlton Avenue, Piscataway, New Jersey 08854
Norfolk Branch, Elvis Presley Fan Club of Great Britian
    Attn: Terry Wortley, 3 Colls Road, Norwich, Norfolk NR7 9QE England
Northampton Branch of OEPFC
    Attn: Helen Brown, 7 Faraday Close, Northampton NN5 4AE England
North Jersey Knights for Elvis
    Attn: Rosemarie Farro, 280 Wilson Avenue, Fairview, New Jersey 07022
The Official Elvis Presley Fan Club of Australasia
    Attn: David Troedson, P.O. Box 341, Niddrie, Victoria 3042, Australia
Official Elvis Presley Fan Club of the Czech Republic
    Attn: Pavel Cernocky, Palaskova 1/1106, 182 00 Prague 8, Czech Republic
Official Elvis Presley Fan Club of Denmark
    Attn: Henrik Knudsen, Postbox 2042, DK-8900 Randers, Denmark
Official Elvis Presley Fan Club of Great Britain and the Commonwealth
    Attn: Julie Mundy/Todd Slaughter, P.O. Box 4, Leicester LE3 5HY, England
Official Elvis Presley Fan Club of Norway "Flaming Star"
    Boks 38, Labertseter, 1101 Oslo, Norway
Oklahoma Fans for Elvis
    Attn: Bill & Judy Wilson, 421 West 6th, Bristow, Oklahoma 74010
    Fax: (405) 525-6049
    E-mail: offe@webtv.net
    The club was founded in 1976.
One and Only King of Rock and Roll Fan Club
    Attn: Bob and Judy Repin, 8010 W. Gregory Street, Norwood Park Township,
    Illinois 60656
One Nation Under Elvis Fan Club
    P. O. Box 3129, Commerce, Texas 75429
    E-mail: bradh@boisdarc.tamu-commerce.edu
    http://www.onenationfanclub.com
Oxford Branch, Elvis Presley Fan Club of Great Britian
    Attn: Jenny de Fraine, 49 Marlborough Road, Grandpoint, South Oxford,
    England OX1 4LW
The Presley Connection
    Attn: Karen Couch, P.O. Box 680444, Prattville, Alabama 36068
    E-mail: preslycnct@aol.com
    http://members.aol.com/PreslyCnct/aboutclub.htm
The Presley Nation Fan Club
    2941 Sunflower Circle East, Palm Springs, California 92262
The Presley-ites
    Attn: John and Kathy Ferguson, 6010 18th Street, Zephyrhills, Florida 33540

Pure Gold Elvis Fan Club
   Attn: Gabriel Rodriguez, P.O. Box 720203, Miami, Florida 33172
   Fax: (305) 552-0052
   E-mail: ELVIZP@aol.com
Quake, Rattle, and Roll
   Attn: Janet Berenson, 3967 Sacramento Street, San Francisco, California 94118
Reflections of Elvis
   14210 Schwartz Road, Grabill, Indiana 46741
Remembering Elvis with TLC in Alabama
   Attn: Linda Harrelson, 725 Cherokee Trail, Anniston, Alabama 36206
Return to Sender
   2501 Barclay Avenue, Portsmouth, Virginia 23702
Rock-a-Hula Baby Fan Club
   Attn: Cle Medler, P.O. Box 1641, Keaau, Puna, Hawaii 96749
Sao Paulo Elvis Presley Society
   Attn: Marcelo E. L. Costa, Rue Santa Branca, 67 Apto, 122-01331,
   040 Sao Paulo, Brazil
See See Rider Fan Club
   Attn: Eric Estep, 4082 Jason Road, Springhill, Florida 34608
Sharing the Memory Elvis Presley Fan Club of Vermont
   Attn: Pharilda Galloway, 99 Hayes Avenue, South Burlington, Vermont 05403
   E-mail: EPFCOFVT@compuserve.com
Sincerely Elvis Fan Club of Michigan
   Attn: Debra Smith, P.O. Box 1384, Midland, Michigan 48641-1384
Smoky Mountains Precious Memories of Elvis Fan Club
   Attn: Vera Wilkinson, 891 Wares Valley Road, Pigeon Forge, Tennessee 37863
Society of Admiration for Elvis Fan Club
   Attn: Teresa Edwards, 411 East Loop 281 Lot 106, Longview, Texas 75605
   (903) 757-5144
   Fax: (903)757-5494
   E-mail: terrye@iamerica.net
   http://www.Members.xoom.com/teenytg/
Snorkling Elvises
   Attn: Otis May, 2832 Seidenberg Avenue, Key West, Florida 33040
Sound of Elvis Fan Club
   Attn: Monika Leone, 3 Reedbeds Cresent Seaton S.A. 5023 Australia
The Spirit Lives On
   Attn: Glenda Ware, 2813 North Sugar Pine Road,Prineville, Oregon 97754
The Star of Elvis Will Shine Forever in Israel Fan Club
   Attn: Becki Erguz, Yehuda Alevi 14/30, Ashdod, Israel

Steadfast, Loyal, and True Official OEPFC
   Attn: Barbara Wilson, 11 Connaught House, Vauxhalls, Wolverhampton WV1
   452 England
Still Rockin' Elvis Fan Club
   Attn: Joe Passos, 200 Gregory Lane, Staten Island, 10314
   E-mail: eprockin@aol.com
   http://www.stillrockin.com
Still Rockin' Fan Club of Georgia
   Attn: Jack Myers, 266 Harmony Grove Road, Lilburn, Georgia 30247
Suspicious Minds Fan Club
   Attn: Julie Banhart, 4610 Owen, Memphis, Tennessee 38122
Swiss Elvis Team Fan Club
   Attn: Marco Guler, Im Maiacher 8/8804, AU, Switzerland
Taking Care of Business Official Elvis Presley Fan Club of South Africa
   Attn: Stevie Godson, P.O. Box 2258, Pinegowrie 2123 South Africa
"Talk About the Good Times" Elvis Fan Club
   Attn: Kelly and Randall Bart, P.O. Box 68361, Schaumburg, Illinois 60168
   E-mail: AlwaysElvis@aol.com
TCB Elvis Presley Fan Club of Virginia
   Box 1158, Glen Allen, Virginia 23060
TCB Fan Club
   2103 West 50th Street, Chicago, Illinois 60609
TCB 4 EAP Fan Club of New York
   Attn: Martin Lockman, P.O. Box 564674, College Point, New York 11356
TCB for Elvis Fan Club
   Attn: Joanne Young, Box 2655, Gastonia, North Carolina 28053
TCB In South Georgia
   Attn: Grace Bledsoe, 1311 North Hutchinson Avenue, Adel, Georgia 31620
Tender Loving Elvis Fan Club
   Attn: Tina Grimes, 1128 Schultz Street, Defiance, Ohio 43512-2947
   E-mail: jtjsmail@bright.net
That's the Way It Is Fan Club of Chicago
   Club Headquarters, P.O. Box 189, Franklin Park, Illinois 60131
Then Now & Forever Elvis Presley Fan Club
   Box 161130, Memphis, Tennessee 38116
Tidskriften Elvis the Official Elvis Presley Fan Club of Sweden
   Attn: Ake Flodin, P.O. Box 4027, S-175 04 Jarfalla, Sweden
To Elvis with Love Fan Club
   Attn: Marek Brada, 101-1001 West Broadway Street, Suite 676
   Vancouver, BritishColumbia V6H 4E4 Canada
   E-mail: elvisfan@rogers.wave.com

Touched by Elvis Fan Club
    Attn: Phyl Gordon, 513 Suber Drive, Virginia Beach, Virginia 23452
Treat Me Nice Official French Fan Club (Club Les Amis d'Elvis)
    Attn: Jean-Marc Gargiulo, B.P 69, 75961 Paris Cedex 20 France
    http://perso.wanadoo.fr/elvispresley/
Tribute to Elvis Fan Club
    Attn: Billie King. P.O. Box 734, Jenva, Louisiana 71342
True Fans for Elvis Fan Club
    Attn: Dot Gonyea, 62 Lowell Street, South Portland, Maine 04106
Unforgettable Elvis Fan Club
    Attn: Linda Leed, 1639A Morningside Drive, Lancaster, Pennsylvania 17602
    Fax: (717) 464-4160
    E-mail: Elvisfanli@aol.com
United Elvis Presley Society
    Attn: Hubert Vindevogel, Pijlstraat 15, B-2070 Zwijndrecht, Belgium
United States Associates of Elvis Presley Fan Club
    5320 D Ave. E #Q-47, Bradenton, FL 34203
Universally Elvis
    Attn: Jordan Ritchie
    E-mail: univlvisfc@aol.com
    E-mail: JELVISSY@aol.com
    http://jordanselvisworld.simplenet.com/index.html
    Jordan's Elvis World online fan club.
Vegetarians Who Like Elvis
    Attn: Ankur Jain, P.O. Box 38566, Germantown, Tennessee 38183
Viva Las Vegas Memphis Fashion
    Attn: Vickie Russell, P.O. Box 161106, Memphis, Tennessee 38186
Walk a Mile in My Shoes
    Attn: Norah Larkin, 13 Sterry Road, Barking, Essex 1G11 9SJ England
Walk a Mile in My Shoes Fan Club
    Attn: Jonathan Long, 512 Dixie Avenue, South Pittsburg, Tennessee 37380
Welcome to Our Elvis World
    Attn: Karen Oberender, 5708 Van Dyke Road, Baltimore, Maryland 21206
We Remember Elvis
    Attn: Priscilla Parker, 1215 Tennessee Avenue, Pittsburgh, Pennsylvania
    15216-2511
    http://ourworld.compuserve.com/homepages/elvis/we.htm
Wild in the Country for Elvis Fan Club
    Attn: Bridgett Elan, P.O. Box 1308, Graham, Washington 98338
The Wonder of You Elvis Fan Club
    Attn: Lynn Beall, 111 Roosevelt Avenue, Glen Burnie, Maryland 21061

Worldwide Elvis Presley Fan Club
   Attn: Curtis Milligan, P.O. Box 2302, Vashon Island, Washington 98070
Worldwide Young Elvis Fans, Inc.
   Attn: Jennifer Sinele, 2905 Stivers, Bryant, Arkansas 72022
You'll Never Walk Alone Fan Club of Israel
   Attn: Ofir Britton, Zalman Aran Street 10/3, Israel 77403
Yours in Elvis Forever Fan Club
   P.O. Box 16677, Memphis, Tennessee 38116
The Young and Beautiful Friends of Elvis Fan Club
   Attn: Megan Murphy, 34 West 29 Street, Bayonne, New Jersey 07002

YOUR ELVIS EDUCATION

Books
E: Reflections on the Birth of the Elvis Faith
   John Strausbaugh
Images of Elvis Presley in American Culture 1977–1997: The Mystery Terrain
   George Plasketes
Elvis People—The Cult of the King
   Ted Harrison
Elvis Culture: Fans, Faith, & Image
   Erika Doss
True Disbelievers: The Elvis Contagion
   R. Serge Denisoff and George Plasketes
Elvis after Elvis: The Posthumous Career of a Living Legend
   Gilbert B. Rodman
Dead Elvis: A Chronicle of a Cultural Obsession
   Greil Marcus

Video
"Mondo Elvis"
"Elvis Presley's America"
"Elvis: He Touched Their Lives"

Web Sites
http://www.geocities.com/~elviscentral/fanclubs
   Fan club listings
http://www.elvispresleyonline.com/html/elvis_fan_clubs.html
   List of fan clubs all over the world
http://www.geocities.com/SunsetStrip/8200/EPEC.html
   Fan club registry

http://www.fansites.com
    Listings of fan sites
http://members.aol.com/just4elvis/circle.htm
    Circle of Memories Annual Elvis Honeymoon Weekend hosted by Elvis Friends
    Hollywood Fan Flub site; E-mail: efh4elvis@aolcom

THE ELVIS AND YOU EXPERIENCE

Elvis fan clubs continue to start up all over the world. No matter where you live or what kind of Elvis Fan you are, being in a fan club can help you get the most out of the Elvis experience.

Join a Fan Club

By far one of the best things about being an Elvis fan is the friendship that develops among fans. Elvis fans are a diverse group of people who feel an instant bond with each other, united by their interest in Elvis. There are many different types of fan clubs, each has its own style. Some have active social calendars while others concentrate on charity work; some have regular newsletters and meetings, others are less active. Choose according to the type of fan you are.

Choose a Local Fan Club

Choose your club for geographical convenience so you can attend meetings and make friends with other local fans. And don't limit yourself only to one. If you can afford the dues, join a variety of clubs. For instance, a good newsletter is one of the best reasons to choose a particular club.

Choose a Favorite Travel Destination Fan Club

If you're planning a trip anytime in the future, why not join an Elvis fan club in your favorite destination? Fan club memberships are fairly inexpensive and come with a lot of benefits, but an unexpected benefit could be joining up with already-made friends when and wherever you travel. Better yet, coordinate your trip with the timing of your new fan club's annual event, dance, or even just a membership meeting.

Choose a Fan Club from Outside Your Home Country

See how the rest of the world sees Elvis. You may have the added advantage of learning or boning up on a foreign language when you receive the newsletter. (Although many foreign clubs do have an English-language version of their publications.)

Start Your Own Fan Club

Here are some ideas to get you thinking about how to go about forming your own club. If you want to go official—and there are tons of advantages—write to:
Patsy Anderson, Fan Relations Manager
Graceland
P.O. Box 16508
Memphis, Tennessee 38186

Choose a Fan Club Name

Select a name that reflects your area of interest or expertise in Elvis like "Rockabilly Rebels for Elvis," "Bikers for Elvis," or "Elvis Trivia Whizzes Fan Club."

Compose a Fan Club Mission Statement

Decide on a mission that your club is committed to and a motto that defines your goals.

Pick a Fan Club Song

There are around 1,000 Elvis songs to choose from so this could be endlessly debated among your club members. Put it to the vote.

Choose a Fan Club Dance

Some clubs have created special dances to specific Elvis songs like a line dance to "The Yellow Rose of Texas" or a rolling conga line to "Frankfurt Special" or a hand waving shuffle to "I Can Help." Choose a song and choreograph your own moves. Of course, once you do, it'll be nice to hold regular club dances.

Decide on a Fan Club Charity

Many clubs choose a charity that Elvis was involved in. Others choose a cause that they feel strongly about. You don't need to limit your giving only to Memphis-based charities. It's also good to choose a local charity wherever you live so the positive legacy of Elvis is spread everywhere.

"The club I belong to—the Elvis Presley Fan Club of Sri Lanka (Ceylon)—was organized by Mr. Jayaratne Perera in the early 1960s. My parents joined me to the club when I was twelve years old in 1967. I've been an active member since then. I got to know Elvis through my English tutor Mr. Regie Abeysinghe when I was eight. My first Elvis song was 'She's Not You' but my favorite one is 'Sylvia.' To keeping the memory of Elvis alive I've devoted most of my time that related to Elvis Presley matters with love and respect."
—Sylvia Perera

Create a Fan Club Newsletter

Here are some ides on what to include:

Profiles of members or a fan-of-the-month series

Names of new members

List of people who are looking for pen pals

List of members who are ill or bereaved and addresses where goodwill messages can be sent

Fund-raising announcements

Photos of club outings and fund-raisers

Thank you letters from charities your club has donated to

Elvis anniversaries for the time period the newsletter covers

Elvis in the media section, where people send in anything they've seen having to do with Elvis

Stories from fans who saw Elvis in concert or met him

Announcements and reviews of the latest CDs, videos, and books

Elvis-related trivia, contests, puzzles, and quizzes

Pictures of members' Elvis rooms, shrines, or artwork

Poems written by members

Upcoming television schedule of Elvis movies

Barter, swap, and sales corner

Classified ads

Offer free memberships for people who bring in other members.

Offer a Membership Kit Upon Joining

Most clubs offer a little something to new members such as a membership card, Elvis stationery, Elvis photos, club button, refrigerator magnets, and photocopied information about Elvis Presley's life and history.

Create a Fan Club Web Site

Web sites are a great way to make connections with other Elvis fans. They can be simple or elaborate affairs. If no one in your club has the necessary computer skills, your local internet access provider should be able to help.

Create Your Fan Club Logo

Design a logo to identify your club. Put the logo and club motto on T-shirts or jackets. You might give them away as promotional items for your club or sell them to your members. When choosing material, keep the heat of a Memphis August in mind. Come out with a new article every so often.

Recruit New Members

Use your web site to recruit new members. Post a message in all the Elvis chat rooms. Take out an ad in your local paper. Create flyers and maybe have an Elvis impersonator pass them out. Get media coverage of fan events. Give a free one-year membership to anyone who brings in other new members. Have family discounts. Award honorary memberships to people who might be goodwill ambassadors for your club.

Try Different Fan Club Activities
Have regular club meetings.
Celebrate Elvis "holidays."
Have fan club movie nights.
Take a fan club road trip.
Organize an impersonator contest.
Go Christmas caroling as a fan club.
Do volunteer work as a club.
Organize regular sock hops.
Create and maintain a cool club web site.
Invite guest speakers to address your club.
Hold Elvis memorabilia swap meets.

Host a Fund-raising Event
Hold auctions and auction off Elvis stuff.
Have garage, lawn, or stoop sales. Let people know that you're raising money for an Elvis-related charity.
Play Elvis Bingo. Fill each box on the bingo grid with the name of an Elvis song instead of letters. Shout out "Elvis" when you win!
Conduct raffles. Use an Elvis-related grand prize like an old Cadillac or a trip to Graceland. Other prizes could be Elvis crafts made by club members or things donated by local businesses.
Hold fund-raising dinners. Serve Elvis' favorite foods.

Raise Money to Send a Fan to Graceland
Give the gift of Graceland to an Elvis fan who can't afford to make the pilgrimage.

Sponsor an International Member Fund
The We Remember Elvis Fan Club raises money to enroll Elvis fans from Eastern Block countries who are unable to afford fan club dues. You might want to start up your own fund to sponsor members for your club or participate in this one:

We Remember Elvis Fan Club
Attn: Priscilla Parker
1215 Tennessee Avenue
Pittsburgh, Pennsylvania 15216-2511
http://ourworld.compuserve.com/homepages/elvis/we.htm

Join with Other Fan Clubs for Charity Fund-Raising

Several fan clubs sometimes join together to combine forces for more challenging charity events that require more people and logistical support. There's strength in numbers.

Attend Fan Events

Circle of Memories
The Elvis Friends-Hollywood Elvis Presley Fan Club hosts a weekend every spring at the "Honeymoon Hideaway," the Ladera Circle, Palm Springs house where Elvis and Priscilla spent their honeymoon after their May 1, 1967, nuptials. For more information, contact:
Bobbie Cunningham
12536 Burbank Boulevard #3
North Hollywood, California 91607
E-mail: efh4elvis@aol.com
http://www.members.aol.com/efh4elvis
The We Remember Elvis Fan Club
This club has a yearly fan convention in Pittsburgh during late April. You may find out more about their event from:
Priscilla Parker
1215 Tennessee Avenue
Pittsburgh, Pennsylvania 15216-2511
http://ourworld.compuserve.com/homepages/elvis/we.htm

The Jailhouse Rockers of California
This club sponsors several events throughout the year. If you are going to be in California, write ahead and see what they have going on. You may contact them at:
Jailhouse Rockers
P.O. Box 16423
Irvine, California 92623-6423
E-mail: Jhrocepfc@aol.com

Portage, Indiana FANtasy Fest
Elvis Fans from Hoosierland hosts a convention every year in the fall. There's a concert, sock hop, buffet meals, Elvis games, auctions, memorabilia dealers, and much more. For more information contact:

Elvis FANtasy Fest
P.O. Box 151
Carmel, Indiana 46032
(800) 283-8687
http://www.porter.CO.Porter.IN.US/

The Annual Elvis Fest, Jamestown, New York
Sponsored by Weisbrod & Son Promotions and Sterling: A Tribute to Elvis Fan
Club, Elvis Fest is held in conjunction with Jamestown. Proceeds go to charity.
More information on this event can be found through:
Dale Weisbrod
1070 Hagerdon Hill Road
Gerry, New York 14740
(716) 287-2134
E-mail: memorylane@madbbs.com
http://www.madbbs.com/~memorylane
http://members.xoom.com/darod/sterling/fest.htm
http://www.madbbs.com/~kado/fest.htm

The Elvis fan clubs throughout Great Britian are incredibly organized, active, and
damn fun too. They have tons of events all year, so if you're going to be there
on business or vacation, do everything you can to find out what's going on at
that time. Here are some contacts in different parts of England there who'll know.

Official Elvis Presley Fan Club of Great Britain
    P.O. Box 4, Leicester LE3 5HY, England
Memphis Mafia Fan Club, Edinburgh Branch of OEPFC
    P.O. Box 710 NWDO, Edinburgh EH4 Scotland
    http://dialspace.dial.pipex.com/memphis.mafia
    E-mail: rcs40@dial.pipex.com
Essential Elvis (UK)
    Andrew Hearn, 62 Shandon Road, Worthing, Sussex BN14 9DX Great Britain
    Terry Bellis, c/o 43 Brownlow Road, New Ferry, Wirral L62 1AU, Great Britain
Elvis Is King Fan Club
    David Trotter, 59 Cambridge Road, New Silksworth, Sunderland SR3 2DQ England
Elvis Presley Fan Club (Northampton Branch)
    7 Faraday Close, Northampton NN5 4AE England
Elvis 2001 Fan Club
    Michelle Rivers, 11, Bondfield Close, Southborough Tunbridge Wells, Kent TN4
    0BF England
    E-mail: Elvisa2001@netscape.net

Elvis Collectors Fair
    For further information, contact:
    OEPFC Herts Branch, 6 Kemps Drive, Northwood, Middlesex HA6 1UA, England

Collingwood, Canada
    For further information, contact:
    Kathy DeNike, Collingwood Rocks with Elvis Fan Club
    (705) 445-9477
    E-mail: fanclub@collingwood.net
Canadian National Elvis Tribute and Convention Orillia
    Orillia, Canada Chamber of Commerce
    (705) 326-4424
    E-mail:orilinfo@orillia.com
    http://www.orillia.com
E. P. Continentals of Florida Annual Elvis Fest
    This event is usually held in February in Orlando.
    Contact:
    Sue Manusazak
    P.O. Box 568082
    Orlando, Florida 32856
    (407) 381-3739 or (407) 889-3696
    Fax: (407) 889-0300
    E-mail: manuszaksb@juno.com
    http://www.jordanselvisworld.simplenet.com/Epcont.htm

Offer Free Memberships in Your Club

Try to offer a free membership from time to time to someone who can't afford it or, if your club has a newsletter, to someone who lives abroad so they can keep in touch with the goings-on in the fan scene in the States.

Find Elvis Pen Pals

Fan club newsletters often feature a section of addresses of fans looking for Elvis pen pals. The magazine *Elvis International Forum* also publishes a list of Elvis pen pals in every issue.

Choose an Official Fan Club Tribute Artist

Although some fans see the existence of Elvis impersonators as an insult to Elvis and want no part of them, some clubs embrace them. A talented and sincere Elvis impersonator can make fan gatherings a lot of fun and also help a club in fund-raising events.

Lobby for a National Elvis Presley Day

"During his all too brief lifetime, Elvis Presley touched the lives and hearts of countless people all over the world. Not only through his musical talents, but also through his concern and compassion for his fellow man—having been a generous and frequent contributor to many unfortunate citizens and numerous charitable organizations. I urge you to recognize the major impact Elvis Presley made on the entire world through his music and his message of faith, hope, and charity."

So goes one part of the list of reasons why Elvis should have a national holiday, to be sent to your representatives in Washington. One fan club is at the fore of this effort: The Presley-ites. You can contact them at:
Nationwide Campaign for Elvis Presley Day
6010 18 Street
Zephyrhills, Florida 33540
(813) 788-9133

Campaign for Elvis to Be Awarded the Presidential Medal of Freedom

The Oklahoma Fans for Elvis are conducting a campaign for Elvis to be named for the prestigious medal. To participate, contact:
Bill and Judy Wilson
Oklahoma Fans for Elvis
421 West 6 Street
Bristow, Oklahoma 74010

Adopt a Child as a Fan Club

Many charities have a program where, for a very small monthly amount, you can sponsor a child in an underprivileged part of the world. It is possible to write to the child and send them extra, small gifts for birthdays and at Christmastime. This would be a great activity for a fan club and would have a real impact on a real child's life that you'll be able to see. It is a good opportunity to introduce following Elvis' example as the motivation for charity.
Christian Children's Fund
2821 Emerywood Parkway
Richmond, Virginia 23294
(800) 394-0707
(800) 776-6767

Feed the Children
As well as child sponsorship, this international nonprofit Christian organization provides food, clothing, educational supplies, medical equipment, and other necessities to needy individuals.

333 North Meridian Avenue
Oklahoma City, Oklahoma 73107-6568
(800) 627-4556
(405) 942-0228
Fax: (405) 945-4177
E-mail: ftc@feedthechildren.org
http://www.feedthechildren.org

Send a Wreath to Graceland from Your Fan Club

Fan clubs arrange to have wreaths delivered to Graceland monthly or at Elvis' birthday and during Tribute Week. Flowers are beautifully displayed around and in the
Meditation Garden. Some local Memphis florists make extraordinary floral creations.
Flowers by Sandy
2015 Union Avenue
Memphis, Tennessee 38104
(901) 276-4495

ELVIS AND CHARITY

Elvis Presley is known for his many talents and accomplishments—he was a prolific recording artist, a successful movie star, a charismatic stage performer. But one of his most enduring and endearing qualities was his generosity and commitment to charity. Giving spontaneously was very much in Elvis' nature. Even as a child whose family was too poor to provide him with many material things, he shared and gave away his own toys to other kids. As a teenager, Elvis saved his earnings from his job as a movie usher to buy a print of Jesus for his parents. He said it was the favorite gift he ever gave anybody. Elvis took great pleasure in seeing the look on people's faces when he gave them a "happy," which was his nickname for a gift. His heartfelt benevolence is part of the reason he's held in such high esteem by his fans. There's no way to know for sure, but it's been estimated that he made approximately $4 billion during his career and gave half of it away. Elvis was more than an entertainer, he was, and continues to be, an inspiration for people to remember those less fortunate than themselves.

Although Elvis became fabulously wealthy, he seemed never to forget what it meant to be poor. He spent the first few weeks of his life in the charity ward of a hospital and it may be based in this sense of vulnerability that he frequently donated to various

Courtesy of Butterfield & Butterfield

The print of Jesus that Elvis bought for his parents when he was 15 years old

Commercial Appeal

Elvis presenting checks totaling $55,000 to Memphis charities on December 17, 1963

medical charities. When he first achieved his extraordinary level of fame, he used it to help raise money and awareness for many causes. He lent his name and image to the American Cancer Society and the American Library Association, among others. He posed for photos while giving blood and getting vaccines. He arranged for the thousands of teddy bears that fans sent him to be distributed to children in hospitals.

One of the reasons Elvis so loved the holidays was because they are the season of giving. In 1961, he started a Christmas tradition of distributing checks to more than 50 charitable organizations, donating more than $100,000 each year. He gave cash and donated many personal items to be auctioned off for charity. In 1964, Elvis purchased the FDR presidential yacht, the *Potomac*, and donated it to St. Jude Children's Research Hospital, which in turn sold it for $55,000. One of his Rolls Royces was auctioned off in 1968 to raise money for a charity that aided mentally retarded children. Sometimes, with his permission, even the bed linens and towels from the hotel rooms he stayed at while on tour were auctioned for charities. (Although we're guessing that many other times, without his permission, his linens were gathered up by others and sold for many reasons other than to give money to charity.)

Although celebrities often make contributions to good causes for the sheen it adds to their image, Elvis frequently gave anonymously. There are countless stories that came to light only after Elvis' death that recount his merciful role to some unfortunate person he didn't know. The best book on this subject, *The Best of Elvis: Recollections of a Great Humanitarian* by Cindy Hazen and Mike Freeman, recalls so many wonderful aspects of Elvis and tells so many touching stories, you will certainly feel like you know him more deeply after reading it. Often upon reading about someone's declining circumstances in the newspaper, Elvis would dispatch one of his men with a check to try to help. He paid off people's debts and mortgages. One time he bought, and personally delivered, a state-of-the-art wheelchair to an old woman who couldn't afford to replace the wheelchair that was stolen from her. We can never really know the full extent of Elvis' charity.

Elvis was even generous to the wealthy. In 1973 he gave his good friend Muhammad Ali an elaborate robe with "The People's Champion" emblazoned on

Elvis presenting a check to McComb, Mississippi, Mayor Johnny Thompson to aid tornado victims

From the collection of Bob Klein

the back. He gave Sammy Davis, Jr., a black sapphire ring worth tens of thousands of dollars. He once said, "Nobody ever thinks to give a rich man a gift."

Among Elvis' most memorable performances were the many benefit concerts he gave throughout his career. In 1956 and 1957 Elvis performed at the Tupelo Fairgrounds in his hometown to raise money for the Elvis Presley Youth Foundation there. On March 25, 1961, Elvis performed a benefit concert at Bloch Arena in Hawaii that raised $65,000 toward the building of the USS *Arizona* Memorial. The famous "Aloha from Hawaii" concert that was watched by around half the world's population in 1973 was a benefit concert that raised more than $75,000 for the Kuiokalani Lee Cancer Fund. Elvis, who as a small child survived a killer tornado that ripped through Tupelo, gave a concert in Jackson, Mississippi, in 1975, that raised more than $100,000 for tornado victims in his home state. A unique feature of all Elvis' benefit concerts was the Colonel's policy that everyone had to buy a ticket, including Elvis and the Colonel. The proceeds from the sale of souvenirs at his concerts often went directly to charity.

For most fans who attended an Elvis concert, the memories of that experience will forever be a treasure. Some lucky fans, however, left the concert hall with a different kind of treasure. At a concert in Asheville, North Carolina, in 1975, Elvis gave out a king's ransom worth of jewelry to audience members. At another concert that year, Elvis took the diamond medallion cross that he wore around his neck and gave it to a five-year-old girl in the audience who reminded him of Lisa Marie. Elvis gave away so much jewelry, he traveled with his own personal jeweler, Lowell Hayes, who carried a portable jewelry mini-mart with him. Elvis bought close to $700,000 worth of jewelry from Hayes during the last five years of his life, most of which he gave away.

Perhaps the major beneficiaries of Elvis' largesse were the friends and family with whom he shared his life. Elvis' infamous entourage, the Memphis Mafia, received lavish gifts of cars, jewelry, houses, vacations, cash bonuses, weddings, and even surgery. Elvis paid for a nose job for George Klein, an intestinal bypass for Lamar Fike, a kidney transplant for his friend and producer Felton Jarvis, even

Elvis Presley Foundation of New York
Fan Club president Joanne Digilio
presenting a check to Le Bonheur
Hospital at the Fan Club Presidents'
Luncheon in Memphis, January 1999

a breast augmentation operation for one of the Mafia wives (upon her husband's request).

Elvis' favorite gift was also one of his own favorite things to buy for himself—a shiny new set of wheels. Elvis and his friends would often visit a car dealership and buy out the entire stock. He didn't just buy cars for his friends, he would buy cars for perfect strangers. On one car-buying spree in Memphis during July 1975, Elvis bought and gave away 13 Cadillacs. When he noticed bank teller Mennie Person admiring his limousine parked in front of the dealership, he bought her a Caddy also and even gave her a check to buy some clothes to go with the car. While vacationing in Colorado, he decided to buy a fleet of cars for some of his police buddies and their wives. Don Kinney, a local DJ, heard about Elvis' splurges and jokingly announced over the airwaves that if Elvis was listening, he wanted a car too. The next day he was the proud owner of a Cadillac Seville compliments of the King. Elvis gave away so many cars that it's become a pop culture cliché. In the 1999 film *Father's Day*, Billy Crystal's character gives Robin Williams's the keys to his car, to which Williams quips, "How *Elvis* of you."

Amazingly, Elvis' spirit of generosity continues to be carried on today. Inspired by Elvis' example, many of his fans have made charity work their raison d'être. Many fan club events are fund-raisers for one cause or another. Every year, especially during Tribute Week, fans from all over the world make donations to the charities Elvis supported. At

The wall of plaques commemorating
contributions made in Elvis' name at
the Elvis Presley Trauma Center

Teddy bears collected for children at the Scottish Rite Hospital

the Elvis Presley Trauma Center in Memphis, a wall is covered with plaques recognizing the philanthropic activities done in his honor by Elvis fan clubs. Patsy Anderson, head of fan relations at EPE, estimates that Elvis fan clubs have generated many millions of dollars to Memphis charities alone since his death. EPE also follows the fans' lead in doing good deeds in Elvis' name. EPE formed The Elvis Presley Charitable Foundation to raise money for scholarship funds and other philanthropic pursuits. In the fall of 1999 EPE, in conjunction with Guernsey's Auction House, conducted an auction of Elvis memorabilia at the MGM Grand Hotel in Las Vegas to raise money to establish a building fund for Presley Place, a transitional housing development that will provide homeless families with up to one year of rent-free housing, child care, and job training. This is a particularly appropriate cause in that Elvis and his family benefited from subsidized housing when they lived at Lauderdale Courts during most of Elvis' high school days in Memphis.

Doing something charitable in honor of Elvis is the perfect way to carry on his humanitarian efforts and protect his legacy. Future generations will not only never forget Elvis' music, but because of the efforts of his fans they'll never forget his tender and kind heart.

ESSENTIAL ELVISOLOGY

Some of the Charities Elvis Contributed To
American Cancer Society
Elvis Presley Youth Center of Tupelo
Arthritis Foundation

Father Flanagan's Boys Town of Nebraska
Braille Institute of America
Foundation for the Junior Blind
Fraternal Order of Police
Goodwill Industries
Junior League
Kidney Foundation
Miles-O-Dimes
Muscular Dystrophy
Oncological Research Foundation
Salvation Army
United Cerebral Palsy
Motion Picture Relief Fund
Bethany Maternity Home
Kui Lee Cancer Fund
St. Jude Children's Research Hospital
Le Bonheur Children's Medical Center
March of Dimes
YMCA

YOUR ELVIS EDUCATION

Books
The Best of Elvis: Recollections of a Great Humanitarian
   Cindy Hazen and Mike Freeman
I Called Him Babe
   Marian Cocke
Elvis: Unknown Stories Behind the Legend
   Jim Curtin
Elvis: A 30-Year Chronicle: Columns, Stories, Articles & Features Exactly as Originally Reported 1954–1983
   Bill E. Burk
Wings of Compassion
   compiled by Evelyn Slayman and the Elvis Presley TLC Fan Club
   May be ordered by contacting: Wings of Compassion, P.O. Box 3598, Cerritos, California 90703-3598.
   E-Mail: wingsofcompassion@mail.usa.com
   http://fly.to/wingsofcompassion

Videos
This Is Elvis
"Elvis: Aloha from Hawaii"

Web Sites
http://www.the-med.com/medfoundation.html
  EP Memorial Trauma Center, Memphis
http://www.netaid.org
  Charity info web site

THE ELVIS AND YOU EXPERIENCE

Give and Ye Shall Receive
When you are generous you receive good karma and personal satisfaction in return. Elvis knew this. It's good for the soul to give, but in some cases it can have actual health benefits also. A recent study demonstrated that donating a pint of blood every three years dramatically decreases the chances of heart attack or stroke.

Contribute to the Charities Sponsored by EPE
EPE sponsors and underwrites several charitable causes under the auspices of the Elvis Presley Charitable Foundation. Their most recent venture is Presley Place. Presley Place will provide 10 to 12 residential units in Memphis for homeless families, up to one year of rent-free housing, child day-care, job training and counseling, financial guidance, and other help they need to break the cycle of poverty and gain self-esteem. Contact Graceland for donation information.

How to Give Stuff Away, the Elvis Way
Elvis gave very necessary *and* very frivolous kinds of gifts. Just be sure that what you give is unexpected and a complete surprise to the recipient. Often, Elvis would be thorough (for instance by taking care of the potential taxes on an expensive gift).

Pay Someone Else's Bill Unexpectedly
Pay a mortgage payment, a utility bill, a telephone bill, something out of the ordinary. You can say that Elvis took care of it.

Sponsor a Local Little League Team
Give them an Elvis-related name like the "Presley Punters," or the "TCB Tigers." Play Elvis music before games.

Donate Wheelchairs

Even better than giving away Cadillacs. Find a nursing home that will accept these donations. Look in your local directory for a wheelchair company nearby. Here are some web sites for wheelchair information.
http://www.the-outlet.com
http://seat.net/healthcare/wheechairs/
  wheelchair.htm

Attend Elvis Impersonator Benefits

Lots of impersonators follow in the King's worthy footsteps by participating in charity events, often performing for free.

Establish an Elvis Presley Scholarship at a Local School

This can be a scholarship for a musically gifted student or any trait that you feel is important to nurture. Maybe at your own alma mater.

> "First I found [Elvis] to be a gentleman and then a gentle man. I found he could be sensitive to small issues. For someone of his stature there is very little for him to notice, ya know? He's so insulated by the people who surround him and by his own popularity. And yet Elvis will still find little things. He'll take the time to be gentle with people."
> —Bill Bixby, in *Elvis: A Biography* by Jerry Hopkins

Give the Gift of Time

Volunteer your time to a worthy cause. Visit nursing homes or foundling hospitals and conduct an Elvis sing-along.

Be a Big Brother or Big Sister

This is a very rewarding and valuable charitable act. It has been amply proven to help the child in numerous ways toward a more successful and happier life. You may,
of course, expose the kid to some Elvis music while you're at it.
Big Brothers and Sisters of America
(215) 567-7000
http://www.bbbsa.org

Sponsor a Child

These are a few of the programs through which you can sponsor a child for a fixed fee every month. This is also an excellent project for a fan club.
Feed the Children
P.O. Box 36
Oklahoma City, Oklahoma 73101-0036

(800) 627-4556
(405) 942-0228
Fax (405) 945-4198
http://www.feedthechildren.org/html/spon.html

The Salvation Army Child Sponsorship Program
For more than 20 years, the Child Sponsorship Program of the Salvation Army
has benefited thousands of children in 103 countries. Call the office nearest you.
Southern Territory: Atlanta, Georgia (404) 728-1314
E-mail: SWWHITE@JUNO.COM
Eastern Territory: West Nyack, New York (914) 620-7237
E-mail: CLSCHOCH@AOL.COM
Central Territory: Des Plaines, Illinois (847) 294-2065
E-mail: OVERSEASBUREAU@USC.SALVATIONARMY.ORG
Western Territory: Rancho Palos Verdes, California (310) 534-6006
E-mail: OHOHRALPH@AOL.COM
http://www.iserv.net/salvarmy/sponsor.htm

Careforce International
Make a difference in the lives of children in need around the world.
(905) 639-8525
Fax: (905) 639-8424
Email: info@careforceinternational.org
http://www.careforceinternational.org/index.html

Child Sponsorship Programs
It is estimated that more than one million Americans currently participate in U.S.
child sponsorship programs that help children around the world. For information:
http://www.interaction.org/development/chsponsr.html

Help Restore the USS *Arizona* Site Plaque
When Elvis heard that there was difficulty raising enough money to erect a memo-
rial for the USS *Arizona*, he undertook it as his cause. In a 1961 benefit concert he
gave in Hawaii, he raised awareness for the cause and $62,000 to kick off the fund-
raising campaign. When the Parks Department took over the management of the
memorial, they removed the plaque about Elvis' contribution. Write to the Parks
Department and request they restore the proclamation and plaque.
Head of Park Service
U.S. Department of the Interior
National Park Service
P.O. Box 37127
Washington, DC 20013-7127

Attend Marian Cocke's Annual Elvis Presley Memorial Charity Dinner

Every year Elvis' friend and nurse, Marian Cocke, hosts a charity dinner during Tribute Week in Memphis. Proceeds from tickets and an auction go to charity. There are always many Elvis intimates in attendance and it is a beautiful evening. For information, contact:
Marian Cocke
784 Pecan Garden Circle
East Memphis, Tennessee 38122
(901) 324-9612.

Donate a Bear to the Teddy Bear Caravan

Every year the Teddy Bear Caravan visits the children at the Scottish Rite Hospital at Christmastime and distributes gifts of teddy bears from Elvis fans. Peggy Sue has been collecting dolls for years and welcomes any contributions for the effort. Tie a picture of Elvis along with your name and address (if you wish) around the neck of a teddy bear and send it to:
Peggy Sue Sosebee
2763 Winding Lane NE
Atlanta, Georgia 30319

Dedicate a Pew or Bench in Elvis' Name at Your Place of Worship

Elvis bought a church pew with his and his cook's Mary Jenkins names on it for her church. This would be a beautiful and lasting honor to bestow.

Establish an Elvis Presley Fellowship at a Local Hospital

Clubs like the We Remember Elvis Fan Club in Pittsburgh have created visiting fellowships at local hospitals. In 1999, they sponsored 15 doctors, nurses, and other medical personnel to study at the Western Pennsylvania Hospital's Burn Unit.

Support the Kind of Charities Elvis Might Have Donated To

There are many extremely worthy charities. We have listed just a handful, many that Elvis gave to and some that were chosen on the basis of their missions. All are very much in the spirit of the charities Elvis was interested in. The National Charities Information Bureau can advise you on the legalities of donating and direct you to the contact information for any charity you're interested in. Call them at (212) 929-6300 or find them on the internet at http://www.give.org. Volunteers of America is another clearinghouse for volunteering information. Call them at (800) 899-0089, (212) 873-2600, or find them at their web site http://www.voa.org.

Elvis Presley Memorial Trauma Center/
Regional Medical Center at Memphis
  The MED Foundation
  877 Jefferson Avenue
  Memphis, Tennessee 38103
  (901) 545-8372
  (901) 545-6787
  E-mail: mrubenstein@med1.the-med.org
Elvis Presley Endowed Scholarship Fund
  In 1979 the University of Memphis cre-
  ated a Distinguished Achievement
  Award in the Creative and Performing
  Arts in memory of Elvis Presley for
  Mid-South artists whose work has
  resulted in national and international
  recognition and influence. It's been
  awarded to Sam Phillips and J. D.
  Sumner among many others. EPE has
  endowed this scholarship fund in
  recognition of their appreciation to the
  university.College of Communication
  and Fine Arts
  University of Memphis
  Campus Box 526546
  Memphis, Tennessee 38152-6546
American Cancer Society
  Write or call for local donation guide-
  lines and information.
  4465 East Genesee Street #253
  Dewitt, New York 13214-2242
  (800) 227-2345
Salvation Army
  (800) SALARMY
  http:www.salvationarmyusa.org
Bethany Maternity Home
  901 Chelsea Avenue
  Memphis, Tennessee 38107
  (901) 525-1837
St. Jude Children's Research Hospital
  P.O. Box 50
  Memphis, Tennessee 38101-9929

  (901) 522-0300
  (800) 822-6344
  http://www.stjude.org
Alive Hospice Foundation
  This was the charity chosen by J. D.
  Sumner's family for people who
  wanted to send a donation instead of
  flowers to his funeral.
  1718 Patterson Street
  Nashville, Tennessee 37203
  (615) 327-1085
American Heart Association
  Attn: Contributions, National Center
  7272 Greenville Avenue
  Dallas, Texas 75231-4596
  (800) 242-8721
  http://www.americanheart.org
The Catalog for Giving
  This catalog describes more than 14
  different inner-city charity projects
  that need funding.
  250 West 57 Street
  New York, New York 10107
  (800) 936-4483
  (212) 765-8212
  Fax: (212) 765-8190
  E-mail: webmaster@
  catalogforgiving.org
  http://www.catalogforgiving.org
Covenant House
  346 West 17 Street
  New York, New York 10011
  (800) 388-3888
Eastern Paralyzed Veterans
Association
  7 Mill Brook Road
  Wilton, New Hampshire 03086
Heart and Stroke Foundation of Canada
  222 Queen Street, Suite 1402
  Ottawa, Ontario K1P 5V9 Canada
  (613) 569-4361

Fax: (613) 569-3278
http://www.hsf.ca/main_e.htm
Humes High School Area Beautification
Program
Elvis Presley International Fan Club
Attn: Georgia King
754 Saffarans Street
Memphis, Tennessee 38107
Le Bonheur Children's Medical Center
50 North Dunlap
Memphis, Tennessee 38103
(901) 572-3000
Leukemia Society of America
600 Third Avenue
New York, New York 10016
(800) 955-4572
Locks of Love
Locks of Love provides quality hair
prosthetics for children under the
age of 18 who have developed long-
term medical hair loss due to serious
illness.
2400 E. Las Olas Boulevard, Suite 399
Ft. Lauderdale, Florida 33301
(888) 896-1588
Fax: (954) 523-8634
http://www.locksoflove.com/

Rock and Roll Hall of Fame and Museum
This hall of fame had their first exhibition of a single artist devoted to
Elvis. They are preserving the legacy
of rock and roll for future generations.
One Key Plaza
Cleveland, Ohio 44144
(800) 349-ROCK
http://www.rockhall.com
Shoes That Fit
Contact this organization to learn
how you can start a chapter of this
program in your community to provide shoes and clothing for underprivileged kids.
112 Harvard Street, Suite 43
Claremont, California 91711
http://www.shoesthatfit.org
Special Olympics
(202) 628-3630
http://www.specialolympicsusa.org
St. Joseph Hospital
Gladys worked as a nurse's aide at
St. Joseph's during the early 1950s.
220 Overton Avenue
Memphis, Tennessee 38105
(901) 577-2700

COLLECTING ELVIS

In 1956 it wasn't possible to buy a pair of Bing Crosby sneakers, Perry Como jeans, or Frank Sinatra coffee mugs. However you could buy Elvis Presley costume jewelry, board games, cosmetics, hats, clothes, gloves, shoes, stationary, pencils, dolls, candy and gum, luggage, perfume, guitars, record players, bookends, wallets, purses, watches, and a load of other things that had Elvis' name and image affixed to them. These days we accept the merchandising of a celebrity as standard practice, but Elvis was the first musical artist to be mass marketed in the modern sense.

No matter what you think of Colonel Parker, Elvis' ethically challenged manager, the man had a knack for making money, and make money he did. During 1956, while just about every teenager in America was listening to "Heartbreak Hotel," the number-one hit in the country, Parker created Elvis Presley Enterprises to be the merchandising branch of the emerging Presley empire. To help sell Elvis to the masses, he recruited Hank Saperstein, the California merchandiser responsible for marketing the then-popular television shows the *Lone Ranger*, *Lassie*, and *Davy Crockett*. Elvis Presley Enterprises' first offering, an Elvis charm bracelet, sold

From the collection of Bob Klein

Merchandiser Hank Saperstein shows Elvis some of the products that would soon be selling in the millions

nearly 400,000 units in a single month. By the end of 1956 EPE had grossed an esti-mated $22 million and, in what would be the model for most future transactions, Parker and Saperstein received the greater bulk of the profits.

In the early days of Elvis' fame, no one had any idea they were acquiring a piece of history when they bought that Hound Dog orange lipstick. They were just making a connection with their idol. But collecting Elvis memora-bilia was not only emotionally rewarding then, it could be potentially lucra-tive now—that is, if an Elvis fan were willing to part with any of it. A $3.98 Elvis doll from 1956 is worth thousands; a 5¢ "I Love Elvis" button can bring more than $100; and a $2.98 Elvis Presley felt skirt fetches more than more than $1,000 these days. Dealers may buy and sell Elvis memorabilia to make a profit, but some of these items, once obtained by a true fan, rarely change hands. They become a permanent part of a collection not to be parted with until extremely hard times or death. This tends to only increase their rarity and value.

Fueled by the unquenchable thirst of his fans for all things Elvis and the appar-ently hypnotic appeal of Elvis' face affixed to almost anything, there's far more memorabilia related to the King than to any other pop star in history. In addition to the EPE merchandise of the fifties, there's a huge amount of RCA marketing material, advertising, and promotional items related to Elvis' films, mementos from the Vegas and touring years, and scores of books and publications.

August 1977 started another era in Elvis collecting. Two days after Elvis' death, Colonel Parker, in a crassly opportunistic maneuver, chose this moment to pres-sure a vulnerable Vernon Presley into signing over to Factors Etc. Inc. global rights to merchandise Elvis-related products. Once again the Colonel was to profit vastly more than anyone, even Elvis' heirs and estate. At the same time, a billion dollar industry was spawned, one that not even Colonel Parker could exercise control over. There was an explosion of merchandise, both sanctioned and bootleg, much of it ill conceived and poorly made. Some of these unautho-rized products, objectionable things like vials of so-called Elvis sweat, belittled Elvis and helped to fuel the perception that his fans would slavishly buy absolutely anything related to the King. This tastelessness helped

John O'Hara

Brian Allward of King Collectibles selling Elvis memorabilia at a fan convention in Memphis

Courtesy of Butterfield & Butterfield

forge an unflattering impression of Elvis and the fan community that lingers to this day.

In July 1981 a court decision ruled that Factors Etc. Inc. had no rights to merchandise the Presley name and Elvis Presley Enterprises, under the guidance of Priscilla Presley and businessman Jack Soden, once again retained those legal rights. In an effort to undo the damage done to the image of Elvis and his fans, they are attempting to exert strict control over the quality of all Elvis memorabilia and any use of Elvis' name or image.

Graceland's catalogs come out five times a year and offer a wide array of Elvis stuff. The expected things like mugs, T-shirts, mouse pads, stationery, umbrellas, bookends, and baseball caps are listed side-by-side with the more far-fetched items like trailer-hitch plugs, gold lamé doorstops, and wind chimes. If fans have any complaint now, it's that Graceland exerts too much control—sometimes stifling the creativity of suppliers seeking licenses to sell more interesting Elvis items.

To Elvis fans, the most coveted type of memorabilia, and understandably the most expensive, is an item that was used, owned, or given as a gift by Elvis. There is a finite amount of actual clothing, jewelry, cars, furniture, and other artifacts from his too-short life. The value of these relics is determined by what someone is willing to pay for them; since these are the most emotionally satisfy-

Megan Murphy

ing, they tend to demand exorbitant prices that only the wealthiest Elvis fan can afford. Most often sold at highly publicized auctions that drive the price up even higher, they're a measure not only of the level of the buyer's devotion but the size of their bank account. Paul McCartney owns the stand-up bass that Bill Black used to lay down the beat

Some of Elvis' furnishings sold at the 1999 Guernsey's auction in Las Vegas

during the Sun Sessions. The Martin D-18 guitar that Elvis played during those same recordings fetched $152,000 at Christie's Auction House in 1993. At an auction conducted by Butterfield & Butterfield in 1994, the actor John Corbett spent $41,400 on Elvis' American Express card and later that same day spent $68,500 on the original physician's record of Elvis' birth. In that same auction, a Pennsylvania businessman paid $321,500 for Elvis' 1969 Mercedes Benz Pullman limousine. The frenzy for collecting a piece of Elvis at times goes way beyond the usual bounds—both of privacy and decency. One of the more bizarre items to be offered for sale was what claimed to be the electrocardiogram paddles used to attempt to revive Elvis at Baptist Memorial Hospital. Elvis and Priscilla's marriage termination and property settlement agreements were offered in magazine ads selling for around $5,500 each.

Of course, almost everyone's Elvis collection starts with the same thing: his music. That first Elvis record, tape, or CD that we purchased was usually our introduction to collecting Elvis. Some people collect Elvis recordings because they just want to hear as much of his music as possible. Elvis had a prolific output and left a spectacular legacy of recordings, both official releases and bootlegs, and collecting it all is an entertaining challenge. Some collectors of Elvis vinyl and 45s treat their collections like the important cultural artifacts that they are. They wouldn't dream of subjecting one of these precious objects to the ravages of a phonograph needle. An original pressing of one of the five Elvis recordings on the Sun Records label in mint condition can be worth thousands of dollars. Even more precious are the demos and discarded acetates from Elvis' many recording sessions.

But short of those, virtually all the music found on the old records can now be found on CD and played to one's heart's content.

Elvis himself was a collector. His passion for acquiring police badges and guns went way beyond any practical need for security to the sheer pleasure of amassing things he was fascinated with. Elvis enjoyed the hunt for the rare item and his fans don't need any encouragement to follow his example. When Elvis died, fans kept $600,000 worth of unused tickets from

Elvis' terry cloth floppy hat

Elvis impersonator perusing collectibles at a Las Vegas fan convention in the Continental Hotel

John O'Hara

his upcoming concert tour. Elvis memorabilia is a part of American history, the ultimate significance of which will be determined by future generations. In the meantime, you might just want a mug with Elvis' picture on it to sip your morning coffee from or you may be compelled to own every song that Elvis ever recorded. You merely have to determine what kind of Elvis collector you are and refer to the resources below to get you on your way.

ESSENTIAL ELVISOLOGY

Some Elvis Memorabilia Sold at Auction
Elvis' birth record from Dr. Hunt's physician's log: $68,500
Elvis' 1977 Cadillac Seville: $101,500
1958 Cobra 427 racing car from *Spinout*: $96,000
Elvis' 1969 Mercedes Benz Pullman limousine: $321,500
"Phoenix" concert belt: $18,400
Macramé concert belt Elvis wore in "That's the Way It Is": $17,250
"Sunburst" concert belt: $10,350
"Thunderbird" stage cape and belt: $50,600
"Burning Love" red wool jumpsuit: $107,000
"Good Luck" stage jumpsuit: $68,500
20-karat gold royal crest ring given to Elvis by the Shah of Iran: $74,000
Elvis' personal TCB pendant: $63,000
Short-sleeved shirt Elvis wore in *Jailhouse Rock*: $13,800
Red jacket Elvis wore in *Double Trouble*: $27,600
Elvis' personal guitar pick: $920
Elvis' RCA recording studio chair: $4,887.50
Elvis' personalized sunglasses: $26,450
Elvis' 8-ounce drinking glass: $218
Number 9 ball from Elvis' billiards table: $1,495
RCA 2000 television from Graceland: $3162.50

Lock of Elvis' hair: $1,035
Elvis' comb: $1,000
Elvis' Martin D-18 guitar used during the Sun Sessions: $152,000
Hagstrom V-2 guitar from the "'68 Comeback Special": $57,500
Elvis' personal Giannini acoustic guitar: $34,500
Poem written by 11-year-old Elvis: $6,325
Elvis' sixth-grade report card: $8,000
Presley family grocery receipt: $1,600
Elvis' draft card: $22,500
Elvis' first piano: $90,000
Elvis' first movie contract: $30,000
Elvis' 1956 personal address book: $9,500

YOUR ELVIS EDUCATION

Books
Presleyana IV
  Jerry Osborne
Elvis! An Illustrated Guide to New and Vintage Collectibles
  Steve Templeton
The Official Price Guide to Elvis Presley Records and Memorabilia
  Jerry Osborne
All the King's Things: The Ultimate Elvis Memorabilia Book
  text by Bill Yenne with Robin Rosaaen's collection
The Elvis Catalog: Memorabilia, Icons, and Collectibles Celebrating the King of Rock 'n' Roll
  Lee Cotton
Elvis Collectibles
  Rosalind Cranor
Elvis Memories and Memorabilia
  Richard Buskin
The Best of Elvis Collectibles
  Rosalind Cranor and Steve Templeton
Solid Gold Elvis: The Complete Collectors Manual
  David Petrelle
  Available from Timewind Publishing, 7756 Silverweed Way, Lonetree, Colorado 80124, or by calling (877) 395-6775
The Goldmine Price Guide to Collectible Record Albums
  editors of *Goldmine* magazine

Elvis in the Post: Catalog and Guide to Elvis Presley International Postage Stamps
  Josephine Woodward
The Official Identification and Price Guide to Rock and Roll
  David K. Henkel
Collectible Magazines: Identification and Price Guide
  David K. Henkel

Web Sites

http://www.elvis-presley.com
  Official Elvis Presley site
http://www.ebay.com
  Auction web site where you can sell or bid on rare and interesting Elvis memorabilia.
http://auctions.amazon.com
  Amazon.com's auction site
http:www.startifacts.com
  Specializes in movie clothes, owned and used guitars, jewelry, autographs of Elvis
E-mail: startifacts@earthlink.net
  (800) 738-6523
http://www.post-age-collectibles.com
  Post-Age Collectibles; records to books to pinball parts
http://www.suite101.com/
  linkscategory.cfm/elvis_presley/5240
  Shopping for Elvis site; links to purchasing sites
http://www.nrmmusic.com
  and http://www.wavesmusic.com
  National Record Marts' site; limited edition collectibles
http://www.elvisshop.demon.co.uk/
  The Elvis Shop, England
http://www.jerryosborne.com/
  Jerry Osborne's site on which you can buy and sell Elvis collectibles

and memorabilia online at Osborne Collectibles.
http://www.worldwideelvis.com
  Paul Dowling's Worldwide Elvis sells Elvis records and CDs and book and CD boxed sets and packages.
  E-mail: wwelvis@gte.net
  (941) 346-1930
http://www.elvispresleyblvd.com
  Auction site for vintage Elvis memorabilia
  E-mail: colonelsnow@prodigy.net
http://www.ggs.com/presley/elvis.html
  Elvis Presley stamps for sale
http://www.starstruckcollectables.com/
  Starstruck Collectibles site
http://www.autographics.com/
  Celebrity autograph dealer's site
http://www.geocities.com/Nashville/
  Opry/4744/epclas2.htm
  Run ads here for Elvis stuff you have for sale and for things you're looking for.
http://www.geocities.com/Nashville/
  Opry/6247/germ_ep.htm
  Jarle Jensen's site; complete German discography
http://www.bluesuedemusic.com/Blue
  Suede/catalog/cat001.htm
  One-stop rock and roll shop

http://www.hollywoodsouvenirs.com/
Hollywood Souvenirs Shop online site

http://www.fridgedoor.com
Elvis magnets for sale

http://www.vipenterprises.com/shoppro/magnetsc.html
Rock and roll refrigerator magnets for sale

http://www.cyberstamps.com/elvis.html
Elvis stamps for sale online

http://www.icscollectibles.com
Elvis stamps for sale or call (800) 606-3018)

http://www.angelfire.com/nj/winstarproducts/page16.html
Elvis photo wall clock for sale

http://www.madstar.com/
Madstar site for magnets, wall rugs, art, more

http://vroom.com/cat/12main.html
Official catalog of rock and roll

http://www.worldprints.com/
Art and poster store

http://www.allwall.com
Elvis posters for sale

http://www.elvispresleyblvd.com
Elvis items for auction; e-mail: colonelsnow@prodigy.net

http://tinpan.fortunecity.com/ashcroft/364/ecotn_mem.htm
Elvis collectibles; e-mail elviscollectible@hotmail.com to subscribe to mailing list

http://www.kingstreasures.com/
Elvis merchandise; collectibles; gifts

http://www.pastnpresents.com/character/elvis.html
Past and Presents' Elvis collectibles

http://www.nightowlbooks.com/
Movie posters and collectibles

http://www.gadgetexperience.com/elvis.htm
Gadget Experience; Elvis Presley clocks, phones, coasters, ceramics, and musical globes

http://www.bright.net/~impala1/index10.htm
Elvis collectibles site

http://www.norwich.net/mody/stuff/ROCKelvis.html
Tom Mody's Elvis stuff; ordering information: (888) 828-MODY

http://www.eclipse-music.com/elvis.htm
Limited edition Elvis head-shaped CDs for sale here

http://www.epcigars.com
Memphis Specialty Cigars for the Elvis Presley cigar with photograph and EPE hologram

http://www.doghaus.com
A display of Elvis collectibles

http://www.post-age-collectibles.com/index.html
Post-age Collectibles

http://tinpan.fortunecity.com/ashcroft/364/
Elvis collectibles

http://freespace.virgin.net/vinyl.music/
Music site; e-mail: vinyl.music@virgin.net

http://www.wholesaleproducts.com/elvispresley.html
Books and music

http://www.diecastnet.com/elvis/elvis/htm
The Elvis Collection; books; CDs

http://members.aol.com/jetdogy/page2/index.htm
Elvis magnets

http://www.allwall.com
    Elvis posters for sale
http://www.barewalls.com
    Elvis posters for sale

THE ELVIS AND YOU EXPERIENCE

Subscribe to Collecting Magazines
Discoveries Magazine
Discoveries is published monthly by Jerry Osborne. In it you'll find tons of extremely rare vinyl and memorabilia advertised.
P.O. Box 1050
Dubuque, Iowa 52004-1050
(800) 334-7165
Fax (800) 531-0880
http://www.collect.com

Goldmine Magazine
Goldmine has an annual Elvis issue. For collectors of records, CDs, and music memorabilia.
700 East State Street
Iola, Wisconsin 54990-2214
(715) 445-2214
Fax (715) 445-4087
http://www.krause.com/goldmine

Autograph Collector Magazine
510-A South Corona Mall
Corona, California 91719
(800) 996-3977

Collecting Magazine
Collecting has a monthly Q&A column by Memphis Mafia member and friend to Elvis Joe Esposito.
510-A South Corona Mall
Corona, California 91719
(800) 996-3977

Go to See Elvis Memorabilia Collections

EP Archives

From automobiles and autographs to backstage passes, this privately owned collection, which is said to be the largest in the world outside of Graceland, has $1,000,000 worth of inventory that is available to rent or purchase.
3261 Maricopa Avenue
Lake Havasu, Arizona 86406
(520) 453-4912

Sierra Sid's Auto Truck Plaza
200 North McCarran Boulevard
Sparks, Nevada 89431
(702) 359-0550

Karl Lindroos
Lindroos has a phenomenal collection of cars, motorcycles, guns, and jewelry also available for lease.
201 East Ocean Avenue, Suite 7
Lantana, Florida 33462
(561) 588-0095
E-mail: k.lindroos@elvis-tcb.com

Buy Elvis Memorabilia and Collectibles

Stores

Graceland Gifts
3734 Elvis Presley Boulevard
Memphis, Tennessee 38116
(901) 332-3322
(800) 238-2000

Memories of Elvis Store
3717 Elvis Presley Boulevard
(across the street from Graceland)
Memphis, Tennessee 38116
(901) 396-1320

Loose Ends Store
Graceland Crossing
3717 Elvis Presley Boulevard #1
Memphis, Tennessee 38116

(800) 44-ELVIS
(901) 396-6401
http://elvistyle.com/Loose%20Ends/
    shop.htm

Happy Memories Collectibles
P.O. Box 1305
Woodland Hills, California 91365
(818) 346-1269

1-Hour Photo Store
3855 Elvis Presley Boulevard
Memphis, Tennessee 38116
(901) 398-6528

Moon Over Miami
Elvis plates
9455 Harding Avenue
Miami Beach, Florida 33154
(305) 865-0735
Fax: (305) 865-1990
E-mail: moonovrmi@aol.com
or flmoe@aol.com

Gifts & Accents
9605 Metcalf Avenue
Overland Park, Kansas 66212
(800) 822-8856

True Legends Inc.
Postcards; T-shirts
6202 SE 145 Street
Portland, Oregon 97236
(888) 554-9400
(503) 760-2677
Fax: (503) 760-3632
http://www.truelegends.com

Country Rock & Roll Store
Stratosphere Tower
2000 South Las Vegas Boulevard
Las Vegas, Nevada 89104
(702) 366-0362
http://www.countryrocknroll.com

Love Saves the Day
119 Second Avenue
New York, New York 10009
(212) 228-3802

Blue Suede Music
Rock and roll shop; Elvis tattoos,
    stickers, pins
3674 Canada Road
Lakeland, Tennessee 38002
(901) 383-1200

Fax: (901) 383-1035
E-mail: info@bluesuedemusic.com.
http://www.bluesuedemusic.com/

The Celebrity Wall
Metal wall plaques of movie posters
    and more
6557 East 38 Street
Tuscon, Arizona 85730
(520) 571-9669
E-mail: posters@tusconlink.com
http://www.tusconlink.com/tvm/posters/
    index.htm

River Records
822 South Highland
Memphis, Tennessee 38111
(901) 324-1757

T. S. Feinarts Company
1626 N. Wilcox, Suite 707
Los Angeles, California 90028
(323) 462-8803
Fax: (323) 462-8579
E-mail: TSFeinarts@aol.com

Antiquities International
3500 South Las Vegas Boulevard
Las Vegas, Nevada 89109
(702) 792-2274

Catalogs

Graceland Mail Order Catalog
Graceland Mail Order
3734 Elvis Presley Boulevard
Memphis, Tennessee 38116
(888) 358-4776

Elvis Presley Mail Order Catalog
(888) ELVIS ROCKS

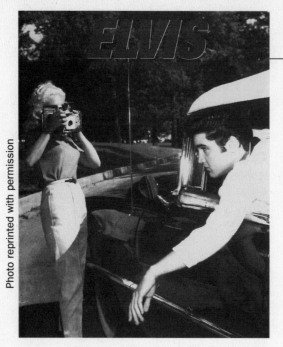

The Graceland catalog, a great source for current Elvis collectibles

9204 Center for the Arts Drive
Niles, Illinois 60714
(800) 828-0118

Bradford Exchange Catalogue
9333 Milwaukee Avenue
Niles, Illinois 60714
(800) 541-8811
Fax: (847) 966-3121

Bradford Exchange in Canada
Collector plates; three-dimensional
    sculpted plates; painted porcelain
    music boxes; Christmas ornaments
40 Pacific Court
London, Ontario N5V 3K4 Canada
(800) 265-1027
Fax: (519) 452-1303

Startifacts
Movie clothes; owned and used guitars;
    jewelry; autographs of Elvis
(800) 738-6523
E-mail: startifacts@earthlink.net
http://www.startifacts.com

EP Archives
3261 Maricopa Avenue,
Lake Havasu, Arizona 86406
(520) 453-4912

Vroom Catalogue
(800) 775-3105

Long Island Treasures
Elvis Christmas ornaments (present
    and past)

This Old House
Roger Bailey
P.O. Box 468
Almont, Michigan 48003
(313) 798-3581

Burk Enterprises Catalog
Box 16792
Memphis, Tennessee 38186
(901) 323-1528
(901) 323-1528

Promised Land Records and
    Collectibles Catalog
P.O. Box 516
Imperial, Missouri 63052
(636) 287-1968
E-mail: plrc1@yahoo.com

Ardleigh Elliott Catalog
They have branches all over the world.

Jim Voesack
1024 N. Hamilton Avenue
Lindenhurst, New York 11757
(516) 226-8078
E-mail: voesack@interport.net
http://www.users.interport.net/~voesack

Danbury Mint
47 Richards Avenue
Norwalk, Connecticut 06857
(800) 426-0373

Franklin Mint
2710 Franklin Center
Pennsylvania 19092
(610) 459-6553

Liberty Mint Catalog
Commemorative coins
P.O. Box 622
Provo, Utah 84603
(323) 962-5069

California Gold
Gold and platinum records such as
"Love Me Tender" and "How Great
Thou Art" framed and mounted with
photos; singles also available.
1951 Old Cuthbert Road, Suite 105
Cherry Hill, New Jersey 08034
(609) 354-9464
Fax: (609) 428-2532

Happy Memories Collectibles
P.O. Box 1305
Woodland Hills, California 91365
(818) 346-1269
Fax: (818) 346-0215

Memphis Memories
P.O. Box 1644

Levittown, Pennsylvania 19058
(215) 269-6949

The Lighter Side Catalog
4514 19 Street Court East
Box 25600
Bradenton, Florida 34206
(941) 747-2356

Idols West
Music, movie, and television memora-
  bilia
P.O. Box 760
Atascadero, California 93423
(805) 464-0127
Fax: (805) 464-0128
E-mail: idolswest@aol.com

Worldwide Elvis
Paul Dowling puts together CDs,
  books, and memorabilia into collectible packaged sets.
Box 17998
Sarasota, Florida 34276-0998
(800) 55-ELVIS
(941) 346-1930
Fax: (941) 346-8139
E-mail: wwelvis@gte.net
http://wwworldwideelvis.com

Graceland Records
Joe Carter
(813) 942-1935
E-mail: Elvistcbix@aol.com

Out of the Ordinary Rock and Roll
  Collectibles
Paul Linke
9821 Eden Avenue
Schiller Park, Illinois 60176
(847) 671-5275

Private Dealers

Aaron Benneian
P.O. Box 820545
Dallas, Texas 75382
(214) 987-4748

John Diesso
197 Engert Avenue
Brooklyn, New York 11222
(718) 389-7042

J&J Collectibles
Palmdale, California
(805) 285-9200

Jim Hannaford
Elvis liquor decanters
(405) 327-3352

Rachel Clark
(252) 492-2691

Ken Bage
421 Atwater Road
Hopewell, Virginia 23860
(804) 458-1089

Helmut Rauch
(847) 692-3330

R. C. Collectibles
Frank and Doris Hobbs
282 Hatt-Swank Road
Loveland, Ohio 45140
(513) 683-4526

John Heath
(870) 739-4003
E-mail: jheath4162@aol.com

Joseph A. Kereta
8335 Winnetka Avenue #156
Winnetka, California 91306
(818) 407-1081

Bob Klein
140-10 84 Drive
Briarwood, New Jersey 11435
(718) 523-5013

Outside the United States

John Hodges
6 Myrtle Avenue
Mayfields, Redditch, Worcestshire,
B98 7EL England

King Collectibles
B. Allward & Associates Inc.
141 King Road
P.O. Box 2792
Richmond Hill, Ontario, L4E 1A7
Canada
(905) PRESLEY
Fax: (905) 773-2842

The Elvis Shop
400 High Street North
Manor Park, London E12 6RH England
(44)181 552 7551
Fax: (44) 181 503 5676
http://www.elvisshop.demon.co.uk/

Elvisly Yours Shop
Trocadero Centre, Piccadilly Circus,
London WIV 7DD England

Curtis Cowen
108 West 22 Avenue
Vancouver, British Columbia, Canada
http://www.cableregina.com/users/ccowan

Check Out the Internet for Elvis Collecting

The internet is the perfect resource to help you in your search for rare and not-so-rare Elvis stuff. In the "Elvis in Cyberspace" chapter there's information about search engines, online auction sites, and all you'll need to know to get your search for Elvis treasure underway.

Where to Get Your Elvisibilia Appraised

Osborne Appraisals by Mail
Jerry Osborne, Syndicated Columnist
Jerry Osborne Answers
Chicago Sun Times
401 North Wabash
Chicago, Illinois 60611
http://www.jerryosborne.com/appraise.htm
(360) 385-1200

Appraisals
Box 255
Port Townsend, Washington 98368

Where to Get Elvis Autographs

Here's where you can find Elvis' and other autographs.
The Album Hunter
P.O. Box 510
Maple Shade, New Jersey 08052
609-482-2273

Heroes & Legends Autograph Dealer
P.O. Box 9088
Calabasas, California 91372
(818) 346-9220
E-mail: heroesross@aol.com

Houle Rare Books & Autographs
7260 Beverly Boulevard
Los Angeles, California 90036
(213) 937-0091

Find Out about Licensing from Elvis Presley Enterprises

If you have an idea or prototype for an Elvis collectible, contact EPE at (800) 238-2010. Unlicensed or bootleg products are illegal so this is the safest way to go.

Tell Graceland What Products You'd Like

Send suggestions to Graceland for the kind of collectibles you'd like to buy. Fans do some complaining about the choice of collectibles; this is a great way to take some action and be heard.

Attend an Auction

Every Elvis-related auction serves as an opportunity not only to acquire Elvis stuff, but a chance for fans to meet each other and share stories about Elvis. These prominent auction houses have sold Elvis items in the past.

Christie's
219 East 67 Street
New York, New York 10021
(212) 737-6076

Sotheby's
1334 York Avenue
New York, New York 10021
(212) 606-7000

Butterfield & Butterfield
220 San Bruno Avenue
San Francisco, California 94103
(800) 223-2854

Guernsey's Auction House
108 East 73 Street
New York, New York 10021
(212) 794-2280
Fax: (212) 744-3638
http://www.geurnseys.com

Attend Fan Conventions

At most fan conventions Elvis dealers set up booths with loads of Elvis stuff, vintage and new. Your local fan club should have information about a convention near you.

Collect an Elvis Relic

There are things that would have little value to anyone other than an Elvis fan: a fallen leaf from Graceland's lawn, a vial of water from the water fountain at the racquetball court in back of Graceland, a pebble from the Circle G ranch. They can't be resold for a profit, but who would ever want to sell them?

Graceland Wines

Graceland Wines produces a wine with an Elvis label. The first vintage was a 1993 Cabernet Sauvignon that has increased in price from $22.50 to upwards of $300. Look in fan publications for their announcements when they have a new vintage for sale.

Where to Get Elvis Cigars

There's an Elvis Presley series of cigars that you can purchase individually or by the box to collect or smoke, if you feel like it. They come in Corona, Robusto, and Churchill sizes and have a photo of Elvis on the band.
Memphis Specialty Cigars
(800) 725-0975
http://www.epcigars.com

Where to Buy Elvis Watches and Timepieces

Hollywood Limited Editions
3380 Commercial Avenue
Northbrook, Illinois 60062
(847) 559-7000
Fax: 847) 559-1060
(800) 323-1413

Abrim Enterprises
Novelty and shaped watches and timepieces with Alfred Wertheimer's photos on them.
383 Fifth Avenue, 2nd Floor
New York, New York
(212) 213-8488
Fax: (212) 213-8490

Collect Elvis Stamps

Some small countries issue Elvis stamps that make beautiful, frameable collectibles. Here are some sources:

"My favorite item is a photo of Elvis giving me a kiss and putting a scarf around me. I tipped the maitre d' so I could sit at the front of the stage during a concert at Sahara Tahoe. During the show, I held up a health club promotional bumper sticker that said I WANT YOUR BODY. Elvis had seen me at shows with the sign before, and he came over to me and said, 'You got it, baby.' That sign became a personal joke between me and Elvis."
—Robin Rosaaen, on the favorite item in her enormous Elvis collection

ICS
Antigua and Barbuda Elvis stamps
3600 Crondall Lane, Suite 100MATQ
Owings Mills, Maryland 21117
(800) 413-0080

Gary Gompf
Souvenir stamp sheets in memory
of Elvis Presley
P.O. Box 4021
Laguna Beach, California
92652-4021
Fax: (949) 496-6951
http://www.gg-s.com/presley/elvis.html

Jamestown Stamp Company
Elvis stamps shown in a free catalog
341 East Third Street
Jamestown, New York 14701
(888) 782-6776
(716) 488-0763
Fax: (716) 664-2211

Elvis Hair For Sale

Kenneth Laurence Galleries Inc. is selling 8 to 10 strands said to have been cut in 1970. They come framed, and with a certificate of authenticity. The cost is approximately $395.00.

Kenneth Laurence Galleries, Inc.
1007 Kane Concourse
Bay Harbor Islands, Florida 33154
(305) 866-3600
(800) 345-5595

From the collection of Bob Klein

ELVIS AND ART

Elvis has been glorified and idolized in every existing art form and medium. He's also been vilified and pilloried. He's been lovingly rendered in fine-art style; irreverently caricatured in cartoons; depicted with near-religious zeal; treated thoughtfully in pop, folk, and primitive art; and written about more than most other popular culture or historic figures. He was also the most photographed man of all time, with the most reproduced human face of the twentieth century. Elvis' image was commercialized and merchandised by Colonel Parker to the nth degree—so much so that the selling of Elvis Presley has been denounced as a capitalist plot.

After the virtual monopoly of machine-made consumer Elvis products, it's great to see the homespun crafts movement thriving out there. So much of the mass-produced stuff is lacking in artistry and beauty. Whatever you think of a needlepointed ELVIS barrette or a quilt made from Elvis T-shirts, there's an emotional component to handmade crafts that gives them real charm. The kinds of crafts you find at fan conventions—no matter how amateurish—really are works of art: they convey a powerful message from the creator to the viewer. The language of the handmade articles generally speaks of the artists' love for Elvis. On the flip side, many other artists merely use Elvis' image as an ironic statement on pop culture.

Laura Levin

Pamela Wood

This statue created by sculptor Eric Parks was unveiled on August 14, 1980. It was eventually moved from its original location on Beale Street to the Memphis Visitors Center.

What got all the creative juices flowing for artists from both of these camps? People want and need to express their feelings when they've experienced a disruption of the norm—when they've been kicked in the head by a blue suede shoe, as Lynn Van Matre a *Chicago Tribune* rock critic called the kind of effect Elvis has. How could this not happen considering the impact Elvis had on the world and the depth of feeling he engendered in people everywhere? And, of course, this *is* what has happened most emphatically to painters, sculptors, writers, poets, lyricists, photographers, embroiderers, web site designers, cartoonists, tattoo artists, musicians, doll makers—even vintners have laid out their feelings for Elvis for everyone to enjoy.

Since, by any measure, Elvis is the most famous of the famous, he's become fair

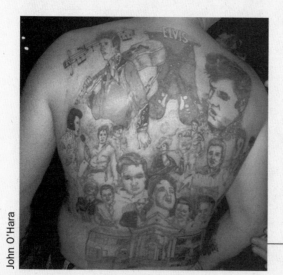

John O'Hara

game for artists who choose to use his image to comment on the society that created him and its judgment for elevating him to the status he achieved. Pop artist Andy Warhol chose a movie pose of Elvis with a gun for a famous series of Elvis paintings, the most impressive of which is *Elvis Eleven Times*, eleven repeated, silver and black panels of the same figure. It is estimated by the Warhol Museum in Pittsburgh to be their most valuable painting. Warhol made a fetish of celebrity, and he was obviously

Some fans themselves are Elvis art

Andrea Lugar designed this statue that stands today at Elvis Presley Plaza on Beale street. It was unveiled in 1997 on the twentieth anniversary of Elvis' death.

sending up Elvis' kind of fame: the commercialism and exploitation. These paintings of Elvis have become among Warhol's most famous works, and Warhol would have loved that.

Everyone knows that the first things that come to mind when talking about Elvis art are the Velvet Elvises and plaster busts, but did you know about the Elvis ballet? We kid you not: the Cleveland San Jose Ballet staged a ballet set to Elvis music choreographed by Dennis Nahat. It's a coming-of-age tale that takes place from the 1950s through the 1970s. Bob Mackie designed the costumes for this charming and unexpected entertainment.

Among the many stereotypes of Elvis fans, would be that of people who are not the greatest connoisseurs of art. Yet, a good portion of fans are marvelously talented and creative when the subject is Elvis; and their creations are very appreciated in the community. One high-profile venue for Elvis art is the Art Contest and Exhibit that Graceland conducts every year. The winning entries are displayed in the Graceland Ticket Office Pavilion during Tribute Week. The artworks are judged in four competitive divisions: craft, nonprofessional, professional, and photography/digital media, and two noncompetitive divisions:— exhibition only and children's. First, second, and third places are awarded in each division.

Some talented fans use the Wall of Love as their canvas

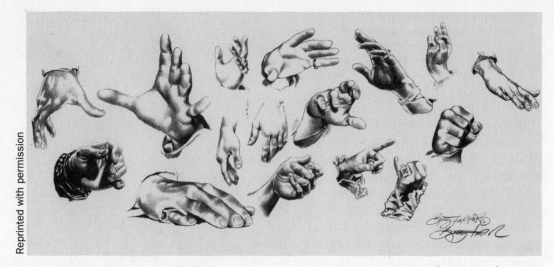

Artist Betty Harper's *Elvis' Hands* study

No matter how flatteringly or unfavorably artists may have portrayed Elvis, photographers who shot him at virtually every point in his career had a plum assignment: they could not take a bad photo of him. When you see a portrait of Elvis by himself looking extraordinarily beautiful you might think, well, that was a good angle, or the photo was well composed and well lit, or the photographer was exceptionally skilled. But to truly appreciate Elvis, look at a picture of him in a crowd or standing with a few other people. You'll notice that while everyone else looks normal, there seems to be a light from heaven shining on Elvis.

The very first professional photos of Elvis were taken at the Blue Light Studio in Memphis. These photos show a soulful young man on the eve of a kind of fame he can't imagine is coming. The next batch of publicity photos were taken by William and Vacil Speer. Some of their shots are of 19-year-old Elvis without his shirt on; he already had "sultry" down pat.

The bulk of Elvis photographers who are known today (and from whom, in some cases, it is possible to acquire photos) were taking pictures of Elvis, usually in concert, during the 1970s. Bob Heis and Keith Alverson both took amazing photos that offer an unexpected glimpse into the real Elvis: playful, passionate, and a committed performer. Ed Bonja took many of the shots used for Elvis' album covers.

Some people, like Bob Heis, Ger Rijff, Jimmy Velvet, Joe Tunzi, Robin Rosaaen, and Linda Everett are famous in the fan world for their vast collections of photos. Lots of fans make an adventure of finding pictures of Elvis they've never seen before and concentrate especially on collecting photos more than anything else. While the universe of Elvis photos is finite, it's still immense, so this hobby provides a real thrill of the hunt. Just think of all those Instamatics snapping away

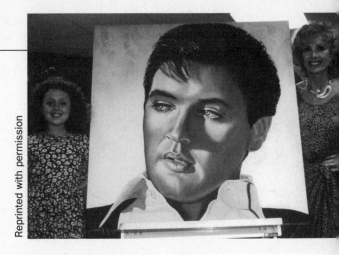

Reprinted with permission

at Elvis; every move he made was captured from a thousand angles.

There's an annual conference on Elvis Presley in Memphis of "fans, scholars, poets, artists, and musicians" organized by the Institute for the Living South that's run by Vernon Chadwick. It's tone is an educational and, perhaps, even intellectual exploration of Elvis. In 1998, the theme was "Elvis and the Dysfunctional Family" with plenty of hand-wringing over the dark side of the story, with speakers such as one who "specializes in the treatment of MICAS [mentally ill chemical abuse patients]." In 1999, the topic was provocative but considerably less dismal: "Elvis in the Oval Office." There were lectures comparing the media coverage of Elvis' death and JFK, Jr.'s; the Clinton/Elvis connection, and more. Although these conferences have been held during Tribute Week when Memphis is packed, they haven't been exactly overrun with fans in the past because the themes they address have been considered insulting or critical of Elvis.

In what other art forms does Elvis turn up? There is an enormous body of fiction and Elvis literature out there, and it expands by the year. Even though Elvis himself never read much fiction, he is the subject of many stories and novels— more often than not, having to do with outlandish sightings or resurrections. Fans are often moved to write poetry about, for, and to Elvis; from the Wall of Love at Graceland to the pages of club newsletters, they express their deepest emotions without inhibition.

So, Elvis Presley, "a dangerous [man] of notorious charisma," as Camille Paglia dubbed him, continues to inspire people to creative endeavors. Every person sees something different in him, so there are still aspects of this man to be explored. We urge you to take a fresh look at things that are not usually considered art—record jackets, movie posters, tea cozies made from Elvis material— to see the art and craft of Elvis artists. Maybe even to buy some. Most of all, we encourage you to make your own.

ESSENTIAL ELVISOLOGY

The World's Largest Velvet Elvis
A nine-by-nine-foot "Velvis" created by David Zweirz.

Elvis at the National Portrait Gallery

When Elvis commissioned a painting of himself to hang at Graceland, he chose Ralph Wolfe Cowan to do it and it became his favorite portrait. Another painting of Elvis painted by this same artist hangs in the National Portrait Gallery in Washington, D.C.

The Mount Rushmore Poll

The results of a poll asking whose face should join the four others carved into Mt. Rushmore was aired on *20/20* on June 2, 1998. John F. Kennedy came in first with Elvis Presley not far behind.

Most-Requested Photo from the National Archives

The Elvis with Nixon photos

The Elvis Stamp Vote Results

Rockabilly Elvis—851,200 votes
Created by Mark Stutzman of Mountain Lake, Maryland

Vegas Elvis—277,723 votes
Created by John Berkey of Excelsior, Minnesota

YOUR ELVIS EDUCATION

Books

The Magic of Elvis through the Art of Betty Harper
  with poetry by Better Harper
Newly Discovered Drawings of Elvis
  Betty Harper
Suddenly and Gently: Visions of Elvis
  Betty Harper
Capturing the Spirit
  Betty Harper
Elvis in Art
  Roger G. Taylor
Everything Elvis
  Joni Mabe
Elvis: A Guide to My Soul
  Isabelle Tanner
Elvis Presley 1956
  edited and designed by Martin Harrison; photography by Marvin Israel

In Search of Elvis: Music, Race, Art, Religion
    edited by Vernon Chadwick
Sex, Art, and American Culture
    Camille Paglia
Life Faces
    commentary by John Loengard (Ben
    Mancuso photo on page 19)
Elvis Rising: Stories on the King
    edited by Kay Sloan and Constance
    Pierce
*The Elvis Reader: Texts and Sources on the
King of Rock 'n' Roll*
    Kevin Quain
The King Is Dead: Tales of Elvis Postmortem
    Edited by Paul M. Sammon
*Images of Elvis Presley in American
Culture 1977–1997*
    George Plasketes
Mondo Elvis: A Collection of Stories and Poems about Elvis
    edited by Richard Peabody and Lucinda Ebersole
Elvis for President
    The Committee to Elect the King: Peter Ginna, David Groff, Wilson Henley,
    Erica Marcus, Richard Marek, Jane Meara, Sharon Squibb, Stephen Topping,
    and James Wade
Great Pop Things: The Real History of Rock and Roll from Elvis to Oasis
    Colin B. Morton and Chuck Death
The Printed Elvis: The Complete Guide to Books about the King (Music Reference
    Collection, No. 75)
    Steven Opdyke

> "Elvis allows us to laugh in what looks like a rare collectivity. Such a situation suggests that we cohere in a way that, in fact, we do not. Some of us laugh because we really do love Elvis and love to see him return and return, happily accepted wherever he appears; others just feel superior to Elvis and his fans."
> —from *Elvis Rising: Stories on the King*, edited by Kay Sloan and Constance Pierce

Web Sites

http://www.katabillups.com
    Kata Billups's Elvis art site
http://www.agt.net/public/truth/elvis.htm
    Terry Ruth's art site; commission
    work, buy T-shirts
http://www.goultralightsgo.com/
    naoki/elvis/
    Naoki Mitsuse's art site

http://www.bigtimedesign.com/
    Elvisian's from Another Planet's art site
http://www.jerryosborne.com/art.htm
    Jerry Osborne's site where you can
    find some of Betty Harper's art for sale
http://torpw1.netcom.ca/%7Esumner/
    elvis.html
    One of the sites where you can
    view Bob Heis's concert photos

http://hometown.aol.com/moody8bl/myhomepage/index.html
Site offering handmade Elvis lawn ornaments for sale

http://www.living-south.com/conf.html
Annual International Conference on Elvis Presley

http://www.allwall.com
Elvis posters for sale

http://www.barewalls.com
Elvis posters for sale

http://www.usps.gov/images/stamps/94/elvis.gif
Elvis stamp gif

http://www.madstar.com/
Madstar site for Elvis wall rugs, art, more

http://www.barewalls.com
Elvis posters for sale

http://torpw1.netcom.ca/~sumner/elvisphotos.html
Elvis photographs on Jumpsuit Junkies

http://homepages.msn.com/HobbyCt/elvis1973/woodornaments.html
Dennis's wood ornament art for sale, also concert photos his uncle took; e-mail him at MOODY8BL@aol.com

http://www.magtechmagnets.com
MagTech photo-magnet backing, magnetic photo pockets for sale

http://members.aol.com/dcleminsr/dan.htm
Dan's Elvis poetry site

http://www.allwall.com
Elvis posters for sale

THE ELVIS AND YOU EXPERIENCE

Get Your Photo Taken at Blue Light Studio

With the same camera and on the same stool where Elvis posed many times in the 1950s. If you're in Memphis for Tribute Week, they can produce your photo fast enough to take home with you.

Blue Light Studio
510 South Main
Memphis, Tennessee 38103
(901) 523-8678

Commission an Elvis Painting

Consider commissioning an Elvis painting by an artist you like or from one of those portrait services near you. You can provide your favorite Elvis photo or rely on the artist's imagination.

Have Yourself Put in a Drawing with Elvis

When you see a charcoal or pastel street artist at a fair, have one draw both you *and* Elvis together.

You Can Buy Elvis Art at these Shops and Galleries

Wake Up Little Suzie
3409 Connecticut Avenue
Washington, DC 20008
(202) 244-0700

America Oh Yes Gallery (by appointment)
P.O. Box 3075
Hilton Head Island, South Carolina 29928
(800) FOLK-ART

Red Piano Too Art Gallery
853 Sea Island Parkway
St. Helena Island, South Carolina 29920
(843) 838-2241

By Hand
100 North Tryon Street, Suite 278
Charlotte, North Carolina 28202
(704) 343-0086

Huey's
77 South Second Street
Memphis, Tennessee 38103
(901) 527-2700

Tutu Tango Art Bar
220 Pharr Road
Atlanta, Georgia
(404) 841-6222

The Primitive Eye Gallery
3234 East Ponce de Leon Avenue
Scottsdale, Georgia 30079
(404) 298-0303

Outside Atlanta
83 East Main Street
Buford, Georgia 30518

"Elvis
If we could have a life-time wish,
A dream that would come true,
We'd pray to God with all our hearts,
For yesterday and you.
A thousand words can't bring you back,
We know because we've tried,
Neither will a thousand tears,
We know because we've cried.
You left behind our broken hearts,
And happy memories too,
But we never wanted memories Elvis,
We only wanted you."
—Author unknown; reprinted from the Pure Gold Elvis Presley Fan Club of South Florida newsletter

(678) 482-5959
Fax: (678) 482-5577
http://www.outsideatlanta.com/

The Living Room
927 Royal Street
New Orleans, Louisiana 70116
(888) 595-8860

Yard Dog
1510 South Congress
Austin, Texas 78704
(512) 912-1613

Primitive Kool
4944 Newport Avenue, Suite A
San Diego, California 92107
(619) 222 0836

La Pop Gallerie
9 Rue des Jardins
94200 Ivry Sur Seine, France
(011 331) 46707034

How Great Thou Art: Photos from Graceland

A traveling exhibition of excellent photographs of 17 years of Elvis fans by Ralph Burns.
D&BA Exhibition Management
Rosemary Seidner, Exhibition Coordinator
3819 Dakota Avenue
Cincinnati, Ohio 45229
(513) 221-6903
Fax: (513) 221-6904

Artists Who Specialize in Elvis

Betty Harper
Betty has made something of a devoted specialty of Elvis portraits; she has done more than 10,000. They range from every period of Elvis' life and delve into every aspect of the man from his moods to his hand movements. Several beautiful books of her Elvis art have been published.
P.O. Box 1416, Hendersonville, Tennessee 37077
(615) 822-4122
E-mail: betjam911@aol.com
Some of Betty's artworks and books may also be purchased at:
Osborne Fine Arts Images
Box 255
Port Townsend, Washington 98368
(800) 246-3255
(360) 385-1200
Fax: (360) 385-6792
http://www.jerryosborne.com/art.htm

Kata Billups
Kata Billups's tender and philosophical pieces—scenes from Elvis' life—are extremely appealing. Her good-natured paintings actually reflect the sort of feelings many fans have for Elvis instead of being a comment on those feelings. Her portable shrines contain tiny scenes from her other works. Julia Roberts, Randy Quaid, Susan Sarandon and Tim Robbins, and Jon Bon Jovi are some of the celebrities who have bought her Elvis works.

Bob Heis

"I'll never forget the first time I got my hands on a real honest-to-God glossy photograph of Elvis Presley. Before that, I had to be content with whatever RCA and Elvis Presley Enterprises supplied. In 1972, I placed an order from a world-famous Elvis photographer named Sean Shaver. I was most pleased when they arrived. And excited. Envious, too. "I had attended many Elvis concerts from 1971 through most of 1974, always taking those Kodak snapshots in which Elvis ended up a little black or white dot (depending on the color of his jumpsuit) in a sea of darkness.

"Over the years, I continued to purchase photographs from others who were quite well known within the Elvis World: in addition to Sean, there was George Hill, Ron Wolf, Joyce Biddy, Len Leech, Keith Alverson, and others. I often thought *I wish I could take photographs like these*. But I didn't know how to spell 'single lens reflex,' much less own one.

"In 1974, I had tickets to two Elvis concerts here in Dayton, Ohio, for October 6. Front row seats for both events. A few days prior to this, I was talking on the telephone with George Hill. George was making quite a name for himself shooting concert after concert, getting stunning results. He asked me if I planned to take photographs in Dayton. I told him I most likely wouldn't, as nothing I ever shot was worth the paper it was printed on. George then laid everything out for me. What kind of camera and various close-up lenses I needed, the proper camera settings, the type of film to use, etc. In essence, I was given a crash course in photography over the telephone in less than an hour. I couldn't wait to get started.

"But this was 1974 and money was tight for a factory worker like myself. I went out and priced the items I needed to follow through with the plan and found out my MasterCard limit didn't go that high. So I began haunting the photo labs and equipment stores looking for someone who might know someone who would perhaps rent me their gear. Lo and behold, I came across Click Camera in Springfield and they did indeed rent what I was seeking. Thus history was about to be written. At least as far as I was concerned.

"From 1974 through and including Elvis' very last concert ever in Indianapolis, Indiana, in 1977, I attended many concerts and shot thousands of photographs. My first effort in Dayton was rewarded with excellent results featuring Elvis wearing the Blue Swirl (sometimes called the Toothpaste) jumpsuit and the fabulous Chinese Dragon jumpsuit. Other efforts were not quite successful but as time passed, practice made perfect."

—Bob Heis, Elvis photographer

PMB 232
1000 Johnnie Dodds Boulevard, Suite 103
Mt. Pleasant, South Carolina 29464
(843) 883-0009
http://www.katabillups.com

Johnny Ace
Atlanta-based artist Johnny Ace makes interesting, intelligent paintings with historical/political/contemporary themes in paint and decoupage on planks of wood. He incorporates text and other images, comments on Elvis' effect and interaction in our culture, into his works.
"Board with Art"
2986 Buford Highway
Duluth, Georgia 30096
(770) 622-9299
http://www.johnnyace.com

Joni Mabe
Joni Mabe is quite well known, even has a book out. Her glitter, collage, and 3D creations are so reverent that they become irreverent. Her art, and this huge installation in particular, are obsessive, glittery, and wildly creative tributes to her infatuation with Elvis Presley. Her work has been described as "glop art." This exhibition, which includes thousands of items, used to travel all over the world and has now found a permanent home.
Joni Mabe's Traveling Panoramic Encyclopedia of Everything Elvis
The Historic Loudermilk Boarding House Museum
271 Foreacre Street
Cornelia, Georgia 30531
(706) 778-2001

Pam Presley Wood
Pamela Wood's thought-provoking works are simple but pack a big punch. Her plaques are intelligent and wry and her boxes are perfect for small Elvis keepsakes or your TCB jewelry. She also makes beautiful Christmas ornaments. She can be reached at:
Fax: (404) 378-8520
E-mail: p.wood@mindspring.com
Her artworks are also carried by Huey's in Memphis.
Huey's
77 South Second Street
Memphis, Tennessee 38103
(901) 527-2700

Barbara McLean
Barbara has won the Elvis Art Exhibit and Contest at Graceland several times. She will reproduce your favorite photo as a painting. She also sells illustrated note cards of her work.
P.O. Box 755
Chesterville, Ontario Canada KOC 1HO
(613) 448-3183
http://roswell.fortunecity.com/blavatsky/114.home.htm

Theresa Baskerville
Celebrity sketch artist from Regina, Saskatchewan, Canada. She specializes in portraits of Elvis that would make a great addition to any memorabilia collection.
http://www.cableregina.com/users/tbaskerville
E-mail: tbaskerville@cableregina.com

Sue Million
924 Poland Avenue
New Orleans, Louisiana 70117
(504) 947-5170

Stephanie Knight
Memphis, Tennessee
(901) 767-7449

Elvis Haiku

I will scream louder
Until he appears onstage
No thrill like Elvis.
—Faye

Elvis Haiku

Memphis Sun burns soul
Sin and Salvation are wed
That's All Right Mama
—Bill Dufour

Randy Toyzini
Lyles, Tennessee
(931) 670-3647

Dianna Magrann
(560) 670-8447

Where to Get Elvis Photos
Keith Alverson
Keith has great quality color concert and candid
backstage photos.
P.O. Box 1666
Palmetto, Georgia 30268

Bob Heis
Bob Heis is well known for his photographs of
the King in concert.
P.O. Box 354
Miamisburg, Ohio 45343-0354
E-mail: BHEISTCB@aol.com

Bob Klein
Bob has a vast collection of Elvis concert shots and candids from every period of
Elvis' life.
140-10 84 Drive
Briarwood, New Jersey 11435
(718) 523-5013

Sean Shaver
Sean puts together beautiful, photo-rich books on Elvis.
P.O. Box 9100
Kansas City, Missouri 64168

Linda Everett
Rare candid shots.
1907 West 39 Street
Vancouver, Washington 98660

Ed Bonja Photo Club
Ed's photos graced many Elvis album covers. He has a yearly photo club: Images of
the King.

Poem written by 11-
year-old Elvis Presley

"Roses are red,
violets are blue.
When a chicken gets
into your house,
You should say shoe,
shoe.
When you get mar-
ried and live in a
shack,
Make your children's
clothes out of 'toe
sacks."

"Elvis is in color even
when the rest of us are in
black and white."
—character in *The Abyss*

Ed Bonja Enterprises
P.O. Box 156
San Dimas, California 91773- 0156
E-mail: ebonja@aol.com

Rosemarie and Len Leech's Photo of the Month Club
Lots of fabulous shots and close-ups taken at 1970s concerts.
P.O. Box 2633
Vincentown, New Jersey 08088
(609) 859-3243

William Speer
William Speer took those incredible early publicity shots of Elvis, when he was 19 years old and on the brink of success.
3500 Barron Street
Memphis, Tennessee 38111
(901) 324-4228

Gloria Pall
Gloria is the *Jailhouse Rock* woman with the famous legs. She has photos for sale of herself and Elvis from that movie.
Showgirl Press
12828 Victory Boulevard #163
North Hollywood, California 91606
Fax: (818) 509-0244
E-mail: glopall@earthlink.net
http://www.gloriapall.com

Have an Elvis Art Contest

Sponsor an art contest through your fan club and run the results in the newsletter. Or propose an Elvis-themed art project for your kid's school class and offer prizes for the winners.

Frame Album Covers for Instant Elvis Art

Elvis' record covers are not exactly renowned for their inspired design, but some are very cool—and there's probably one or two that have sentimental value for you. It's a great way to use the sleeves if the record itself is shot. You can buy square frames that are the exact size of record covers from the company below.
Worldwide Marketing Associates
956 South Bartlett Road, #270

Bartlett, Illinois 60103
(800) 640-0306
http://www.albumframes.com

Make Your Own Elvis-Picture Magnets or Postcards

MagTech makes adhesive magnetic backing to which you can adhere any picture, photo, or cutout of Elvis you like. (They also make adhesive postcard backing so you can make your own postcards from any photo.)
MagTech
10850 Switzer, #111
Dallas, Texas 75238
(800) 278-9458
Fax: (214) 340-4983
http://www.magtech.com

Frame Elvis Stamps

Some countries, like Antigua and Barbuda, issue beautiful painted portraits of Elvis on postage stamps. You can purchase these from:
ICS/Elvis Stamps
3600 Crondall Lane
Owings Mills, Maryland 21117
(800) 340-3666

Play Card Games with Elvis Playing Cards

Piatnik of America sells Elvis cards, but only wholesale: there's a $100 minimum order. So get together with some other members of your fan club and buy a few decks.
Piatnik of America
362 South Avenue
New Canaan, Connecticut 06840
(800) 962-3468
Fax: (203) 972-0713
E-mail: orders@piatnik.com

Make a T-Quilt

Got more T-shirts than you'll ever be able to wear? This company sells a pattern for making quilts out of T-shirts.
T-Quilt Pattern
14 Sunrise Point Court
Lake Wylie, South Carolina 29710
(803) 831-2455

"This obsession gave me a subject that has been a big part of my work and it seems [Elvis] is even a part of my immediate family. My life has been dedicated to preserving his memory...."
— Joni Mabe, Elvis artist

Create a "FanFic" Section on Your Web Site
If you have an Elvis web site up and running or have the know-how to create one, why not devote a section to fan fiction about Elvis? Ask for contributions from people who visit the site and post them for everyone to read.

Visit the 24-Hour Church of Elvis
A Portland artist has created what she calls "A Gallery of Art for the Smart." The tone of the Elvis installation is snide, but you may find it interesting to see other sides of the subject.
720 S.W. Ankeny
Portland, Oregon 97205
(503) 226-3671
http://www.churchofelvis.com

Elvis Presley Statues around the World
EPE commissioned a statue of Elvis from artist Andrea Holmes Luger and it can be seen at the Welcome Center near Mud Island in Memphis. The Elvis statue that is at the intersection of Beale and Main streets in downtown Memphis was created by sculptor Eric Parks. Carl Romanelli created the Hilton Hotel statue in Las Vegas. There's sculptures of Elvis in London and in Tel Aviv at the Jerusalem Inn. The Memories of Elvis Fan Club of Auckland, New Zealand, has raised money and has a statue.

See Elvis in Wax
Movieland Wax Museum
7711 Beach Boulevard
Buena Park, California 90620
(714) 522-1154

Hollywood Wax Museum
3030 West 76 Country Boulevard
Branson, Missouri 65616
(417) 337-8277

Vermont Wax Museum & Store
RR 11
Manchester Center, Vermont 05255
(802) 362-0609

Myrtle Beach National Wax Museum
1000 North Ocean Boulevard

Myrtle Beach, South Carolina 29577
(843) 448-9921

Royal London Wax Museum
16 Street and Atlantic Avenue
Virginia Beach, Virginia 23450
(757) 491-6876

Madame Tussaud's Wax Museum
Venetian Casino Resort
3355 Las Vegas Boulevard South
Las Vegas, Nevada 89109
(877) 883-6423
(702) 733-5000

> "Finally managed to find a suitable place for my velvet Elvis. I've put him at the bottom of our stairway from our lounge to our laundry and rumpus room. It is dark down there without the light on and it looks hauntingly beautiful with the face staring out of the darkness. Yum...."
> —Alex, New Zealand fan

Enter the Graceland Art Contest and Exhibit

The deadline is usually around July 31. For art contest entry form and directions, write or call Graceland at (800) 238-2010 or (901) 332-3322.

Visit the Andy Warhol Museum to See *Elvis Eleven Times*

117 Sandusky Street
Pittsburgh, Pennsylvania 15212
(412) 237-8300

ELVIS AND STYLE

I f Elvis had been just an extraordinarily talented singer and recording artist, he still would have had a major influence on popular, cultural, and musical history. But of course, he was much more than that. Elvis was an audiovisual experience. Millions of people enthusiastically responded to his music and voice when they first heard it on the radio in 1956. But when he appeared on television that same year, America got a good look at him for the first time and an entire culture was seduced, smitten, or outraged. No one had ever seen anything quite like him and no one was unmoved one way or the other. For many, it was love at first sight. He was an ideal of classic male beauty and many people to this day consider him the best-looking man who ever lived. So potent were Elvis' unearthly good looks and shockingly original sense of style that the response to them set in motion an upheaval, the effects of which are still felt to this day. Never before was there a male pop star who was such an overtly sexual presence. Women wanted him and men wanted to be like him.

Elvis was genetically blessed with a combination of his parent's best qualities. He inherited his father's square jaw, lusty head of hair, blue eyes, and lopsided grin.

A very young Vernon and Gladys Presley in a photo on display at Graceland

John O'Hara

From the collection of Bob Klein

From his mother he inherited something darker and more soulful, the perpetually pouting lips, the brooding gaze of the eyes. Elvis was a mixture of two opposing forces, the light and the dark. He descended from Northern European stock mixed with the melting pot of the New World, including both Cherokee and Jewish blood. Although fate gave Elvis the raw material for his extraordinary beauty, it was Elvis who molded himself into the enduring icon he became. Elvis knew how to make the most of what he had; before heading to Hollywood he had his nose worked on, his skin buffed, and his teeth capped.

One of the most provocative things about Elvis was his startlingly original personal style. His clothes, his hair, the way he moved—were the result of an instinctive grasp of the visual. In the beginning he didn't have a fashion consultant, movie studio, or style guru to guide him— his choice of hairstyle and garb were strictly his own. The look he created was an expression of who he was and who he wanted to be. From Hillbilly to Movie Star to Cowboy to Superfly to Superhero.

Elvis grew up in overalls, the uniform of the dirt poor. Perhaps because of that he had a lifelong aversion to blue jeans. They were too ordinary, and Elvis was far from ordinary. He knew he was different from other people and he announced that difference to the world by the way he dressed. He craved attention and he knew how to get it because he understood the power of a costume both on stage and in life.

From the collection of Bob Klein

Elvis with buddies Buzzy Forbess and Farley Guy at Lauderdale Courts, fall 1954

Early on, as if in anticipation of being famous, Elvis carefully crafted his image. While his high school classmates conformed to the wholesome, dull styles of the early fifties teenager, Elvis' favorite clothing store was Lanksy's, a store catering to a primarily hip, black Beale Street musician clientele like Junior Parker and Rufus Thomas. Amid the crew cuts, blue jeans, and penny loafers, Elvis appeared in two-tone bolero jackets and pegged black pants with stripes down the side. His trademark flamboyance was not always well received. In fact, until he started to sing in public, Elvis was known to his classmates as the quiet guy with the wild clothes.

Elvis' hair was also a distinguishing characteristic since his school days when, Elvis lore maintains, he was sometimes bothered, even accosted, by classmates wanting to cut off his long, slicked, and expertly coifed hair. His hair was the King's crown. He's said to have spent an inordinate amount of attention to it, combing and fussing until he turned it into a kinetic sculpture that danced provocatively when he moved. It's become so linked to his image that it almost has an identity of its own: "The Elvis Head." Say the word *sideburns* and only one person immediately comes to mind. Elvis realized intuitively the power of his hair when he dyed his natural sandy blond locks to the deep black hue that became an integral part of his trademark look. Just as it was bold for a man to dye his hair, Elvis would sometimes enhance his eyes with

From the collection of Bob Klein

Elvis modeling the Bill Belew-designed gold lamé suit for his parents in the living room at the Presley's Audubon Drive home

makeup. Reporters covering some of his early performances were quick to point out those times when his mascara would run, as if this was a challenge to their idea of manhood. But Elvis' look was intended to challenge. He wanted to shake things up and shake they did.

When Elvis first started performing, his everyday wardrobe of bold patterns and loud colors doubled as the stage costume we're all so familiar with—the look of the Hillbilly Cat: the draped jackets, the pegged pants, the velvet shirts. He dressed as if he were always ready to hop on stage at a moment's notice. When Scotty Moore met Elvis for the first time, he was shocked that Elvis showed up dressed in pink and black. Those colors became a favorite combination of Elvis'. If rock and roll had a flag, there's little doubt about what its colors would be.

When Elvis started reaping the rewards of his success, he indulged his passion for fashion both on stage and off. He admired the showmanship of Liberace whom he met and befriended when he played Vegas early in his career. Elvis wanted to follow the country music tradition of dressing as differently from your audience as possible, so in 1957 he hired Nudie Cohen to make what was to become one of Elvis' signature outfits—the gold lamé tuxedo. Nudie Cohen was a Hollywood designer responsible for some of the flashy stage costumes worn by many of the big names in country music. (Hank Williams was buried in a Nudie stage outfit in 1953.) Although he wore it for very few appearances, this suit has remained the quintessential image of Elvis as the golden idol of the fifties.

In the spring of 1958, a new color started to dominate the Presley wardrobe: olive drab. Being drafted forced Elvis into an abrupt change in personal style.

From the collection of Bob Klein

Elvis' detractors were eagerly anticipating the famous military haircut that would rob him of some of his power. Elvis himself anticipated the big change by getting several progressively shorter haircuts in the weeks prior to his induction to lessen the shock to the system. What the bullies had failed to do at Humes High, Uncle Sam did instead. But when shorn of his hair and forced into the anonymity of a uniform, Elvis lost none of his beauty. Instead he looked amazingly good and, as always, he knew it. Elvis chose to wear his uniform while on leave in Paris and back home in Memphis, although he would have been free to dress in civilian clothes. Part of the reason he looked so great in his uniforms is that they were

Nancy Sinatra giving Elvis a welcome home gift of shirts on behalf of her father, Frank, during a press conference following Elvis' discharge from the army

often brand new. He bought scores of uniforms and they were maintained in peak condition by members of his entourage.

When Elvis got out of the army he was 15 pounds lighter than when he went in, his hair was back to its natural blond color and crafted into a gravity-defying pompadour, his manner was more continental and subdued. He actually wore cummerbunds. Within a few days of being back home he dyed his hair back to its "poured-tar black." The gold lamé jacket was resurrected and worn for a few more concerts (this time combined with black pants) before being finally retired in 1961, when Elvis gave what was to be his final live performance for the next eight years.

When Elvis started making movies and stopped performing live, his personal style was heavily influenced by the costume designers of the films he worked on. He had little outlet to express himself within the confines of whatever character he was playing. Because his film characters were often modeled on elements from his own life, his film wardrobe of motorcycle outfits, boating caps, tight-waisted mod suits, and Beatle boots were pretty much what Elvis wore in his own life. One of the styles from Elvis' life that never made it to his onscreen wardrobe was the elaborately embroidered caftans that he sometimes wore during the years of his spiritual quests.

Another influence on Elvis' style during part of the movie years was his acquisition of the Flying Circle G ranch in Walls, Mississippi. Whatever he was doing Elvis always dressed the part, and when he

Elvis, in *Roustabout*

Sandi Miller

Elvis on his favorite horse, Rising Sun

bought the 163-acre cattle ranch as a place to ride he went whole hog on Western wear. He became a real-life Marlboro man with cowboy hats and custom chaps and holsters. There's a famous photograph of a young very Elvis and his cousin Gene smith posing as cowboys at a fair in Tupelo. During the Circle G period Elvis got to play dress up and live the cowboy life with all the trappings for real.

In 1968 Elvis returned to live performance in the career-revitalizing Singer television special (commonly referred to as the "'68 Comeback Special"). Working with designer Bill Belew for the first time, Elvis chose to make his return in a head-to-toe skin-tight black leather outfit. It was modeled after a Levi's denim jacket with a heightened Napoleonic collar that covered what Elvis thought was his embarrassingly long neck. The vision of Elvis in that outfit, sweating and staring directly into the camera, is another of the indelible images that have become one of the icons of the Elvis World. The collaboration with Bill Belew triggered a burst of creativity both in Elvis' stage outfits and personal wear. It was Belew who introduced scarves into Elvis' wardrobe. With input from Elvis, he designed customized karate *gis*, the tuxedo he wore to receive his award from the Jaycees, and the jumpsuits and stage outfits he wore in Vegas and while on tour that have become synonymous with Elvis' later years.

The jumpsuits are a dividing issue among fans. To some, the jumpsuits are associated with Elvis' decline. They see them as emblematic of Elvis' excesses. The

Courtesy of Butterfield & Butterfield

Costume sketch for Bill Belew-designed jumpsuit

Fringe jumpsuit

negative image of Elvis, overweight and in failing health, that's burned in people's minds is always that of him in a jumpsuit. When the U.S. Post Office let people choose between Rockabilly Elvis or Jumpsuit Elvis, the voters rejected the jumpsuit image. When the media referred to the stamps as "Young Elvis" or "Fat Elvis," they encouraged the false associations so often made with the jumpsuit. The image on the rejected stamp is actually based on the "Aloha from Hawaii" concert during which Elvis weighed only 165 pounds, the lightest he ever was as an adult. For that concert, Elvis wanted to wear something that said "America" and the American Eagle jumpsuit from "Aloha" has indeed become a symbol of America to the rest of the world.

On the other hand, many fans see the jumpsuit as uniquely Elvisian. Some study the jumpsuits—they've named them all—and there are even web sites devoted to them. When they talk about a specific concert, they always mention which jumpsuit was worn. Elvis had nearly 300 of these magical costumes. They were made of wool gabardine from Milan and mostly Austrian and Czechoslovakian stones purchased in Paris. The genesis of the jumpsuit began with Elvis' return to the Vegas stage. Elvis asked Bill Belew to make a stage outfit based on a karate *gi*. In July of 1969, Elvis took the stage in a black two-piece outfit open at the chest and tied at the waist with a sash. A high collar and a scarf covered his neck. This eventually evolved into the one-piece, elaborately embroidered, bejeweled and studded stage costumes. The outfits

Elvis in his signature EP sunglasses with prescription lenses

Sandi Miller

reflected who Elvis had become. He was a living legend. He *was* a King. The jump-suits became an integral part of each show: at some point in many concerts he would stand at center stage, spread out his cape with his arms, and share his resplendence as thousands of camera flashbulbs lit the recording of the spectacle. The scarves became another important part of the ritual. At every show Elvis would work the crowd dispensing sweat-infused scarves to the women crowding the stage trying to get a kiss.

Looking back, it seems amazing that Elvis had the stones to wear some of the outfits he did. In the *New York Times* review of Elvis' Madison Square Garden performance he was described as "a prince from another planet." Shortly before the end of his life, after having pushed the boundaries, Elvis and Bill Belew were planning the next stage in the evolution of the jumpsuit. Not only would it sparkle in the stage lights, it would be equipped with laser beams. It sounds pretty outlandish, but you know Elvis could've pulled it off.

During the seventies, the line between Elvis' stage costumes and real-life clothes blurred even more. Elvis knew he was "on stage" even during those times when he would venture out from behind the walls of Graceland, so he was always "in costume." When he went to Washington on his personal mission to meet President

Caped leather and suede coat from Elvis' Superfly period

Courtesy of Butterfield & Butterfield

"Elvis is not a god, but we worship him because he is Elvis." —Sam Phillips

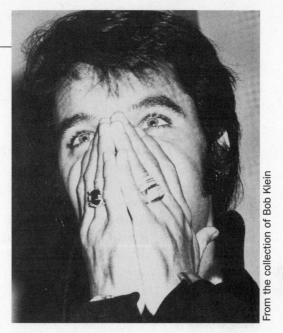

From the collection of Bob Klein

Nixon, he was dressed in a purple crushed-fur outfit with an Edwardian collar and cape. He looked "like a vampire" according to Jerry Schilling, who accompanied him to the Oval Office. Even Nixon commented on the wildness of his clothes. Elvis replied, "Mr. President, you've got your show to run and I've got mine." He started to accessorize his outfits with gold-headed canes and he carried police flashlights. He wore medallions, expensive jewelry, and long Superfly coats. He was even said to wear a turban on occasion. The tinted custom sunglasses that he almost always wore during these years were not just the affectation of a star; they were a necessity. Elvis needed prescription lenses for nearsightedness, but with his sense of style he succeeded in making the sunglasses a signature accessory to the Elvis look.

At home, especially in the later years, he tended to dress for comfort in running suits and police coveralls. He spent a good deal of time in pajamas and bathrobes. Elvis was plagued with sleeping disorders his whole life. He battled insomnia and had bouts of sleepwalking called "action nightmares." Raised on the high-fat diet of the rural South, Elvis also had a life-long battle with his weight. He routinely gained weight between his films and public appearances and would then try to shed it before the next. As his metabolism slowed, he found it increasingly difficult to lose the excess pounds. To combat both of these problems, and aided by doctors willing to do anything for their famous client, Elvis fell into a pattern of prescription drugs that no doubt contributed to his health problems and his early demise.

Perhaps because he was so beautiful, he was and continues to be viciously ridiculed for having gained weight. Those envious people not lucky enough to be as physically gifted as Elvis was, seem to take great pleasure in focusing so much attention on his decline. Particularly in the years after his death, the media placed an unkind and disproportionate emphasis on Elvis' failing appearance. That focus seems to be changing now that we can view his entire career in retrospect. People are just as likely to remember Elvis as that whip-thin Hillbilly Cat or brooding Adonis in black leather. If anything, the decline and unnecessarily

ELVIS AND STYLE **341**

early death of one of the world's most stunning physical specimens should remain as a cautionary tale to everyone of the importance of maintaining a healthy lifestyle.

ESSENTIAL ELVISOLOGY

Voted Most Handsome at Humes High in Elvis' Class, 1953
Thomas Eugene Bernard

Elvis' Sunglasses
Optique Originals, Las Vegas
Dennis Roberts Optical Boutique, Los Angeles
Foster Grant
Nautic, Germany
Renauld, USA

His Sizes
January 1, 1957
(Gold lamé suit measurements)

Neck	15½"
Chest	42"
Waist	32"
Sleeve	31½"
Inside seam	17½"
Pant inseam	32"
Hat size	7½"
Shoe size	10½
Height	5'11"

March 7, 1967

Neck	15¾"
Chest	42"
Waist	34"
Sleeve	31½"
Inside seam	17½"
Pant inseam	31½"
Hat size	7¼"
Shoe size	11D
Height	5'11"

Courtesy of Butterfield & Butterfield

Elvis' Smile

Decatur, Alabama, pediatrician Dr. Jeffrey Hull said Elvis' snarl-smile was the result of a birth defect called "asymmetric crying facies." Explains Hull, "A baby looks fine until it smiles or cries…." According to Hull, Sylvester Stallone has this same congenital defect. Not!

Some of Elvis' Stage Outfit Names

Elvis in dragon jumpsuit

Adonis	Gypsy
Aloha Eagle	Gypsy Alpine
American Eagle	I Got Lucky
Andre	Inca Gold Leaf
Aqua	Indian
Aztec Calendar	Indian Feather
Blue Bicentennial	King of Spades
Black Eagle	Light Blue Flowers
Black Fireworks	Mad Tiger
Black Flying	Matador
Black Matador	Memphis
Black Pyramid	Mermaid
Black Way Down	Mexican Sundial
Blue Aztec	Nail-Studded
Blue Braid	Now Jumpsuit
Blue Eagle	Owl Jumpsuit
Blue Leaf	Peacock
Blue Nail	Double Peacock
Blue Prehistoric Bird	Phoenix
Blue Rainbow	Double Phoenix
Blue Swirl	Porthole
Blue Tiffany	Rainbow Swirl
Burning Love	Rainfall
Caped Fringe	Red Eagle
Chain	Red Ladder
Cisco Kid	Red Flower
Claw	Red Lion
Conchas	Rhinestone
Dark Blue Aztec	Saturn
Dark Blue Gypsy	Second Pontiac
Dragon	Silver Eagle
Flame	Snowflake
Flower	Spanish Flower
Fringe	Spectrum

Starburst Planet
Sundial
Sunlight
Superman
Tiffany
Today
V-Neck
Western
White Way Down

White Bicentennial
White Eagle
White Fireworks
White Flying
White Pearl
White Prehistoric Bird
White Pyramid
White Spanish Flower
White Target

Elvis' Jewelers

Schwartz & Ableser Jewelers
   Beverly Hills, California
Harry Levitch Jewelers
   Memphis, Tennessee
Lowell G. Hays and Sons Jewelers
   Memphis, Tennessee

Elvis Footwear

White Chelsea boots
Continental gaiters
Vedi boots
San Remos boots
Florshiem
Renegades

Elvis Accessories

Belts
Buckles
Capes
Sunglasses
Canes
Flashlights
Guns

Elvis' Costume Designers

Nudie Cohen
Edith Head
Sy Devore
Lambert Marks
Bill Belew

Elvis' Valets

Marvin (Gee Gee) Gamble
David Leach
James Caughly
Rick Stanley
Richard Davis
Al Strada
Billy Smith

What Was on Elvis' Bathroom Shelves

Colgate toothpaste
Brut cologne
Neutrogena soap
Schick Flexamatic razor
L'Oréal Excellence blue-black hair dye
Lady Clairol blue-black
Dristan
Super Anahist
Contac
Sucrets
Blistex
Feenamint gum
Eye drops

Elvis' Hair Stylists

Blake Johnson
    Blake's Coiffures
    Memphis, Tennessee
Jim's Barbershop
    Memphis, Tennessee
Homer "Gil" Gilliland
    Personal hairdresser; Elvis gave him his gold lamé coat.
James B. Peterson
    The barber who gave Elvis the army haircut.
Herr Leutzer
    Salon Jean Hemer
    Germany
Karl-Heinz Stein
    Haircutter at Ray Barracks
    Germany
Norman Richards
    Beverly Hills stylist
Victor Honig
    Cut Elvis' hair in the early '60s
Sal Orifice
    From Jay Sebring's Salon, Los Angeles
Patty Perry
    Los Angeles haircutter and unofficial
    Memphis Mafia member

> "When Elvis reached his teens, he … grew his hair long and added sideburns. Elvis favored the ducktail look and knew if he went to a barber shop, the barber might take it upon himself to cut his hair in the popular crew cut style. As a result, Elvis chose to go to the local beauty parlor instead."
> —Jim Curtin, from *Elvis: Unknown Stories behind the Legend*

Larry Geller
   Elvis' spiritual adviser, friend, and hairdresser

Elvis' Hair Color

Most hard-core fans know that Elvis' gorgeous head of hair started out sandy blond and that he dyed it black after his film career was underway. Why black? Theories vary from Elvis having been influenced by Tony Curtis or Roy Orbison to Captain Marvel.

Elvis' Plastic Surgeons

Dr. Maury Parks
   This Hollywood plastic surgeon operated on both Elvis' and his friend George Klein's noses in the fifties.
Dr. Asghan Koleyni
   This Memphis plastic surgeon performed plastic surgery on Elvis on June 15, 1975, at Mid-South Hospital.

Other Physicians and Nurses

Dr. William Robert Hunt
   Tupelo physician present at Elvis' birth.
Edna Robinson
   Midwife at Elvis' birth
Dr. Charles Clarke
   Memphis physician who attempted to save Gladys's life in 1958.
Dr. Max Shapiro
   Los Angeles dentist

Dr. Thomas Newman
   Las Vegas physician, nicknamed "the Flash."
Dr. Sidney Boyer
   Las Vegas eye, nose, and throat doctor.
Dr. Elias Ghanem
   Las Vegas physician
Dr. Larry Wruble
   Memphis gastroenterologist

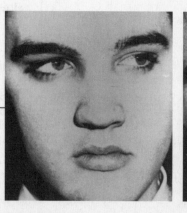

Elvis before plastic surgery on his nose. The results of the surgery can be seen in a photo at right taken years later.

Dr. David Meyer
  Memphis opthamologist
Dr. Daniel Brady
  Memphis cardiologist
Dr. Leon Cole
  Los Angeles physician gave Elvis
  "acupuncture treatments."
Dr. Gerald Starkey
  Denver police surgeon
Dr. John Nash
  Elvis tried to persuade him to per-
  form a gastrointestinal bypass.
Dr. Lester Hofman
  Memphis dentist
Dr. Robert E. Kinsman
  Los Angeles dentist who made caps
  for Elvis in the fifties.

Dr. M. E. Gorsin
  Los Angeles physician who treated
  Elvis after his concussion.
Dr. George Elerding
  Radiologist who X-rayed Elvis after
  his concussion.
Dr. George Nichopolous
  Elvis' personal physician
Marion Cocke
  Baptist Memorial nurse
Tish Hinsley
  Resident nurse at Graceland
Kathy Seamon
  Day nurse at Graceland

YOUR ELVIS EDUCATION

Books

Elvis: Photographing the King
  Sean Shaver
Elvis: His Life in Pictures
  text by Todd Morgan with Laura Kath
Elvis
  text by Dave Marsh; art direction
  by Bea Feitler
Elvis: The Rebel Years
  Ger Rijff
*The Official Elvis Presley Fan Club
Commemorative Album 1935–1977*
  edited by Julie Mundy
*Unseen Elvis: Candids of the King
from the Collection of Jim Curtin*
  Jim Curtin
Elvis: His Life in Pictures

  text by Todd Morgan with Laura
  Kath
Elvis: A Celebration in Pictures
  Charles Hirshberg and the editors
  of *Life*
Elvis + Marilyn
  Geri DePaoli
If I Can Dream
  Larry Geller
Elvis Immortal
  introduction by Glen Campbell
I Called Him Babe
  Marion Cocke
Elvis: The Concert Years 1969–1977
  Stein Erik Skar
Rare Elvis
  Sid Shaw

*Elvis Presley: The Official Auction
Catalog from the Archives of
Graceland*
   compiled by Guernsey's Auction
   House

One Hundred Years of Western Wear
   Tyler Beard
Sexual Personae
   Camille Paglia

Video
Elvis '56: In the Beginning

This Is Elvis

Web Sites
http://secure.elvis-presley.com/
   cgi-bin/-store2/perlshop.cgi
   Elvis jewelry
http://www.grafisk-consult.no/
   flamingstar
   Lots of '50s, '60s, and '70s photos
   on the Flaming Star of Norway Fan
   Club web site
http://www.inos.com/users/
   pebbles/elvis photo kingdom.htm
   Personal web site with photo gallery
htpp://www.neosoft.com/~kcderr/
   elvis/elvis.html
   Elvis Is Still #1; Big Bad Bob's tribute site
http://www.geocities.com/SunsetStrip/
   8200/books.html
   Jumpsuits web sites

http://wsrv.clas.virginia.edu/~acs5/
   elvis.html
   Elvis lives in Evil Levis; many
   photos of E
http://members.tripod.com/
   ~Crazy_Canuck/index.html
   The Canuck's Elvis Pages; go to
   Jumpsuit Junkies section
http://www.freehomepages.com/ecs/
   photo4.html
   Mike Keating's photo page
http://www.discountshirts.com
   Elvis T-shirts for sale at a discount
http://ourworld.compuserve.com/
   homepages/elvis/stamp.htm
   Elvis stamp story site

THE ELVIS AND YOU EXPERIENCE

See Some of Elvis' Wardrobe
Graceland
Many important items from Elvis' wardrobe are displayed here: the gold lamé
tuxedo, the leather suit from the "'68 Comeback Special," army uniforms, stage
costumes, jewelry, and more.

Rock and Roll Hall of Fame and Museum
They have rotating exhibits that feature Elvis' clothing.

One Key Plaza
Cleveland, Ohio 44144
(888) 764-ROCK
http://www.rockhall.com

Sierra Sid's Auto Truck Plaza
This truck-stop museum contains some of
Elvis' jewelry.
200 North McCarren Boulevard
Interstate 80, Exit 19
Sparks, Nevada 89431
(702) 359-0550

> "... I realized that there was nothing hipper or cooler than Elvis. He had *created* cool with that withering sneer of his, and anybody who said Elvis wasn't cool was like a rebel priest denying the God that gave him life."
> —Chet Williamson, from his essay "Double Trouble," in *The King Is Dead*

How to Look Like Elvis

The only way to really look like Elvis would
be to have been born to Gladys and Vernon.
Seeing as that's not how your planets aligned, you have limited alternatives.

Your Elvis Wardrobe

Part of what made Elvis *Elvis* was his sense of fashion, so one of the easiest ways
to emulate him is to dress like him. There's a lot of looks to choose from, since
he was a bit of a dandy.

Some Different Elvis Looks

The Wild One: Biker Elvis
Soldier Boy Elvis: Ladies love a man in uniform.
The Hawaiian Beach Boy Look: Fun in the sun
Superfly Elvis: Bad, bad Elvis
Master Tiger Elvis: Everybody was kung fu fighting

Recreate an Elvis Movie Wardrobe

The "baseball suit" of *Clambake*, the red-striped jacket from *Speedway*, the
Roustabout leather motorcycle outfit, the Hawaiian shirts of *Blue Hawaii*: watch
the videos and go shopping or start sewing.

Shop at Antique Clothing Stores

There are antique and vintage clothing stores in almost every community. Not
only can you find Elvis-era clothes from the '50s, '60s, and '70s, but you can find
some great bargains.

Sandi Miller

From the collection of Sandi Miller

Elvis wearing one of his more flamboyant fringe stagesuits during a performance at the L.A. Forum, November 14, 1970

Sandi Miller posing with the same Elvis' fringe suit on its way to the dry cleaners the day after the L. A. Forum concerts

Shop Where Elvis Shopped

Although the original building is now occupied by Elvis Presley's Memphis Restaurant, Lanksy's is still in business in the lobby of the Peabody Hotel just a few blocks away. Bernard Lansky still comes to the store each morning and is glad to talk to Elvis fans.

Lansky Brothers
Peabody Hotel
149 Union Avenue
Memphis, Tennessee 38103
(888) 303-8257
Fax: (901) 525-1476
E-mail: hal@lanskybros.com
http://www.lanskybros.com

Laura Levin

Use Elvis's Dry Cleaner

Kraus Dry Cleaners
(branches throughout the city)
Memphis, Tennessee
(901) 528-0400

Suggested Uses for Gold Lamé

Elvis had a tuxedo made of this oh-so-showbiz fabric. You don't have to limit yourself to that. Make something unexpected like gold lamé curtains or gold lamé underwear.

Jewelry, the Elvis Way

Elvis' first jewelry purchase was a diamond horseshoe ring. His favorite stone was, what else, Tiger's Eye. Fans may want to own one of the bejeweled lightning-bolt TCBs that Elvis gave to his inner circle. You are inner circle, aren't you? Here is a list of Elvis' jewelers that are still open for business and carry some Elvis-related items.

Harry Levitch Jewelers
5100 Poplar Avenue, Suite 111
Memphis, Tennessee 38137
(901) 761-1188

Lowell G. Hays and Sons Jewelers
4872 Poplar Avenue
Memphis, Tennessee 38117
(901) 767-2840

Lee Ableser of Schwartz & Ableser
251 North Beverly Drive
Beverly Hills, California
(323) 274-3088

Your Elvis Makeover

Getting an Elvis Haircut

Find a haircutter who specializes in haircuts of the fifties to seventies. Sometimes it's best to find a place that's been open since then. Bring a photo of your favorite

"Once he hit it really big, he came in more often and, no, he never bought me out. Every time he dropped by he wanted something different.... People would ask, 'Elvis, where are you buying your clothes?' And he would say 'Lansky's.' We did a lot of mail-order sales because of him. He was a real sharp dresser. Real neat. His clothes looked great on him. He was clean as Ajax. I mean, really nice. We would get new merchandise in and we would load it into a truck and I would have my son drive it out to Graceland for Elvis to look at. When the truck came back, it was empty. Elvis had taken all of it."
—Bernard J. Lansky of Lansky Brothers Men's Shop, Elvis' main clothier in Memphis from *Elvis: The Official Auction Catalog* from the October 1999 Guernsey's auction. (The original site of Lansky's at 126 Beale is now occupied by Elvis Presley's Memphis Nightclub and Restaurant. Lansky's can be found just around the corner in the lobby of the historic Peabody Hotel.)

"Elvis 'do." Try to meet a member of a rockabilly band or an Elvis impersonator and ask who cuts their hair. It was said that Elvis used three different kinds of hair oils to achieve his signature look: Butch Wax for the front, a Rose Oil hair tonic for the top, and Vaseline for the sides.

The Sideburns

There's wide a range of choices, from the sharp and subtle sideburns of the fifties to the massive muttonchops of the seventies.

Dye for Elvis

Elvis used L'Oréal Excellence blue-black.

Choosing a Wig

Less of a commitment than a 24-hour Elvis Head, and that may be a good thing.

The Elvis Smile

With the recent advances in cosmetic dentistry, this is one of Elvis' few facial features that you actually have a good chance of replicating. Just bring a photo of your favorite Elvis smile to a skilled cosmetic dentist and let him get to work on your choppers.

Go to E's Podiatrists

Drs. Gold and Cook
3804 Elvis Presley Boulevard
Memphis, Tennessee 38116
(901) 396-2277

Elvis' Favorite Smokes

Elvis would often have a little cigar in his mouth, not only because he liked them, but it looked mad cool, too. Here is a list of the brands he was known to smoke.
Hav-a-Tampa Jewels
Rum Crooks
Villager Kiels
Roi-tan
El Producto diamond tip

Re-create an Elvis Photo Shoot

Choose your favorite Elvis portrait and have yourself photographed in the same pose. When you're in Memphis, you can even have yourself photographed by the exact same camera that shot some of Elvis' earliest publicity shots.
Blue Light Studio
510 South Main
Memphis, Tennessee 38103
(901) 523-8678

Retouch Your Photo to Resemble Elvis

If your photo doesn't make you Elvis-like enough, there are simple photo retouching programs on many home computers that could give it a digital nudge in the right direction. It's a lot more practical than plastic surgery.

Get an Elvis Tattoo

Getting an Elvis-related tattoo is a dramatic statement that announces your fandom to the world in indelible terms. For most fans, Elvis is a lifetime commitment anyway. His face is a power

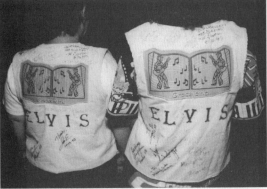

Elvis fans in handmade outfits

ful image to be permanently inked on your body. A talented tattoo artist should be able to render anything you want. Some other suggestions are the TCB logo, the karate patch, or Elvis' Hell on Wheels army insignia.

Wear an "Elvis in Concert" Jacket

Just call for a mail-order catalog from Graceland for this and many other items of clothing. Call them at (888) 358-4776.

Make Elvis T-Shirts

There's no end to the variety of Elvis T-shirts out there. Why not make your own? Many places that sell T-shirts can very inexpensively print your favorite Elvis photo on a shirt. Be creative; use an obscure photo. Combine a photo of you and Elvis together.

Create an Elvis Outfit

Elvis fans often express their devotion through their clothes. It's also an easy way to meet other Elvis fans. Sew a TCB patch onto a jacket or wear some

blue suede shoes and see all the Elvis friends you'll meet.

Wear an Elvis Watch
Make your watch face your favorite face. "Elvis: The Wertheimer Watch Collection" is a novelty series of watches with Alfred Wertheimer's famous 1956 black-and-white photos on the faces. Elvis' signature is on the interior of the band and they come with a booklet of Elvis photos.
Abrim Enterprises, Inc.
383 Fifth Avenue, 2nd floor
New York, New York 10016
(212) 213-8488
Fax: (212) 213-8490

Wear Elvis Belt Buckles, Lapel Pins, Money Clips, and Key Rings
C&J Manufacturing Company
440 East 3 Street
Carlstadt, New Jersey 07072
(201) 438-2411
E-mail: LBlake2498@worldnet.att.net

Use Donna Presley Early and Patsy Anderson Cosmetics
Donna Presley Early, Elvis' cousin, and Patsy Anderson, fan club liaison at Graceland, have created a makeup and skin-care line called Arbonne International.
Donna Presley Early and Patsy Andersen
P.O. Box 587
Wynne, Arkansas 72396
(870) 238-0242
(888) 235-8470
E-mail: donnap@ipa.net
http://www.presleyd.com

Donate Clothing to Charity
Donate your old Elvis T-shirts and kill two birds with one stone: provide clothes for those in need and turn them on to Elvis.

Help Someone Dress for Success
Dress for Success is an organization that helps people in need of clothing for job interviews or work. Elvis knew how important it was to dress for the part; help someone else do it.
Dress for Success Worldwide
19 Union Square West
New York, New York 10003
(212) 989-6373
http://www.dressforsuccess.org

Return to Slender
When Elvis needed to lose weight, his program often consisted of extremes of fasting and exercise. Sometimes he would live on nothing but artificially sweetened Jello. To lose weight before the "Aloha" concert, he embarked on a regimen that included the injection of hormones found in the urine of pregnant women. Dr. Nick had him on a liquid protein diet at another time. These particular methods are not recommended.

Exercise to Elvis Music
Who wants to sweat with Richard Simmons when you can sweat with Elvis! Persuade your aerobics instructor to use Elvis music. Or listen to Elvis on your Walkman when you work out.

Dance to Elvis Music

Whether you're out somewhere pumping coins into a jukebox or just dancing in front of your mirror at home, moving to Elvis music is the preferred method of burning calories.

Exercise Elvis-Style

Elvis couldn't exactly be described as an athlete, but he was a sportsman and loved to be active. Burn calories off the way Elvis did.

Karate
Racquetball
Football
Roller-skating
Swimming
Horseback riding
Water-skiing
Performing kick-ass concerts

Buy a Fur from the Same Store where Elvis Shopped

The store where Elvis bought furs as gifts for lady friends is still in business and there's even a few old salesmen with stories.

King's Furs
4568 Poplar Avenue
Memphis, Tennessee 38117
(901) 767-5464

Tanning the Elvis Way

Elvis liked to sit in the sun around the pool at Graceland with an electric fan blowing on him. And when he needed a deep and even tan, such as for his role in *Blue Hawaii*, the director Hal Wallis recommended he get it with a Hanovia ultraviolet tanning lamp.

Where to Buy Posters and Photos of Elvis

Jerry Ohlinger's Movie Material Store Inc.
242 West 14 Street
New York, New York 10011
(212) 989-0869

YOUR ELVIS SHRINE

Human beings of all cultures and from every corner of the earth have created shrines throughout history. We have felt the need to erect buildings and monuments, designate hills or piles of stones, or simply dedicate corners of our dwellings to figures who have captured our imaginations, who have made us realize the existence of something spectacular outside of ourselves. At these sites we have dedicated our devotion to those who have inspired our love and awe. And Elvis fans are no different.

Many Elvis fans have created a special place, or whole room, in their homes where they can display, and let the world know of, the appreciation and love they feel for Elvis. And as with totems, talismans, and temples of the past, the concept of the Elvis shrine is essentially the same: to put people in touch with something marvelous and incomprehensible and to serve as a focal point for the emotions they feel. And the emotions felt by those who actually create Elvis shrines sometimes go as far as reverence and adulation. For the vast majority, however, it is a sense of abiding affection and respect for Elvis that motivates them to keep a shrine in their homes. Those feelings may be exclusively for Elvis' music, and it could be argued that a painstakingly collected

Artist Kata Billups's painting *Elvis Praying in the Pink Bedroom*

record or CD collection might
be considered a sort of shrine
as well. Whatever the intention, the end result is certainly
a staggering number of personal Elvis shrines throughout
the world. In *E: Reflections on
the Birth of the Elvis Faith*,
John Strausbaugh estimates
"... they must number in the
tens of thousands throughout the United States, England, Europe, and beyond....
Nothing remotely on the scale of this adoration has been accorded any mere sec-
ular hero in this, or perhaps any, century."

Whether it's the Elvis-festooned office that inspires the ad agency copywriter,
or the Elvis bust that brings comfort to the woman who prays near it, or the
seven-foot portrait of Elvis that graces Eddie Murphy's bedroom—the question
must be asked: exactly when did the fans' collections of Elvis stuff start being
considered, and called, shrines? Certainly, millions of people had collections of
Elvis memorabilia long before he passed on, so what is it exactly that imbues a
collection of artifacts with a sense of specialness beyond their value, or with any
meaning at all, for that matter?

Just as with religious shrines, it's primarily the intent. If we yearn for *and achieve*
a connection, if we seek *and
find* inspiration, if we desire
comfort *and feel pleasure* when
in our Elvis rooms, then these
mere collections are transformed into something greater.
The Velvet Elvises, Bradford
Exchange plates, Elvis Presley
Boulevard street signs, and the
countless photos of Elvis him-

Mary and Bud Stonebraker's
living room tribute to Elvis in
the house they bought near to
Graceland

Mike Schreiber

self, take on the meaning we ascribe to them and give us something in return. This freaks some people out.

"Elvis is God," is the provocative opening of John Strausbaugh's *E: Reflections on the Birth of the Elvis Faith*. "Not the One True God of a monotheism like Islam, Judaism, or Christianity, but a modern pagan god, one of the thousands whom people have worshipped throughout existence, across many cultures." Does this explain, or are there even any explanations, why so many people spend their time, invest their money, enlist their creativity, in some cases go so far as to devote a whole room in their homes, to honor and celebrate Elvis? Absolutely not. To outsiders this conclusion is used for a shorthand explanation of what the fans are about. But as virtually every Elvis fan will tell you, there is no religious basis for their connection to Elvis. As with everything else to do with Elvis, most explanations, if any may be offered, are deeply personal and mysterious. The shrine trend may have started as a response to Elvis' death, as a way to make sure his memory would never die. It may be that all the incredible things Elvis makes people feel become even more powerful when given focus in a specific place and through specific objects. Or it may be that to have an Elvis shrine is just plain fun and makes people feel good. The impulse to create a shrine is one that even Elvis felt; not a shrine to himself of course, but in his own bedroom at Graceland he kept a large framed photo portrait of his mother, Gladys, and several images of Jesus. These were much more than mere images to him, and he surely sought comfort from them.

Since there are many who shudder at the religious aspects of the very nature

Pamela Wood in her Elvis room

Photo reprinted with permission

"I became an Elvis fan in the late 1980s, later in life—my early years took me elsewhere. I became a fan by listening to his music while commuting for my job, and my fandom evolved from there. Because my son was grown and out of the house, his bedroom gradually became Elvis' room, and has evolved into a space filled with special things. I have a number of pieces of folk art, the most elaborate and favorite being a five-foot shrine and a large Graceland dollhouse. I have chosen my favorite/unusual photos and hung them on the wall chronologically—one wall for each decade—ceiling to floor. They tell the story of Elvis' life, showing important events, periods, and symbols. The fourth wall is filled with photos of Elvis with a person or place important to him, next to a picture of me with the same person or in the same place. Doing this is the next best thing to having been there, and is one way for me to get to know him better and to help create what his life was like. I enjoy spending time in this room and taking in what I see. The major connection to Elvis for me is identifying with him on a very personal level: How could someone as wonderful as Elvis externally have the difficulties he had internally? If Elvis has these problems and is a good person, and I have similar problems, I can be okay, too. There is saying: You can't judge someone's insides by his/her outsides. We all have judged Elvis to be bigger than life and to be perfect. We all know he was not perfect, but we love him anyway, just as I know I am not perfect and want to be loved anyway."

—Pamela Wood

of any shrine, it's important to understand that a shrine to Elvis is rarely a real altar nor does it actually have spiritual undertones. In most cases, Elvis rooms or shrines are an amassed collection of Elvis-significant objects, artfully and lovingly tended and displayed. It seems ironic, however, that the same people who wouldn't bat an eyelash at seeing a den with walls covered in baseball pennants and posters, or a framed portrait of President Kennedy with a burning candle in front of it, automatically bristle at the thought of a shrine to Elvis. It is hard for us to understand why. Elvis shrines play a sometimes meaningful, but most often playful, role in the lives of many Elvis fans.

When creating their Elvis shrines, fans have given their artistic talents and imaginations free rein. Historically, shrines were designed to arouse every one of the senses and, ideally, your Elvis shrine should have the same effect. Think lighting, scent, and sound; incorporate unanticipated touches; imagine the feeling Elvis had when he got the inspiration for the Meditation Garden. (See "Spirituality and Gospel.") A spectacular shrine bestows on Elvis the immortality he deserves.

John O'Hara

Paul Macleod inside Graceland Too,
Holly Springs, Mississippi

ESSENTIAL ELVISOLOGY

Graceland Too—One of the Ultimate Shrines

Set aside the time to stop at Graceland Too if you are traveling between Memphis and Tupelo for any reason. This shrine-like museum to Elvis' memory is a most worthwhile detour. Paul Macleod, who's been described as Elvis' number-one chronicler, has been collecting Elvis memorabilia, recordings, costumes, and photos since he was 13. To quote him, "If it's not pertaining to Elvis, we don't keep it on this property." And he, along with his son Elvis Aaron Presley Macleod, welcomes the public to their wall-to-wall, floor-to-ceiling, house-wide shrine to the King 24 hours a day, 365 days a year. The hour-and-a-half tour costs $5. If it's not too crowded, they'll play bootlegs and barter collectibles and regale you with stories collected during a lifetime's devotion to Elvis. You'll come away with some awesome shrine ideas.
200 East Gholson Avenue
Holly Springs, Mississippi 38655
(601) 252-7954
Fax: (601) 252-1918

YOUR ELVIS EDUCATION

Books
Everything Elvis
  Joni Mabe
All the King's Things: The Ultimate Elvis Memorabilia Book
  Richard Michaels and Bill Yenne
Elvis World
  Jane and Michael Stern
E: Reflections on the Birth of the Elvis Faith
  John Strausbaugh

John O'Hara

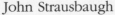
Graceland Too

Altars Made Easy: A Complete Guide to Creating and Using Your Own Sacred Space
   Peg Streep

Video
A Thousand Points of Elvis (1991)
   produced by George King

Web Sites
http://www.yall.com/culture/art/patty/shrine.html
   Exhibition and insightful text by photographer Patty Carroll of many personal Elvis shrines she has photographed

http://www.elimpersonators.com/shrines.html
   Photographer Patty Carroll's site of shrines and Elvis collections

http://www.andrewlane.com
   Purchase church materials such as candles, altar cloths

http:www.web-net.com.cut-it-out/index.html
   E-mail: jonthomp@freewwweb.com
   Purchase shrine decorations;
   Kathleen Trenchard (210) 225-6009

http://www.dizzy.library.arizona.edu/images/folkarts/papflowers.html
   Purchase and get ideas for shrine decorations from other cultural traditions

http://www.mit.edu:8001/activities/41West/Elvis.html
   MIT shrine to Elvis

http://www.maui.net/~designs/spirithouse/
   Purchase a home or garden hand-crafted shrine from Hawaii and use it as the centerpiece of a tiki-theme shrine.

http://www.coolpage.com/aries/articles/altarp/htm
   Information about creating personal altars

http://www.ccimports.com/public/0RetBG.htm
   Get ideas for three-dimensional shrines from other cultural traditions.

http://members.aol.com/ElvisAronP/Elvis1.html
   EP Shrine site

THE ELVIS AND YOU EXPERIENCE

Make Your Own Elvis Shrine
There are several recurring traditional themes and objects to be found in almost all Elvis shrines. They're not obligatory, but they do make up the powerful iconography that these shrines are famous for. (See "Collecting Elvis" for ideas and sources for many of these items.)

The Ubiquitous Elvis Bust

Usually made of plaster, brightly painted or pristine all-white, the life-size Elvis bust is the most frequently used centerpiece of the personal Elvis shrine. These are most often made in Mexico and are inexpensive and easily found in garden supply or plaster statue shops. Busts made of other materials, such as bronze, and in many sizes also exist and can be found at flea markets, garage sales, and fan conventions.

Other *Objets d'Elvis*

Here again, there are many traditional objects that are often associated with Elvis Rooms.

Concert scarves

Leis

Bradford Exchange plates

Ardleigh & Elliott music boxes

Framed photos

Buttons

Candles

Some Unconventional Props

Use objects that have an Elvis association or things that he surrounded himself with. Fifties, sixties, and seventies vintage stuff is a good start.

Microphone

Cigar: Hav-a-Tampa, Cigarillo, or
    Villager Kiel brand

Gun (a toy gun might be best)

Motorcycle or car parts

Motorcycle helmet

Yachting cap

Car keys

Guitar and pick

Juicy Fruit gum

Tiny replica of Graceland

Elvis' army division insignia

Models of cars

Models of army vehicles

Models of airplanes

TCB jewelry

Old 45s (or your first Elvis music,
    even if it was an 8-track)

RCA's nipper dog figurine

Relics from Graceland

Police department badges

Elvis' karate patches

Rig Your Shrine with Sound

Place your stereo speakers in your Elvis Room or on either side of your shrine (or even just place a small tape recorder behind it), load up the Elvis music, and enjoy your favorite songs while gazing at Elvis.

Rig Your Shrine with Lighting

Elvis loved being in the spotlight and your shrine is a good place to shine one on him.

Dedicate Your Shrine to a Specific Era or Theme

If you have a definite preference, say Rockabilly Elvis over Vegas Elvis, why not concentrate on adorning your shrine with objects from a specific period of Elvis' (and your) life. How about a Hawaiian mood? Leis, tropical or tiki decorations, pictures of Elvis in a bathing suit, terry cloth hat, anything blue or "Aloha" concert related.

Locations for Your Shrine

In Your House

Ideally, an Elvis shrine, if you can spare the space, would be a whole room. A full room shrine will be the envy of all your friends.

Your Kitchen

This may be the easiest to accomplish since there are so many products to fill your kitchen with: Elvis mugs, glasses, plates, napkins, spoon rests, kitchen towels, and those hundreds of refrigerator magnets.

"After finally gaining an extra room when my eldest son moved away from home, I got my long-awaited Elvis Room. I have so many things in my collection that I can't even display them all at once. It consists of things that I have collected since I was eight years old, from my first album, *Elvis: The TV Special*, to the Pepsi bottles created to commemorate his last birthday. If it says Elvis, has his picture, or is related to Graceland, I buy it! I have Elvis in my blood, anything and everything Elvis, that is my passion."
—Teresa Guest, president of the Society of Admiration for Elvis Fan Club

Your Bedroom

Bedrooms, more than anywhere else, suit the purposes of an Elvis room. Surround yourself with pillows, blankets, bedspreads, Elvis-material curtains, walls covered with Elvis. Sweet dreams.

Your Bathroom

This is a small space that can be generously decorated with memorabilia. Some well-placed photos could make that relaxing bath an occasion to remember.

An Old Refrigerator

That defunct refrigerator you were going to throw out would make a good self-contained shrine.

An Old (Preferably Shot-Out) Television Set

Elvis loved television and it played a major part in the beginning of his career. It may be where you first saw him, so having a shrine in one would be especially poignant. If you can find a vintage, cabinet-type television set, it would make a great conversation piece.

A Closet

If you aren't ready to share Elvis with the world, you can place your shrine/collection in an extra closet. This has the added advantage of being lockable and, if it's a walk-in, affording you some privacy while at your shrine.

At the Office

Office and other "public" shrines may also be used as a departure point for conversation and conversion. (See "Elvis in Cyberspace" for tips on Elvisizing your computer.)

Your Car or Mobile Home

Elvis adored to drive. Mount a little Elvis statue on your dashboard and take him along on your next road trip.

Exotic Shrines

You can purchase handcrafted, exotic shrines from different cultures and traditions. A spirit house made in Maui would be an interesting setting for your Elvis shrine since he loved Hawaii and spent many good times there.
Bill Ernst
Design Solutions
Fax: (808) 878-6644
http://www.designexcellence.com
http://www.maui.net/~designs/spirithouse/

Use a Genuine Shrine or Icon Case to House Your Elvis Shrine

Phoenix Studio is a small wood shop that designs and builds real prayer and contemplative furniture.
Phoenix Studio
Attn: Michael Shea
P.O. Box 6024
Annapolis, Maryland 21401
(800) 683-7904
E-mail: phoenix@maryland.net
http://www.doubleclicked.com/phoenix/home.html

Exterior Shrines

If you really want to share Elvis with the world, you don't have to confine him to the inside of your home. Any outdoor space you have access to (lawns, yards, terraces, fire escapes) would make a great location for an Elvis shrine. Elvis busts can be found in element-resistant concrete from certain garden supply centers that can also give you directions on weatherproofing whatever else you want to place outdoors at your shrine.

If you can run a natural gas outlet, you can make an eternal flame like the one in the Meditation Garden at Graceland. Incorporating a fountain modeled after that one would be a soothing and peaceful touch. Planting a tree or creating a topiary or floral tribute at your shrine would be a beautiful and long-term gesture in Elvis' honor. You can train ivy into a lightning-bolt, tiger, or guitar shape, or even into the letters *EP* or *TCB*. You may want to install a motion sensor to protect your outdoor Elvis shrine from burglars and varmints.

Obtaining and Displaying an Elvis Relic

When visiting Graceland or Elvis' birthplace in Tupelo, try to pick up a leaf, blade of grass, or pebble from the ground to place at your shrine. Please do not defoliate the area to accomplish this. The "relic" you choose may be enclosed in a glassine envelope or, better yet, in a shadowbox frame. This is a frame that has some depth to it and is the perfect way to preserve and display any precious three-dimensional article. These are available from Exposures, a company that specializes in photographic and archival materials. Thumbing through their great catalog will give you other ideas for displaying your collection.

Exposures Catalog
One Memory Lane
P.O. Box 3615
Oshkosh, Wisconsin 54903-3615
(800) 222-4947
(920) 231-4886
Fax: (920) 231-6942

Keep a Shrine Guest Book

Have a small blank-paged, tiger-print-covered journal kept open at your shrine so you and friends can record feelings while visiting there.

Scents for Your Shrine

Brut Cologne
Douse a concert-type scarf with the cologne Elvis wore and drape it around your Elvis statue's neck.

Incense
Select fragrances that remind you of Elvis or his songs: roses, rain, Christmas scents. They may also have an aromatherapy effect on you.

Put Your Shrine on the Internet
Share your shrine with the world over the internet by setting up a shrine cam. (See "Elvis in Cyberspace" chapter for ideas.)

Animate Your Shrine
Place your shrine on a turntable or, for the less electronically inclined, a lazy Susan. Generating movement will give it vitality.

Traveling Shrines
You can create a shrine that can be taken with you when you travel by placing a favorite photo or object in a small decorated box. Pack it in your suitcase so you can have the comforts of Elvis wherever your travels may take you. Several Elvis artists make small decorative Elvis-themed boxes that would be ideal for this purpose.

Pamela Wood
Pamela Wood designs custom-made, hand-decorated boxes that are hip and slightly irreverent but still reflect a love for Elvis. Contact her for the names of stores that are currently carrying her work.
776 North Parkwood Road
Decatur, Georgia 30030
Fax: (404) 378-8520
E-mail: p.wood@mindspring.com

Kata Billups
Kata Billups's Elvis art is extremely original, tender, and humorous. She makes boxes that could serve as traveling shrines or be artwork themselves. And she makes a portable shrine triptych that can fit into your briefcase or suitcase and go wherever you go, or stay on your wall as a permanent shrine.
PMB 232
1000 Johnnie Dodds Boulevard, Suite 103
Mount Pleasant, South Carolina 29464
(843) 805-7774
http://www.katabillups.com

ELVIS IMPERSONATORS

The very existence of Elvis impersonators is one of the most controversial subjects among Elvis fans. The Elvis world is clearly split into two camps. To some fans impersonators are a fun way to remember Elvis and get even a small taste of what it was like to experience him in person; other fans, however, see them as a mockery and as part of the reason Elvis is so often trivialized as a hackneyed, pop-culture joke instead of being treated as the gifted artist he was. Even the name itself is controversial. There are some who refuse to be called Elvis impersonators. They prefer to be called Elvis tribute artists, Elvis illusionists, Elvis stylists, Elvis performers, Elvis actors, Elvis authenticators, or Elvis replicators.

Elvis impersonators (or EIs as they're sometimes referred to in fan slang) existed throughout Elvis' career. As early as 1956, Nancy Kozikowski, a junior high school student in New Mexico, performed as Elvis. Dave Ehlert began in 1967, Wade Cummings in 1968, and Rick Saucedo in 1972. Elvis himself was amused by it all and saw the fun in it. In May of 1976 he even invited impersonator Douglas Roy to perform onstage for him for a few minutes at the Lake Tahoe Horizon. Elvis was said to laugh along with everyone else in the country at comedian Andy Kaufman's impersonation of him on *Saturday Night Live*. But during his lifetime, Elvis impersonators were a seldom-seen novelty act. With the real Elvis constantly touring the United States—giving a concert every three days on average—there

An Elvis Impersonator with Elvis in Los Angeles. Elvis is the one on the right.

Sandi Miller

Elvis impersonator contestants jamming together on stage at 1998 Portage, Indiana, FANtasy Fest

was little demand for an impersonator. Why settle for an imitation when you could get the real thing?

After his death in 1977, the phenomena exploded. The demand was suddenly there and hundreds of singers, entertainers, and devoted fans started careers as Elvis impersonators to fill the void left by Elvis' passing and spawning a cottage industry that continues to grow to this day. One estimate puts the number of EIs worldwide at 3,000, another at 10,000. Whatever the number, it seems to grow unabated so that now the Elvis impersonator has become as accepted and ubiquitous a part of our culture as Elvis himself. Today there's nothing unusual about an EI appearing on a cruise ship, at a wedding, or a corporate event. They frequently pop up in advertising campaigns and in the plotlines of movies and television shows. No longer on the fringe, they are now a part of the mainstream and have become American icons in and of themselves. At the 1984 Olympics in Los Angeles, Elvis impersonators were part of the festivities. On July 4, 1986, 200 EIs performed en masse as part of the centennial celebration at the Statue of Liberty. Two years later, a delegation of EIs took part in the 1988 Olympics in Seoul, Korea. A pre-fame Quentin Tarrintino played an Elvis impersonator on an episode of *Designing Women* in 1989. Even the January 1993 Clinton Inauguration had an Elvis float filled with Elvis look-alikes, exploiting the many Elvis references made by the candidate during that presidential election.

This plethora of imitators is utterly unique to Elvis. When was the last time you heard about a Frank Sinatra or a Jerry Garcia imitator? Even if someone was inclined

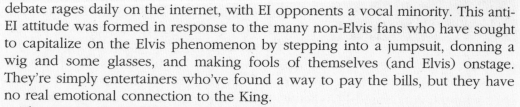

Mike Schreiber

to imitate those other two pop stars, would they find an audience? The popularity of Elvis impersonators is, if nothing else, certainly a testament to the popularity of Elvis and of how much he is missed.

Although the culture at large seems to have accepted the EI, there is a sizable percentage of Elvis fans who are vehemently dead set against the idea. Their love of Elvis is inversely proportional to their hatred of EIs. To some Elvis purists, an EI is seen as a vulture making a living by lampooning a man they view in almost reverential terms. The debate rages daily on the internet, with EI opponents a vocal minority. This anti-EI attitude was formed in response to the many non-Elvis fans who have sought to capitalize on the Elvis phenomenon by stepping into a jumpsuit, donning a wig and some glasses, and making fools of themselves (and Elvis) onstage. They're simply entertainers who've found a way to pay the bills, but they have no real emotional connection to the King.

They exaggerate Elvis' foibles in pursuit of the cheap laugh. The film *Honeymoon in Vegas* is a good example of the EI as a buffoon archetype. The entire film reinforced the image of Elvis impersonators as a bunch of losers and freaks, the butt of jokes. The fans who take offense at EIs have good reason to feel this way when they see some of the portrayals of Elvis that focus on clichés of food consumption, drug references, and other eccentricities. This form of imitation is far from flattery. More people today have seen Elvis impersonators than the real Elvis live. The parody image threatens to replace the image of the real man.

Although there are those EIs whose acts damage Elvis' image, there are many more whose performances are sincere tributes. They want to recreate some of the magic and charisma that

Impersonators at Stan Mayo's Las Vegas Elvis convention

John O'Hara

John O'Hara

Chris Young, veteran EI, giving tips to Quentin Flagg, the next generation

was part of every Elvis concert. To enjoy Elvis, a person can listen to an Elvis record or watch an Elvis movie, but one way to experience the excitement and spontaneity of a live show is to see someone else perform live.

Many EIs are true fans who are motivated by the best of reasons and the great majority of Elvis impersonators fall into this category. Part entertainer, part historian, they are students of Elvisology and they do their homework. They endlessly study his recordings and master subtle nuances of inflection. They review his films and scrutinize the bootleg videos of his many performances to soak up the look, the voice, the moves, the cool. They try to mimic his walk, his laugh, the way he holds his hands. They memorize his stage banter. They respond to shouts from the audience with the anticipated Elvis retort. Some of them even drink water like Elvis did (with his hand facing his body). Elvis is a language that they've learned to speak fluently.

Elvis had to invent himself as he went along; he had no template to follow. His impersonators have an advantage in that they've had 20-odd years to study the films and recordings of Elvis' 23-year career. Some impersonators have been doing Elvis longer than Elvis did Elvis. Some of the new generation of EIs, many of whom started as children, already have 5 or 10 years of performance experience under their belts before they reach 19, the age at which Elvis' professional career started.

There are two main classifications of good impersonators: sound-alikes and look-alikes. The sound-alikes are limited either by their lack of a physical resemblance to Elvis or just choose to concentrate only on Elvis' music. One of the best of these is Ronny McDowell who sang all the Elvis songs on the soundtracks of both *Elvis*, the TV movie starring Kurt Russell, and *Elvis and the Beauty Queen,* starring Don Johnson. Jimmy (Orion) Ellis was also considered by some to be a sound-alike. In a publicity stunt around the peak of the Elvis-is-alive hysteria, Shelby Singleton, the person who bought Sun Records from Sam Phillips, released several records by Ellis on the Sun label with the implication that it was Elvis. The vocal similarity was enough to fool some people. More recently James Brown, a Belfast, Northern Ireland, EI, released an album of Nirvana, Bob Marley, and other contemporary artists singing in the style of EP. Elvis was always a great

Frankie Castro with Elvis' nurse, Marion Cocke

John O'Hara

interpreter of other people's songs. The sound-alikes give an indication of what Elvis might sound like if he were recording today.

The best EIs combine elements of both sound and vision. They strive for a photo-realistic approach that requires a minimal suspension of disbelief. They dress in accurate recreations that cost thousands of dollars each of Elvis' stage wardrobe. They grow and style and dye their hair into the perfect Elvis Head. They seek out people who personally knew Elvis to gain some insight into their subject. Some EIs perform with the same musicians and vocalists who performed with Elvis. Rick Saucado performed for 17 weeks with the Jordanaires and D. J. Fontana on Broadway and then toured the country. Charlie Hodge, Elvis' right-hand man on stage, has even performed with EIs, handing them water, feeding them scarves, and catching their guitars. If an EI can't get the real people, then they just recreate them with performers impersonating the Jordanaires, the Blue Moon Boys, J. D. Sumner and the Stamps, or the TCB Band. There are even EI events at which people impersonate characters from Elvis' life such as Priscilla, Vernon, Gladys, and the Colonel.

On one level, Elvis is the world's easiest entertainer to imitate. Elvis' look was so original—the black hair, the jumpsuits, the sunglasses, the sideburns—that when anyone puts on the outfit he's instantly identifiable. Elvis realized the power of the costume. His stage costumes were designed to transform him from a mortal man to a King. For the EI, it transforms him from a mortal man to an Elvis. The costume is the most important element in the transformation process. Reproductions of the best Elvis costumes can cost more than five grand but, then again, what would you expect a magic suit to cost?

It may be easy to dress like Elvis, but it's difficult to physically resemble the man whom many people consider the best-looking man who ever lived. Many of the large men with black hair and caped superhero outfits at EI events resemble Superman as much as Elvis. Some EIs have gone so far as to have plastic surgery. Although people may look on this as a bit extreme, everyday people visit plastic

Elvis tribute artist Steve Davis performing at the annual Elvis tribute held at Blueberry Hill restaurant and club in St. Louis, Missouri. Behind him are people portraying Vernon, Gladys, Lisa Marie, Uncle Vester, and even Michael Jackson.

surgeons to improve their looks, often with photos of a pop star's face that they want to emulate. Why not try to look like the most handsome man in the world?

Some EIs specialize in a specific Elvis era, sometimes by choice and sometimes because of limitations. Fifteen-year-old EIs can do a mean Rockabilly Elvis but can't pull off the Vegas Elvis until they get some more testosterone in their system. Some of the Vegas Elvises would have a hard time convincing anyone that they're a 19-year-old rebel. The three periods of Elvis—Rockabilly Cat, 1968 Comeback Black Leather Elvis, and Majestic Vegas Elvis—are the usual categories of Elvis portrayal. The most versatile of EIs are those who can pull off all three. These days EIs are getting creative and continue to add other Elvises to their repertoire—GI Blues Elvis in full army uniform and Movie Star Elvis dressed in the wardrobe from a specific movie are starting to show up at contests. Sometimes EIs will re-create a specific Elvis performance like the "Aloha from Hawaii" concert or the "unplugged" rehearsal pit segment of the "'68 Comeback Special."

Who are these people? The stereotype portrayed in the media is that of lost souls so lacking in their own identity that they must adopt someone else's. They're often portrayed as eccentric nut cases living a delusional fantasy life. As usual, the reality is something other than this ignorant and elitist view. EIs are more often sincere Elvis fans who are expressing their passion for Elvis and his music and sharing it with those who feel the same way.

Extremely talented West Coast impersonator Dean Z in his GI Blues costume

Travis Morris, Johnny Thompson, and Irv Cass illustrate three different phases of Elvis' career

John O'Hara

Some see themselves as actors with a juicy role. When Kurt Russell played Elvis in the 1979 TV movie *Elvis*, he was impersonating Elvis and doing a damn good job of it, too. Russell landed an Emmy for the role. To perform as Elvis is a no less valid choice than Richard Widmark touring as Will Rogers or Hal Holbrook performing as Mark Twain. But if someone chooses to portray Elvis, they're labeled as a loon. Of course, if those actors stayed in character after the show, that would be a different story.

There are those EIs who stay in character 24 hours a day, but they are a very rare few. (There are also people who stay in character as Napoleon all day.) Sometimes if an EI has made the commitment to an Elvis Head, the characteristic black hair and sideburns that instantly announce "Elvis!" to the world, people just assume he's in character. The 24-hour Elvis Head can be a problem for some professional EIs who'd like to limit how many times they have to hear "Yo Elvis" every day. Some EIs affect an Elvis-nullifying disguise of a hat and wrap-around shades.

Every good Elvis impersonator who steps onto a stage first has to overcome the stigma created by all the bad ones. It's hard to witness a good EI performance and not feel the fun and positive energy that these shows generate. They have the feeling of revival meetings, and skeptics who experience a good show are often converted.

Although EIs are disliked by some Elvis fans, there are many others who have embraced the phenomenon wholeheartedly. Many EIs have their own fan clubs that travel with them in a caravan of cars and buses to lend support at every contest. They sell their own memorabilia. People save the towels they use, the glasses they drink from, the sheets they sleep on, and even make deals with their hairdressers to have access to their hair. During the scarves and kisses part of the show, they approach

John O'Hara

Las Vegas Elvis impersonator Brendan Paul, off duty and trying to remain incognito

John O'Hara

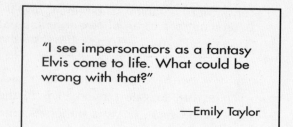

"I see impersonators as a fantasy Elvis come to life. What could be wrong with that?"

—Emily Taylor

the stage and swoon as they would if they were being kissed by Elvis himself. Most entertainment requires the suspension of disbelief, and some fans are willing to meet this fantasy half way.

Graceland at first was opposed to the existence of Elvis impersonators. Claiming to be protecting Elvis' image, they even sued a few of the more successful ones for copyright infringement and licensing fees. But now, just about the only Elvis impersonators who pay a licensing fee are the ones who jump out of planes. EPE has since given up the fight against this grass roots movement and now recognize EIs as an inevitable part of the Elvis community.

In addition to performance venues in casinos, cruise ships, and music clubs around the world, there are also contests held around the country. Many of the contests are fan club sponsored benefits for charity. One of the best ways to enjoy the EI experience is at one of these contests. The competition adds an edge to the show. It's part *Star Search*, part beauty pageant, part magic show, and a lot of fun to compare the EIs. Elvis himself got his start in the music business by competing in contests and talent shows. Many contests end with an onstage jam with all the contestants. The sight of multiple Elvis' from different eras performing together is a mind-boggling spectacle.

One of the most important EI contests is the Images of Elvis contest held in Memphis during Tribute Week. Although this is the mother of all Elvis impersonator contests, the organizers also have a January contest and regional contests throughout the year. Images was started in 1981 by Dr. E. O. Franklin, Elvis' former veterinarian, who still runs the Desoto County Animal Clinic in Southaven, Mississippi. Many careers have been launched after winning or placing in this high-pro-

John O'Hara

Dean Z performing in Vegas for fans all too willing to suspend disbelief

John O'Hara

file contest. The contest begins one week before the Candlelight Vigil with EIs from all over the world competing. The judges rate the EIs on four qualities: 50 percent on vocal abilities, 15 percent on appearance, 15 percent on audience appeal, and 20 percent on stage presence. There seemed to be a marked preference for the Vegas Elvis over all others until 1990 when Kevin Mills from New Jersey was the first Young Elvis to win the contest. In 1992, Mori Yasumasa, a Japanese impersonator, was the first non-American to win.

There are also alternative impersonators. They are not trying to re-create the Elvis experience so much as interpret it. And sometimes that interpretation is quite broad. El Vez, a.k.a. Robert Lopez, created his Mexican-American Elvis with the Elvettes, a backup group of singers named Lisa Marie and Priscillita, and Hispanic versions of Elvis songs. There's even a lesbian EI, Elvis Herselvis, backed by a band called the Straight White Males. Dread Zepplin is a band led by an Elvis impersonator named Tortelvis who covers Led Zepplin songs sung in Reggae style in Elvis' voice. Some of these alternative EIs are just vocal impressionists doing a loose interpretation of Elvis' style. Not satisfied to "accurately" re-create Elvis, they filter him through their own persona. They are running Elvis software on their non-Elvis hardware.

What will happen to EIs in the future? Is it a short-lived phenomenon that will die out as Elvis fans do? Or will it continue to regenerate as new, younger fans discover Elvis? Will impersonating Elvis evolve into a unique American form of entertainment? There will come a time when there will be no people left alive who have seen the real Elvis perform and impersonators will bear an even more onerous responsibility of carrying on a cultural tradition. EIs can also give

John O'Hara

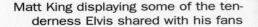

Matt King displaying some of the tenderness Elvis shared with his fans

Larry Travis performing poolside at the Circle of Memories Honeymoon Hideaway weekend annual fan gathering at Elvis' Palm Springs home, May 1999

John O'Hara

us a chance to look at some of the great "what ifs" about Elvis. If he were alive today, what would he be wearing? What would he be singing? What would Elvis be like as an old man? There will be a legion of entertainers to show us the possibilities.

ESSENTIAL ELVISOLOGY

Actors Portraying Elvis

When an actor portrays Elvis, he's basically being an Elvis impersonator. Here are some notable Elvis portrayals.

Kurt Russell
  Elvis the Movie
Val Kilmer
  True Romance
Don Johnson
  Elvis and the Beauty Queen
Dale Midkiff
  Elvis and Me
David Keith
  Heartbreak Hotel
Michael St. Gerard
  Great Balls of Fire and "Elvis: The Early Years"
Andy Kaufman
  Saturday Night Live
Eddie Murphy
  Saturday Night Live
Nicholas Cage
  Wild at Heart (1990)

Stephen Jones
  Mystery Train (1990)
Peter Dobson
  Forrest Gump (1994)
Larry Seth
  Elvis Lives (Broadway play)
Martin Shaw
  Are You Lonesome Tonight? (London production)
Tim Whitnall, Shakin' Stevens, James Proby
  Elvis Stage Show (London theatrical production)
Alex Courtney
  Elvis and the Colonel
Rick Peters
  Elvis Meets Nixon
Pete Wilcox
  Dudes

The EPIIA Creed

The Elvis Presley Impersonators International Association is a nonprofit organization that drafted the following code of behavior for Elvis impersonators in order to maintain professionalism and high standards.

1. I have an obligation to all associations, groups, and businesses who purchase my entertainment services, and to provide those services in a professional and ethical manner.
2. I have an obligation as an Elvis performer in all my personal, business, and social contracts, to be conscious of my image and what I represent and to conduct myself accordingly.
3. I will provide leadership and direction in continuing the music and style of Elvis while lending strength and direction to the growth of the activity as a great world-class entertainment media in "continuing the legacy of the King."

Dos and Don'ts of Impersonating Elvis

Do study Elvis trivia. Know your subject.

Do copy Elvis' best qualities. Be polite, be humble, be helpful, be sincere.

Don't take it too far. Only one person was meant to be Elvis 24 hours a day, and he died in 1977.

Do wear your natural hair if possible. If you're follicularly challenged, a wig might be necessary but a full head of natural hair, dyed unnaturally black, is best. Use Lady Clairol blue-black or L'Oréal Excellence blue-black.

Do wear the best costume you can afford. It's an investment in credibility.

Don't wear the costume off stage. No real pro would think of walking around Graceland in his stage clothes.

Do perform for charity events as often as possible. It's both good policy and good practice for paying gigs.

An impersonator in the Meditation Garden committing what some fans consider to be a major faux pas, wearing a stage costume while at Graceland

Laura Levin

Don't wear sunglasses the entire time you perform. Elvis didn't. Too many impersonators use them as a crutch.

Do practice historical accuracy: generally try to keep the song, your costume, and your hair in the same era.

Do have a sense of humor. Elvis didn't take himself too seriously so you definitely shouldn't either.

Don't give an autograph as Elvis Presley unless your name has been legally changed to Elvis Presley. Which brings us to another don't.

Don't change your name to Elvis Presley.

Past Winners of the Images of Elvis Contest

1987—Glenn Bowles
1988—Michael Hoover
1989—Clay Smith
1990—Kevin Mills
1991—Doug Church
1992—Mori Yasumasa
1993—Ray Guillmette, Jr.

1994—Steve Chappell
1995—Chris Young
1996—Mike Albert
1997—Darren Lee
1998—Travis Morris
1999—Irv Cass

Books

Biggest Elvis
   P. F. Kluge
The King & I: A Little Gallery of Elvis Impersonators
   photographs by Kent Barker; text by Karin Pritikin
Stark Raving Elvis
   William McCranor Henderson
Impersonating Elvis
   Leslie Rubinkowski
I, Elvis: Confessions of an Elvis Impersonator
   WIlliam McCranor Henderson
All the King's Knights
   Rebecca Polston
E: Reflections on the Birth of the Elvis Faith
   John Strausbaugh
Return to Sender: The First Complete Discography of Elvis Tribute and Novelty Records, 1956–1986
   Howard F Banney
The Impersonators Guide Book
   Ed and Jackie Franklin
   To order call (601) 342-4899 or e-mail: JFrank1037@aol.com.

Video

"It's Good to Be King"
  Tom Petty Music Video
"Leaving Las Vegas"
  Sheryl Crow Music Video
Legends
Finding Graceland
High Tide
Aria
Dudes
Elvis' Grave
Into the Night
Rockula
Mondo Elvis: The Real Life Rites and Rituals of the King's Most Devoted Fans
Honeymoon in Vegas
David Susskind Show
  All-Elvis Impersonator show
Man on the Moon
  The Andy Kaufman bio-pic starring Jim Carrey
"The Night of 1000 Elvises"
  TBS Special
Almost Elvis
"Viva Elvis"
  British documentary interview with Butch Polston, Images of Elvis contest
"Elvis U.S.A"

Dick Clark's 1978 television special starring the nation's top impersonators
The Gong Show 1978
  All Elvis Impersonators show
The Last Precinct
  An NBC show from the early '80s in which an impersonator named Pete Wilcox plays an Elvis look-alike cop with Elvis hairdo and uniform altered to look like a jumpsuit. He arrests people with comments like, "You have the right to remain silent, *baby.*" And he sings to the prisoners in jail.
Sledge Hammer
  In the episode "All Shook Up," to catch a murderer who's been offing Elvis impersonators, the detective poses as an Elvis impersonator.
The New Twilight Zone
  An Elvis impersonator goes back in time to meet Elvis and ends up replacing him.
Civil Wars
  The pilot episode concerns a person who becomes an impersonator and faces divorce.
Geraldo
  EI show

Web Sites

http://www.geocities.com/~arpt/eiw.html
  Elvis impersonators web ring
http://www.elvisimpersonators.com
  Almost Elvis: Elvis impersonators and their quest for the crown
http://www.elimpersonators.com
  Patty Carroll's gallery of Elvis impersonators
http://members.aol.comelvez.com

El Vez: the Mexican Elvis site
http://www.style-beauty-barber.com/elvis.htm
  '50s, '60s, and '70s Elvis wigs; style, beauty, and barber supply company
http://www.elvis-extraganza.com/impersonator.html
  Gallery of impersonators
http://members.aol.com/nudeelvis/

National Association of Amateur
Elvis Impersonators
http://roswell.fortunecity.com/
blavatsky/114/home.htm
Canadian Elvis Tribute artists
http://www.geocities.com/Hollywood/
Location/9999
William Maurice, Ontario Canada
http:www.impersonators.de
German EI web site
http://www.members.aol.com/
ronmcfan/ronnie.htm
Ronnie McDowell & the Rockits site;
concert schedule, audio
http://www.thedreamking.com
Trent Carlini's web site
http://www.tsf.net/personal/saucedo
Rick Saucedo's web site
http://www.flyingelvi.com/
Flying Elvi, Las Vegas
http://hometown.aol.com/elvisdeman/
fan/index.html
Jeff, a young impersonator's site
http://www.du.altawixa.de/telecom/
Marco Knappe, Teddy Elvis
http://www.kingtracks.com/
King Tracks; Elvis music, CDs, and
cassettes

http://www.tune1000.com
Karaoke site
http://www.bigbadelvi.com/
The Fresno Christmas Caroling Elvis
Impersonators site
http://www.elvis-extravaganza.com/
Elvis extravanganza
http://www.elimpersonators.com/store.
html
Patty Carroll's site; Elvis impersonator playing cards and pens for sale
http://www.pcostume.com/
Professional Costumer web site
http://www.pcostume.com/elvis/
The Elvis Impersonator Connection
site; scarves, belts for sale
http://www.imperialpalace.com
Imperial Palace Hotel in Las Vegas,
Legends in Concert and the Antique
and Classic Auto Collection
(800) 634-6441
(702) 731-3311
http://mglinks.com/elvis.htm
Krewe of Elvis Marching Club of
New Orleans

THE ELVIS AND YOU EXPERIENCE

Be In or Attend an Impersonator Performance or Contest

This is a list of venues and contacts from whom you can get information about
entering, or viewing, performances and contests across the States and Canada.
Images of Elvis International Competition
Memphis, Tribute Week
Doc and Jackie Franklin
8330 Highway 51 North
Southaven, Mississippi 3871

(601) 342-4899
E-mail: jfrank1037@aol.com

Images of Elvis Regional Competitions

Shreveport, Louisiana
    Dianne Patrick
    (318) 996-6102
    E-mail: dianne@jewel-paula.com
Monroe, Louisiana
    Gene Shaw
    (318) 323-5847
    (318) 396-5194
LaCrosse, Wisconsin
    Mark Viner
    (608) 781-7755
    or
    Ronny Craig
    (608) 785-7464
Hamilton, Ohio
    Taylor Lawrence
    P.O. Box 34
    Minerva, Kentucky 41062
    (606) 882-2072
Grand Rapids, Michigan
    Bonnie Lee
    P.O. Box 363
    Howard City, Michigan 49329
    (888) 746-9368
    (616) 937-6946
    E-mail: showcase@pathwaynet.com
    http://www.showcase-ent.com
Cedar Bluffs, Iowa
    Johnny Ray Gomez
    Bluffs Run Casino
    2701 23 Avenue
    Council Bluffs, Iowa 51501
    (800) 238-2946 ext. 1743
    (712) 323-2500
    Fax: (712) 322-9354
Fargo, North Dakota

    Gary Weber
    (701) 282-2650
    Fax: (701) 282-2487
Portland, Oregon
    Jamie Goetz
    17438 SE Haig Drive
    Portland, Oregon 97236
    (503) 760-2416
    Fax: (503) 760-8227
Springfeild, Illinois
    Fred or Nora Puglia
    Perfect Impressions Entertainment
    (217) 793-3733
Augusta, Georgia
    Steve Chappell and Danny Haywood
    May be contacted through Images.
South Bend, Indiana
    Dottie Skwiat
    Gerald Productions
    16615 Gerard Street
    Granger, Indiana 46530
    (219) 272-0426
South Bend, Indiana
    Cindy Amador
    (219) 288-0223
Annual Tribute to the King of Rock
and Roll
    Tribute Week
    Alfred's Restaurant
    197 Beale Street
    Memphis, Tennessee 38103
    (901) 525-3711
Viva Las Vegas
    Stan Mayo
    P.O. Box 341232
    Los Angeles, California 90034
    (310) 815-1962
Grand Elvis Tribute
    Junior Talley
    Galesburg, Illinois
    (309) 734-2289

Photo reprinted with permission

Trent Carlini, Elvis look-alike and sound-alike, one of the best in the business

Legends in Concert
    On Stage Entertainment, Inc.
    Las Vegas, Nevada
    (702) 253-1333
Elvis National Competition
    Tropicana Casino
    Brighton Avenue & Boardwalk
    Atlantic City, New Jersey 08401
    (609) 340-4000
Memories Theatre
    2141 Parkway
    Pigeon Forge, Tennessee
    (800) 325-3078
    (423) 428-7852
Visions of Elvis Impersonator Contest
    Bossier City, Louisiana
    Dianne Patrick
    (318) 996-6102
    E-mail: dianne@jewel-parla.com
South Central Regional EP Contest
    Monroe, Louisiana

Gene Shaw
    (318) 323-5847
    (318) 396-5194
National Elvis Impersonator Contest
    Phil De Angelo
    (609) 625-2021
Canadian National Elvis Tribute and
Convention
    Orillia, Canada
    Chamber of Commerce
    (705) 326-4424
    E-mail:orilinfo@orillia.com
    http://www.orillia.com
Elvis Fest
    Jamestown, New York
    Weisbord and Son Promotions
    http://members.xoom.com/darod/
    sterling/fest.htm
    http://www.madbbs.com/~kado/
    fest.htm
The IIAC Annual Convention Contest
    Jerome Marion
    (708) 297-1234
Collingwood Elvis Festival
    Kathy DeNike
    P.O. Box 2346, R.R. #2
    Collingwood, Ontario, Canada L9Y 3Z1
    (705) 444-1162
    (705) 445-0221
    Fax: (705) 445-6858
    E-mail: kdenike@bmts.com
    E-mail: chamber@georgian.net
    http://www.collingwood.net/elvis
World Championship Elvis
Impersonator Contest
    Paul Recht
    71 North Willett Street
    Memphis, Tennessee 38104

E-mail: prairiesquid@iname.com
http://members.accessus.net/
~gboyd/index.html

Night of 100 Elvises
Baltimore, Maryland
Carol Carroll
P.O. Box 231
Glyndon, Maryland 21071-0231
(410) 494-9558 in Maryland
(888) 494-9558
Fax: (410) 833-8991

The Sabre Room
8900 West 95 Street
Hickory Hills, Illinois
(708) 598-1200

Portage Annual FANtasy Fest
Usually held in October, this fund-aiser for the Special Olympics is a con-cert and contest, fan convention, and sock hop with buffet meals, Elvis games, auctions, and memorabilia deal-ers. It is sponsored by Portage Elvis Fans, TCP Memorial Benefit Committee, and Elvis Fans from Hoosierland.
3179 Driftwood Court
Carmel, Indiana 46033
(800) 283-8687

(219) 926-2255
http://www.porter.CO.Porter.IN.US/

Showcase Entertainment Annual Elvis Contest
Bonnie Lee
P.O. Box 363
Howard City, Michigan 49329
(888) 746-9368
(616) 937-6946
http://www.showcase-ent.com
E-mail: showcase@pathwaynet.com

Holiday Star Theatre
Merrilville, Indiana
(219) 769-6311

Legends Theater
301 Business Highway 17 South
Surfside Beach, South Carolina 29575
(843) 238-7827
(800) 960-7469

Foxwoods Resort Casino
Foxwoods has an Elvis impersonator performing twice a year.
I-95, Route 2
Mashantucket, Connecticut 06339
(800) 752-9244
http://www.foxwoods.com

See Some EIs on Video

Of course the whole point is to see a show live, but watching an EI contest or showcase on tape is a good way to get to know who some of the players are. If you can't make it to an EI contest, you can sometimes order a videotape from the promoters of the shows. Call them for information about ordering videos.

Almost Elvis: Elvis Impersonators and Their Quest for the Crown

One of the best videos you can get to bring you up to speed on who's who in the EI world is *Almost Elvis*, a documentary film on the state of the art in Elvis Impersonation directed by John Paget. The producers traveled to Elvis imper-sonator contests and venues all around the country and filmed the up-and-com-ing as well as the big names of the business.

Almost Elvis
Blue Suede Films
P.O. Box 502
Olympia, Washington 98507
(360) 570-5000
E-mail: bluesuedef@aol.com

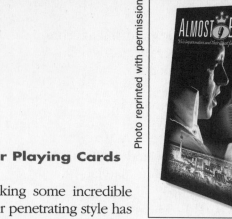

Where to Get Elvis Impersonator Playing Cards and Pens

Photographer Patty Carroll has been taking some incredible pictures of Elvis impersonators, and in her penetrating style has created works of art (and sociology!). These photo cards as well as impersonator pens can be purchased through Kings Kards.

Kings Kards
2505 West Chicago Avenue
Chicago, Illinois 60622
E-mail: patty@suba.com
http://www.elimpersonators.com

Get a Thompson Eliminator

This piece of electronic equipment strips the vocal tracks from recorded music.

How to Find Out about the Images of Elvis Newsletter and Videos

Images of Elvis hosts contests across the country and they have an organized and professional operation. They make professional quality videos of all their performers every year and these videos are available for purchase. They also publish an impersonator newsletter. For more information contact:

Images of Elvis
Dr. E. O. Franklin and Jackie Franklin
8330 Highway 51 North
Southaven, Mississippi 38671
(601) 342-4899
Fax: (601) 342-4622
E-mail: Jackief@concentric.net

Start Your Own Elvis Impersonator Benefit Contest

Choose a Charity

A local charity is best. That way it's easier to get support from the community. Choose an Elvis-related charity.

Choose a Venue

Rent a theater or club or even a high school gym. You could even stage it from the back of a flatbed truck parked at parking lot (like Elvis did).

Choose Your Elvises

Use the hiring guide in this chapter. Or place an ad in your local paper for contestants. Or post something on the Internet in one of the Elvis chat rooms.

Promote Your Contest

Some media will contribute advertising space or airtime to help promote charity benefits. Try and tie in with local oldies radio stations. Contact Elvis fan clubs in your area.

Impersonating Colonel Parker

If you can't impersonate Elvis, why not help manage an EI? Be a Colonel Parker impersonator, but do a better job.

Elvis Impersonator Booking Agents

Elvis Entertainers Network
Nance Fox, Manager
She represents some of the best EIs
   across the States, even abroad:
   Frankie Castro, Johnny Thompson,
   Doug Church, Irv Cass, Travis
   Morris, Michael Kennedy, Jerome
   Marion, and Joe Tirrito among
   them.
16545 Bruce Road
Lockport, Illinois 60441
(630) 953-5280
(877) 837-3444
E-mail: info@elvisentertainers.com
E-mail: NanceFox@aol.com
http://www.elvisentertainers.com/
Showcasing for Elvis
   Bonnie Lee, Producer
   P.O. Box 363
   Howard City, Michigan 49329
   (888) 746-9368

(616) 937-6946
E-mail: showcase@pathwaynet.com
http://www.showcase-ent.com
Classique Productions
   Linda and John Collins
   711 Glenwood Springs Avenue
   North Las Vegas, Nevada 89030
   (702) 639-6550
   (888) 409-6550
   E-mail: clasique@ix.netcom.com
   http:www.classique-productions.
   com
Perfect Impressions Entertainment
   154 Seminole Drive
   Springfield, Illinois 62704
   (217) 793-3733
Denise Dody
   1416 West Juniper Street
   Ontario, California
   Gerald Productions
   (219) 272-0426

Sandon Entertainment
  RR#1
  Southampton, Ontario, NOH 2L0
  Canada
  (519) 797-2413
  Fax: (905) 476-6977
Powderblue Productions
  97 Lake Drive North Unit #4
  Keswick, Ontario, LAP 1AP Canada
  (877) 777-2281
  Fax: (905) 476-6977
Sandra Galysh
  (519) 797-2414
  E-mail: djhill@swbi.net

Curtis Cowan
  A talent agency for impersonators
  and look-alikes and also an Elvis
  memorabilia collector.
  108 West 22 Ave.
  Vancouver, British Columbia, V5Y
  2G1 Canada
  E-mail: ccowan@cableregina.com
  http://www.cableregina.com/
  users/ccowan
Jane Mathers Management
  230 West Summit Avenue
  Haddonfield, New Jersey 08033
  (609) 795-1843
  (609) 795-4223

Suggested Occasions for Impersonator Appearances

Reunions
Corporate events
Bachelorette parties
Weddings
Anniversaries
Store openings

Block parties
Car shows
Lodge meetings
Benefit functions
Church festivals
County fairs

Hire an Impersonator for Your Own Funeral

Pay in advance and choose your own songs.

How to Get Started as an Impersonator

Sing in Your Shower

For the benefit of everyone, it's the best place to begin. Also, the bathroom gives you that cool echo effect of the Sun years.

Study Concert Footage

In addition to *Elvis on Tour* and *Elvis, That's the Way It Is*, the two concert movies, there are hundreds of bootleg videos of Elvis' performances to study.

Try Karaoke

Karaoke is basically the first step for most people who want to sing like the King. There are karaoke machines on which you can tape your performances as well.

King Tracks
    P.O. Box 944
    Goodlettsville, Tennessee 37070
    (615) 851-1532
    Fax: (615) 851-1820
The Pros Karaoke
    1800 Byberry Road Suite 1401
    Huntingdon Valley, Pennsylvania 19006
    (800) 843-776
    (215) 914-1505
Elvis Karaoke songs and related software
    http://www.midikar.com
Elvis Karaoke and Gallery
    http://www.geocities.com/Nashville/Stage/5447/index.html

> "I see [Elvis impersonators] as the functional equivalent of priests, because the role of the priest is to continue the tradition, to bring believers together and to act in place of the messiah, the founder or the guru."
> —Professor Joseph Kotarba, University of Houston

Be Elvis on Halloween

Be Elvis once a year. Have an all-Elvis costume party and let everyone be a King for a day.

Choose Your Elvis

Elvises come in all sizes; choose which one fits you best. Some years you might want to be Rockabilly Elvis. Other years you can be the '68 Comeback Elvis.

Creating the Elvis Head

To dye your hair is a big commitment. A good wig will suffice if you're not ready to make the jump.

It's all about being the best Elvis you can be.

John O'Hara

Learn an Elvis Stage Soliloquy

Not only should you learn to sing like Elvis, you should practice speaking like him. Get a copy of "Having Fun Onstage with Elvis." It's a half hour of nothing but stage intros and tomfoolery onstage with Elvis.

Choosing a Stage Name

Many EIs choose their names from Elvis' movie characters and combine it with their own names. Here's a list of Elvis' movie character names.

Clint Reno	Mike Edwards	Mike McCoy
Deke Rivers	Mike Windgren	Ted Jackson
Vince Everett	Josh Morgan	Scott Hayward
Danny Fisher	Jodie Tatum	Guy Lambert
Pacer Burton	Lucky Jackson	Greg Nolan
Tulsa McLean	Charlie Rogers	Steve Grayson
Glenn Tyler	Rick Richards	Joe Lightcloud
Chad Gates	Johnny Tyronne	Jess Wade
Ross Carpenter	Rusty Wells	Walter Hale
Toby Kwimper	Lonnie Beale	Dr. John Carpenter
Walter Gulick	Johnny	

Elvis Impersonator Suppliers

Costumes

B&K Enterprises
  P.O. Box 2057
  Clarksville, Indiana 47131-2057
  (812) 256-2687
  Fax: (812) 256-3650
Professional Costumer
  Janet Tingle
  2505 Henderson Springs Road
  Pigeon Forge, Tennessee 37863
  (423) 429-4106

Fax: (423) 429-1846
http://www1.shore.net/~ikrakow/
elvis.html/
Beverly Knight
  Douglasville, Georgia
  (770) 942-5950
Shelly Naples
  (708) 839-0188
  E-mail: Shelnaples@aol.co

Concert Belts

Mike McGregor Custom Jewelry
& Leatherwork
  793 Highway 7S
  Oxford, Mississippi 38655

(601) 234-6970
Route 4, Box 195
Oxford, Mississippi 38655

B&K Enterprises
  P.O. Box 2057
  Clarksville, Indiana 47131-2057

(812) 256-2687
Fax: (812) 256-3650

Where to Get Scarves
E. P. Scarfs
Scarves to fit any budget, from one scarf to a thousand.
American Trilogy (red/white/blue) mixed set.
Elvis in Concert (cream/powder blue) mixed set.
All Shook Up (pink/black) mixed set.
Viva Las Vegas (green/orange/purple/gold) mixed set.
E-mail: ep2001@webtv.net

Dawn Marie's Show Scarves
(219) 759-1472

Study Elvis' Movements for Verisimilitude
Beyond the jumpsuit and the voice, there are plenty of things you can do to make your act better. When you watch Elvis videos, pay special attention to:

The hand gestures
The Elvis tongue moves
The Tiger Man walk
Mastering the Elvis lip
The guitar throw
The scarf toss

> "Humility, patience, kindness, and respect are the Presley qualities I strive for."
> —Steve Chappel,
> Elvis impersonator

Get the Hair Right
Custom-made hairpieces can be mail-ordered. You send them a photo of the hairdo or cut you would like and the measurements of your head—and they produce a fine hairpiece. If you're in New York City, you can go there in person.
Top Priority Hairpieces
174 Fifth Avenue
New York, New York 10010
(212) 206-6785

Make Your Own Costume
Amazon Patterns
Jumpsuit with bellbottoms pattern
(800) 798-7979

Don't Forget the Music

Find real time, excellent quality tapes and CDs with lyrics booklets included from:

King Tracks
P.O. Box 944
Goodlettsville, Tennessee 37070
(615) 851-1532
Fax: (615) 851-1820
E-mail: kingtrks@bellsouth.net
http://www.kingtracks.com/

Frankie Castro
    707 West 180 Street
    New York, New York 10033
    (212) 928-4117
Rich Wilson
    P.O. Box 65
    Huguenot, New York 12746
    http://visitweb.com/ELVIS
    http://www.geocities.com/Nashville/
    4402/
Gene DiNapoli
    6927B 215 Street
    Flushing, New York 11364
    E-mail: genedin@aol.com
Kevin Mills
    New Jersey
    (609) 829-6641
Tony Grova
    T. G. Productions
    P.O. Box 134
    Ringwood, New Jersey 07456-2030
    (973) 835-7585
    E-mail: zoomjob@aol.com
    http://www.tonygrova.com
Tulsa McLean
    E-mail: Tulsa_Mc@webtv.net
David Faria
    http://www.impersonators.de
Dave "Elvis" Sneddon
    Lakewood, New Jersey

http://www.impersonators.de
Sterling Pollaro
    Book through Dale Weisbrod
    1070 Hagerdon Hill Road
    Gerry, New York 14740
    (716) 287-2134
    E-mail: memorylane@madbbs.com
    http://www.madbbs.com/
    ~memorylane
Jeff Stanulis
    Long Island, New York
    (516) 541-7412
Floyd King
    Book through Colonel Jack Management
    191 Front Street
    New York, New York 10038
    (212) 943-4137
Mike Bryant
    (916) 773-3144
Mark Reno
    Book through Jane Mathers
    Management
    230 West Summit Avenue
    Haddonfield, New Jersey 08033
    (609) 795-1845
    Fax: (609) 795-4223
    E-mail: mathersmgt@aol.com
Robert Washington
    Alice Dickey Enterprises
    112 Romano Road

Jamie Aaron Kelley in front of the mobile home he and his family use to get from gig to gig

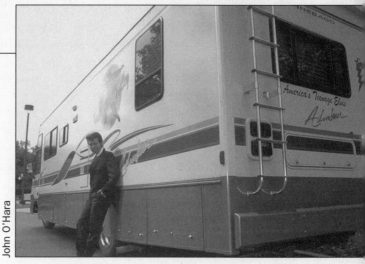

John O'Hara

Elvis Impersonator Hiring Guide

Northern and Eastern United States

South Portland, Maine 04106
(207) 799-2500
E-mail: ADickkey@aol.com

Jim Barone
Westfield, New Jersey
E-mail: jim@jimbarone.com
http://www.jimbarone.com/about.
html

Craig Newell
(609) 361-2349
E-mail: CRAIG2001DJ@webtv.net
http://community1.webtv.net/
CRAIG2001DJ/THCRAIGNEWELL
ELVI/

Amy Beth
Rob Friday, Agent
Entertainment Unlimited
64 Division Avenue
Levittown, New York 11756
(516) 735-5550

Bobby Granville
P.O. ox 5646674
College Pt., New York 11356
E-mail: TCB4EAP.aol.com

Mid-West

Jamie Aaron Kelley
718 West Mamie Eisenhower Avenue
Boone, Iowa 50036-4007

King-of-the-Hill Productions
(515) 432-4332 (also works as Fax)
E-mail: musicman@tdsi.net

Travis Morris
P.O. Box 335
Winthrop Harbor, Illinois 60096
(847) 746-3189
E-mail: blewshew@aol.com

Rick Saucedo
(630) 393-2405

Steven Davis and the TCB Band
St. Louis, Missouri
(618) 372-4155

John O'Hara

Jamie travels with his father, fellow impersonator Larry Kelly, and the rest of the family as support crew

Johnny Thompson
   (630) 953-5280
   http://www.swiftsite.com/Johnny
   Elvis
Irv Cass
   (616) 684-2746
Dave "Elvis"
   Branson, Missouri
   (800) ELVIS-95
Doug Church
   (616) 979-1191
John Rossi
   Woodale, Illinois
   (708) 766-2886
Joe "Elvis" Tirrito
   Tinley Park, Illinois
   (708) 430-4423
Matt King
   24376 Hopkins
   Dearborn Heights, Michigan
   48125
Brian Brenner
   P.O. Box 340636
   Beavercreek, Ohio 45434
   (937) 235-0167
   E-mail: brianbrennershow@
   prodigy.net
Quentin Flagg
   328 W. Church Street
   Argos, Indiana 46501
   (219) 892-5852
   E-mail: quentinflagg@hotmail.com
Chesiree Bellvano
   Akron, Ohio
   (330) 762-KING
Sherman Arnold
   13632 Pardee
   Taylor, Michigan 48180
   (734) 374-0032
   http://www.community1.webtv.net/
   Elvis3577/ShermanArnold/

David Pasco
   1230 Stewart Road
   Salem, Ohio 44460
   (330) 332-5914
Gary Stone
   Evangelical Elvis Impersonator
   Cincinnati, Ohio
   (513) 867-1007
   E-mail: gstone2814@aol.com
   http://hometown.aol.com/gstone
   2814/index.htm
John Carpenter
   Booking: Lookkapypy@Hotmail.
   com
   E-mail: Markerdeb@aol.com
Rick Ardisano
   (847) 895-3075
   (708) 456-1011
Rick Dunham
   Springfield, Illinois
   (888) 784-5587
Eric Erickson
   P.O. Box 1263
   Travers, Michigan 49685
   (616) 922-5077
Scott Alan
   Farmington Hills Michigan
   (248) 225-1964
   E-mail: TCB4EP@aol.com
   http://members.aol.com/TCB4EP/
   index6.html
David E. Presley
   (760) 956-7341
   http://www.geocities.com/
   BROADWAY/2545
Mike Albert
   Columbus, Ohio
   (800) 985-4586
   (614) 798-8990
   Pager: (614) 985-4586
   E-mail: Ann@etribute.com

Pager: (614) 985-4586
E-mail: Ann@etribute.com
Ryan Pelton
  Columbus, Ohio
  (614) 470-2751
  http://www.ryanpelton.com
Chris T. Young
  (219) 362-2775
  E-mail: CTYElvis1@Prodigy.net
  http://members.aol.com/ctyelvis
Jim Vanhollebeke
  Can-o-van-o-gram Records
  19367 Poinciana
  Redford, Michigan 48240
  (313) 534-1414
  E-mail: canovan@oeonline.com
  http://www.oeonline.com/~canovan
Dave "Green King" Pyle
  environmental Elvis
  (312) 666-2426
  E-mail: grnelvis@mcs,net
  http://www.greenelvis.com
Michael Kennedy
  (312) 391-0823

West

Brendan Paul
  Las Vegas, Nevada
  (702) 450-9548
  Pager: (702) 667-2090
  (818) 366-6938
Gene Lane
  Box 181
  Shingle Springs, California 95682
  (530) 622-0395
  (916) 622-0395
Robert Manis
  855 East Twain, Suite 123–400
  Las Vegas, Nevada 89109
  (702) 361-8544
Jim LeBoeuf

Las Vegas, Nevada
  (702) 457-1560
Steve Connolly
  P.O. Box 27703
  Las Vegas, Nevada 89126
  (702) 453-0411
Ed Abayari
  Whittier, California
  (562) 699-7508
Tom Yokoyama
  11835 South Street
  Cerrites, California 90703
  (562) 926-4934
Elvis Charlie Hodge
  2190 Prater Way #16
  Sparks, Nevada 89531
David "The Polynesian King" Lomond
  Eugene, Oregon
  (541) 334-0219
  E-mail: david@davidlomond.com
  http://www.davidlomond.com
  elima.html
Mike Bryant
  Roseville, California
  (916) 773-3144
C. J. Charlton
  Las Vegas, Nevada
  (702) 658-2598
Thierry Pham
  17831 Kensington Avenue
  Cerritos, California 90701
  (213) 404-3954
  (213) 387-7166
Harry Shahoian
  California
  (626) 462-7066
Steve Mason
  Las Vegas, Nevada
  (702) 432-0855

Jeremy M. Pierce
  (209) 323-0330
Paul Butler
  (765) 644-8185
Tom J. Triplett
  12333 Colfax Highway
  Grass Valley, California 95945
  (916) 272-2322
Dean Z
  (805) 946-8862
  E-mail: DeanZ@Prodigy.net
Darrin Race
  Las Vegas, Nevada
  (702) 891-5284
  Pager: (702) 590-2824
Michael Conti
  (702) 892-9888
Chance Tinder
  http://sony.inergy.com/viva2001/
Raymond Michael
  4987 Hollyglen Court
  Moorpark, California 93021
  (562) 690-6607
  (805) 529-6490
Wilma Green
  P.O. Box 1183
  Diamond Springs, California 95619
  (415) 378-5429
Ken Yuvienco
  16621 Eccles Street
  North Hills, California 91343
  (818) 894-7264
David "Jesse" Moore
  15613 South Maple Grove Road
  Molalla, Oregon 97038
  Fax: (503) 668-5555
  E-mail: 1elvis@molalla.net
  http://www.rdrop.com/users/larry/
Steve Sogura
  P.O. Box 654
  Ravensdale, Washington 98051
  (425) 413-0924

Mark Reno

Paul Thorpe

Raymond Michael

Lil Raymond
Michael

Steve Davis

Steve Connolly

Photos reprinted with permission

"My name is Robert Washington. I've been an Elvis Fan for as long as I can remember. Probably my first association with him was from TV, then on records. For me, just seeing him was all it took. I mean even for a guy, I thought he was great looking and boy could he sing. He could dance, got all the women, he just had it all. Being young, it was easy to be bowled over by all this, so you can see the performing just didn't happen overnight. It's been around for a long time.

"During my high school years, I started wearing my hair like his, buying his records, and just listening, learning the words to his songs. But I didn't have a clue on just how many of them he had recorded.

"As for my own singing, it basically came fairly easy. Sure, I did practice a lot, but I'm from the South (Missouri, that is), so the accent was already there. I think being African-American also helped because, if you remember, most people thought Elvis was Black when "That's Alright Mama" came out in '54 on the radio.

"So, putting all these things together made me the 'Elvis Performer' that I am today. I do this out of respect for *The Man* who really changed my life.

"There are a lot of references nowadays of Elvis, on TV and radio, but it always seems to be in the joking manner. It upsets me sometimes, but I always say 'Listen to the music because it will never let you down.'

"It was his music in the beginning and it will always be his music in the end.... It will never let you down, so I'll keep singing his songs ...."

—Sincerely, Robert Washington

Barry Beatty
  Tenino, Washington
  (360) 264-6304
Sonny Boline
  7083 Rhapsody Lane
  Las Vegas, Nevada 89119
  (702) 270-8221
James Clark
  San Francisco Bay area
  http://www.jgcproductions.com/
El Vez
  P.O. Box 26405
  Los Angeles, California 90026
  E-mail: elvezco@aol.com
  http://members.aol.com/elvezco/
  main.htm

Bookings:
Tom Windish at the Billions Corporation
833 West Chicago Avenue
Chicago, Illinois 60622
(312) 997-9999
Fax: (312) 997-2287
http://www.billions.com
E-mail: windish@billions.com
or
Rachel Cohen
Cadence Arts Network
10516 Clarkson Road
Los Angeles, California 90064
(310) 838-0849
Fax: (310) 838-1922
E-Mail: CadnceArts@aol.com

http://www.dance90210.com/
cadence.html

Flying Elvii
7910 Bermuda Road
Las Vegas, Nevada 89123
(702) 896-9420
http://www.flyingelvi.com

South

Daniel Young
DanMar Productions
6480 Michael Way
Douglasville, Georgia 30135
(770) 947-2355
Fax: (770) 947-2156
http://homel.gte.net/young123/

Darrell Dunhill
(561) 340-3922
E-mail: Lisa.dunhill@attws.com

Rick Marino
Jacksonville, Florida
(904) 641-8973

John "Elvis John" Newinn
Houston, Texas
(281) 589-8133

Roger Perry
Talbott, Tennessee
(423) 471-0116

Kenny Wyatt
3533 Kallaher
Memphis, Tennessee 38122
(901) 452-0081

Gary Friedrich
Little Rock, Arkansas
(501) 758-3037

"I think that the responsibility of an Elvis impersonator is to meet and talk with people who are not fans and explain who Elvis was and what he had done, and dispel the bad rumors. This is how I 'TCB' for the man who gave so much to the world: Monsieur Elvis Presley."

—Elvis Jr., Belgian EI

John O'Hara

Among Daniel Young's many talents is the ability to play the piano. Some of Elvis' best vocal performances were given while he sat at the piano and Daniel's show faithfully re-creates some of those moments.

The very popular Atlanta-based Daniel Young performing for his many fans

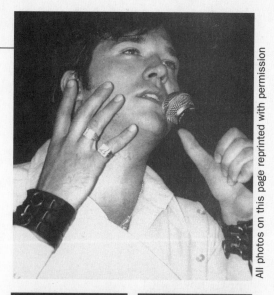

Joel Harris
    3313 Gondolier Way
    Lantana, Florida 33462
    (561) 642-8894
J. R. King
    Jack Kimbro/B. R. Productions
    200 Birch Street
    Paducah, Kentucky 42001
    (502) 443-2525
Chris McDonald
    109 Lake Emerald Drive #302
    Fort Lauderdale, Florida 33309
    (954) 341-6005
    E-mail: cmacdo1188@aol.com
    http://chrismacdonaldselvis.com/
Michael "Black Elvis" Burnett
    Northwest Florida
    Ruth Flint, Manager
    E-mail: blackelvis@usa.net
Michael Hoover
    Virginia Beach, Virginia
    E-mail: show@michaelhoover.com
    http://www.michaelhoover.com
Steve Chappel
    Augusta, Georgia
    E-mail: schappel3@aol.com
    http://www.members.aol.com/
    schappel1/

Southwest

Jim Wilson
(520) 742-2031
    E-mail: SKA8Elvis@aol.com
Rich Butler
    1811 West Eagle Crest Place
    Oro Valley, Arizona 85737
    (520) 575-8709
    E-mail: RVRBUTLER@worldnet.att.net

All photos on this page reprinted with permission

Brendan Paul   Jeff Stanulis

Chris MacDonald   Brian Brenner

Canada

Paul "Officer Elvis" Bentham
    (905) 318-0496
    E-mail: officerelvis@sprint.com
Luc "Paramount Presley" Bisonetter
    (905) 684-1674
Eddy Prince
    Niagara Falls, Ontario, Canada
    (905) 937-5135
Jay Zaniard
    (416) 247-1786
Barry Moyle
    (519) 767-2377
    Fax: (519) 767-6732
Sal "Selvis"
    (416) 438-4001
Douglas Roy (sang with Elvis)
    (905) 356-5171
    (905) 371-6725
Kid Elvis and the Elvis Family Band
    Ernie Rodgers, EAR Productions,
    Manager,
    (705) 788-0909
The Graceliners
    117 Morton Avenue
    Brantford, Ontario, Canada N3R 2N9
Curtis Cowan
    108 West 22 Avenue
    Vancouver, British Columbia,
    Canada V5Y 2G1
    (604) 874-7880
    E-mail: Ccowan@cableregina.com
    http://www.cableregina

Europe

Franz "Elvis Jr." Goovaerts
    401 Avenue Paul Pastur
    6032 Charleroi, Belgium
    (71) 55-34-84

Chance Tinder

Jim Van Hollebeke

Dean Z

Paul Butler

Jeremy Pierce

Frankie Castro

Paul Thorpe
  180 Gassiot Road
  Tooting, London SW178LE England
Deke Rivers
  E-mail: deke.elvis@breathemail.net
  http://users.breathemail.net/deke.
  elvis/index.htm
Robert McCarthy
  Wales
  Elvis Entertainers Network
  (630) 953-5280
  (877) 837-3444
Lou Jordan
  England
  (44) 1-81 303-0798

Floyd King   Irv Cass

"The fact that Elvis is so popular
dead, and so widely imitated
after death, suggests to me that
the presence of Elvis is very com-
forting to people and, in fact,
that deep down many people
love him in the true sense of the
word."
     —Mark Gottdiener, from *In Search
                             of Elvis*

Elvis Junior   Jerome Marion

Michael Kennedy   Leo Days   Sterling Pollaro   Joel Harris

Steve Murphy

Travis Morris

Matt King

Robert Washington

Elvis John

Tony Grova

Jamie Aaron Kelley

Larry Travis

Gary Stone

Shawn Barry

William Maurice

Pasquale Ferro

AT HOME WITH ELVIS

When Elvis finished shooting a movie in Hollywood, he usually wasted little time before he and his gang headed back home to Memphis in a caravan of vehicles. On one of these cross-country road trips, Elvis was at the wheel of his customized motor home listening to the radio as he drove through the night. Just outside of Little Rock they started to pick up Elvis' disc jockey friend George Klein's radio show. George was playing the new Tom Jones song called "The Green, Green Grass of Home," a sentimental ode to the pleasures of going home. When the song was over, Elvis pulled over to a phone booth and had one of his men call the radio station to request the song be played again. The DJ obliged, of course, dedicating it to a "friend who is coming home." Elvis liked the song so much he spent the rest of the trip requesting it be played over and over until he pulled into the gates of his precious Graceland. The song had struck a nerve in Elvis because the concept of home meant so much to him.

Because of the instability of his impoverished youth, Elvis lived in more than a dozen different places before he bought the house on Audubon Drive in Memphis, the first house his family owned. A year later, when he purchased Graceland,

John O'Hara

Graceland

401

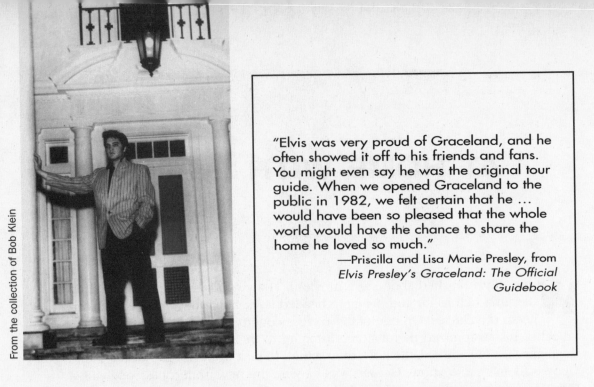

"Elvis was very proud of Graceland, and he often showed it off to his friends and fans. You might even say he was the original tour guide. When we opened Graceland to the public in 1982, we felt certain that he ... would have been so pleased that the whole world would have the chance to share the home he loved so much."

—Priscilla and Lisa Marie Presley, from *Elvis Presley's Graceland: The Official Guidebook*

he knew he had found the place where he would put down roots. It was his home from the age of 22 until his death 20 years later. Graceland became a part of who he was. It was his safe harbor from the slings of life. It was both a symbol of his success and his refuge from the demands of that success. Above all, Graceland was the fulfillment of the audacious promise Elvis had made to his parents as a boy to someday buy them a mansion.

Graceland is a two-story house built of stone brought from Tishomingo County in Elvis' home state of Mississippi. It's set on a hilltop with a row of pin oaks leading up to the house, and sweet gums, sycamores, weeping willows, and magnolias growing all across the 13.8 acres of land. The front door is framed by four columns supporting a classical pediment. It seems inspired by the southern plantation esthetic made popular again by *Gone With the Wind,* and perhaps it was. It was built in 1939, the same year that epic film captured the country's imagination.

Originally a 500-acre farm established in 1861 by S. E. Toof, the publisher of the Memphis newspaper the *Commercial Appeal,* it was named Graceland—which you must admit rolls off the tongue a lot better than Toofland—after his daughter Grace Toof. In 1939, Dr. Thomas D. Moore and his wife Ruth, who was Grace's niece, commissioned the house to be built. When Mrs. Moore sold it to Elvis, he decided the name was just too perfect to change. To the heart of that poor boy from Tupelo, Graceland was a miracle, a gift of God's good grace.

Elvis was in Hollywood filming *Love Me Tender,* his first movie, when he called his parents and instructed them to look for a place in the country, maybe even a

View from Graceland mansion facing
Elvis Presley Boulevard

John O'Hara

farm. When Vernon and Gladys were first showed the property and home, it was being used for prayer meetings by the Graceland Christian Church, surely a good portent to the religious couple. The day Elvis finally saw it, one of the first things he did after walking through the front door was to sit at the piano in the music room and play a few notes. He immediately responded to the house and bought it on March 25, 1957, for $102,500.

As soon as Elvis bought Graceland, he began a series of renovations. His mother, Gladys, and interior decorator George Golden assisted him, but the King had final say in all work done on his castle. Perhaps in keeping with his desire for a farm, among the first additions was a chicken coop. He had a pink Alabama fieldstone wall built to surround his property and bought and installed custom-built decorative gates for $3,052. As the meeting place of his fans, the Music Gates and the Wall of Love have become two of the more famous features of Graceland. He lit the house with blue and gold spotlights and the driveway was strung with blue lights like an airport runway.

Decorating and redecorating his dream house became a lifelong hobby for Elvis, and the house went through many different styles and color schemes over the years. The only changes Elvis was reluctant to make were of those things that reminded him of his mother. He even hesitated to replace a windowpane accidentally broken by Gladys shortly before her death. Dee Stanley, the second wife of Elvis' father, was banished from Graceland when she tried to impose her own design ideas, changing the drapes Gladys had chosen, while Elvis was away shooting a movie. Renovations over the years caused the house to grow from 10,266 square feet to its current 17,552 square feet.

Elvis was proud of his home and enjoyed showing it off to friends and often to fans as well. When Graceland was opened to the public on June 7, 1982, his estate was carrying on a tradition started by Elvis himself. Now, each year, approximately 750,000 people come from all over the world to Memphis to tour this place that was so close to his heart.

When you step through the front door of Graceland, you cross the threshold into the emotional ground zero of the Elvis world. This foyer is where Elvis' casket lay in state for viewing and above this very spot is the room where he died.

To the left is the dining room and to the right is the living room and music room. It was here where Elvis' funeral took place. The current blue, gold, and white scheme was chosen during the restoration made after Elvis' death; it never existed in precisely this form while Elvis was alive. The room is actually a mixture of furnishings from different years and is an approximation of the Graceland of the 1960s.

In 1977, at the time of Elvis' death, the house was in its spectacular red period, the result of Elvis' last major redecorating outburst in 1974. Red carpets, red walls, red drapes, red everything. The red period gained notoriety because it was often mentioned by journalists covering the funeral. In his hateful "biography" of Elvis, Albert Goldman really jumped on the whole red thing. His mockery of Elvis' taste in interior decorating is *said* to be part of the reason Graceland was remodeled before it was opened. It's thought that the present, more subdued, color scheme makes a better first impression than the antebellum bordello look it had. Another possible reason for the change, it is said, is that Priscilla Presley, who's most responsible for the restoration, didn't want the design sensibility of Linda Thompson (Elvis' girlfriend in 1974) to be the one that would be immortalized and forever associated with Elvis.

The stairs that lead from the foyer to the second floor are closed to the public and off-limits to all but select members of the Graceland staff. Even in Elvis' day the stairs were the absolute dividing line between the King's inner sanctum and the rest of the world. Because the upstairs is where Elvis died, it remains a place of mystery and great fascination to his fans. Until the upstairs is opened to the public, and it's unlikely that it ever will be, the only way to get a glimpse of it is in the opening of the documentary *This Is Elvis*.

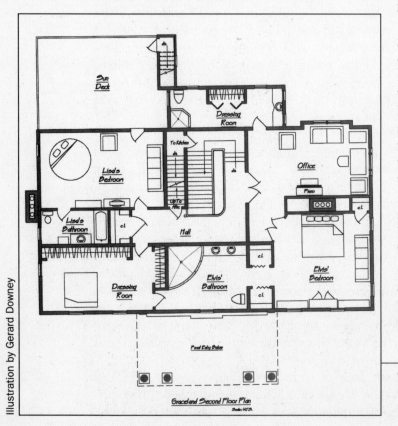

Illustration by Gerard Downey

The approximate layout of the off-limits second floor of Graceland

The forbidden second floor of Graceland consists of Elvis' bedroom, bathroom, wardrobe room, and office. There's also another bath and dressing area that was used by his girlfriend du jour and Lisa Marie's gold and white bedroom and bathroom. Elvis' bedroom is behind the two upper windows to the right of the entrance as you face the front of the house.

In 1993, the tour was expanded to include the kitchen and, on Mother's Day in 1998, Gladys's bedroom was opened to the public. Until that time both were still being used by Elvis' aunt Delta Mae Biggs who lived at Graceland from 1967 until her death. Gladys's bedroom was restored to the way it was in 1958 when she died.

Perhaps the most infamous and memorable room in the mansion is what is now referred to as the Jungle Room—a title coined by the tour guides and never used during Elvis' day, when it was simply known as the den. Originally an open patio, it was enclosed in the early 1960s and the indoor waterfall was added in 1965. The three air conditioners in the room always kept it at the very unjungle-like temperature that Elvis demanded. It's got wood paneling on the walls and green shag carpeting on the floors and ceilings and it was filled with an assortment of Polynesian fake-fur-upholstered furniture with wooden arms carved in animal and totem figures. Elvis bought the furniture in 1974 during a 30-minute shopping spree at Donald's Furniture store. Some say he bought it because it reminded him of Hawaii, a favorite and special place in his life. Another version is that he bought the furniture as a practical joke on his father. Whatever his motivation, the room does forever reinforce the Elvis–Hawaii connection. It was used as a recording studio in 1976 when all of *From Elvis Presley Boulevard, Memphis, Tennessee* and six songs from *Moody Blue* were recorded here. Because the

"Elvis' house
has balls."
—Michael St.
Gerard, actor
who played Elvis
in "Elvis" on ABC

John O'Hara

Jungle Room represents the fun, spontaneity, and exuberance of Elvis, it's a definite favorite among his fans. It's appropriate that the man who so convincingly could sing "I'm the king of the jungle, they call me the tiger man" should have such a room.

A mirrored staircase leads downstairs into two other rooms designed entirely for leisure. Memphis interior designer Bill Eubanks, with input from Elvis and Linda Thompson, redesigned the TV room and the poolroom in 1974. Both rooms used to have windows but they were sealed off to create an environment well suited to Elvis' nocturnal habits. The TV room's walls, ceiling, fireplace, and bar are fully mirrored and the blue and smiley-face-yellow wall graphics echoes Elvis' TCB logo. Mounted in one wall are three televisions that today constantly play tapes representing some of Elvis' favorite viewing: Kubrick's *Dr. Strangelove* on one, a Johnny Carson show from the seventies on another, and a Clint Eastwood Western on the third. A jukebox mounted in the wall was wired for sound to the whole house and held 100 records.

Across from the TV room is the poolroom. It features a mixed bag of nostalgic decorations that might have been found in many cocktail lounges in the 1970s. Its ceiling and walls are covered in nearly 400 yards of red paisley fabric tufted into the center of the room. A Tiffany-style stained glass lamp hangs over the pool table. Reproductions of red Louis XV chairs stand in the corners. A tear in the pool table's surface is left unrepaired, giving it that Memphis Mafia roughhouse lived-in look.

The only other part of the main house included in the tour is the trophy room. Originally, it was also a porch that Elvis had enclosed to house an elaborate slot car track. After he grew bored with that diversion, he turned it into a room to display the many awards and plaques he had received. When Elvis received the award as "One of the Ten Outstanding Young Men" of our nation on January 16, 1971, he chose this room to host a reception for his fellow honorees. Today, the trophy room is a museum of Elvis artifacts that contains parts of his gun and police badge collections, clothing and stage costumes, awards, and many mementos from fans.

Behind the main house at Graceland are several other buildings. Directly behind the house, Elvis' father, Vernon, had an office where business affairs and fan mail were handled. Thanks to Vernon's famous fru-

The trophy room, at Graceland

John O'Hara

gality, almost everything is original and unchanged since 1957. A videotape of the press conference Elvis gave at his father's desk March 8, 1960, the day after his homecoming from the army, plays on a loop on a monitor in the room.

Next to the office is a smokehouse that Elvis and his friends used as a shooting range. Although Elvis did a lot of shooting on police and professional ranges, his extensive arsenal saw a lot of action at Graceland also, occasionally with creative targets such as automobiles. And the careful observer can still find the hole of a wayward bullet that pierced the slide of Lisa Marie's swing set in front of the smokehouse.

In the fields behind the house stands the barn. In 1966, Elvis bought Priscilla a horse named Domino. That started Elvis on a horse-buying spree that eventually became the motivation to buy his own ranch. Elvis had a favorite horse named Rising Sun and so the barn was dubbed "House of the Rising Sun." Today, Rising Sun is buried in the pasture facing, of course, the rising sun. Descendants of some of the original horses still live in those fields behind Graceland.

The racquetball court is yet another building behind the main house. In 1975, Elvis commissioned the 2,240-square-foot building so he could indulge his growing interest in the then-popular sport. Elvis played here just hours before he died. It was on the Schimmel piano in the lounge of this building that Elvis sang his last song, "Blue Eyes Crying in the Rain." The racquetball court itself has been converted into another awards showcase

"The happiest we ever saw Elvis was when he first bought that ranch. He had some horses down there and he was exercising, and he looked great, and he felt great. As I remember, he even let his hair go back to its natural color for a while. He walked in one day and he had a tan, and we couldn't get over how good he looked. We just stood there and stared at him. Finally, he broke into a smile and said, 'Shall we dance?'"

—Ray Walker of the Jordanaires, from *Elvis Aaron Presley: Revelations from the Memphis Mafia*

Elvis in cowboy gear near the barn behind Graceland

Sandi Miller

John O'Hara

Graceland pool

room. Here you can see the amazing Wall of Gold presented to the Presley estate in August 1992 by RCA and the Recording Industry Association of America. One hundred eleven different gold, platinum, or multiplatinum records cover the walls along with a nine-foot-tall etched-glass award from RCA recognizing Elvis as the greatest recording artist of all time.

Next to the bean-shaped pool (not guitar-shaped contrary to many people's expectations) is the last and most poignant part of the Graceland tour, the Meditation Garden. In the mid-sixties, Elvis had the Meditation Garden built as a place for contemplation. It's said that he was inspired by the lake shrine of the Self-Realization Fellowship in Los Angeles, a 12-acre garden with statues of Jesus, Buddha, Gandhi, and other spiritual leaders that he had visited as part of his spiritual quests.

The garden's centerpiece is a circular twelve-foot pool with five single jets of water and a larger one in the middle all lit by colored floodlights. Behind the fountain is a curved wall of Mexican brick with four stained-glass windows. In front of the wall are eight columns set in a half circle supporting a wooden trellis; at the center of the columns is a statue of Jesus given to Elvis as a gift from his inner circle.

Because of security threats to the original grave site, Vernon Presley had the bodies of Elvis and Gladys moved from Forest Hill Cemetery and reinterred here in the garden on the night of October 2, 1977. Today Elvis, his mother, his father, and his grandmother are all buried here, and a small plaque commemorates Elvis' stillborn twin, Jessie Garon. On November 27, 1977, the garden was opened to the public and today is the only part of Graceland that can be visited free of charge for a portion of every day. Little did Elvis know when he built this garden that millions of people would someday come to this place for the same reason he did, to quietly contemplate his extraordinary life.

Although Graceland was the home that was closest to Elvis' heart, there are other places he lived that were important in his life. To understand Graceland's significance to Elvis, you have to go back to the beginning and consider the other places he had lived.

The shotgun shack in Tupelo where
Elvis was born

The shotgun shack in Tupelo where
Elvis was born

John O'Hara

He was born in a 15-by-30-foot shotgun shack in Tupelo, Mississippi. Built by Vernon with help from his father, Jessie, and brother, Vester, in 1934, the house still stands after 60-plus years of floods and the occasional tornado. It has two perfectly square rooms, only 450 square feet altogether, with a tiny porch in front. Vernon borrowed $180 for supplies from local landowner Orville Bean to build the house. It has since been restored into a dollhouse-like cottage with fresh paint, curtains, and landscaping, but when Elvis lived here it was considerably more primitive. They burned oil lamps for light, pumped water by hand, and used an outhouse. While Vernon was in prison for forgery, Gladys was evicted when she was unable to keep up with the house payments. This humble beginning instilled in Elvis the burning need for a home that he couldn't be thrown out of. Elvis was known to drive down to Tupelo in the middle of the night and park near the house with his lights out and stare at that shack in wonder. The fact that this house could fit into his living room at Graceland would never cease to amaze him.

Another important home in Elvis' life was the apartment at Lauderdale Courts, a public housing complex built in 1938 as part of Roosevelt's New Deal that offered subsidized housing to families making less than $3,000 a year.

John O'Hara

This is the doorway Elvis walked
through every day he lived at
Lauderdale Courts apartments

The Presleys paid $35 a month for apartment 328, a two-bedroom, first-floor apartment at 185 Winchester. This is where Elvis lived for most of his formative high school years. Beale Street, and its many influences on his personal style and music, was within walking distance. It was here, more or less, that Elvis became Elvis. Elvis would sit on the steps and sing and play the guitar. These walls witnessed Elvis rehearsing for his dream. It gave him a stable home for three years straight, the longest he and his family had ever stayed in one place up until then. When the Presley's income increased, they were forced to leave on January 7, 1953. It was yet another home they were forced out of, ironically this time for a slight rise in the family's fortunes. The Courts were scheduled for demolition in 1997 but were saved by organized fan action. The fight is still being waged to preserve Lauderdale Courts and so far the people who want to preserve this landmark are winning.

Within only three years of leaving public housing, the Presleys moved to another important home in their saga. On May 11, 1956, with the money from his first movie deal, Elvis bought his first house on 1034 Audubon Drive in a tree-lined upper-middle-class neighborhood. It was a pastel green wood-frame ranch-style house with black shutters, brick trim, and a gray tile roof. It had a patio in the back and a carport for Elvis' growing collection of vehicles. It was an up-to-the-minute American suburban dwelling of its time and that time was the 1950s. This is the house where Elvis lived when he achieved stardom. It was in the living room of this house that his parents watched his Ed Sullivan appearances while most of the rest of America did also. Although they lived here less than a year, the house was well documented by the photographer Alfred Wertheimer who accompanied Elvis from one of his Ed Sullivan appearances in New York back home to Memphis. He shot 3,800 black-and-white photos, many of them taken in this house. Those images of a young and still-innocent Elvis show him enjoying the first fruits of his success and sharing it with his parents. A photo of Gladys handing Elvis a freshly ironed pair of underwear as he prepares for a concert is one of the more memorable shots.

Elvis spent much of his time on the road that year. While he was traveling he

John O'Hara

Audubon Drive home

John O'Hara

would often buy a lamp or something else for the house and bring it back to Gladys. She wanted Elvis to spend more time at home and, perhaps impressed by his flair for home decorating, suggested he settle down and open a furniture store. He had a huge swimming pool and changing room put in behind the house. And to pamper his mother, he even bought two deluxe Mixmasters, one for each end of the kitchen so Gladys wouldn't have to walk as far.

As Elvis' stardom increased, the house became overrun with fans and visitors. Venders sold popcorn in the street. Even when Elvis wasn't there fans knocked on the door to ask if they could have some water from the pool or blades of grass from the lawn. Eventually, Elvis' neighbors resented the disruption of their peaceful suburban existence. They were said to be upset by Gladys hanging her wash on the line in the backyard and the stream of "hillbilly" relatives. They tried to buy Elvis' house and, maybe in defiance of being told to leave yet another home, he offered to buy their houses instead. Finally Elvis conceded that he needed more privacy anyway and made the last move of his life, to Graceland. Today, the Audubon house is owned by Mike Freeman and Cindy Hazen, Elvis fans and authors of *The Best of Elvis* and *Memphis Elvis-Style*. They are in the process of affectionately restoring Elvis' first home to its 1950s "Elvis-just-stepped-out-for-a-spin" condition.

In 1967, Elvis was driving through the countryside about 10 miles away from Graceland over the Mississippi border, when he spotted a 50-foot-high concrete

"I wish my boy would stop right now, buy a furniture store, and get married."
—Gladys Presley

cross in a distant pasture and fell in love with the place. This inspired him to purchase the property, a 163-acre ranch called Twinkletown Farms, and finally satisfy his desire for a place truly out in the country. He renamed it the Circle G Ranch and moved his entourage, their families, and his horses there. He bought dozens of mobile homes and a fleet of pickup trucks and tractors and tried to turn the place into a commune. For him, it was a perfect retreat from Hollywood and he was thrilled to move back to Mississippi. The peacefulness and back-to-nature activities soothed him. Elvis enjoyed his time at the ranch riding horses in God's country, as he called it. He enjoyed it so much, he didn't want to leave; he spent many happy days playing cowboy with his friends. Elvis and Priscilla spent part of their honeymoon there, preferring to stay in one of the mobile homes instead of the main house. It is speculated that Lisa Marie may have been conceived in that mobile home. Privacy again became an issue and Elvis was forced to build a 10-foot-high wooden fence around the property to keep the fans at bay. He ended up selling the ranch 2 years after the purchase when he grew tired of it and it had become too much of a financial burden.

Elvis had some homes on the West Coast that were also of note. For most of the sixties he divided his time between his Graceland and California. For the most part, his homes in Hollywood were bachelor pads that functioned as hotels. He lived in five different houses in the hills of Hollywood. He lived at 565 Perugia Way from 1960 until 1965 with the exception of the summer of 1963 when he briefly moved to a different house for a few months and then returned. It was in this house, that had once belonged to the Shah of Iran, that Elvis played host to the Beatles on August 27, 1965. This place, witness to that amazing event in pop music history, was demolished in 1990 and a new home was built in its place.

In 1965, Elvis moved to 10550 Rocca Way and lived there until 1967. It was a one-story ranch that now has been remodeled into a stately Tudor. In 1967, Elvis bought his first house in Los Angeles on 1174 Hillcrest Road in the Trousdale Estates section of Beverly Hills. Even today people scrawl messages on the iron gate of this house. It's become a sort of West Coast Wall of Love. In late 1967, Elvis and Priscilla moved to 144 Monovale Drive in Holmby Hills. Elvis made his last six films during the time he lived in this house. This is also where he lived when made the famous "'68 Comeback Special." After the divorce, Priscilla lived here and Elvis returned to Hillcrest.

After being introduced to Palm Springs by the Colonel, who owned a residence there, Elvis would often retreat from Hollywood to one of his two houses in that desert resort.

Sandi Miller

Elvis and his men at 10550 Rocca Place house in July of 1967. Among the fleet of vehicles is Elvis' customized Greyhound bus.

The "West Coast Wall of Love" at 1174 Hillcrest Road

In 1965, Elvis commissioned a 15-room house to be built at 845 Chino Canyon Road. This was the only house that Elvis actually had built. In 1967, he also briefly leased a 5,000-square-foot futuristic house on a cul de sac at 1350 Ladera Circle. It was here that Elvis spent his wedding night with Priscilla and for that reason this house has been nicknamed the Honeymoon Hideaway.

Mike Freeman and Cindy Hazen in the kitchen at Audubon Drive displaying the very same stove where Gladys baked her special treats for her son

"To fully appreciate Graceland you have to see where Elvis came from. Within four years time Elvis moved from a public housing project to his mansion on the hill. In less time than that, in only three years, he was able to buy a house for his mother on Audubon Drive. Every day, we imagine him in this house—in our house—grabbing a bite to eat in the kitchen, horsing around with his friends, kissing his mother goodnight. His life that year, in many was, was as ordinary as our own, filled with family, friends, and common activities, but it was filled with unlimited possibility too. The evidence of how extraordinary his life was is in the little things: Gladys's modern appliances, a kitchen stereo speaker, star-shaped lights in the game room, the added third bath. Elvis was constantly improving the house and making it his own, and his family's, as if he intended to live here forever. He might have if fame hadn't intervened. He became too famous for this serene little neighborhood and before long he moved to Graceland which became his refuge. For us, Audubon Drive was his dream. And now it is ours too, to keep alive and preserve for the future."

—Cindy Hazen and Mike Freeman, authors of *The Best of Elvis: Recollections of a Great Humanitarian* about their home, Elvis' first-purchased home http://www.elvistyle.com

All these other homes notwithstanding, it's the Graceland/Elvis association that is inextricable. No other celebrity is so closely identified with one specific home and it's because of this that Graceland has become as important to his fans as it was to Elvis, and a palpable connection to him. It was a real home and there was plenty of life in it. A home like any other—with Easter eggs hunts; monkeying around with friends on the back lawn; cozy, good meals at the kitchen table; harmonizing around the piano. *Elvis lived here* and this is what you feel when you're there. That Graceland is open to visit is one of the many perks that EPE has provided for Elvis' fans. If you can make it there, by all means, *go*.

ESSENTIAL ELVISOLOGY

The Architects
Furbringer and Ehrman designed Graceland in 1938.

The Realtors
Virginia Grant
Hugh Bosworth

Law Office that Handled the Closing on Graceland
Evans, Petree and Cobb

Graceland's Interior Designers
George Golden
Worked with Gladys and Elvis decorating Graceland in 1957. He had decorated Sam Phillips's house. He used to advertise his services with a roving flatbed truck that carried model rooms.
Abe Saucer
Designed the music gates.
Don Johnson
Custom-made furniture for Graceland in the fifties.
Bernie Grenadier
Brother-in-law to Memphis Mafia member Marty Lacker. He built the Meditation Garden and the Jungle Room waterfall.
Bill Eubanks
A partner in McCormik-Eubanks Interior Design, Inc., he designed the TV room and the poolroom.

Suppliers

Goldsmith's Department Store

Both Elvis and his mother shopped here for furnishings. It is still doing business at Oak Court, 4545 Poplar Avenue, Memphis, Tennessee. (901) 766-4199.

Donald's Furniture Store

The infamous Jungle Room furniture was purchased here.

Duck's Carpets

The blood red carpet of 1974, the Jungle Room, and kitchen carpeting, as well as many other generations of carpeting came from this store. They are still doing business as Duck's Flooring Center at 3685 Kirby Parkway, Memphis, Tennessee. (901) 363-2871.

Laukhuff Stained Glass of Memphis

They designed the peacocks in the music room, the "Tiffany" lamp over the pool table, and the stained glass around the front door. They're at 2585 Summer Avenue and they can reproduce the peacocks (in any size) and ship them to you or do any custom design you're interested in. (901) 320-9206.

Doors, Incorporated

The famous Music Gates were installed by John Dillars, Jr. They are still in business and located at 911 Rayner Street in Memphis. (901) 272-3046.

Belvedere Lighting

Elvis bought three chandeliers here on August 16, 1974. Two were of Italian cut glass in the Maria Theresa design and one was Strauss crystal. The shop is now at 3120 Village Shops in Memphis. (901) 757-1012.

Rex Billiard Supply Company

This company supplied the pool table in the basement. It's located at 634 Minor in Memphis. (901) 323-4180.

Central Home Improvement Company

They installed Graceland's wall-mounted television sets.

Palmer Ornamental Iron Works

They supplied the ironwork on the doors and windows at Graceland. They're located at 1439 North Willett Street in Memphis. (901) 726-6874.

Paddock of California

Elvis commissioned the Graceland swimming pool from Paddocks.

Elvis' China Pattern

Buckingham by Noritake
They can be reached at:
(888) NORITAKE
Fax: (847) 228-5104
http://www.noritake.com
http://www.discontinuedchina.com/noritake.htm

Places Where Elvis Lived

Tupelo

306 Elvis Presley Drive
  The house Elvis was born in; street was formerly called Old Saltillo Road.
510 1/2 Maple Street
  Elvis and Gladys moved in with her cousin Frank Richards and his wife after being evicted from Elvis' birthplace.
Reese Street
  Elvis, Gladys, and Vernon lived here from 1940 to 1941 with Vernon's brother, Vester, who was married to Gladys's sister Clettes.
Kelly Street
  Rented apartment
Berry Street
  In August 1945, Vernon bought a house from Orville Bean but was forced to leave it less than a year later after missing a payment.
North Commerce Street
  This is where Elvis' grandmother Minnie first moved in with the family.
Pascagoula, Mississippi
  The young family lived in a one-room cabin for a few months while Vernon worked in the nearby shipyard.
Mulberry Alley
  Near the city dump and the tracks.
1010 North Greene Street
  Their last home in Tupelo was near the slaughterhouse.

Memphis

Washington Avenue Boarding House
  Where the family first settled in Memphis.
572 Poplar Avenue
  They shared a bathroom with three other families and cooked on a hot plate.
185 Winchester Street, Lauderdale Courts
  They lived in this federally funded housing project until being evicted.
698 Saffarans Street
  This two-room apartment was the family's third home in Memphis.
462 Alabama Avenue
  This is where Elvis was living when he graduated from high school and made his first recording at Sun.
2414 Lamar Avenue
  Rented four-room house from late 1954 to mid-1955.

John O'Hara

"My husband Bud and I have been Elvis fans most of our lives. It got rekindled when an impersonator came to San Antonio. I became involved in making some of his costumes and the first one didn't fit just right so the impersonator sent it back to me. That suit became the first of the jumpsuits I have made for my daughter, my husband, and myself.

Well, Bud looked pretty good to me in the suit so I told him he should learn to sing too, which he did. Then he gave me an ultimatum: well, now that I can sing, it's move to Memphis or give up Elvis. So here we are just over the fence from the back of Graceland."

—Mary Stonebraker, Memphis

1414 Getwell Road,
  Rented house, mid-1955 to May 1956.
 1034 Audubon Drive
  Suburban ranch house, May 11, 1956, to March 1957. This was their last house before Graceland.
3764 Elvis Presley Boulevard
  Graceland. While Elvis was alive, the road Graceland is on was called Highway 51. Elvis always called it "51."

Elvis' Hollywood Homes
(See "Motion Picture Elvis.")

YOUR ELVIS EDUCATION

Books
Memphis Elvis-Style
  Cindy Hazen and Mike Freeman
Elvis Presley's Graceland: The Official Guidebook
  Elvis Presley Enterprises
Graceland: The Living Legacy of Elvis Presley
  Chet Flippo with introduction by Todd Morgan
Elvis: His Life in Pictures
  text by Todd Morgan with Laura Kath

"The red furniture was picked out by Elvis, liked by Elvis, and bought by Elvis, not Linda [Thompson]. It was done in '76 [sic] and they looked antiquish or like something you'd find in a bordello. That was Elvis' taste: gaudy!"
  —Marty Lacker, commenting on the red period at Graceland on alt.elvis.king

Elvis Presley Boulevard: From Sea to Shining Sea, Almost
  Mark Winegardner
Graceland: Going Home with Elvis
  Karal Ann Marling
Elvis Presley's Graceland Gates
  Harold Loyd
How Elvis Bought Graceland: Exactly as It Happened
  Virginia Grant
The Field Guide to Elvis Shrines
  Bill Yenne
Over the Fence: A Neighbor's Memories of Elvis
  Sara Erwin
  (Can be ordered through Sara Erwin, Box 161334, Memphis, Tennessee 38186 for $10 plus $3 S&H.)
The Inventory of the Estate of Elvis Presley
  edited by Richard Singer

Video
This Is Elvis
  (The only known footage of Elvis' bedroom and upstairs at Graceland.)
Elvis Presley's Graceland
  hosted by Priscilla Beaulieu Presley
If Walls Could Talk
  This Home and Garden Network Production focuses on Elvis' home at 1034 Audubon Drive in Memphis.

Web Sites
http://www.elvis-presley.com
  Graceland's web site
http://elvistyle.com/elvistyl.htm
  Elvis-style by Memphis Explorations
http://www.hup.harvard.edu/Graceland
  /graceland.page.html
  Graceland: Going Home with Elvis site

http://elvistyle.com/Audubon%20Drive/
audubon.htm
1034 Audubon Drive site; Elvis' home in 1956

THE ELVIS AND YOU EXPERIENCE

Visit Graceland
(Refer to "The Pilgrimage" chapter.)

Tips on Photographing Graceland

As long as you don't use a flash you can take as many photos as you like while you're on the tour. Use high-speed, light-sensitive film. Tripods are not allowed either so buy or rent a monopod to steady your camera. This will increase your chances of getting sharp pictures in the low light. Don't forget to bring extra batteries. Take plenty of photographs and use them for inspiration. Remember, Elvis is in the details.

Plant a Tree from Graceland

You can buy a direct offspring from the very trees of the Graceland estate. Plant them in your yard or garden and make a piece of Graceland part of your own home. Every 1- to 3-foot sapling comes with an outdoor planting kit: greenhouse tube, stake, fertilizer, instructions, and a lifetime replacement guarantee. There's a choice of pin oak, sweet gum, weeping willow, and sycamore trees. To accompany the sycamore trees, a granite plaque with Elvis' gold-leafed signature is also offered for sale. Contact American Forests' Famous & Historic Trees at:

American Forests
8701 Old Kings Road
Jacksonville, Florida 32219
(800) 320-8733
Fax: (800) 264-6869
E-mail: info@historictrees.org
http://www.americanforests.org

Try to Emulate the Lawn at Graceland

Briggs & Stratton Top Ten Lawns List evaluates lawns on overall appearance; lawn and garden maintenance and care philosophy; and use of green space to enhance or complement the look, visual appeal, and significance of the site—and Graceland's beautiful lawn made their list! Graceland's maintenance staff is headed by Jimmy Gambill and the lawn is a mixture of Bermuda and zoysia grasses.

Re-create an Element of Graceland in Your Home

Build your own Jungle Room, with Polynesian furniture and a waterfall. Or a Meditation Garden with a fountain and stained glass. Or a TV room with three TVs.

Commission Some Stained Glass from Elvis' Supplier

Hire the same company that made Elvis' stained glass. In addition to the work done at Graceland, they also created the stained glass windows in the Elvis Presley Chapel in Tupelo. Commission an Elvis-related piece.

Laukhuff Stained Glass of Memphis
2585 Summer Avenue
Memphis, Tennessee 38112
(901) 320-9206

Build a Replica of Graceland
A few fans have already done it. If you can't afford to build it full size, then build a smaller version.

Visit Miniature Graceland
Kim and Don Epperly built this doll-sized Elvis world that includes re-creations of Elvis' birthplace, his church in Tupelo, the Roanoke Coliseum (where Elvis had been scheduled to appear eight days before he died), and Graceland (with Meditation Garden, Music Gates, garage filled with cars, pool, barbecue). Ten thousand guests come each year. Admission to this outdoor exhibition is free.
Miniature Graceland
605 Riverland Road Southeast
Roanoke, Virginia 24014
(504) 563-5847

Visit "Little Graceland"
The owner of Little Graceland, Simon Vega, served in the army with Elvis in Germany. He has a put together a museum of Elvis Presley memorabilia. In front of his house is a replica of the Graceland wall and the Music Gates. He even has a small-scale replica of Elvis' birthplace in Tupelo constructed on his property. Since August of 1993, Simon has held an annual Elvis Festival in August and a birthday celebration in January, with live music, food and beverages, a look alike contest, and a sing-along contest. He sometimes showcases Elvis Impersonators as part of the festivities. The museum is open Saturday and Sunday from 9 A.M. to 5 P.M. and other times by appointment. It's located on West Ocean Boulevard in downtown Los Fresnos.
Little Graceland
E. Highway 100
P.O. Box 94
Los Fresnos, Texas 78566
(956) 233-5482

Simon Vega posing in front of the "Music Gates" at his home, Little Graceland

Mary O'Hara

Mary O'Hara

Build Your Own Graceland Dollhouse

If you make dollhouses, why not turn your talents to a tiny replica of Graceland? Here's a good place to start for the raw materials: Hobby Builders Supply
P.O. Box 620876
Doraville, Georgia 30362
(800) 926-6464
E-mail: hbs@miniatures.com
http://www.miniatures.com

Build Your Own Wall of Love

Use pink Alabama fieldstone as in the wall around Graceland or something that resembles it. Encourage people to write on it.

Have a Replica Made of the Music Gates

Bring photos of the music gates to a custom metalwork shop near you. The gates at Graceland were manufactured by The Veterans Ornamental Iron Works of Phoenix, Arizona.

Look for '50s, '60s, and '70s Artifacts for Your Decor

Ideally, you should try to pick up some decorating items while you visit Memphis. Flashback specializes in retro furniture, clothing, and accessories from the 1930s to the 1970s, and since it's in Elvis' hometown, they'll have things that were bought at the same stores where Elvis and his mother shopped. And who knows ....
Flashback
2304 Central Avenue
Memphis, Tennessee 38104
(901) 272-2304

The Salvation Army
When not in Memphis, try exploring your local Salvation Army. It's like visiting a museum of cultural archeology specializing in the recent past.

The Elvis Window Treatment
Whenever Elvis checked into a hotel room, an advance team would cover the windows with aluminum foil. A quick, easy way to Elvisize your windows and also one way to insulate a room against light and heat.

Make Elvis Lampshades
Housewares stores sell plain white shades that you can decorate with Elvis photos, cutouts, or pins, or cover in Elvis fabric. Make sure to get information on safety and heat-resistance of the materials.

Elvis and Trailers
Trailers had a special place in Elvis' heart; he even chose to spend part of his honeymoon in one. He bought dozens of trailers for Graceland and the Flying Circle G ranch. Why not get one and put it on your property. House your relatives, friends, or flunkies. Or make it into your Elvis Room.

Some Trailers Elvis used

Stylemaster Mobile Homes
While stationed at Fort Hood, Elvis stayed in a mobile home in Killeen, Texas, supplied by this company in exchange for promotional photographs.

Woodcrest Trailer
Elvis bought this 1975 model three-bedroom double trailer for his cousin Billy Smith to live in behind Graceland.

Help Provide Shelter for the Needy
The perfect charity to reflect Elvis' concern for home and heart is Habitat for Humanity, which helps build first homes for families. Also, Presley Place has recently been formed by Elvis Presley Charitable Foundation as transitional housing for people trying to make a go of it. In addition to a place to live for one year, they provide vocational training and other help.
Habitat for Humanity International
P.O. Box 1167
Americus, Georgia 31709-9951
(912) 924-6935 ext. 552
http://www.habitat.org

Presley Place
Contact Graceland about making donations.

Recreate Elvis' Tupelo Birth House

Building a two-room shotgun shack is a lot less ambitious than building a mansion on a hill but, in a lot of ways, equally satisfying. Use it as a guest house or Elvis Room to store your memorabilia collection.

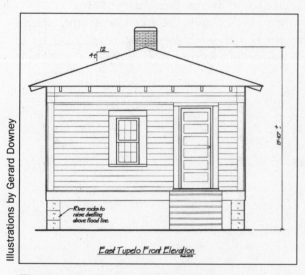

The simple façade of the house

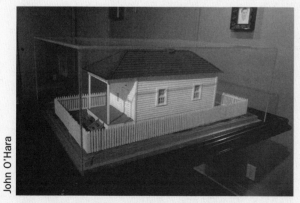

A model of Elvis' Tupelo house in Graceland Museum

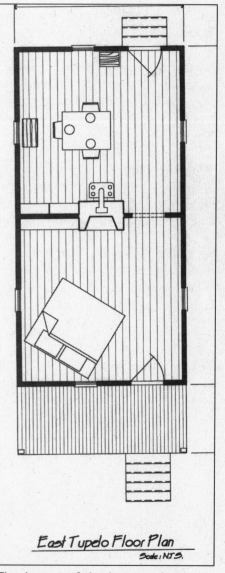

The layout of the house where Elvis was born

Move to Memphis

Write or call for Memphis apartment list-ings in:

Memphis Apartment Blue Book
4746 Spottswood Avenue, Suite 347
Memphis, Tennessee 38117
(901) 323-5207
(877) 323-5207
Fax: (901) 323-5242

"I'm going to keep Graceland as long as I possibly can."
—Elvis Presley, 1960

Get a Reproduction of Elvis' Graceland from Danbury Mint

A masterful, perfectly detailed sculpture of Graceland, the front lawn and drive-way, and the Wall of Love is available for purchase. It measures 8 1/2 by 7 by 2 1/4 inches. Here's the contact information to get further details:

The Danbury Mint
47 Richards Avenue
P.O. Box 4960
Norwalk, Connecticut 06860
(800) 426-0372
E-mail: customerservice@danburymint.com

ELVIS AND FAMILY

Elvis' close relationship and interdependence with his family was probably the single most significant factor in shaping who he was. He wanted never to be far from his kin and he lived by choice with several members of his family until the day he died. Throughout his career Elvis took care of a large brood of aunts, uncles, cousins, and more distant relations than this, employing them as gatekeepers, valets, bodyguards, and aides-de-camp. They served as a link to his childhood and were some of the only people he felt he could trust to love him as Elvis the *man*, not Elvis the *image*. In the rural South, families traditionally maintain tight bonds as a survival mechanism against a harsh and challenging existence. Elvis' early poverty was more easily endured with the warmth and kinship of his extended family, and when he became rich and famous he went out of his way to share his good fortune with them in return.

As every fan knows, Elvis was born in a shotgun shack at around 4:35 on the morning of January 8, 1935, in Tupelo, Mississippi. He was one of twin boys born to Vernon Elvis Presley and Gladys Love Smith Presley. Elvis' brother, Jesse Garon, thought to be an identical twin, was stillborn. Elvis entered the world with the closest bond one person could possibly have to another, as a twin having shared the same womb. With the death of his brother, he lost that bond. He

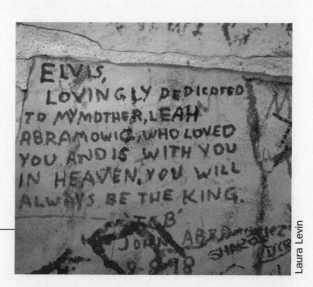

Graffiti from the Wall of Love

Laura Levin

Author's collection

Gladys and Vernon Presley

was said to mourn the loss of his twin all his life and often visited the unmarked grave in Priceville Cemetery in Tupelo where the little Jesse is buried.

The death of one twin heightened the preciousness of the survivor and an unseverable, powerful relationship formed between Gladys and Elvis. The physician present at the birth, Dr. William Robert Hunt, insisted that Gladys and Elvis be admitted to the Tupelo Charity Hospital, where they spent the first three weeks of Elvis' life recovering together from the difficult delivery. The experience left Gladys with a zeal to protect and cherish her son that intensified as she got older.

The bond between Gladys and her son was further cemented during Vernon's absence when Elvis was a toddler. In May of 1938, Vernon was sentenced to three years in prison for tampering with a check. Gladys and three-year-old Elvis were forced to move in with Gladys's cousin, Frank Richards, and his family. While Vernon was incarcerated, mother and child made frequent five-hour bus trips to Parchman State Penitentiary where Vernon was serving his sentence. Gladys spent much of these early years with Elvis seeking solace in the First Assembly of God Baptist Church. It was while in his mothers' protective arms that Elvis first heard the gospel music that he loved so much and became one of his primary musical influences. During this period, Elvis and his mother developed their own language of baby talk that they used all their lives. Their favorite term of endearment for each other was "Satnin'." It was from a made-up song Gladys used to sing, "Mama's little baby has satnin' skin" to the tune of "Shortnin' Bread."

Thanks in part to Gladys's efforts, Vernon was released before his full sentence was up. He had a hard time being the breadwinner after he got out of prison and he relied on the help and support of family. The Presleys were forced to move a few more times until they were again taken in by family members, this time Vernon's brother Vester and his wife

Laura Levin

Memorial marker for Jesse Garon in Meditation Garden at Graceland

Gladys Presley, the mother Elvis loved so much. It became increasingly rare to see her smile like this for a photo as she neared the end of her life.

Clettes, who was also Gladys's sister. When the Presleys moved to Memphis in search of a better life, they were joined in their migration by Gladys's brother Travis, his wife, Lorraine, and their sons Bobby and Billy. Initially, they all lived together in Memphis until Vernon, Gladys, and Elvis moved into their own apartment at Lauderdale Courts.

The one exception to this tight-knit and supportive clan was Vernon's father, Jessie Presley. He was the hard-drinking, philandering husband of Minnie Mae Hood by whom he sired five children. J. D., as he was called, was tough on Vernon to the point of cruelty. He was quick to point out his son's flaws and reluctant to extend a helping hand. Instead of posting bail for his son when he was awaiting trial, J. D. let Vernon cool his heels for six months in the local jail in order to teach him a lesson.

When Jessie Presley finally deserted Minnie Mae, she moved in with her son Vernon and his little family. She lived with them for the rest of her life. J. D. moved to Kentucky, remarried, and had little contact with his previous family. When Elvis became famous, J. D. tried to capitalize on his grandson's popularity. He appeared on the television show *I've Got a Secret* and even recorded a record, which included such Presley "hits" as "The Billy Goat Song" and "Swinging in

This photo of the Presley family singing together hangs today on the wall in the same spot where it was shot at Audubon Drive

From the collection of Bob Klein

the Orchard." Although J. D. was the only family member Elvis rarely spent time with, Elvis did buy his grandfather a new car, a television set, and other gifts.

After Minnie Mae came to live with Elvis and his family, she became the most important woman in his life in addition to Gladys. Elvis nicknamed her "Dodger," supposedly because of her quick reflexes at dodging a projectile that Elvis threw at her as a child. Though, Elvis' Aunt Nash claims that Dodger was actually a shortened version of Elvis' mispronunciation of the word grandmother as *granddodger*. Minnie Mae was a witness to Elvis' entire life. She was present at his birth and lived with him for most of his years, not only at each of the Presley homes in Memphis but at Fort Hood and in Germany, also. She was there the day Elvis met Priscilla in Bad Nauheim; she grilled up five bacon sandwiches for Elvis to eat as the two sat and spoke in the kitchen for the first time. At Graceland, she watched Priscilla grow from a teenager to the woman who became Elvis' wife. She consoled Elvis after his divorce and was there at his death. The nearly six-foot tall, sunglasses-wearing granny was a straight shooter who told Elvis exactly what she was thinking. She was one of the few people who spoke her mind to Elvis and he depended on and loved her for that.

Gladys continued to be what some have called overprotective of Elvis even after he was a teenager. If she insisted on walking Elvis to school, it wasn't only to protect her baby boy but to ensure that he went to school every day to get the education she never got. When her son's career started to take off, Gladys was filled with pride. She loved to hear his name on the radio. While Elvis showered his whole family with gifts, he especially spoiled his parents. He bought them new clothes, cars, and houses and loved taking care of his "babies" as he called his parents.

To Gladys, Elvis' success brought some happiness, but mostly anxiety. It was the fulfillment of her dream of success for Elvis, but it also separated her from her son in a way she never could have anticipated. Gladys instinctively distrusted Colonel Parker and worried herself sick while Elvis was out touring. She had good reason to worry about his safety. At one concert she attended, she witnessed firsthand a mob of frenzied fans trying to claw their way to Elvis onstage.

Gladys, Elvis, and Vernon Presley

From the collection of Bob Klein

She waded into the crowd in an attempt to protect her son asking those around her, "Why are you trying to kill my boy?"

When Elvis was on the road, Graceland was a lonely place for Gladys. She would sometimes bring a chair down to the front gate and sit with her brother Travis, the security guard there, and reminisce about simpler times. As a result of her worries and loneliness, she began to increase her drinking and gain weight. Like her son would do years later, she took diet pills to help her lose some of the weight and this contributed to her other health problems.

The biggest blow to Gladys came when Elvis was drafted. She couldn't bear the thought of him stationed overseas, facing what she perceived as the perilous life of a soldier. Elvis entered the army and was stationed at Fort Hood, Texas, for training, but as soon as he could, he sent for his family. Gladys, Vernon, Dodger. They all lived together off base first in a trailer, then in a rented house in nearby Killeen. During this time, Gladys's health continued to deteriorate until she was sent back to Memphis to be diagnosed by her own doctor. She was admitted to Methodist Hospital with what was most likely acute hepatitis. Elvis was given emergency leave and rushed to her bedside. On the night of August 15, 1958, at 3:30 in the morning, after Gladys had insisted that Elvis go home to get some sleep, a ringing phone awakened everyone at Graceland. Elvis said he knew what the news was before he answered the phone. He rushed back to the hospital to join his father, who was wailing over Gladys's lifeless body.

Elvis' response to his mother's death was an unashamed, candid expression of grief, the likes of which had rarely been witnessed from a public figure. The Colonel treated Gladys's death as a just another public relations event and photo op for his client. With insensitivity and customary lack of taste, the Colonel let the press cover Elvis' mourning as enthusiastically and as crassly as they did his military induction. Parker had the gates of Graceland opened to a small army of reporters and photographers so they could record Elvis' gut-wrenching sorrow. The Colonel saw this as another opportunity to further manipulate Elvis' image from the young rebel who outraged decent people to the young soldier who loved his mother. If he was trying to create empathy for Elvis, it worked. At Gladys's funeral, Elvis could barely control himself. None were unmoved by his

Gladys and Vernon's first-floor bedroom at Graceland

John O'Hara

profound grief. His devotion to his mother and his heartbreak at her death only endeared Elvis to his fans even more and won the sympathy of many others who couldn't help but feel sorry for the young man who suffered such a loss. Graceland received more than one hundred thousand sympathy cards. Gladys's death was a heartbreak that affected Elvis for the rest of his life. In remembrance of her, Elvis made sure that flowers were delivered to her grave once a week until the day he died. You can see Gladys's bedroom today at Graceland; it's restored to the way it was during her time there, complete with the poodle wallpaper in the bathroom. It was opened to the public, appropriately enough, on Mother's Day in 1994.

Shortly after returning to active duty, Elvis was shipped overseas and Vernon and Dodger joined him in Germany to live off base together as he adjusted to life without his mother. Much to Elvis' dismay, Vernon had his own method of adjusting to life without Gladys. He met Davada "Dee" Stanley, the wife of an army sergeant, and fell for her. Elvis thought Vernon's rebound was a little too quick and refused to attend their wedding on July 3, 1960, on their return to the States. In spite of Elvis' unhappiness with the situation, he welcomed Vernon, his new bride, and her three young sons into his home as was his tradition with family. Elvis treated his new stepbrothers, Ricky, David, and Billy, as if they were really his own brothers. Vernon's new wife crossed the line, however, when she took it upon herself to redecorate Graceland while Elvis was in Hollywood shooting a movie. When he returned, he found that Dee had removed some of Gladys's original decorations and tried to put her own stamp on his personal space. That very day a moving truck appeared outside the mansion and Dee's days living inside Graceland were over. Elvis eventually relocated Vernon and his new brood to a house around the corner on Dolan Drive, which abuts the back of Graceland. Years later, on May 5, 1977, Elvis was more than happy to pay the quarter-million-dollar divorce settlement when Vernon and Dee parted ways. Elvis' stepbrothers, however, remained on the scene as flunkies until the end of his life. At that time, Dee Stanley sealed her role as a

"Goodbye, darling, goodbye. I love you so much. You know how much I lived my whole life just for you."
—Elvis, at his mother's funeral

Sandi Miller

Dee Stanley and Priscilla at Priscilla's baby shower at Graceland

pariah in the Elvis community when she sold a story to the *National Enquirer* claiming that Elvis and his mother had had an incestuous relationship. It still stands as the most outrageous attempt by an "insider" to capitalize, without regard to any sense of decency, on an association with Elvis.

Elvis started his own family when he married his long-time, live-in love, Priscilla Beaulieu, on May 1, 1967. Exactly 9 months later—to the day, on February 1, 1968—Elvis' only child, Lisa Marie Presley, was born at Baptist Memorial Hospital. She weighed 6 pounds 15 ounces, and was 20 inches long at birth. If it had been a boy, they planned to name him John Baron Presley. Elvis spoiled his only child with inappropriate gifts of furs and jewels. He loved having a family, but not necessarily being a family man. Disillusioned or unhappy in his marriage for reasons we will never know, Elvis treated it as a part-time job. While he was on the road, he was "single"; when he was home, he was married. In early 1973, Priscilla left him and they were divorced in October of that year. They shared joint custody of Lisa Marie and she would often spend time at Graceland with her father. It was during one of these stays in August 1977 that Elvis passed away. Elvis was described by those closest to him as not ever being quite the same after the divorce. The idea of marriage and family were of paramount importance to him, and he must have suffered because this part of his life hadn't been as successful as others.

There is plenty of interest in Lisa Marie in the fan world. She is undeniably her father's daughter, a sort of "female Elvis." She's a mysterious figure and seldom makes public appearances or interacts with the fans. Like her mother, she's

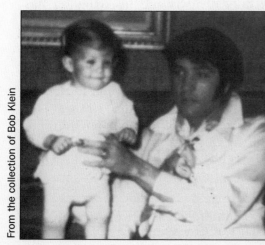

From the collection of Bob Klein

Elvis with Lisa Marie

From the collection of Bob Klein

an ardent Scientologist. On October 3, 1988, she married Daniel Keough, a musician and fellow Scientologist. They were married by a Scientologist minister and honeymooned on a Scientology cruise. Their marriage produced two children, Danielle Riley and Benjamin Storm, but ended in divorce.

Lisa Marie's biggest claim to fame so far, in addition to being the daughter of the King of rock and roll, has been to have been the wife of the King of Pop. As if scripted by a tabloid newspaper owner, Lisa Marie married Michael Jackson in the Dominican Republic on May 26, 1994. The marriage was brief and, not surprisingly, produced no children. It boggles the mind to think of what the product of that union would have been. There were many rumors as to the reasons for the mysterious pairing, but very few people must know what their motivations were.

There has always been speculation about whether or not Lisa Marie has inherited any of Elvis' musical talent. Fans who were present at the debut of the "Elvis in Concert" show during Tribute Week in 1997 were stunned to see Lisa Marie sing a duet of "Don't Cry Daddy" with her father (on video). If there were any dry eyes in the house at the end of that performance, we didn't see them. When Priscilla asked if everyone wanted to see it again, the response left no doubt and it was immediately shown a second time. The duet of Elvis and his daughter has become a popular bootleg at fan conventions, but the fans soon won't have to rely on bootlegs to hear Lisa Marie perform. She has signed a contract with Java Records, a division of Capital, to release her first album. As of this writing, Lisa Marie's debut is scheduled some time in the year 2000.

After Elvis died, Vernon moved back to Graceland. On October 2, 1977, he had

Sandi Miller

Lisa Marie Presley in her customized golf cart at Graceland

Vernon and his son

the bodies of Elvis and Gladys moved from Forest Hills Cemetery to the Meditation Garden at Graceland where they were reinterred, together again for eternity. Vernon never said much publicly, but he did do one interview for the January 1978 issue of *Good Housekeeping* in which he speaks of son and his sense of loss. Vernon died not long after this on June 26, 1979, and was also buried in the Garden. Elvis' grandmother Dodger had lived up to her nickname by dodging death the longest of all the members of the clan. She died on May 8, 1980, at the age of 86 and was also buried with her son's family. Even in the end, Elvis' family was reunited as that basic Presley family unit—Elvis, his mother, his father, and his grandmother. At the site there is even a small memorial plaque for the Jesse, the twin brother who no one ever knew. The family that lived together and joined together in defense against the outside world, now rests together in the place they all called home.

The love that Elvis so obviously felt for his family is part of the reason why Elvis is so loved himself. To so many fans, Elvis almost feels like a family member. When they visit Graceland and get together with each other, they often talk about the strong feeling of family that exists in the Elvis world. The Elvis "family" is truly following the example left by Elvis.

ESSENTIAL ELVISOLOGY

Vernon's Birthday
April 19, 1916

Gladys's Birthday
April 25, 1912

Fans visiting the Presley family's final resting place in the Meditation Garden at Graceland

THE FAMILY TREE

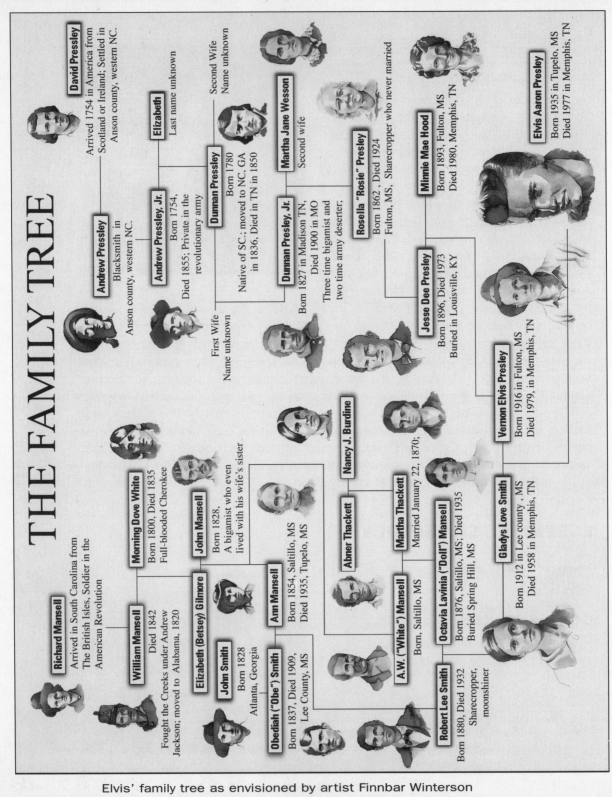

David Pressley
Arrived 1754 in America from Scotland or Ireland; Settled in Anson county, western NC.

Andrew Pressley
Blacksmith in Anson county, western NC.

Elizabeth
Last name unknown

Andrew Pressley, Jr.
Born 1754, Died 1855; Private in the revolutionary army

Dunnan Pressley
Born 1780
Native of SC.; moved to NC, GA in 1836, Died in TN in 1850

First Wife
Name unknown

Second Wife
Name unknown

Martha Jane Wesson
Second wife

Dunnan Pressley, Jr.
Born 1827 in Madison TN, Died 1900 in MO
Three time bigamist and two time army deserter;

Rosella "Rosie" Presley
Born 1862 , Died 1924
Fulton, MS, Sharecropper who never married

Minnie Mae Hood
Born 1893, Fulton, MS
Died 1980, Memphis, TN

Jesse Dee Presley
Born 1896, Died 1973
Buried in Louisville, KY

Vernon Elvis Presley
Born 1916 in Fulton, MS
Died 1979, in Memphis, TN

Elvis Aaron Presley
Born 1935 in Tupelo, MS
Died 1977 in Memphis, TN

Richard Mansell
Arrived in South Carolina from The British Isles, Soldier in the American Revolution

William Mansell
Died 1842
Fought the Creeks under Andrew Jackson; moved to Alabama, 1820

Morning Dove White
Born 1800, Died 1835
Full-blooded Cherokee

John Mansell
Born 1828,
A bigamist who even lived with his wife's sister

Elizabeth (Betsey) Gilmore

John Smith
Born 1828
Atlanta, Georgia

Ann Mansell
Born 1854, Saltillo, MS
Died 1935, Tupelo, MS

Obediah ("Obe") Smith
Born 1837, Died 1909,
Lee County, MS

Nancy J. Burdine

Abner Thackett
Born, Saltillo, MS

Martha Thackett
Married January 22, 1870;

A.W. ("White") Mansell
Born, Saltillo, MS

Octavia Lavinia ("Doll") Mansell
Born 1876, Saltillo, MS; Died 1935
Buried Spring Hill, MS

Robert Lee Smith
Born 1880, Died 1932
Sharecropper, moonshiner

Gladys Love Smith
Born 1912 in Lee county , MS
Died 1958 in Memphis, TN

Elvis' family tree as envisioned by artist Finnbar Winterson

Illustration by Finnbar Winterson

Vernon and Gladys's Wedding Day
June 17, 1933

Lisa Marie's Birth Stats
Born 5:01 P.M. February 1, 1968
Weight: 6 pounds 15 ounces
Length: 20 inches
Delivered by Dr. T. A. Turman

Lisa Marie's Nicknames
"Buttonhead"
"Yisa"
"Little Fuhrer" (dubbed by Lamar Fike)
"Gumbernickel" (dubbed by Linda
   Thompson)

Elvis' Grandchildren
Danielle Riley Keough
   Born May 29, 1989
Benjamin Storm Keough
   Born October 21, 1992

Some Elvis Relatives Who Lived or Worked at Graceland
Vernon Presley
   Elvis' father, worked as Elvis' manager.
Vester Presley
   Elvis' uncle, worked security at the front gate.
Donna Presley Early
   Elvis' first cousin, spent summers at Graceland.
Nashval Presley Pritchett
   Elvis' paternal aunt, lived in a mobile home behind Graceland.
Delta Mae Presley Biggs
   Elvis' paternal aunt, lived at Graceland until her death in 1993.
Patsy Presley
   Elvis' double first cousin, worked in Vernon's office.
Minnie Mae Presley
   Elvis' paternal grandmother.

John O'Hara

"We travel, as a family, to Memphis twice a year and we just love it! Reuniting with our friends through Elvis is well worth the 1,200 miles we endure annually. As club president of the only Miami Dade County fan club in Florida, I take pride in continuing Elvis' legacy and generosity. We correspond with several fan clubs and exchange ideas. We are glad our daughters are growing up in such a positive atmosphere. We have been kindly referred to as the Elvis Family and we get a kick out of it."
—Gabe, Betty, Gabriela, and Alexandra Rodriguez

Elvis with his cousin Billy Smith

Sandi Miller

Karen Sue Pritchett
  Elvis' cousin, worked at
  Graceland after Elvis' death.
Earl Pritchett
  Husband of Elvis' cousin, Karen
  Sue. He worked at Graceland for
  more than 20 years.
Buddy Early
  Donna Presley's husband,
  worked security at Graceland.
Billy Smith
  Elvis' cousin, lived in a mobile
  home behind Graceland.
Gene Smith
  Elvis' cousin, lived in the garage
  apartment at Graceland.
Travis Smith
  Elvis uncle, lived in a house behind Graceland that Elvis himself eventually
  bulldozed.
Lillian Smith
  Elvis' aunt, worked in the office.
John Smith
  Elvis' uncle, worked as a gate guard.
Harold Loyd
  Elvis' cousin, worked as a guard at Graceland.

The Last Presley to Live at Graceland
Delta Mae Presley Biggs
  Lived at Graceland until her death in July 1993.

> "They like my boy."
> —Gladys

Glossary of Elvis- and Gladys-Speak
Butch = milk
Toophies = teeth
Yittle = little
Yuv = love
Duckling = water
Sooties = feet
Boocups = a lot

Iddytream = ice cream
Bellywash = Pepsi
Happies = gifts
Nungin' = young one
Lather = sugar and cream for coffee
Satnin' or Sattnin' = a term of endearment

YOUR ELVIS EDUCATION

Books

Elvis and Gladys
Elaine Dundy
Early Elvis
Bill E. Burk
A Presley Speaks
Vester Presley as told Deda Bonura
One Flower While I live
Nash Pritchett
Last Train to Memphis
Peter Guralnick
Careless Love
Peter Guralnick
Elvis Presley's Graceland Gates
Harold Loyd
*Elvis Up Close: In the Words of Those Who
Knew Him Best*
edited by Rose Clayton and Dick Heard
Precious Memories
Donna Presley Early and Edie Hand, with Lynn Edge
Elvis My Dad: The Unauthorized Biography of Lisa Marie Presley
David Adler and Ernst Andrews
The Inner Elvis: A Psychological Biography of Elvis Aaron Presley
Peter Witmers
That's All Right, Mama: The Unauthorized Life of Elvis' Twin
a novel by Gerald Duff
Return to Sender: The Secret Son of Elvis Presley
Les and Sue Fox
Elvis Presley Calls His Mother after the Ed Sullivan Show
Samuel Charters
Caught in a Trap
Rick Stanley with Paul Harold
Elvis: We Love You Tender
Dee Presley, Billy, Rick, and David Stanley as told to Martin Torgoff
Life with Elvis
David Stanley
Shake Rag: From the Life of Elvis Presley
Amy Littlesugar and Floyd Cooper

> "I think if Priscilla or Lisa were involved a little more in the public they would not be so misunderstood. I think that is what upsets most fans. I hear that they are involved more than the fans know but shy away from the limelight. If that is so, I would respect them more for not taking the light away from Elvis."
>
> —Megan

Video

"*Elvis*" (ABC)
20/20 (ABC)
  Barbara Walters interview with Lisa Marie
  and Michael Jackson
"The Presleys: Rock-and-Roll Royalty"
  Family Channel *Famous Family* series

> "Elvis has always been there. I always expected him to be a part of American culture that I would share with my children."
>
> —Dave Marsh,
> from his book *Elvis*

Web Sites

http://www.geocities.com/~arpt/az/
  Elvis Presley Encyclopaedia
http://www.infinet.com/~bands/index.html
  Stacy's Lisa Marie web page

http://members.aol.com/LisaMariP2/
  lisamarie.html
  Lisa Marie shrine
http://www.women-celebrities.com/
  celebs/lisamariepresley.html#lisa
  Lisa Marie Links site

THE ELVIS AND YOU EXPERIENCE

Turn Your Kids on to Elvis

Elvis is good family entertainment. Children respond to him in a positive way. His movies are basically as wholesome as Saturday morning cartoons. You could give your kid a copy of *Shake Rag: From the Life of Elvis Presley* by Amy Littlesugar and Floyd Cooper. It's an illustrated children's book that tells the story of Elvis' childhood and his discovery of his passion for music. Or get a copy of *Elvis Sings for Children and Grown Ups Too,* a collection of Elvis songs that kids will love.

Practice Nepotism at Every Opportunity

Hire your relatives as often as possible. Make sure they're qualified, though. Elvis could have found a better money manager than his father, Vernon.

Take an Elvis Family Tree Road Trip

Trace Elvis' family tree. You can start off in Scotland and then trace his family's path across the southern United States (not on the same road trip). Seek out cemeteries where his ancestors are buried. Make tracings from the headstones or take photographs. It's a lesson in American history since Elvis was one of those great mixtures that occur here: Cherokee, Scottish, Jewish....

Find Out If You're Related to Elvis

A genealogist has claimed to have traced Elvis' family tree back to Oprah Winfrey. Who knows, maybe you're related to Elvis! The internet has many genealogical sites to help you start your search. Also, the Mormon Church in Salt Lake City has one of the most extensive genealogical databases on the planet that is available for research.

Write to Lisa Marie
Lisa Marie can receive mail through the Graceland Communications Department. They'll acknowledge your letter and it will be kept for her until she next visits Graceland.

Use Elvis-Speak at Home with Your Family
Elvis and Gladys had their own special words for things. Use some of the terms with those close to you. Think of it as a secret code.

Nickname Your Relatives
Call your grandmother "Dodger" (even if her reflexes aren't so good.) Call your mother "Satnin'."

Have a Family Reunion Picnic
Get your family together for a reunion on a regular basis. Play Elvis music. Serve Elvis food. Sing together.

Name Your Child in the Smith/Presley Family Tradition

Obediah	Sayles	Effie	White
Delta Mae	Lavinia	Dunnan	Rosella
Minnie Mae	Calhoun	Milege	Jessie
Doll	Travis	Dukie	Rhetha
Vester	Lafeyette	Senna	Levalle
Truitt	Nashville Lorene	Jehru	
Gains	Clettes	Octavia	

Honor Your Mother
Don't just take her out for Mother's Day, take her out on Gladys's birthday, April 25, too.

Make a Donation to St. Joseph Hospital
Gladys worked as a nurse's aide at St. Joseph's during the early 1950s.
St. Joseph Hospital
220 Overton Avenue
Memphis, Tennessee 38105
(901) 577-2700

Start the Kids Off with Their Own Elvis CD

Blue Suede Music online rock and roll shop sells many products for the younger fan including temporary Elvis tattoos and stickers; but best of all, they sell an *Elvis Sings for Children* CD. You can reach them online or write to them at:

Blue Suede Music
3674 Canada Road
Lakeland, Tennessee 38002
(901) 383-1200
Fax: (901) 383-1035
E-mail: info@bluesuedemusic.com
http://www.bluesuedemusic.com/

Elvis Paper Dolls

Dover Publications came out with an Elvis cutout paper doll book a while back. It's a collectible now, but still not that expensive. Buy two if you see the book for sale, and let the kids play with one of them.

"Elvis not only got me with his music but he also turned me on to music in general. My Mom, who is from Tennessee, was on board with the entire 'Elvis thing.' My Dad said he thought Elvis was just a fad. My Dad is a very smart man, but he missed on this one big time."
—Steve Braun

"... We have virtually ambitionless Vernon with his bad back whose most imaginative vocational aspirations for his only son consist of a stable, well-paying job ('I never knew a guitar player that was worth a damn.') and Gladys, aged beyond her years by thankless domestic chores and hard living in general. Neither have any hope for a better future, and both are resigned to reality as they understand it. Elvis is the one who dares to dream. ('I was the hero in the comic books, folks.') He's the one who refuses to accept reality, first as a youth, and later, long after 'every dream I've ever dreamed has come true a million times.' Reality for him consists of tedium, humility, and boredom. Now, if he can just stand the slight odor of sulfur and brimstone that comes part and parcel with Tom Parker, he also has the chance not only to realize his own outsized ambitions, but to improve greatly the circumstances of the only other people who have ever cared about him...."
—Cathy, on alt.elvis.king

ELVIS AND ROMANCE

While millions of girls were kissing their souvenir photos of Elvis, the ones who got to buss those lips in person all had superlative things to say about the way Elvis kissed. "Elvis was a great kisser. When we played spin the bottle, we always hoped the bottle would land on him," revealed Billie Wardlaw in Bill E. Burk's wonderful book *Early Elvis*.

In her tender and affectionate account of their teenage relationship, *Elvis in the Twilight of Memory*, June Juanico wrote, "Elvis was a wonderful kisser. How do you describe soft lips, slightly parted, not too much, but just perfect. And he sometimes opened his mouth about three inches—sucked off part of my nose." Elvis loved to neck and he was obviously pretty creative about it. The raves go on and on.

Elvis launched what were to become his legendarily romantic ways like all other young kids: with innocent childhood and teenage crushes. He passed notes, went on walks, and serenaded his youthful sweethearts with doleful ballads and love songs. In the hope of winning her heart, Elvis sang with his guitar under Billie Jean Wardlaw's window in Lauderdale Courts where they both lived during junior high and high school. (Elvis sang *to* all and *with* some of the women he was romancing—Anita Wood and Linda Thompson can actually be heard harmonizing along with Elvis on some of the various "home recordings" that have been released.)

From the collection of Bob Klein

Author's collection

Elvis with Magdelen Morgan, Tupelo

His high school pals remember that Elvis didn't participate in bumptious locker-room conversations about girls. It wasn't only because he was so shy; Elvis was respectful, even protective, of the girls he went out with—a real gentleman. He always preferred confiding in his female friends, anyway.

Within a short time after graduating high school, Elvis had recorded "That's All Right," and with its success on the radio he started touring and performing around the South in what was essentially the first rock and roll band. At 19, Elvis was gorgeous and exciting as sin itself. He was on top of the world and enjoying every moment of it.

It's easy to imagine that the fun-loving and playful Elvis we all know from his movies and stage performances was the same when he was alone with a woman. According to June Juanico, one of the girls he went with steadily during the mid-fifties, when the record player or radio played a song with a strong bass line, Elvis would grab her, put one hand on her forehead and the other on her stomach, and play her like an upright bass.

When Elvis made it to Hollywood in 1956, his offscreen love life started out rather inauspiciously with an innocent but decapitating crush on Deborah Paget, the actress from *Love Me Tender*. Elvis' character doesn't win her heart in the movie or in real life and their relations were innocent only because Elvis' feelings were not reciprocated. In Deborah Paget, Elvis felt he had found the perfect woman, certainly in terms of looks.

"I consider [Elvis] a menace to young girls."
—Hedda Hopper

From the collection of Bob Klein

After a few years of making films, Elvis was drafted into the Army and then stationed in Germany. There he met, and fell hard for, a young teenager named Priscilla Beaulieu whose army dad was also stationed nearby. She was shy, but poised, and incredibly beautiful—Elvis couldn't get over just how lovely she was and he talked about her beauty with everyone who would listen. (Oddly enough, Priscilla looked a good deal like Deborah

Paget.) When Elvis got back to the States, he somehow arranged with Priscilla's parents for their teenage daughter to join him in Memphis. The story was that Priscilla would be living, chaperoned by Elvis' father, in his home near Graceland, but everyone has admitted this wasn't precisely the case. She came over from Germany, moved into Graceland, and finished high school as the "live-in Lolita" of Elvis Presley.

Everyone who was in Elvis' life has a version of the sequence of events that led to how their marriage finally came to be. Priscilla wrote *Elvis and Me* in 1985 to tell her side. Lamar Fike, a friend who was with Elvis from the beginning of his career to the end of his life, has said that Elvis would have had more fun catching bowling balls with his teeth than getting married. Mary Jenkins, one of Elvis' favorite cooks, tells the story (she's got lots of great ones, by the way) of seeing Elvis depressed and downcast over his upcoming wedding. When he told her how unhappy he was, she says she told him that he could either be a man and say he wasn't going to go through with it, or he could be a man and go through with it. And Suzanne Finstad wrote a fascinating and detailed book about Elvis and Priscilla's courtship and marriage. What we do know for certain is that after waiting for several years Elvis and Priscilla married in a roughly eight-minute ceremony at the Aladdin Hotel in Las Vegas. They made it official on May 1, 1967, with a three-and-a-half-carat diamond (designed by Harry Levitch) and a kiss. Elvis' bride was treated to "The Hawaiian Love Song" as he carried her over the threshold. Nine months later to the day, on February 1, 1968, at 5:01 P.M., their daughter Lisa Marie was

Sandi Miller

From the collection of Bob Klein

Elvis and Priscilla on their wedding day

Sandi Miller

born at Baptist Memorial Hospital. She was named after Colonel Parker's wife, Marie Mott Ross Parker. If she had been a boy, Priscilla says they would have named him John Baron.

The saddest aspect of the failure of their marriage, perhaps, was that Elvis and Priscilla didn't connect on any of the planes that were important to either of them. She naturally wanted some privacy in her marriage, but those ubiquitous Memphis Mafia guys were always underfoot. Intimacy for the couple was compromised by the ever-present fans, the Colonel, and the moat built around Elvis by his entourage—just as it had been during all those years leading up to the marriage. Priscilla must have been hurt to see that this was the way Elvis wanted things. And whether or not she should have known what she was getting into as many have argued, Elvis' many betrayals can't have been a picnic for her. As for Elvis, if his goal in choosing Priscilla initially as a teenager was to guide her formation into his ideal woman and perfect mate, then his plan failed. As the years passed, he did not find the partner he wanted in his wife. When his spiritual leanings led to a consuming obsession and full-time quest for deeper knowledge, Priscilla didn't display much, if any, interest. She was antagonistic toward his endless spiritual reading and studies and reportedly worked to sabotage Elvis' connection with his good friend and

Sandi Miller

Elvis and Priscilla in Palm Springs the day after their marriage spiritual brother, Larry Geller. Eventually she participated in the destruction of Elvis' spiritual book collection. Looking back, her now famous allegiance to and belief in Scientology seems somewhat ironic.

Elvis was complex and even difficult as a partner and it seems that he was impenetrable even to Priscilla, if her autobiography is an indication of how well she understood him. To their credit, they remained excellent friends, always had good communications, and shared in the raising of their daughter.

Most female Elvis fans look at Priscilla through green eyes. It's understandable enough that they would be envious of the woman who became Mrs. Elvis Presley and shared her days … and nights … with him for many years. And, of course, she bore the child Elvis loved so much.

Most of all, fans are galled when Priscilla is referred to in the press as Elvis' widow. Since they were divorced when he died, she isn't his widow in legal terms. Among the various grudges against her are the way she conducts the business of Elvis' estate, that she keeps his name, that she doesn't show up in person for Tribute Week events, and even the way she wears her hair.

On the other hand, there are many supporters of Priscilla among the fans. They feel she's always been in a bind she could never win—when she married him *and* when she divorced him. She was vilified first as the girl who claimed Elvis' heart and then as the woman who broke it by walking away.

On the Hollywood front during the sixties, Elvis wooed and won several of his beautiful costars and even the occasional wardrobe mistress. Most famously, Elvis lived a real-life love story with Ann-Margret who performed with him in *Viva Las Vegas*. In her book *My Story,* Ann-Margret wrote of their love for each other and subsequent lifelong friendship. He had nicknamed her "Rusty Ammo" after her screen name in *Viva Las Vegas*, Rusty Martin. To Ann, Elvis was "strong, gentle, exciting and protective," but he didn't like equally strong or aggressive women. They appeared to many observers to be genuinely in love. Ann-Margret, who had been dubbed the Female Elvis because of her awesome energy and sex appeal as a performer, seemed to be a good match

Author's collection

Elvis and Ann-Margret in *Viva Las Vegas*

Sandi Miller

Elvis and one of the dancers he met while making his "'68 Comeback Special"

for Elvis. But their relationship couldn't last. Priscilla was waiting for Elvis back at Graceland. And Ann was committed to continuing her career, which didn't precisely fit in with Elvis' idea of the little woman. Their friendship remained strong, and every time Ann opened a show Elvis sent her a guitar-shaped floral arrangement. When she didn't receive one for her opening night in mid-August 1977, she knew something was wrong. She found out the next day that Elvis had died. Ann and her husband came to Elvis' funeral in Memphis.

The Memphis Mafia divided Elvis' women into two categories. "Lifers" were the women with whom Elvis had serious longer-term relationships, such as Anita Wood, Priscilla, Ann-Margret, Sheila Ryan, Barbara Leigh, and Linda Thompson. His dalliances were nicknamed "Queen for a Day."

With women he cared about, Elvis could be tenderly, even poetically, romantic. Or he could indulge in an affectionate sort of baby talk. He made up nicknames for everyone including girlfriends that ranged from "Pee Pee Britches" to "Nungin" and "Satnin'"—all terms he got from his mother.

When Elvis dated a woman, he wowed her in more ways than by just being Elvis. His generosity was phenomenal and many ended up with cars and

"Elvis will be around as long as there are women."
—Kay Wheeler, 1956, Dallas fan club president

Photo reprinted with permission

Carol Jacobs and Elvis liplocked in Las Vegas, 1971

jewelry. Elvis was known to have private phone lines installed in his girlfriend's homes so they'd know it was him calling and more important, he would never get a busy signal. Inevitably it became known as the Elvis hot line.

What woman wouldn't want to be with him? What man wouldn't want to be him? Oh, all right, you can probably find a couple of people *somewhere* who don't fit these categories—but it's safe to say that Elvis was one of the most desirable men who ever lived. It may sound thrilling, but when you think about it a little more, it sounds like a burden as well. How would a woman know if she's in love with the real man or the outer appeal—and how would he know? Elvis was very troubled by the idea that he could never really know for sure if was loved for who he really was and he sometimes shared these concerns with friends.

From a woman's point of view, we know what the love story was about. Elvis was physically beautiful; talented beyond measure; and sexy, sensitive, and vulnerable, potent and strong. Imagine kissing the most famous face in the world, coming to after receiving the most exciting kiss of your life and you're staring into the loveliest smiling blue eyes. You're staring at Elvis!

What about his perspective? Many woman have described themselves when they met Elvis as weeping, speechless, quaking, awestruck. It may sound like a charge, but those conditions are not very conducive to meaningful interaction. Desire, adoration, fantasy, projection—Elvis wasn't only the recipient of all these, in a way he was the target of them as well.

Of course it was Elvis himself who had pulled the stopper on women's sexuality. With his sexually powerful persona and his highly charged performances, Elvis gave women something to respond to and with his own defiant and unapologetic attitude, he made it all right not to hold back. So how did everyone handle all the excitement? Well, "He … was both *Elvis* and Elvis," as Joyce

> "[Elvis] had his old boyish grin on his face and his hands were behind his back. 'Sit down, Sattnin', and close your eyes.' I did. When I opened my eyes, I found Elvis on his knees before me, holding a small black velvet box. 'Sattnin',' he said. I opened the box to find the most beautiful diamond ring I'd ever seen. It was three-and-a-half karats, encircled by a row of smaller diamonds, which were detachable—I could wear them separately. 'We're going to be married,' Elvis said. 'You're going to be his. I told you I'd know when the time was right. Well, the time's right.' He slipped the ring on my finger. I was too overwhelmed to speak; it was the most beautiful and romantic moment of my life."
> —Priscilla Beaulieu Presley, on Elvis' marriage proposal from *Elvis and Me*

Bova, who dated Elvis in the early '70s, explained in her book *Don't Ask Forever*. Meaning that he was the legendary performer who was truly larger than life but he was also still just Elvis, a man who had a great gift and desire to put people around him at ease.

What type of women did Elvis like? They ranged from petite and kittenish to tall and slender. He liked dark hair and complexions ... and fair-skinned blondes when he was with them. He liked wide-set, large eyes and button noses. And he liked makeup artfully applied and clothes dressy and extravagant. He liked Chanel No. 5. Requisites were femininity and good humor. And like almost all men of his generation, he had a great deal of respect for women who guarded their virginity and those who expected to stay at home with the kids and casseroles.

Whether or not it's true that Elvis followed up many of the concerts he gave during the 1950s with a romantic encounter and cut a swath through the landscape of Hollywood starlets in the 1960s, he appears to have slowed down from about 1967 on. Many of his relationships were unconsummated or briefly sexual and then friendly encounters. There are dozens of stories of Elvis disappearing into a hotel bedroom with several women and when the door was opened later the scene was of Elvis reading the Bible to them. Linda Thompson, who lived with Elvis in the early seventies, said of him, "Elvis had a great capacity for love, which I think is commendable. You know, he was not nearly as promiscuous as people might assert. There were a lot of women friends that Elvis had, even when he was with me, and they truly were just friends."

It is noteworthy that not one of the paternity suits brought against Elvis ever proved to be true. Elvis fought them quietly and with dignity by vol-

"I felt a responsibility toward him and toward the whole world, too. I felt that this is someone the world loves. I adored him beyond description, but I also felt so many other people loved him that I wanted to take good care of him for everybody."
—Linda Thompson, in an interview for *The Inner Child* by Peter Whitmer, Ph.D.

Elvis and Ginger Alden

From the collection of Bob Klein

unteering for blood tests and cooperating legally. The contention that Elvis fathered any children other than Lisa Marie is simply not true.

Linda Thompson and Elvis met on July 26, 1972. He was in the middle of his divorce, and he found a great friend and love in her. Linda understood Elvis and, in virtually everyone's opinion, he made a grave mistake by not marrying her. She had a sense of humor on a par with Elvis' and laughter was one of the hallmarks of their time together. She mothered Elvis too; when he wasn't feeling well Linda slept with her hand on his chest so she could feel him breathe. When Linda finally opted out after several years, it wasn't because they had fallen out of love with one another. She could no longer take Elvis' lifestyle and was saddened by his self-destructive behavior.

"You're burning a hole through me." With this fateful pickup line, Elvis introduced himself to a Miss Traffic Safety titleholder named Ginger Alden on November 29, 1976. Ginger was the last live-in girlfriend that Elvis had, and she was there at the time he died.

Fans can learn about Elvis' as a romantic partner from a few sources whose veracity may reasonably be questioned and a few whose experiences are told from their extremely subjective, and in some cases imaginary, perspective only. The Memphis Mafia guys in various exposés and tell-alls paint a fairly seamy picture, dwelling on the sexploits and sheer volume. Maybe they were motivated by envy or simply a knack for seeing the tawdry side of things, or maybe they were goaded by the prospect of more book sales to embellish the stories from Elvis' love life. Other sources are a smattering of books and word-of-mouth tales by women who actually did know Elvis and a few accounts by women who apparently *wish* they had known him. Needless to say, not much of it would hold up in court.

Elvis' life was filled with romance in all its manifestations. He was a man who had a great

> "Elvis is still in my life. He is everywhere at home and next Sunday his music is going to be the soundtrack at my wedding. Yeah, I'm going to marry this Valentine's Day in Lake Tahoe!"
>
> —Francesc Lopez

capacity to give love and a very human need to receive it. But even though millions upon millions of women fell in love with him and were willing to show it, his life was filled with heartbreak and unhappiness also. For that reason, when Elvis sang a love song, you knew he really meant it—he was really singing from his heart.

Laura Levin

ESSENTIAL ELVISOLOGY

Some of the Women in Elvis' Life

We're not making any claims whatsoever here. We're just saying that these women have been "linked romantically" with Elvis. Some of them, as very good friends, he discussed the Bible with and some of them knew him in a biblical way. Some were flirtations and nothing more and some were long-term, serious girlfriends.

Carol Ballard
    In Tupelo; Elvis was nine.
Eloise Bedford
    Childhood girlfriend
Magdelen Morgan
    In Tupelo
Betty McMann
    1950–1951
Billie Wardlaw
    Lauderdale Courts girlfriend
Regis Wilson Vaughan
    Senior prom date, 1953
Tammy Young
    High school
Dixie Locke
    Memphis sweetheart, met Elvis in church January 1954
Patty Philpot
    Memphis, mid-fifties
Anita Carter
    Singer with the Carter Sisters, 1955–56

Barbara Pittman
    She also recorded at Sun Records
Sharon Wiley
    Mid-fifties
Carolyn Bradshaw
    Folksinger on *Louisiana Hayride*

Sandi Miller

A very mod Priscilla

June Juanico
  Serious early girlfriend
Wanda Jackson
  Decca recording artist, 1955
Marilyn Evans
  Las Vegas showgirl, 1956
Judy Spreckles
  Spring 1957
Andrea June Stevens
  Won a date with Elvis through *Hit Parade* magazine contest
June Blackman
  Summer 1956, costar in *Blue Hawaii* and *Kid Galahad*
Diana Dors
  British sex kitten
Natalie Wood
  Actress
Kate Wheeler
  1956
Joan Brasher
  A former Miss Nevada
Kitty Dolan
  Tropicana singer
Sandy Preston
  Dated Elvis in Vegas in 1956
Jayne Mansfield
  Actress, fall 1956
Yvonne Lime
  Actress 1956–57, *Loving You*
Anita Wood
  Serious Memphis girlfriend, nicknamed "Wittle Beadie"
Rita Moreno
  Actress, 1957
Venetia Stevenson
  Dated Elvis in 1957 and 1958
Mamie Van Doren
  1957
Tempest Storm
  Stripper, 1957

Sandi Miller

Priscilla looking positively shagadelic in the '60s

"Elvis, you had great taste in women. Priscilla is a babe."
—Graffiti from the Wall of Love, from *Dear Elvis: Graffiti from Graceland*

From the collection of Bob Klein

Linda Thompson and Elvis

Dottie Harmony
  Las Vegas showgirl
Joan Bradshaw
  Winter 1957
Anne Neyland
  Dated during filming of *Jailhouse Rock*
Sherry Jackson
  Actress from the *Danny Thomas Show*
June Wilbank
  1958
Lillian Portnoy
  She kissed Elvis as he shipped out to Germany.
Barbara Hearn
  Actress from *Loving You*
Dolores Hart
  Actress from *Loving You* and *King Creole*, 1958; she later became a nun.
Jeanne Carmen
  B-movie actress, 1958
Carol Connors
  Singer from the Teddy Bears, 1958
Bobbie Gentry
  Singer
Heli Priemel
  Dated Elvis in Germany; nicknamed "Legs"
Siegrid Schutz
  Summer 1959, in Germany
Vera Tschechowa
  German actress, dated E in Munich
Margrit Buergin
  Worked as his secretary in Germany; nicknamed "Little Puppie"
Anjelika Zehetbauer
  Nightclub dancer from Germany
Jane Clarke
  Lido Club dancer

Linda Thompson

Nancy Parker
  Lido Club dancer
Sue Anderson
  In Germany
Patti Parry
  Honorary Memphis Mafia member
Kathy Gabriel
  1958, Miss Ohio
Hannah Melcher
  Miss Austria
Sherry Jackson
  Actress, 1959–60
Carolyn Frazer
  Girlfriend who introduced E to Continental suits, March 1960
Juliet Prowse
  GI Blues costar
Bonnie Bunkley
  Dated E in the spring of 1960
Nancy Sharp
  Flaming Star wardrobe assistant, 1960
Sandy Ferra
  Dated E in 1960
Connie Stevens
  Actress, 1961
Hope Hathaway
  Chorus girl, 1961

Yvonne Craig
    Kissin' Cousins costar
Cheryl Holdridge
    Starlet
Sharon Hugueny
    Actress, dated E in 1963
Shelley Fabares
    Favorite costar of three films,
    1965–67
Vicky Meyerlink
    Dated during filming of *Clambake*
Jackie Deshannon
    Singer and songwriter, mid-1960s
Barbara Bonner
    Dated E in the 1960s
Ann-Margret
    Viva Las Vegas costar, 1964
Deborah Walley
    Spinout costar
Cybill Shepherd
    1966, actress and former Miss
    Teenage America
Joyce Bova
    Met in 1969; wrote *Don't Ask
    Forever*
Barbara Leigh
    1970
Vicki Peters
    Dated E in 1971
Carol Connor
    Songwriter, 1972
Sandra Zancan
    Las Vegas showgirl, Summer 1972
Linda Thompson
    One of the great loves of Elvis' life.
    Linda spent a good part of the '70s

with him as a girlfriend *and* friend;
Miss Memphis State, Miss Liberty
Bowl, runner-up Miss USA.
Ann Pennington
    1974
Diane Goodman
    Miss Georgia, 1972
Mindi Miller
    Model, 1975–76
Jo Cathy Brownlee
    1975, hostess of the Memphis
    Grizzlies football team
Mallessa Blackwood
    Elvis gave her a Grand Prix on their
    first date.
Ann Helm
    Follow That Dream costar
Nancy Sinatra
    Friend of Elvis though rumored to
    be more
Tina Louise
    Actress
Sheila Ryan
    Dated Elvis in 1974
Piper Laurie
    Actress
Tuesday Weld
    Costar romance
Kathy Westmoreland
    Singer who toured with Elvis in the
    1970s
Alicia Kerwin
    1977, bank teller
Ginger Alden
    Miss Mid-South, Miss Traffic Safety

Priscilla's Nicknames
"Beau"
"Cilla"
"Priscilla–illa"

Songs Elvis Sang to Priscilla the Night They Met

"Rags to Riches"

"I Asked the Lord"

"The End"

Elvis and Priscilla's Divorce

The marriage ended during the winter of 1972. On February 23, 1972, at the age of 28, Priscilla moved out of Graceland. The settlement was $1.7 million and $8000 per month for 10 years. The official divorce was granted in October of 1973.

Priscilla's Film and Television Appearances

Titanic Too: It Missed the Iceberg (2000)

"Breakfast with Einstein" (1998)

Melrose Place TV series

Naked Gun: From the Files of Police Squad! (1988)

Naked Gun 2 1/2: The Smell of Fear (1991)

Naked Gun 33 1/3: The Final Insult (1994)

The Adventures of Ford Fairlane (1990)

Love Is Forever (1983) TV

Dallas (starting in 1978) TV series

Those Amazing Animals (1980); cohost on television series

Spin City TV series

Touched by an Angel TV series

Tales from the Crypt "Oil's Well That Ends Well" (1989)

The Fall Guy (1981)

Tony Orlando TV special

Some of Priscilla's Post-Elvis Male Friends and Boyfriends

Mike Stone

Terry O'Neill

Robert Kardashian

Richard Gere

Mike Edwards

Marco Garibaldi (She is presently still with Garibaldi.)

Priscilla's Nickname for Elvis

"Fire Eyes"

Ann-Margret's Nickname for Elvis

"Scoobie"

Linda Thompson's Nicknames for Elvis

"Bunting"

"Button"

Linda Thompson's Film and Television Appearances

Bare Exposure (1993)

The Bodyguard (1992)

Robocop 2 (1990)

Three on a Meathook (1972)

Hee Haw (1969)

CHIPS (1977)

Ginger Alden's Film Appearances

Lady Grey (1980)

Living Legend (1980)

Ginger Alden's Nicknames

"Gingerbread"

"Chicken Neck"

YOUR ELVIS EDUCATION

Books

Elvis and Kathy
    Kathy Westmoreland
Don't Ask Forever: My Love Affair with Elvis
    Joyce Bova as told to William Conrad Nowels
Are You Lonesome Tonight? The Untold Story of Elvis Presley's One True Love—and the Child He Never Knew
    Lucy de Barbin and Dary Matera
Child Bride
    Suzanne Finstad
Priscilla, Elvis and Me: In the Shadow of the King
    Michael Edwards
Elvis Up Close: In the Words of Those Who Knew Him Best
    edited by Rose Clayton and Dick Heard
Elvis: In the Twilight of Memory
    June Juanico

Elvis and Me
    Priscilla Beaulieu Presley with Sandra Harmon
Priscilla and Elvis
    Caroline Latham
Ann-Margret: My Story
    Ann-Margret
Long Trip from Omaha
    Joe Esposito
The Lady Is a Vamp
    Tempest Storm
The Complete Book of Dallas
    Suzy Kalter
Cybill Disobedience: How I Survived Beauty Pageants, Elvis, Sex, Bruce Willis, Lies, Marriage, Motherhood, Hollywood
    Cybill Shepherd with Jim Jerome
Twas the Night I Met Elvis
    Gloria Pall (Available from Showgirl Press, 12828 Victory Boulevard #163, North Hollywood, California 91606. Fax: (818) 509-0244 or http://www.gloriapall.com/

Video

"Elvis and the Beauty Queen" (NBC 1981
Rare Moments with the King
    Documentary, with film of the wedding kiss
"Elvis and Me"
June Juanico's *Lost Love* film

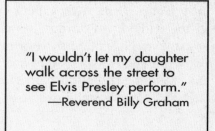

"I wouldn't let my daughter walk across the street to see Elvis Presley perform."
—Reverend Billy Graham

Web Sites

http://elvis-is-still-the
 king.simplenet.com/Personals_Page/
 Personals.html
 For love matches and pen pals
http://members.aol.com/ElvisPLovr/
 prissy.html
 Priscilla Presley shrine

http://www.carasso.com:80/roger/
 vegawed.html
 Getting married Elvis style web site
http://greggers.granitecity.com/elvis/
 women/
 Elvis' Women, in the movies, that is
http://www.geocities.com/~arpt/az/
 Elvis Presley Encyclopaedia

THE ELVIS AND YOU EXPERIENCE

Give Elvis' Favorite Flowers to Your Lover

Elvis loved roses. There's even a rose named after him. A Small hybrid red rose named "Elvis" was developed by W. Whit Wells in 1981 and was registered by the American Rose Society. It's light red with touches of white at the base of the petals.
The American Rose Society
P. O. Box 30,000
Shreveport, Louisiana 71130
(318) 938-5402
Fax: (318) 938-5405
E-mail: ars@ars-hq.org
http://www.ars.org/

Choose Your Own Special Elvis Love Song

Elvis' music is the perfect soundtrack for a love affair no matter what shape it's in. There are dozens and dozens of Elvis love ballads to choose from.

Elvis at Your Wedding

The best way to include Elvis in your wedding ceremony is to play him singing your favorite, most romantic song while you walk down the aisle or have your first dance. "Can't Help Falling in Love" and "Hawaiian Wedding Song" are a few of the traditional favorite Elvis wedding songs among fans. Some people choose to have an Elvis impersonator perform, officiate, or actually give the bride away. Why not choose songs that are a little more unconventional for your ceremony and wedding reception party? Here follows a list of songs that will touch people and give them a smile or two.

"Always on My Mind"
"I Got a Feelin' in My Body"
"I Got a Woman"
"I Got Lucky"
"I Love Only One Girl"
"I'm Yours"
"I Want You, I Need You, I Love You"
"Kiss Me Quick"
"Let It Be Me"
"Love Coming Down"
"Love Me Tender"
"Love Me Tonight"
"Make Me Know It"
"My Happiness"

"One Night of Sin"
"Playing for Keeps"
"Pledging My Love"
"Power of My Love"
"She Wears My Ring"
"So Glad You're Mine"
"Steamroller Blues"
"The First Time Ever I Saw Your Face"
"The Next Step Is Love"
"Today, Tomorrow and Forever"
"Tonight Is So Right for Love"
"True Love Travels on a Gravel Road"
"Unchained Melody"

Getting Married at Graceland

It's possible to have not only your wedding ceremony but reception as well right across from the Graceland mansion! Graceland hosts weddings in most of their shops and museums. They offer full catering and event-planning services. (Packages may include private evening tours of the mansion and other Graceland sites.)
Graceland Special Events Department
(800) 238-2010
(901) 344-3146

Getting Married at the Elvis Presley Chapel in Tupelo

Hundreds of couples have been married at the Elvis Presley Chapel in Tupelo.
Elvis Presley Chapel
306 Elvis Presley Drive
Tupelo, Mississippi 38801
(601) 841-1245

Other Elvis-Themed Places Where You Can Get Married

Viva Memphis Wedding Chapel
Tommy Foster performs an exciting wedding ceremony at this chapel in Memphis in case the mood strikes you while

Pamela Wood

Fans often marry and honeymoon in Memphis

you're there on your pilgrimage. He's an Elvis artist and Memphian with many wonderful stories. The Viva Memphis Wedding Chapel is a fun place to visit even if you don't have marriage plans.
Reverend Tommy Foster
2174 Young Avenue
Memphis, Tennessee 38104
(901) 272-7210

Viva Las Vegas Wedding Chapel
Elvis stylist Ron deCar officiates at many different themed weddings. Top of the line is the "Blue Hawaii" package complete with hula bridesmaids. You can be picked up at your hotel in a pink '64 Cadillac and driven to the chapel.
1205 Las Vegas Boulevard South
Las Vegas, Nevada 89104
(800) 574-4450
(702) 384-0771
E-mail: wedsing@ix.netcom.com
http://www.vivalasvegasweddings.com

Las Vegas Weddings
Elvis fans will love this shrine decorated in honor of the King with Elvis stained glass windows, guitar candelabra, the King's framed gold records, and to top it off, an Elvis impersonator, will perform the ceremony and sing Elvis' most memorable tunes.
2770 S. Maryland Parkway, Suite 416
Las Vegas, Nevada 89109
(888) 30-MARRY
(702) 737-6800
Fax (702) 737-8989
E-mail: info@lasvegasweddings.com
http://www.lasvegasweddings.com/guide.htm

"Do you promise to adopt each other's hound dog, and never to step on each other's blue suede shoes, and to always be each other's teddy bear?"
—Wedding vows offered by Ron DeCar, Elvis impersonator, performing the ceremony at the Viva Las Vegas Wedding Chapel in Las Vegas

"It was no picnic being his wife ... nor being a girlfriend—not to him or any of the people who worked for him. But I think Priscilla and any woman entering into a relationship with him knew that from the get-go. Just my opinion."
—Fan, on the Internet

Graceland Wedding Chapel, Las Vegas

Photo reprinted with permission

An Elvis Wedding
1605 Franklin Avenue
Las Vegas, Nevada 89104
(702) 384-0771
(800) 574-4450
E-mail: wedsing@ix.netcom

Graceland Wedding Chapel
619 Las Vegas Boulevard South
Las Vegas, Nevada 89101
(702) 474-6655

The Little White Chapel
1301 Las Vegas Boulevard South
Las Vegas, Nevada 89019
(800) 322-LOVE
http://www.iwedu@
    alitlewhitechapel.com

Getting Married in Hawaii

Have a Genuine Blue Hawaii Wedding
Couples can get married in the same place where Elvis' *Blue Hawaii* movie wedding took place. Elvis also stayed at this hotel (in cottage 56) while filming and vacationing on other occasions.
Coco Palms Resort
4241 Kuhio Highway
Kapaa, Hawaii 96746
(808) 822-4921

Take an Elvis Honeymoon

Whether you're newlyweds or just want to feel like it.
The Bahamas
    Elvis and his new wife spent part of their honeymoon in Nassau at the Paradise Island Hotel.

The bed where Elvis and Priscilla spent part of their honeymoon

John O'Hara

Honeymoon Hideaway house, Palm Springs

John O'Hara

Elvis and Priscilla in Hawaii

Sandi Miller

The Trailer Option

Elvis and Priscilla spent part of their honeymoon in a trailer at the Walls, Mississippi, property, the Circle G Ranch. Lamar Fike shared the trailer with them.

The Honeymoon Hideaway

Elvis and Pris also spent part of the honeymoon in this rented house at 1350 Ladera Circle in Palm Springs. It's now referred to by fans as "The Honeymoon Hideaway." This home is available for events.

Hawaiian Love Idyll

Hawaii as a Honeymoon destination is a no-brainer. Elvis always loved to visit these special islands and it's easy to see why.

Visiting Graceland for Your Honeymoon

Many Elvis fans make a trip to Graceland as part of their honeymoon. For Elvis fans in love, Memphis can be a very romantic place.

Have an Elvis Fantasy Night

Have your man dress or talk like Elvis for the night, or surprise your woman with her Elvis fantasy. Or relive a steamy night from the '50s when Elvis was first having his effect by dressing up for a romantic evening in lingerie from that time.

Elvis' Favorite Lingerie

None of that traditional froufrou lace and silk for Elvis; he was known to appreciate simple white cotton panties.

Write a "Love Letter" to Elvis

While you can't send your message *directly to* Elvis, you do have a few different ways to express yourself. Go to Memphis and put your sentiments on the Wall of Love surrounding Graceland. Write poems dedicated to him for your fan club newsletter.

Write a Letter to Priscilla

There aren't many men who don't appreciate Priscilla's exquisite beauty. She receives mail at Graceland, if you want to tell her so. The Communications Department will acknowledge your letter and it will be kept for her until she next visits Graceland.

Bring Elvis into Your Bedroom

Recreate Elvis' bedroom décor. He slept on a nine-foot-square bed with a black quilted headboard. He had two televisions mounted in the ceiling over it. Even if you don't want to go to that extreme, you can get Elvis sheets, pillows, or pajamas. Some pillows and afghans are available for sale at Graceland, but you can make your own bed linens with Elvis material. Your

Bob Klein

> "I am 18 and in Iowa so I never got to see Elvis. I would like to believe I could have made Elvis happy and content, and not been like Priscilla. But isn't that every female Elvis fan's dream? I know I would have proudly stood by such a man, famous or not. But maybe I don't really know what it would be like, I can only imagine it in my dreams."
>
> —Lynn

local photo shop can give you information on having Elvis images silk-screened onto your pillows. For a special cold-night treat have a hot water bottle covered with Elvis material.

Keep Elvis Close to Your Heart

You probably don't need any instructions on how to do this. But if you want to do this quite literally, you can put a tiny photo of Elvis in a locket around your neck.

See the House Elvis Bought for Linda Thompson

1254 Old Hickory Road
Memphis, Tennessee 38116

See the House Elvis Bought for Ginger Alden

4152 Royal Crest Place
Memphis, Tennessee 38116

Fall in Love with Someone Who Shares Your Love for Elvis

The internet is a great place to meet other fans—and you never know what could form between two people who share Elvis. These sites have sections where you can write up an Elvis "personal" and see the ones left by others:

http://elvis-is-still-the-king.
    simplenet.com/Personals_Page/
    Personals.html
http://members.aol.com/Kingbee25/
    personals.html

Everywhere fans meet, friendships are formed. It may be possible to make a love connection, too. So go to conventions and other fan events. If there are none near, organize your own Elvis dance party.

There's also a phone dateline for Elvis fans where you just might meet someone who has the same passion for Elvis that you do. You can listen to the recordings made by people who've called in to find a mate and leave a message if one intrigues you, or you can even make your own recording. This service costs $2.95 per minute.

(900) 884-1400, extension 814

Priscilla's Boutique from the Seventies

Bis and Beau
9650 Santa Monica Boulevard
Beverly Hills, California

Suggested Songs of Heartbreak

Elvis' music accompanies us through all our moods, including when we really just want to wallow. These are all sad songs, but Elvis' voice will make you feel better anyway.

"The Last Farewell"

"Wearin' that Loved-on Look"

"You Gave Me a Mountain"

"Your Cheatin' Heart"

"You've Lost that Lovin' Feelin'"

"After Loving You"

"Big Love, Big Heartache"

"Blue Eyes Crying in the Rain"

"Heartbreak Hotel"

"Hurt"

"I Can't Help It (If I'm Still in Love with You)"

"I Forgot to Remember to Forget"

"I'll Never Fall in Love Again"

"I'm Gonna Sit Right Down and Cry (Over You)"

"I'm Left, You're Right, She's Gone"

"I'm So Lonesome I Could Cry"

"It Keeps Right on a-Hurtin'"

"It's Over"

"I've Lost You"

"My Baby Left Me"

"My Baby's Gone"

"Old Shep"

"Only the Strong Survive"

"Return to Sender"

"Separate Ways"

"She's Not You"

"Take Good Care of Her"

"Tender Feeling"

"That's When Your Heartaches Begin"

"When Elvis brought me around him (as charismatic, wonderful and charming as Elvis was), I really didn't like all the guys and the people who swarmed around him. Don't get me wrong, I was flattered. I liked the private Elvis ... when he was just being himself. Unfortunately, his stardom and lifestyle didn't allow him to always be that guy for very long. How different he acted when you were alone with him."
—Beverly, on the internet

"I have been an Elvis love and fan since 1956 when 'Love Me Tender' was sung by him and I have loved Elvis tender ever since and still do. If I had ever met him when he was alive he would still be married to me. Elvis never found a woman who would dedicate herself to him but I would have done that. We are perfect for each other."
—Elizabeth "Betty" Zogob

Pamela Wood

An Elvis couple at Graceland

"Using endearing terms like 'little us' was his way of being affectionate. His mother had raised him on this sweet talk and Elvis spoke it with those he cherished.... In moments of intimacy he would switch to third-person address: Him yuvs you and her yuvs him."
—Priscilla Beaulieu Presley, from *Elvis and Me*

Laura Levin

Another couple brought together through Elvis

"Elvis' date said, 'Elvis is only reading the Bible to them.' We snuck up to the door and watched, and that's what he was doing. So many times I saw that happen."
—Journalist Frank Lieberman's anecdote about Elvis being in a bedroom with several girls, from *Elvis: The Final Years*

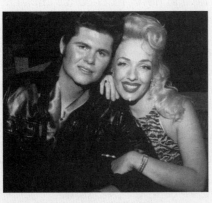

Photo reprinted with permission

Elvis impersonator Robert Manis and his wife, Marilyn Monroe

ELVIS AND FRIENDSHIP

The day after Elvis died, the headline of the *Memphis Press-Scimitar* read, "A Lonely Life Ends on Elvis Presley Boulevard." This may have been essentially true, in spite of the fact that Elvis was known to surround himself constantly with a posse of friends. It was a statement about the isolation that Elvis endured while being the center of attention for nearly every moment of his adult life. As the most famous man in the world, he must frequently have questioned the motives of those who wanted to be his friends; as a result, he surrounded himself with people he was most comfortable with. He preferred the unpretentious sort he had grown up with and didn't involve himself with overtures of friendship and requests for meetings by the show biz elite.

Elvis was a fun-loving, good-natured, and affable man who, even if he had never reached his amazing level of stardom and wealth, would certainly have attracted a large circle of friends. By virtually all accounts he was a kind and sensitive person who was proud of the fact that he was raised to be considerate of other peoples' feelings. His many close and loyal friendships were an important part of his life and reveal a lot about Elvis as a person.

From the collection of Bob Klein

Elvis with one of his few Hollywood pals, Sammy Davis, Jr.

Red West, Elvis, Jerry Schilling,
Lamar Fike, Joe Esposito

From the collection of Bob Klein

His classmates at L. C. Humes High School in Memphis are said to have thought of him as a loner, a strangely dressed, long-haired misfit outside any of the school's social cliques. In reality, Elvis was just a shy country boy alone in a new city whose unusual style was not only a way of expressing himself but a way of getting attention. Sometimes that attention proved to be a problem. When cornered in the boys' restroom by some bullies who were intent on cutting Elvis' hair, a burly football player by the name of Bobby "Red" West came to his defense. Red and Elvis became lifelong friends and Red continued to act as his bodyguard until 1976.

When Elvis barnstormed through the country in the early part of his career, he was often accompanied, for protection and companionship, by Red or one of his own cousins, Gene or Junior Smith. Because Elvis' fans were so physically demonstrative, he needed to be isolated from the public after the performances and confined himself to one anonymous hotel room after another. He hated being alone, so out of necessity Elvis constantly surrounded himself with friends, family, and flunkies.

Elvis' entourage of playmates and protectors eventually came to be known as the Memphis Mafia. In the early sixties, Elvis provided identical black mohair suits and dark sunglasses to all the guys. Emerging from long black limousines with an assumed air of power and position, they resembled nothing so much as gangsters. And with most of them packing pistols under those mohair suits, they seemed to fit the bill. Another nickname for the group was "El's Angels." They received this moniker because they roared through the streets of Memphis and L.A. on an Elvis-purchased

Sandi Miller

Elvis and Joe Esposito

Jerry Schilling on his Triumph 650

fleet of motorcycles. The Memphis Mafia was made up of Elvis' relatives, school chums, army buddies, athletes, fellow karate enthusiasts, and people who just struck his fancy at the spur of the moment. Its membership varied from year to year with some members on the scene for only a few months and others for as many as 17 years. Some would leave the group for a while and return years later. They were a shield of familiarity that helped insulate Elvis from the outside world.

Some of the Memphis Mafia were salaried employees who were assigned a specific duty in the kingdom. They functioned as valets, chauffeurs, bodyguards, stuntmen, roadies, sparring partners, bookkeepers, personal assistants, gofers, and of course "talent" scouts looking for young women. They weren't paid much, but they had fringe benefits that would make any young man happy. The guys received gifts of cars, jewelry, and houses; cash bonuses; all-expense-paid vacations; access to women *way* out of their league; and a ringside seat at one of the more interesting lives of this century. They were on constant, 24-hour call and had to be ready for any adventure that Elvis decided to embark on with little or no notice. Several of them even lived with him at Graceland much to the dismay of Elvis' privacy-starved wife, Priscilla. It was a fraternity based on fun, devoted to satisfying the whims and wishes of one man.

Elvis' wealth allowed him to indulge any desire and his constant companions got

Elvis and entourage December 28, 1970, displaying their police badges or, in cop talk, "flashing their tin"

to share in those indulgences. For the most part, life with Elvis consisted of ceaseless parties, practical jokes, fireworks battles, football games, watermelon-seed-spitting contests, cross-country road trips, amusement parks, all-night movies, gunplay, fisticuffs and the general pursuit of good times. But life in the Memphis Mafia had its dark side. Elvis had a temper he would sometimes vent on those around him. Many of his crew were fired after some blowup only to be hired back later—the offended party often receiving an apology from Elvis in the form of an expensive gift.

There were also confrontations within the group itself. Jealousies arose as the courtiers competed for the favor of their King. Some members of the group were, more or less, Colonel Parker's spies, reporting to Elvis' morally challenged manager any of Elvis' excesses that might jeopardize the gravy train. The Colonel did much to foment divisions within the group. When Elvis got married, the Colonel handled the wedding preparations and excluded some of the group, causing a rift that left several of Elvis' closest friends deeply and permanently offended.

The Memphis Mafia was essentially a boys' club whose membership wasn't interested in having female members. One exception was Patty Perry, a Los Angeles hairstylist who met Elvis on Sunset Boulevard. She partied and traveled to Vegas and Memphis with Elvis and the guys and was looked on as the little sister of the group. Elvis often befriended his female fans in a similarly innocent fashion. He seemed to be able to drop his tough guy façade and reveal his vulnerable side to women in a way he couldn't and didn't with his macho chums.

Sandi Miller

Elvis and Sonny West on the set of *It Happened at the World's Fair*

From the collection of Bob Klein

Red West, Elvis, and Joe Esposito

Elvis and Charlie Hodge

A lot of controversy and animosity surrounds the Memphis Mafia in the Elvis fan world. In his 1982 book, *Elvis*, Dave Marsh called the Memphis Mafia "toadies and stooges … buffoons, yes-men, gold-diggers and dull thugs … the most small-time sidekicks that any great man has known." A bit harsh, but also representative of the reaction that fans have to certain members of the group.

Some of the people who were close to Elvis wrote or contributed to books that capitalized on their association with Elvis at the cost of his reputation. The two most offensive tell-all books were *Elvis, What Happened?* by writer Steve Dunleavy with Red West, Sonny West, and Dave Hebler and Albert Goldman's notoriously hateful *Elvis,* fabricated with Lamar Fike's cooperation.

In 1976, charter member of the Memphis Mafia Red West, his cousin Sonny West, and karate black belt Dave Hebler were unceremoniously fired by Vernon Presley. The reason given was their overzealousness in protecting Elvis by treating some of his fans as their personal piñatas. Their rowdiness was costing too much in lawsuits. After 17 years of service, Red was sent packing with two weeks severance pay. Elvis didn't even say goodbye. The wounded trio retaliated by penning a no-holds-barred, no-feelings-spared account of their time with Elvis. Although they claim they were motivated by the desire to shock Elvis out of his self-destructive behavior by exposing it to the world, many fans believe the book contributed to Elvis' premature death and are unwilling to give them the benefit of the doubt. Elvis died two weeks after *Elvis, What Happened?* was published. He was tormented in his last days by the betrayal of his former friends. There are even a very small number of people who believe Elvis committed suicide on the night before he was scheduled to begin a tour rather than face his fans.

Another Memphis Mafia member considered persona non grata by many Elvis fans is Lamar Fike. Lamar, who had been with Elvis from 1956 until the very end, provided the raw material for author Albert Goldman's 1980 book. This vile piece of character assassination revealed more about the author's personal hang-ups than it did about Elvis. Yet the book became a huge bestseller and is probably the single thing that is most responsible for contributing to the negative image of Elvis and the disproportionate focus on his personal problems by some in the media. Although Lamar can't be faulted for the tone of Goldman's slimy rantings against Elvis, many fans regard his connection to the project reason enough to question his loyalty to his "friend."

Today the Memphis Mafia and others of the inner circle serve as a valuable resource for Elvis fans. They were witnesses to history and are a living link to Elvis. The story of Elvis' life is best told by those who lived it with him and although some of the versions of that story don't agree, the spirit of Elvis can be found somewhere among all the tales. Many of them have written or participated in books or videos about their years with Elvis. Some of them attend fan conventions, operate web sites, and hang out in internet news groups to make themselves accessible to fans. George Klein, a friend from Elvis' high school days, hosts a Memphis Mafia

Elvis, Sam Thompson, and Joe Esposito

Keith Alverson

Richard Davis being interviewed in May of 1999 about his days with Elvis

John O'Hara

Elvis, Linda Thompson, Sonny West, and Red West

From the collection of Bob Klein

Sandi Miller

"I was lucky enough to be around at a time and place when it was easy for fans to have access to this man, this man who had a gentle soul and warm heart that beat inside a beautiful body. He was such a complex person that I don't think even he knew himself at times. This man was Elvis Presley.

"Maybe he considered me a friend, maybe he didn't. I don't want to make it sound like it was more than it was but neither will I downplay it. Elvis was a very special individual and an even more special entertainer. I'm not speaking from a talent and music aspect (I don't need to), I mean that he didn't *think* he was special! Don't get me wrong, he'd strut his stuff, pat himself on the back, and occasionally brag but it always came back to 'Why me?' or 'I don't understand what the big deal is.'

"Elvis, of course, was close to most of the guys (the Mafia), some more than others and different ones at different times. But to assume, as some do, that he was not close to any other people is wrong. In some cases I believe he was more candid with those who were *not* in the inner circle. A lot of times it was the fans who he got to know over the years, and there were quite a few of them that Elvis enjoyed talking to. And boy could he talk!! … and talk … and talk … sometimes in excruciating detail, which was really annoying if you happened to be dead tired and just wanted to go to bed and he was only on the second volume of the Encyclopedia Britannica! (Okay—I'm exaggerating.) Elvis *did* discuss many things with many people obviously. Things that might even surprise the boys. The entire 'star' thing escaped him and he couldn't really comprehend what fans saw in him or why. Of course that is *exactly* why the fans loved him so much.

"Life did not stop for Elvis when the Memphis Mafia retreated to their rooms. They usually stayed up until he retired but not always! There were times when he'd be the only one up or times when it would be down to only one of the guys and Elvis would dismiss him. He'd say, 'Leave us alone, I think I'll be okay.' Guess he felt safe enough to know he wasn't going to be attacked!! This was the lead-in to some of our many conversations over the years about his 'situation.' One-on-one conversations that in some cases lasted for hours. He talked about a lot of things including the entourage, the fans, his life, his marriage, his career. He wasn't telling me what he thought I wanted to hear either. Some people don't give him half the credit he deserves. Elvis could be *brutally* frank and he was at times. He also had a very clear picture of what was going on around him even if he didn't always act on the situation in his best interest.

"I think, because he didn't like confrontations and he often had his father or Joe handle the unpleasant stuff for him in his personal and business life, that he's gotten the reputation at times for not being able to speak his mind. Wrong!"

—Sandi Miller, friend of Elvis

reunion in Memphis during Tribute Week where several members of the group gather and relive the glory days.

For a good part of his career, Elvis became so familiar with the fans who gathered outside his various homes and followed his concert schedule, that the fan–star business was sometimes dropped and genuine friendships formed. This unique relationship with his fans was so close that he often treated them as his friends and welcomed their friendship in return. Enjoying a break from the smothering Memphis clan, he shared meals and confidences with these fans—and got to reveal a very different Elvis than when he was around the guys.

Elvis often said the most important quality he required of a friend was loyalty. How appropriate it is that one of the things that distinguishes the Elvis Fan from any other fans is their powerful and undying loyalty. Some Elvis fans think of themselves as "Elvis friends" because they know their loyalty will never waver and they feel a sense of friendship with Elvis.

ESSENTIAL ELVISOLOGY

The TCB Necklace
Designed by Lee Abeleser of Schwartz-Abeleser Jewelers in Beverly Hills. It was given by Elvis to his close friends. To women, he gave TLC necklaces, indicating tender loving care. (Children got mini-versions).

Courtesy of Butterfield & Butterfield

Elvis' Friends' Nicknames for Him
"Big E"
"Crazy"

Memphis Mafia Christmas Gift 1965
In 1965, some of the Memphis Mafia chipped in and commissioned John McIntire, an instructor at the Memphis Academy of Arts, to create a statue of Jesus as a Christmas gift to Elvis. It stands today in the Meditation Garden of Graceland looking down on Elvis' grave.

John O'Hara

The Tree of Life Pendant
As a birthday gift from his inner circle in 1965, Elvis was given a gold pendant inscribed with

the names of some of his friends. The design was a family tree with "Elvis Presley" engraved on the trunk. On the branches were the names of the people who gave it to him: Billy Smith, Harry Levitch, Alan Fortas, Joe Esposito, Richard Davis, Mike Keeton, Red West, Larry Geller, Jerry Schilling, and Marty Lacker. Above the tree was inscribed, "Like a tree planted by the water that bringeth forth fruit in his season." On the other side was inscribed, "And ye shall know the truth and the truth shall set you free," in English, Hebrew, and Latin.

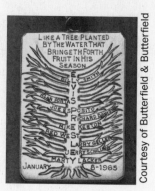

Memphis Mafia Salaries
$250 per week in '60s
$425 per week in '70s
Plus tons of benefits

Other Names for the Memphis Mafia
"El's Angels"
"Presley Punks"
"The CBs" (Cherry Busters)

The Memphis Mafia
The Memphis Mafia was a fluid group whose roster changed over the years and its membership is, therefore, open to some debate. Some members were short-timers, others were lifers. Some left and came back numerous times. The line between friend and employee was blurred. Some of the group had specific jobs while others were just traveling companions. The name Memphis Mafia is trademarked by Marty Lacker, Lamar Fike, Billy Smith, Red West, and Sonny West. For the purposes of this list we deviated from the strict definition of the Memphis Mafia and included people who were close to Elvis or shared a part of his life with him as a friend.

Billy Smith
   Nicknamed "Mighty Mouth." Elvis' first cousin and perhaps his closest friend. Billy and his wife lived in a trailer behind Graceland.

Elvis and the boys on the set of *Stay Away Joe*

Gene Smith
    Nicknamed "El Gino Stone." Elvis' eccentric cousin accompanied him to Hollywood in the early days.
Carroll "Junior" Smith
    Elvis' cousin accompanied him to New York when Elvis did the *Steve Allen Show*. He died in 1960 after an all night bout of drinking.
Bobby "Red" West
    Nicknamed "the Dragon." Red was a charter member of the Memphis Mafia. Elvis met Red at Humes High where Red became his protector. He worked as bodyguard for Elvis until 1976. He was the coauthor of *Elvis, What Happened?*

He appeared in many of Elvis' movies and even wrote some of his songs. Red became an actor after leaving the MM. He recently had a bit part as a boat captain in the film *I Still Know What You Did Last Summer*. Other film credits include *Roadhouse* and *Natural Born Killers*.
Delbert "Sonny" West
    Nicknamed "The Eagle." Cousin of Red West. Responsible for vehicle maintenance and security. Fired by Vernon in 1976. He was one of the coauthors of *Elvis, What Happened?* He is currently a used car salesman.
George Klein
    Nicknamed "GK." George met Elvis at Humes High where he was senior class president. He became a disc jockey at WHBQ in Memphis. Elvis was George's best man at his wedding. GK introduced Elvis to Ginger Alden.
Alan Fortas
    Nicknamed "Hog Ears." He was a football star for an opposing high school in Memphis. George Klein introduced him to Elvis in 1958. He started as a bodyguard during filming of *King Creole* and was was ranch manager of the Circle G ranch. In Elvis' "'68 ComebackSpecial," Alan is seen playing the tambourine in the "unplugged" part of the show.
Cliff Gleaves
    Cliff was a rockabilly singer and former DJ who served as Elvis' gofer while Elvis filmed *Love Me Tender* in 1956. He was a good-natured free spirit who joined Elvis in Germany replacing Red West.
Mike Keaton
    Fellow member of the first Assembly of God Church. Married to a woman named Gladys. Started in 1964.

Louis Harris

Short-time member from 1957 to 1958. He accompanied Elvis to the second Tupelo homecoming concert.

Lance LeGault

Fellow rock and roll singer from Louisiana who met Elvis at the Crossbow nightclub in Los Angeles. He was Elvis' movie double and participated in the "'68 Comeback Special."

Marty Lacker

Nicknamed "Moon." Marty met Elvis at Humes High. He and his wife Patsy lived at Graceland from 1960 to 1967. He functioned as bookkeeper and occasional clothing designer. He designed Elvis' wedding tux and was co-best man at Elvis' wedding. Today he describes himself as a publisher and a bum.

Lamar Fike

Nicknamed "Mr. Bull," "Buddha," and "The Great Speckled Bird." In 1956 Lamar used to hang out in front of the house at Audubon Drive. Eventually he was invited in and befriended by Elvis. He even tried to enlist in the army when Elvis was drafted but was turned down because he was 4F. He lived with Elvis and his family in Germany. He performed many functions for Elvis, including lighting technician, driver, and bodyguard. He collaborated with Albert Goldman on *Elvis* and because of that is still persona non grata to many Elvis fans.

Nick Adams

One of Elvis first Hollywood friends. He met Elvis while Elvis was shooting *Love Me Tender*. He died of a drug overdose in 1968.

Bitsey Mott

Colonel Parker's brother-in-law. He traveled with Elvis from 1955 to 1956.

Charlie Hodge

Nicknamed "Slewfoot," and "Waterhead." Elvis met Charlie in 1956 while touring through the south. Years later their paths crossed again while both men served together in the Army. He lived at Graceland for 17 years. A fellow musician, Charlie was Elvis' right-hand man on stage, supplying Elvis with his scarves and water. He played himself in the 1979 *Elvis* the TV movie.

Joe Esposito

"Diamond Joe," also nicknamed "The Brain," met Elvis in Germany while both were serving in the army. He functioned as Elvis' tour manager, accountant, and all-

Charlie Hodge and Elvis in Hawaii

around right-hand man. He was co-best man at Elvis' wedding.

James Caughley
Nicknamed "Hamburger James" and "The Brow." He worked as valet and general lackey for Elvis. He was another source of information for Goldman's book.

Arthur Hooten
Nicknamed "Arturo Van Hooton" and "Arthritis." A short-term member of the group from the mid-fifties. His mother had worked with Gladys at Britlings Cafeteria.

Raymond Sitton
Nicknamed "Chief." A six foot three inch 300-pound gate-person who was invited by Elvis into the group for a short time.

Jimmy Kingsley
He met Elvis in Memphis. He and Richard Davis were hired as personal aides by Elvis in the bathroom of Elvis' Bel Air home and he started working on *It Happened at the World's Fair*. He committed suicide in 1989.

Marvin "Gee Gee" Gambill, Jr.
Married to Elvis' cousin Patsy Presley. Worked as chauffeur and valet beginning in 1967.

Larry Geller
Nicknamed "Guru" by Elvis and "Swami" and "Rasputin" by other Memphis Mafia members. He was working as a hairstylist at Jay Sebring's Salon in California when he was summoned to be the personal hairstylist to Elvis in April of 1964. Essentially banished by the Colonel in 1967, he rejoined the MM in the mid-seventies. Larry was a sort of spiritual adviser to Elvis and helped assemble his collection of spiritual books. He has written several excellent books about Elvis' spiritual search. He played himself in the 1979 *Elvis* television movie.

Billy Stanley
Nicknamed "Charles Manson." Elvis' stepbrother. Son of Vernon's second wife, Dee Stanley.

Rick Stanley
Elvis' stepbrother. Son of Vernon's second wife, Dee Stanley. Arrested in 1975 for forged prescriptions. He later became a minister

David Stanley
Elvis' stepbrother. Son of Vernon's second wife, Dee Stanley. He worked security at Graceland. He later became an evangelist.

"When I saw Elvis in concert in 1976, I don't think I ever heard him sing any better. He gave me chill bumps many times during that evening. And of course, that was the last time I saw Elvis, the best friend I really never knew."

—Steve Braun

Richard Davis
Nicknamed "Broom" or "Beer Brain." Elvis met the fun-loving and good-natured fellow Southerner while Richard was working at the Memphian Theater. He served as Elvis' personal valet from 1962 to 1969.

Jerry Schilling
Nicknamed "Milk." Elvis first met Jerry in Memphis in 1954 while playing touch football. He played college football for Arkansas State University (he was the only one in the inner entourage who went to college). He joined the group in 1964. Jerry was with Elvis when he met Nixon. After Elvis' death, he served as creative affairs director for the Presley estate.

> "I am thankful for all the wonderful friends, from all over the world, that I have made by being an Elvis Fan. Through our love for him, he brought many of us together."
> —Bobbie Cunningham, Elvis Friends Hollywood Fan Club

David Hebler
Fifth-degree black belt and former student of Ed Parker. He served as bodyguard from 1972 until 1975. He was one of the coauthors of *Elvis, What Happened?*

Al Strada
Worked for Elvis from 1972 until Elvis' death. It was Al who was summoned by Ginger Alden when she discovered Elvis' lifeless body on August 16, 1977.

Patty Perry
The "little sister" of the Memphis Mafia, Patty was a hairdresser who met Elvis in L.A. She is considered to be the only female member of the Memphis Mafia.

Dean Nichopoulos
Dr. Nick's son. Dean started to work for Elvis in 1974. He was a personal aide and worked security.

Dick Grob
Nicknamed "Grob the Fox." A former fighter pilot and Palms Spring police sergeant. He was head of security at Graceland for seven years starting in 1969.

Sam Thompson
Brother of Linda Thompson, Elvis' mid-seventies girlfriend. Sam worked security for Elvis. He later became a judge.

The Elvis Presley Enterprises Football Team

Elvis organized his own football team in Hollywood during the 1960s. They

> "If you really want to please me, search for God and the truth."
> —Elvis, to his friends in the Memphis Mafia

played at De Neve Park in Bel Air, Los Angeles. Not to be confused with Elvis' favorite team, which was the Cleveland Browns.

Ricky Nelson	Robert Conrad	Dean Torrence
Max Baer, Jr.	Pat Boone	Ty Hardin
Gary Lockwood	Gary Crosby	Lee Majors

YOUR ELVIS EDUCATION

Books

Elvis: Intimate and Rare
  Joe Esposito

Elvis Aaron Presley: Revelations from the Memphis Mafia
  Alanna Nash with Billy Smith, Marty Lacker, and Lamar Fike

Good Rockin' Tonight: Twenty years on the Road and on the Town with Elvis
  Joe Esposito and Elena Oumano

Elvis: Portrait of a Friend
  Marty and Patsy Lacker and Leslie Smith

Elvis, from Memphis to Hollywood: Memories from My Twelve Years With Elvis Presley
  Alan Fortas and Alanna Nash

Me 'n' Elvis
  Charlie Hodge with Charles Goodman

Elvis on Tour: The Last Year
  Sam Thompson

My Life with Elvis
  Beckey Yancy and Cliff Linedecker

Elvis' Man Friday
  Gene Smith

Elvis Up Close: In the Words of Those Who Knew Him Best
  edited by Rose Clayton and Dick Heard

Elvis, What Happened?
  Red West, Sonny West, Dave Hebler as told to Steve Dunleavy

Elvis' Search for God
  Larry Geller

The Truth about Elvis
  Larry Geller and Jessie Stearn

If I Can Dream: Elvis' Own Story
  Larry Geller
  To order any of Larry's books call (800) 905-8367 or (615) 896-1356) or e-mail: orders@ greenleafpublications.com.

The Elvis Conspiracy?
  Dick Grob

Print run of *Elvis, What Happened?*

Initial press run: 400,000 copies
Six hours after E's death: an additional 250,000 copies
By the end of that week: an additional 2,000,000 copies

Video

All the King's Men
Red West, Sonny West, Marty Lacker, Billy Smith, Lamar Fike
Widely available for purchase, and you can visit their web site at:
http://www.memphismafia.com/king/

My Home Movies of Elvis
Joe Esposito's home movies from his years with Elvis. Because of certain legal restrictions, this video can't be sold in the United States so you'll have to have a friend or fellow Elvis fan outside of the country get it for you. It's available from Elvisly Yours, P.O. Box 315, London NW 10 England. http://www.elvisly-yours.com/

The Elvis I Knew by Charlie Hodge

Elvis: A Portrait by His Friends

Web Sites

http://www.memphismafia.com
Memphis Mafia's home page
http://memphismafia.com
Official Memphis Mafia web site
http://www.geocities.com/Hollywood/
Bungalow/4660/index.html
Elvis and Joe Esposito home page

http://www.elvistyle.com/richard.htm
Richard Davis's site
http://www.geocities.com/~arpt/az/
Elvis Presley Encyclopedia

THE ELVIS AND YOU EXPERIENCE

Memphis Mafia Contact Information

Many of Elvis' friends are still in contact with Graceland and a letter will be forwarded to them if you send it there.

Richard Davis
Elvistyle
P.O. Box 757
Southhaven, Mississippi 38671
E-mail: Richard@Elvistyle.com
Marty Lacker
E-mail: moonooo@aol.com
Charlie Hodge
Memories Theater
2141 Parkway

Pigeon Forge, Tennessee 37863
(800) 325-3078
(423) 428-7852
http://memoriestheatre.com/
Charlie.jpg
Joe Esposito
E-mail: Joe@JoeEsposito.com
Larry Geller
E-mail: Gell@earthlink.com

Meet the Memphis Mafia

Many of Elvis' friends make guest appearances at fan conventions and fan club gatherings all over the world where they regale Elvis fans with their stories of the King.

George Klein's Annual Memphis Mafia Reunion

Elvis' long-time friends and associates gather to reminisce and answer questions. Held every year during Tribute Week. For location and information, ask Graceland for a Tribute Week schedule.

> "There have been so many *facts* written about Elvis and all too often they are not true. It must be terribly difficult for anyone truly interested in his life to sort the whole thing out."
>
> —Marty Lacker, from *Portrait of a Friend*

Hear the Memphis Mafia's Side of the Story

The boys have a series of videos out with scenes of them in the present reminiscing interspersed with great footage of Elvis.

All the King's Men Videos Titles
The Secret Life of Elvis
Rocket Ride to Stardom
Wild in Hollywood
The King Comes Back
Collapse of the Kingdom
The Legend Lives On
http://memphismafia.com

> "I can find eight people to jump up and get me a coke, but I have very few friends."
>
> —Elvis Presley

Give TCB Jewelry to Your Inner Circle

And of course TLC jewelry to your lady friends. You can order it from the Graceland catalog. More expensive, better quality jewelry can still be bought at these two Memphis Jewelry stores where Elvis did business.

Lowell G. Hayes and Sons
4872 Poplar Avenue
Memphis, Tennessee 38117
(901) 767-2840

Harry Levitch Jewelers
5100 Poplar Avenue
Memphis, Tennessee 38137
(901) 761-1188

> "We were ... offered every conceivable enticement to either take a gift to Elvis, meet him, be allowed onstage to get a kiss, get a scarf, etc."
>
> —Ed Parker, on being Elvis' bodyguard, from *Inside Elvis*

Be a Memphis Mafia Impersonator

Find an Elvis impersonator and offer to be part of his entourage. Keep your "Elvis guy" safe from any overzealous fans. Wear a replica of the red jacket worn by security and the inner circle while on tour. Or wear matching outfits of black mohair suits and sunglasses. Use Memphis Mafia nicknames: "Slewfoot," "Buddha," "Mr. Milk," "Lardass," "Hacker," "The Brow," and "Kahuna" are just a few that were used in the original MM. Engage in roughhousing and general tomfoolery. Go roller-skating, have water fights, play mud football, conduct fireworks battles, have shaving cream fights, and do anything as long as it's fun and slightly juvenile.

The Memphis Mafia Fan Club

There's a very active fan club in Edinburgh, Scotland (a branch of the Official Elvis Presley Fan Club of Great Britain). They're not affiliated with the Memphis Mafia *in any way*, but they're an extremely fun bunch.
Memphis Mafia Fan Club
P.O. Box 710 NWDO
Edinburgh EH4 Scotland
http://dialspace.dial.pipex.com/memphis.mafia
E-mail: rcs40@dial.pipex.com

Study Acting with Red West

Red West runs an acting school in Memphis. Call for a schedule of classes and other information.
The Red West Actors Studio
(901) 385-7885

Fill Up Your Shopping Cart at the Memphis Mafia Store

You can buy T-shirts, beer steins, baseball caps, beer coolers, mouse pads, and more from an MM catalog.
Memphis Mafia Store
P.O. Box 26277
San Diego, California 92196
http://www.memphismafia.com

Make Friends with Other Elvis fans

This is a no-brainer. It is impossible to spend any time in the Elvis world and not make many good friends.

"He never changed over the years. Elvis was the real thing."
—Larry Geller,
Elvis' good friend

ELVIS AND FOOD

Does anyone know what Julio Iglesias's favorite sandwich is, or what Mick Jagger eats for breakfast? Does anyone care? Apparently not; but when it comes to Elvis there is an endless fascination with the details and quirks of his dietary habits that has no parallel with any other celebrity. No other person, living or dead, has more than a half-dozen cookbooks based on his personal eating habits. Elvis had what quaintly used to be called a healthy appetite for what we now know are unhealthy foods. He indulged this appetite with little restraint. The particulars of Elvis' diet are so well known by now that even a Kalahari bushman could tell you that Elvis had a hankering for fried mashed banana and peanut butter sandwiches.

The man who could have afforded to hire a kitchen staff of the world's best chefs and stock his pantry with the most expensive and delectable comestibles, chose instead to eat the simple comfort foods that he ate as a child in his native South. He associated the plain cooking of his mother and grandmother with the welcoming safety of a loving and protective family. Even though he was occasionally exposed to other cuisines throughout his life, his tastes could not be described as experimental. In Germany, he

Sandi Miller

Elvis enjoying his favorite drink,
Mountain Valley Water

John O'Hara

tried and enjoyed broiled bratwurst; in Hawaii it was Polynesian flavors and barbecue that appealed to his taste buds. Notwithstanding these few forays, exotic or fancy dishes held no appeal to Elvis. Instead, he opted for pork chops, cheeseburgers, or burnt bacon sandwiches on rye toast slathered with mustard every time.

It wasn't just what he ate, it's also how he ate that people find interesting. According to some of his childhood friends, Elvis had his own personal utensils that he carried with him, opting to use these even when he ate in other people's homes. As an adult he would sometimes eat the same meal for months in a row. For a while it was mashed potatoes, tomatoes, sauerkraut, and that crisp bacon he loved, all mixed together. Another time it was meat loaf for what some friends reported to be six months on end. Once it was pound cake topped with canned peaches that captured his fancy for a long period. He was so particular about his food that when he was stationed in Germany he bought an extensive kitchen to prepare meals in the field for himself and his regiment.

Although Elvis used the barbecue pit at the Circle G ranch for many traditional cookouts with family and friends, he is also remembered for the more unusual eating habit of consuming plain hamburger or hot dog buns—straight from the package—that he tied to his saddle so he could eat while horseback riding.

It may be easy to judge Elvis in retrospect but, to be fair, times were very different then. It was a prehealth-conscious America that Elvis was born into, and in those days guys who ate "heartily" were considered manly and very few people concerned themselves with heart-healthy regimens. And when you consider these two facts—Mississippi is the state with the most overweight people (32 percent of the population), and Memphis has the lowest sales of vitamins in the United States—you begin to realize the

John O'Hara

The kitchen at Graceland

environment that was familiar to him. And those figures are for today, so you can imagine what it was like in the 1940s and 1950s when Elvis was growing up. So, perhaps, people are riveted to Elvis' food peccadilloes because they reflect their own. We empathize with him because we know he struggled with his weight like many of us do. We know he loved food and would have been better off resisting some of the temptations, again like the rest of us.

Eating the foods that Elvis ate is one of the easiest ways to experience something that he loved. With the exception of some southern regional favorites like crowder peas or corn pone, there's nothing at all exotic about the ingredients of the Elvis diet and your local supermarket probably carries them all.

Author's collection

ESSENTIAL ELVISOLOGY

Elvis' Cooks

Gladys Presley
Elvis' mother raised him on southern cooking; the main ingredient was plenty of love.

Minnie Mae Presley
Elvis grandmother took over after Gladys died.

LaNelle Fadal
The wife of Elvis' friend in Texas who cooked him homemade meals while he was in basic training.

Ursula Eggers
Family friend who cooked German food for Elvis in Memphis.

Mary Jenkins, one of Elvis' favorite cooks, shares Elvis stories with impersonator Irv Cass at a fan convention

John O'Hara

The scene of much activity, the stove at Graceland

John O'Hara

Alberta Holman Brown
   Worked as maid and cook at Audubon Drive. She was nick-named "Alberta VO5" by Elvis.
Mary Jenkins
   Daytime cook at Graceland from 1963.
Pauline Nicholson
   Day shift maid and cook at Graceland from 1963 until 1977.
Alvena Roy
   Cook at Bel Air homes and Graceland from 1963. Cooked midnight supper for the Beatles visit, Elvis' wedding, and the celebration in honor of Lisa Marie's birth.
Christine Strickland
   Cook at Graceland, mid-sixties.
Nancy Rooks
   Maid and cook at Graceland from 1967 on.
Daisy Mae Williams
   Cook at Graceland.
Lottie Tyson
   Night-shift cook at Graceland.
Bernard and Rene Sinclair
   Butler and cook at the Hillcrest home in Los Angeles.

Elvis' Favorite Drinking Water
Mountain Valley

Fool's Gold Sandwich
This is the sandwich that motivated Elvis and a group of his friends to fly the *Lisa Marie* from Memphis to Denver just so they could pick up some "takeout" from the Colorado Gold Mine Company restaurant. (This restaurant is no longer in business.)
A whole loaf of bread
Creamy peanut butter
Grape (or blueberry) jelly
Well-cooked bacon
Slice a loaf of bread lengthwise and hollow it out. Smear and pile other ingredients inside. Deep-fry (we're not sure how!) the whole damn thing. Wash down with Champagne or Perrier.

Some of Elvis' Favorite Foods and Snacks

Crowder peas
Pork chops
Extra-crisp bacon
Biscuits
Baked beans
Meat loaf
Fried chicken
Grits
Hot dogs
Corn pone
Beefsteak tomatoes
    (thickly sliced)

Lemon meringue pie
Cherry angel food cake
Ice cream sodas
Jello
Pepsi
Milk
Pineapple juice
Banana pudding
GreenGatorade
    (on stage)
Peach soda
Nehi

Peppermint candy
Hawaiian Punch
Strawberries
Strawberry milkshakes
Spinach
Bacon burgers
Hash brown potatoes
Barbecued pork pizza
Spanish omelets
Reese's Peanut Butter
    Cups
Juicy Fruit gum

Foods that Were Always Stocked at Graceland

Hot dogs
Sauerkraut in cans
Ground meat
Hamburger rolls
Potatoes
Onions
Pickles
Mustard

Biscuit fixings
Bacon (thin sliced)
Several bottles of milk
Half-and-half
Peanut butter
Shredded coconut
Fresh fruit

Vanilla and chocolate
    ice cream
Fudge cookies
Juice oranges for
    squeezing
Banana pudding fixings
Meat loaf fixings
Brownie fixings

Midnight Supper with the Beatles

Broiled chicken livers wrapped in bacon
Sweet and sour meatballs
Deviled eggs

Fresh cracked crab
Assorted cold cuts and cheeses
Fruit

The Presley Wedding Banquet

Ham and eggs
Southern fried chicken
Roast suckling pig
Clams Casino
Fresh poached salmon
Eggs Mignonette
Oysters Rockefeller

Smoked salmon
Turkey with gravy and stuffing
String beans
Stuffed tomatoes
$3,500 six-tier wedding cake
    decorated with white pearls
    and red hearts

Favorite Christmas Dinner for Elvis

Ham salad
Potato salad

Meat loaf
Hot rolls

Monkey bread
(Traditional turkey dinner for everyone else)

A Dish from Elvis Presley's Memphis Restaurant

This downtown Memphis restaurant serves lots of Elvis' favorite foods like banana pudding and other good down-home-style cooking. The mood is always friendly and fun and it's a must stop if you go to Memphis. Where else will you be able to play pool on the same table that Elvis and the Beatles played in 1964? It's run by EPE/Graceland and they've done a wonderful job here.

126 Beale Street
Memphis, Tennessee 38103
(901) 527-6900

Elvis' Fried Pickle Chips
    1 10- to 12-ounce jar of thinly sliced hamburger dill pickles
    corn meal

Shake excess vinegar off the pickle slices and dredge them in corn meal. Shake off excess meal and deep fry in 360-degree oil until golden brown. Serve with Honey Dijon Mustard dipping sauce.

Honey Dijon Mustard Dipping Sauce
    1 cup mayonnaise
    1 pinch cayenne pepper
    2 tablespoons honey
    1 1/2 teaspoons cider vinegar
    2 tablespoons Dijon mustard

Mix all ingredients together well. Place dip in small bowl in center of serving plate and arrange Elvis' Fried Pickle Chips around the dip.

John O'Hara

"In one dream, he comes to me and says, 'Mary, I wanna come stay with you. I wanna rest. Can I rest at your house?' And I say, 'Mr. Elvis, you know you can come to my house any time. You're always welcome."
    —Mary Jenkins, Elvis' cook at Graceland

One of Elvis' Favorite Southern "Sides"
Corn Bread "Soaks"

    2 cups white cornmeal
    1 cup all-purpose flour
    1 tablespoon sugar
    1 teaspoon salt

    4 teaspoons baking powder
    1 egg
    Milk

In a mixing bowl, combine all of the dry ingredients. Add eggs and enough milk to make a smooth batter. Pour the batter into a warm, well-greased bread pan. Bake at 425 degrees for about 25 minutes or until golden brown. Makes one loaf. Dunk corn bread into buttermilk for a yummy snack that Elvis enjoyed immensely.

YOUR ELVIS EDUCATION

Books
Presley Family Cookbook
  Vester Presley and Nancy Rooks
The Presley Family and Friends Cookbook
  Donna Presley Early, Edie Hand, Darcy Bonfils, Ken Beck, and Jim Clark
Fit for a King: The Elvis Presley Cookbook (Alvena Roy's recipes)
  Elizabeth McKeon, Ralph Gervitz, and Julie Bandy
Memories Beyond Graceland Gates
  Mary Jenkins and Beth Pease
Are You Hungry Tonight? Elvis' Favorite Recipes
  Brenda Arlene Butler
The I Love Elvis Cookbook
  Elizabeth Wolf-Cohen
The Wonder of You: Elvis Fans Cookbook
  R&M Crafts & Reproductions Cookbook
The Life and Cuisine of Elvis Presley
  David Adler

Video
The Burger & the King: The Life and Cuisine of Elvis Presley, Cinemax

Web Sites
http://members.aol.com/mompac/
  recipe.htm
  An Elvis recipes site

http://www. epmemphis.com
  Elvis Presley's Memphis Restaurant
  and Nightclub site

THE ELVIS AND YOU EXPERIENCE

Eat Where Elvis Ate
The Gridiron
  This classic burger joint, open since 1954, is a real piece of local history. It serves a special Elvis cheeseburger with pimento cheese. It's open 24 hours a day and is just a few minutes' walk from Graceland.

4101 Elvis Presley Boulevard, Memphis
(901) 396-9869

Piccadilly Cafeteria
Elvis hung out and ate here; not to mention, Priscilla modeled at fashion shows at this chain in the 1960s.
3968 Elvis Presley Boulevard, Memphis
(901) 398-5186

K's Restaurant
Originally called K's Drive-In, this favorite of Elvis' still serves the same menu as when he drove in in his old green Lincoln Zephyr, years before fame struck.
166 East H. Crump Boulevard, Memphis
(901) 948-3127

McDonald's
Linda Thompson once convinced Elvis to go with her to this McDonald's to prove to him that he could go out in public without being mobbed. A patron saw the two of them eating at a table and approached Elvis. "I'm sick and tired of you people pretending to be Elvis," he said to the King. To which Elvis replied, "I am Elvis." Linda ended the conversation with Elvis, "Oh George, stop fooling around."
4237 Elvis Presley Boulevard, Memphis

Sun Studio Café
Originally called Taylor's Café, this is where Sam Phillips and the Sun Studio recording artists Roy Orbison, Jerry Lee Lewis, Johnny Cash, and of course Elvis, would have a nosh while taking a break from changing musical history next door.
710 Union Avenue, Memphis
(901) 521-0664

Mac's Kitchen (formerly Chenault's)
This is a completely different restaurant from where Elvis frequently dined. Elvis threw parties there for friends and family.
1402 Elvis Presley Boulevard South, Memphis
(901) 946-3387

> "I had too much praise, too much flattery and fawning over and I needed to remember me: who I was, where I came from. One time I called a relative in Tupelo. It was Christmas and they were havin' dinner. I asked, 'What?' and she was kind of quiet, then said, 'Meat loaf.' I was ... shocked as we'd had the best, you know, turkey, ham, steak, everything. She said that it was near the first and they'd run out of money so they just had meat loaf. It hurt me. And so, I ate meat loaf for about eight months, every night, so I'd remember where I came from and to remind me of how many people were unable to have what I did. It was kind of a penance...."
> —Elvis Presley

Pizza Hut
    Elvis ate here and there's Elvis music on
    the jukebox and wall decorations noting
    his visits.
    4290 Elvis Presley Boulevard, Memphis
    (901) 332-1150
Leonard's Pit Barbecue
    The original location is closed, but you
    can still taste that classic Memphis barbe-
    cue that Elvis loved at the new Leonard's,
    which is decorated in a Memphis 1950s
    theme.
    5465 Fox Plaza Drive, Memphis
    (901) 360-1963
Marlowe's Ribs and Restaurant
    Just down the road from Graceland, this
    was a regular eating spot for Elvis and,
    these days, for a lot of the Graceland staff
    and fans. Free shuttle bus and food deliv-
    ery to Graceland area hotels.
    4381 Elvis Presley Boulevard, Memphis
    (901) 332-4159

> "Maybe your fans and critics cast a disapproving glance at your form in your later years. But not me, because I understood. That's why I know the angels are whipping up heavenly delights for you every day and I sure hope you're enjoying every morsel. My only prayer is that you'll save me a seat at your table when my time is at hand."
>
> —letter from Molly McKay to Elvis, from *Letters to Elvis*

Coletta's Italian Restaurant
    About as exotic a dining experience as it got for Elvis. Some of his favorites
    were barbecued pork pizza and the ravioli and lasagna. These favorite dishes
    of his are still served. Priscilla was known to stop by to get take-away dinners
    from them. See owner Jerry Coletta for great stories and special care as an Elvis
    Fan.
    1063 South Parkway East, Memphis
    (901) 948-7652
Broadway Pizza
    Elvis frequented Broadway for pizza while in Memphis. Memorabilia and
    framed locks of Elvis' hair are on display.
    2581 Broad Avenue, Memphis
    (901) 454-7930
Johnnie's Drive-Inn
    Specializing in BBQ and burgers, Johnnie's looks much as it did as when Elvis
    went there as a kid who lived nearby. Lots of Elvis photos decorate the walls.
    908 East Main, Tupelo
    (601) 842-6748

The Elite Café
   Elvis ate here with Eddie Fadal when he was stationed at Fort Hood in Texas.
   They have Elvis photos all around (especially in the ladies room).
   On the Circle
   Waco, Texas 76702
   (254) 754-4941
Formosa Café
   7165 Santa Monica Boulevard
   Los Angeles, California 90046
   (323) 850-9050

Restaurants with Elvis Themes or Decor

Elvis Presley's Memphis Restaurant
   126 Beale Street
   Memphis, Tennessee 38103
   (901) 527-6900
   Fax: (901) 529-0980
Hard Rock Café
   They have an enormous collection of rock memorabilia.
   315 Beale Street
   Memphis, Tennessee 38103
   (901) 529-0007
Tupelo McDonald's
   There are collages, photos, and etched glass renderings of Elvis everywhere
   you look. And, of course, McDonald's cuisine.
   372 South Gloster Street
   Tupelo, Mississippi 38801
   (601) 844-5505
Anna's Steakhouse
   This restaurant, located in suburban
   Memphis, has the world's largest col-
   lection of Humes High School memo-
   rabilia that was donated by various
   Humes alumni. The restaurant runs
   "Humes Nights" where classmates and
   contemporaries of Elvis come and
   meet and share great stories with fans.
   The Humes High gatherings are the

Anna, owner of Anna's Steakhouse

John O'Hara

fourth Friday of every month and there's usually a special one during Tribute Week every year. The owner, Anna, went to many Elvis movie nights at the Memphian Theater and has a few good stories to tell herself.

7424 Stage Road
Bartlett, Tennessee 38133
(901) 383-9989

Celebrity Room

This restaurant has a groovy Elvis Room.

7515 Brook Road
Richmond, Virginia
(804) 266-3328

Blueberry Hill

This restaurant and club has a permanent Elvis room with a 24-foot-long display case filled with memorabilia. Twice a year, on Elvis' birthday in January and during Tribute Week in August, Blueberry Hill has an Elvis celebration that includes performances by not only Elvis impersonators but people who impersonate Vernon, Gladys, Lisa Marie, and even Elvis' horse, Rising Sun. That's right, Elvis' horse! There is also a room called the Duck room named after Chuck Berry's famous duck walk. Chuck Berry, hometown boy, performs here once a month.

6504 Delmar Street
St. Louis, Missouri 63130
(314) 727-0880

Country Star American Music Grill

This Elvis Room is at this Las Vegas strip restaurant.

3724 Las Vegas Boulevard South
Las Vegas, Nevada 89109
(702) 740-8400

The Hound Dog Hole

The Embassy cafe uses kitchen equipment purchased by Elvis and left behind when he finished his military service in Germany. So if you're ever in Kazakhstan....

United States Embassy
Almaty, Kazakhstan

Peanut Butter & Co.

"The Elvis" sandwich is at the top of the menu, and by far the most requested, at this New York City café.

240 Sullivan Street
New York, New York 10012
(212) 677-3995
http://www.peanutbutterco.com

Azteca Restaurant

A Mexican restaurant and bar in Orange County that has rare Elvis memorabilia and often features Elvis impersonators as entertainment.

12911 Main Street

Garden Grove, California 92840

(714) 638-3790

http://www.angelfire.com/az/crooners

Jack Astor's

This is a chain of restaurants in Canada and the U.S. that has an Elvis tribute booth decorated with Elvis stuff in every locale (of course it's the biggest booth). Call for the location near you.

(905) 681-2997

The Jungle Room

This restaurant and bar is owned by brothers Kriss and Scott Arbury who were lucky enough to see Elvis in concert in 1972 when they were young boys. A huge painting of Elvis on a Harley covers one of the exterior walls. Guitars and other memorabilia are displayed.

3167 Roswell Road

Atlanta, Georgia 30305

(404) 364-9149

Yesterdave's Diner

This place is loaded with Elvis memorabilia. They have an Elvis wall mural plus it's a great place to eat. The owner has purchased several Elvis-owned items that are displayed.

10601 Montgomery Northeast Boulevard

Albuquerque, New Mexico 87111

(505) 293-0033

The Elvis Inn, Jerusalem

The Elvis Inn in Israel is home to a vast collection of Elvis memorabilia, as well as a fully stocked Elvis jukebox playing all Elvis, all the time. The Inn has more than 1,000 Elvis posters from movies, concerts, and album releases.

E-mail: amir420@internet-zahav.net

Jerusalem–Tel Aviv Highway, Neve Ilan Exit

P.O. Box 6095

Jerusalem 91060 Israel

(02) 534-1275

Fax: (02) 534-1371

http://www.bestjerusalem.co.il/food/cafe/elvis/

Elvis Wines

Graceland Napa Valley Wines

This vineyard produces a very passable wine every year with a beautiful Elvis label. To collect or enjoy.

(888) 472-235

Always Elvis Frontenac—Blanc D'Oro

Italian white wine licensed by Boxcar Enterprises in 1979. This wine originally sold for $4.00 and is now considered a valuable collectible.

Take a Food Road Trip

You might not want to fly hundreds of miles for a sandwich like Elvis did, but any road trip you take motivated by food would be a very Elvisian experience.

Have a Luau

Get out your grass skirts and your Hawaiian shirts! Invite all your friends, give each one a lei, put on the soundtracks to the Hawaiian-themed Elvis movies, and fire up the barbecue. Rock a hula baby.

Take a Southern Cooking Class

Find a cooking or adult continuing education class that teaches how to prepare southern regional "delicacies" like Elvis enjoyed his whole life.

Have an Elvis-Style Picnic

Serve lemonade and Elvis fare, followed by a round of skeet shooting and Elvis sing-alongs.

Have a Clambake, Gonna Have a Clambake!

Although Elvis himself disliked seafood, having a clambake makes a great excuse to throw an Elvis-themed beach party, preferably in Hawaii. And, of course, you should actually "do the clam."

Keep a Refrigerator in Your Bedroom

Elvis had a small refrigerator in his bedroom at Graceland. Save yourself a trip to the kitchen for those TV-time snacks.

Where to Get Authentic Ingredients

The Lee Bros. Boiled Peanuts Catalog. This mail-order catalog sells many uniquely southern specialties including Poke Salad. No fooling.

(843) 720-8890

http://www.southernfood.com

E-mail: webmaster@southernfood.com

Carry Your Meal in an Elvis Lunch Box

Available from Starstruck Collectibles
http://www.starstruckcollectables.com/

Eat Black-Eyed Peas on New Year's Eve

Elvis, in keeping with Southern tradition, always ate black-eyed peas on New Year's for good luck in the coming year. Most years it seemed to work for him; see if it works for you.

Collect Russell Stover Elvis Collectible Candy Tins

Eat the chocolate, save the tin.

Bring Elvis' Diet into the Twenty-First Century

Cooking Light magazine takes recipes submitted by readers and turns them into healthier and lighter versions. You can try food from Elvis' fare and still be eating smart.
To subscribe:

Cooking Light
P.O. Box 830549
Birmingham, Alabama 35282
(800) 336-0125,
E-mail CookingLight@time-inc.com

To submit a recipe:

Lighten Up
Cooking Light
P.O. Box 1748
Birmingham, Alabama 35201

Help Feed the Less Fortunate

Elvis liked food and he liked to help people. Contributing to a charity that feeds the needy is a natural.
Citymeals-On-Wheels USA
355 Lexington Avenue
New York, New York 10017
(212) 687-1234
http://www.citymeals.usite.net

Eat with Elvis

Eat your meals on the Elvis Presley 16-piece dinner set. It includes 4 each of $10\frac{1}{2}$-inch dinner plates, salad plates, bowls, and 10-ounce mugs. Five-piece completer set includes sugar bowl and creamer, oval serving platter, serving bowl, 10½-inch straw dispenser, double-sided chrome napkin dispenser, and a salt and pepper shaker set. Available from the Graceland Catalog: (800) 238-2000.

Drink from Elvis Mugs
This company offers 11-ounce ceramic mugs with several different Elvis photo designs for sale. Several mug styles are also available from the Graceland catalog and stores.

Classico San Francisco Inc.
15-B Koch Road
Corte Madera, California 94925
(800) 872-2737
(415) 927-8488
Fax: (415) 927-8477
E-mail: classicosanfransicso@worldnet.att.net
http://www.classicosfus.com

> "My grandmother cooks all my favorite dishes. You know, good, simple foods."
> —Elvis Presley

ELVIS AND ANIMALS

Picture Elvis with his arms around a curvy costar. Picture him prowling a small stage in that incredible black leather outfit. Picture him hitting those final amazing notes of "How Great Thou Art." Now picture Elvis on the lawn behind Graceland playing tug-of-war with a puppy. It's not the first image we have when we think of Elvis, but it's a real one from his personal life, and one that reveals a glimpse of Elvis' warmth, tenderness, and playfulness.

Elvis loved animals and had dozens of pets of all kinds. It was probably Gladys who instilled in Elvis the desire to have lots of life around him; she certainly shared a love of animals and nature. At the Audubon Drive house where the Presleys lived after Elvis' first burst of success, they housed a spider monkey that Elvis had bought on an impulse. Little Jayhew wrought a lot of havoc but, even so, was the first of many simians Elvis welcomed into his various homes. Gladys even wanted to keep chickens at Audubon, but that didn't wash with the neighbors in this middle-class section of Memphis.

When Elvis finally got his mansion and the roughly 14 acres of property that surrounded it, he—and Gladys while she was alive—could indulge in building a veritable zoo. Over the years this zoo included many dogs, cats, horses, ponies, donkeys, monkeys, and birds of all kinds:

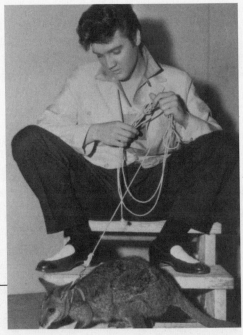

Elvis with a baby wallaby, a gift from Down Under fans

From the collection of Robin Rosaaen

peacocks, a Mynah bird, ducks, turkeys, and, last but not least, Gladys's chickens. A fan from Down Under, who knew of Elvis' love of animals, once sent a baby wallaby to Graceland.

During the summer of 1962, Elvis bought a 3½-foot-tall, 40-pound chimpanzee named Scatter. All the stories about Scatter's antics have given him a special place in history as Elvis' most famous pet. Scatter developed the habit of drinking along with Elvis' guests at parties, looking up women's dresses, and following them into the bathroom. With all this monkey business, he became the center of attention. Scatter was more than a pet; he was a full-fledged member of the Memphis Mafia. One of his more colorful exploits was when Elvis' friend and driver Alan Fortas would place the chimp on his lap at the wheel of Elvis' Rolls Royce. When someone would drive by, Alan would hunker down and there would be Scatter, dressed up in a chauffeur's cap and outfit, appearing to drive through the streets of Los Angeles. Years later, after Scatter had died, Elvis told Kathy Westmoreland that the flamboyant primate had been his best friend.

In 1966, Elvis bought a horse named Domino for Priscilla and when he saw how much fun she was having riding, he had to get one for himself. And, as with many of the things that gave Elvis pleasure, he wanted to spread it around. Elvis bought a passel of horses for the whole Memphis Mafia. All of a sudden the property at Graceland didn't seem so big anymore and the search was on for a ranch. Elvis found a beautiful spread in Walls, Mississippi, that he named the Circle G. Many of his friends have been quoted as saying that Elvis was at his happiest while there. Ranching, horseback riding, and cowboying suited Elvis extremely well. Seeing him full of life and enjoying his ani-

Horses grazing at Graceland, 1999

John O'Hara

Sandi Miller

mals made the time on the ranch wonderful. Mike McGregor, who started out as a ranch hand and took care of the stable and horses at Circle G, often told the story of how the birth of any animal on the ranch was attended by Elvis and friends and treated as a special occasion and cause for celebration.

To the general public, because of some of his more popular hit songs, Elvis is most often associated with hound dogs and teddy bears; but the animal Elvis himself identified with was the tiger. His karate name, given to him by Kang Rhee, one of his karate instructors, was Master Tiger and Elvis delighted in decorating Graceland with paintings, sculptures, and drawings of tigers. He even had several jumpsuits made with a tiger motif. Coincidentally, his Humes High School mascot was a tiger. When Elvis sang those incredibly sexy lyrics, "They call me the tiger man," it had special meaning to him. He *was* the Tiger Man.

Elvis was so attached to some of his animals that whenever one would die while he was on the road no one would tell him about it until he returned. Perhaps the one story that best illustrates Elvis' love of animals was his desperate efforts to save the life of his dog Getlo. In August of 1975, Getlo, a beautiful Chow, developed life-threatening kidney problems. Elvis spent tens of thousands of dollars to fly the dog to Boston for treatment. Getlo stayed at the Copley Plaza Hotel where he was treated for two days before being transferred to a veterinary hospital. After two months of treatment, Getlo returned to Graceland and died not long after in spite of Elvis' efforts.

The first song Elvis played in public was "Old Shep"—an ode to a dying dog. School pals remember Elvis often singing this song and many shed a tear at this early example of Elvis' raw talent. Because of his genuine love of animals he was able to invest real emotion in the song, a quality that would become one of his trademark talents in years to come. Elvis lovers are often pet lovers also and all over the world there's many a cat, dog, hamster, or iguana that answers to the name "Elvis."

ESSENTIAL ELVISOLOGY

The Presley Menagerie

Dogs

Woodlawn
  Childhood dog
Muffy Dee
  Tupelo dog
Boy
  White mutt lived at Audubon
Sweetpea
  Gift for Gladys in 1956
Duke
  Gladys's poodle, named after John Wayne
Littlebit
  Toy poodle, gift for Anita Wood
Sherlock
  Basset hound, used for RCA publicity in the fifties
Baba
  Collie
Getlo
  Chow that Elvis went to great lengths to save
Honey
  Poodle, gift for Priscilla for Christmas 1962
Muffin
  Great Pyrenees
Snoopy
  Great Dane
Brutus
  Great Dane

Stuff
  Aunt Delta Mae's black poodle at Graceland
Teddy Bear of Zixi Pom Pom
  Poodle, gift to Elvis in Germany
Cherry
  Poodle, also in Germany
Foxhugh
  Maltese, from Linda Thompson
Edmund
  Pomeranian with Elvis when he died
Ninja
  Doberman, Priscilla's dog after the divorce
Nipper
  The dog on the RCA trademark; Elvis kept a statue of Nipper in his bedroom.

Honey, one of the dogs Elvis gave as a gift to Priscilla

Poodle wallpaper in Gladys's bathroom, at Graceland

Priscilla and Baba, her Collie

Priscilla and one of Elvis' Great Danes

Cats

Fluff
  From Elvis to Lisa Marie
Puff
  From Elvis to Lisa Marie

Wendell
  Named after costar Wendell Corey

Laura Levin

Mike McGregor worked for Elvis at Graceland taking care of his horses and doing leatherwork

Monkeys

Jayhew
  Spider monkey
Scatter
  Chimpanzee bought from Memphis TV personality Captain Bill Killebrew
Bambi
  Squirrel monkey
Jettu
  Chimpanzee
Jimbo

Horses

Rising Sun
  (originally named Midget's Vandy)
  Palomino is buried at Graceland
Pokey Dunit
Keno
Memphis
  Member of the stable during the 1960s
Bear
  Tennessee walking horse
Domino
  Priscilla's quarter horse
Beauty
Baret
Lady
Conchita's Gold
  Quarter horse
Yankee Revenge
  Black stallion
Mare Ingram
  Named after Memphis mayor, Bill Ingram
(Colonel) Midnight Sun
  Vernon's horse, Tennessee walker

Scout
Butterscotch
  Alan Fortas's palomino
Star Trek
Traveler
  Tennessee walker, Jo Smith's horse
Flaming Star
Buckshot
  Charlie Hodge's horse
Whirlaway
  Chestnut/sorrel horse
Spurt
  Sorrel horse
Guy
  Bay horse
Thundercloud
Sheba
  Jerry Schilling's wife's horse
Cutter's Bill
  Sorrel horse
Sun Down
Big Red
  Red West's mount
El Poco

Model
   Alan Fortas's horse
Boogaloo
   Shetland pony for children to ride

Cattle

18 head of Santa Gertrudis

Birds

Mynah bird
Turkeys (one was named Bow-Tie)
Peacocks
Chickens
Ducks

Elvis' Veterinarian

Doc Franklin took good care of Elvis' animals and his clinic is still open. Doc is now also famous for conducting the Images of Elvis contests throughout the country and in Memphis during Tribute Week.
Ed Franklin
Desoto County Animal Clinic
8330 Highway 51N
South Haven, Mississippi 38671
(601) 342-4899

Elvis' Animals in His Movies

When you watch these movies again, look out for Elvis with his owns pups.
Paradise Hawaiian Style
   Elvis's collie, Baba, got a part in this movie.
Live a Little, Love a Little
   The Great Dane is played by Elvis' dog Brutus.

Elvis in *Live a Little Love a Little* costarring with one of his Great Danes, Brutus

Books
Elvis Aaron Presley: Revelations from the Memphis Mafia
   Alanna Nash with Billy Smith, Marty Lacker, and Lamar Fike
Elvis, from Memphis to Hollywood: Memories from My Eleven Years with Elvis Presley
   Alan Fortas and Alanna Nash

Video
This Is Elvis

THE ELVIS AND YOU EXPERIENCE

Name Your Pets From the Presley Menagerie
Rising Sun, Scatter, Sweetpea, Getlo, and Foxhugh are but a few. It's a fun insider wink among Elvis fans and some of the names are pretty imaginative.

Get a Hound Dog
A little obvious, but a constant reminder of Elvis nonetheless.

Get a Monkey
Add a mischievous monkey to your household, but learn from Elvis' experience with Scatter and try to teach him better manners. And by all means keep him away from the liquor cabinet.

Get a Mynah Bird and Teach It Elvis Phrases
Elvis' mynah bird was taught by some of the Mafia pranksters to say "Elvis, go to hell" and other rude phrases. You can teach yours something a little more positive.

Build an Elvis-Style Doghouse or Birdhouse
Make a façade of the Graceland mansion to cover the front of your animal's dwelling. Or build a scaled-down version of the Tupelo shotgun shack where Elvis was born. The proportions make a perfect doghouse and the little house will be a reminder of Elvis' humble beginnings. Refer to the blueprints in "At Home with Elvis."

Dress Your Pet as Elvis on Halloween
It's amazing what sideburns and sunglasses can do for other species. This is a fun thing to do on Halloween. There's even a white jumpsuit for dogs, with dangling arms that hold a guitar, available from:
Celebration Fantastic Catalog

104 Challenger Drive
Portland, Tennessee 37148
(800) 235-3272
Fax: (800) 260-9360
Compass Marketing
115 Coastline Road
Sanford, Florida 32771
(407) 330-9060

> "Animals don't hate and we're supposed to be better than them."
>
> —EAP

Create an Elvis Aquarium
Stock it with catfish ... hepcat fish, of course. Display your waterproof collectibles here. Apply photos of Elvis waterskiing or surfing to the outside of the back glass of the aquarium. And what better place for a Hawaiian theme?

Go Horseback Riding
Elvis loved riding horses and all the cowboy trappings that went with it. Buy a horse if you can. If not, at least get the outfit. Elvis bought a lot of his riding supplies at Southern Leather in Memphis (901) 774-0400.

Give a Pet as a Gift
Elvis loved to give animals as gifts to his friends and loved ones. If you do this, make sure the pet is going to someone who is prepared to love and take care of it.

Stay in the Same Hotel as Elvis' Dog
In the attempt to save his dog Getlo's life, Elvis had him flown to Boston for treatment. This is where the dog stayed for two days while being treated.
Fairmount Copley Plaza
138 St. James Avenue
Boston, Massachusetts 02116
(617) 267-5300
(800) 527-4727

Adopt or Rescue a Pet Who Needs a Home
No matter what kind of house you live in, it'll seem like Graceland Mansion to an animal in need of a home. There are lots of dogs and cats out there who'd be happy to be your Teddy Bear. Most breeds of dogs now have their own rescue foundations and there's always your local ASPCA, Bide-a-Wee, or Humane Society.

Donate to Animal Charities
Many Elvis fans may not want to, or may not be able to, have a pet in their home but you can always extend a little bit of your love the way Elvis did—by giving to charity.

ASPCA
(American Society for the Prevention of
Cruelty to Animals)
424 East 92 Street
New York, New York 10128
(212) 876-7700
http://www.aspca.org
Humane Society of the United States
P.O. Box 97049
Washington, DC 20077-7066
Canine Companions for Independence
This nonprofit organization trains dogs to be live-in helpmates for adults and
children with physical disabilities. It is the brainchild of Charles (creator of
Peanuts) and Jean Schulz.
National Headquarters
P.O. Box 446
Santa Rosa, California 95402-0446
(800) 572-2275
(707) 577-1700
http://www.canine-companions.org/
Heifer Project International
This extraordinary charity enables you to
provide a heifer, goat, pig, sheep, chick-
ens, bees, or even a water buffalo to a family or community somewhere in the
world. These animals provide dairy, farm help, wool, income, eggs, honey,
transportation, and good old fertilizer. And your gift multiplies, quite literally,
as the family who received it then passes the offspring animals to others in
need. We think Elvis surely would have understood, since he started out as a
poor country boy himself, the value of this extraordinary charity to the lives of
people in poverty.
P.O. Box 808
Little Rock, Arkansas 72203-0808
(800) 422-0474
(501) 889-2014
Fax: (501) 376-8906
National Education for Assistance Dog Services
This organization trains service and hearing dogs who can help people who
are deaf or in wheelchairs to lead a more independent life. These assistance
dogs bring security, freedom, independence, and relief from social isolation to
their human partners.

> "[Scatter] was an exhibi-
> tionist, in the manner of
> all chimpanzees."
> —Peter Guralnick's tactful
> description of Elvis' pet
> Scatter, from *Careless Love*

> "... and now I can't even
> feed my chickens. It's sup-
> posed to be bad for his
> image."
> —Gladys Presley

P.O. Box 213
   West Boylston, Massachusetts 01583
   (978) 422-9064
   http://chamber.worcester.ma.us/neads/index.htm
Guide Dogs for the Blind, Inc.
   P.O. Box 151200
   San Rafael, California 94915-1200
   (415) 499-4000
   (800) 295-4050
   http://www.guidedogs.com/
Operation Critters
   Attn: Mary Etta Duncan
   P.O. Box 3774
   Coos Bay, Oregon 97420

Sponsor a Handicapped Cat or Dog

This 40-acre shelter in Minnesota takes in unadoptable, aged, and handicapped pets and provides lifelong, tender loving care for them. They accept one-time donations or, better yet, you can actually sponsor a specific animal.
Home for Life Animal Sanctuary
P.O. Box 847
Stillwater, Minnesota 55082
(800) 252-5918
Fax: (612) 223-5963
E-mail: lisa@jmalaw.com
http://www.homeforlife.org

Donate a Wheelchair for a Handicapped Dog

These companies make pet wheelchairs and mobility aids for crippled dogs. Because Elvis both loved animals and was known for having spontaneously given wheelchairs to those in need, this is an appropriate and unique way to help out these animals. Contact your local animal rescue societies to find out about a dog in need.

K-9 Carts
   P.O. Box 160639
   Big Sky, Montana 59716
   (406) 995-3111
   Fax (406) 995-3113
   http://www.k9carts.com

Doggon' Wheels
   P.O. Box 6147
   Bend, Oregon 97708
   (888) 7-DOGGON
   Fax: (888) 2-DOGFAX
   E-mail: doggon@doggon.com
   http://www.doggon.com

ELVIS AND THE ARMY

When Elvis received his draft notice from Memphis Draft Board #86 on December 19, 1957, he feared it would mean the end of the dream he had been living since his career started its spectacular ascent. Would the rocket be stopped in mid-flight? No one knew at the time if rock and roll music was to be just another short-lived preoccupation among teenagers and Elvis would drop off the radar screens of the fickle youth market while he was out of circulation.

Of course, as we now know, his fears were unfounded and the opposite proved to be true. Elvis' military service didn't end his stardom, it transformed it. After faith-fully and ungrudgingly fulfilling his duty serving in General Patton's old outfit, he returned to the States as a veteran of the Cold War, a red-blooded, patriotic, all-American boy. This former "threat to the nation" was now one of its defenders and a role model for its youth. His appeal vastly broadened as he earned the respect of many of his former critics. And of course, no one ever looked better in a uniform.

Elvis' military service did more than radically transform the public's perception of him; it forever altered his perception of himself. It was while performing his mili-

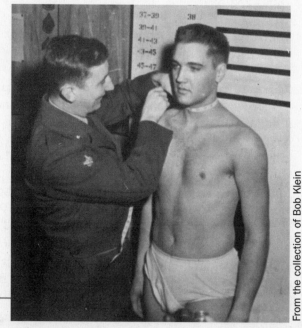

From the collection of Bob Klein

Measuring up for the U.S. Army

"To his great credit this young American became just another GI Joe.... I for one would like to say to him yours was a job well done, Soldier."
—Tennessee Senator Estes Kefauver's tribute to Elvis, read into *The Congressional Record*

tary service that he experienced some of the most significant events of his life. During this time he lived away from home in a different culture for the first time; he suffered the heartbreaking loss of his mother; he met the girl who was to become his wife; he met several people who would become loyal, lifelong friends; he was introduced to the martial arts; and, according to many, he was first exposed to prescription drugs. In telling Elvis' life story, respected biographer Peter Guralnick chose Elvis' induction into the army as the turning point that signaled the end of the "Rise of Elvis Presley." The change in Elvis as a result of his service was so profound that John Lennon was moved to pontificate that "Elvis died when he went into the army." Although that statement is pure hyperbole it indicates how crucial this rite of passage was to both Elvis' life and career.

After receiving a 60-day deferment so he could finish filming *King Creole*, Elvis' military career began on March 24, 1958, when he was sworn in as a member of the United States Army and assigned the serial number 55310761. Elvis turned down all offers of special privileges and soft assignments so he could fulfill his duty like every other ordinary soldier. The army was forced to draw up a special plan called "Operation Elvis" to deal with the logistical problems of treating one of the world's biggest stars as just another recruit. His induction process and medical checkup at Kennedy Veteran's Hospital in Memphis was of course

From the collection of Bob Klein

aggressively exploited by Colonel Parker. The publicity bonanza the Colonel planned let the media follow Elvis from his tearful goodbye with his parents to the cutting off of his famous hair—even to his being examined in his skivvies by military physicians. After a few days of orientation at Fort Chaffee, Arkansas, Elvis was sent to Fort Hood, Texas, for basic training. He was assigned to Company A, Second Medium Tank Battalion, Thirty-seventh Armor, Second Armored Division.

Two weeks into basic training, Eddie Fadal, a disc jockey who had met Elvis in 1956 while working at KRLD in Dallas, visited him at Fort Hood. Fadal offered his home in Waco as a nearby getaway for Elvis and even built an addition onto his house with a bedroom decorated in pink and black to accommodate him. Elvis gratefully took advantage of the offer and spent many weekends there with friends singing around the piano in this home away from home. As soon as basic training was completed, Elvis sent for his family to join him in Texas and live with him off base in Killeen. At first they lived in a rented three-bedroom trailer, but when that proved to be too small he rented a house from Judge Chester Crawford at 906 Oak Hill Drive in the middle of town.

While Elvis was undergoing training as a tank crewman, his mother Gladys's health started deteriorating until she was forced to return to Memphis to be treated by her physician, Dr. Charles Clarke. On August 12, Elvis was granted an emergency leave to go to Memphis and be with his mother. Two days later, on August 14, Gladys died in room 688 of Methodist Hospital, just after Elvis had left for the evening to get some sleep following a long bedside vigil. His anguish at losing his mother was overwhelming. He spent the rest of his leave mourning her loss and reported back to Fort Hood on August 25. For the first time in his life he felt truly alone, and according to all accounts he mourned her for the rest of his life.

From the collection of Bob Klein

Fellow soldier and friend Charlie Hodge and Elvis

Elvis' house at Goethstrasse

Caroline Van Hijfte

On September 19 Elvis left Texas on a troop train headed for the Military Ocean Terminal in Brooklyn, New York. On the train he met a fellow musician and southerner, Charlie Hodge. Charlie's attempt to comfort Elvis earned him a place as a lifelong friend and confidant. Elvis held a 45-minute press conference before boarding the *General Randall*, his troopship bound for Germany. At the press conference he held a book called *Poems that Touch the Heart* that had been given to him by a fellow soldier. It would be hard for anyone watching that footage not to feel empathy for the humble and sincere young man who lost his mother and was now reluctantly about to leave his country for the first time.

Elvis arrived in Bremorhaven, Germany, on October 1 to the cheers of 1,500 German fans and a horde of press. He took a troop train to Friedburg where he was stationed at Friedberg Kaserne, Ray Barracks, bunk #13, barracks 3707. He was transferred to First Medium Tank Battalion 32nd Armored Company D and assigned as a jeep driver for Reconnaissance Platoon Sergeant Ira Jones. His father and grandmother, along with Red West and Lamar Fike, arrived on October 4 and checked into the Ritter's Park Hotel in Bad Homberg. Two days later they moved to Hilbert's Park Hotel in Bad Nauheim. Still dissatisfied with their accommodations, they settled into the Hotel Grunewald, a hotel catering to a moneyed, mostly elderly clientele taking advantage of the nearby health spa.

While on maneuvers in Grafenwohr near the Czech border, Elvis met and dated Elisabeth Stefaniak, a nineteen-year-old German girl whose stepfather was a U.S. Army sergeant stationed at the military base there. He offered her a job as personal secretary and she later joined him in Bad Nauheim. It was also on these maneuvers that Elvis is reputed to have been exposed by a superior officer to amphetamines for the first time for the purpose of keeping him awake while on guard duty during the long winter nights. On one of these bitterly cold nights, Elvis even had a brush with death when he nearly succumbed to carbon monoxide poisoning as a result of a faulty heater in his jeep.

The Hotel Grunewald's management soon grew irritated with hosting the young superstar who enjoyed staging raucous water pistol duels, fireworks battles, and shaving cream fights with his friends in the corridors of the staid hotel. His family and entourage moved from the hotel, settled into a rented three-story, five-bedroom house at Goethestrasse 14, and stayed there until their departure from Germany. Each day, dressed in spit-polished boots and a perfectly pressed uniform (thanks to his friends Lamar and Red), he'd drive off to the base in his BMW 507 sports car, dubbed "Der Elviswagon" by the German press. At night, the house became a mini Graceland where Elvis and his friends gathered around a rented piano singing gospel and entertaining frauleins.

In March 1957, accompanied by Red and Lamar, Elvis took a three-day leave to visit Munich where he spent time with Vera Tschechowa, an 18-year old actress whom he had met while doing publicity shots for the March of Dimes. They visited the striptease club, the Moulin Rouge. This excursion has been well documented in a book of photographs entitled *Private Elvis*. They show Elvis cavorting with showgirls and strippers like any other soldier on leave might have done, but receiving considerably more interest from the women. Seven months later Elvis, his two "bodyguards" Red and Lamar, and fellow soldiers Charlie Hodge and Rex Mansfeild visited Munich again. This time they stayed for only two days before heading on to Paris where they checked into the Prince de Galles Hotel. Each evening they gorged themselves on the Parisian nightlife, carousing through a half-dozen nightclubs before returning back to the hotel accompanied by whichever showgirls had turned their heads. They were having so much fun they stayed longer than originally planned and instead of taking the train back from Paris Elvis hired a limo to speed them back to Freidburg so they could report back to their barracks in the nick of time.

September 13, 1959, was a portentous day for Elvis. It was on that day that his friend Currie Grant, an airman stationed at nearby Weisbaden air force base, brought a pretty little 14-year-old girl named Priscilla Beaulieu to the house on Goethestrasse. Elvis was instantly smitten with her and from that point on they saw each other almost every night. Elvis wasn't the only Presley to fall in love while in Germany. Vernon, Elvis' father, met Dee Stanley, the wife of an army sergeant and mother of three children. Their whirlwind romance, so soon after the death of Gladys, was a source of great annoyance— even pain—to Elvis.

Another important character in Elvis' life appeared at this time. Joining Elvis and his buddies for their weekly touch football games was a Chicago native named Joe

From the collection of Bob Klein

Vernon and Elvis Presley in Germany

National Archives

"Hey, Elvis, watch where you point that thing!"

Esposito. Elvis took a liking to the diminutive yet charismatic young soldier. So much so that "Diamond Joe," as he came to be known, later became Elvis' road manager and right-hand man and remained so until the day Elvis died.

After first being exposed to karate during basic training at Fort Hood, Elvis took up the sport in earnest while in Germany. He studied under Jurgen Seydel, "the father of German karate." On his second trip to Paris he even brought Master Seydel with him along with buddies Cliff Gleaves, Lamar, and Joe Esposito, who first displayed his organizational skills by handling the financial logistics of the trip. This trip differed from Elvis' earlier Parisian bacchanal in that in addition to making the rounds of the nightclubs, he now spent his days studying karate with a Japanese karate master introduced to him by Jurgen Seydel.

On the day before Elvis left Germany, he held a press conference at Ray Barracks Enlisted Men's Club attended by more than 100 reporters. Interestingly, among the people in the crowd was Air Force Captain Marion Keisker MacInnes, the same Marion Keisker who was working at Sun Studios in Memphis the day that Elvis strolled in to record his first record. Elvis, always mindful of giving credit where credit was due, acknowledged Marion by saying that they wouldn't be having this press conference if it weren't for her.

The next day Elvis boarded a C-118 military air transport at Frankfurt's Rhine-Main Airport and after waving goodbye to a tearful Priscilla in the crowd left Germany for the final time. The plane made a two-hour refueling stop at Prestwick Airport in Scotland where Elvis greeted fans and signed autographs. When his plane left Scotland it would be the last time he was ever to set foot in Europe.

His plane landed in a dramatic snowstorm at McGuire Air Force Base near Fort Dix, New Jersey. Elvis held another press conference where he was greeted by Nancy Sinatra, who presented him with a gift from her father, Frank, who was scheduled to host the "Welcome Home, Elvis" television special later that month.

He boarded a luxurious private rail car on the end of the Tennessean, the train that would carry him back to Memphis like a conquering hero returning home. Along the route Elvis would emerge and wave from the back of the train to the

Elvis giving a press conference at the end of his tour of duty on March 7, 1960

crowds of fans who gathered at every stop. It was obvious that in the case of Elvis' fans, absence had indeed made the heart grow fonder.

Shortly after Elvis returned home, he gave another press conference in his father's office behind the main house at Graceland. A video of Elvis answering questions at that press conference can be seen as part of the Graceland tour in the same room where it took place. Elvis' "soldier boy" period makes him stand apart from other entertainers. It's almost inconceivable to picture any other rock star at the height of his fame risking it all by putting aside his career, allowing his hair to be shorn, and performing a dreary or potentially dangerous stint as an ordinary GI. The qualities that made Elvis a good soldier—courage, honor, discipline, self-sacrifice, leadership—are among the qualities that many Elvis fans love and admire in him.

Elvis is seen as an emblem, a representation, of America itself for a lot of reasons, not the least of which is the image in our mind's eye of a beautiful young man in uniform doing his duty just like any other rank-and-file soldier. Elvis' association with America's military continues even today. When U.S. soldiers wanted to mark their presence on the battlefield in the Persian Gulf War, they chose an interesting phrase to paint as graffiti everywhere they passed. On walls and vehicles all over the theater of operations was written "Elvis was here."

ESSENTIAL ELVISOLOGY

Elvis-Related Military Bases
Fort Chaffee, Arkansas
   Where Elvis got the famous military haircut.
Fort Hood, Texas
   Elvis underwent basic training here.
Military Ocean Terminal, Brooklyn, New York
   Elvis departed to Germany from here.
Friedburg Army Base, Ray Barracks, Germany
   Elvis was stationed here in barracks 3707, bunk #13.

Prestwick Airforce Base, Scotland
Elvis' plane made a brief refueling stop here on its way back to America.
McGuire Air Force Base, New Jersey
Elvis' plane landed here on his return to the States.
Fort Dix, New Jersey
Elvis was discharged here.

Battalion Motto
"Victory or Death"

Rank at the End of His Tour of Duty
Sergeant E5

Division Nickname
"Hell on Wheels"

Elvis' Monthly Army Pay
$83.20—Private
$99.37—Private First Class
$122.30—Specialist Fourth Class

Selective Service Number
40-86-35-16

Serial Number
53310761

Elvis' Outfits
March 28, 1958–September 17, 1958
  U.S. Army
  Company A
  Second Medium Tank Battalion
  Thirty-seventh Armor
  Third Armored Division

October 1, 1958–March 2, 1960
  U.S. Army
  Company D
  First Medium Tank Battalion
  Thirty-second Armor
  Third Armored Division

From the collection of Bob Klein

Medals Elvis Was Awarded
Marksmen badge for M2 carbine
Sharpshooter badge for .45 caliber pistol

Sharpshooter badge for M1 rifle
Good Conduct ribbon

Elvis' Superior Officers
Sergeant William Norwood
  His boot camp instructor
Sergeant Ira Jones
  Elvis was assigned as Sergeant Jones' driver.

Lieutenant William J. Taylor, Jr.
  His executive officer
General Richard J. Brown
  His commanding officer

Some of Elvis' Army Romances
Lilian Portnoy,
  Kissed him right before he got on the boat
Vera Tschechowa
Venetia Stevenson
Janie Wilbanks,
  Memphis girl who visited him in Germany

Margit Buergin
Priscilla Beaulieu
Elisabeth Stefaniak
Siegrid Schutz
Ingrid Sauer

Important Elvis Army Dates
December 10, 1957
  Received draft notice
March 24, 1958
  Reported for induction
March 25, 1958
  Barber James Peterson gives Elvis
  his famous military haircut.
Nov 27, 1958
  Promoted to private first class

June 1, 1959
  Promoted to specialist fourth
  class
January 20, 1960
  Promoted to sergeant
March 5, 1960
  Discharged

YOUR ELVIS EDUCATION

Books
Elvis the Soldier
  Rex Mansfield and Elisabeth Mansfield
Elvis in the Army: The King of Rock 'n' Roll as Seen By an Officer Who Served with Him
  William J. Taylor, Jr.
Soldier Boy Elvis
  Ira Jones as told to Bill E. Burk

Der Elvis
   Gary Paul Gates
Child Bride: The Untold Story of Priscilla Beaulieu Presley
   Suzanne Finstad
Elvis and Me
   Priscilla Presley and Sandy Harmon
Me 'n Elvis
   Charlie Hodge, with Charles Goodman
Operation Elvis
   Alan Levy
Private Elvis
   Diego Cortez
Elvis, Like Any Other Soldier
   1958 Second Army Division Yearbook
Private Presley: The Missing Years—Elvis in Germany
   Andreas Schroer
Poems that Touch the Heart
   A. L. Alexander
Elvis in der Wetterau (in German)
   Heinrich Burk

Video
GI Blues
The Lost Elvis Home Movies
   Scenes of Elvis's visits to his friend Eddie Fadal's house in Waco while he was stationed at Fort Hood, Texas. To order call (877) 567-8358.
Elvis en Service (in French)
   Translation: Elvis in the Army

Recordings
Elvis Sails
   A recording of a press conference that took place before Elvis sailed to Germany on the United States Troop Transport Ship, the U.S.S. *General George M. Randall* (T-AP-115).

Web Sites
http://www.go-army.com
   For army recruiting, the main web site
http://www.hood-pao.army.mil/
   Official Fort Hood site

http://www.hoodmwr.com/
   Unofficial Fort Hood site

THE ELVIS AND YOU EXPERIENCE

Join the Army
Request Elvis' outfit.

Re-create His Army Uniform
Your local Army-Navy store is a good source.

Wear His Army Insignia
A Hell on Wheels patch is an instant nod to Elvis fans.

Wear Elvis Dog Tags
When Elvis was in the army, replicas of his dog tags were popular among his fans. To find a pair, refer to the "Collecting Elvis" chapter.

Get Photos of Elvis in the Army
The National Archives and Records Administration
   Still Picture Branch, NWCS, Room 5360
   8601 Adelphia Road
   College Park, Maryland 20740-6001
   (202)-501-5000
The Library Of Congress
   Prints and Photographs Division
   Washington, DC 20540
   http://lcweb2.loc.gov/pp/pphome.html
Love 4 Elvis Fan Club
   (800) 732-93333

Do Something Nice for a Soldier
Send some Elvis CDs to a soldier stationed overseas. Become a pen pal. Contact the U.S.O. for information.

Make a Donation to the U.S.O
Elvis contributed money to the U.S.O. to provide recreational facilities for soldiers serving in Vietnam. Make a similar contribution to this organization in his name.

Take the Military Elvis Tour
See some of the places associated with Elvis' army days.

The United States

Fort Hood, Texas
> Elvis lived here with his family while he trained at Fort Hood.
> 906 Oak Hill Drive
> Killeen, Texas 76541

Waco, Texas
> Elvis spent many weekends visiting his friend Eddie Fadal while serving at nearby Fort Hood.
> The Eddie Fadal House
> 2807 Lasker Avenue
> Waco, Texas 76707
> (254) 776-5388

Germany

Hilberts Park Hotel
> Elvis and his crew were asked to leave after only a few days.
> 2-4 Kurstrasse
> 61231 Bad Nauheim, Germany
> (311) 316-318-319

Hotel Gruenwald
> Elvis and his boys lasted only a few months here before being asked to leave.
> 10 Terrassenstrasse
> 61231 Bad Nauheim, Germany
> (49) 6032-2230

14 Goethestrasse
> Elvis lived in this private house for most of the time he was in Germany.
> 61231 Bad Nauheim, Germany

Elvis Presley Platz
> Freidberg, Germany

Useful German Phrases

"Where is Elvis Presley Plaza?"
> "Wo ist der Elvis-Presley-Platz?"

906 Oak Hill Drive

Mary O'Hara

2897 Lasker Avenue

Mary O'Hara

A monument in a small park near the Hotel Gruenwald commemorates Elvis' time in Germany

Caroline Van Hijfte

A closer look at the monument

Caroline Van Hijfte

"Where is Elvis Presley's house?"
   "Wo ist das Haus von Elvis Presley?"
"Did you ever meet Elvis?"
   "Haben Sie Elvis jemals getroffen?"
"Do you know anyone who met Elvis?"
   "Kennen Sie jemanden der Elvis getroffen hat?"
"Which Elvis stamp did you prefer?"
   "Welche Elvis-Briefmarke mochten Sie am liebsten?"
"Are you Elvis' love child?"
   "Sind Sie Elvis' Kindder Liebe?"

Paris Elvis-Style

Re-create one of Elvis' military leaves in Paris. Spend a few days ogling showgirls and studying karate. Here are some of the places where he and his friends did their carousing.
Folies-Bergere
   32 Rue Richer
   Paris, 75009 France
Casino de Paris
   19 Rue de Clichy
   Paris, 75009 France
Lido
   116 Avenue de Champs-Elysees
   Paris, 75009 France
Moulin Rouge
   82 Boulevard de Clichy
   Paris, 75018 France

Elvis in Scotland

Elvis' plane had a brief refueling stop here at Prestwick Airforce Base on its way back to America. A plaque commemorates this, the only time Elvis set foot on the British Isles.

Buy a Jeep
When Elvis wasn't behind the wheel of his BMV 507, he was driving an olive green Willys Jeep. Paint the numbers 20976607 on the side like Elvis' jeep.

Give Donations to Veterans' Causes
Disabled American Veterans
P.O. Box 14301
Cincinnati, Ohio 45250-0301

If You Must Go into Battle, Wear an Elvis Good Luck Charm

There's been a long-standing tradition among some Elvis fans serving in the military to wear an Elvis T-shirt or piece of Elvis TCB jewelry when going on a mission.

Get the History of the *Randall,* Elvis' Troop Ship

Seaweed's Ships Histories brings "Elvis the Veteran" into

National Archives

your home through the history of the ship that Private Presley departed on from New York, bound for Bremerhaven, West Germany. The history is on fine parchment paper (8 by 11 inches) and is suitable for framing. The photo of the ship is a glossy black and white. They also offer never-before-released photos of Elvis taken while he was serving his country in Bremerhaven, Germany. Each official action photo shows Elvis conducting his military duties. Photos can be purchased separately or in the Collector's Series. One dollar from each order will be donated to homeless veterans in Elvis' name.

Seaweed's Ships Histories
P.O. Box 154
Sistersville, West Virginia 26175-0154
(800) 732-9333
Fax: (304) 652-1523
E-mail: uss-seaweed@uss-seaweed.com
http://www.uss-seaweed.com/elvis.htm

"What I do ... care a great deal about, is how Elvis Presley did his assigned job and how he related to others in his unit. He pulled his weight. He used his head and did his job well. He was one of us. He cared about us. And he got back the respect and friendship he gave everyone else. In several instances I saw sparks of leadership in Elvis that made me think he could have induced men to follow him into combat, just as his music caused millions of young people to follow him."
—William J. Taylor, Jr., from *Elvis in the Army*

ELVIS AND FIREARMS

There's a great story often repeated by members of the Memphis Mafia by those who were there and in that damn-I-wish-I-had-been-there style by those who weren't. One night while Elvis was in Washington, D.C., he decided to get out of his limo in a dicey neighborhood. He was wearing the famous diamond-, ruby-, and sapphire-studded gold belt that he had received as an award from the International Hotel. A small group of unsavory characters gathered around him. Elvis noticed them eyeing the gold belt. He pulled back his coat so that they all could get a good look at it. "This means I set the all-time attendance record at the International Hotel," he told them. He then pulled his jacket even farther back to display his gun in its holster. "And this means I get to keep it."

Gun-toting badasses, on both sides of the law, have played a colorful role in our popular imagination. Our movies, our collective dreams, are dominated by stories of gunslingers: the cowboy, the gangster, the tough-guy cop. A good many of our heroes run around with guns. Elvis saw himself in this light—the good guy with the gun, Dirty Harry, James Bond. It was important, and later maybe necessary, for Elvis to be a tough guy.

Forrest L. Bobo was a young clerk at the Tupelo Hardware Store when Gladys Presley brought her son to the store in January 1946 to buy him a birthday present. The way Bobo tells the story, Gladys had to persuade Elvis to choose that now-famous first guitar because

Elvis playing gunslinger as a boy

From the collection of Bob Klein

520

what he really wanted was a gun. In the rural American South where Elvis grew up, there was nothing out of the ordinary about a young boy wanting a gun. Luckily for Elvis fans everywhere, though, he settled for the guitar. But he never did lose that gun lust.

Elvis was a controversial figure right from the beginning of his career when his performances were deemed to be contributing to juvenile delinquency and the corruption of female virtue. He received death threats on a regular basis during the 1950s. Billy Smith, Elvis' cousin, says that Elvis used to keep a .22 caliber revolver in his room to protect himself even in those days. When someone becomes famous, they become a target; Elvis' fame was unprecedented—and so was the threat. If he was going to be a target, though, he was determined to be one who was ready to shoot back.

But Elvis' interest in guns went beyond the need to defend himself. More than mere protection, guns represented independence and self-reliance and perhaps of greatest significance to Elvis: *badness.* He was, to put it mildly, a gun enthusiast. He collected rare and interesting firearms. As a fully legal badge-carrying deputy of several police departments, Elvis was permitted to carry concealed weapons. And he didn't hesitate to take advantage of that opportunity, often packing two or more guns at a time on his person—once, wearing five guns when he showed up to be best man at Memphis Mafia member Sonny West's wedding.

There was something about the power and mystique of guns that captivated Elvis. He experienced that power on March 22, 1957. A marine named Herschel Nixon tried to pick a fight with Elvis over a girl. Elvis pulled out a movie-prop pistol and scared the marine off. (More involving guns and another federal employee named Nixon later.)

Elvis' military career also influenced his relationship with firearms. A soldier is never far from his gun. Elvis spent time on shooting ranges both for required military training and for fun. He even got a taste of firing the 99mm M48 tank gun. In basic training at Fort Hood, he scored third in his platoon in marksmanship.

National Archives

Elvis posing with an M48 tank gun

John O'Hara

The shooting range in the smoke-house behind Graceland

Basically, the same thing that fueled Elvis' interest in karate fueled his interest in guns. As effective as karate is, it's no match for what is sometimes referred to as gun-fu, the ultimate martial art. At an exhibition at Kang Rhee's dojo in Memphis, Elvis did a demonstration of defense techniques against an assailant with a gun at close range. Then he stepped back about five feet to demonstrate defense techniques from a longer distance. He got down on his knees and put his hands together in the prayer position. He said that's the only way you can defend against a gun from that distance.

His gun collection was a more than just something to admire; it was meant for use on a daily basis. The smokehouse behind Graceland was converted into a shooting range and Elvis and the Memphis Mafia would spend hours pumping lead into targets. He didn't confine his shooting to the range, however. Elvis was notorious for "creative" target practice, occasionally displaying a dangerously cavalier attitude about firearm safety. It is a testament to his good luck that Elvis never accidentally shot anyone. But there was a close call or two. In one incident, Elvis' gun accidentally discharged sending a ricocheting bullet around the room until, spent, it hit Dr. Nick's chest, leaving him bruised but feeling fortunate to be alive.

John O'Hara

There were times in Elvis' life when, sequestered by his fame, his television became his main link to the outside world. It's little wonder that it often became a target of his scorn and his bullets. If Elvis became displeased with the programming, he turned it off with a gunshot to the screen—remote control Elvis-style. A hemorrhoid

If you look closley you can see a hole from an errant bullet that punctured Lisa Marie's slide and is still left unrepaired commercial was shot with a turquoise-handled Colt .45. Robert Goulet's television appearances took more than a few rounds from Elvis' .22 Savage.

In Las Vegas, in August 1970, the FBI was called in because of some very credible kidnapping and death threats. Security was tightened, an ambulance was put on standby outside the casino, and Elvis even wore a special monitoring device on his wrist. He started to pack a gun while on stage, often wearing a Derringer in his boot, sometimes one in each boot. Some people might think this was a bit extreme but as John Lennon's assassination proved to the world ten years later, Elvis' fears were not groundless.

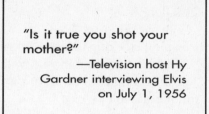

"Is it true you shot your mother?"
—Television host Hy Gardner interviewing Elvis on July 1, 1956

When Elvis made his famous spur-of-the-moment visit to President Nixon, he flew on a commercial flight. At first he was not allowed to board the plane with his guns, but the pilot intervened. This was, after all, Elvis Presley. Elvis' choice of a gift for President Nixon, which he was carrying, was a WWII commemorative Colt .45 with seven silver bullets.

Owning a gun is understandably a controversial issue. Although we recommend you get to know Elvis by getting to know the things he loved, some people want no part of guns and have no interest in sharing Elvis' enthusiasm for them. On the other hand, there are many fans who cherish their right to legal firearms and enjoy exercising it in a safe and responsible manner.

ESSENTIAL ELVISOLOGY

The Presley Arsenal over the Years

Erma Waffenfabrik-Erfut 36.54 mm rifle

Winchester 12-20-gauge pump action rifle

Remington .22-caliber Speedmaster rifle model 552

Flite King Riot model k-10 high standard shotgun
  TCB logo in gold on both sides of grip with EP and lightning bolt on both sides of shotgun barrel

Belgian Browning 20-gauge shotgun

Wishco K6 Erlangen .25-caliber automatic pistol model 11
  Carried in boot occasionally for Vegas engagements

Hi-Standard Duramatic automatic pistol M101
  Black metal with brown plastic grips

Smith & Wesson modern revolver .38 special model 60
  With wooden grip and ivory inlay on one side.

Smith & Wesson .38-caliber revolver
model 36
  With wood grips
Browning stocking-top six-clip pistol
  Polished steel snub-nosed with
  pearlized butt. Good boot pistol.
Antique gambler's pistol
  Chrome-plated with six-shot barrel
Antique double-barreled pinfire pistol
  Silver metal with a checkered plastic grip and ring at bottom
Old-style Spanish percussion rifle
  Flintlock resembling a musket
Marlin .22-caliber single-shot bolt-action target rifle
Colt .22-caliber Derringers
  Short dueling pistols, nickel plated.
  Each handle is inlaid with EP in 18
  karat gold. Elvis sometimes packed
  one in his boot and the other in the
  small of his back
Fabrique Nationale Browning .25-caliber automatic pistol
  Carried by Elvis in his boot. Once
  fell out while he was motorcycle
  riding
Mauser 9 mm short automatic pistol
Colt Woodman's .22-caliber automatic
  long pistol
Ruger .357 single-action pistol
Cobra .38-caliber snub-nosed revolver
  With 14 karat gold TCB logos on
  Rosewood grip
Hi -Standard .22-caliber automatic pistol, Field King model
Savage lever-action carbine rifle
  With wood grip
Antique service pistol
  Metal octagonal barrel, flintlock
  with brass trimming with hammer
  shaped like a griffin

(*top to bottom*) Smith & Wesson.38 Special model #60, Smith & Wesson model 36 .38 caliber revolver

(*top to bottom*) Ruger .357 single action pistol, Colt Python .357 Magnum revolver, Colt Cobra .38 caliber snub nose revolver

Smith & Wesson .357 Magnum model 66; silver metal with customized wood grips.

Savage .22-caliber single-shot bolt-action, model 4C
  With wood grip
Colt Python .357-caliber Magnum revolver
  With gold inlays of a bighorn sheep, a bison, a ram, a bear, and a bobcat; engraved by Frederick Wilhelm Heym Company, Germany.
Savage .32-caliber automatic pistol
  With Native American profile on both sides of grip
Browning 9 mm automatic pistol
Colt Frontier Scout 22-caliber
  Magnum revolver single-action
  Walnut grip with gold inlays of EP and TCB on either side
Walther PPK 7.65 mm double-action pistol
  Also James Bond's favorite gun
Walther Kurz PPK 9 mm
  "Elvis" was engraved on the silver barrel; TCB medallion in the wooden stock.
.22-caliber breech break revolver
Remington .22-caliber rifle
  With plastic handle
Colt Automatic .22-caliber pistol
  Gilded
Pietro Baretta 9 mm
  Gilded with mother-of-pearl handle; purchased from Blake Edwards
Colt .45
  Commemorative pistol 1917–1967
Remington Five Fourteen .22-caliber short bolt-action rifle
Stevens .22-caliber bolt-action target rifle
  Buckhorn Model 56
Winchester model 42 410 gauge shotgun
Colt AR-15 model SPI.223-caliber rifle

Colt single action frontier scout .22 magnum nickel-plated revolvers

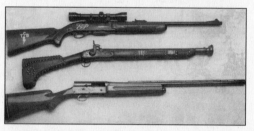

(*top to bottom*) Remington model 742 Woodmaster Rifle, Spanish style percussion rifle, Belgian Browning 20 gauge shotgun

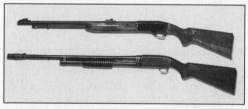

(top to bottom) Winchester 12-20 gauge pump-action rifle, Remington .22 caliber Speedmaster Rifle model 552

.30-caliber carbine rifle
  Walnut handle and stock, government issue
Howa Armalite model AR-180 5.56 mm
  Japanese

Winchester 30-30
Embossed with six flags
Low Stack commemorative rifle
Japanese automatic rifle
With walnut handle
Carl Hauptmann-Ferlach
German rifle
Remington 22gauge shotgun model 1100
Remington Woodmaster rifle model 742
Wooden butt decorated with gold initials EP and TCB logo
Modern .30-caliber
With walnut handle
Universal sawed-off carbine
Colt Python .357-caliberMagnum revolver
Dark gray metal with checkered wood grips
Remington XP-100 221 Fireball handgun
Japanese Frontier Derringer double-barreled pistol
General Nathan Bedford Forrest .22 caliber revolver
With brass barrel and rosewood handle
Continental miniature dueling pistols
With ebony handles with ivory tips
Crossman .454 semiautomatic BB repeater
German officer's 9 mm Luger automatic
Navy revolver
With walnut handle
Colt .22-caliber single-action revolver
With mother-of-pearl handle
Ruger Black Hawk .44-caliber revolver
Ruger Black Hawk .30-caliber revolver
Black metal with wood grips

(*top to bottom*) Belgian Browning 20 gauge shotgun, Flight King riot model K-10 high standard shotgun, Remington .22 caliber Speedmaster rifle model 552

All photos this page courtesy of Butterfield & Butterfield

Colt .22 caliber short derringer dueling pistols

Colt Python .357 magnum revolver, M101 Duramatic automatic pistol, Smith & Wesson .38 Special model 60

Associates Trooper .357-caliber Magnum revolver
Wood handle inset with pennies
M.B.A. Associates Metal Mark 1 model B 13 mm Tyrojet
Thompson submachine gun
Colt .38-caliber Detective Special
Silver metal with checkered brown plastic grips
Smith & Wesson .38-caliber Special pistol
With walnut handle
Great Western Arms Company Derringer dueling pistols
With mother-of-pearl handle
Black Hawk .357
With walnut handle
Smith & Wesson .357-caliber Magnum pistols
With walnut handles and engraved barrels
Smith & Wesson .357-caliberMagnum pistols Model 66
Silver metal with wood grips inlaid with 14 karat gold TCB logo

The Army Weapons
M1 Rifle
M3 .45-caliber grease gun
90 mm M48 tank gun
3.5-inch rocket launcher
.45-caliber automatic pistol
.30- and .50-caliber jeep-mounted machine guns

Army Firing Range Proficiency
Qualified Sharpshooter—M1 Rifle, 45-caliber pistol
Qualified Marksmen—M2 carbine

Arms Suppliers to the King
Sears at Southland Mall

Courtesy of Butterfield & Butterfield

Engraved Colt Python .357 magnum revolver

Smith & Wesson .69-caliber automatic pistol
Colt .45 chrome-plated WWII commemorative
Given as a gift to Nixon.. On the gun is inscribed WWII Commemorative European/African Middle Eastern Theatre, December 11, 1941–May 7, 1943.: North Atlantic, Tunisia, Sicily, Plusto, Anzio, Normandy, Bastogne, Remagen, and Berlin.

National Archives

From the collection of Bob Klein

Memphis, Tennessee
Kerr's Sporting Goods Store
  Los Angeles, California
Taylor's Gun Shop
  Southaven, Mississippi
Tiny's Gun Shop
  Palm Springs, California
Frontier Gun Shop
  Palm Springs, California

The Elvis Wedding Arsenal

At Sonny West's wedding, Elvis was not only the best man, he was the best-armed man. Usually it's only the father of the bride who might be carrying so much firepower at a wedding. Although he was persuaded not to carry his police flashlight to the altar, this is what he was packing during the ceremony:

  2 gold-plated .45-caliber pistols in shoulder holsters
  1 pearl-handled pistol in waistband
  1 pearl-handled pistol in small of his back
  1 Derringer in boot

Where Did Elvis Shoot?

Graceland smokehouse shooting range
Circle G Ranch
Memphis indoor shooting range
Memphis police shooting range

Beverly Hills police shooting range
Palm Springs police shooting range
More or less anyplace else he wanted

Favorite Targets

Televisions
Chandeliers
Drinking glasses
Light bulbs
Light switches
Cars

Toilets
Snakes
Swing set
Ice maker
Flashbulbs floating in pool

YOUR ELVIS EDUCATION

Books
Graceland
  Chet Flippo
Elvis: The Final Years
  Jerry Hopkins
Elvis, What Happened?
  Red West, Sonny West, Dave Hebler with Steve Dunleavy
Elvis Aaron Presley: Revelations from the Memphis Mafia
  Billy Smith, Marty Lacker, and Lamar Fike with Alanna Nash
Elvis in the Army: The King of Rock n Roll as Seen by an Officer Who Served with Him
  William J. Taylor Jr.
The Concealed Handgun Manual: How to Choose, Carry, and Shoot a Gun in Self-Defense
  Chris Bird

Video
All the King's Men
Elvis

Web Sites
http://www.nixonlibrary.org
  Nixon Library site
http://www.nwlink.com/~timelvis/elvis
  gun.html
  Sierra Sid's Auto Truck Plaza:
  The Guns of Elvis! site

http://www.elvis-tcb.com/memorab.htm
  Karl E. Lindroos collection
http://www.nra.org
  National Rifle Association

THE ELVIS AND YOU EXPERIENCE

Visit an Elvis Gun Exhibit
These museums and collections contain some Elvis guns.
Graceland
  The trophy room at Graceland has the largest number of Elvis' guns displayed
  in any one place.
The Nixon Library
  Exhibit 119 of this museum is the chrome-plated Colt .45 with wooden handle
  and seven silver bullets that Elvis gave to Nixon during his famous visit to the
  White House.

18001 Yorba Linda Boulevard
Yorba Linda, California 92886-3949
(714) 993-3393
http://www.nixonfoundation.org
http://www.nixonlibrary.org

Sierra Sid's Auto Truck Plaza
Formerly known as "Guns of Elvis," this truck-stop museum contains three of Elvis' guns:
Colt .38 with a quick-draw holster
Ruger Blackhawk.44 Magnum with ivory grip
Gold-engraved Smith & Wesson .38 Special with a two-inch barrel
200 North McCarren Boulevard
Interstate 80, Exit 19
Sparks, Nevada 89431
(702) 359-0550
http://www.nwlink.com/~timelvis/elvisgun.html

Karl E. Lindroos Collection
This is one of the largest privately owned collections of Elvis memorabilia in the world. He has several of Elvis' guns including:
Smith & Wesson .38: Elvis shot his yellow Pantera with this gun.
Derringer .22-caliber: One of the boot guns.
201 East Ocean Avenue, Suite 7
Lantana, Florida 33462
(561) 588-0095
E-mail: k.lindroos@elvis-tcb.com
http://www.elvis-tcb.com

Mike McGregor Custom Jewelry & Leatherwork
A much-beloved friend of Elvis, Mike McGregor passed away in early 1999. His store and museum will be kept open by his wife and son. Some of Elvis' guns are displayed in their Elvis Memorabilia Collection Gallery.
793 Highway 7 South
Oxford, Mississippi 38655
(662) 234-6970

Promote Gun Safety

Elvis had a few near misses that illustrated the wrong way to handle a gun. Before handling any gun get proper safety training and a Basic Firearms Safety Certificate. Most shooting ranges offer courses as do local NRA chapters. They also sell handbooks and videos on safety and instruction. For information on NRA safety courses contact their Training Department at:
National Rifle Association of America

11250 Waples Mill Road
Fairfax, Virginia 22030
(703) 267-1430
(800) 672-2582
http://www.nra.org.

Buy One of Elvis' Guns

An Elvis gun is a highly coveted collectible. They can be found through auctions and private collectors. Special rules apply to the sale of firearms, so check with your local authorities. See "Elvis in Cyberspace" for a list of auction sites on the internet.
Butterfield & Butterfield
Auction house that has sold Elvis' guns and other memorabilia in the past.
Arms and Armor Department
220 San Bruno Avenue
San Francisco, California 94103
(415) 861-7500 ext. 550

Buy a Gun at the Tupelo Hardware Store

Okay, the Tupelo Hardware Store no longer sells guns—but if they ever do again, go and get the gun Elvis had wanted. And don't let your mother talk you out of it.

Buy a Replica of an Elvis Gun

Check "The Presley Arsenal" for suggestions. You can buy a similar gun and then have it customized by a gunsmith like Elvis did. It doesn't even have to be a real gun; it could be a gun-shaped cigarette lighter.

Wear a Holster

Keep your wallet or Walkman in it; it's a look. Elvis often used a custom-made white leather holster. For cowhide holsters and accessories contact:
Kramer Handgun Leather, Inc.
P.O. Box 112154, Dept. GAH
Tacoma, Washington 98411
(800) 510-2666
http://www.kramerleather.com

Visit a Gun Range

A professional licensed gun range is the safest place to do some shooting and you'll probably have many different guns to choose from. Consult the Presley Arsenal list and choose a gun like one of Elvis'. For even more fun create customized targets.

A target made from the likeness of the late Albert Goldman makes a satisfyingly disrespectful target for Elvis fans

Illustration by Finnbarr Winterson

Go Skeet Shooting

Use Michael Jackson records or other appropriate disc-shaped objects.

How to Shoot a Television

Shooting a television set, for that matter shooting anything indoors, is a potentially dangerous activity. Elvis sometimes took big chances. You shouldn't. Shooting a television is a very Elvis thing to do and a lot of fans would get a big kick out of it. But it should only be done with the right precautions.

Contact a Shooting Range

Find a shooting range near you. Tell the manager of the shooting range what you'd like to do. The manager is very possibly already an Elvis fan and will understand.

Find a Dispensible Television

If you're planning to upgrade to a better television, then this is a great way to get rid of your old set. Televisions are thrown out on a regular basis so be on the lookout for one. Your local Salvation Army is another great source of televisions, most of them being the proper 1960s to 1970s vintage. An RCA 2000 console would be ideal. If the set works, try and hook it up to a VCR. Or you can play a tape of Robert Goulet singing to enhance your shooting experience.

Courtesy of Butterfield & Butterfield

Choose Your Gun

Avoid shotguns and rifles; this is strictly a handgun thing. Elvis was known to favor a turquoise-handled Colt .45 automatic or a .22 Savage for "telecide."

An RCA 2000 once owned by Elvis

Make It a Fan Club Fund-raiser

You can raffle off tickets to see who gets to shoot the television. Give the proceeds to a gun-related charity, like a bulletproof vest fund for your local police department.

Use a Dart Gun

Keep a dart gun near your television. If anything displeases you, you know what to do. Not as much fun as a real gun, but it won't be as dangerous or as costly.

Use Your Remote Control

Every time you turn off your television just shout out *"Bang!"*

Try the Water Pistol Alternative

Elvis also liked water pistols. They're much safer, unless of course you shoot your television with one.

Play War

Elvis used to stage twice-yearly epic fireworks battles. He and his entourage would put on helmets, goggles, leather jackets, and gloves and then attack each other in a firefight until they ran out of ammo. It is exactly what you shouldn't do with fireworks, but that may be why it appealed to Elvis.

Buy Fireworks Where Elvis Bought His

Atomic Fireworks
West Memphis, Arkansas
(870) 735-1753

Play Paintball

It didn't really exist in an organized way during Elvis' time, but you know he would have just loved it. It's a very Elvis kind of game.

Subscribe to Gun Magazines

It will scare your mailman and maybe that's a good thing. There are many to choose from, here's one:
Handguns
P.O. Box 56195
Boulder, Colorado 80322
(800) 800-4486
(303) 678-0354

ELVIS AND
LAW ENFORCEMENT

When Elvis was chosen by the United States Jaycees as one of the Ten Outstanding Young Men in America in 1970, he considered it a tremendous honor and source of pride. He was questioned by the selection committee at a closed-door meeting before the presentation as to what other career path he might have chosen if he hadn't become an entertainer. Elvis said he probably would have gone into law enforcement. It's irresistible to imagine Officer Elvis pulling you over for speeding.

Elvis was a hard-core cop buff his whole life. One of the things you'll start to notice when you look at photos of Elvis in public at any point in his career is that somewhere in so many of the photos there are police nearby. Quite often the only thing separating Elvis from a mob of clawing fans was that "thin blue line." Elvis came to depend on a police presence in his life and it was only natural that he would form an affinity with the people protecting him. He developed close relationships and made friends with law enforcement officers all over the country.

He was on especially good terms with the police in Memphis. Captain Bill Woodward of the Memphis Police Department became a friend and mentor to the young Elvis. When Elvis was on army leave immediately after the death of his mother, the Tennessee Highway Patrol sent a police helicopter to Graceland to give him flying lessons to try and cheer him up. For the rest

A pin given to Elvis by some of his law enforcement pals

Elvis being protected by the boys in blue

From the collection of Bob Klein

of his life he would often drop in around the holidays to visit his pals at various police stations.

On September 21, 1964, Shelby County (Tennessee) Chief Deputy Sheriff Bill Morris gave Elvis an honorary badge and title. True to form, Elvis had the badge set with rubies and diamonds. He became an avid collector of police credentials, badges, and paraphernalia. Six years later, on October 9, 1970, no longer satisfied with honorary titles, Elvis persuaded Shelby County Sheriff Roy Nixon to commission him as a special deputy with full powers. He was promoted to the rank of Memphis Police Captain on February 10, 1976. Although Elvis was genuinely enthralled by the whole mystique of police work, there was a pragmatic side to all this as well. The police credentials enabled Elvis to carry and transport his firearms legally, which was something he saw as necessary for the protection of himself and his family.

In addition to Memphis, Elvis had particularly close ties to the Los Angeles, Denver, and Palm Springs police departments. Wherever he went Elvis would be offered honorary badges by the local police, but he always tried to finagle a real one. He'd ask to be put on the force for a salary of a dollar a year and even occasionally accompanied some of his cop buddies on patrol. He once contributed $7,000 to the LAPD police community relations program to buy special flak jackets for explosive-sniffing dogs, uniforms for the police marching band, and toys for needy children. He received a gold commissioner's badge from Chief Edward Davis in appreciation.

One of his Los Angeles police friends, LAPD narcotics officer John O'Gradey, introduced him to Paul Frees, an actor who specialized in voice-overs—the Pillsbury Doughboy and Captain Crunch being two of his creations. O'Gradey revealed to Elvis that Frees also worked as an undercover federal narcotics agent. When

From the collection of Bob Klein

Backstage with his guardians

Elvis saw Free's Bureau of Narcotics and Dangerous Drugs badge, it started him on an obsessive quest to acquire that badge for himself. That quest would eventually lead him on one of his most notorious adventures to the highest office of the land.

On December 19, 1970, Elvis left Graceland by himself and traveled on American Airlines under the pseudonym John Carpenter. After spending a few hours in Washington, D.C., he flew on to Los Angeles where he enlisted Memphis Mafia member Jerry Schilling as a participant in his grand mysterious scheme. While in flight from Los Angeles back to Washington, he penned a letter to President Nixon proclaiming his patriotism and requesting a meeting. After dropping the letter off with a stunned guard at the visitor's gate of the White House, Elvis checked into the Washington Hotel using the alias Colonel Jon Burrows. He met with Deputy Director John Finlator of the Bureau of Narcotics and Dangerous Drugs who refused his request for the federal agent badge. His disappointment changed to euphoria when he received the news that the White House had called and the meeting with Nixon was arranged.

Accompanied by Jerry Schilling and Sonny West, who had been summoned to Washington as extra security, Elvis met with Nixon in the Oval Office. After small talk about family and fashion, they commiserated about the drug problem facing the nation and Elvis made an offer to help in any way he could. He showed Nixon photos of Priscilla and Lisa Marie and displayed part of his col-

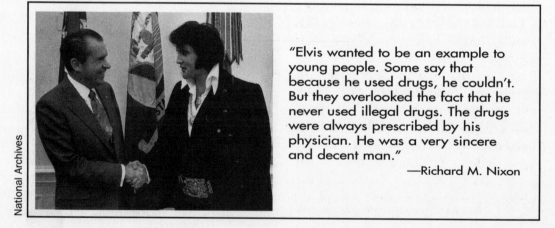

"Elvis wanted to be an example to young people. Some say that because he used drugs, he couldn't. But they overlooked the fact that he never used illegal drugs. The drugs were always prescribed by his physician. He was a very sincere and decent man."

—Richard M. Nixon

From the collection of Bob Klein

lection of badges. With Nixon firmly under the influence of the famous Presley charm, Elvis made his request for the BDNN badge he wanted. Nixon gave his permission and made the arrangements. Elvis was so thrilled to get his new badge, he spontaneously hugged Nixon. Although the famous meeting was well documented in a book by presidential aide Egil "Bud" Krogh, it's a shame that the infamous Nixon taping system was not yet operational. The tape of the Nixon–Presley meeting would be a wildly sought-after bootleg recording among Elvis fans and students of presidential history. The photos from their historic meeting are by far the most requested items from the National Archives. Elvis' BNDD badge was one of his most prized possessions and he carried it with him the rest of his life.

On December 30 he was back in Washington, this time accompanied by a group of eight others including former sheriff Bill Morris. He visited the National Sheriff's Association and toured FBI headquarters. He had hoped to meet with J. Edgar Hoover but was informed that the FBI head was out of town. Elvis wanted to volunteer his services to the Bureau as an undercover agent. In an attempt to impress the FBI agents he met with, he referred to Hoover as "the greatest living American" and claimed to have read two of Hoover's books about the Communist menace. (Elvis *really* wanted that badge!)

Elvis identified with his "fellow officers" so much that he participated in some of their rituals and traditions, such as attending the funeral of a fallen comrade. In Denver in January 1976, Elvis attended the funeral of

Sandi Miller

While touring, Elvis would go out of his way to meet with police officers and talk shop

Sandi Miller

Elvis posing backstage with the man

Detective Eugene Kennedy, the brother of Denver Vice Squad Captain Jerry Kennedy, one of Elvis' friends on the force. Out of respect, Elvis wore a Denver police captain's full dress uniform.

The Denver funeral wasn't the only time he incorporated police paraphernalia into his wardrobe. His custom-jeweled badges would sometimes be worn as part of one of his elaborate belt buckles. And his DEA jumpsuit was his favorite outfit while flying on the Lisa Marie. At one point in his life he carried a police flashlight almost everywhere he went. As the best man at Sonny West's wedding, Elvis had to be talked out of carrying the 15-inch flashlight up to the altar.

Elvis admired and respected police and the police admired and respected him in return. When Elvis drove out of the Graceland gates, it would be reported on the Memphis police radio and he'd be tracked through the city. A patrol car was never far away in case the King might need help. When you look at the photos of Elvis' funeral, you notice the police again holding the crowds back one last time as the hearse containing Elvis' body passes them by. Only this time, in these photos, all the police are saluting.

Commercial Appeal

Elvis "on the job" at the scene of a traffic accident   March 27, 1976

Because of the connection between Elvis and law enforcement, he still holds a special place in the hearts of many police. A lot of police officers are Elvis fans and a few have even become impersonators. Elvis' admiration and support of the police is often emulated by Elvis' fans. Elvis knew it's a good thing to be friends with Johnny Law. As Elvis fans, we think it's a good tradition to continue.

ESSENTIAL ELVISOLOGY

Elvis' Lawyers
Ed Hookstratten
Charles Davis

Some of Elvis' Law Enforcement Titles
Honorary Deputy Sheriff, Shelby County ID#39
Deputy Sheriff, Shelby County
Honorary Policeman, Monroe, Louisiana
Special Deputy Sheriff, Shelby County, Badge 6, ID#293
Lieutenant, Denver Police Department
Investigator, Colorado Organized Crime Strike Force
Captain, Memphis Police Department
Federal Narcotics Officer
Deputy U.S. Marshall

Some of Elvis' Police Friends
Edward M. Davis, LAPD chief
Bill Morris, Shelby County sheriff
Roy W. Nixon, Shelby County sheriff
Guy Harris, Tupelo police sergeant
Bill Mitchell, Lee County sheriff
Jack Kelly, former head of the Los Angeles Office of the Federal Drug Enforcement Agency
John O'Gradey, former LAPD narcotics detective
Ron Pietrefaso, Denver police detective
Jerry Kennedy, Denver vice squad captain
Dr. Gerald Starky, Denver police physician
Dick Grob, former Palm Springs police officer
Sam Thompson, circuit court judge
Fred Woodward, Memphis police captain

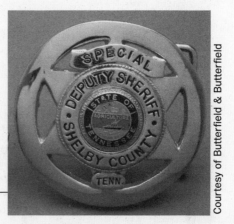

Courtesy of Butterfield & Butterfield

Elvis' special deputy badge belt buckle

The Text of Elvis' Letter to Nixon

Dear Mr. President,

First I would like to introduce myself. I am Elvis Presley and admire you and have great respect for your office. I talked to Vice President Agnew in Palm Springs three weeks ago and expressed my concern for our country. The drug culture, the hippie demonstrations, the SDS, Black Panthers, etc. do not consider me as their enemy or as they call it the establishment. I call it America and I love it. Sir, I can and will be of any service to help the country out. I have no concern or motives other than helping the country out. So I wish not to be given a title or an appointed position. I can and will do more good if I were made a federal agent at large, and I will help out by doing it my way through my connections with people of all ages. First and foremost I am an entertainer, but all I need is the federal credentials. I am on the plane with Senator George Murphy and we have been discussing the problems that our country is faced with. So I am staying at the Washington Hotel room 505-506-507. I have two men who work with me by the name of Jerry Schilling and Sonny West. I am registered under the name of Jon Burrows. I will be here for as long as it takes to get the credentials of a Federal Agent. I have done an in-depth study of drug abuse and communist brainwashing techniques and I am right in the middle of the whole thing where I can and will do the most good. I am glad to help just so long as it is kept very private. You can have your staff or whomever call on me anytime today, tonight or tomorrow. I was nominated this coming year one of America's ten most outstanding young men. That will be in January 18 in my hometown of Memphis, Tenn. I am sending you the short autobiography about myself so you can better understand their approval. I would love to meet you just to say hello if you're not to [sic] busy.

Respectfully,
Elvis Presley

P.S. I believe that you Sir were one of the top ten outstanding men of America also. I have a personal gift for you also which I would like to present to you and you can accept it or I will keep it for you until you can take it.

Elvis' handwritten letter to President Nixon on American Airlines stationery

YOUR ELVIS EDUCATION

Books
The Day Elvis Met Nixon
  Egil "Bud" Krogh
Elvis, What Happened?
  Red West, Sonny West, and Dave Hebler as told to Steve Dunleavy
Elvis Presley, Richard Nixon and the American Dream
  Connie Kirchberg and Marc Hendrickx
Elvis: Top Secret: The Untold Story of Elvis' Secret FBI Files
  Earl Greenwood and Kathleen Tracy
Elvis: The Secret Files
  John Parker
O'Gradey: The Life and Times of Hollywood's No.1 Private Eye
  John O'Gradey and Nolan Davis
The Elvis Conspiracy?
  Dick Grob
The Drugged Nation
  John Finlator
Masters of Deceit: A Study of Communism
  J. Edgar Hoover
J. Edgar Hoover on Communism
  J. Edgar Hoover

Videos
Elvis and Nixon, HBO   *All the King's Men*

Web Sites
http://www.nara.gov/exhall/nixonelvis/   http://www.fbi.gov
  nixmain.html   Access the complete FBI file on Elvis
  The Nixon/Elvis photos   http://www.fbifile.com
ftp://sunsite.unc.edu/pub/   How to obtain your own FBI files
  multimedia/pictures/presidential/
  Photo of Elvis and Nixon gift

THE ELVIS AND YOU EXPERIENCE

Visit Related Museums and Exhibitions
Graceland
Quite a few of Elvis' badges and police credentials are on display in the trophy room.

Memphis Police Substation

This informal Memphis law enforcement museum displays some Elvis police memorabilia. It's part of a working police station so it's open 24 hours a day.
159 Beale Street
Memphis, Tennessee 38103
(901) 525-9800

The Nixon Library

This museum has several items commemorating the famous meeting of Elvis and Nixon.
18001 Yorba Linda Boulevard
Yorba Linda, California 92886-3949
(714) 993-3393
http://www.nixonfoundation.org
http://www.nixonlibrary.org

Become a Cop

It was Elvis' second choice as a career. The job comes with good benefits, the respect of your fellow citizens, and a collection of cool cop stuff that Elvis would have loved.

Join the Auxiliary Police

Get cool cop stuff without quite the same commitment.

Make Friends with a Cop

It's always a good policy to be on the right side of the law and Elvis knew it.

Attend Law Enforcement Conventions

Elvis sometimes attended these conventions. It's the best way to meet fellow cop buffs and find cop collectibles.

Re-create Elvis' Trip to Washington

Fly to Washington

Book your flight on American Airlines like Elvis did. (800) 433-7300. You're no longer permitted to fly under an alias, but feel free to introduce yourself as Dr. John Carpenter (Elvis' alias) to anyone you meet. While on the plane, write a letter to the

Elvis posing near one of his Bel Air homes with a Los Angeles police officer patrolling the area

Sandi Miller

President on airline stationery requesting a meeting. Offer to help with some national problem that is close to your heart.

Visit the White House and Drop Off Your Own Letter to the President

Register at the Hotel Washington

515 15th Street, N.W.
Washington, DC 20004
(202) 638-5900
Check into the hotel under the name Jon Burrows, the alias Elvis used. Stay in room 505, 506, or 507. The hotel is just a block away from the White House but Elvis, of course, took a Lincoln limo to get there. Wait here for your reply from the President. Don't be too surprised if you don't hear back; after all, only Elvis could pull something like this off.

Visit the Bureau of Narcotics and Dangerous Drugs

Now called the Drug Enforcement Administration
The DEA Museum
700 Army Navy Drive
Arlington Virginia
Washington, DC 20537
(202) 307-3463

Visit FBI Headquarters

Federal Bureau of Investigation
Washington Metropolitan Field Office
601 4th Street, N.W.
Washington, DC 20535-0002
(202) 278-2000
http://www.fbi.gov/homepage.htm

Visit the National Law Enforcement Association

888 16th Street, N.W.
Washington, DC 20006
(202) 835-8020
http://www.sheriffs.org/

"The only possibility in the United States for a humane society would be a revolution with Elvis Presley as leader."
—Phil Ochs, singer and composer

National Archives

Get a Copy of the Nixon-Elvis Photos

These are the most requested photos in the National Archives. 'Nuff said. The Nixon Project
National Archives
(301) 713-6950
http://www.nara.gov/exhall/nixonelvis/nixmain.html

Get a Copy of Elvis' FBI Files

Contact this office and request Elvis' files:
Federal Bureau of Investigation
Records Management Division/U.S. Department of Justice
Freedom of Information—Privacy Acts Section
Washington, DC 10535
Subject requested: Elvis Aron Presley
Freedom of Information Act
(Title 5, U.S. Code, Section 552)

Buy a Retired Police Car

Every police force sells off their old cars as they replace them with new ones. Although the insignias are removed, they still retain that cop feel and sometimes you can get a real bargain.

Start Your Own Police Paraphernalia Collection

Some police products can only legally be sold to actual police, so stay within the law. Here are some places to order badges and patches and other cop stuff.
NIC Law Enforcement Supply Catalog
   500 Flournoy Lucas Road, Bldg. #3-I
   P.O. Box 5950
   Shreveport, Louisiana 71135
   (888) 642-0007
Gulf States Distributors
   6000-A E. Shirley Lane
   Montgomery, Alabama 36117
   (800) 223-7869
   (334) 271-2010
   Fax: (334) 279-9267

Courtesy of Butterfield & Butterfield

Elvis' Mag-Lite police flashlight, Memphis police dress uniform vest, and assorted badges

Subscribe to Police and Police Buff Magazines
There are a lot of specialized magazines not only for actual cops but for aficionados of law enforcement as well. Look for the following magazines at your newsstand:
The Police Marksman
American Police Beat
Law Enforcement Product News

Carry a Police Flashlight
Elvis occasionally carried a black metal Kel-Light Industries 15-inch police flashlight almost as a fashion accessory. In some cases it may seem very practical (at night) and in some cases it may seem very peculiar (at a wedding).

Get a Flashing Emergency Light for Your Car
Elvis loved the blue magnetic police lights that can instantly turn any car into a more *Starsky and Hutch* experience.

Get a Police Scanner
Elvis used to listen to his police radio to find out where the action was and to check up on his friends on the force. It's very entertaining. It's like an audio-only version of the ultimate cop-buff TV series *Cops*.

Make a Contribution to Your Local Police Department
Most police forces will gladly accept donations to buy bulletproof vests, to purchase and train K-9 officers, for police widow and orphan funds, or for community programs. Make your donation in Elvis' name. Elvis often donated to the Fraternal Order of Police and other police charities.

Make a Contribution to Police K-9 Corps
Two things Elvis loved were animals and police. This charity combines both of those interests by raising and training K-9 police dogs and providing them to police forces.
North American Police Work Dog Association
Jim Watson, NAPWDA Secretary
4222 Manchester Avenue

Elvis flashes his credentials as he poses with his "fellow officers"

Perry, Ohio 44081
(888) 4CANINE
Fax: (440) 259-3170

Get a Jailhouse Rock Shirt

Although Elvis always was on the right side of the law, one of his more memorable movie roles was as a jailbird. Vince Everett, prisoner #6240, was Elvis' character in *Jailhouse Rock*. You can buy a prison denim work shirt with his name and serial number at the Graceland shops, from their catalog, or from Vroom Catalog at (888) 762-5111.

"I've also tried to help the guys in law enforcement around the country. They're on the front lines."
—Elvis Presley

From the collection of Bob Klein

ELVIS AND
THE MARTIAL ARTS

O ne of Elvis' great obsessions was his passion for karate. By his own admission his love of karate was second only to his love of music. From the moment he was introduced to it during his military service, he maintained an unflagging interest in studying and promoting the martial arts. The elaborate katas or karate routines that he incorporated into his stage shows have left us with some of the most memorable images we have of Elvis. It was a big part of who he was and how he saw himself. Elvis was a real-life superhero and a superhero needs super powers.

Elvis had good reason to learn how to defend himself. As a student at Humes High School he was sometimes picked on because of his unusual looks and style. One version of Elvis lore maintains that his friendship with Red West, schoolmate and future member of the Memphis Mafia, started when Red came to his defense during one of these altercations.

Early in his career, when Elvis, Scotty, and Bill were touring the country, there were many times when a jealous boyfriend or envious tough guy tried to challenge the young King. On October 18, 1956, Elvis got into a fistfight with two attendants at a Memphis gas station after one of them slapped him in the back of the head. Elvis decked

Elvis performing a karate demonstration while on stage in Las Vegas 1974

From the collection of Sandi Miller

Elvis faces his gas station adversaries in a Memphis city court on October 19, 1956

his assailant, who then pulled a knife on him. Police arrived in time to break it up, charging all three men with assault and battery and disorderly conduct. Elvis was acquitted in court the next day, but the incident no doubt left a lasting impression on him.

While undergoing basic training at Fort Hood, Texas, Elvis witnessed a judo or jujitsu demonstration that planted the seed of his lifelong obsession. Later, while stationed in Germany, he began studying under Juergen Seydel, an expert in shotokan karate. Rex Mansfield, another soldier and fellow Memphian, was a frequent sparring partner.

Karate was such a passion for Elvis that during one of his army leaves to Paris he and his entourage, now including Juergen Seydel, visited Club Yoseiken, a karate dojo run by Tetsuji Murakami. He trained toward his brown belt with Master Tetsuji for four days.

Elvis received his first-degree black belt on March 21, 1960, from Hank Slamansky, an ex-marine. Slamansky taught the martial art known as chito-ryu. At the time, Elvis was one of only about 100 Americans who held a black-belt title. That same year, during a demonstration at the Beverly Wilshire Hotel in Los Angeles, Elvis met Ed Parker, a Hawaiian kenpo karate instructor. Parker would become one of Elvis' instructors and bodyguards in the seventies and would play an important role in Elvis' personal life as well.

Elvis was a pioneer in exposing karate to a wider audience. Since the Elvis movie formula required the obligatory fight scene, Elvis made a point of incorporating the then little-known art into his films. Not since James Cagney in *Blood on the Sun* were martial arts seen by an American audience. In the film *Roustabout*, for example, three bullies accost Elvis. After dispatching two of them with some martial art moves, the third guy backs off as if Elvis has magic powers. "That's

Elvis' Kenpo karate necklace

The teacher and the student, Ed Parker and Elvis

karate!" the thug says as he retreats. To prepare for his role as a boxer in *Kid Galahad,* he trained with Mush Callahan, former world junior welter-weight boxing champion who said he thought Elvis had the talent to fight professionally. On the set of his films Elvis often entertained the crew by breaking boards and giving demonstrations.

Karate eventually became part of Elvis' live performances as well. In the "'68 Comeback Special," the "Big Boss Man" sequence for the first time combined karate and dance. From that point on, Elvis integrated karate katas into his stage shows in Las Vegas and subsequent tours. The stage karate was mostly kenpo, a flamboyant style that incorporated elaborate rotational hand techniques taught to him by Ed Parker, then working as one of his bodyguards. Elvis even affixed a kenpo logo to one of his favorite guitars to help promote awareness of the martial art. People all over the world were exposed to kenpo because of the thousands of photos of Elvis with that guitar on stage. During one performance in Las Vegas he did a karate exhibition for close to 20 minutes running. Summoned on stage during a Tom Jones show, instead of singing he performed a flamboyant karate demonstration to the delight of Tom's fans.

At another Vegas performance Elvis got to demonstrate some actual sparring. On February 18, 1973, four men jumped on stage and rushed Elvis. A melee broke out among the men and security with Elvis himself knocking one of the men off the stage into the audience where he smashed a table. Elvis told the audience, "I'm sorry ladies and gentleman … I'm sorry I didn't break his goddamned neck is what I'm sorry about! If he wants to shake my hand, that's fine. If he wants to get tough, I'll whoop his ass!" The audience gave Elvis a lengthy and exuberant standing ovation.

Elvis on the set of *Kid Galahad*

Sandi Miller

Elvis deplaning from the *Lisa Marie* while wearing his karate *gi*

Elvis financed the American Karate Team's tour of Europe in 1974 and purchased each fighter's custom-made red, white, and blue *gi* or uniform. Perhaps his most ambitious attempt at promoting the martial arts was his involvement in the never-completed film project *The New Gladiators*. The documentary film was conceived by George Waite, a black belt student of Ed Parker's. Elvis offered full financial backing and planned to narrate and appear in the film. He wrote a 10-page outline for the film in which he sums up his karate philosophy: "The real meaning of karate, helping a person help himself." Two 20-minute reels of film were shot of Elvis demonstrating his karate expertise. A few minutes of this footage can be seen in *This Is Elvis*, the documentary made after Elvis' death.

Elvis encouraged his inner circle to study martial arts. He even persuaded Priscilla to study and she eventually attained green belt status. A pre-movie-star Chuck Norris was one of her instructors. An even more significant instructor in Priscilla's training was Mike Stone, an international grand champion introduced to the Presleys by Ed Parker during a karate tournament in Hawaii. Ironically, Priscilla and Stone became lovers and their romance was one of the factors that led to Priscilla's divorce from Elvis.

Red West became so involved in the sport he even opened his own school, the Tennessee Karate Institute. Elvis was featured in an ad for the school claiming TKI to be the place where he trained while in Memphis. Elvis did train there on occasion, at one point taking an intensive three week refresher course with Bill "Superfoot" Wallace. But his main instructor in Memphis was a Korean tae kwon do master named Kang Rhee. Kang Rhee taught a system called pasaryu, meaning "all systems into one."

Kang Rhee became one of the more important instructors toward the end of Elvis' life,

Photo courtesy of Kang Rhee

Master Kang Rhee with Elvis at Kang Rhee's dojo in Memphis

Prettiest men alive: Elvis with Muhammad Ali in Las Vegas. Ali is wearing a Bill Belew-designed robe with "People's Champion" embroidered across the back, which was a gift from Elvis.

From the collection of Bob Klein

occasionally touring with him and teaching other members of Elvis' entourage. Kang Rhee and Elvis became good friends. Together they designed the karate emblem worn by Elvis on his *gi* and it was Kang Rhee who gave Elvis the karate name "Tiger Man." According to Master Rhee, Elvis taught him more than he taught Elvis. He still teaches in Memphis and Elvis fans often visit his dojo.

In Madison, Wisconsin, on June 24, 1977, just weeks before he died, Elvis was being driven from the airport to his hotel when he saw two men ganging up on a service station attendant. He ordered his driver to stop and jumped out of the car to confront the two attackers. Elvis assumed a menacing karate stance and said he would take on both men. His presence was enough to avert the fight; the situation ended without incident and everyone even posed for photos together. But if things had gone differently, Elvis knew he could take care of himself. He'd had more than 20 years of martial arts training since his last fight in a gas station.

ESSENTIAL ELVISOLOGY

Karate Names

Tiger: Elvis	Eagle: Sonny West
Ox: Kang Rhee	Cobra: Charlie Hodge
Cougar: Jerry Schilling	Lion: Joe Esposito
Dragon: Red West	Bull: Lamar Fike

Elvis Movies with Martial Arts Sequences

GI Blues	*Follow that Dream*
Wild in the Country	*Kid Galahad*
Blue Hawaii	*Roustabout*

Keith Alverson

Elvis, the tiger man, in tiger jumpsuit with Kenpo logo on his guitar

Elvis signing an autograph; note the Kenpo patch on his jacket

Sandi Miller

Harum Scarum   *Elvis: That's the Way It Is*
Elvis on Tour   *This Is Elvis*

The Karate Movie Treatment

Elvis wrote a brief treatment to convey his vision of the Karate film he wanted to produce and star in. Here's an excerpt from his ten-page handwritten screenplay:

"Ending of Picture—on a remote hill, the camera is on close up of Elvis as he stands in fighting stance. The camera zooms back as he does a middle punch with a key up and we see what looks like every Karate instructor in the world doing the moves with him. He then does the Lord's Prayer in Indian sign language as a soft wind gently blows around him. The picture ends with 'The Beginning' written across the screen."

Elvis' Karate Titles

8th degree black belt—Pasaryu Karate, Tae Kwon Do
8th degree black belt—Kenpo

The TCB Oath

Elvis wrote this on a torn envelope while flying on his private plane, the *Lisa Marie*.

"More self-respect, more respect for fellow man. Respect for fellow students and instructors. Respect for all styles and techniques. Body conditioning, mental conditioning, meditation for calming and stilling of the mind and body. Sharpen your skills, increase mental awareness for all those who might choose a new outlook and personal philosophy. Freedom from constipation. TCB TECHNIQUE All techniques into one. Elvis Presley, 8th applying all techniques into one."

Elvis Customized *Gi*

Designed by Bill Belew, it was a Tokado brand *gi* modified by the IC Costume Company, Hollywood, California.

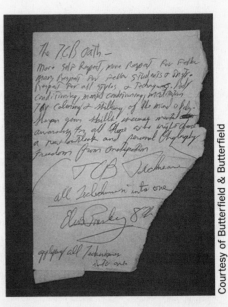
Courtesy of Butterfield & Butterfield

The TCB Karate Patch

Designed by Elvis and Kang Rhee at the Las Vegas Hilton in 1973, the TCB patch stands for taking care of business quickly though faith, spirit, discipline, and endurance. The red ball represents the earth. The seven stars represent the universe. The lightning bolt represents speed and efficiency. Inside the red ball is the oriental character for endurance. It means that you can channel all the energies of the universe by having faith, spirit, discipline, and endurance.

Courtesy of Kang Rhee

The Crown Fist Patch

"The fist represents the martial arts, the crown represents champions, and the map of the U.S. represents the world as we know it." —Kang Rhee

The Martial Arts Elvis Studied

Shotokan
Chito-Ryu
Kenpo
Pasaryu—a combination of karate, kung fu, and tae kwan do.

Karate Instructors

Juergen Seydel—in Germany
Tetsuji Murakami—in Paris for four days at Club Yoseiken
Hank Slamansky—former U.S. Marine, awarded Elvis his first Black Belt
Ed Parker—father of American Kenpo
Bill Wallace—at the Tennessee Karate Institute
Al Holcomb—in Memphis
Wayne Carmen—in Memphis
Kang Rhee—in Memphis

Favorite Sparring Partners

The Memphis Mafia

Priscilla's Instructors

Kang Rhee—in Memphis
Chuck Norris—in Los Angeles
Mike Stone—in Los Angeles

Courtesy of Kang Rhee

Elvis sparring with a fan in
Los Angeles

Sandi Miller

YOUR ELVIS EDUCATION

Books

Elvis' Karate Legacy
  Wayne Carmen
*Karate—The Art of "Empty Hands
Fighting"*
  Hidetka Nishyama and Richard C.
  Brown
Elvis and Me
  Priscilla Presley
Elvis the Soldier
  Rex Mansfield
Inside Elvis
  Ed Parker
Infinite Insights of Kenpo (Volumes I to V)
  Ed Parker
The Zen of Kenpo
  Ed Parker
The Original Martial Arts Encyclopedia: Tradition, History, Pioneers
  John Corcoran and Emil Farkas with Stuart Sobel
Elvis and Bobbie
  Linda Jackson and Vera Jane Goodin

Video

The New Gladiators
Elvis: The Karate Years

Web Sites

http://www.uga/edu/cuda/tigerman.html
  Elvis and the martial arts; Shane
  Peterson's site
http://www.stanford.edu/group/
  kenpo-faq.html
  Kenpo FAQ Site

http://www.elvis.com.au/tcb/night.htm
  "Night Fever In Vegas;" Elvis delivered a lengthy monologue on karate during this show.
http://www.wushuboy.com/wv/fame/htm
  International Karate and Kickboxing Hall of Fame

THE ELVIS AND YOU EXPERIENCE

Attend Karate Tournaments and Exhibitions

It's a good way to get exposed to the world of the martial arts that Elvis loved so much without having to break a sweat or take a blow. Contact the dojo nearest you for information about local tournaments. Some years there have been Elvis Presley Karate Tournaments as part of Tribute Week in Memphis.

Study Karate

Elvis said at several concerts that just about anybody could take up karate in one form or another. So, gain some insight into Elvis while getting excellent exercise for both body and mind. You don't have to commit yourself to getting a black belt; most schools offer special introductory classes. Try to sample all the different forms that Elvis studied and then see which style most suits you. Your local phone book should have many listings for karate schools, or dojos. For more information or to find a dojo near you that teaches one of the disciplines Elvis studied, you can contact these organizations:

Sandi Miller

World Tae Kwon Do Federation
   635 Yuksamdong,Kangnamku
   Seoul 135-080, Korea
   (822) 566-2505 or 557-5446
   Fax: (822) 553.4728
   E-mail: wtf@unitel.co.Kr
United Kenpo Karate Association
   P.O. Box 5225
   Babylon, New York 11707
   (516) 669-7132
   http://www.upcyber.com/up/ukka
Worldwide Kenpo Karate Association
   1400 B Riesterstown Road
   Pikesville, Maryland 21203
International Chito-Ryu Karate Federation
   Chito Ryu Hombu Dojo
   Tsuboi 1119-5
   Kurokami-machi
   Kumamoto, Japan 860-0861
   (96) 343-1723
   Fax: (96) 346-1649
   http://www.chebuctos.ns.ca/~ab333/cnet/world-dojo.html

United States Chito-Ryu Karate Federation
Yoseikan So-Honbu
22 Martin Street
Covington, Kentucky 41011
(606) 291-7232
E-Mail: info@chito-ryu.com
http://www.chito-ryu.com/ welcome.html

The Best Elvis-Related Dojo

Kang Rhee Institute

For fans of Elvis and the martial arts there could be no better instructor in the world than Kang Rhee. Kang Rhee still teaches in Memphis and this man of honor welcomes Elvis fans to his dojo, which has moved from its original downtown location to a mall in the suburbs. When you meet him in person you see he's aged imperceptibly since the photos of him and Elvis that hang on the wall were taken more than 25 years ago. Master Rhee is happy to meet with fans, pose for photos, and discuss Elvis. You can buy Elvis karate photos, or one of the famous TCB patches. He also offers instructional books and videos on Pasaryu, the martial art form he created and taught to Elvis.

If you're up to it, you should schedule a class with the master himself. Kang Rhee is one of the dwindling direct links between the fan and Elvis. It's a thrill to study from the master who taught the King even if it's only for one class. In addition to karate, Master Rhee also teaches taekuk, a combination of tai chi, yoga, and hang sun. It's a much gentler form of exercise and a great way to relieve all that stress of shopping for Elvis souvenirs. Before you go to the dojo, always phone ahead for the best time to visit and to make an appointment.

Kang Rhee Institute
706 North Germantown Parkway
Cordova, Tennessee 38108
(901) 757-5000
Fax: (901) 757-5040
E-mail: kchoi@memphis.edu
For a catalog and to order
merchandise:
Kang Rhee
P.O. Box 2466
Cordova, Tennessee 38088

Kang Rhee

John O'Hara

Order a Custom Elvis *Gi*

Have a *gi* made like Elvis'. Even if you don't study martial arts, you can just wear it around the house. Elvis' *gi*, designed by his costume designer Bill Belew, was a Tokiado brand purchased at Nozawa Martial Arts Supply Company, Los Angeles, and modified by the I. C. Costume Company of Hollywood, California. Elvis also wore a Bear Brand black *gi* made by Sampson Trade Manufacturing, Seoul, Korea.

Where Elvis Got His Martial Arts Supplies

Martial Arts Suppliers
Los Angeles, California
(310) 836-8833

Courtesy of Butterfield & Butterfield

Make Up Your Own Elvis Stage Kata Dance

The elaborate dancelike movements that Elvis often performed on stage were often improvised. Improvise your own when dancing to his music. It gets the blood flowing. A spontaneous kata exhibition loosens you up nicely. Try it. There's even a bootleg video called *Kung Fu Fighting* featuring more than an hour of Elvis doing nothing but karate moves onstage. Beats the hell out of Tae Bo.

Make an Elvis Fight Scene Tape

Rent some of the Elvis movies that feature him doing karate and edit together a fight scene tape. Study it for the moves.

Choose a Karate Name for Yourself

Elvis was "Tiger." Choose an animal you think appropriate to your own image.

Learn to Break Boards

Elvis used to break boards to pass the time on movie sets. It's not as hard as you think and, man, does it impress your pals. Some hints: Use ¾-inch-thick clear pine cut into 8-by-10-inch pieces with the grain of the wood perpendicular to the length and not the width. Bake the boards in the oven before breaking. The drier the board, the easier it is to break. Get professional instruction before you try it.

Sponsor a Karate Tournament

To honor Elvis' role in advancing and promoting the popularity of martial arts, approach a dojo that teaches one of Elvis' styles and offer to sponsor an Elvis memorial karate tournament. Buy some trophies, have some special patches made, and advertise the event. Request that some of the katas be done to Elvis music. It's a great thing to do as a fan club fund-raiser.

Design Your Own Karate Patch

Elvis designed his own karate patch; so can you. You don't even have to study karate. You can make special karate-style patches for your fan club that express your own vision of Elvis as a martial artist. Listed below is one company that can make them. Minimum custom order is about fifty.

Asian World of Martial Arts
11601 Caroline Road
Philadelphia, Pennsylvania 19154-2177
(800) 345-2962
Fax: (800) 922-2962

Contribute to Kang Rhee's Annual Fund-Raiser

Master Rhee produces an annual charity fund-raiser for St. Jude Children's Research Hospital in Memphis. For further information contact his dojo at (901) 757-5000.

Collect Elvis' Fighting Star Card

Elvis was one of 50 martial artists featured in this series of Martial Arts Masters. This is a collectible and you'll have to search for it. See "Collecting Elvis" for pointers.

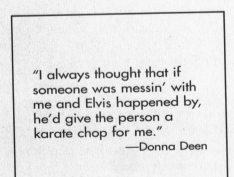

"I always thought that if someone was messin' with me and Elvis happened by, he'd give the person a karate chop for me."
—Donna Deen

From the collection of Bob Klein

ELVIS AND
THE MOTOR VEHICLE

Who's the first person you think of when you hear the word *Cadillac?* You probably said Elvis—and not just because you're reading this book. Almost everyone else would too. One reason may be that the pink Cadillac he bought during his first flush of success is the most famous car in the world. But even though Cadillacs held a special place in his heart, his passion for the internal combustion engine was not confined to any one make, or even type, of vehicle. He bought, drove, and gave away an astronomical number of cars, motorcycles, golf carts—just about anything that burned gas and rubber. For these reasons Elvis and the motor vehicle are forever enmeshed both in image and reality.

Elvis' father, Vernon, placed him behind the wheel of a pickup truck for his first driving lesson and right there, at the age of nine, the groundwork was laid for a lifelong obsession. Later, while in high school, like every other teenager in America, Elvis longed for a cool set of wheels. What he got instead was a $35, beat up, old green 1941 Lincoln Zephyr. Because they knew how important that first car was to Elvis, Gladys and Vernon raised the money in spite of the family's financial difficulties. His classmates remember the old Zephyr well; most days after

Sandi Miller

Elvis at the wheel of his
Rolls Royce

559

From the collection of Bob Klein

Elvis on his Harley Davidson K Model

school they helped Elvis push-start it and he would offer a ride home in return for their effort.

When fame struck and Elvis first exploded on the scene, his day job was driving the delivery truck for Crown Electric and, because of that, Elvis was first introduced to the world as a Memphis truck driver. The very first major purchase made with his newfound riches was, of course, a car. In an article written by Elvis for Rod Builder and Customizer magazine in 1956 entitled "Rock and Roll Drag," he admits that one of his earliest desires was to own a hot rod. When the money started rolling in, so did the cars and bikes: Cadillacs, Harleys, Lincolns, even a three-wheeled German Messcherschmitt. They were the favorite toys of the boy who suddenly could have anything he wanted.

Because they were symbols of success and represented style, mobility, and the thrill of being able to leave the past behind in a cloud of dust, cars were much more than mere transportation to Elvis. They were a physical manifestation of his dreams. And Elvis liked to share his dreams.

It is well known that a new set of wheels was his gift of choice—to people he cared about, to his employees, even to total strangers. His car-buying sprees are legendary. Sometimes the gift of one car would cause a chain reaction that ended with Elvis depleting the stock of a Cadillac or Lincoln showroom in one fell swoop. Because he was impressed with the handling of Memphis Mafia member Jerry Schilling's Triumph 650 motorcycle after taking it out for a spin, he decided to buy one for everyone in his entourage. That same

Sandi Miller

Elvis receiving delivery of nine Triumph 650 motorcycles in 1966 at his Bel Air home

Elvis' customized Greyhound bus leaving Hollywood for the trip back to Memphis

Sandi Miller

day nine motorcycles were delivered to Elvis' Los Angeles home. He and his boys would roar around Bel Air, earning them the moniker "El's Angels." After one exuberantly generous period in the mid-seventies, Elvis was presented with a plaque by Bob Brown, salesmen at Madison Cadillac in Memphis, that read "World's Best Car Buyer." Inscribed on it were the names of 31 people to whom Elvis had given a car.

Even when Elvis was stationed in Germany he was able to indulge his love of being behind the wheel. He was assigned as a jeep driver and his duties included scouting around the German countryside, conducting reconnaissance, and maintaining his vehicle. Being part of a military unit whose motto was "Hell on Wheels" was the perfect assignment for a motorhead like Elvis.

Elvis loved a long road trip. He thought nothing of driving cross-country and did it regularly with great joy. During one three-month period in the spring of 1954, he and his bandmates Scotty Moore and Bill Black logged more than 25,000 miles driving from one small venue to another, with Elvis doing most of the driving. Later, when his film career required three trips a year from Graceland to Hollywood, he and the Memphis Mafia would take the 2,300-mile excursion in a customized Greyhound bus. It was Elvis, wearing his yachting cap and racing gloves, who insisted on being behind the wheel of the 40-foot-long D'Elegance coach as it cruised across the Southwest.

Many of Elvis' movies reflected his interests. Script-writers often created plots that portrayed Elvis' character piloting a speeding car, boat, or motorcycle. These Technicolor tributes have helped reinforce our image of Elvis at the wheel. A clause in his

Elvis and Linda Thompson riding one of Elvis' supertrikes in Memphis

Sandi Miller

movie contracts provided that the studio would be required to send a limo to pick him up each morning to bring him to the set. Elvis enjoyed driving so much, he insisted on driving his own car. The limo would carry his script.

Even though he could indulge himself with the most expensive cars in the world, his love affair with wheels wasn't just limited to luxury cars and slick motorcycles. One year as a Christmas present Priscilla gave Elvis a slot car set. He liked it so much he built an addition onto Graceland, now the trophy room, to house a larger set. When they vacationed in Aspen, instead of skiing Elvis and his friends took to the slopes at night in a posse of snowmobiles. The approximately 14 acres of Graceland often functioned as a speedway and bumper car arena for supercharged golf carts and go-carts. He drove everything from dune buggies to tractors and bulldozers. There were few moving vehicles that Elvis did not enjoy.

To Elvis, driving was pure pleasure. It was therapy. He did, quite simply, love to drive—the pure fun of it, the speed and the freedom. He dug being in control. Under the cloak of night he could slip out of Graceland in one of his Elvismobiles and hit the road with his own thoughts and savor some hard won privacy. Or he could dress incognito in a helmet and leather suit and cruise by himself on his Harley, one of the few times he could be alone and anonymous. For Elvis, riding a motorcycle wasn't a rebellious adolescent phase he passed through. He continued to ride until the end of his life. He never outgrew his need for speed. He was a restless soul who couldn't be still. On the eve of his death someone shot the last photograph of the most photographed person in the world. Appropriately, it shows him at the wheel of his 1973 Stutz Blackhawk, one of his all-time favorite cars.

A car is a perfect place for Elvis fans to listen to his music. The acoustics are usually superior and you can play it as loud and as long as you like without apology. You want to play "That's All Right" fourteen times in row? Well, that's all right! And because Elvis loved driving so much, his music is the perfect soundtrack for when you're behind the wheel. His voice harmonizes well with the purr of an engine and the hum of the road.

ESSENTIAL ELVISOLOGY

The Presley Motor Pool
This is just a partial list of motor vehicles owned, used, or given away by Elvis.

1937 Plymouth Coupe—green
  The car the Presleys drove from
  Tupelo to Memphis.
Late '40s Ford F-100 pickup truck
  Elvis drove this truck when he
  worked for Crown Electric.
1941 Lincoln Zepher two-door—light
green
  Bought by Vernon for $175 in the
  summer of 1951; Elvis' first car.
1950 Lincoln—black
  Elvis bought this for his family to
  use while he was on the road.
1951 Lincoln Cosmopolitan—tan
  Had the words "Elvis Presley Sun
  Records" painted on the side.
1950 Chevrolet one-ton truck
  Used by Elvis to drive around
  Memphis anonymously.
1954 Chevrolet Bel Air—gold and
white
  Elvis toured the south in this,
  Scotty Moore's wife's car.
1954 Ford Crown Victoria—pink and
white
  The first pink car bought for
  Gladys and Vernon.
1954 Cadillac four-door—pink and
white
  Tennessee plate #2-d-35218; it
  burned on the road between Hope
  and Texarkana in June 1955.
1954 Cadillac Eldorado convertible—
yellow
1954 Cadillac Series 75 Fleetwood
limousine—yellow
  Originally blue, he had it painted
  yellow; once used to haul poultry
  to Graceland.
1955 Cadillac Fleetwood 60
Special—pink and white

1955 Cadillac Fleetwood 60 Special

1956 Lincoln Continental Mark II

BMW 507

1962 Lincoln Continental

1960 Cherry Red Convertible MG

1966 Silver Cloud III Rolls Royce

Cobra 427 used in Spinout

1967 Ford Ranchero 51500

The car Elvis bought for his mother. He never sold it or gave it away. It's still at Graceland.

1956 Lincoln Mark II Tudor—white

1956 Plymouth station wagon
Gift to his parents

1956 Messerschmitt mini-car—black and white
Imported German three wheeler. Elvis traded it for a three-hour shopping spree for clothes at Lansky brothers.

1956 Lincoln Premiere—lavender
He traded in his 1954 yellow Cadillac, but returned the next day to retrieve it.

1956 Cadillac Eldorado Biarritz
Originally white, Elvis had it painted the color of squashed grapes.

1956 Ford
Gift to Anita Wood

1957 Cadillac Limousine—black

1957 Cadillac Eldorado Seville
Two-door hardtop

1957 Isetta Coupe sports car—red
Christmas gift to the Colonel

1957 Chrysler Imperial convertible

1957 Ford Fairlaine—red and white
Gift to J. D. Presley, Elvis' grandfather

1958 Lincoln Continental convertible—red
Purchased June 4, 1958

1958 Cadillac limousine—black
As Elvis got on the bus to leave for Fort Chaffee he said, "goodbye you long black son of a bitch" to this car.

1958 BMW 507 Sport Coupe—white
Originally white, Elvis had it painted red. Germans named it "Der Elviswagon."

1958 Cobra 427—white
Elvis drove this car in *Spinout*.
Volkswagen Beetle
Elvis bought this for the guys to
use in Germany.
1958 Mercedes Benz 300 sedan—
black
Totaled by Vernon and Elisabeth
Stefaniak in Germany
1960 Lincoln Continental—yellow
Gift to Elisabeth Stefaniak
1960 Cadillac convertible—maroon
1960 Chrysler station wagon—white
Used to tow the speedboat and
haul luggage
1960 Lincoln Continental Mark V—
black
1960 MG convertible—red
Seen in *Blue Hawaii*; later bought
for personal use
1960 Willys Jeep—pink
Used by security at Graceland
1960 Chrysler New Yorker station
wagon—white
Used to tow the speedboat and
haul luggage
1960 Series 75 Fleetwood limousine—white
Customized by George Barris, it
toured the country in 1965; now
in the Country Music Hall of Fame
in Nashville.
1962 Lincoln Continental—white
with gold top
On display at Graceland, this car
has suicide doors.
1962 Mercury Comet
Four-door station wagon
1963 Chevrolet Corvair—red
Priscilla's graduation present; later
sold to Alan Fortas for one dollar

Priscilla with a 1966 Oldsmobile
Toronado

Sandi Miller

1974 Scout Jeep

Megan Murphy

1971 Mercedes Benz 280 SL roadster

John O'Hara

Elvis in his Mercedes limo in Los Angeles.

Courtesy of Butterfield & Butterfield

1969 Mercedes Benz 600 limo

Cadilac Eldorado 1968

1976 Lincoln Continental limo

1962 Ford Thunderbird convertible—white
Elvis returned it after problems with wheel spokes.

1963 Buick Riviera—white
Elvis once used this car to smash the gates of Graceland.

1964 Buick LeSabre
Gift to Pauline Nicholson, one of Elvis' cooks

1964 Cadillac limousine—black

1960 Rolls Royce Silver Cloud II—black
Interior was upholstered in gray cloth.

1966 Ford Bronco—white

1966 Oldsmobile Toronado convertible—red

1966 Oldsmobile Toronado convertible—white
Tennessee plate b1-6048

1966 Cadillac Eldorado convertible—black

1966 Pontiac station wagon—black

1966 Lincoln limousine—black
Gift from the Colonel

1966 Chevrolet Impala convertible—white
Elvis gave this to Gary Pepper; originally it was George Klein's car.

1966 Cadillac convertible—yellow
Gift to George Klein

1966 Chrysler Imperial Le Baron—black
Displayed at the Imperial Palace, Las Vegas

1964 Rolls Royce Silver Cloud II—white
Blue leather seats; auctioned for charity in 1968

1966 Mustang—blue and white

Gift to Annette Day, costar of
Double Trouble
1967 Ford Ranchero 5L 500
   Elvis bought a fleet of these
   during his ranching period.
1967 Chevrolet El Camino
   The other vehicle of choice at the
   Circle G
1967 Cadillac Coupe de Ville—red
1967 Ferrari Spyder Custom SAE
A67—black
1968 Chrysler station wagon—white
1968 Cadillac Fleetwood—midnight
blue
1968 Cadillac Fleetwood—black
   One of Vernon's rides
1968 Cadillac Eldorado Coupe—
green
   On display in the Memphis Rock
   Cafe in Cairns, Queensland,
   Australia
1968 Cadillac Eldorado Coupe—
gold
1968 Cadillac Eldorado Coupe—
black
1968 Mustang—red and white
   Gift to Priscilla's brother, Danny
1968 Lincoln Continental Mark II—
black
1969 Lincoln Continental Mark III—
cream and black
1969 Cadillac Fleetwood—burgundy
and black
   Gift to director Norman Taurog
1969 Mercedes-Benz Grand 600 limousine—blue
   Six-door, Der Grosse Pullman
1970 Mercedes-Benz Grand 600 limousine—silver
   Black leather interior

Elvis receiving delivery of a new limo

1977 Lincoln Mark V

1977 Cadillac Seville

1977 Chevy Siverado

1970 Mercury Cougar
  Gift to Colonel Parker
1970 Lincoln Continental Mark III
1970 Cadillac Coupe de Ville—copper
  Gift to Mike McGregor
1970 Mercedes-Benz 280 SL—silver
1970 Mercedes-Benz 280 SL
  Gift to Shelby County Sheriff
  William Morris
1971 Mercedes-Benz 280 SL—white
  One of Priscilla's cars
1971 Cadillac Sedan de Ville—black
  Given to the parents of Linda
  Thompson
1971 Stutz Blackhawk Coupe—black
  Elvis purchased the first one ever
  manufactured.
1971 Stutz Blackhawk Coupe—white
  Gift to Dr. Elias Ghanam
1972 Cadillac station wagon—cream
with black vinyl top
  Purchased from Center City
  Cadillac, Philadelphia
1972 Datsun Z—white
  Gift to Sandra Zancan
1972 Mercury Marquis
  Wedding gift to Dick Grob

Elvis signs an autograph from his car

1972 Chevrolet Camaro—blue with
white vinyl top
  Gift to Sheila Ryan
1973 Stutz Blackhawk Custom—
black
  Red leather interior with gold trim;
  this was the last car he ever drove.
1973 Pontiac Grand Prix—green
  Gift to Marty Lacker's wife, Patsy
1974 Cadillac Eldorado—white
  Gift to Kang Rhee; it tours with the
  Harrah's auto collection.
1974 Lincoln Continental Mark IV—
black
1974 Lincoln Continental Mark IV—
silver
1974 Lincoln Continental Mark IV—
blue
  Gift to Linda Thompson
1974 Lincoln Continental Mark IV—
maroon
  Gift to Billy Smith
1974 Stutz Blackhawk Custom—
black
  Red-leather interior with gold trim
1974 Lincoln Continental Mark IV—
dark blue
  Gift to Marty Lacker
1974 Pontiac Ventura
  Gift to Nancy Rook
1974 International Scout Jeep—yellow
1974 Mercedes-Benz 450 SLC
1974 Cadillac Fleetwood
Brougham—white
  Gift to Ed Parker
1975 Cadillac Eldorado—gold and
white
  Gift to Mennie Person
1975 Cadillac Eldorado convertible—
black
  Gift to Red West

1975 Cadillac Eldorado—maroon
   Gift to Joe Esposito
1975 Cadillac Eldorado—black
   Gift to Larry Geller
1975 Cadillac Eldorado—white
   Gift to Jerry Schilling
1975 Cadillac Eldorado—white
   Gift to Alan Fortas
1975 Cadillac Eldorado—white
   Gift to Richard Davis
1975 Cadillac Coupe de Ville—gold
with black top
   Gift to Vester Presley
1975 Dino Ferrari 308 QT4 Coupe—
black
1975 Pantera Didamasa 265—yellow
   Once shot by Elvis
1975 Pontiac Grand Prix—white
   Gift to Malessa Blackwood
1975 Pontiac Lemans
   Gift to Portia Fisher, realtor
1975 Pontiac Bonneville
   Gift to Mary Jenkins, Elvis' cook
1975 Lincoln Continental Mark IV
Coupe—silver
   Gift to David Hebler
1975 Cadillac Seville—blue
1976 Cadillac Seville—black
   Gift to Don Kinney, Denver TV
   host
1976 Cadillac Seville
   Gift to Ron Piestrofaso, Denver
   police detective
1976 Cadillac Seville
   Gift to Dr. Lester Hofman, Elvis'
   dentist
1976 Cadillac Eldorado—green
1976 Cadillac Eldorado Coupe—light
blue
   This was a vacation car Elvis kept
   in Denver. He would fly in, then

drive this to get to Aspen. It's now
part of the Imperial Palace Car
Museum in Las Vegas.
1976 Pontiac Grand Prix—white on
white
   Gift to Marion Cocke, one of Elvis'
   nurses
1976 Pontiac Trans Am—white
   Gift to Mindi Miller
1976 Lincoln Continental limousine—white
   Gift to J. D. Sumner
1976 Lincoln Continental Mark IV—
   white on blue
   Gift to Denver police captain Jerry
   Kennedy
1976 Lincoln Continental Mark V, 1st
   Edition
1976 Lincoln Continental Mark IV—
brown on brown
   Gift to Denver police physician
   Starkey
1976 Lincoln Continental Mark IV—
white
   Given as a gift to a go-go girl from
   T. J.'s in Memphis
1976 Chevrolet Corvette
   Gift to Lamar Fike
1976 Chevrolet pickup, Custom
   Deluxe
1976 Cadillac Seville
   Gift to Ginger Alden
1976 Cadillac Seville—crystal blue
1977 Lincoln Continental Mark V—
white on white
   Given as a gift to Ginger Alden
1977 Cadillac Sedan de Ville—gold
with white top
1977 Triumph TR6
   Gift to Ginger Alden
1977 Datsun 240z

Sandi Miller

Elvis in his dune buggy

Photo courtesy of Ron Eliot

Elvis on his 1956 Harley Davidson K

Gift to David Stanley
1977 Cadillac Seville—burgundy and silver
  With white leather interior; the last Cadillac Elvis ever bought
1977 Chevrolet Silverado
  Nicknamed "2001" by Elvis

Dune Buggies

Dune buggy—bright green
  With Porsche engine
Dune buggy—black
  With 1600cc Volkswagen engine; bought from Liberace

Sandi Miller

1966 Harley Davidson Electraglide

Motorcycles

1956 Harley Davidson K—red and white
  Elvis' first motorcycle
1957 Harley Davidson Hydroglide FLH—black and chrome
1965 Honda Dream 350
  Priscilla's first motorcycle
1965 Triumph Bonneville 650
  Elvis bought a veritable fleet of these in L.A. so the Memphis Mafia could ride together.
1966 Harley Chopper—red with black flames

Karl Lindroos

1976 Harley Davidson Sportster

1966 Harley Davidson Electraglide—
blue and white
1973 Rupp Trike
  With two-stroke snowmobile
  engine
1973 Supertrikes—black, red, and
blue
  1600 cc, 65-horsepower, three-
  wheelers custom-made by Super
  Cycle with Volkswagen engines
  from a kit by Stires Kits, California
1976 Harley Davidson Sportster—
black
  Bought in Marina Del Ray; his last
  bike
1976 Harley Davidson Electraglide—
red, white, and blue
  Bicentennial edition
1976 Harley Davidson Electraglide—
black

Motor Homes

1959 Greyhound VL 100 D'Elegance
Coach
  Customized by George Barris; Used
  for Memphis-to-Hollywood cross-
  country trips

1962 Dodge House Car Motorhome—
black and white
  Used sometimes as dressing room
  on location; Customized by Jimmy
  Sanders in Florida; Elvis once skillfully drove it down a mountain at
  high speed after the brakes went
  out.

Tractors

John Deere Diesel 4010
John Deere International
Easy Flow
Case Tractor

Snowmobiles

Yamaha
Johnson
1969 Jetstar Cycle 440
  Converted to a grassmobile

Golf Carts

Harley Davidson 770
  Customized by Super Cycle,
  Memphis
Grand Prix Golf Cart

Elvis' Chauffeurs
Joseph Wehrheim
  Drove for Elvis in Germany; former chauffeur of William Randolph Hearst
"Sir" Gerald Peters
  Former chauffeur to Winston Churchill, he owned London Towne Livery
  Service in Los Angeles.
Ben Guervitz
  Chauffeured Elvis when he visited Washington, D.C.
Al Golub
  Owner of Chicago Limousine, he chauffeured Elvis' Chicago excursions.

The Presley Marine Fleet

Glasspar Citation Speedboat, 16 feet
 75 horsepower Johnson outboard; powder blue; named "Karate"
Chris Craft Century Coronado Speedboat, 21 feet
 Used on the set of *Follow that Dream* in Florida; it was powered by a 325-horsepower Cadillac Crusader engine.
USS *Potomac*, presidential yacht
 Purchased and then donated to St. Jude Children's Hospital

"The World's Greatest Car Buyer"

Elvis was given an award by one of the auto dealers with whom he frequently did business. The dealer made a plaque that listed some of those people for whom Elvis bought cars. These are the names as they appeared on the plaque.

Patsy Lacker	Marty Lacker	Portia Fisher
Jo Smith	Marvin Gambill	Maggie Smith
Vernon Presley	Patsy Gambill	Katherine Jackson
Vester Presley	Loraine Pritchett	Alfred Strada
George Klein	Richard Davis	Mary Jenkins
Barbara Klein	Aunt Delta	Paul Shafer
Linda Thompson	Sonny West	David Leach
Billy Smith	Red West	Jo Smith
Billy Stanley	Jeanne Lemay	Elias Ghanem
David Stanley	Myrtle Fisher	
Ricky Stanley	Herbert Smith	

Customizers

George Barris
 "King of the Kustomizers" in West Hollywood. This master of the art worked on many of Elvis' vehicles including the "Solid Gold" 1960 Cadillac limo and the Greyhound bus conversion.
Luther Robert's Van Mann Inc.
 This Elkhart, Indiana, customizer worked on a van for Elvis.
Super Cycle
 This Memphis bike shop custom-built two of Elvis' trikes and supercharged his golf carts.

The Motor Vehicle in the Elvis Movie

To see Elvis behind the wheel, check these movies out.

Viva Las Vegas	*Spinout*
Clambake	*Roustabout*
Speedway	*GI Blues*

YOUR ELVIS EDUCATION

Books

Cars of the Stars
George Barris and Jack Scagnetti

Barris 1950 Customs
George Barris

The Elvis Atlas: A Journey through Elvis Presley's America
Michael Gray and Roger Osborne

The Field Guide to Elvis Shrines
Bill Yenne

Roadside Elvis: The Complete State-by-State Travel Guide for Elvis Presley Fans
Jack Barth

Fifties Flashback: The American Car
Dennis Adler

Standard Catalog of American Cars 1946-1975 (4th Edition)
Ron Kowalke and Beverly Rae Kimes

Web Sites

http://members.tripod.com/~cool59/elvis.html
Elvis' Cadillacs site

htpp://www.neosoft.com/~kcderr/elvis/elvis.html
Elvis Is Still #1; Big Bad Bob's tribute site

> HONK IF YOU
> LOVE ELVIS
> —Elvis Bumper Sticker

THE ELVIS AND YOU EXPERIENCE

Wheels were a big part of Elvis' life and they're probably a big part of your life too. The time you spend behind the wheel is a great time to enjoy the King. Whether you're a biker or you drive a minivan, Elvis can enhance your experience of the road no matter what your ride is.

See Some of Elvis' Cars and Motorcycles

The Graceland Automobile Museum

A separate building in the Graceland complex contains a collection of Elvis' vehicles. The museum includes a recreation of a 1950s drive-in movie theater that shows a short video with movie clips (made by Steve Binder, producer of the "'68 Comeback Special"). Several of Elvis' bikes and trikes are on display. A replica of his 1956 Hydraglide built by Memphis motorcycle shop Super Cycle is also displayed.

Elvis' 1966 Electraglide on display at the Murdo Pioneer Auto Museum

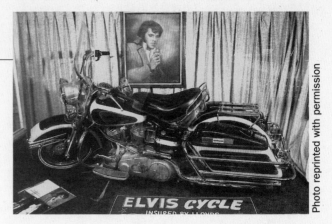

The Country Music Hall of Fame Museum
The famous 1959 George Barris-customized, gold-plated Cadillac Fleetwood limo that toured the country can be seen here.
Four Music Square East
Nashville, Tennessee 37203
(615) 256-1639
(615) 255-5333

Murdo Pioneer Auto Museum
One of Elvis' Harleys is here.
Exit 192 on I-90
503 Fifth Street
Murdo, South Dakota 57559
(605) 669-2691

The Karl E. Lindroos Collection
This vast collection of Elvisibilia has many vehicles including Elvis' '62 Dodge motor home, his '66 Chevy Impala, his last Harley, his '77 Chevy Silverado, a white on white Lincoln Mark V, and a '74 Mercedes 450 SLC. Elvis' last Harley is here.
201 East Ocean Avenue, Suite 7
Lantana, Florida 33462
(561) 588-0095
E-mail: k.lindroos@
elvis-tcb.com
http://www.elvis-tcb.com

The Imperial Palace Auto Collection
Inside the Imperial Palace Hotel and Casino is an auto

1966 Chrysler Imperial on display at the Imperial Palace

collection that includes Elvis' Black '66 Imperial and a light blue '76 Cadillac Eldorado Coupe.
3535 Las Vegas Boulevard South
Las Vegas, Nevada 89109
(702) 794-3174 ext. 3665
Harrah National Auto Museum
The white 1973 Cadillac Eldorado Custom Coupe that Elvis gave to karate instructor Kang Rhee is displayed here.
10 Lake Street
Reno, Nevada 89501
(775) 333-9300

Buy One of Elvis' Cars
A car once owned, purchased, or used by Elvis has tremendous value. One good thing, there's a lot of them out there in the hands of private collectors. But be prepared to spend some serious cash. They often turn up at auctions or are advertised over the internet. Classic car magazines also run listings of dealers and merchants. Happy hunting.
http://www.ClassicCars.com

Pay the Toll for the Car Behind You
Give the toll-booth person enough money to pay the toll for the car behind yours. Tell 'em Elvis did it.

Subscribe to Car Magazines
Classic Automobile Register
Hachette Filipacchi Magazines, Inc.
1633 Broadway
New York, New York 10019
(800) 280-5712
Road & Track and *Car & Driver*
Dept. N, P.O. Box 1757
Newport Beach, California 92663
(800) 914-5656

ELVIS BOUGHT ME
THIS CAR
—Elvis Bumper Sticker

Buy a Replica of an Elvis Car
Even though Elvis bought hundreds and hundreds of cars, they're still a finite commodity. Why not just buy a similar car? Use the list in this chapter and start looking. The Ferrari or the Stutz Blackhawk might be out of your reach, but the 1976 Cadillac Seville or a 1974 Pontiac Ventura may not be. Used car lots everywhere are filled with cars that have Elvis potential. Have it painted or customized

to be like one of Elvis' cars. If it doesn't run, consider making it part of your out-door Elvis shrine.

Buy a Small-Scale Replica of an Elvis Car
You might not want a vintage Cadillac or Lincoln cluttering up your garage. Get a model of an Elvis car instead. Make it part of your shrine.

Rent a Replica of an Elvis Car
The problems associated with owning a vintage car may be daunting for some of the less mechanically inclined, but there are other solutions. Renting one of the types of cars that Elvis owned is a great way to simulate something that Elvis enjoyed. It's a memorable thing to do while making a trip to Memphis, Las Vegas, or Los Angeles.

Buy a Car from One of Elvis' Dealers
You can still buy a car from one of these Elvis-related dealers. Not all dealers are at their original locations where Elvis shopped.

Hull-Dobbs Ford
  The original location, at the intersection of Third and Gayoso Avenues, is now a parking lot. Renamed Dobb's Ford, it's currently located at 2515 Mt. Moriah Road, Memphis.
  (901) 362-6364
Madison Cadillac
  Originally named Southern Motors at the intersection of Union and Danny Thomas Boulevard, it's now called Cadillac of Memphis and has moved to 2177 Covington Pike, Memphis.
  (901) 373-7373
Schilling Lincoln-Mercury
  Originally called Fox Gate Lincoln and located at 987 Union Avenue, it's now located at 2660 South Mendenhal Road, Memphis.
  (901) 794-4000
Robertson Motors Inc.
  Elvis bought some Mercedes here. It was originally called Autorama. It's located at 2950 Airways Boulevard, Memphis.
  (901) 345-6211
Oakley Keesee Ford
  Elvis bought an entire fleet of Ford Rancheros for the Circle G ranch from these guys. They, of course, have fond memories of Elvis. 7925 U.S., Highway 64, Memphis.
  (901) 382-5555

Dress Elvis-Style when You Drive

No matter what he was doing Elvis loved to dress the part, and driving was no exception.

Driving Cap

A dark blue motorcycle cap with a gold embroidered star on the front or any yachting cap will do.

Driving Gloves

When Elvis took the wheel for a cross-country journey he always had his special leather racing gloves.

Sunglasses

If you don't have the guts to wear those Elvis shades in public, then wear them in the relative privacy of your car. You can even have them fitted with prescription lenses.

Black Leather Suit

Motorcycle riding is the best excuse to dress up like Elvis from the "'68 Comeback Special." You can enjoy the thrill of wearing tight black leather and yet actually appear practical and safety conscious.

Helmet Options

Have "Lucky" painted on the front like Elvis had in *Viva Las Vegas*. Not a bad word to have emblazoned on the device designed to protect your noggin.

Elvisize Your Car

Get Vanity Plates

"Elvis" and its many variations are probably already taken. Try a more creative Elvis reference. Be obscure.

Use an Elvis Key Chain

The Graceland gift shops and catalogs have plenty to choose from. Or make your own by putting your favorite Elvis photo into a key chain made to hold photos.

Elvis' jumpsuit from *Speedway* made by Hinchmen of Indianapolis

Elvis' black Harley Davidson cap with white vinyl visor

One of Elvis' helmets from *Viva Las Vegas*

Mount a Plastic Elvis Bust on Your Dash

Make Elvis your patron saint of driving. It might keep you safe and guide your path. His presence may even ward off car thieves.

Use Elvis Bumper Stickers

The gift shops near Graceland offer a wide variety or you could just make your own. But don't use HONK IF YOU LOVE ELVIS unless you like the sound of horns.

John O'Hara

Elvisize Your Upholstery

Blue suede is, of course, a given. Green shag carpeting à la the Jungle Room might be nice.

Paint Your Car

Elvis often bought a car then had it painted. The shade of pink he preferred was "Studebaker pink." He's said to have once squashed a handful of grapes against a car and said, "That's the color I want." Try that at your local auto paint shop and see what happens.

Give Your Car a Nickname

Elvis called his 1977 Silverado "2001." Fans' cars covered with Elvis bumper stickers and window decals often get dubbed as "Elvismobiles."

The King's Kustomizer

George Barris is Hollywood's most famous car designer. His company, Barris Kustom Industries, is responsible for creating many of pop culture's unique cars. The Monkee-mobile, the Green Hornet's Black Beauty, the Munster Hot Rod Hearse, and all three Batmobiles are among his creations.

John O'Hara

A subtle TCB logo lets the world know you're an Elvis fan

Elvis hired him to customize the gold-plated 1960 limousine and his converted Greyhound tour bus. Elvis was so close to Barris that when the underage Priscilla first visited Elvis in Los Angeles, she at first stayed at the Barris's home so her parents would trust that she was being chaperoned. You can have your car customized by BKI if you have the money. Or you could just buy one of the many plastic models of his cars produced by AMT model company.

Barris Kustom Industries
  10811 Riverside Drive
  North Hollywood, California 91602
  (818) 984-1314
  (323) 877-2352

Give Away a Car Elvis-Style

To a Friend

When Elvis gave a car to someone he said, "I want you to do nothing but drive the car." Elvis often paid the insurance costs also. If you give someone a car, try to take care of all paperwork, registration, and tax matters. Contact your local Department of Motor Vehicles and find out the correct procedures for your area.

To a Charity

There are several charities willing to accept your old car as a donation. You get to give away a car and get a tax deduction too. They'll even come and pick it up for you.

To a Stranger

Give a car to an Elvis fan at the gates of Graceland. It should be a fan club tradition.

Elvis' Favorite Motorcycle Shop

Super Cycle in Memphis is a mecca to motorheads and Elvis fans from all over the world. Elvis had a biker streak in him ever since his teen rebel days of the '50s. He did a lot of business here, often dropping by on one of the trikes that he bought from owners Ron Eliot and his brother Lew. Elvis visited Super Cycle just two weeks before his death. In addition to the trikes and motorcycles, Elvis bought a fleet of golf carts here and had them souped up for maximum speed. Super Cycle built the replica of the 1957 Hydraglide that is currently exhibited at Graceland. They can build one for you, too, if you can afford it. But you better act quickly. Ron and his brother Lew still work at Super Cycle, but not for much longer. During Tribute Week in 2002, the 25th anniversary of Elvis's death, the Eliot brothers plan to hold an auction selling off their entire stock which includes many rare Elvis-related items. If you can't afford one of the bikes, maybe you can afford a set of spark plugs or a new gas tank. The auction will be your last chance to buy something, but until then you can stop by and pick up a souvenir to put on your own bike back home.

Super Cycle
624 Bellevue Boulevard
Memphis, Tennessee 38104
(901) 725-5991

Rent a Hog

Elvis had many motorcycles over the years but his favorites were always Harley Davidsons. If you don't want to own one, you can at least rent one if you have a motorcycle license and feel what Elvis felt gliding down the road on that magnificent machine. For information on nation-wide rentals:

Harley Davidson Rental
(888) 916-7433
http://www.hogrent.com

Take an Elvis Road Trip

Go down the same road as Elvis, literally. Drive a route that Elvis often did. Or take a driving tour of any Elvis-related sites in your vicinity. Use one of the Elvis travel guide books listed in this chapter to help you choose a route.

The Elvis Presley Memorial Highway

Highway 78 from Tupelo to Memphis This is the road that took Elvis out of Tupelo when his family drove the '39 Plymouth Coupe to Memphis. If you re-create this ride, make sure you stay on the old road as much as possible to see what Elvis saw. Listen to your

John O'Hara

Ron Eliot of Super Cycle with one of the Harley's built at his shop

John O'Hara

Super Cycle

Photo courtesy of Ron Eliot

Elvis on the day his 1957 Harley FLH was delivered

Karl Lindroos

Elvis' 1962 Dodge Motorhome used for many cross-country trips

favorite Elvis music or listen to the music that was playing in Elvis' head as he looked out the window. Play bluegrass, Hank Williams, or gospel. Later in his life Elvis used to slip out of Graceland and take this drive back to Tupelo, sometimes in a nondescript panel truck. This is probably the most perfect stretch of road in the world to drive any Elvis-type vehicle.

From Your Home to His Home

A good many of the people visiting Graceland for Tribute Week drive into Memphis. The drive to Graceland is a classic American road trip no matter where you start from. When you consider how much Elvis loved driving, it makes sense that when you visit Graceland you go by car. And if it's a classic car, all the better.

Memphis to Vegas

Take a Greyhound bus or motor home to simulate how Elvis covered the route.

Memphis to Hollywood

Elvis' route was west on Route 40 through Little Rock, Oklahoma City, Amarillo, Albuquerque, and Flagstaff, into Southern California and then Route 10 into Los Angeles. He would travel by night and sleep during the day.

L.A. to Vegas

Both places are a good source of vintage vehicles and motor home rentals.

L.A. to Palm Springs

This is the route that Elvis and the guys took when they wanted to split out of Hollywood and blow off some steam at their desert hideaway.

Hollywood to Memphis

These 2,300 miles were probably Elvis' favorite stretch because it was the ride home to Graceland. Play "The Green Green Grass of Home" over and over as you approach Memphis like Elvis once did. He would usually make a pit stop at a Holiday Inn off route 66 in Albuquerque. Elvis' personal directions for this trip as written by him were: "Go 66 then San Bern to Barstow to Oklahoma City— Tennessee left on 77 go to 62 turn left go 62 to 266 to 64 to 65 to 70 to Memphis." If you get lost, blame it on Elvis.

Drive the "Follow That Dream" Parkway

This is a road in Florida that was named in honor of the Elvis movie filmed in the area. It consists of part of US 19 and State Rt. 40.

Re-create the Early Tour Days

When Elvis was starting out, he crisscrossed the Southwest with Scotty and Bill, their instruments strapped to the top of the car. Research one of the early tours and drive part of the route. Play no music later than the year that tour happened. Re-create what was playing on the car radio circa 1955. Shooting fireworks out of the window as Elvis did is optional.

Use a Guitar Case as Luggage

Strap a stand-up bass guitar case to the roof of your car or a guitar case to your motorcycle. Put whatever you want in it. Even if you fill it with dirty laundry people will think you're a cool cat.

Race Slot Cars

Elvis built an addition to his house just to contain a huge slot car set. You may not want to go that far, but a small set as part of your Elvis room might be cool. Use cars Elvis would have liked.

Make a Stage from a Flatbed Truck

In the early days, Elvis often performed from a flatbed truck. Next time you have

Elvis on a motorcycle date, June 30, 1972

Commercial Appeal

an outdoor event and you need a quick Elvisian stage, find someone with a flatbed or rent one.

Go on a Motorcycle Date

Elvis used to love to go motorcycle riding with a girl on the back seat. Invite someone special along for a ride. It's very exciting to have something powerful and dangerous between your legs. Share it with someone special.

Go to a Speedway

A disproportionate amount of Elvis' movie plots had him winning "the big race." Go to a racetrack near you and cheer for the driver who looks the most like Elvis. Or better yet, visit the racetrack where *Speedway* was filmed.
Charlotte Motor Speedway
    P.O. Box 600
    Concord, North Carolina 28026
    (704) 455-3216

See the Elvis Racing Team Cars

The only two racing cars with an Elvis theme are now part of the automobile museum at Graceland. These two cars, covered in Elvis imagery, have hurtled down the raceway at ungodly speeds. Elvis would have loved it.
The Elvis Edition Miller Nascar
    Driven by Rusty Wallace
The Elvis Edition Castrol NHRA Funny Car
    Driven by John Force

Get a Model of the Elvis Racing Cars

Nascar and NHRA Collectibles
    P.O. Box 2878
    Glen Allen, Virginia 23058
    (804) 264-4491
    E-mail: annscott.enterprises@erols.com
    http://www.diecastnet.com/elvis/elvis.htm

Get an Elvis Driver's License

You can find a mock-up of an Elvis driver's license at the shops across the street from Graceland, in catalogs, and on various sites on the Internet.
http://www.tucsonlink.com/tvm/posters/license.htm

ELVIS AND AIR TRAVEL

Suppose you're sitting around with some friends reminiscing about a particularly tasty meal you all once had in a restaurant in another state a thousand miles away. If you're a normal person, you savor this fond memory and you leave it at that. If you're Elvis, you fire up your private jet, pile everyone on board, and go for some serious "take out." That's what happened on October 10, 1976, when Elvis was hanging out at Graceland and someone mentioned how delicious those Fool's Gold sandwiches were from the Colorado Gold Mine Company restaurant in Denver. Accompanied by the ever-present Memphis Mafia and a few law enforcement buddies, Elvis flew from Memphis to Denver where his plane was met by the restaurant owners Buck and Cindy Scott who delivered 22 Fool's Gold sandwiches and a case of champagne and Perrier. After touching down on the runway long enough for the pickup, the *Lisa Marie* turned around and headed back to Memphis. Cost of the meal—more than $30 thousand. Elvis required instant gratification and having his own personal air force was one of the things that made that a reality.

Elvis took his first plane flight on March 23, 1955, when he flew from Memphis to New York to audition for *The Arthur Godfrey Show*. His mother, Gladys, ever vigilant about Elvis' safety, was beside herself with worry and her concern was not entirely unfounded. The next year, on April 14, 1956, while flying from Amarillo to Nashville, Elvis and his band mates Scotty and Bill had a close call in a small twin-engine plane that was forced to make an

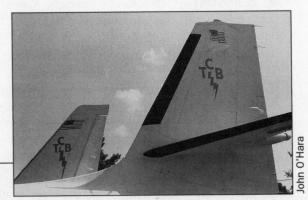

The *Hound Dog II* and *Lisa Marie*, at the Graceland complex

John O'Hara

From the collection of Bob Klein

emergency landing. After that, Elvis tried to avoid air travel until the demands of his tour schedule required he cover a lot of territory in a short amount of time and flying became a necessity.

In the seventies, when Elvis started touring again, he would charter planes on a regular basis, occasionally using Hugh Hefner's Playboy jet. In 1975, Elvis purchased the *Lisa Marie,* a huge Convair 880 that formerly belonged to Delta Airlines. Elvis had it customized as a flying Graceland, with a queen-size bed (fitted with an FAA-required seat belt across its width), a videotape system linked to four televisions, a stereo system with 52 speakers, and a conference room finished in teak.

When Elvis' daughter Lisa Marie turned nine years old, it was only fitting that her birthday party take place on the plane that bore her name. And when she wanted to see snow for the first time in her life, Elvis just cranked up the big jet and they were off to the mountains.

Elvis also owned a smaller plane, a nine-passenger Lockheed Jetstar that required a shorter runway than the lumberig *Lisa Marie.* Named the *Hound Dog II,* it was piloted by the appropriately named Milo High. With two planes at his beck and call, Elvis and his entourage could travel from Graceland to anywhere to do a show and never have to see an unfamiliar face.

After Elvis' death, both planes were hastily sold by Vernon Presley to raise

Photo reprinted with permission

Sandi Miller

Elvis boarding the *Lisa Marie* followed by his father, Vernon

John O'Hara

A fan's floral tribute to the *Lisa Marie*

Pamela Wood

money for the cash-strapped estate. Larry Flynt of *Hustler* magazine fame bought the Jetstar. In 1984, the *Lisa Marie* and *Hound Dog* were repurchased by the estate and returned to Graceland. With its wings removed for transport, the *Lisa Marie* was paraded down Elvis Presley Boulevard to much fanfare. Today, both planes sit across the street from Elvis' mansion at a replica of a small airport terminal and can be visited as part of the Graceland tour. They represent Elvis' desire to be able to travel on his own terms: whenever he wanted, for whatever reason, and in his own inimitable style.

Sandi Miller

ESSENTIAL ELVISOLOGY

Elvis Presley Airlines

The Lisa Marie

"Hound Dog I"
General Dynamics Convair 880
Call sign N880EP
Seats 28 passengers
Cruising speed 615 mph
Ceiling 41,000 feet
Range 4,050 miles
Length 129 feet, 4 inches
Wingspan 120 feet
Tail height 36 feet 3 inches

The *Lisa Marie* Flight Crew

Elwood David, captain
Ron Strauss, copilot

Jim Many, flight engineer
Carole Boutilier, stewardess

The *Lisa Marie's* First Flight

The maiden flight of the Convair 880 as the *Lisa Marie* took place on November 27, 1975, from Memphis to Las Vegas.

The *Lisa Marie's* Last Flight

Ft. Lauderdale to Memphis in February 1984.

The *Hound Dog II*

Lockheed Jetstar model 329
Call sign N777EP
Seats 9 passengers
Cruising speed 550 mph
Ceiling 45,000 feet

Range 3,000 miles
Length 60 feet 6 inches
Wingspan 54 feet 6 inches
Tail height 20 feet 6 inches

The *Hound Dog* Flight Crew

Milo High, captain

Other Pilots

Henry Cannon, the husband of Minnie Pearl, used to pilot chartered light planes for Elvis in the 1950s.

Other Elvis Planes

Grumman Gulfstream g-1
  A gift to Colonel Parker who refused to accept it.
Aero Jet Commander
  Elvis only owned it for two weeks. He sold it to Wayne Newton.
Dessault Falcon
  Bought in November of 1976 as an investment.
The Playboy Jet
  Rented by Elvis for touring in the 1970s.
The *Christina*
  Frank Sinatra's Lear jet. Elvis and Priscilla flew from Las Vegas to Palm Springs for their honeymoon on this plane. The *Christina* crashed in 1976, killing Frank Sinatra's mother.

YOUR ELVIS EDUCATION

Books

The King on the Road: Elvis Live on Tour 1954 to 1977
  Robert Gorden
Elvis Aaron Presley: Revelations from the Memphis Mafia
  Billy Smith, Marty Lacker, and Lamar Fike with Alanna Nash
Elvis: the Concert Years 1969-1977
  Stein Erik Skar
Elvis on Tour: The Last Year
  Sam Thompson
The Elvis Conspiracy?
  Dick Grob
The Elvis Atlas: A Journey through Elvis Presley's America
  Michael Gray and Roger Osborne
Graceland: The Living Legacy of Elvis Presley
  Chet Flippo

Video
Elvis on Tour

Web Sites
htpp://www.neosoft.com/~kcderr/elvis/elvis.html
  Elvis Is Still #1; Big Bad Bob's tribute site

THE ELVIS AND YOU EXPERIENCE

Take the Elvis Airplane Tour

The *Lisa Marie* and the *Hound Dog II* sit across the street from Graceland at the north end of Graceland Plaza. From the gold sink in the bathroom to the King's FAA-required seat-belted bed, Presley Airlines is something that should not be missed. Open seven days a week, year round, except New Year's Day, Thanksgiving Day, and Christmas Day.

The *Lisa Marie*'s flight map

The Perfect Flight Suit

When flying, Elvis often wore his blue pajamas covered by a Drug Enforcement Administration jumpsuit. Very Practical. Very Elvis. You can order your own from one of the sources listed in the "Elvis and Law Enforcement" chapter.

Bring a Walkman and Elvis Tapes With You When You Fly

Elvis' gospel music is the ideal music to listen to when you're 30,000 feet above the earth. It's glorious and soothing music, and if the plane goes down there's no better soundtrack an Elvis fan could have at the end.

Courtesy of Butterfield & Butterfield

Thank Your Flight Crew When Your Plane Lands

As you walk by the cockpit say "Thankyouverymuch," to the crew as you deplane.

Get Group-Discount Tickets on Elvis-Related Travel

Most airlines offer group rates on travel prices. Always try to take advantage of this if you are traveling as a club or with at least ten other Elvis friends. We've listed American because that's the airline Elvis chose the few times he flew commercially and Northwest because they fly direct to Memphis from many major American cities.

American Airlines Group and Meeting Travel
  (800) 433-1790
Northwest Airlines Meeting Services
  (800) 328-1111

Ask for a Tribute Week or Impersonator Discount Airfare

Some airlines flying to Memphis offer special discounts for Elvis fans during Tribute Week. Be sure to ask the airline you'll be taking. American Airlines once offered discounted tickets to anyone who showed up dressed as Elvis on certain Elvis-related dates. If you have a jumpsuit, you can ask if they're doing it on your travel dates. Call for details.

American Airlines (800) 433-7300

Charter a Plane

A great thing to do as a fan club outing or with a group of friends. A Convair 880 or a Lockheed Jetstar would, of course, be best. Christen the plane Lisa Marie for the day. Fly to someplace for a meal then fly back. Play Elvis music and movies.

Build a Model of an Elvis Plane

Suspend it with fishing line over your shrine.

Elvisize Your Luggage

Stick Elvis bumper stickers or glue photos of Elvis on your luggage. When your bag makes its way around the luggage carousel it'll be easier to pick out. People handling your luggage will automatically "treat it nice." Also, you'll smoke out all the other Elvis fans as you walk through the airport.

Give Away a Plane Ticket to Memphis

It's hard to imagine a better gift for a fellow fan who might otherwise not be able to visit Graceland. Fan clubs can offer the ticket as a raffle prize. It's a fine way to raise money for an Elvis-related charity.

Sandi Miller

Elvis deplaning into a limo that met the *Lisa Marie* on the tarmac

ELVIS AND MONEY

Elvis' relationship with money was a story of extremes, of abject poverty and spectacular wealth. His transformation from pauper to King is an element of his life story's lasting appeal. Elvis' rise to riches is the most popular American success story since Abe Lincoln went from a log cabin to the White House. Elvis was born in a two-room shack, delivered by a doctor who was paid for his services by welfare. He spent the first three weeks of his life in the charity ward of the Tupelo Hospital.

The lean years in Tupelo, which were never far from his mind, served to make Elvis appreciate his wealth all the more. His success was sudden and drastic—the most fun way to achieve it. Elvis lived out his own (and his fans') fantasies of instant gratification and conspicuous consumption. He was a real-life Richie Rich using his money to indulge his every whim and to amuse, and help, all those around him. In spite of his childhood poverty, Elvis never hoarded his money. He spent it like it fell out of the sky because, for him, it did. He burned through his money, confident of his ability always to be able to replace it.

Although Elvis' personal motto was "taking care of business," in financial matters he did anything but. Elvis never actually knew how much he was making and didn't care. As long as he had enough money to buy whatever he wanted and do whatever he wanted,

Diamond and 14k gold TCB necklace

From the collection of Bob Klein

Elvis and Andreas Cornelius van Kujik aka, "Colonel Tom Parker"

he was uninterested in the financial details. His one concern was that there should always be $1,000,000 in his (no interest!) checking account at all times. It was important to Elvis to always be a millionaire.

Perhaps because he struck it rich while still a very young man, his attitude toward money remained unsophisticated and blissfully unrealistic. He ceded all dealings concerning his career to his manager, Colonel Parker, very much to his fiscal detriment. Elvis kept roughly 22¢ out of every dollar he earned during much of his career. The IRS, his agent William Morris, the merchandisers, and the Colonel ate up the rest.

These days, most entertainers who find themselves in a similar position of newfound wealth employ a team of professionals to assist them with financial planning, investments, and tax matters. Because Elvis trusted no one outside of his family with his financial affairs (with the exception of Colonel Parker—which was like trusting the henhouse to the Tasmanian devil), the man he chose to manage his money was his father, Vernon. Unfortunately, Vernon had a seventh-grade education and his most creative financial dealing before working for Elvis was forging the figures on a check for a hog transaction so he could make an extra $36. For this, Vernon spent time in prison. Not exactly the kind of guy who should be managing millions.

Because of that experience, Vernon had a fear of the government. The Colonel exacerbated things by strongly urging that he allow the IRS to calculate and prepare

John O'Hara

his son's income taxes. As a result, Colonel Parker was known to boast, Elvis paid more income tax than any other individual in the United States. And of all the millions Elvis gave to charity in his lifetime, none of it was taken as a tax deduction.

Vernon's office, at Graceland

The Colonel continues to be a figure of some controversy in the Elvis world. The question of how much of Elvis' success was due to the Colonel and how much was the inevitable result of Elvis' raw talent continues to be debated. Though most fans do believe that after the first couple of years or so of his career, Elvis could've been managed better by his pet chimp.

Early in Elvis' career the Colonel was successful in exposing him to larger audiences. But once the world got a taste of Elvis, it was his magic appeal not the Colonel's manipulations that made millions of people loyal fans. The Colonel is considered by some people to be a marketing genius and by others in Greil Marcus's words as "the most overrated man in show business." Parker often bragged, "When I met Elvis Presley he had a million dollars worth of talent. Now he has a million dollars." To his credit, he didn't hide the fact that he was all about money and really nothing else.

"From a strictly Marxist-Leninist viewpoint, [Elvis Presley] is a typical example of capitalist exploitation."
—*Harper's*, April 1957

It is an understatement to say that Colonel Parker was not a patron of the arts. He was a carny, a former dogcatcher, a department store Santa Claus, a bush-league promoter, a problem gambler, an all-around huckster, and a secret illegal immigrant, and his business dealings reflected that background. He sold not only "I Like Elvis" buttons during the fifties, but also "I Hate Elvis" buttons at twice the price. Parker was largely responsible for Elvis' uninspired movie career in the sixties. He didn't care about the quality of the product as long as people kept buying it. And buy they did. Elvis was the highest paid actor in Hollywood and because of that, Parker was the highest paid manager. For the first 11 years of their relationship, Parker made 25 percent on all gross earnings; in 1967 that went up to 50 percent. In order to line his pockets even faster, he became the master of the side deal. His fee as "technical adviser" on every Elvis movie is just one example. Many more side deals were under the table. After all the side fees and commissions were collected—and the expenses were deducted from Elvis' take—Parker usually made more than Elvis did.

Parker was born Andreas Cornelius van Kujik in Breda, Holland, and illegally immigrated to America where he served in the U.S. Army. Initially, Andreas dubbed himself "colonel" although he never legitimately achieved that rank. Later he was given the honorary title of colonel in the Southern tradition as a reward for doing favors for a politician. His illegal immigrant status may be one of the reasons he turned down world tours that would have brought Elvis to wider audiences and even more international acclaim. In 1973 he proposed a concert that would be broadcast by satellite around the world. The "Aloha from Hawaii" television special was his creative solution on how to cash in on Elvis' worldwide appeal while saving his own bacon by not risking exposure by traveling outside the country.

The Colonel even, in effect, turned down the offer for Elvis to perform at the Nixon White House. He insisted Elvis be paid $25,000, although tradition dictates that no one gets paid to perform at the White House, the honor alone being enough. But Parker insisted that, "My boy don't perform for free." Money was more important than honor, or anything else it seems, to the Colonel.

At one point Elvis refused to make any more movies and rejuvenated his career with a triumphant television special in 1968, often referred to as the "'68 Comeback Special." Realizing where his strength lay, Elvis made the decision to start performing live again. This period of his career started a pattern of regular engagements in Las Vegas and tours around the country. Parker saw nothing improper about negotiating with the very casino that he owed massive gambling debts to. As a result, the deals Parker cut for Elvis in Vegas (one written on a hotel tablecloth) were tinged by a flagrant conflict of interest.

From 1969 to 1977 Elvis performed in concert well over 1,000 times. Even on the day of his death he was scheduled to start yet another 12-city tour. Touring became a quick way to get "now money," as the Colonel liked to call it. Elvis sincerely loved to tour because it brought him into personal contact with his most loyal fans. But Elvis toured ceaselessly not just because he enjoyed it, he had to or he'd have gone broke. In spite of the regular cash flow, there were times when Elvis was spending it even faster than he was making it. In one day he spent close to $100,000 on pickup trucks for himself and his friends so they could ride around on his ranch. On another day he bought 14 Cadillacs and gave them all away. One month he spent $38,000 on guns. When Elvis toured, his personal jeweler Lowell Hayes traveled with him accompanied by a stash of jewels for

From the collection of Bob Klein

"The mean streak in Parker saw kids who were idolizing his client as a multitude of marks who only deserved to be short-changed and humiliated."
—Dick Vellenga, from *Elvis and the Colonel*

> "Whenever Elvis appeared at the Hilton, all those nice little flyers and flags and decorations were put up by some hotel personnel and a lot of fans who happened to be around. We worked our butts off putting that stuff up, sorting menus, postcards, and heaven knows what else. After working, working, working, for several days prior to Elvis' openings, we got our reward … drum roll … *a pancake breakfast!!!* When we told Elvis, he howled and said, "Yeah, that would be the Colonel all right!!"
>
> —Sandi Miller, a friend of Elvis' during the '60s and '70s

Elvis to choose from and give away. In the last five years of his life Elvis bought close to $700,000 of jewelry from Hayes. He gave jewelry to members of the audience and his band on a regular basis.

In March of 1973, Parker sold the rights to all the songs Elvis recorded before that date (nearly 700) to RCA for around $5.4 million. Elvis' take of that money was roughly $1.35 million, most of which went to Priscilla to satisfy her divorce settlement. Of course, Parker's take was considerably more than his client's. As a result of shortsighted, self-serving, and ethically questionable deals like that, when Elvis died he left behind an estate worth less than $7 million. By comparison, John Lennon, who died 3 years after Elvis, left a fortune of $200 million.

"Elvis didn't die. The body did. We're keeping up the good spirits. We're keeping Elvis alive. I talked to him this morning and he told me to carry on," Colonel Parker told reporters after Elvis' death. Parker attempted to continue to keep his hold on his client even after death. He tried to act as if nothing had changed. Before Elvis was even in his grave, Parker negotiated a deal with Elvis' grieving father, Vernon, that once again gave him the lion's share of Elvis' posthumous income.

On August 24, 1977, Elvis' last will and testament was read. He left the bulk of his estate to Lisa Marie and conspicuously nothing to Priscilla. Vernon was appointed as sole executor of the estate. In 1979, after Vernon's death, a probate court was to appoint Vernon's successor. In May 1980, during a review by Judge Joseph Evans, a Memphis entertainment lawyer named Blanchard L. Tual was appointed legal guardian of Lisa Marie, giving him powers to investigate the tangled financial relationship between Elvis and the Colonel. One of Tual's conclusions was that Parker's dealings with Elvis went beyond all reasonable bounds of industry standards. Tual wrote in his report that Elvis was "naïve, shy and unassertive" while Parker was "aggressive, shrewd and tough." The report stated that the Colonel "handled affairs not in Elvis' but *his own best interests.*"

In response to the report, a lawsuit was filed against Parker by the Presley Estate. Parker finally admitted his true identity and used it to his advantage by claiming that he could not be sued in an American court since he was not an American citizen. Instead of a long and expensive legal battle, the estate settled out of court and Parker gave up all claims to Elvis for a final payment of $2 million.

Even from beyond the grave Elvis has not lost his ability to generate money at an incredible rate. Elvis Presley Enterprises is a well-oiled marketing machine led by Priscilla Presley and Jack Soden. Today, the sale of licensing fees, Elvis merchandise, and tickets to tour Graceland continues unabated, creating an annual income of more than $100 million. Since his death roughly 500 million of his recordings have been sold generating about $4 billion. And the "Elvis in Concert" tour that went around the world sold out in virtually every venue where it was booked.

Some fans are at odds with the way EPE runs things. One fan, Bill DeNight, president of the Burning Love fan club protested what he saw as their exploitation of Elvis and his fans by driving a van painted with anti-EPE slogans back and forth in front of Graceland during Elvis events. He refers to Graceland as Greedland and some fans tend to agree.

> "The sad part is that the demands the Colonel made on Elvis would not have stood up in any court; Elvis just didn't know it. And who could he turn to? What genius at Graceland could advise him? In fact, I believe you can only have a management contract for two years at a time, so their whole arrangement was not even legal. Elvis could have not only stepped away at any time, he could have sued the @#$@ out of the Colonel."
> —Yummy, commenting on the Colonel's demand for millions when Elvis tried to break ties with him, on elvis@coollist.com

EPE did win a precedent-setting court case a few years ago, which established that the estate and heirs of a public figure own licensing rights after his or her death. Prior to that court decision, an estate and heirs had rights to what the celebrities produced during their lifetimes (music, movies, and so on), but licensing rights ended at death. What this means is that, legally, EPE actually does own Elvis and all the rights to license his name and image.

The continuing financial success of EPE might ultimately be good for the fan. As long as Graceland remains profitable, and with plans to greatly expand the physical Graceland complex there is every indication that it will, EPE will be more likely to keep it open to the public as the focal point of the Elvis world.

ESSENTIAL ELVISOLOGY

Elvis' Social Security Number
409-52-2002

Elvis' Bank
National Bank of Commerce
Memphis, Tennessee

Elvis' Bank Account Number
011-143875

Elvis' Checking Account Balance at the Time of His Death
$1,055,173.69

Elvis' Accountants
Joseph A. Hanks
Spain and Fisher

Some of Elvis' Pre-Fame Jobs
Precision Tools
   In June 1951, Elvis made artillery shells. He was fired after a month for lying about his age. He returned two years later to work for a short time.
Loews State Theater
   He worked as an usher for about a month in the spring of 1952 until he was fired for fighting with a fellow employee.
Upholsteries Specialties
   He started working here in August of 1952.
Marl Metal Manufacturing
   In September of 1952, he helped build dinette tables. After two months Gladys made him quit this job because it was interfering with school.
M. B. Parker Machinist Shop
   He worked here in the summer of 1953.
Crown Electric
   He drove a truck as an electrician's apprentice from November 1953 until the fall of 1954. This was to be his last job outside of entertainment.

Vernon's Annual Salary
Delivery truck driver, L. P. McCarty
   $1,080
Stock clerk, United Paint Company
   $1,608
Elvis' business manager
   $75,000

Elvis' first American Express card

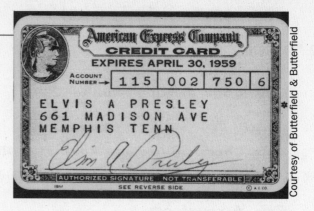

Elvis' Last American Express Card Number
029 756 417 1 800AX

The First Elvis Credit Card
Elvis Presley was the first person ever featured on a credit card when Leader Federal Savings and Loan of Memphis issued an Elvis card in 1988.

Elvis Economics
During the 1992 presidential election, President Bush coined this phrase to refer to Clinton's fiscal policies claiming it would lead the nation "to the 'Heartbreak Hotel.'"

Elvis' Attorney
Ed Hookstraten

Elvis' Estimated Lifetime Income
$4.3 billion

Elvis' Nickname for the Colonel
"The Admiral"

YOUR ELVIS EDUCATION

Books
Elvis and the Colonel
  Dirk Vellenga with Mick Farren
Up and Down with Elvis: The Inside Story
  Marge and Tucker Crumbaker
My Boy Elvis: The Colonel Parker Story
  Sean O'Neal
Elvis Inc.
  Sean O'Neal
The Inventory of the Estate of Elvis Presley
  edited by Richard Singer

The Elvis Syndrome: How to Avoid Death by Success
    John Q.Baucom

Video
"Elvis and the Colonel: The Untold Story"

Web Sites
http://www.a2zlasvegas.com/games/progressive/elvis.html
    IGT's ELVIS Vision slot machine
http://www.inos.com/users/pebbles/easy_come_easy_go.html
    Becky's site; Elvis slot machine info page

THE ELVIS AND YOU EXPERIENCE

Use Elvis Checks
Here's a company that makes Elvis picture checks and address labels. It will make paying your bills infinitely more tolerable.
Checks in the Mail
2435 Goodwin Road
New Braunfels, Texas 78135
(830) 609-5500
Fax: (830) 609-6510
(800) 733-4443
http://www.checksinthemail.com

Choose an Elvis-Related Secret Pin Code
E-L-V-I-S might be a bit obvious (therefore taken), but you can choose any arcane Elvisiana as your code.

Write Elvis Phrases on Your Paper Money
Spread the message. Some fans write "Elvis Lives," "I Love Elvis," or "TCB" on their dollar bills to keep Elvis in circulation. But we would never recommend this. That would be illegal. But of course, we can't stop you.

Play Elvis Slots
Some casinos have Elvis-themed slot machines that play video and audio of Elvis every time you win. Elvis fans can hear the sweet sound of Elvis combined with the sweet sound of coins cascading from the machine. To buy one of these slot machines for your home contact:
C. J.'s Casino Emporium

4625 Wynn Road, Suite A-21
Las Vegas, Nevada 89103
(888) 257-5687
(702) 257-2220
Fax: (702) 257-2223
http://www.cjslots.com

Make Elvis-Related Investments

Of course, the most fun and often best-performing Elvis investment is in collectibles, but there are other ways to invest your money in things Elvis-related. Become a shareholder in companies that are a part of Elvis history or will be a part of his future. Take stock in Elvis.

Open an Account at Elvis' Bank

Start a Christmas Club savings account in Memphis. Make a deposit once a month by mail. You can use it as a Tribute Week slush fund account for whenever you visit Graceland.

National Bank of Commerce
3338 Elvis Presley Boulevard
Memphis, Tennessee 38116
(901) 346-6100

> "Dear Colonel, Words can never tell you how my folks and I appreciate what you did for me. I've always known and now my folks are assured that you are the best, most wonderful person I could ever hope to work with. Believe me when I say I will stick with you through thick and thin and do everything I can to uphold your faith in me. Again, I say thanks and I love you like a father. Elvis Presley"
> —November 22, 1955, telegram from Elvis to Colonel Parker

Lobby for Elvis' Face on Currency

Hey, we were able to get him on a stamp! Why not on some money? Other countries have artists on their currency, why not America? Enough with the dead presidents.

See Where Colonel Parker Lived

Parker died on January 21, 1997, at the very ripe old age of 87, so he is no longer at either of these

National Bank of Commerce, 3338 Elvis Presley Boulevard

John O'Hara

homes. If you pass by, please do not disturb the current occupants.
Palm Springs home
   1166 Vista Vespero Drive North
   Palm Springs, California 92262
Tennessee home
   1221 Gallatin Road
   Madison, Tennessee 37863

> "When he started he couldn't even spell Tennessee. Now he owns it."
> —Bob Hope

Order the Elvis Presley Estate Inventory Book

Find out about Elvis' property and financial assets, stockholdings, artist royalty rights, cars, trophies, awards, furniture, paintings, and gun collection at the time of his death. Call R. J. Publishing for pricing and ordering information at (800) 353-4221.

Apply for an Elvis Presley Credit Card

Elvis Presley Foundation Charitable Credit Card
The Elvis Presley Foundation offers a credit card. There's no annual fee and every purchase you make with the Elvis Presley Visa credit card generates a contribution to the Elvis Presley Charitable Foundation to do good works for less fortunate and homeless people—at no additional cost to you. Using the card gives you a 10 percent discount on Graceland Platinum Tour Admission and all catalog purchases, souvenir and gift shop merchandise, Heartbreak Hotel room rates, and Elvis Presley's Memphis restaurant meals and merchandise. For an application call Graceland at (800) 238-2000 or visit this web site: http://www.webapply.com/elvis/

The Union Planters Bank Elvis Credit Card
The Union Planters Bank offers an Elvis credit card. You receive an *Elvis in Hollywood* video when you begin using your card.
Bank Card Center
P.O. Box 1165
Memphis, Tennessee 38101-9774

> "Hi Babies, Here's the money to pay the bills. Don't tell no one how much money I sent. I will send more next week. There is a card in the mail. Love, Elvis"
> —Telegram from Elvis to his parents

ELVIS IN CYBERSPACE

Where can you go to hear Elvis music, see Elvis film clips, look at Elvis photos by the thousands, buy Elvis memorabilia, books, movies, CDs, and souvenirs and get to know other Elvis fans? Well, there's Graceland, of course. But now there's a another meeting place for fans from all over the world where you can trade Elvis stories and stock up on Elvis goodies and it sits right on your desktop. The internet, the world's largest coffee klatch, attracts Elvis fans with its limitless offerings and provides them the opportunity to form a genuine community.

The internet has been well utilized by Elvis fans; because his appeal is global, this makes perfect sense. Since people with similar interests can easily find each other, fans use their computers to meet other fans, communicate with each other, plan to meet in Memphis, and keep in touch in between fan gatherings. They meet people from across the globe in Elvis newsgroups, on bulletin boards, in chat rooms, and via e-mail loops, and find they have this incredible thing in common. An appreciation for Elvis is the best good will generator we've ever found.

People who knew him and many fans agree that computers are something Elvis would have really dug. What fun it is to think that if Elvis were alive today, he would be surfing the

Elvis fans who've met each other on the internet getting together in a Memphis restaurant, many meeting each other in person for the first time

Photo reprinted with permission

602

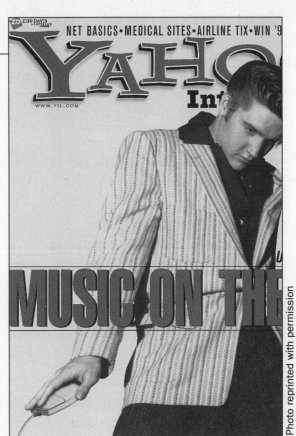

NET BASICS • MEDICAL SITES • AIRLINE TIX • WIN '9

YAHO Int

WWW.YIL.COM

MUSIC ON THE

Photo reprinted with permission

web and hanging around on the internet with his fans. Considering Elvis' propensity for gadgets and toys, it's reasonable to imagine that every room at Graceland would be rigged up with a computer. Elvis could lurk in the chat rooms and newsgroups dedicated to him and see what was being bandied about. It would have been great if Elvis could enjoy all the effort, talent, and creativity that have gone into the web sites dedicated to him and his music. But best of all, Elvis could have had contact with fans, heard how much he is loved and appreciated, and continued the playful, joking, and generous-hearted communication he had with them while he was alive.

So even though you won't run into Elvis himself when you log on, you will find an immeasurable number of sites dedicated to every conceivable aspect of his life and career. There are sites about his music and lyrics, movies, cars, costars, jumpsuits, concerts, ex-wife and daughter, and friends, all created and run by individuals who want to share their ideas and expertise with the world (not to mention the multitude of sites by companies with Elvis products to sell).

Fans keep his memory alive in cyberspace with discussions and occasional arguments about Elvis news, documentaries, books, and new music releases. They share their pleasure in his songs and his beauty, and they reminisce and grieve together over the loss of him. So by all means get to a computer if you're looking to locate rare Elvis collectibles, find out next month's lineup of Elvis' movies on television, see artwork about Elvis, or post your own. Make friends with Elvis fans in different parts of the world. Elvis brought an estimated one billion people together to watch the Aloha concert, and he's doing nothing less these days on our computers.

ESSENTIAL ELVISOLOGY

Graceland's Web Site
Graceland has a very interesting web site that is a must-see for every fan—and since it is always being updated and has all the latest news, you'll learn something every time you go.
http://www.elvis-presley.com

Elvis Has His Own Smileys
&:-)
5:-)

YOUR ELVIS EDUCATION

Books
Elvis after Elvis: The Posthumous Career of a Living Legend
   Gilbert B. Rodman
Images of Elvis Presley in American Culture 1977–1997
   George Plasketes

CD ROMs
Virtual Graceland: Your Personal Tour of Elvis' Life and Home (2 CD-ROM set)
  http://www.virtualgraceland.com

Recommended Web Sites
http://www.elvexpages.com
   Lex's Elvis Presley Page and ELVEX
   site; also Ringmaster of the "Won't
   You Wear My TCB-ring" webring at
   http://www.casema.net/~arpt/
   tcbring.html
http://jordanselvisworld.simplenet.com/
   index.html
   Jordan's Elvis World and the world's
   largest Elvis music library

Virtual Graceland CD ROM

Photo reprinted with permission

"I became an Elvis fan when I was five years old. It's hard to explain how one becomes a fan; it is almost destiny! My parents were not fans until I became one, the opposite of what most people think—*I made them fans*—not the other way around! From when I was five until December 1996, it was very hard to get up-to-date Elvis news or keep in touch with other fans. That is, until I hooked up to the internet! When I first came online, I searched for as many Elvis sites as I could but there weren't many. The first Elvis site I came across was Willem's CD Collector's Page (http://www.noord.bart. nl/~kaauw/index2.html). Willem's pages influenced me so much I decided to start working on a web page of my own.

"In early 1997, my site, Jordan's Elvis World, started out as a newsletter, basically a collection of links to other Elvis sites, and reviews of new releases. I wanted to put something on the site that *nobody* else had.... There was some new software called RealAudio and I decided to do the impossible—open up the first Elvis online music library where fans could listen to Elvis music they couldn't get anywhere else. The response was great, and the amount of material I could use was infinite. Today my site contains Many Many Many more albums of rare material you can listen to. In fact, it's the world's *largest* Elvis Music Library! Also, my site's been ranked #1 by other online fans (thanks)!!

"Running my web site is definitely a labor of love, and in the process I have met many wonderful people from all over the world and made many close friends, and many are from different countries! I have also been invited to several Elvis events throughout the world, which is really exciting!

"I am now president of the 'Universally Elvis' Fan Club (http://jordanselvisworld.simplenet.com/univelvismain.htm) and you can become a member online. I think that being an Elvis Fan is the greatest thing in the world, and I wouldn't give it up for *anything*!"

—Jordan Ritchie, http://jordanselvisworld.simplenet.com/index.html

http://www.noord.bart.nl/~kaauw/import20.html
Dutch import site
http://www.noord.bart.nl/~kaauw/index2.html
Willem's Kaauw's For CD Fans Only
http://www.geocities.com/~arpt/ieteng/216inl.html
Ger Rijff's It's Elvis Time; jumpsuit-free zone

http://www.uio.no/~ovene/
Oven Egeland's Elvis Is Still Active In Norway site
http://members.tripod.com/~Crazy_Canuck/elvisworld.html
Claude the Canuck's Elvis Pages
http://www.biwa.ne.jp/~presley/
Haruo Hirose's Elvis World of Japan
http://apachelvis.simplenet.com/
Pete Smith's Apache Elvis site

http://elvistelegraph.findhere.com/
   Online weekly Elvis newsmagazine
http://www.geocities.com/
   bourbonstreet/quarter/5733
   Elvis site with guitar chords
http://metalab.unc.edu/elvis/
   elvishom.html
   The Unofficial Elvis home page

http://www.kolumbus.fi/samini/
   Sami's Elvis page; the Finnish Elvis
   site
http://www.presley.de/
   First German Elvis pages
http://www.people.virginia.edu/
   ~acs5d/elvis.html
   Elvis Lives in Evil Levi's

Elvis Links Sites

http://www.sunsite.unc.edu/elvis/
   elvlinks.html
   Elvis Links
http://www.fansites.com/elvis_
   presley.html
   Elvis Links, fan sites
http://metalab.unc.edu/elvis/elvlinks.html
   Huge list of Elvis links
http://users.aol.com/petedixon/links.html
   Elvis links
http://www.nwlink.com/~timelvis/
   Disgraceland—A Thousand Points
   of Elvis

http://perso.wanadoo.fr/ch.jouanne/
   liens.htm
   Christophe Jouanne's links page
http://www.washingtonpost.com/
   wpsrv/style/longterm/elvis/elvis.htm
   News; articles; links
http://www.blackstump.com.au/king.
   htm
   Black Stump's Elvis links page
http://www.4elvis.com/
   4Elvis.com site

Elvis Presley Database and Information Web Sites

http://www.geocities.com/~arpt/az/
   Elvis Presley Encyclopaedia
http://www.uio.no/~ovene/facts.html
   Downloadable Elvis database
http://www.uio.no/~ovene/program.html
   Database program and datafile
   available for sale
http://www.geocities.com/SunsetStrip/
   8200/books.html

Bibliography of books in print
http://users.aol.com/petedixon/elvis/
   index.html
   Elvis Presley database
http://www.tourette.demon.nl/
   The Elvis Presley internet database
http://friko2.onet.pl/gd/piowal/
   Elvis Presley index page

Computer-Related Sites and Elvis Downloadables

http:www.xs4all.nl/~mouwen/elvis/
   Elvis Presley theme page

http://www.sunsite.unc/edu/elvis/
   download.html
   Elvis in the Machine

http://www.elvis.findhere.com
  Elvis theme page
http://www.members.tripod.com/
  ~wbroekman
  Wouter Broekman's Elvis the King;
  software, information, games
http://aloha.bizland.com
  Aloha themes; wallpaper; startup
  screens; screensavers

http://galttech.simplenet.com/
  ssheaven/e0077.html
  Screen Saver Heaven's slide-show
  format Elvis screensaver
http://www.gallery.com
  Elvis screensaver

Online Sources for Books, Music, and Films
http://www.virginmega.com
http://www.amazon.com
http://www.barnesandnoble.com
http://www.borders.com
http://www.powells.com
http://www.dealpilot.com

http://www.geocities.com/SunsetStrip/
  8200/books.html
  Bibliography of Books in Print
http://members.aol.com/sndzgood/
  Soundzgood Records and
  Memorabilia

More Elvis Sites
http://ourworld.compuserve.com/
  homepages/elvis/
  Bringin' It Back—The Elvis Presley
  e-zine
http://www.elibrary.com
  Electric Library; do a search for
  Elvis articles
http://www.angelfire.com/il/
  CHICAGOSTYLEHOMEPAGE
  Elvis Chicago Style fan club home page
http://www.nwlink.com/~timelvis.ne
  ws.html
  Elvis newsgroups
http://www.geocities.com/SunsetStrip/
  8200/events.html
  Elvis events calendar
http://www.elvispresleyonline.com/
  html/elvis_daily_update.html
  Daily Elvis update
http://www.centuryalpha.com/~yannone/
  Eddie Fadal's Elvis museum

http://www.stealthware.interspeed.
  net/elvis.html
  Elvis site
http://members.aol.com/elvanic1/
  page24/index.htm
  Elvis Aron Presley site
http://www.geocities.com/Broadway/
  Stage/3349/
  Elvis4ever
http://www.geocities.com/Nashville/
  Opry/4744/
  Elvis classifieds; find items to buy,
  sell, or trade
http://www.fansites.com/elvis_
  presley.html
  ElvisPresley@Fansites.com links
  page
http://www.freeyellow.com/
  members4/zhazam/
  Elvis for Trade

http://w1.866.telia.com/~u86600188/
elvis/index2.html
Elvis Internet Times
http://wsrv.clas.virginia.edu/~acs5/
elvis.html
Elvis Lives in Evil Levis
http://listen.to/elvis-presley-superstar
Elvis Presley Superstar
http://www.epmemphis.com/
Elvis Presley's Memphis
http://www.angelfire.com/la/
judydees/elvis.html
Elvis Remembered
http://www.geocities.com/Nashville/
Stage/1762/index.html
Elvis Rocks the Big Apple
http://www.geocities.com/Nashville/
Stage/5447/
Elvis sing-along
http://members.aol.com/ElvisRebel/
Home.html
Elvis the King of Rock n Roll
http://home.sol.no/~tlidsoe/Link_page. html
Elvis: The Las Vegas Years
http://www.angelfire.com/sc/
novakhomesite/index.html
Elvis P's second home
http://elvistyle.com/elvistyl.htm
Cindy Hazen and Mike Freeman's
Elvistyle site; take a virtual tour of
Elvis' life
http://www.elvis.com.au/index.htm
For Elvis Fans Only
http://oscar.teclink.net/~elvisgto/
Graceland Too
http://www.eoni.com/~soultone/elvis.
html
Graceland: Coming Right up!
http://members.aol.com/simplyhill/
elvis2.html
My Elvis

http://tor-pw1.netcom.ca/~sumner/
elvis.html
Paul's Elvis Page
http://www.blackdogweb.com/elvis/
Rare Elvis
http://members.aol.com/mompac/
elvis.htm
Rockin' with Elvis
http://www.dsr.kvl.dk/~jakobpo/
Surfin' Safari with Elvis
http://www.geocities.com/Nashville/
8605/index.html
The Elvis Presley Diary
http://members.aol.com/ElvisAronP/
Elvis1.html
The Elvis Presley Shrine
http://www.aha.ru/~hse/
The first Russian Elvis site
http://home.eznet.net/~bigtoast/
The King's corner
http://come.to/tigerman
Tigerman Elvis
http://www.grafisk-consult.no/
flamingstar/menys.html
Flaming Star; Norway site
http://www.worldwideelvis.com/
wwemain.htm
Worldwide Elvis
http://www.ioa.com/~gwynn/
Elvis
RadioMe.htm
Elvis, Radio and Me
http://www.members.xoom.com/
livingsouth
Institute for the Living South;
Vernon Chadwick
http://www.vegaslounge.com/elvis/
index.htm
Elvis Slept Here
http://www.geocities.com/SunsetStrip/
Backstage/2175/

Elvis Meets Tom—Jones, that is,
with plenty of RealAudio
http://www.worldwideelvis.com/
ELVISNET; online fan club
http://www.pathfinder.com/people/
960819/photogallery/king00.html
People magazine's Elvis site;
RealAudio and tons of photos
http://www.metronet.com/~elvis/
personal/elvis.html
Mike Hernandez's personal Elvis
site; lyrics, trivia, photos
http://home7.inet.tele.dk/elvis/index.
htm
Elvis Unlimited site
http://www.nwlink.com/~timelvis_
news.html
Newsgroups
http://www.geocities.com/Nashville/
Opry/6247/germ_ep.htm
Jarle Jensen's site; a complete
German EP discography
http://www.precious-elvis.com
Precious Memories
http://www.the-med.com/
medfoundation.html
EP Memorial Trauma Center
http://www.elvis-tcb.com/museum
Florida EP Museum
http://www.elvispresleyonline.com/
Elvis Presley Online
http://www.elvispresleyonline.com
Paul Jaffee's Elvis online site
http://chelsea.ios.com/~hkarlin1/
welcom.html
First Presleyterian Church
http://www.elvistcb.com
Hutchinson Records & Collectibles
http://www.chron.com/voyager/
elvis/trivia.html
Trivia contest

http://www.geocities.com/Hollywood/
Studio/4382/
Judy's Elivs Presley Blvd.
http://sunsite.unc.edu/elvis/elvishom.
html
Original unofficial Elvis home page
http://w1.866.telia.com/~u86600188/
elvis/index.html
Elvis Internet Times; The Elvis
Presley Album and Singles Page
http://w1.383.telia.com/~u38300150/
Sweden's Greatest Elvis Site
http://www.rockhall.com/induct/
preselvi.html
Rock and Roll Music Hall of Fame
Elvis site
http://www.churchofelvis.com/
24-hour Church of Elvis
http://worldwideelvis.com/inter.htm
Worldwide Elvis
http://www.tv-now.com/stars/
elvis.html
TV-Now monthly television schedule for Elvis Presley
http://members.aol.com/
kingzimage/main.html
The Kings Image
http://members.aol.com/mkolajtowi/
index.html
Elvis Is Still the King
http://ourworld.compuserve.com/
homepages/BrettMallard/
Elvis Presley forum on
CompuServe
http://ourworld.compuserve.com/
homepages/Nolet_M/
Welcome to my world
http://www.dsr.kvl.dk/~jakobpo/
On a Surfin Safari with Elvis
Presley

http://www.torget.se/users/e/ELViSiss/
   Elvis Aron Presley: King of rock
   and roll
http://www.geocities.com/Nashville/
8575/
   Elvis: The King Rocks On
http://members.aol.com/tcb4eap/
index.html
   TCB4EAP's home page
http://userzweb.lightspeed.net/
~mimii/elvis/index.htm
   Elvis Presley in concert
http://home.wxs.nl/~hruyter/
   Elvis Presley site
http://home.wxs.nl/~chris.senden/
elvis_presley.htm
   Elvis Presley site
http://www.presley.de/elvis/
multimedia/ra/index.htm
   Elvis Real Video & Audio page
http://musik.freepage.de/andre/index
german.html
   Keep Him In Mind: Elvis Presley
http://www.elvis.com.au/
   For Elvis Fans Only
http://altern.org/elvis1/
   Elvis, une voix
http://hem2.passagen.se/epresley/
index.html
   Elvis Presley—King of Rock n
   Roll!
http://www.fortunecity.com/tinpan/
floyd/597/
   Elvis in Hawaii
http://www.legendsofmusic.com/
ElvisPresley/
   Elvis Presley's tribute headquarters
http://www.elvis.com.au/tcb/
   Elvis Presley: That's the Way It Is
http://www.uio.no/~ovene/
   Elvis Is Still Active in Norway

http://www.geocities.com/Bourbon
Street/Quarter/5733/
   Elvis: Electrifying!
http://www.geocities.com/Nashville/
Stage/5447/
   Elvis Sing Along
http://worldwideelvis.com/inter.htm
   Worldwide Elvis
http://come.to/Keep-Him-In-Mind
   Andre Mester's site
http://users.aol.com/petedixon/elvis/
lyric1.html
   Song lyrics
http://wsrv.clas.virginia.edu/~acs5d/
elvis.html
   EP, the Man, the Music, the King
http://biobase.dk/users/example.html
   EP WWW home page, Denmark
http://www.geocities.com/
~mygraceland/
   The Sights and Sounds of the King
http://www.pathfinder.com/people/
sp/elvis/index.html
   Essence of Elvis
http://userzweb.lightspeed.net/
~mimii/elvis/form.htm
   Add your own impressions and
   comments if you have seen Elvis
   in concert and check out the other
   comments from people who saw
   him.
http://www.bigtimedesign.com/elvis.
dir/elvisian.html
   Elvisians from Another Planet
http://users.aol.com/elvisnet/index.
html
   Elvisnet EP Fan Club
http://elvistyle.com/elvistyl.htm
   Memphis Elvis Style; Memphis
   Explorations

http://www.gomemphis.com/elvis/
elvis.html
The *Commercial Appeal* Elvis
Archives
http://www.geocities.com/SunsetStrip/
8200/EPEC.html
Fan club registry

http://www.neosoft.com/~kcderr/
elvis/elvis.html
Elvis Is Still #1

THE ELVIS AND YOU EXPERIENCE

Tips on Searching for Elvis in Cyberspace

A good start for finding Elvis in the machine is with search engines set up to do just that. Here are sites you can use to launch into cyberspace. There'll be a lot of overlap but each will also list many different sites.

Search Engines

http://www.altavista.com
http://www.askjeeves.com
http://www.dogpile.com
http://www.eblast.com
http://www.excite.com
http://www.goto.com
http://www.hotbot.com

http://www.infoseek.com
http://www.looksmart.com
http://www.lycos.com
http://www.theminingcompany.com
http://www.northernlight.com
http://www.snap.com
http://www.yahoo.com

Elvis Newsgroups

Newsgroups are posted conversations that you don't need to subscribe to, you can just visit. There are quite a few where you'll find Elvis mentioned with varying frequency.
http://www.dejanews.com
To locate information on newsgroups with instructions on how to use them

alt.elvis
alt.elvis.sighting
alt.elvis.king

Alt.elvis.king is a relatively tight group—not too much spam and porn—where you'll find several Elvis intimates and many people who are really knowledge-able about Elvis' music and history. This is an extremely active site with great dialogue and lively disagreements. It ranges from lovefest to slugfest; affec-tionately referred to as aek.

These two are much less active than aek and have a somewhat different thrust. If you don't want your posts lost in the maelstrom of aek, you might consider going here.

There are other newsgroups where you can find discussions about Elvis, but they are not dedicated solely to him:

rec.music.rock-pop-r+b.1960s
rec.music.rock-pop-r+b.1950s
alt.fan.elvis-presley
rec.music.rock-pop-r+b.1970s

rec.music.beatles
alt.gossip.celebrities
alt.music.lyrics

Mailing Lists, Loops, and Chat Rooms

There are many mailing lists and loops that you can subscribe to. The messages are then sent to you as e-mails and you can participate in the ongoing conversation or post new messages for everyone on the list to read.

http://www.liszt.com
   To find information on mailings lists
http://www.egroups.com
   Will also have info on lists
elvis@coollist.com
   One of the best lists is elvis@cool-list.com, which is a good meeting place for fans. To subscribe, visit http://www.geocities.com/SunsetStrip/Alley/8250/eml.html

There is an Elvis chat room at Delphi and you can find information about joining at http://www.suite101.com/welcome.cfm/elvis_presley. They usually chat on Mondays and Saturdays but can use the room anytime.
http://jordanselvisworld.simplenet.com/jchatroom.htm
   The Official Elvis Presley Chatroom
http://www.talkcity.com/chat
   Download EZTalk Pro and it will give you information on entering specific chatrooms. The Elvis room is #elvispresley, port 6667, server chat.talkcity.com

http://www.talkcity.com/help/Pro/
   For info on EZTalk Pro program
http://www.suite101.com/welcome.cfm/elvis_presley
   Elvis chatroom and discussion groups
http://www.ForumOne.com
   To find information on discussion groups and forums
http://elvis-is-still-the-king.simplenet.com/Personals_Page/Personals.html
   Meet other fans on this bulletin board for a pen pal, friendship, or more....
http://www.elvis-online.de
http://www.presley.de
http://www.elvispages.com
http://www.elvispages.de
http://www.elvispage.de
http://www.elvis-pages.de
http://www.elvisweb.de
http://www.elvisboard.de
http://www.elvisnet.de
   Bulletin boards where you can post anything Elvis related.

Web Rings

http://www.webring.com
   For information about web rings
http://www.webring.org
   For information about web rings
http://www.geocities.com/SouthBeach/Port/8910/Elvis.html
   E-mail: JDSWL@webtv.net
   Elvis Remembered Web Ring

The TCB-Ring (written by Lex Raaphorst)

The "Won't You Wear My TCB-ring" web ring was founded in 1996. The web ring system makes it possible to link subject-related web sites into a circle. There's a "next" button at the bottom of each web page and when you press it you travel form site to site and eventually finish where you started. There are also options to list the sites in the ring or to choose from the next, or previous, five sites. In general any Elvis-related page is welcome in the ring, but David Troedson (my co-ringmaster) and I do check every page before we add it. It is possible to customize the ring in a way that any member is able to add a new site, but I didn't choose for that option, because I want to keep track of the quality (although, of course, quality is pretty subjective).

I got a lot of complaints from people who didn't like the intrusion of impersonator sites on the TCB-ring so I started a separate web ring for them. Occasionally we delete a page because of complaints about the contents or because it's not working anymore. Currently there are more than 150 pages in our web ring, which generate over 67,000 hits during a two-month period. It's very nice to "lead" this ring because it is obviously very much appreciated by all members.

Elvis Scores: The Elvis Scores is a system where people can vote for Best of the Net and favorite songs, album, and movie. I keep track of it all in order to prevent multiple votes by the same person and any other manipulations. The "Best of the Net" section is the biggest success. The system measures the viewer's overall impression of the various web sites (for design and content) and keeps score of the votes. A lot of people just give two tens, which is the highest rating. This doesn't make the list as lively as it should be. In my opinion there are only a few pages that deserve a maximum score for only one of the categories (design/contents), not even to mention both categories. But that's the way people are ... giving just two tens because it's about Elvis. A big difference is noticeable between American and European votes: American votes are almost always two tens. European visitors are more critical.

Import Top 20: This third list you can vote on is the best we have. Because people are really dedicated to their votes for the best imports and bootlegs, and get feedback from the system (automatically) every month, they are willing to update their votes pretty often. The list is linked directly to the files in Willem Kaauw's huge bootleg archive, so people can check the contents (and often reviews) of the bootlegs. http://www.casema.net/~arpt

Lex's Elvis Presley page; Ringmaster of the "Won't You Wear My TCB-ring" webring at http://www.casema.net/~arpt/tcbring.html

Elvisize Your Computer
If you can't wait for Apple to come up with a new flavor, you'll just have to paint your computer pink and black. You can buy an Elvis mousepad or even create your own.

Program Elvis Sound Cues into Your Computer
When you turn it off:
    "Elvis has left the building."
When you turn it on:
    "Let's get real, real gone for a change."
As an alert sound:
    "Thankyouverymuch."

Build Your Own Fan Site on the Net
A web site can be a sort of Elvis shrine that you share with the world. Surf around and see what other people have done—and then bring your own special touch to a new site. Some internet services have free online web-page builders that are especially set up to help you create your own fan site. This is the twenty-first century way to share your feelings and knowledge about Elvis. Contact your internet service provider for details.

Software to Download Elvis Music
In order to be able to hear music on your computer, you should download RealAudio from http://www.realaudio.com.

Create an Elvis Web Cam Site
Web cameras can be set up on any Elvis-significant area in the world. Consider sharing your own Elvis shrine with the world by setting up a shrine-cam. Remember though, the more activity, the more interesting the site.

Lobby for a Graceland Cam

Petition Graceland to add a live-feed video view of the music gates or the Meditation Garden on the Graceland web site. That way fans can visit Elvis and Graceland anytime they want.

Choose an Elvisian Screen Name

You'll have to be a bit creative to choose something that's not already taken.

Get an Elvis E-Mail Address

At http://www.funmail.co.uk you can get an e-mail address with the word *Elvis* in it such as yourname@elvislives.co.uk or other customized Elvis addresses. To find Elvislives, click on "famous people/TV and movie." Go to the Funmail site for further information and instructions.

Broadcast Your Elvis Event Live on the Internet

LiveOnTheNet.com (http://www.liveonthenet.com), is a streaming media entertainment webcast and broadcast network that features live concerts, interactive chats, movies, and more. LiveOnTheNet.com enables viewers to access hundreds of concerts and events on-demand through the internet's richest searchable event archives. All LiveOnTheNet.com events are distributed via RealSystem G2 technology from RealNetworks and are available for any recent version of Microsoft Internet Explorer, Netscape Navigator, and AOL browsers. Contact Jim Felfder at: LiveOnTheNet.com

  (800) 840-8638 ext. 7025
  E-mail: jim@liveonthenet.com

Create Your Own Elvis Poll on FreeVote.com

FreeVote.com is a free service on the internet that everyone is welcome to use. Customized voting booths can be created by absolutely anyone with very little effort and web surfers can come in and vote for the items you have listed with just a click of a button. You can get opinions on any Elvis-related issue you can think of. Go to http://www.freevote.com for information on how to set up your own poll page.

Search Magazine and Newspaper Sites for Any Elvis Archives

Most big magazines, newspapers, and news agencies have archives at their web sites. Do a search for old articles and photos of Elvis. (Try *People* magazine, CNN, and *Entertainment Weekly* to start.)

Send an Elvis E-Mail Card to a Fellow Fan

There are many greeting card sites on the net where you can select and send e-mail Elvis cards to your friends and fellow fans. Some can be enhanced with music and personalized messages.

Free Cards for Music Lovers
  Online Elvis cards with music
  http://www.musicfanclubs.org/
  meredithbrooks/postcard/
  Corbis e-card
  Choose your card and customize it.
  http://www.corbis.com/
Elvis Slept Here
  A large selection of cards
  http://www.vegaslounge.com/
  elvis/postcards.html
123 Greetings
  Elvis photo and cartoon cards
  available with music
  http://www.123greetings.com/

American Greetings
  One of the largest on the net with
  lots to choose from
  http://www.americangreetings.com
Sparks.Com
  Choose from several Elvis-related
  cards
  http://www.sparks.com
The Elvis Presley Fan Club
  This is one of the best Elvis greeting
  card centers. There's ten different
  Elvis poses to choose from as well
  as background, text colors, and
  sound bites from various Elvis songs.
  http://www.elvispresley.cjb.net/

The Internet and Elvis Collecting

Online Auctions

http://www.ebay.com/elvis
Ebay is an auction web site that acts as middleman to bring together buyers and sellers. They charge the sellers a small fee when the transaction is completed. It's the place to buy sell or talk about Elvis collectibles. Even if you don't have anything to buy or sell, it's a great way to meet other Elvis fans in their specialized chat rooms.

"Rockin' Robin" Rosaaen runs eBay's Elvis area. The owner of one of the worlds largest private collections of Elvis memorabilia, she's appeared on Geraldo, Oprah Winfrey, and other talk shows featuring her extensive collection. She advises anyone wanting to buy or sell Elvis items to register with the special Elvis Priority Code AM-01-0001. Just go to the web site click the icon for new users and eBay will explain the procedures and rules.

http://auctionwatch.com
This is a clearinghouse site for auction information; you can do your initial searches from here.

Other Online Auction Sites

http://auctions.amazon.com
http://auctions.yahoo.com/
http://www.utrade.com
http://auction.icollector.com
http://www.elvispresleyblvd.com
   E-mail: colonelsnow@prodigy.net
http://www.ozemail.com.au/~spinauctions
http://www.bazar.fr
   French site, different items than found in the States
http://www.gmbid.com/
   Georges Marciano Luxury online auction site
http://www.bid.com

The Elvis and You Web Site

We've set up a web site to introduce you to, escort you around, and share with you all aspects of the Elvis fan scene. The Elvis and You site is also your portal to the wealth of Elvis-related information and fun to be had in cyberspace. You'll find links to recommended web sites, updated listings of fan events, an Elvis tribute artist hiring guide, and all sorts of late-breaking news from the Elvis World. You'll also find giveaways, trivia contests, and even downloadable coupons for some of the goods and services mentioned in the book.

   We also hope you'll use the site to contact us with corrections and updates to the information in this book for use in future editions. Of course, every possible effort has been made to ensure the most recent and accurate information, but contact information and URLs will change over time and we ask you to let us know.

   http://www.elvisandyou.com

"If he were alive, maybe he'd read all the good stuff we are saying about him on the internet and come out of hiding and come visit us."
—Fan, on the internet

ELVIS IN THE FUTURE

What does the future hold for Elvis? What future can he possibly have, you may be asking? Well, with Elvis gone his future will be what his fans make for and with him. Will they continue to buy and listen to his music, visit Graceland, respond to him the way they have never stopped doing since 1954, persist in loving him on the incredible scale that they do? In death he is still inextricably linked to his fans. What happens from now on is up to them and, in a way, it's about them. The fans understand this is essentially all that's left and it is surely one of the reasons they are so protective of Elvis' image and vigorous in defending him. In *Dead Elvis* Greil Marcus wrote, "When [Elvis] died, the event was a kind of explosion that went off silently, in minds and hearts; out of that explosion came many fragments, edging slowly into the light, taking shape, changing shape again and again as the years went on." And this is true—the aftershocks of that explosion have been accumulating ever since and are exactly what has given Elvis a future.

Elvis affected the fans in a way that they weren't accustomed to and certainly didn't expect. In exchange, fans—and others, too, for that matter—have not only kept Elvis' memory very much alive thereby ensuring him a future beyond death, but have kept the flame burning and given him a very lively afterlife and genuine immortality.

People are very curious about what Elvis might have gone on to do had he lived. It may have been that Elvis and the Colonel had really reached the

Graffiti on the Wall of Love, at Graceland

John O'Hara

Larry Geller sharing some stories of his Elvis experiences with a generation X Elvis fan in Palm Springs

John O'Hara

end of the line together and there was discussion about changing managers at long last. Speculating on the benefits to Elvis of such a move is a pleasure. And Larry Geller, a close and good friend to Elvis, has said that Elvis had spoken to him about turning more toward producing rather than performing. There were some projects that had been kicking around for a while such as making a movie to promote karate. There even was some banter about plans to create a spiritual resort or retreat in Egypt.

Elvis had many interests and it is possible he would have thrown his influence behind any one of them by producing a film or endorsing other creative ventures. A common prediction among those close to him was that Elvis might have moved into doing more and more gospel music and phased out popular and rock music altogether. Might Elvis have toured less, done commercials, gone on to be one of those permanent Vegas acts like Wayne Newton, or simply retired and turned toward the family life he obviously wanted on some level? It can probably be assumed that Elvis would have resumed doing exciting things, with his career, musically, or with his life when he got inspired. He was a wildly inventive and prodigiously talented man and on many occasions we witnessed his artistry downright change the points of the compass. If Elvis had lived, it's exciting to think that he would have done it again—several times: Oscar winning dramatic actor, talk-show host, Reagan-appointed ambassador to Germany, phil-anthropist, professional fund-raiser, NRA spokesman, middle square on *The Hollywood Squares*, costar in a Jackie Chan martial arts buddy cop movie? Really sadly, we'll never know....

In many ways, Elvis is more popular now than when he died. There is a sense of permanence to his presence in our culture. Certainly enough time has passed to prove that his enduring popularity is neither a fad nor a phenomenon that is going away anytime soon. His music and his image are still

"One of my last conversations with him, he was saying, 'What is this all about? How are people going to remember me? They aren't going to remember me.' He said, 'I've never done anything lasting.'"
—Kathy Westmoreland, from *Child Bride*

very much with us—an image that has even been somewhat rehabilitated. The daily reality of the Elvis references all around us, in magazines and on television, is not just about the 1970s Elvis, suffering and sad, as it was when he died. Instead, there is a sort of global view of his career that has become the reality, which is considerably more positive. Elvis was bound to look, and fare, better and better in retrospect because we are able to see the enduring significance of his whole life (not just the end). The cultural and emotional impact he had on so many more people than was ever suspected and so much more strongly, was relatively undetectable while he was alive.

Even though Elvis fans exist in all age groups nowadays, what can we expect to happen when Elvis' first crop of fans—those who've been in it since the 1950s— also leave this earthly realm? Are they his best standard bearers? Will the interest in Elvis decrease with each successive generation, or will future generations also be seduced by his glorious appeal? We think the latter will prove true. It's been demonstrated a million times over since 1977 with new crops of fans all over the world who weren't even alive at the time of Elvis' death. Half of the people visiting Graceland are under 30—which means they were in their early teens and younger when Elvis died. Certainly this younger age group represents the most active Elvis fans on the internet. These factors alone offer a rather promising prognosis for Elvis' popularity to continue well into the next century at the very least.

Of course, RCA and BMG have a great deal to do with Elvis' future as well. Certainly the popularity of Elvis' music is still very strong and it continues to sell phenomenally well. More recently, in an effort to make available recordings that everyone hasn't heard already, private, home, and live recordings from concerts have been released. Also, there seems to be a desire to head off the bootleggers and release CDs that will be of interest to the collectors. This appears to be the trend for the foreseeable future.

Then there's EPE. They definitely have plans for the future, but it's impossible to know specifically what they are. There is speculation about an Elvis theme park in some part of the world (maybe Japan? maybe near Graceland?!) and about further expansion of the Graceland complex. They've already expanded the public tour by adding several additional rooms and areas of the grounds. With recent additions such as the kitchen and Gladys's bedroom, virtually the entire first floor and basement rooms may now be visited. Of course, there's the controversy about whether or not the second floor, which includes Elvis' bedroom and private dressing room, will be added to the tour in the future. Graceland is also in the process of creating a be-all and end-all, multi-installment television/video documentary about Elvis' life and career.

There have been some outlandish, science fiction assertions and theories about Elvis' future in the new millennium. Some fans predict he will be resurrected. There's been discussion about the possibilities of cloning. And what about those radio waves that

One of the next generation of Elvis fans

John O'Hara

have been departing Earth since the 1950s? Will some alien civilization discover Elvis' voice? Maybe we should be including some Elvis music on those deep-space probe launches, just in case.

How about *our* future involving Elvis? We already have his music coming through our computers. Potentially, in years to come, there'll be every note of music he ever recorded, by request, any time, available for our pleasure. Maybe we'll hear it through the Elvis music chip implanted in our heads. Perhaps there'll be a computer-generated, special-effects virtual Elvis and he could finally star in some of those movies he had to pass up. There are silver and golden anniversaries coming up—and eventually it will be 500 years from the day Elvis died. Who'll be there in the Meditation Garden remembering him then? If we pass down our enthusiasm for him, perhaps it will be our own descendants. But in imagining a future for him, really only one thing is absolutely certain; there'll only ever be one Elvis Presley and, in our hearts, we'll carry him into the twenty-first century.

ESSENTIAL ELVISOLOGY

Elvis' Face on Mars
The September 20, 1988, issue of *The Sun* claimed that a statue of Elvis was found on Mars. We think this may be the best excuse for funding a manned mission to Mars we've ever heard.

YOUR ELVIS EDUCATION

Books
Elvissey
  Jack Womack
Dead Elvis
  Greil Marcus
Mostly Harmless
  Douglas Adams

> "Two thousand years from now they'll still be hearing about Elvis Presley."
> —Wolfman Jack

Armageddon: The Musical
    Robert Rankin
The King Is Dead: Tales of Elvis Postmortem
    edited by Paul M. Sammon
Images of Elvis Presley in American Culture 1977–1997
    George Plasketes
Unfinished Lives: What If? Marilyn Monroe, Elvis Presley, John F. Kennedy, Judy Garland, James Dean, Natalie Wood, Montgomery Clift, Arthur Ashe
    Michael Viner, Les Whitten, and Anthony Heald

THE ELVIS AND YOU EXPERIENCE

Influence Elvis' Future Legacy
Keep those fires burning! Make donations and do good works in Elvis' name. Promulgate good will by wearing an Elvis T-shirt or jewelry. Play Elvis' music on your car stereo or boom box real loud and expose new people to Elvis.

Pass the Torch of Burnin' Love to Future Generations
Provide in your will for your Elvisibilia to go to a museum, school, library, or to your family's next generation. Look into donating a glass front showcase also.

Join ACE (Americans for Cloning Elvis)
Go to this web site to sign ACE's petition in support of having Elvis cloned: http://www.geocities.com/Vienna/1673

Make an Elvis Time Capsule
Include some items from your Elvis collection for the benefit of future generations. Bury it in your backyard.

Name a Star Elvis
It's possible to "buy" a star and name it whatever you want. If *Elvis* is already taken, try something else Elvis related. These companies register a name and issue a certificate to you of an actual star out there in the Solar System.
The Millennium Chronicle
    15913 Three Palms Drive, Suite 102
    Hacienda Heights, California 91745
    http://www.off-planet.com/millennium/index.html
The International Star Registry
    24 Highbury Grove
    London N5 2DQ England
    (441) 71 226-6886

Phone (U.K only) 0800 212 493
Fax: (441) 71 226 8668
E-mail: orion@starregistry.co.uk

Propose Renaming Pluto "Planet Elvis"
Come on, who really likes the name Pluto anyway.

Construct a Robot Elvis
We can't think of a better person to model the perfect android on. This kind of thing requires special skills so if you've got 'em, why not put your creativity to work. The Colonel commissioned the construction of nine jump-suited robots as a promotional gimmick for the "Aloha from Hawaii" and some Las Vegas concerts. They were models SPA-1 and SPA-7 and constructed by Quasar Industries of Hackensack, New Jersey.

Write Science Fiction Involving Elvis
Many magazines feature short stories with alternate history, interdimensional, fantasy, or paranormal themes. If you have written an unusual story involving Elvis, submit it for publication to:

Millennium Magazine
    Review Editor
    3507 Tully Road, Suite E2-130
    Modesto, California 95356
    http://www.gnp1.com/magazine/
    scifi.htm
Romance and Beyond Magazine
    Briada Press
    3527 Ambassador Caffery Parkway,
    Suite 9
    Lafayette, Louisiana 70503
    E-mail: RBeyond@aol.com

The Magazine of Fantasy & Science Fiction
    Mercury Press
    P.O. Box 1806
    Madison Square Station
    New York, New York 10159
    Fax: (212) 982-2676
    E-mail: gordonsf@aol.com
    http://www.fsfmag.com

The UFO Connection
There's a fan club called Elvisians from Another Planet and they have a pretty cool web site at:
http://www.bigtimedesign.com/

Computer-Generated Elvis
Spielberg made it appear that dinosaurs lived again. Movie makers of the future please take note.

WHAT WE CAN LEARN FROM ELVIS

Elvis Presley was, during his lifetime, and has continued to be, beyond death, a source not only of pleasure but of inspiration to people from all walks of life. He somehow reached into the heart of so many of us all over the world and changed its beat.

The story of Elvis' life and accomplishments gives people hope. He shows us that if you believe in yourself you can rise from the most meager beginnings to become a king. At the same time, he shows us that even a king's life is not without trials and tragedy.

A greater knowledge of Elvis' life provides fans with a road map to their own lives. He is a guide, both of goals to aspire to and some pitfalls to avoid. But most important, he teaches us to live life fully, to smile magnificently, to dance with abandon, to laugh heartily, to love passionately, and to dream without limits.

There's a lot we can learn from this dreamer whose dreams came true.

Follow your dreams.
Have fun.
Do it your way.
Think big.
Cut loose.
Turn on the charm.
Take the time to do the job right.
Seek the truth.
Have a good sense of humor.
Be a good kisser.
Don't be impressed with status.
Be a prankster.
Don't be afraid to change your hair color.

> "I owe so much to Elvis. There was something incredibly inspiring about him. He pushed right to the limit of his potential, always himself, always trying to be the best he could be. When I had doubts, he made me feel like trying a little harder."
> —Betty Harper, Elvis artist

Leave your job and find another one if you're not happy.
Be careful with guns.
Don't put blind trust in your doctor.
Don't put blind trust in people who manage your money.
Give the best you've got.
Admit when you're wrong.
Take care of business in a flash.
Be polite.
Be good to your parents.
Be generous.
Take care of your family.
Don't take things too seriously.
Don't be afraid to be different.
Don't live the unexamined life.
Study martial arts.
Choose your friends carefully.
Eat a balanced diet.
Read contracts before you sign them.
Take responsibility for your actions.
Don't ever be afraid to ask for help.
Find refuge in music.
Seek solace in meditation.
Never give up on your goals.
Cry if you want to.
Protect your karma.
Rip it up.
See the world while you have the chance.
Remember your friends.
Do what you can to help.
Sing out.
Give wholeheartedly.
Remember where you came from.
Respect your elders.
Stay true to yourself.
Respect authority.
Question authority.
Destroy the status quo.
Don't be afraid to get your hair messed up.
Get out of the house more.

> "There are those who claim that [Elvis'] final acquiescence proves that the American dream is a nightmare, but they're wrong. What Elvis Presley's story really proves is that all dreams become nightmares unless they're carefully nurtured."
> —Dave Marsh, in his book *Elvis*

> "We are here to honor the memory of a man loved by millions. Elvis can serve as an inspiring example of the great potential of one human being who has strong desire and unfailing determination.... But Elvis was a frail human being. And he would be the first to admit his weaknesses. Perhaps because of his rapid rise to fame and fortune he was thrown into temptations that some never experience. Elvis would not want anyone to think that he had no flaws or faults. But now that he's gone, I find it more helpful to remember his good qualities, and I hope you do, too."
> —part of Pastor C. W. Bradley's eulogy at Elvis' funeral

Trust your instincts.
Respect the law.
Be home for Christmas.
Patch it up, baby.
Don't forget to remember to forget.
Don't be cruel.
Shake, rattle, and roll.
Love tenderly.
Believe.
Keep singing the song.

Sandi Miller

"So now let's have a tremendous
hand for a very nice person."
—Ed Sullivan